Horrorshows

THE A~TO~Z OF HORROR IN FILM, TV, RADIO AND THEATER

GENE WRIGHT

Facts On File Publications
New York, New York • Oxford, England

HORRORSHOWS

Library of Congress Cataloging in Publication Data
Wright, Gene
    Horrorshows.
    1. Horror films—Dictionaries.   2. Horror-television
programs—Dictionaries.   3. Horror radio programs—
Dictionaries.   I. Title.
PN1995.9.H6W74   1985   791.43′09′0916   83-9016
ISBN 0-8160-1014-5

Printed in the United States of America

10 9 8 7 6 5 4 3 2 1

CONTENTS

ACKNOWLEDGMENTS

The author wishes to thank his many friends in the American film industry for generously giving of their time and resources. Especially helpful were The American Academy of Motion Picture Arts and Sciences, The Museum of Modern Art, The Theater Collection of the New York Public Library, The Museum of Broadcasting and the British Film Institute. The works used for researching this volume are listed in the bibliography at the back of this book, but particularly useful were *An Illustrated History of the Horror Film* by Carlos Clarens, a seminal work on the subject, and *Living in Fear* by Les Daniels, an entertaining and informative overview of horror in the mass media.

A special note of gratitude must go to Michael and Barbara Tomlin and Robert and Rebecca Elfant for their help and insights; and to Jamie Warren, the editor of this volume, who no longer lives in terror.

Introduction

Watching horror movies is an experience that can trigger a range of reactions. For most of us they are good escapist fun, a shriek-filled roller coaster ride through the labyrinthine, dimly lit back streets of the imagination. On a more profound level horror stories can prod primitive depths of the psyche and thus provoke a primal scream that allows the viewer to cast off the real demons, if only for a while. The impulse to witness and reflect on pain, corruption, oppression and death (the ultimate horror) may account for the unflagging loyalty of buffs who have long ago lost their capacity to be genuinely unsettled.

Some stay away from horror films because they find them *too* terrifying or because they consider them to be a shoddy and inferior genre. Others, echoing complaints heard throughout the history of the genre, posit contemporary chillers as contributing to social disorder by dwelling on the ugly, terrible and violent.

Whatever one thinks of them, horror stories have always been popular and have a long and generally honorable history. In ancient Greek dramas, for instance, people are gutted, boiled alive and eaten by their neighbors. Parents kill their children and children slaughter their parents. During the Middle Ages the most popular stories were the lives of the saints, which recounted in graphic detail the gruesome tortures suffered by good Christians. Complementing these tales were the works of medieval artists who depicted the tortures of hell, complete with rotting corpses crawling with worms. And many fairy tales are actually horror tales: Consider the wife-murderer Bluebeard, for example, and "Hansel and Gretel," whose wicked witch attempts to cannibalize two helpless children.

As a genre, horror is a relatively recent invention, having arrived soon after the novel itself, in the mid-18th century. The first tale written for the thrill of it was inspired, as were so many to follow, by a nightmare. The dreamer was Horace Walpole, a wealthy and eccentric English aristocrat with a nostalgia for the past who devoted his fortune to the construction of a medieval castle on his estate, Strawberry Hill. Walpole's novel, *The Castle of Otranto* (1764), mixed equal parts of madness, murder and family mayhem in a castle setting similar to his own and thereby established a formula for many works of supernatural fiction.

The novel helped spark a demand for Gothic horror novels, which flourished during the Victorian era. Out of this flowering came the genre's great seminal works: Mary Shelley's *Frankenstein* (1818), Edgar Allan Poe's macabre stories and his famous horror poem *The Raven* (1845), Robert Louis Stevenson's *The Strange Case of Dr. Jekyll and Mr. Hyde* (1888) and Bram Stoker's *Dracula* (1897).

Today the most popular medium for horror is the movies. Most of us like to enjoy fabricated frights in a theater, seated like anonymous participants in a seance, lost in the darkness and filled with anticipation. We suspend our disbelief as the filmmaker manipulates our repressed desires and psychological struggles with an arsenal of techniques, devices, color, sound, words, editing, music and special effects.

Although it was once a popular live entertainment, horror has rarely found an adequate voice on the contemporary stage. Words speak louder than actions in the theater, and playwrights prefer to appeal to the intellect rather than manipulate the emotions. Moreover, the theater lacks the cinema's technical resources for approximating fantasy *frissons* of the printed page. Non-literary horror still exists in the theater, usually hidden in the trappings of a mystery thriller.

There are some macabre stories, however, that defy translation to any media. For example, the qualities that make the works of Edgar Allan Poe and H. P. Lovecraft so heart-thumping have yet to be adequately translated to the screen. And Ambrose Bierce and M. R. James, two of our most talented story writers, continue to frustrate the imagination of filmmakers. These writers communicate an almost untranslatable feeling of dread that can only be bridged by direct communication between author and reader.

Radio drama was probably the most versatile medium for conveying horror to a mass audience. Like film, radio could either underplay sensation and aim at a queasy uneasiness or bludgeon the audience with vivid, breathtaking shocks. But unlike film, radio had no technical limits since the screen that created the images was inside the listener's own head. By detouring around the visual aspect of reality, radio overcame film's limitations and could depict interior monologues and fantastic scenes beyond the capability of the camera. Unfortunately, this impressive tool was sent to an early death by the arrival of television in the 1950s.

Conversely, horror and commercial television have always been uneasy bedfellows. Censorship, budget limitations and the nature of the medium itself conspire to undermine televised tales of terror. TV's censor-moralists forbid the showing of explicit gore, pain or torture (except in newscasts) but allow titillating sex and certain types of violence, both of which are only incidental to horror. And since most TV horror is cast in an anthology format, the genre has never been popular with a mass audience. Television is primarily an advertising medium geared to the largest possible audience, and ratings show that home viewers prefer series with a continuing cast of characters seen from week to week.

Appropriately, the acknowledged father of the horror film was a dabbler in the black arts named Georges Melies. Born in 1861, Melies was a stage magician who performed in his own theater in Paris. He began experimenting with film, then a novelty, as an optical illusion to include in his magic act, and eventually switched to fantasy filmmaking. Although his movies are sketchy and primitive by today's standard, they are significant in that they introduced special effects and several horror archetypes to the screen. These include the vampire, in *The Devil's Castle* (1896); the ghost, in *The Haunted Castle* (1897); and the alien monster, in *A Trip to the Moon* (1902).

While the horror film is largely an American phenomenon, its roots in fact lie in the cultural soil of Germany, a country where fantasy has been nourished by centuries of legend, tradition and myth. The first true cycle of genre movies began in that country with the release of Robert Wiene's *The Cabinet of Dr. Caligari* in 1920. The film's stylized acting and bizarre story and sets created a convincing nightmare world which made it a success around the world. Its three central characters—a mad scientist, a monster who is his slave and a girl who is kidnapped by the monster— became an eternal triangle copied by hundreds of later shockers.

Horror was slow arriving in the United States, where scares for their own sake were thought to be evil influences on the minds of movie-goers, and were often attacked from pulpits all over the country. The Edison Company made a version of *Frankenstein* in 1910 and there were a few early versions of *Dr. Jekyll and Mr. Hyde*, but most American studios were content with mysteries featuring clutching claws emerging from trapdoors or hooded villains skulking through shadowy hallways. Moments of sheer terror could only be presented in a moral context, usually as a vision of Dante-esque punishments that awaited dope fiends, fornicators and other wanton types. The German sensibility began to filter through to Hollywood, noticeably in Lon Chaney's popular silent films *The Hunchback of Notre Dame* (1923) and *The Phantom of the Opera* (1925), both of which featured human grotesques.

By the late 1920s many talented members of the German film industry had emigrated to the United States, where the next great horror cycle would take place. With them they brought their superior technical skill, a knowing attitude toward the sinister and supernatural, and a lexicon of subjects that continue to characterize the horror film. These include masks and waxworks (*Mystery of the Wax Museum, House of Wax, Friday the 13th*), artificial life (*The Golem, Frankenstein*), possession (*The Mummy, The Exorcist*), dismemberment (*The Hands of Orlac, Mad Love, The Hand*) and Beauty and the Beast (most genre films).

Coinciding with the German invasion of Hollywood was the arrival of sound, which would have a sweeping effect on filmmaking in general and horror in particular. While the silent film was capable of considerable subtlety, it limited the effectiveness of genre movies. With dialogue and sound effects, horror was infinitely more convincing. Suspicion and fear were more powerfully evoked when underlined by dialogue and vocal inflection, and the audience's tension was formidably increased by such sounds as rustling draperies and by unexpected noises and screams.

The leader of the so-called golden age of the American horror film was Universal studios, run by the German-born Carl Laemmle. Universal dominated the field during the 1930s and made legends of Boris Karloff and Bela Lugosi, who were known for the rest of their lives for their roles during this decade.

In these early films American xenophobia dictated that all monsters be foreign. Settings were usually ruined castles and fogbound moors, reeking of corruption and even sexual perversion, and these could only be found in the Old World. The innocents who faced these terrors were usually played by American actors, while the great ghouls were European.

Horror began leaving the mythic in the early

1940s when filmmakers shifted emphasis to the human antagonist. One of the first of these was the Wolf Man, who was both hero and villain (and the American scion of a European family). At about the same time Val Lewton brought horror into the mid-20th century with a series of low-budget scarers, such as *Cat People* (1942) and *The Seventh Victim* (1943), that focused on the psychological horrors of the mind. Lewton placed the unseen, unimaginable force in ourselves and found it no less terrifying.

Since then the popularity of the horror film has come and gone in cycles, and has redefined itself with each rebirth. After a brief postwar hiatus, horror was co-opted by the science fiction B movie, always faster than the mainstream movie to reflect the spirit of the times. After Hiroshima the country's screens were filled with giant insects, mutant lizards and fun-house aliens from outer space that could glut, zap and erase people and things in one terrible convulsion.

Apocalyptic anxieties were reflected in *Invasion of the Body Snatchers* (1956), a key work of the period which brought to the horror film an unsettling contemporary paranoia. In the film no one is who he appears to be, not even familiar loved ones and one's own children. Anyone may be the alien under his normal exterior. And in *Psycho* (1960), a milestone film that casts a long shadow over the genre, Alfred Hitchcock unleashed on the world the unlikeliest of monsters—a docile Norman Bates, who loved his mother so much that he killed to keep her by his side. Finding supernatural monsters was no longer necessary, Hitchcock told us, since the human animal has so many of its own to choose from.

Meanwhile, the B studios were pumping new blood into the old Gothic staples, but now they were filmed in garish Technicolor. Freed of the constraints of censorship, Britain's little Hammer studio began a cycle of revamping the old chestnuts of the 1930s and 1940s with equal doses of violence, sex and explicit gore. Many of these starred Peter Cushing and Christopher Lee, who returned year after year increasingly drenched in movie blood. In the United States, Karloff, Peter Lorre and Vincent Price found themselves back in demand, while at AIP, Roger Corman found his niche turning out a popular series of Poe-inspired quickies, often presented with a knowing wink.

During the late 1960s and early 1970s, the counterculture's spirited interest in the occult paved the way for a new series of diabolical mainstream horrors that began with Roman Polanski's *Rosemary's Baby* (1968). The idea that Satan was living among us in human form appealed to a generation of movie-goers who had lived through the Charles Manson murders, political assassinations and the Vietnam war. The apex of this trend came with the release of *The Exorcist* (1973), a movie blockbuster that found evil in the unlikeliest of places—an innocent 12-year-old virgin. As a genre influence, however, the film is significant primarily for extending the limits of on-screen gore and profanity rather than for its supernatural hocus pocus. With the arrival of *The Exorcist*, stomach-turning special effects became a fact of movie life, a turn of events verified by millions of viewers who lined up to see *Jaws* (1975), an old-fashioned monster movie cleverly retooled by Steven Spielberg.

The trend toward explicit genre violence reaches back to Hitchcock's *Psycho* (which showed much less than the viewer thought he saw), but was officially inaugurated by George Romero's *The Night of the Living Dead* (1968). Made in Pittsburgh for pennies, the film played on the underground circuit for years. It still manages to shock and provoke with its cannibalistic carnage and almost comic depiction of a man-eat-man world where no one cares about anyone else and logic is beside the point. Also stirring in the backwaters of cinema were a handful of hard-core "splatter" movies distinguished mainly for their red-neck sadism but which gained a following among those who delight in sheer outrageousness (bad-movie buffs have their own set of values). Borrowing from these wellsprings, Tobe Hooper stitched together *The Texas Chain Saw Massacre* (1974), an homage to irrationality that some still consider the ultimate gore film.

When mainstream Hollywood turned to a series of expensive science fiction comic books, spawned by the mega-hit *Star Wars* (1977), horror seemed to be as cold as the Frankenstein Monster's cadaver. The announcement of the genre's demise proved to be premature, however, when John Carpenter's independently made *Halloween* (1978) was released by Universal, the studio that had produced the old horror classics. The big hit of the year, *Halloween* spawned *Friday the 13th* (1980) and a host of lesser imitations, all of which featured a crazed slasher who killed without remorse and in the most graphic manner imaginable.

Most of these new filmmakers, like Carpenter, David Cronenberg, Wes Craven, Sean Cunningham, Joe Dante and others, had been raised on and trained in the tradition of genre movies. Their films naturally found their inspiration in what had gone before as well as in their own contemporary realities. Providing the innovative twists on mangling bodies in these films is a generation of makeup "stars": Rick Baker, Dick Smith, Tom Savini, Rob Bottin, Carl Fullerton, Craig Reardon and others.

Much has been written about the escalating gore and violence of this new trend in horror, and the lack of subtlety and dramatic cohesiveness (although *Halloween* is a well-made film in the traditional sense). Parents fear that their children are being subverted, and moralists fear that the simulated violence will spill out into the streets. But viewers—not critics—determine the kinds of film that are made, and young audiences have always been given exactly what they ask for.

There is no simple explanation for the arrival of repulsively graphic violence. In order to scare audiences, movies—which deal in hyperbole—have always had to stay several steps ahead of reality. Ultimately, these films probably have the effect of expunging violence by deadening the memory of it. For better or for worse, the post-1978 horror film has emptied the old cliches of the mythic and replaced them with the primitive and hypnotic.

These films manipulate the nervous system more than the brain and stoke anxieties more than emotions. The voracious and unkillable monster is today a lunatic who could be any person on the street. You are not asked to identify with the characters, only to participate in the film's addictive psychotic energy and be swept along by the physical sensation—the horrible thrill of it all. It may not be art, but it is what genre cinema is all about.

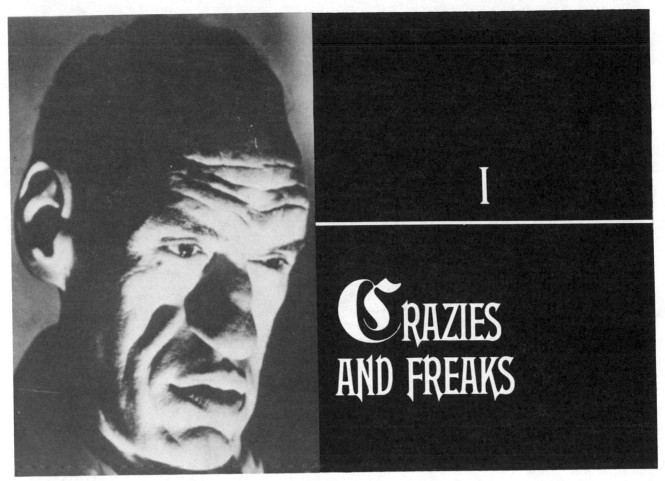

I

Crazies and Freaks

The Brute Man: Rondo Hatton, one of Hollywood's ugliest men, introduces The Creeper.

Of all the abnormal creatures that have stalked the horror film, the most anxiety producing are the human freak and the human fiend. The former is, of course, a physical "monster" afflicted with a biological mishap, and the latter is his mentally unhinged counterpart. Both disturb us profoundly because they touch on our fear of being so different that we don't belong and by reminding us that it is only the thin veneer of appearance and sanity that renders us "normal." Crazies, who also represent the violent chaos of nature, embody the repressed urges we all fear in ourselves.

In the case of freaks, the cinema attaches to this signifier a confusion of values that equates physical aberration with evil and terror (in real life this confusion becomes dangerous and evil in itself). During the silent era, Lon Chaney made a specialty of portraying physical misfits, often with great compassion, born perhaps from the ostracization of his parents, who had been stigmatized for being deaf. Later, director Tod Browning cast real misfits in his early sound film FREAKS, which so shocked

audiences that it was withdrawn from release for years.

Today the physically deformed are no longer cruelly exploited (witness the decline in carnival sideshows), and recent films such as the *The Elephant Man* (1980) and *The Mask* (1985) eschew playing on our morbid fantasies and fears in favor of sharing the precarious and bitter experience of being an odd-man-out. The "other" is more likely to be a science-created monster or a grotesque space alien. The most memorable freak of recent years is Darth Vader, villain of the *Star Wars* series, a misshapen cyborg whose damaged organs and limbs have been replaced with machine parts.

Crazies, on the other hand, have come into their own. This subgenre can be traced back to early silent films based on the career of the unidentified psychopathic killer known as Jack the Ripper. But it was Alfred Hitchcock's PSYCHO (1960) that launched the current trend, which hit its stride with the release of HALLOWEEN (1978) and a subsequent flood of "teenie-kill" pictures. Today, the mad

1

killer has supplanted the vampire and werewolf as the horror film's preeminent threat. The monster is now ourselves.

This state of affairs seems particularly appropriate to the declining years of the 20th century, which has seen two world wars, several attempts at genocide, a brutal callousness to human suffering and, closer to home, several assassinations and a constant supply of mass murderers. Mindless sadism and murder have intruded into the order of things, which have gone "helter skelter," in the words of Charles Manson and his gang of followers, who murdered seven people in a two-day spree in August 1969.

Since art imitates life, it shouldn't be surprising (as it is to many film critics) that the horror movie has shifted its focus from the timeless supernatural to the psychotic and instant. In most of these films the general plot is the same. A group of young people is trapped in an isolated spot where an unidentified killer stabs, hacks, minces or dices them one by one. These scenes, accomplished by state-of-the-art makeup effects, are nearly as explicit as hardcore splatter films (see Splatter), the difference being that the Motion Picture Association of America requires studios to flashcut grislier slayings to get an R rating and avoid the deadly X label (and consequent limited bookings).

Much has been written about the lack of characterization and complexity in current slasher movies and their near-disregard of forging an artistic link between audience and filmmaker. In truth, they offer little narrative suspense and very little identification, but both considerations are beside the point. These films have broken with the genre's historical past and tread upon the old cliches with a manic, anarchistic energy that is only interested in the effect produced. The terrible mysteries of man's psyche are the subject matter, and anyone in the films—as in real life—could be the murderer. This uniquely contemporary subgenre is less interested in engaging the brain than the nervous system, and, judging from the pleasurable shrieks of helpless audiences, it succeeds awesomely.

ARSENIC AND OLD LACE

Film   1944   U.S. (Warner Bros.)
118 minutes   Black & white

Still one of the funniest horror comedies ever, this whirlwind farce takes place in the cozy Brooklyn home of two charmingly crazy old ladies who poison lonely old men with elderberry wine. Their assumption is that the men would prefer to be dead. The women inter them in their basement with the help of their harmless off-the-wall nephew, who thinks he's burying yellow fever victims in the Panama Canal. Into this well-organized menage walks nasty nephew Jonathan with a few corpses of his own. Karloff played the role in the Broadway play on which the film is based, but was unavailable for the movie, so Raymond Massey was cast instead. The script cleverly refers to this casting change by having Massey undergo plastic surgery at the hands of Peter Lorre and emerge as a Karloff lookalike. Whenever the resemblance is commented on by one of the characters, Massey becomes murderously angry. The romantic lead is Cary Grant, in his only genre movie.

CREDITS

Director/Producer Frank Capra; *Screenplay* Julius J. and Philip G. Epstein, based on the play by Joseph Kesselring, with Howard Lindsay and Russell Crouse; *Photographer* Sol Polito; *Makeup* George Bau, Perc Westmore; *Music* Max Steiner

CAST

Cary Grant, Josephine Hull, Jean Adair, Raymond Massey, Peter Lorre, Priscilla Lane, Edward Everett Horton, Jack Carson, James Gleason

THE AVENGING CONSCIENCE

Film   1914   U.S. (Mutual)   92 minutes
Black & white (silent)

From the beginning, American moviemakers looked to Poe as a rich source of filmable, and copyright free, genre material. In the early 1900s there were *Sherlock Holmes and the Great Murder Mystery*, based on Poe's "The Murders in the Rue Morgue," and *Lunatics in Power*, Thomas Edison's comedic reworking of "The System of Dr. Tarr and Professor Fether." The most significant of these early efforts is *The Avenging Conscience*, directed by cinema pioneer D.W. Griffith on the eve of his greatest achievement, *The Birth of a Nation*.

The plot, described by Gilbert Seldes as a story of "tragic love in the midst of terror," weaves elements from "The Tell-Tale Heart" and "The Black Cat" and elaborates on them with subtitles from "Annabel Lee," "The Bells" and other Poe verses. A young man murders his rich uncle because he won't let him marry, then walls up the old man inside a fireplace. In a scene that Poe might have scripted, the obsessed hero watches a spider devour a fly trapped in its web, after which an ant kills the spider. Although the film is silent, Griffith evokes the illusion of sound with his rhythmic cutting of a scene in which the young man, overcome with guilt, hears his uncle's heartbeat in the pendulum of a clock and the tapping of a policeman's foot. Griffith's all-American moralizing is out of sync with Poe, however, and the ending is a typical period copout—straight horror wasn't acceptable at the time—revealing it all to have been a dream.

CREDITS

Director D.W. Griffith; *Photographer* G.W. Bitzer

CAST

Henry B. Walthall, Blanche Sweet, Mae Marsh, Spottiswoode Aitken, Ralph Lewis

The Beast with Five Fingers: Robert Alda and Andrea King attempt to convince Peter Lorre that he's seeing things.

THE BEAST WITH FIVE FINGERS

Film   1947   U.S. (Warner Bros.)   88 minutes
Black & white

A dead pianist's hand seemingly returns from the grave to murder the man's secretary. Peter Lorre, who had starred in the 1935 "hand" movie MAD

LOVE (see Mad Scientists), is the bald amanuensis, eyes bulging in terror of the tenacious hand. The beast pulls itself across the floor, yanks apart a bookshelf and trips through a left-hand solo of Bach's *Chaconne* on a grand piano. Lorre tries to nail the wiggling monstrosity to the floor, but it nevertheless manages to crawl up to his throat. Director Robert Florey, who had helmed MURDERS IN THE RUE MORGUE (1932) (see Mad Scientists), intended the story to be a *Caligari*-like hallucination, but Warners decided straight horror was passe and added comic relief. As a result Florey disowned the film, but it's still gruesome enough to be worth seeing. (Luis Bunuel reportedly helped with the hand effects.) The film was the era's last important horror feature; the genre was put on hold until the 1950's.

The idea was updated in a five-finger exercise titled *The Hand* (1981), directed and written by Oliver Stone. This time the hand belongs to cartoonist Michael Caine, who loses it in an accident near his Soho studio. A figment of his psychopathic male-chauvinist imagination, the hand—the one he draws with—follows him to Vermont for some murder and mayhem. Although more graphic and in color, this one can't match *Mad Love* and *Beast* for sheer creepiness.

CREDITS

Director Robert Florey; *Producer* William Jacobs; *Screenplay* Robert Siodmak, based on a short story by William Fryer Harvey; *Photographer* Wesley Anderson; *Special Effects* William McGann, Henry Koenekamp; *Music* Max Steiner

CAST

Peter Lorre, Robert Alda, Andrea King, Jr., J. Carrol Naish, Victor Francen, Charles Dingle

BEDLAM

Film   1946   U.S. (RKO)   79 minutes
Black & white

Lewton's innovative formula was showing signs of fatigue by now, and after *Bedlam* he turned to other genres. Burdened with dialogue and literary narrative, the film lacks the fluid dramatic consistency of his best work. Still, there's a lot to recommend it, especially Karloff as the cruel master of St. Mary of Bethlehem Asylum of London and the 18th-century *mise-en-scene* inspired by Hogarth's engraving of Bedlam (plate no. 8 of *The Rake's Progress*). A young man is suffocated to death under a coat of gold paint—long before *Goldfinger*—and Karloff gets an appropriate comeuppance at the hands of mistreated inmates, who build a brick wall and bury him alive.

CREDITS

Director Mark Robson; *Producer* Val Lewton; *Screenplay* Mark Robson, Carlos Keith (Val Lewton); *Photographer* Nicholas Musuraca; *Art Directors* Albert S. D'Agostino, Walter E. Keller; *Special Effects* Vernon L. Walker; *Music* Roy Webb

CAST

Boris Karloff, Anna Lee, Billy House, Richard Fraser, Glenn Vernon, Jason Robards, Sr.

BLACK CHRISTMAS

U.S. titles: Silent Night, Evil Night; Stranger in the House

Film   1974   Canada (Film Funding/Vision IV)
97 minutes   Color

This Canadian slasher effort, set in a sorority house, anticipated the arrival of horror films tailored to an increasingly younger audience. Like HALLOWEEN (1978) and company, it speeds cleverly through a tried-and-true scenario while adding a few jolts of its own. The suspense derives from the fact that we know, but the sorority sisters don't, that a homicidal maniac is skulking in the attic.

CREDITS

Director/Producer Robert Clark; *Screenplay* Roy Moore; *Photographer* Reginald Morris; *Art Director* Karen Bromly; *Music* Carl Zitter

CAST

Olivia Hussey, Margot Kidder, Keir Dullea, John Saxon, Art Hindle, Andra Martin

THE BRUTE MAN

Film   1946   U.S. (PRC)   58 minutes
Black & white

Universal quite rightly handed over this decelerated melodrama to poverty row's PRC for release. The anomalous Rondo Hatton, the real-life victim of a bone disease, plays an accidentally disfigured madman nearly redeemed by his love for a blind pianist.

CREDITS

Director Jean Yarbrough; *Producer* Ben Pivar; *Screenplay* George Bricker, M. Coates Webster; *Photographer* Maury Gertsman; *Art Directors* John B. Goodman, Abraham Grossman

CAST

Rondo Hatton, Tom Neal, Jane Adams, Donald McBride, Peter Whitney

A BUCKET OF BLOOD

Film   1959   U.S. (AIP)   65 minutes
Black & white

Walter Paisley, a busboy in a beatnik hangout, wins renown as a sculptor and gets to meet girls by murdering patrons and molding their bodies with clay. Roger Corman tossed off this witty skit on a budget of only $50,000 during a five-day improv session with his actor friends. The premise is lifted from THE MYSTERY OF THE WAX MUSEUM, but the Southern California setting, with its jukeboxes, coffee houses and poetry-spouting beats, completely alters the mood. Dick Miller is engagingly wimpy as Paisley, who goes from distress to delight when an accidental murder points the way to wealth and fame. Corman's triple play sends up his own quickie films, the art world (his sculptures look prophetically like George Segal's pop-art plastercasts of the 1960s) and, above all, teen thrillers of the 1950's.

CREDITS

Director/Producer Roger Corman; *Screenplay* Charles B. Griffith; *Photographer* Jack Marquette; *Art Director* Daniel Haller; *Music* Fred Katz

CAST

Dick Miller, Barboura Morris, Anthony Carbone, Ed Nelson, Bert Convy, Julian Burton

THE BURNING

Film   1982   U.S. (Filmways)
90 minutes   Color

Another one of those teen-torture flicks made in the wake of HALLOWEEN (1978). Kids at camp scare dumb caretaker Cropsy with a maggoty skull and he falls into a campfire. Returning five years later, the badly scarred Cropsy—now a crazy freak—comes at a new generation of campers with his trademark shears. After Cropsy gets chopped up and burned, a counselor tells the kids that "his spirit lives on," leaving the way open for an as-yet unmaterialized sequel.

CREDITS

Director Tony Maylan; *Screenplay* Peter Lawrence, Bob Weinstein; *Story* Harvey Weinstein, Tony Maylan, Brad Grey; *Photographer* Harvey Harrison; *Music* Rick Wakeman

CAST

Shelley Bruce, Brian Matthews, Leah Ayres, Brian Backer, Larry Joshua, Jason Alexander, Ned Eisenberg

Carrie: Mousy Sissy Spacek throws a telekinetic temper tantrum.

CARRIE

Film   1976   U.S. (United Artists/Red Bank)
98 minutes   De Luxe color

Poor Carrie! She's a mousy high school nerd whom nobody likes. Frightened when she begins to menstruate in the girls' gym, Carrie silently endures the taunts and laughter of her classmates, who pelt her with tampons. The girls are punished by a teacher, prompting them to devise a prank that involves rigging a class election so that she and the hunkiest boy in the school will be named king and queen of the senior prom. When she steps up to collect her crown, a bucket of pig's blood sloshes over her head, eliciting one of the most terrible temper tantrums in movie history.

What her tormentors don't know is that the strange, shy girl has awesome telekinetic powers. Dripping blood, Carrie moves in slow-motion and sets the place on fire. Surveying the blazing gym with a wide-eyed stare which suggests both pain and anger, she takes care of would-be escapees by causing their cars to crash. When she goes home to her fanatically religious mother, Carrie is questioned not about the fire and carnage but about whether she has lost her virginity. Convinced the girl has sinned, Mom stabs her with a butcher knife, and before she dies Carrie aims every knife at the house into her mother's body.

A big box-office hit, the film was De Palma's breakthrough into the major leagues, and it established Stephen King's reputation as a genre novelist. His book was little known until after the movie was released. De Palma cheats quite a bit by staging events that are impossible to deduce from the evidence on the screen, and the plot doesn't bear close scrutiny. But he knows how to catch viewers off-guard, and you'll have a hard time staying in your seat. The film concludes with an old-fashioned trick ending that works remarkably well, and one that De Palma reused in *Dressed to Kill* (1980). Piper Laurie and Sissy Spacek superbly caricature their roles as mother and daughter

CREDITS

Director Brian De Palma; *Producer* Paul Monash; *Screenplay* Lawrence D. Cohen, based on the novel by Stephen King; *Photographer* Mario Tosi; *Art Directors* William Kenney, Jack Fish; *Special Effects* Gregory M. Auer; *Music* Pino Donaggio

CAST

Sissy Spacek, Piper Laurie, Amy Irving, William Katt, John Travolta, Nancy Allen, Betty Buckley, P.J. Soles, Sidney Lassic

THE CAT AND THE CANARY

Film   1927   U.S. (Universal)   84 minutes
Black & white (silent)

Spooky old houses were popular on Broadway during the early years of the Jazz Age, and some of the earliest Hollywood horror movies were made from stage plays. First came *The Bat* (1921), by mystery writer Mary Roberts Rinehart and Avery Hopwood, which duplicated its success as a silent movie in 1926 (but not as the 1959 remake with Vincent Price). Even better is the following year's *The Cat and the Canary*, based on a play by John Willard, whose influence can be seen in Universal's classic THE OLD DARK HOUSE (1932) and scores of similar films.

Directed by Germany's Paul Leni in his American debut, the film has the relatives of a hypochondriac millionaire gathering in his cobwebbed mansion to attend the reading of his will. Laura La Plante is named as sole heir, with the stipulation that the estate be passed to a second relative if she becomes mentally unstable. During the night, Laura is badly shaken by a hairy hand that reaches out from behind her bed and by a corpse which falls from a secret panel. Meanwhile, a murderous lunatic called The Cat has escaped from a nearby asylum. It's all a plot to drive her mad, of course, and the mystery is solved with the coming of daylight. The murderer is indeed The Cat, who is also the second heir. Leni's spooky expressionist lighting and mobile, all-seeing camera counterbalance the tongue-in-cheek, typically American story. The camera snakes ominously through the house's empty corridors and abruptly shifts to the murderer's point of view, an effective cinematic trick still relied on by genre filmmakers. Although its comedy has dated, the film was one of the first to combine laughs with thrills, a formula that endures to this day.

In 1931 Rupert Julian made the first sound version of the play—titled *The Cat Creeps*—with Helen Twelvetrees, Raymond Hackett and Jean Hersholt. (A 1946 poverty-row feature with this title bears no relationship to Willard's play.) Still enjoyable is Paramount's 1939 remake, with wisecracking Bob Hope in his first important starring role. Director is Elliott Nugent, and the cast includes Paulette Goddard, Gale Sondergaard and George Zucco. Hope and Goddard also appeared in a comedy old-house follow-up, THE GHOST BREAKERS (1940) (see Zombies). The most recent *Cat and the Canary* is former softcore filmmaker Radley Metzger's 1978 British camp blunder, whose impressive cast includes Dame Wendy Hiller, Edward Fox and Wilfrid Hyde-White.

CREDITS

Director Paul Leni; *Screenplay* Robert F. Hill, Alfreda Cohn, based on the play by John Willard; *Photographer* Gilbert Warrenton; *Art Director* Charles D. Hall

CAST

Laura La Plante, Creighton Hale, Gertrude Astor, Forrest Stanley, Edmund Carewe, Flora Finch, Tully Marshall

CAULDRON OF BLOOD

Also titled: Blind Man's Bluff

Spanish title: El Colleccionista de Cadaveres/The Collector of Cadavers

Film   1967   Spain/U.S. (Hispaner/Weinbach)
101 minutes   Color

Released in the U.S. in 1971, this rehash of THE MYSTERY OF THE WAX MUSEUM (1932) fails to come alive despite the presence of one of the screen's great horror stars. Karloff, playing a blind sculptor supplied with framework skeletons by his murderous wife, subbed for Claude Rains, who became ill during filming and died that year.

CREDITS

Director Edward Mann (Santos Alcocer); *Producer* Robert D. Weinbach; *Screenplay* John Nelson, Edward Mann, Jose Luis Mayonas; *Photographer* Francisco Sempere; *Special Effects* Therese Pathe; *Makeup* Manolita Garcia Fraile; *Music* Ray Ellis

CAST

Boris Karloff, Viveca Lindfors, Jean-Pierre Aumont, Rosenda Monterus, Jacqui Speed

CHAMBER OF HORRORS

Film   1966   U.S. (Warner Bros.)
99 minutes   Color

A mass killer escapes capture by amputating his hand, and terrorizes Baltimore, circa 1880. He's tracked down by amateur sleuths who operate a wax museum featuring effigies of famous murderers. Supposedly based on Warner's HOUSE OF WAX (1953), this pilot for a would-be TV series was deemed too gruesome for television, so it was released instead to theaters, where it wasn't horrific enough. The studio added a ballyhooed "Fear Flasher" (a strobe light effect) and "Horror Horn" noisemaker which proved more unnerving than anything in the film. These were subsequently removed for TV showings.

CREDITS

Director/Producer Hy Averback; *Screenplay* Stephen Kandel; *Story* Stephen Kandel, Ray Russell; *Photographer* Richard Kline; *Art Director* Art Loel; *Makeup* Gordon Bau; *Music* William Lave

CAST

Patrick O'Neal, Cesare Danova, Laura Devon, Wilfrid Hyde-White, Tony Curtis, Jeanette Nolan, Marie Windsor

THE CLIMAX

Film   1944   U.S. (Universal)
86 minutes   Color

The box-office bonanza of Universal's THE PHANTOM OF THE OPERA (1943) inspired this nearly forgotten spinoff, filmed on the same sets and featuring the same leading lady. This time out Susanna Foster is mesmerized by Svengali-like Boris Karloff, the opera house doctor, who lives with the embalmed corpse of his wife, a prima donna he murdered ten years before. Karloff (in his first color film) and company are great fun to watch, but the suspense is bearable.

CREDITS

Director/Producer George Waggner; *Screenplay* Curt Siodmak, Lynn Starling; *Play* Edward Locke; *Photographer* Hal Mohr, W. Howard Greene; *Music* Edward Ward

CAST

Boris Karloff, Susanna Foster, Turhan Bey, Gale Sondergaard, Thomas Gomez, Scotty Beckett

CRESCENDO

Film   1969   G.B. (Hammer)   95 minutes
Technicolor

A young woman writer visiting the widow of a famous composer becomes involved with his handsome son. When the son begins acting strangely, she discovers there are actually two sons, identical twins, one of whom is insane. Alan Gibson drives home the shocks with a sledgehammer, but we've been through it before with PSYCHO (1960) and other Hammer thrillers such as *Taste of Fear* (1961), *Maniac* and *Nightmare* (1963).

CREDITS

Director Alan Gibson; *Producer* Michael Carreras; *Screenplay* Jimmy Sangster, Alfred Shaughnessy; *Story* Alfred Shaughnessy; *Photographer* Paul Beeson; *Art Director* Scott MacGregor; *Music* Malcolm Williamson

CAST

Stefanie Powers, James Olson, Jane Lapotaire, Margaretta Scott, Joss Ackland

THE COMEDY OF TERRORS

Film   1963   U.S. (AIP)
88 minutes   Pathecolor   Panavision

Hollywood's fearsome foursome get together for the first and only time to goose the kind of movies that made them famous. Peter Lorre and Vincent Price, the Laurel and Hardy of horror, are bumbling New England morticians, circa 1890, who attempt to drum up business by doing in senile old Boris Karloff and pesty landlord Basil Rathbone. The plan backfires, however, setting up a surprise ending and a few moments of enjoyable slapstick. Making his comedy debut, director Jacques Tourneur (*Cat People, Night of the Demon*) seems ill at ease with the form, and he's prone to let his actors have more fun than the audience. If the sets look familiar, it's because they were previously used in THE PREMATURE BURIAL and other AIP Poe features.

CREDITS

Director Jacques Tourneur; *Producers* James H. Nicolson, Samuel A. Z. Arkoff; *Screenplay* Richard Matheson; *Photographer* Floyd Crosby; *Art Director* Daniel Haller; *Special Effects* Pat Dinga; *Music* Lex Baxter

CAST

Vincent Price, Boris Karloff, Peter Lorre, Basil Rathbone, Joe E. Brown, Joyce Jameson, Buddy Mason, Beverly Hills

The Comedy of Terrors: An all-star reunion with, from left, Boris Karloff, Basil Rathbone, Peter Lorre and Vincent Price.

CUJO

Film 1983 U.S. (Warner Bros.) 97 minutes
CFI Color

You might have second thoughts about your loyal pooch after viewing this filmization of Stephen King's best-seller. Dee Wallace, the mother in *E.T. The Extra-Terrestrial* (1982), and son Danny Pintauro find themselves trapped in a stalled Ford Pinto for two days by a formerly gentle St. Bernard, turned into a feral killer by a bite from a rabid bat. The dog, covered in blood, drool and snot, is the cinema's most fearsome canine since Fox's version of Conan Doyle's *The Hound of the Baskervilles* (1939). King's attempt to portray the dog as a projection of our darker fears isn't especially apt since the dog itself is a victim, but the film is suspenseful and genuinely terrifying. Director Lewis Teague previously helmed the likable tongue-in-cheek *Alligator* (1981), scripted by John Sayles, in which a baby gator flushed into the sewer grows into a monster which feeds on passersby through storm drains.

CREDITS

Director Lewis Teague; *Producers* Daniel H. Blatt, Robert Singer; *Screenplay* Don Carlos Dunaway, Lauren Currier, based on the novel by Stephen King; *Photographer* Jan De Bont; *Production Designer* Guy Comtois; *Music* Charles Bernstein

CAST

Dee Wallace, Daniel Hugh-Kelly, Danny Pintauro, Christopher Stone, Ed Lauter, Bill Jacoby, Kaiulani Lee

THE DEAD ZONE

Film 1983 U.S. (Paramount) 103 minutes
Technicolor

You'd expect a scarier movie from the tandem talents of novelist Stephen King, director David Cronenberg and producer Debra Hill of the HALLOWEEN series. Jeffrey Boam's script faithfully recounts King's story of a young schoolteacher named Johnny Smith, who wakes up from a long accident-induced coma with the paranormal gift of seeing into the future. King makes this occult cliche work by depicting Johnny as a contemporary Everyman who, rather than becoming the traditional megalomaniac, reluctantly accepts the responsibility of his strange new power. Christopher Walken is a mesmerizing Johnny, and Martin Sheen lends support as an apocalypse-bound politician whose psychosis turns Johnny into a man of action. With the exception of one murder and a ritual suicide, the film eschews genre conventions in favor of greater socio-political horrors, which seem less pretentious on the printed page.

CREDITS

Director David Cronenberg; *Producer* Debra Hill; *Screenplay* Jeffrey Boam, based on the novel by Stephen King; *Photographer* Mark Irvin; *Production Designer* Carol Spier; *Special Effects* John Belyeu; *Music* Michael Kamen

CAST

Christopher Walken, Brooke Adams, Tom Skerritt, Martin Sheen, Herbert Lom, Anthony Zerbe, Colleen Dewhurst, Nicholas Campbell, Geza Kovacs

DEMENTIA 13

G.B. title: The Haunted and the Hunted

Film 1963 U.S./Ireland (AIP/Filmgroup)
81 minutes Black & white

Old memories inhabiting an Irish castle inspire an axe murderer to finish off a noble old family. A polished rhinestone that almost passes for the real thing, from whiz kid filmmaker Francis Coppola (before he added the Ford and succumbed to bloated subjects and budgets). "Roger wanted . . . sort of a copy of PSYCHO," Coppola recalls, "with some kind of terrible knife killing scene thrown in. So I wrote the script to order."

CREDITS

Director/Screenplay Francis [Ford] Coppola; *Producer* Roger Corman; *Photographer* Charles Hannawalt; *Art Director* Albert Locatelli; *Music* Ronald Stein

CAST

William Campbell, Bart Patton, Luana Anders, Mary Mitchell, Patrick Magee, Eithne Dunn

LES DIABOLIQUES

Also titled: Diabolique, The Fiends

Film 1954 France (Filmsonor)
114 minutes Black & white

American critics thought this film too shocking for words (and Pauline Kael still does), and the public turned out in record numbers, for a foreign-language movie. Simone Signoret and Vera Clouzot as, respectively, the mistress and wife of a principal of a boy's school, join forces to murder the intolerable bastard. Dumping his body in a lake, the women discover it missing when they come to retrieve it, leading to a series of hauntings by the dead professor which may or may not be figments of the wife's overwrought imagination. The melodramatic plot is a bit arthritic by now, but the bathtub finale still packs a high-voltage jolt. A harbinger of things to come, *Les Diaboliques* is a seminal work of Henri-Georges Clouzot, who has been called the French Hitchcock.

CREDITS

Director/Producer Henri-Georges Clouzot; *Screenplay* Henri-Georges Clouzot, G. Geronimi, based on the novel *The Woman Who Was No More* by Pierre Boileau and Thomas Narcejac; *Photographer* Armand Thirard; *Music* Georges Van Parys

CAST

Simone Signoret, Vera Clouzot, Charles Vanel, Paul Meuerisse

THE FALL OF THE HOUSE OF USHER

Film 1948 G.B. (GIB Films) 70 minutes
Black & white

This is an atmospheric, arty and ultimately disappointing version of the famous Poe story about a young woman buried alive by her brother, the last of the Usher line. Neither the cast nor the crew are up to the demands of translating Poe to the screen. For a more successful attempt, see Roger Corman's HOUSE OF USHER.

CREDITS

Director/Producer/Photographer Ivan Barnett; *Screenplay* Kenneth Thompson, Dorothy Catt, based on the story by Edgar Allan Poe; *Music* De Wolfe

CAST

Gwendoline Watford, Kay Tendeter, Irving Steen, Lucy Pavey, Gavin Lee

FEAR IN THE NIGHT

Film   1972   G.B. (Hammer)   85 minutes
Technicolor

A young woman, recovering from a nervous breakdown, claims she was attacked by a hooded maniac, but no one will believe her—and things go from bad to worse. Derivative, but good prickly fun set in a deserted boy's school, with a few nice plot twists.

CREDITS

Director/Producer Jimmy Sangster; *Screenplay* Jimmy Sangster, Michael Syson; *Photographer* Arthur Grant; *Art Director* Don Picton; *Music* John McCabe

CAST

Judy Geeson, Ralph Bates, Joan Collins, Peter Cushing, Gilliam Lind

FREAKS

Film   1932   U.S. (MGM)   64 minutes
Black & white

Still a *cause celebre*, this atypical MGM product was conceived as the studio's answer to Universal's recent genre hits. "Give me something that will out-horror *Frankenstein*," studio head Irving Thalberg reportedly said to director Tod Browning, then riding the crest of the wave for his adaptation of *Dracula* (see VAMPIRES). Browning, a circus buff who had previously helmed MGM's *The Unknown* (1927), in which Lon Chaney had his arms amputated for the love of Joan Crawford, set to work with a contingent of real-life sideshow freaks and delivered to order. After a woman ran screaming from a California preview, the studio recut the film, but it still seemed unbearably grue-

Freaks: Tod Browning, center, directs a cast of real-life anomalies.

some. Many distributors refused to book it, and MGM consigned the film to its vaults for more than 20 years.

Seen today, *Freaks* is still unsettling, primarily for the exploitive way it uses its anomalous players. The cast includes Randian, the Hindu Living Torso; Josephine-Joseph, the half-man, half-woman; Martha, the Armless Wonder; the Hilton Siamese Twins, and various pinheads and dwarfs. Until the last 20 minutes or so, the film is a tragic love story about a likable midget (Harry Earles) who forsakes his true love to marry a normal-sized trapeze artist (Olga Baclanova). She's only interested in his money and plots to poison him with the help of her lover, the carnival's strongman. When the freaks find out, they plot a fitting revenge on the scheming couple.

As in Hitchcock's later *Saboteur* (1942), Browning's freaks are noble and self-sustaining and not the pathetic misfits we take them for. (Echoing popular sentiment, a character calls them "monstrosities that should have been killed at birth.") It is the "normal" woman and her lover who are the true freaks for forsaking their humanity and preying on people they mistakenly assume to be helpless. The woman's suggestions of the midget's sexual inadequacy have already made us dislike her, and by the time the denouement comes we're set up for a catharsis of justifiable violence—one that is equaled only in Sam Peckinpah's *Straw Dogs* (1972).

While the performers pinion the strongman against a hot stove and make him cry out in pain as they kill him (a scene suggesting castration was eliminated), the armless, legless human torso slithers through the mud of a thunderstorm gripping a knife in his teeth. Brought back from her attempted escape into the woods by a circle of crawling and hopping freaks, the trapeze artist is suitably punished by making her "one of us." Browning falters somewhat at this point. Having previously identified with the freaks, we now see them as vile monsters and identify with the culprits who are, after all, like us. But the final scene is one of horror's great moments. As the camera dollies into her sideshow cubicle, we see that the woman has become a legless, scarred and feathered creature known as The Feathered Hen.

CREDITS

Director/Producer Tod Browning; *Screenplay* Willis Goldbeck, Leon Gordon, Edgar Allan Woolf, based on the novel *Spurs* by Tod Robbins; *Photographer* Merrit B. Gerstad; *Art Director* Cedric Gibbons

CAST

Wallace Ford, Leila Hyams, Olga Baclanova, Roscoe Ates, Harry Earles, Henry Victor, Daisy and Violet Hilton, Koo-Koo, Zip and Pip

Friday the 13th, parts I and II: Low-budget "teeny-kill" shockers become the dominant mode.

FRIDAY THE 13th

Film   1980   U.S. (Georgetown/Paramount)
95 minutes   Color

An unabashed swipe of the precedent-setting HALLOWEEN (1978), this crudely produced but suspenseful low-budgeter made movie history by becoming the first protosplatter film to be released by a major Hollywood studio. Paramount spent millions on an advertising campaign, and the film became as much of a crowd pleaser with the under-25s, who comprise the majority of today's moviegoers, as its far superior model. Victor Miller's script takes place at the by-now familiar Camp Crystal (also known as Camp Blood), where several gruesome murders had occurred 20 years before. Six happy-go-lucky teens are just getting settled in, when Jason Voorhees shows up. A vengeful mama's boy in a hockey mask, Jason begins hacking, chopping and perforating the nice, dumb kids in some diabolically clever ways (including a giant drill which skewers one boy through his bunk bed). The plot is gauze-thin, but it's meant only as a medium for getting from one gore scene to the next. Filmmaker Sean Cunningham—who co-scripted Wes Craven's sadistic *The Last House on the Left*—takes a light-hearted approach to the carnage, and there's never a dull moment.

Curiously, this film was singled out by critics and moralists during the early 1980s as being virulently anti-female. In fact, *Halloween*, although less gruesome, takes a harsher attitude toward its female victims. While its sexual politics are by no means exemplary, *Friday the 13th* dispatches its male victims with equal abandon. And heroine Adrienne King gets to lop off her pursuer's head with the killer's own machete. Both films, however, spawned a contagion of splatter and protosplatter quickies in which a woman is abused both as killer and victim. The most notorious of these are I SPIT ON YOUR GRAVE (1980) (see Splatter); *Mother's Day* (1980), a tale of two rapists who eat from slop buckets and are dispatched by two beautiful campers armed with a can of Draino and an electric carving knife; and *Slumber Party Massacre* (1982), a T&A feature written, surprisingly, by feminist Rita Mae Brown and directed and produced by Amy Jose. In this one the females become crazed murderers themselves, after suffering at the hands of a mass murderer armed with a battery-operated drill which pulps through eyeballs, brains and various body parts.

Like the Frankenstein Monster, Jason seems to be unstoppable, and the teen-age body count has continued to mount in four sequels. These include *Friday the 13th Part II* (1981), directed by Steve Miner and scripted by Ron Kurz; *Friday the 13th Part III—In 3-D* (1982), directed by Steve Miner and written by Martin Kitrosser and Carol Watson; *Friday the 13th—The Final Chapter* (1984), directed by Joseph Zito and scripted by Barney Cohen; and *Friday the 13th—A New Beginning* (1985), directed by Danny Steinmann and written

by Martin Kitrosser, David Cohen and Steinmann. The latest—and best—sequel introduced a young protege of the finally departed Jason.

CREDITS

Director/Producer Sean Cunningham; *Screenplay* Victor Miller; *Photographer* Barry Abrams, Peter Stein; *Special Makeup Effects* Tom Savini, Taso Stavrakis; *Special Effects* Steve Kirshoff; *Sound Effects* Ross-Gaffney; *Music* Harry Manfredini

CAST

Betsy Palmer, Adrienne King, Jeannine Taylor, Robbi Morgan, Kevin Bacon, Harry Crosby, Laurie Bartram, Mark Nelson, Peter Brouwer, Walt Gorney

GRIP OF THE STRANGLER

U.S. Title: The Haunted Strangler

Film   1958   G.B. (Producers Assoc.)
78 minutes   Black & white

Karloff adds some spice to this clever but clumsily handled Jekyll/Hyde tale. He's a turn-of-the-century British novelist who becomes a mad killer while researching a series of gruesome murders committed 20 years before. Turns out he was the original strangler.

CREDITS

Director Robert Day; *Producer* John Croydon; *Screenplay* Jan Read, John C. Cooper; *Photographer* Lionel Baines; *Art Director* John Elphick; *Special Effects* Les Bowie; *Makeup* Jim Hydes; *Music* Buxton Orr

CAST

Boris Karloff, Tim Turner, Jean Kent, Vera Day, Anthony Dawson, Elizabeth Allen

HALLOWEEN

Film   1978   U.S. (Universal)   91 minutes
Color

A box-office sensation, this independently produced slasher movie pointed horror in a new direction by supplanting the mythic with nerve-wracking shocks and special effects. Enormously influential, it spawned an ongoing cycle of bloodier imitations,

Halloween: An unkillable madman called The Shape stalks Jamie Lee Curtis and Donald Pleasence.

few of which have approached director John Carpenter's sense of style and grasp of technique.

The plot is tissue thin: Michael, a mad killer, escapes from a mental hospital where he has been confined for 15 years, and returns to the small Illinois town where he grew up. As a child he had knifed his sister after seeing her make love to a local boy. Back home, three teenage girls spark his distant memory and he stalks them one by one on Halloween night. What makes the viewer leap out of his seat is the way Carpenter tells it. We are given only enough information about the characters to make us care about them, at which point the violence begins.

Carpenter's speciality is the delayed shock, which is often accompanied by a red herring. After arousing our fear that something terrible is about to happen, he will often apply a Val Lewton touch, like a hand coming from out of the frame to grab a probable victim (it turns out to be a harmless friendly gesture). He then relaxes the tension and, when we are lulled into a sense of false security, he strikes. The suspense builds slowly but inexorably, and we are hardly aware that nothing much happens until the full-scale frenzy of the final reel.

Carpenter hired director Rick Rosenthal to helm *Halloween II* (1981), which is a class act but not quite up to its predecessor. The action picks up on the night when the original *Halloween* left off. Jamie Lee Curtis has been sedated in a hospital room and left all alone, prompting the "boogeyman" to arrive and begin killing off the nurses and doctors. Carpenter produced with Debra Hill and wrote the score with Alan Howarth.

Last in the series (so far) is *Halloween III: Season of the Witch* (1982). Director-writer Tommy Wallace opted for a new plot that has nothing to do with the original. Dan O'Herlihy struggles with a confused script that casts him as a maker of children's Halloween masks who plans to annihilate anybody wearing them via a concealed explosive device. The gross-out effects include a boy's head exploding in a shower of roaches, rattlesnakes and insects. Maker of the clever masks is Don Post, who in fact owns a company which manufactures children's masks. John Carpenter and Debra Hill produced.

CREDITS

Director/Music John Carpenter; *Producer* Debra Hill; *Screenplay* John Carpenter, Debra Hill; *Photographer* Dean Cundey; *Production Designer* Tommy Wallace; *Makeup* Erica Ulland

CAST

Donald Pleasence, Jamie Lee Curtis, Nancy Loomis, P.J. Soles, Charles Cyphers, Kyle Richards, Tony Moran, Will Sandin

HANDS OF THE RIPPER

Film   1971   G.B. (Hammer)   85 minutes Technicolor

The sins of Jack the Ripper are visited on his daughter, who went round the bend watching Dad slaughter Mom in the bathtub. Tantalizing Angharad Rees of TV's *Poldark* disembowels with gusto, and the direction and period details are up to Hammer's standards. Ms. Ripper's genre sisters include DRACULA'S DAUGHTER (1936) (see Vampires), *Daughter of Dr. Jekyll* (1957) and *Frankenstein's Daughter* (1958).

CREDITS

Director Peter Sasdy; *Producer* Aida Young; *Screenplay* L.W. Davidson, based on a story by Edward Spencer Shew; *Photographer* Kenneth Talbot; *Art Director* Roy Stannard; *Special Effects* Cliff Culley; *Music* Christopher Gunning

CAST

Angharad Rees, Eric Porter, Keith Bell, Dor Bryan, Derek Godfrey

HOMICIDAL

Film 1961 U.S. (Columbia) 87 minutes Black & white

People are being hacked to death by a maniac with a butcher knife, and the finger of suspicion points to a strange brother and sister living with their invalid mother. If you haven't seen PSYCHO (1960), you might be entertained; if you have, you'll guess the plot. Gimmicky filmmaker William Castle provided a 45-second "fright break" to allow the fainthearted to go for popcorn.

CREDITS

Director/Producer William Castle; *Screenplay* Robb White; *Photographer* Burnett Guffey; *Art Director* Cary Odell; *Music* Hugo Friedlander

CAST

Glenn Corbett, Jean Arless, Patricia Breslin, Eugenie Leontovich, Alan Bunce; *Narrator* William Castle

HORRORS OF THE BLACK MUSEUM

Film 1959 G.B. (Herman Cohen) 95 minutes Color Anamorphic

A burned-out crime writer hypnotizes his researcher and creates a murderer to provide himself with plenty of material. Routine gore out of the Hammer mold, with some clever murder scenes (one via binoculars fitted with springed daggers) that steal the show.

CREDITS

Director Arthur Crabtree; *Producer* Jack Greenwood; *Screenplay* Aben Kandel, Herman Cohen; *Photographer* Desmond Dickinson; *Art Director* Wilfred Arnold; *Makeup* Jack Craig; *Music* Ken Jones, Gerard Schurmann

CAST

Michael Gough, June Cunningham, Graham Curnow, Shirley Ann Field, Geoffrey Keen

HOUSE OF USHER

Also titled: The Fall of the House of Usher

Film 1960 U.S. (AIP/Alta Vista) 85 minutes Eastmancolor CinemaScope

Previously known more for his speed than for his style, Roger Corman was rewarded for his profitable teenage potboilers with a $200,000 budget and a lengthy three-week schedule. With a reverence for Poe and an eye to Hammer's recent Gothic successes, Corman assembled a first-rate team of veteran and new talent to bring to life Poe's most haunting story of the undead. "The Fall of the House of Usher" (1839) had been filmed previously by France's Jean Epstein in 1928 and by American collaborators James Watson and Melville Webber in 1933. There was also a 1948 British version and two television adaptations. (The first (1958) starred actor-turned-horror-novelist Tom Tryon, and the second (1979) featured wild-eyed Martin Landau.) This adaptation, by Richard Matheson, is relatively faithful to the short story, and Corman evokes a convincing facsimile of Poe's subtle feeling of psychological dread.

The House of Usher: Vincent Price explains the family curse to his sister and her fiancee (Myrna Fahey and Mark Damon.).

Vincent Price, ascending to Karloff's vacant throne as the prince of devils, gives a low-key performance as Roderick Usher, tortured by an old family curse which drives him to burying his sister alive while she is in a trance. The young woman claws open her coffin with bleeding fingers, and comes back emaciated to seek vengeance. In her death agony, she clutches her brother to her, while the House of Usher splits apart and sinks into a lightning-streaked black marsh. An unprecedented success (for AIP), the film gave a contemporary emphasis to Gothic horror by concentrating on self-destructive madness rather than evil imposed by outside supernatural forces. Moreover, Corman's small budget worked to the film's advantage by forcing him to shoot "tight" on a small sound stage, which gave the secluded house a suitably claustropobic feeling.

As a result of *Usher,* Corman began to be taken seriously by film critics, and he embarked on his famous Poe series. The young lovers, included for audience identification, were dispensed with since Corman concluded that viewers preferred to identify with the anti-heroics of Price. Subsequent titles include: THE PIT AND THE PENDULUM (1961); THE PREMATURE BURIAL (1961); TALES OF TERROR (1962) (see Anthologies); THE RAVEN (1962) (see Mad Scientists); THE HAUNTED PALACE (1963) [actually a Poe title with a Lovecraft story], THE MASQUE OF THE RED DEATH (1964) and THE TOMB OF LIGEIA (1964) (see Ghosts, Demons and Witches).

CREDITS

Director/Producer Roger Corman; *Screenplay* Richard Matheson, based on the story by Edgar Allan Poe; *Photographer* Floyd Crosby; *Art Director* Daniel Haller; *Special Effects* Ray Mercer; *Makeup* Fred Philipps; *Music* Les Baxter

CAST

Vincent Price, Mark Damon, Myrna Fahey, Harry Ellerbe, Bill Borzage, Mike Jordan

HOUSE OF WAX

Film   1953   U.S. (Warner Bros.)   88 minutes
Warnercolor   3-D

When television began to lure away moviegoers in the early 1950's, Hollywood came up with several innovative formats to give audiences some-

thing they couldn't get at home. The first of these was 3-D, which provided a realistic illusion of depth. Viewers soon tired of having things thrust at them from the screen, and the nuisance of wearing paper stereoscopic glasses was hardly worthwhile for seeing films that were otherwise second-rate. By 1954 the fad had run its course, and Hollywood settled on more conventional wide-screen processes such as CinemaScope.

The best of the 3-D films were horror films, where jolting visual images are a tool of the trade. *House of Wax,* while far from a masterpiece, shows what film can do short of physically assaulting an audience. A remake of Warner's THE MYSTERY OF THE WAX MUSEUM (1933), it stars Vincent Price, establishing himself as a major fiend, although his real fame would come later with AIP's Poe series. Disfigured in an accident in his wax museum, sculptor Price goes berserk, kills people, dips them in wax—and unveils a new work of art. The big scene comes when the heroine hits him in the face and breaks his Vincent Price mask, the same one he would wear in *The Abominable Dr. Phibes* (see Mad Scientists), revealing his horribly

House of Wax: Sculptor Vincent Price's wax museum is destroyed by fire.

scarred face. Some of the depth effects merely startle and titillate: a carnival barker roller-skating forward and batting a Ping-Pong ball at the camera; can-can dancers kicking their legs off the screen. But others are authentically frightening: the sculptor swings by a rope into the sleeping heroine's room; the hero chases him through the shadowy streets of turn-of-the-century New York.

While the film is entertaining shown flat, it's best enjoyed in its original 3-D and stereophonic sound track, the latter an equally depth-producing sound perspective introduced to accompany the new screen formats. The success of *House of Wax* prompted Warners to follow with the stereoscopic *Phantom of the Rue Morgue* (1954). The films signaled the reemergence of traditional Gothic horror—which gained a visceral new excitement in color—a genre that had been on hold since Warners' THE BEAST WITH FIVE FINGERS (1947).

CREDITS

Director Andre de Toth; *Producer* Bryan Foy; *Screenplay* Crane Wilbur, based on a story by Charles Beiden; *Photographers* Bert Glennon, Peverell Marley; *3-D Consultant* Lothrop Worth; *Art Director* Stanley Fleischer; *Makeup* Gordon Bau; *Music* David Buttolph

CAST

Vincent Price, Frank Lovejoy, Phyllis Kirk, Carolyn Jones, Paul Picerni, Roy Roberts, Charles Buchinsky (Charles Bronson, playing Igor)

THE HUNCHBACK OF NOTRE DAME

Film   1923   U.S. (Universal)   108 minutes Black & white (silent)

Victor Hugo's popular classic *Notre Dame de Paris* (1831) has been a perennial favorite of filmmakers. First came France's *Esmerelda* (1906) and *Notre Dame de Paris* (1911), followed by *The Darling of Paris* (1917), a Theda Bara vehicle shot in the U.S. in 1917. This is the first major movie version, and it's still worth seeing for Lon Chaney's epic performance as the hunchback Quasimodo. A gargoyle come to life, Quasimodo is a bellringer in medieval Paris who falls in love with a beautiful gypsy girl, Esmerelda, as much an outcast as he. The story's motif is the fairy tale of the Beauty and the Beast, with Quasimodo being ridiculed and tortured by the mob to save the life of his unrequited

The Hunchback of Notre Dame (1923): Lon Chaney as the bell-ringer Quasimodo, the role that made him an international star.

love. Edward T. Lowe's script avoids the downbeat ending of the novel, however, establishing a precedent for future adaptations.

Chaney is the personification of the lovesick Quasimodo, whose body, Hugo writes, "might have been described as a twisted grimace. His huge head bristled with stiff red hair; between his shoulders was an enormous hump which had a corresponding projection in front; his legs were so strangely made that they could touch only at the knees . . . his feet were immense and his hands monstrous." Chaney's makeup, which took him three and a half hours to apply, required the actor to strap himself into a painful harness with a rubber hump that prevented him from walking upright. One of Hollywood's first historical spectacles, the film captivated audiences and critics, and was selected as one of the 10 best films of the year. But except for Chaney, it seems creaky and quaint today, and compares unfavorably with RKO's 1939 remake (see listing below).

CREDITS

Director Wallace Worsley; *Producer* Carl Laemmle; *Screenplay* Edward T. Lowe, Jr.; *Adaptation* Perley Poore Sheehan, based on the novel *Notre Dame de Paris* by Victor Hugo; *Photographers* Robert Newhard, Tony Kornman

CAST

Lon Chaney, Patsy Ruth Miller, Ernest Torrence, Raymond Hatton, Norman Kerry, Kate Lester, Winifred Bryson, Nigel de Brulier

The Hunchback of Notre Dame (1939): Charles Laughton and Maureen O'Hara in the classic screen version of Victor Hugo's novel.

THE HUNCHBACK OF NOTRE DAME

Film   1939   U.S. (RKO)   117 minutes
Black & white

Charles Laughton is outstanding as the lonely, misshapen Quasimodo in this realistic, brutally grotesque near-masterpiece. Scriptwriters Bruno Frank and Sonya Levien envision the world of King Louis XI as it probably was: the poor are exploited by the rich, repression is commonplace and enlightenment has yet to overcome blind superstition.

Daring for its time, the film shows men being pilloried and boiled alive in hot oil. Quasimodo's hunchback is mercilessly exposed to a foaming crowd while he is savagely whipped in a scene more horrific than Chaney's 1923 version. As in Tod Browning's FREAKS (1932), the villain of the piece is not the deformed outsider but the ugly xenophobia of "normals" that isolates him from the human community.

One of RKO's most expensive productions (it cost nearly $2 million), the film bears the hallmark of Hollywood expertise at its most accomplished.

The Breughlish sets of Van Nest Polglase, the period costumes, the camerawork, lighting, and especially the direction of German expatriate William Dieterle vigorously support a perfectly matched, talented cast. Although the film was somewhat overshadowed by *Gone with the Wind*, released the same year, it was a popular and critical success. Laughton's makeup—the equal of Chaney's—was designed by the brothers George and R. Gordon Bau, using their revolutionary new foam latex. The porous sponge rubber looks, feels and wrinkles like skin, and can be applied with a tissue-thin edge. The Bau's formula soon established a new makeup standard for the industry.

Subsequent versions of Hugo's *Notre Dame de Paris*, all titled *The Hunchback of Notre Dame*, include a forgettable 1956 French-Italian co-production directed by Jean Delannoy, with Anthony Quinn and Gina Lollobrigida: a 1976 BBC-TV adaptation directed by Alan Cooke and starring Warren Clarke and Michelle Newell; and a well-crafted British TV version scripted by John Gay, with Anthony Hopkins as a subtly defined Quasimodo.

CREDITS

Director William Dieterle; *Producer* Pandro S. Berman; *Screenplay* Sonya Levien, Bruno Frank, based on the novel *Notre Dame de Paris* by Victor Hugo; *Photographer* Joseph H. August; *Art Director* Van Nest Polglase; *Special Effects* Vernon L. Walker; *Makeup* George and R. Gordon Bau, Perc Westmore; *Music* Alfred Newman

CAST

Charles Laughton, Maureen O'Hara, Cedric Hardwicke, Thomas Mitchell, Edmund O'Brien, Alan Marshal, Walter Hampden, George Zucco

I DRINK YOUR BLOOD

Film   1971   U.S. (Cinemation)   83 minutes Color

A good, grisly proto-splatter film which deserves a better title. Reminiscent of NIGHT OF THE LIVING DEAD (1968) (see Zombies), it follows a group of Mansonoid hippies to a small town whose farm animals have rabies. The dropouts eat rabid meat pies, handed out by a kid who wants to get rid of them, and they turn into zombielike marauders. Director Durston and cinematographer Demarecaux evoke a Ray Bradbury-like imagery, remarkable under their reduced circumstances. Released on a double bill with I EAT YOUR SKIN (see Zombies), a zombie flick of interest only to terrible makeup buffs.

CREDITS

Director/Screenplay David Durston; *Producer* Jerry Gross; *Photographer* Jacques Demarecaux; *Art Director* Charles Baxter; *Music* Clay Pitts

CAST

Bhaskar, Jadine Wong, Elizabeth Marner-Brooks, Ronda Fultz, George Patterson, Riley Mills, Iris Brooks

JACK THE RIPPER

Film   1958   G.B. (Mid Century)   84 minutes Black & white

In 1960 American showman Joseph E. Levine picked up this minor Hammer-style thriller and promoted it into a big moneymaker with a million-dollar advertising campaign that emphasized the film's graphic violence. The governor of New Hampshire wanted to ban it because of the gleefully gruesome disembowelment scenes and a socko color ending in which the Ripper, identified as a famous surgeon, hides in an elevator shaft and gets squashed under a descending cabin. The 1976 *Jack the Ripper*, a Swiss-French co-production directed by Jesus Franco, hewed no closer to the facts, even though the film is infinitely more brutally detailed. In it, Klaus Kinski portrays the Ripper as a sexual psychopath who rapes his victims while he's killing them.

The real-life Ripper committed his five murders in the late summer and autumn of 1888 in the notorious Whitechapel slums of London. All his victims were prostitutes, grabbed from behind, their throats slit from ear to ear. There was no sexual assault, but each had her abdomen laid open (the intestines of one were thrown over her shoulder like a carrying strap) and some organs were surgically removed. The murderer wrote at least three letters to authorities identifying himself as Jack the Ripper, and to prove he was the genuine article he even enclosed a piece of kidney from his latest victim. The killings ended as mysteriously as they had begun, and the Ripper remains the most famous uncaught murderer of all time. Speculation continues as to his identity, and some scholars believe the evidence points to Edward, duke of Clarence, grandson of Queen Victoria and an heir to the Crown of Great Britain.

Jack the Ripper: From right, clockwise: **Jack the Ripper** (1960); Christopher Plummer as the legendary detective Sherlock Holmes inspects a prostitute's corpse as James Mason (Dr. Watson) and Frank Finlay stand by in **Murder by Decree** (1979); physician Anthony Quayle examines a victim in **A Study in Terror** (1965).

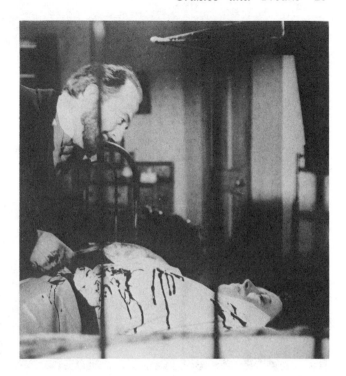

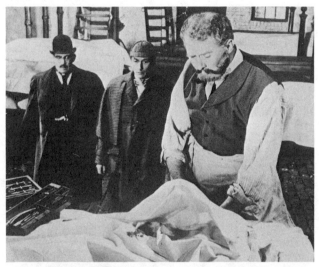

The mystery has had an endless fascination for filmmakers, whose fanciful depictions of the un-known murderer served as prototypes for a later generation of mad slashers. The Ripper first came to the screen in Paul Leni's 1924 tri-parter DAS WACHSFIGURENKABINETT (see Anthologies). Next came Alfred Hitchcock's *The Lodger* (1926), an adaptation of the novel by Marie Belloc Lowndes, filmed again as *The Phantom Fiend* (1935), *The Lodger* (1944) and *The Man in the Attic* (1953). Louise Brooks fell in love with the Ripper in G.W. Pabst's *Pandora's Box* (1928), and Sherlock Holmes and Dr. Watson deduced his identity in *A Study in Terror* (1965). DR. JEKYLL AND SISTER HYDE (1971) (see Mad Scientists) used the Ripper as an

alibi, and his daughter inherited the scalpel in HANDS OF THE RIPPER (1972). American television found him prolonging his youth with the organs of his victims in "Yours Truly, Jack the Ripper," a 1961 episode of the THRILLER (see Anthologies) series; and *Kolchak: The Night Stalker* placed him in modern-day Chicago in a 1974 lead-off episode titled "The Ripper." The latter idea was the plot device of the 1979 film *Time After Time*, which had Jack the Ripper fleeing Victorian London in H.G. Wells's Time Machine for contemporary San Francisco and feeling very much at home there.

CREDITS

Directors/Producers/Photographers Robert S. Baker, Monty Berman; *Screenplay* Jimmy Sangster; *Music* Stanley Black

CAST

Ewen Solon, Eddie Byrnes, Lee Patterson, Betty Mc-Dowell, John Le Mesurier

M

Film 1931 Germany (Nero) 118 minutes
Black & white

Fritz Lang was holding a mirror up to his times when he made this grimly realistic expressionist

M: Fritz Lang's child-murderer (Peter Lorre) stalks a prospective victim.

film, his first with sound. The Depression had created near-anarchy in Germany, and Lang feared that the Nazis were about to step into the breach and install a criminal new order. The film's protagonist is a psychopathic child murderer, played to frothing perfection by Peter Lorre in his debut role. Unable to stop himself but repulsed by his perversion, the whistling, moon-faced killer compulsively snatches unsuspecting little girls off streets in full daylight and later adds their shoes to a hoard in his closet. Because police are unable to catch him, mass hysteria results, prompting the underworld to join forces with the law to restore order to their disrupted illegal activities.

Lang's higher horrific purpose is to show what can happen to a society demoralized by a sense of helplessness and a breakdown of law and order. His point was made even before the film's release, when death threats from anonymous Nazis convinced him to change the title from *The Murderer Is Among Us* to *M*, which stands for *Morder*, murderer in German. Modeled after a true-life child-murderer in Dusseldorf, the role catapulted Lorre to fame and also typecast him forever. The cinema's first homicidal psychopath, *M* established the precedent for a later generation of innocuous-looking killers. (Joseph Losey made an unaffecting remake of the film in England in 1951.)

CREDITS

Director Fritz Lang; *Screenplay* Thea Von Harbou, Paul Falkenberg, Adolf Jansen, Karl Vash; *Photograper* Fritz Arno Wagner; *Art Directors* Karl Vollbrecht, Emil Hasler; *Music* Adolf Jansen

CAST

Peter Lorre, Otto Wernicke, Gustav Grundgens

MACABRE

Film   1958   U.S. (Allied Artists)   73 minutes Black & white

Gimmick filmmaker William Castle lured the unsuspecting to this tepid tale of burial alive by offering $1000 (to be paid by Lloyd's of London) in case of "death by fright of any member of the audience." Which only goes to prove there are worse things.

CREDITS

Director/Producer William Castle; *Screenplay* Robb White, based on novel *The Marble Forest* by Theo Durant; *Photographer* Carl E. Guthrie; *Art Directors* Jack T. Collins, Robert Kinoshita; *Special Effects* Jack Rabin, Irving Block, Louis DeWitt; *Makeup* Jack Dusick; *Music* Lex Baxter

CAST

William Prince, Jacqueline Scott, Jim Backus, Ellen Corby, Philip Tonge, Susan Morrow

THE MAN WHO LAUGHS

Film   1928   U.S. (Universal)   61 minutes Black & white (silent)

The great German director Paul Leni followed his horror comic THE CAT AND THE CANARY (1927) with this sober costume drama set in the 17th century. Genre star Conrad Veidt is Gwynplaine, the victim of a horrible mutilation inflicted as a punishment on his father: his mouth is carved into a huge, obscene and permanent smile. Gwynplaine goes on to become a popular clown known as "The Man Who Laughs," and after many in-

The Man Who Laughs: The smile has been permanently carved into Conrad Veidt's face.

trigues finds out who he really is. Veidt's makeup, originally intended for Lon Chaney, is a must-see.

CREDITS

Director Paul Leni; *Screenplay* J. Grubb Alexander, based on the novel by Victor Hugo; *Photographer* Gilbert Warrenton

CAST

Conrad Veidt, Mary Philbin, Olga Baclanova, Brandon Hurst, George Siegmann, Zimbo the Dog

THE MOST DANGEROUS GAME

Also titled: The Hounds of Zaroff

Film 1932 U.S. (RKO) 63 minutes
Black & white

Bored with stalking tigers and leopards on his private Malay island, a great white hunter imports the most dangerous game of all—the human animal. Whenever he's in the mood, the self-indulgent Count Zaroff scuttles passing yachts and, after providing dinner and a good night's sleep, orders the survivors into the jungle armed with only a knife and a sporting four-hour head start. Into his net falls the tall resourceful Rainsford, who has no intention of joining the ghoulish trophies on the walls of Zaroff's game room. Outwitting him by animal stealth and human cunning, Rainsford kills the bloodhounds and servants one by one, and ultimately bags the count with his own lance.

A pet project of the producers, both big-game hunters, the film is dominated by Leslie Banks' scene-stealing performance as Zaroff, first in a long line of sybaritic movie sadists. Described as a sort of warm-up exercise for KING KONG (1933) (see Monsters), it was shot on the same Skull Island sets. Cooper, Schoedsack, Creelman, Wray, Armstrong and Max Steiner, composer of the rousing score, made this one while the ape's special effects were being completed. The story has been reprised many times, on radio and television, and in three remakes, the first two of which changed Zaroff validly into a German Nazi who imagined himself a member of the master race. *A Game of Death* (1945), directed by Robert Wise, which included footage from the 1932 original, was followed by *Run for the Sun* (1956), shot in South America in Technicolor by Ray Boulting. In the latter film, survivor Richard Widmark is almost as ruthless as villain Peter Van Eyck. The war had narrowed the boundary lines between good and evil, and the hero could now give as good as he got. Last and least comes *Bloodlust* (1961), directed by Ralph Brooke.

CREDITS

Directors Ernest B. Schoedsack, Irving Pichel; *Producers* Merian C. Cooper, Ernest B. Schoedsack; *Screenplay*

The Most Dangerous Game: Joel McCrea and Fay Wray turn the tables on human-game hunter Leslie Banks.

James A. Creelman, based on a short story by Richard Connell; *Photographer* Henry Gerrard; *Art Director* Carroll Clark; *Special Effects* Linwood C. Dunn, Harry Redmond, Jr., Lloyd Knechtel, Vernon L. Walker; *Makeup* Wally Westmore; *Music* Max Steiner

CAST

Joel McCrea, Fay Wray, Leslie Banks, Robert Armstrong, Hale Hamilton, Noble Johnson, Dutch Hendrian, Steve Clemento

MURDERS IN THE RUE MORGUE

*Film   1971   U.S./Spain (AIP)   86 minutes
FotoFilm color*

A vitriol-throwing maniac terrorizes Paris's famous Theatre du Grand Guignol, where the performers are staging a no-holds-barred version of Poe's short story, "The Murders in the Rue Morgue" (which in fact was one of the theater's most popular attractions). Because the victims had all done business with the company, the finger of suspicion points to theater owner Jason Robards. This is the fourth film to bear Poe's title, and it has less to do with the author's story than with THE PHANTOM OF THE OPERA. Despite a zestful beginning and an elegantly mounted production, it fails to sustain its initial suspense and quickly runs out of steam. Best of the lot remains Universal's 1932 classic (see Mad Scientists).

CREDITS

Director Gordon Hessler; *Producer* Louis M. Heyward; *Screenplay* Christopher Wicking, Henry Slesar; *Photographer* Manuel Berenguer; *Production Designer* Jose Luis Galicia; *Makeup* Jack Young; *Music* Waldo de los Rios

CAST

Jason Robards, Herbert Lom, Christine Kauffmann, Adolfo Celi, Lilli Palmer, Michael Dunn

THE MYSTERY OF THE WAX MUSEUM

*Film   1933   U.S. (Warner Bros.)   73 minutes
Technicolor*

The quintessential mad sculptor movie, with Lionel Atwill in his finest hour as the demented Ivan Igor, owner of a popular wax museum. Hideously scarred and driven mad by an arsonist's fire, Atwill opens a new museum in New York stocked with horror displays that are actually human bodies dipped in wax. As much a mystery thriller as it is a genre film, *Mystery* includes an abundance of superfluous characters and more comic relief than is necessary. But the performances are first-rate, Anton Grot's thirties' Gothic sets are imaginatively macabre, and Fay Wray gets to let loose one of her famous screams as she pounds apart Atwill's facelike mask and reveals the horror inside it.

This is the second genre film shot in Technicolor—the early two-strip process—the first being Warner's DR. X (1932) (see Mad Scientists). Believed lost for more than 20 years, the film turned up in the late 1960s in Jack Warner's personal vault. Duplicates were made of the mint-condition print for television showings, but these lack the blazing reds of the fire scenes and the ghoulish greens of the boiling wax, and the effect is of a tinted black-and-white movie. Warners remade the story during the 3-D craze of the 1950s as HOUSE OF WAX, with Vincent Price reprising the Atwill role. The studio's subsequent CHAMBER OF HORRORS (1966) is nominally based on the film.

CREDITS

Director Michael Curtiz; *Producer* Henry Blanke; *Screenplay:* Don Mullaly, Carl Erickson, based on the play *Waxworks* by Charles S. Belden; *Photographer* Ray Rennahan; *Art Director* Anton Grot

CAST

Lionel Atwill, Fay Wray, Glenda Farrell, Frank McHugh, Allen Vincent, Holmes Herbert, Monica Bannister, Edwin Maxwell

NEXT OF KIN

*Film   1983   G.B. (SIS/Filmco/Miracle)
86 minutes   Eastmancolor*

The old stalk-and-slash routine, with an interesting switch: the mad killer is an old lady and her victims all live in a rest home. Lots of glossy gore and an excess of generic Hitchcockian "quotes."

CREDITS

Director Tony Williams; *Producer* Robert Le Tet; *Screenplay:* Michael Heath, Tony Williams; *Photographer* Gary Hansen; *Art Directors* Richard Francis, Nick Hepworth; *Music* Klaus Schulze

CAST

Jackie Kerin, Alex Scott, John Jarratt, Charles McCallum, Gerda Nicholson

NIGHT HAIR CHILD

Film   1971   G.B. (Leander)   89 minutes
Movielab

Cherubic 12-year-old Mark Lester kills his mother, then tries to seduce blonde stepmom Britt Ekland while trying to pin the murder on Daddy. It's all very weird and distasteful, although Lester has his moments as an incestuous child psychotic.

CREDITS

Director James Killy; *Producer* Graham Harris; *Executive Producer* Harry Alan Towers; *Screenplay* Trevor Preston; *Photographers* Luis Cuadrado, Harry Waxman; *Music* Stelvio Cipriani

CAST

Mark Lester, Britt Ekland, Hardy Kruger, Lilli Palmer, Harry Andrez, Conchita Montez, Collette Jack

THE NIGHT HAS EYES

U.S. title: Terror House

Film   1942   G.B. (Associated British-Pathe)
79 minutes   Black & white

Cozy Gothic thriller by way of *Jane Eyre*, with a young James Mason looking alternately sinister and romantic as he spellbinds a young woman who arrives at his lonely house on the Yorkshire moors in search of her vanished friend. Gunther Krampf's camera frames the familiar proceedings with an artist's eye, notably in a scene in which two women are stranded in a foggy, quicksand-lined wilderness during a violent thunderstorm. The horror shots are kept to a minimum, but you won't be disappointed.

CREDITS

Director/Screenplay Leslie Arliss; *Producer* John Argyle; *Photographer* Gunther Kampf; *Art Director* Donald Sutherland; *Music* Charles Williams

CAST

James Mason, Mary Clare, Wilfrid Lawson, Joyce Howard, John Fernald, Tucker McGuire, Dorothy Black

THE OBLONG BOX

Film   1969   G.B. (AIP)   91 minutes
Eastmancolor

AIP's 11th borrowing of a Poe title stars Vincent Price as a 19th-century neurotic distressed by the insanity of his brother, whom he had inadvertently buried alive. Lee, wasted in a lesser role, is a surgeon looking for a body to experiment on. Director Gordon dwells on the nastier aspects of sibling rivalry and provides a barely adequate number of medium to well-done shudders. Some of the footage reportedly belongs to cult favorite Michael Reeves, who died of an overdose of barbiturates that year.

CREDITS

Director/Producer Gordon Hessler; *Screenplay* Lawrence Huntington; *Photographer* John Coquillon; *Art Director* George Provis; *Music* Harry Robinson

CAST

Vincent Price, Christopher Lee, Alastair Williamson, Hilary Dwyer, Rupert Davies, Sally Geeson, Peter Arne

THE OLD DARK HOUSE

Film   1932   U.S. (Universal)   74 minutes
Black & white

Who can resist a cast and a setting like this? Charles Laughton, Raymond Massey, Melvyn Douglas, Gloria Stuart, Ernest Thesiger and four others are forced to spend a stormy night in a spooky old house presided over by brutish butler Boris Karloff. No blood is spilled but there are plenty of startling moments, especially after Karloff sets free the family pyromaniac (Brember Wills) and begins skulking through secret passageways and turning up where least expected. It's played for chuckles as well as chills, with Karloff sneaking into the liquor cabinet as often as possible while keeping a glassy eye on blonde Gloria Stuart.

A standout in the distinguished ensemble is Eva Moore as a bun-haired spinster who invokes the word of God at the drop of a hat. (She just happened to be in Hollywood at the time, visiting with her daughter Jill Esmond and son-in-law Laurence Olivier.) Also exceptional is Ernest Thesiger as the prissy sixtyish son of the 102-year-old lord of the manor. His contempt seems to come off the screen as he takes a drink of gin and says, "It's my only weakness," a line he repeated as the wicked Dr. Pretorius in BRIDE OF FRANKENSTEIN (see Monsters). Knowingly directed by James Whale on the heels of his immensely profitable FRANKENSTEIN (1931) (see Monsters), this is the quintessential old house movie. The ornate, trickily twisted house (the long shots are miniatures) was later rented out to Hollywood "B" studios for a number of lesser thrillers. William Castle/Hammer did a remake in 1963. See also THE CAT AND THE CANARY.

CREDITS

Director James Whale; *Producer* Carl Laemmle, Jr.; *Screenplay* Benn W. Levy, based on the novel *Benighted* by J.B. Priestley; *Photographer* Arthur Edeson; *Makeup* Jack Pierce

CAST

Boris Karloff, Melvyn Douglas, Charles Laughton, Lilian Bond, Gloria Stuart, Ernest Thesiger, Raymond Massey, Eva Moore, John Dudgeon, Brember Wills

THE OLD DARK HOUSE

Film   1963   G.B. (Castle/Hammer)
86 minutes   Color

Almost universally condemned for being inferior to the 1932 classic, this color remake, taken on its own terms, is an effective tongue-in-cheek thriller. Scriptwriter Dillon has speeded up the proceedings by recasting Priestley's story in the mold of Agatha Christie's whodunit, *Ten Little Indians*, and having the manorhouse guests being murdered throughout the night. The casting of TV comedian Tom Poston as the pivotal character is a mistake, but there are some good full-blown bits from Britain's most eccentric character actors, and director/producer Castle gives us a neat twist at the finale.

CREDITS

Director William Castle; *Producers* William Castle, Anthony Hinds; *Screenplay* Robert Dillon; *Photographer* Arthur Grant; *Production Designer* Bernard Robinson; *Special Effects* Les Bowie; *Music* Benjamin Frankel

CAST

Tom Poston, Robert Morley, Joyce Grenfell, Peter Bull, Janette Scott, Mervyn Johns, Fenella Fielding, Danny Green

PARANOIAC

Film   1962   G.B. (Hammer/Universal-International)
Black & white   CinemaScope

A suicidal heiress falls victim to a greedy sibling attempting to drive her insane with a hooded spectre and the reappearance of their dead brother. One of the first PSYCHO (1960) imitators, with old pro Freddie Francis deftly alternating intrigue with gore and capping it all with a surprise twist ending.

CREDITS

Director Freddie Francis; *Producer* Anthony Hinds; *Screenplay* Jimmy Sangster; *Photographer* Arthur Grant; *Art Director* Bernard Robinson, Don Mingaye; *Special Effects* Les Bowie; *Music* Elisabeth Lutyens

CAST

Janette Scott, Oliver Reed, Alexander Davion, Maurice Denham, Sheila Burrell

PEEPING TOM

Film   1959   G.B. (Powell/Anglo-Amalgamated)
109 minutes   Eastmancolor

A *cause celebre* in its time, this cult film so outraged British critics that one suggested that the distributor "flush it swiftly down the nearest sewer." The story matter-of-factly details the career of an attractive young bachelor who works as a focus-puller for a movie company and earns extra money by taking pornographic photographs. A psychopathic sadist by night, he picks up prostitutes and films their dying agony as he murders them, the only way he can achieve sexual release. Finally trapped by police in his studio, he turns the camera on himself and offers his neck to the murder weapon—a blade that emerges from the tripod.

Although there is a minimum of blood and graphic violence in the film, what's so unsettling is the sympathetic portrayal of the killer. As with Norman Bates in PSYCHO, released the following year, the true villain is a parent; the man's father had subjected him to filmed experiments in human reactions to fear (which he screens early in the story). Seen today, *Peeping Tom* is still effective in the perverse way it invites us to enjoy the film while involving us in the deeper voyeurism of the young cameraman's deadly obsession. Director Powell—known for such early British color films as *The Red Shoes* (1948)—sees the viewer of cinematic brutality as being as guilty as the filmmaker, a point of view that anticipated critics of a later generation of horror stylists. (See Splatter.)

CREDITS

Director/Producer Michael Powell; *Screenplay* Leo Marks; *Photographer* Otto Heller; *Art Director* Arthur Lawson; *Music* Brian Easdale

CAST

Carl Boehm, Anna Massey, Moira Shearer, Maxine Audley, Esmond Knight, Shirley Ann Field, Nigel Davenport, Michael Goodliffe

PERSECUTION

Also titled: The Terror of Sheba

Film   1974   G.B. (Tyburn)   96 minutes Eastmancolor

Lana Turner, on a typical clothes-horse binge, follows her aging Hollywood sisters into the low-budget loony bin. Turner digs into her role as a castrating mom obsessed by a shady past, apparently unaware of the nasty parody of her image in countless women's pictures. *Persecution* marked the genre debut of Tyburn Films—a company formed by Kevin Francis, son of director Freddie—which hoped to mine the Hammer formula.

CREDITS

Director Don Chaffey; *Producer* Kevin Francis; *Screenplay* Robert W. Hutton, Rosemary Wootten; *Photographer* Ken Talbot; *Music* Paul Ferris

CAST

Lana Turner, Ralph Bates, Trevor Howard, Olga Georges-Picot, Suzan Farmer

THE PHANTOM OF HOLLYWOOD

TV film   1974   U.S. (MGM)   74 minutes Color

At heart a Hollywood in-joke, this perfunctory remake of THE PHANTOM OF THE OPERA takes place in a Hollywood movie studio about to be demolished for a real estate development. Hiding among the sets and costumes for more than 30 years is a disfigured actor, who weaves a plot of devilish revenge against the executives who made the sale. Movie buffs will enjoy the tour of MGM's famous back lot, which vanished forever soon after the film was made.

CREDITS

Director/Producer Gene Levitt; *Screenplay* Robert Thom, George Shenk; *Photographer* Gene Polito; *Art Director* Edward Carfagno; *Makeup* William Tuttle; *Music* Leonard Rosenman

CAST

Jack Cassidy, Skye Aubrey, Jackie Coogan, Broderick Crawford, Peter Haskell, Peter Lawford, John Ireland, Kent Taylor, Corinne Calvet, Billy Halop, Regis Toomey, Bill Williams

THE PHANTOM OF THE OPERA

Film   1925   U.S. (Universal)   94 minutes Black & white, with Technicolor sequences   (silent)

Lon Chaney still thrills as the mysterious masked Phantom, even if the film is as dated as a tintype and distanced by the lack of sound. The Phantom, as everyone knows by now, is an acid-scarred music lover who lives in a grotto beneath the Paris Opera, terrorizing singers and audiences who displease him. Virginal Mary Philbin, beauty to his beast in the durable fairy-tale plot, plays a young chorus singer coached backstage by a patient, disembodied voice belonging to you-know-who. When the girl is denied her big chance in favor of a famous soprano—in spite of the Phantom's warning—he saws through the chain holding the auditorium's massive chandelier, and it crashes into the audience.

Universal reported that many women fainted during the sexually charged scene when Philbin, overcome by curiosity in the Phantom's lair, rips away his mask and reveals his disfigured, cadaverous face. Chaney's makeup, the most horrifying yet seen, required, among other appliances, the wearing of extremely uncomfortable pin-shaped wires to up-tilt his nose and open the nostrils, and jagged false teeth attached to prongs to shape his mouth into a skeletal grin. Also effective are the two-strip Technicolor sequences, a novelty then, used for ballet and opera sequences and the costume ball, where the Phantom appears dressed as the Red Death.

Phantom's influence can be seen in Universal's subsequent horror series, in which the leading characters are sympathetic villains who usurp the

The Phantom of the Opera: Above, from left: Lon Chaney originated the role in the 1925 silent film. Claude Rains was a more elegant music-lover in the 1943 color remake. Opposite: Herbert Lom was a one-eyed Phantom in the 1962 British version.

dramatic function of the nominal hero by being both protagonist and antagonist. For the record, Chaney directed many of his own scenes after director Rupert Julian was dismissed following a dispute and replaced by Edward Sedgwick. In 1929 Universal added several scenes (directed by Ernst Laemmle and written by Frank McCormack) and released the film as a part-talkie.

CREDITS

Director Rupert Julian; *Producer* Carl Laemmle; *Screenplay* Elliott J. Clawson, Raymond Schrock, based on the novel by Gaston Leroux; *Titles* Tom Reed; *Photographer* Charles Van Enger; *Color Sequences* Milton Bridenbecker, Virgil Miller; *Art Directors* E. E. Sheely, Sidney M. Ullman, Ben Carre

CAST

Lon Chaney, Mary Philbin, Norman Kerry, Arthur Edmund Carewe, Gibson Gowland, Snitz Edwards, John Sainpolis

THE PHANTOM OF THE OPERA

Film   1943   U.S. (Universal)   92 minutes
Technicolor

In reshaping its old chestnut to accommodate the talents of baritone Nelson Eddy, star of a series of MGM operettas, Universal excised most of the story's mythic erotic horror in favor of standard forties romance. Claude Rains is in fine form as an elegantly sinister Phantom who terrorizes the Paris Opera, but he's reduced to a secondary role in a film which demands a strong central performance. Chaney's Phantom wouldn't have suffered the indignity of playing a father figure to his soprano protegee and being vanquished by Eddy's posturing blond hero. Still, the film has its moments, and the dazzling chandelier scene is superior to the original. One of the first genre features to be shot in Technicolor, it won Oscars for photography and set design. Universal used the same sets for THE CLIMAX, a sequel of sorts, starring Boris Karloff as the new house spook.

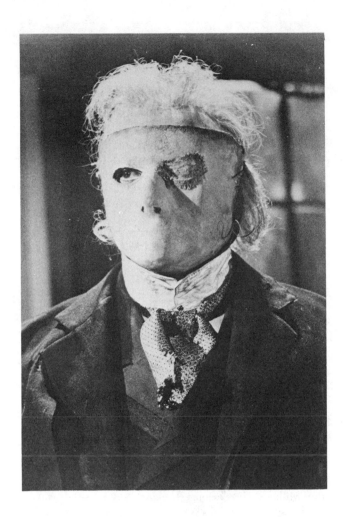

Lom isn't very scary in his cloth mask, and director Fisher seems to have been captivated by Universal's 1943 movie (even though the setting has been changed to London). In a 1983 made-for-TV version of the story, the action takes place in turn-of-the-century Budapest, with Maximilian Schell competing for last place with Lom.

CREDITS

Director Terence Fisher; *Producer* Anthony Hinds; *Screenplay* John Elder (Anthony Hinds), based on the novel by Gaston Leroux; *Photographer* Arthur Grant; *Art Director* Bernard Robinson, Don Mingaye; *Makeup* Roy Ashton; *Music* Edwin Astley

CAST

Herbert Lom, Heather Sears, Edward De Souza, Michael Gough, Thorley Walters, Ian Wilson

PHANTOM OF THE PARADISE

Film   1974   U.S. (20th Century-Fox)
91 minutes   Movielab

It's not a bad idea to recast THE PHANTOM OF THE OPERA as a musical set in a neon rock palace. But how do you play it: as a thriller, as a parody of horror films, or as a sendup of the music business? Director Brian De Palma can't make up his mind, so he opts for all three possibilities. The result is a glitzy pastiche restlessly shifting focus like an out-of-control kaleidoscope. The music is passable, but it's unlikely that anyone would want to steal a hit song from the Phantom, whose disfigurement (cleverly imagined) was caused by a record press.

CREDITS

Director/Screenplay Brian De Palma; *Producer* Edward R. Pressman; *Screenplay* Larry Pizer; *Production Designer* Jack Fisk; *Special Effects* Greg Auer; *Choreographers* Harold Oblong, William Shephard; *Songs* Paul Williams

CAST

Paul Williams, Jessica Harper, William Finley, George Memmoli, Gerrit Graham, Archie Hahn, Jeffrey Comanor, Harold Oblong

CREDITS

Director Arthur Lubin; *Producer* George Waggner; *Screenplay:* Eric Taylor, Samuel Hoffenstein, based on the novel by Gaston Leroux; *Photographers* Hal Mohr, W. Howard Greene; *Art Directors* John Goodman, Alexander Golitzen; *Musical Director* Edward Ward

CAST

Nelson Eddy, Claude Rains, Susanna Foster, Jane Farrar, Edgar Barrier, Miles Mander, Hume Cronyn, J. Edward Bromberg, Fritz Leiber

THE PHANTOM OF THE OPERA

Film   1962   G.B. (Hammer)   84 minutes
Technicolor

There's less operatic warbling in this second sound version of the old Lon Chaney classic and more time for mayhem up in the flies. But Herbert

THE PIT AND THE PENDULUM

Film   1961   U.S. (AIP/Alta Vista)
85 minutes   Pathecolor   Panavision

Following the unexpected box office returns of HOUSE OF USHER, Corman embarked on a series of Poe "adaptations," beginning with this artfully padded version of Poe's tale of the Spanish Inquisition. Matheson's script has a young nobleman visiting Vincent Price's castle to find out the truth about his sister's death. He ends up strapped to a board in madman Price's torture chamber, under the swinging pendulum described by Poe in AIP's advertising poster: "It was designed to cross the region of the heart . . . It would return again and again . . . Down and still it came down!"

What's still remarkable about the film is its heady atmosphere of Gothic terror, with cobwebbed castles, violent thunderstorms, moldering dungeons and screams of helpless victims punctuating the darkness. Corman, quite rightly, credits much of the film's success to art director Daniel Haller and cameraman Floyd Crosby. Working on an expanded but still miniscule budget, Haller removed the catwalks and ran his sets up to the ceiling of the soundstage, giving the illusion of enormous depth and height. Crosby's fluid camerawork and creative use of lenses made the sets appear to be even larger, and his handling of the cheap Pathecolor process exploited its inherent ghoulish tendency to greens and purples, notably in the dream sequence (which became a staple ingredient of the series). Perhaps the most frightening moment in the film (for its day) came with the on-screen exposure of the decaying, parchment-skinned corpse of a woman who had been buried alive—a milestone of sorts which advanced the cause of explicit movie horror.

CREDITS

Director/Producer Roger Corman; *Screenplay* Richard Matheson, based on the short story by Edgar Allan Poe; *Photographer* Floyd Crosby; *Art Director* Daniel Haller; *Special Photographic Effects* Larry Butler, Don Glouner; *Special Effects* Pat Dinga; *Makeup* Ted Coodley; *Music* Les Baxter

CAST

Vincent Price, John Kerr, Barbara Steele, Luana Anders, Anthony Carbone, Patrick Westwood

THE PREMATURE BURIAL

Film   1961   U.S. (AIP)   81 minutes
Eastmancolor   Panavision

Former matinee idol Ray Milland joined Corman's exclusive horror club for this inadvertently parodic Gothic thriller. Milland, afflicted by spells of catalepsy, is obsessed with the idea of being mistaken for dead and buried alive, so he builds a crypt outfitted with fail-safe devices and an abundant supply of food. When the inevitable burial occurs, the devices don't work of course. Milland, an otherwise capable actor, is hilarious as the terror-stricken nobleman, pulling bell ropes that won't ring, turning handles that fall off doors, and trying to find the secret passageway he had previously installed. The title is lifted from a Poe essay and the script is based on "The Tale of Illusion." Television's THRILLER (see Anthologies) also adapted the story in 1961, with the same title.

CREDITS

Director/Producer Roger Corman; *Screenplay* Charles Beaumont, Ray Russell, based on "The Tale of Illusion" by Edgar Allan Poe; *Photographer* Floyd Crosby; *Art Director* Daniel Haller; *Music* Ronald Stein

CAST

Ray Milland, Hazel Court, Richard Ney, Heather Angel, Alan Napier, John Dierkes

PSYCHO

Film   1960   U.S. (Paramount)
109 minutes   Black & white

Still the definitive slasher movie, despite HALLOWEEN, FRIDAY THE 13TH and all their teen-torture spinoffs. You know the story: Janet Leigh has stolen some money from her boss. She drives away to join her lover and ends up in a small motel located near a creepy Gothic mansion. Nice guy Norman Bates (Tony Perkins), the son of the motel owner, fixes her some sandwiches and she decides to take a shower before bed. Next day she will return the money. She looks through the shower curtain and sees the figure of a matronly woman approaching. Gasp! Before she can comprehend what's happening, a knife plunges into her naked body again and again. Her blood ebbs into the bathtub drain.

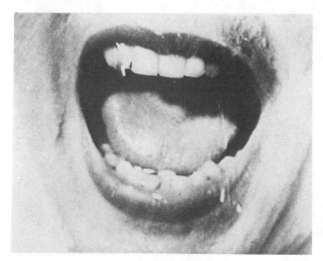

Psycho: "Mother" pays a surprise call on Janet Leigh in Hitchcock's unforgettable shower scene.

Hitchcock has pulled the rug from under our feet. After we've identified with and cared for the heroine for nearly half the movie, she's suddenly out of the film. Dead. Finished. We've been denied one of the basic conventions of storytelling, so we transfer our loyalties to poor nebbishy Norman. He has to clean up the bathroom and protect his mother, and we begin to root for him. It's another one of Hitchcock's tricks, of course, since we have no reason to believe the old lady doesn't exist. The shots of the woman's bedroom and a high-angled scene of her mad, knife-wielding rush into the hall are so cleverly designed that we never wonder why we haven't seen her face. We have no way of knowing that Norman is a smothered mama's boy who mummified the woman's body rather than be parted from her (he's an amateur taxidermist). He had long ago become her murderous alter ego.

Hitchcock filmed this black joke in record time on the set of his TV series ALFRED HITCHCOCK PRESENTS (1955–60) (see Anthologies), using speedy TV techniques. The famous shower scene—in which the knife never penetrates Leigh's flesh—took the longest to complete: seven days for 70 shots, spliced together with the elegance and speed of a new Ferrari. ("Mom" was actually Perkins's stand-in; the actor was appearing in a Broadway play at the time.) *Psycho's* antecedents reach back to Fritz Lang's M (1931) and Hitchcock's own insidious charmers of *Shadow of a Doubt* (1942) and *Strangers on a Train* (1951). The film's source is Robert Bloch's novel of the same title, which was inspired by the gruesome career of Ed Gein, a handyman/babysitter in Plainfield, Wisconsin. A quiet, diminutive oddball, Gein made headlines in the late 1950s when he confessed he had been robbing graves, dismembering the bodies and tanning the skins. He eventually killed two women because they resembled his dead mother, with whom psychiatrists said he had an abnormal love. Diagnosed as a chronic schizophrenic, he was committed to an institution where he died in 1984 at the age of 77. Two other films based on Gein are *Deranged* and THE TEXAS CHAIN SAW MASSACRE (see Ghouls).

CREDITS

Director/Producer Alfred Hitchcock; *Screenplay* Joseph Stefano, based on the novel by Robert Bloch; *Photographer* John L. Russell; *Art Directors* Joseph Hurley, Robert Clatworthy; *Titles* Saul Bass; *Special Effects* Clarence Champagne; *Makeup* Jack Barron, Robert Dawn; *Music* Bernard Herrmann

CAST

Anthony Perkins, Janet Leigh, John Gavin, Vera Miles, Martin Balsam, John McIntyre, Simon Oakland, Frank Albertson, John Anderson, Mort Mills

PSYCHO II

Film   1983   U.S. (Universal)
113 minutes   Technicolor

Oh my god! After more than 20 years in a mental hospital, Norman Bates has been declared sane, and he's back at the tacky Bates Motel and the old Victorian house he shared with his mother. "Mom" promptly swings back into action, terrorizing poor Norman (Anthony Perkins) and offing a few people with a butcher knife. Helping poor Norman find the real killer is pert young Meg Tilly, daughter of old nemesis Vera Miles, who wants to send sister Janet Leigh's killer back to the asylum. Not on hand is Leigh's old lover John Gavin (who was in real life serving as Ronald Reagan's ambassador to Mexico).

As much a camp homage as a rip-off, the film impressively recreates the house—which is as important as Norman—from the original sets and props. The shower head, last used in John Carpenter's *The Thing*, was stolen during preproduction. Australian director Richard Franklin, a USC film school graduate, quotes entire sequences from the first movie and copies lighting effects and camera angles. Tom Holland's script keeps the corkscrew surprises coming, but the plot works itself into a corner, and the final twist is a cheat in that the film offers no previous evidence for it. Hitchcock probably would have axed the full-frontal gore. Director Franklin and executive producer Bernard Schwartz got the film on the strength of their Australian-made *Roadgames* (1982), a Hitchcockian story of a trucker (Stacy Keach) on the trail of a murderer who stores his female corpses in a refrigerated van. Also in the cast of *Roadgames* is Jamie Lee Curtis.

CREDITS

Director Richard Franklin; *Producer* Hilton A. Green; *Screenplay* Tom Holland, based on characters created

Psycho II: Norman Bates goes home to Mom in the long-delayed sequel.

by Robert Bloch; *Photographer* Dean Cundey; *Production Designer* John W. Corso; *Music* Jerry Goldsmith

CAST

Anthony Perkins, Vera Miles, Meg Tilly, Robert Loggia, Dennis Franz, Hugh Gillin, Claudia Bryar, Robert Alan Browne

REPULSION

Film	1965	G.B. (Compton/Tekli)
104 minutes		Black & white

Polanski's shattering study of homicidal madness owes a debt to Hitchcock's PSYCHO (1960) and to the superb performance of Catherine Deneuve, hitherto called upon to play blank-eyed ingenues. Deneuve is a Belgian manicurist living in contemporary London who, repressed and lonely, breeds a man-hating psychosis in which she imagines she is being brutally raped. Repelled by the sounds of creaking springs and the gasps and moans of two lovers in the next apartment, she goes berserk and savages two male visitors with a straight razor. Polanski is perhaps too clinical in his approach and the girl's motivation is never made clear (our only clue to her madness is a smiling family photograph displayed on her dresser). But these are minor quibbles.

In 1976 Polanski wrote, directed and starred in a somewhat similar film, *The Tenant*, which features Shelley Winters, Melvyn Douglas and Isabelle Adjani. One of Polanski's most personal films, it's a Kafka-esque meditation on identity, with Polanski playing a Polish nonentity named Trelkovsky who moves into the Paris apartment of a woman who has killed herself. Driven into paranoia because he has no friends and neighbors hate him, he begins to believe that the woman is beginning to possess him. He obsessively smokes her brand of cigarettes, drinks her brand of chocolate, and finally dresses in her clothing, until the transformation finally becomes reality.

CREDITS

Director Roman Polanski; *Producer* Gene Gutowski; *Screenplay* Roman Polanski, Gerard Brach; *Photographer* Gilbert Taylor; *Art Director* Seamus Flannery; *Music* Chico Hamilton

CAST

Catherine Deneuve, Yvonne Furneaux, Ian Hendry, John Fraser, Patrick Wymark, Valerie Taylor, Helen Fraser

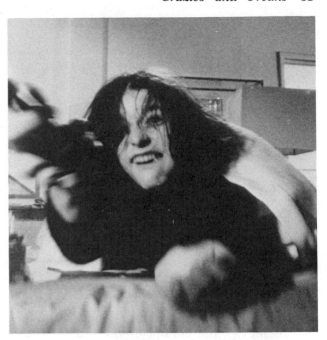

Sisters: Margot Kidder is a demented Siamese twin in Brian De Palma's homage to Alfred Hitchcock.

SISTERS

Also titled: Blood Sisters

Film	1972	U.S. (Pressman-Williams)
92 minutes		Color

No one can do a Hitchcock "homage" like moviepoid Brian De Palma, and this is one of his best. Filmed on Staten Island on a budget that wouldn't have paid for a Hollywood limousine service, *Sisters* features pre-Lois Lane Margot Kidder as a Siamese twin separated from her sister, who seems to be a schizo murderer. When reporter Jennifer Salt witnesses one of the killings through her window, police visit the apartment but find no evidence of the crime. What follows is improbable but hair-raising and paced nicely by witty sendups of the police, bureaucracies and TV game shows. De Palma acknowledges his debt to *Rear Window* (1954) in using a score by Bernard Herrmann, who wrote the music for several Hitchcock films.

CREDITS

Director/Story Brian De Palma; *Producer* Edward R. Pressman; *Screenplay* Brian De Palma, Louisa Rose; *Photographer* Gregory Sandor; *Production Designer* Gary Weist; *Music* Bernard Herrmann

CAST

Margot Kidder, Jennifer Salt, Charles Durning, Lisle Wilson, Barnard Hughes, Bill Finley, Mary Davenport

TARGETS

*Film   1968   U.S. (Paramount)
90 minutes   Pathecolor*

Working with only leftovers, Peter Bogdanovich parlayed this long shot into a major career. *Targets* came about because Karloff owed producer Roger Corman two days' work when a previous project wrapped ahead of schedule. Assigned by Corman to stitch together a film with the star, Bogdanovich came up with a tandem plot that casts Karloff as Byron Orlock, a great horror star who wants to pack it in because people are no longer scared by horror movies (he comments that the horrors of real life are far worse). Meanwhile, across town, Bobby Thompson, a taciturn Vietnam veteran, has inexplicably shot to death his wife, his mother and a delivery boy. After killing several passers-by from an oil-tank tower, he escapes to the stage of a drive-in theater currently playing a horror film starring Orlock (the scenes are outtakes from Corman's THE TERROR [see Ghosts, Demons and Witches]). Orlock, there to promote the film, disarms Bobby, who is confused by the actor's flickering on-screen image.

An impressive debut film, considered Bogdanovich's most powerful work, *Targets* derives its impact from the anomalous killing sprees that have become almost commonplace today. (Robert Kennedy was shot the year the film was made; two years before Charles Whitman climbed to the University of Texas bell tower and killed and wounded 46 people.) While Bogdanovich only hints at the root causes of such violence (a stifling family life that never allowed Bobby to mature), he makes a strong argument for gun control. When police announce that a sniper is loose in the drive-in theater, for instance, car trunks fly open, revealing enough guns to fight a small war. In such an environment, Bogdanovich says, we are all targets. The film ingeniously bridges the gap between Gothic and modern horror, and it's a fitting wind-up for Karloff, who finally got to play the hero.

CREDITS

Director/Producer/Screenplay Peter Bogdanovich; *Story* Polly Platt, Peter Bogdanovich; *Photographer* Laszlo Kovacs

CAST

Boris Karloff, Tim O'Kelly, Nancy Hsueh, Peter Bogdanovich, James Brown, Sandy Baron, Arthur Peterson

THE TENANT

See: Repulsion

The Terror: May McAvoy meets a fiendish hooded criminal called The Terror in the first genre sound movie.

THE TERROR

*Film   1928   U.S. (Warner Bros.)   82 minutes
Black & white*

During the late 1920s the public began to tire of silent films. The enormous popularity of radio—which arrived after cinema—had whetted their appetite for voices and music, and they responded enthusiastically to Warner's part-talkie *The Jazz Singer* (1927). Warner followed with two all-talkies, *The Lights of New York* and *The Terror*, the latter of which is the genre's first sound film. An adaptation of a London play by Edgar Wallace, it is essentially an old house thriller about a hooded murderer attempting to abduct the heroine from secret passageways.

To demonstrate its Vitaphone system (which consisted of synchronized disks), the studio did away with printed credits and had the refined voice of Conrad Nagel read the names of cast and crew. The advertised "spine-tingling" effects consisted mostly of organ music, creaking doors, howling winds and May McAvoy's lisps and screams. No better than what had been seen in countless silent melodramas, even though it brought a new dimension to cinematic terror, the film was a flop. Hollywood's echoing scream of terror would ultimately be released in 1931 with Bela Lugosi's DRACULA (see Vampires). Warner made a sequel of sorts, *Return of the Terror* (1934), a routine mad scientist story with J. Carroll Naish. In 1938 British director Richard Bird filmed a remake of the original film.

CREDITS

Director Roy del Ruth; *Screenplay* Harvey Gates, from a play by Edgar Wallace; *Photographer* Barney McGill

CAST

May McAvoy, Edward Everett Horton, Louise Fazenda, Matthew Betz, Alec B. Francis, Holmes Herbert

TERROR IN THE WAX MUSEUM

Film   1973   U.S. (Bing Crosby Enterprises) 94 minutes   De Luxe

A murder mystery set in a London wax museum, circa 1900, with figures of Jack the Ripper, Lizzie Borden (and her mother, of course), Bluebeard, Attila the Hun and other legendary figures seemingly coming to life. Director Fenady has little feeling for the old traditions, and it's an el-cheapo production, but there are plenty of famous old horror faces to identify, and you may enjoy it as a trivial pursuit.

CREDITS

Director George Fenady; *Producer/Story* Andrew J. Fenady; *Screenplay* Jameson Brewer; *Photographer* William Jurgensen; *Production Designer* Stan Jolley; *Makeup* Jack H. Young; *Music* George Duning

CAST

Ray Milland, Elsa Lanchester, Maurice Evans, Broderick Crawford, Louis Hayward, John Carradine, Shani Wallis, Patric Knowles, Lisa Lu, Don Herbert

TERROR TRAIN

Film   1980   Canada (Triple T)   97 minutes Color

The victim of a fraternity hazing gets even by slashing some obnoxious preppies holding a masquerade party aboard an express train. With a passenger list that includes character actor Ben Johnson, magician David Copperfield and horror princess Jamie Lee Curtis, you'd expect a thrilling trip, even if the terrain is a bit familiar. But the only goosepimply sequence is when the maniac chases Curtis through the train. It's not HALLOWEEN, only April Fool's Day.

CREDITS

Director Roger Spottiswoode; *Producer* Harold Greenberg; *Screenplay* T. Y. Drake; *Photographers* Rene Verzier, Al Smith, Peter Bensison; *Production Designer* Glenn Bydwell; *Special Effects* Josef Elsner; *Makeup* Alan Friedman, Joan Isaacson, Michele Burke; *Music* John Mills-Cockle

CAST

Ben Johnson, Jamie Lee Curtis, Hart Bochner, David Copperfield, Derek MacKinnon, Sandee Currie

THEATRE OF BLOOD

Film   1973   G.B. (Cineman/United Artists) 102 minutes   De Luxe

Acting very much like THE ABOMINABLE DR. PHIBES (1971) (see Mad Scientists), Vincent Price grins and grimaces as a thin-skinned Shakespearean actor who can't tolerate bad notices. Faking his suicide, he decides to murder the snobbish critics who savaged his latest performance, using methods adapted from scenes in Shakespeare's plays. With the help of his faithful daughter Diana Rigg—who matches Price line for line—he polishes them off in a series of gruesome scenes that are often as terrifying as they are hilarious. Film critics, apparently forewarned, applauded this one.

CREDITS

Director Douglas Hickox; *Producers* John Kohn, Stanley Mann; *Screenplay* Anthony Greville-Bell; *Photographer* Wolfgang Suschitzky; *Production Designer* Michael Seymour; *Special Effects* John Stears; *Music* Michael J. Lewis

CAST

Vincent Price, Diana Rigg, Ian Hendry, Coral Browne, Jack Hawkins, Robert Morley, Diana Dors, Milo O'Shea, Harry Andrews, Robert Coote, Dennis Price, Michael Hordern, Arthur Lowe

TOWER OF LONDON

*Film   1939   U.S. (Universal)   92 minutes
Black & white*

An atmospheric, full-blooded retelling of Shakespeare's *Richard III* which strips the play bare of almost everything but its horror elements (of which there are no shortage). Basil Rathbone is impressively sinister as the duke of Gloucester, plotting and murdering his way to the throne with the help of Mord (Boris Karloff), the court's bald, clubfooted executioner. Director Rowland N. Lee stages the film as a historical pageant of 15th-century England, and seems to relish every drowning, beheading, stabbing and smothering of two small children. Karloff lingers in the memory begging to fight in battle because "I've never killed in hot blood before." Vincent Price, who would play Richard in the 1962 remake, appears briefly as the duke of Clarence, before being drowned in a barrel of wine.

CREDITS

Director/Producer Rowland N. Lee; *Screenplay* Robert N. Lee; *Photographer* George Robinson; *Art Director* Jack Otterson; *Musical Director* Charles Previn

CAST

Basil Rathbone, Boris Karloff, Ian Hunter, Barbara O'Neil, Vincent Price, Nan Grey, John Sutton, Leo G. Carroll

TOWER OF LONDON

*Film   1962   U.S. (Admiral/United Artists)
79 minutes   Black & white*

Roger Corman interrupted his Poe cycle to toss off this remake of Universal's 1939 film. Cast and crew are his AIP standbys, with Vincent Price, featured as Clarence in the earlier film, overplaying Richard III, England's notorious crippled king. The low budget is all too apparent, and despite a transfusion of graphic violence and ghostly apparitions, Corman hits the mark only occasionally.

CREDITS

Director Roger Corman; *Producer* Gene Corman; *Screenplay* Leo V. Gordon; *Dialogue Director* Francis Ford Coppola; *Photographer* Arch R. Dalzell; *Art Director* Daniel Haller; *Music* Michael Anderson

CAST

Vincent Price, Joan Freeman, Michael Pate, Robert Brown, Justice Watson, Sara Selby, Richard McCauly

WHAT EVER HAPPENED TO BABY JANE?

Film   1962   U.S. (Warner-Seven Arts/Associates and Aldrich)   133 minutes   Black & white

Too old to play romantic leads, movie *grande dames* Bette Davis and Joan Crawford rejuvenated their sagging careers by appearing in this low-budget surprise hit as two batty Hollywood rejects. Davis, outfreaking glamour queen Crawford in a grotesque white makeup, is Baby Jane, a child star of 40 years ago planning a comeback in her patent leather tap shoes and blonde Mary Pickford curls. Crawford is her invalid sister Blanche, whose own budding movie career had been cut short by an automobile accident, apparently caused by Jane. Holed up ever since in a gloomy old house, the pair begin to stir up old resentments, with Blanche finding herself at the mercy of the jealous, sadistic Jane. What little violence there is is mostly suggested (Jane serves Blanche her pet canary and a dead rat for dinner). But the two ladies grab the overlong script by the throat and supply more than enough *frissons.*

Although credited with spawning a series of horror *Whatevers* starring fading leading ladies, *Baby Jane* was anticipated 12 years earlier by Gloria Swanson as the past-obsessed movie queen Norma Desmond in Billy Wilder's *Sunset Boulevard.* (Richard Corliss calls the film "the definitive Hollywood horror movie.") Shot in a Los Angeles TV studio on a "B" picture budget—with the stars taking a percentage instead of a salary—*Baby Jane* earned so much money that Robert Aldrich made a more expensive follow-up in 1964. Originally titled *What Ever Happened to Cousin Charlotte?*, the film was released as *Hush . . . Hush, Sweet Charlotte*, with Davis cast as an aging Southern belle who believes her axe-murdered fiancee has returned to haunt her 37 years after the fact. Behind the DIABOLIQUE-type plot to drive her mad—and collect a fortune—is cousin Olivia de Havilland, subbing for an ailing and sorely missed Joan Crawford.

What Ever Happened to Baby Jane? Joan Crawford, left, and Bette Davis as spiteful sisters trapped in the past. In the sequel, **Hush . . . Hush, Sweet Charlotte**, right, Olivia de Havilland subbed for Crawford.

Davis's subsequent genre (or near-genre) films include *The Nanny* (1965), *The Anniversary* (1965), BURNT OFFERINGS (1976) (see Ghosts, Witches and Demons) and *Return From Witch Mountain* (1978). Her TV films include *Madame Sin* (1972), *Scream, Pretty Peggy* and THE DARK SECRET OF HARVEST HOME (1978) (see Vampires). Crawford's films include *Strait-Jacket* (1964), *I Saw What You Did* (1965), *Berserk!* (1967) and *Trog* (1970). She also appeared in the TV movie NIGHT GALLERY (1969) (see Anthologies) in an episode directed by Steven Spielberg.

CREDITS

Director/Producer Robert Aldrich; *Screenplay* Lukas Heller, based on the novel by Henry Farrell; *Photographer* Ernest Haller; *Art Director* William Glasgow; *Special Effects* Don Steward; *Makeup* Jack Obringer, Monty Westmore; *Music* De Vol

CAST

Bette Davis, Joan Crawford, Victor Buono, Anna Lee, Barbara Merrill (Davis's daughter), Maidie Norman, Marjorie Bennett

WHEN A STRANGER CALLS

Film 1979 U.S. (Melvin Simon) 96 minutes
Color

A baby-sitter is terrorized by phone calls from a homicidal maniac who, she discovers, is somewhere in the house. Cut to seven years later, when the killer is released from an asylum. After slaughtering an aging barfly in the back streets of Los Angeles, he locates the baby-sitter, who has since become a mother herself. Carol Kane and Colleen Dewhurst are very good as, respectively, the baby-sitter and the barfly, and there are several heart-stopping scenes. But the plot is clumsily handled, and by humanizing the killer filmmakers Steve Feke and Fred Walton—who expanded their superior 20-minute short *The Sitter*—seriously undermine the essence of the film.

CREDITS

Director Fred Walton; *Executive Producers* Melvin Simon, Barry Krost; *Screenplay* Steve Feke, Fred Walton; *Photographer* Don Peterman; *Production Designer* Elayne Barbara Ceder; *Special Effects* B & D Special Effects; *Makeup* Bon Mills; *Music* Dana Kaproff

CAST

Carol Kane, Charles Durning, Colleen Dewhurst, Tony Beckley, Rachel Roberts, Ron O'Neil

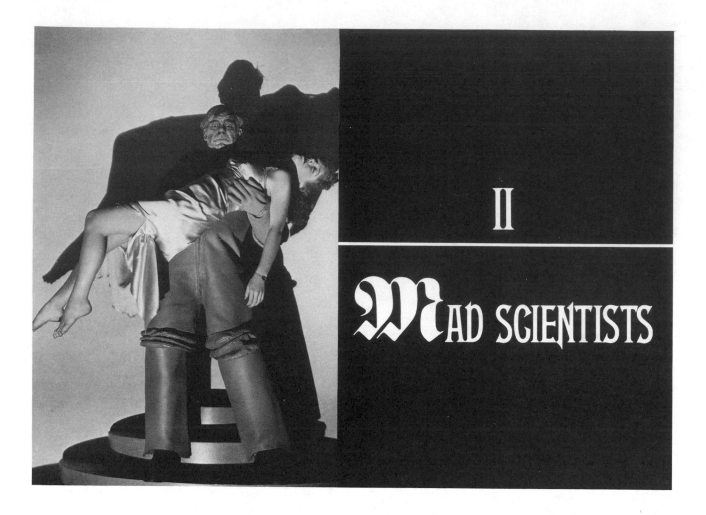

II MAD SCIENTISTS

A staple of the horror film from the earliest days of cinema, the mad scientist is an obsessive, antisocial experimenter with the wild desire to revolutionize the processes of life. Eyes aglow, the mad scientist usually makes his startling breakthrough in painful isolation at the expense of his sanity, which is further undermined by the ridicule of medical colleagues. His one saving grace, Isaac Asimov points out, is his beautiful daughter, which he unfortunately doesn't always have.

The character, an outgrowth of 19th-century mistrust of science, is an updated Prometheus, the ancient Greek Titan who was punished for giving knowledge to mankind by having his liver torn out by a vulture. The image of the mad scientist comes from medieval alchemists, mesmerists and magicians. Alchemy, a precursor of modern chemistry, was aimed chiefly at discovering the philosopher's stone, which was believed to transmute base metals into gold and, when dissolved as an elixir, to confer eternal youth. The laboratories of such alchemists as Albertus Magnus and Paracelsus were

filled with arcane apparatus, furnaces, skeletons and glass tubes of colorful infusions—all standard furnishings in the mad scientist's secret lair. Another influence is the bona fide medical researcher of later centuries who was compelled to buy his cadavers from the "resurrection men," covered in the chapter Ghouls.

Mad scientists appear in both horror and science fiction films, which are often the same thing. But, generally, the horror film is after a gut reaction rather than a cerebral one, and its science is used to alarm rather than enlighten. Seminal mad scientists—who belong to both categories—are Dr. Frankenstein, Dr. Jekyll, Dr. Moreau and the Invisible Man. The sin of pride led Dr. Frankenstein to play God and create an artificial man (listed under Monsters), just as it prompted Dr. Jekyll to swallow his own self-splitting hallucinogenic chemicals. "The study of Nature makes a man at last as remorseless as Nature," declared Dr. Moreau, whose incredible hubris and scalpel-magic painfully transformed animals into men. Each perished at the hands of his creation, which, like so many of mankind's accomplishments, was cast in the image of human imperfection.

The visual style of mad scientist movies was defined by the German cinema (as was so much of early Hollywood moviemaking), which produced such masterworks as ORLACS HAENDE (1925). Americans proved to be as fascinated by quasi-medical chillers as Germans, and the 1930s and 1940s saw a cycle of films in which deranged doctors, either for revenge or to become ruler of the world, continued their unspeakable vivisections. The medical dismemberments of horror movies were always performed in gleaming surgeries in glossy, metallic black and white, in ways that thrilled and frightened audiences.

The key actors during this period were Boris Karloff, Lionel Atwill, George Zucco and Bela Lugosi. Karloff, who began his career playing tormented monsters, stands out from the rest because of his superior acting skill and his uncanny ability to seem both threatening and trustworthy. With his deep, slightly lisping voice and gangling, finely tuned body, Karloff is the quintessential mad scientist. During the 1950s, the scalpel and forceps were passed to Vincent Price and Peter Cushing, whose surgeries were often performed in color and stomach-turning detail.

Now largely a camp menace, the mad scientist was seriously undermined by Peter Sellers as *Dr. Strangelove* (1963), a wheelchair-bound nuclear scientist whose self-animated right hand—like Dr. Orlac's—can't help offering a Nazi salute. The mad scientists of today are the collective forces of progress, whose failures—the possibility of a nuclear holocaust, excessive chemical pollution, nuclear radiation and overpopulation—are discussed in the category Cataclysmic Disasters.

ABBOTT AND COSTELLO MEET THE INVISIBLE MAN

Film   1951   U.S. (Universal-International)
82 minutes   Black & white

The comedy team play detectives who give H.G. Wells's invisibility potion to a framed client, allowing him to find the real murderers. Agreeable flimflam, brightened by John P. Fulton's invisibility effects, the last time they were used.

CREDITS

Director Charles Lamont; *Producer* Howard Christie; *Screenplay* Frederic I. Rinaldo, John Grant, Robert

Abbott & Costello Meet Dr. Jekyll and Mr. Hyde: Karloff plays the two-faced doctor for slapstick.

Lees; *Photographer* Bernard Herzbrun, Richard Riedel; *Special Effects* David S. Horsley; *Makeup* Bud Westmore; *Music* Joseph Gershenson;

CAST

Bud Abbott, Lou Costello, Arthur Franz, Nancy Guild, Sheldon Leonard, William Frawley

THE ABOMINABLE DR. PHIBES

Film   1971   G.B. (AIP)   94 minutes
Movielab

If Busby Berkeley had directed a horror movie, this might have been it. Vincent Price, working that old camp magic, is a deformed genius seeking revenge against a team of surgeons he blames for the death of his wife. Their executions are artfully—and horribly—arranged according to the ten plagues of Egypt. There's a marvelously inventive art deco laboratory, a robot dance band, borrowings from famous genre films, and knowing cliche dialogue—which has gotten funnier with the passage of time. In the finale, Phibes, who eats and speaks through a tube in his throat, joins his wife in a matching coffin and embalms himself to the

The Abominable Dr. Phibes: "Love means never having to say you're ugly."

amplified strains of "Somewhere Over the Rainbow."

The film was so popular that it prompted a sequel, *Dr. Phibes Rises Again*, released a year later. Also directed by Robert Fuest (who made a name for himself with the horror-oriented TV series *The Avengers*), it gave Price his first and only continuing genre character. Journeying by boat to Egypt, Phibes sets out to find the lost River of Life to revive the corpse of his wife, which he has brought with him. When he discovers that several fellow passengers are archaeologists on the same quest, he narrows the field with the same malicious elan displayed previously. (One voyager is stuffed into a huge bottle and labeled "Not Wanted on Voyage," and another is squeezed to death in an accordionlike bed.) Slogan of the series was "Love means never having to say you're ugly," a play on the catch phrase of the forgotten superhit of the early 1970s, *Love Story*.

CREDITS

Director Robert Fuest; *Producer* Louis M. Heyward; *Screenplay* James Whiton, William Goldstein; *Photographer* Norman Warwick; *Production Designer* Brian Eatwell; *Special Effects* George Blackwell; *Makeup* Trevor Cole-Rees; *Music* Basil Kirchen

CAST

Vincent Price, Joseph Cotten, Hugh Griffith, Terry-Thomas, Virginia North, Aubrey Woods, Susan Travers, Caroline Munro

THE APE

Film   1940   U.S. (Monogram)
61 minutes   Black & white

Karloff, in a gentler mood, is a selfless M.D. who develops a medicine that will cure a young girl's polio. To obtain the key ingredient, human spinal fluid, he dresses in a gorilla suit—with a syringe pocket—and calls on the town nasties. Karloff finished his Monogram contract with this low-energy vehicle.

CREDITS

Director William Nigh; *Producer* Scott R. Dunlap; *Screenplay:* Curt Siodmak, Richard Carroll, based on the play by Adam Hull Shirk; *Photographer* Harry Neumann; *Musical Director* Edward Kay

CAST

Boris Karloff, Maris Wrixon, Henry Hall, Gertrude Hoffman, Gene O'Donnell

THE ASPHYX

Film   1972   G.B. (Glendale)
99 minutes   Color

Did you know that the human body possesses an "asphyx," a demonlike spirit that escapes at the moment of death? Talented actor Robert Stephens helps suspend disbelief playing an Edwardian researcher who traps his own asphyx in a box, with the intention of staying alive forever. The trick ending is a good one.

CREDITS

Director Peter Newbrook; *Producer* John Brittany; *Screenplay* Brian Comport; *Idea* Christina Beers; *Photographer* Freddie Young; *Art Director* John Stoll; *Special Effects* Ted Samuels; *Music* Bill McGuffie

CAST

Robert Stephens, Robert Powell, Jane Lapotaire, Ralph Arliss, Alex Scott, Fiona Walker

THE AWFUL DOCTOR ORLOFF

Film   1961   France/Spain (Rosson)
86 minutes   Black & white
Released 1964 U.S. (Sigma III)

Beautiful young women fall victim to a deranged plastic surgeon who peels off their skin to graft on his disfigured wife. *Awful* is the word for it.

CREDITS

Director/Screenplay Jess Franco; *Producer* Serge Newman; *Photographer* Godfredo Pacheco; *Music* Pagan and Ramirez Angel

CAST

Howard Vernon, Diana Lorys, Conrado San Martin, Marin Silva

BEACH GIRLS AND THE MONSTER

Film   1965   U.S. (U.S. Films)
70 minutes   Black & white

A shabby drive-in exploiter pegged to AIP's *Beach Blanket* series. Director Jon Hall, Hollywood's former sarong king, is a sight as a paunchy, seaweed covered brute who chases surfing beauties.

CREDITS

Director Jon Hall; *Producer* Edward Janis; *Screenplay* Joan Gardner; *Music* Frank Sinatra, Jr.

CAST

Jon Hall, Sue Casey, Dale Davis, Walker Edmiston, Arnold Lessing

BEN

Film   1972   U.S. (Bing Crosby Productions)
94 minutes   Color

Ben, the popular superintelligent rodent of WIL-LARD (1970), gets title billing in the sequel. After a reprise of the previous film's ending, Ben makes friends with another introverted misfit, a little boy invalided by a heart condition, who passes the time writing songs. Conflict is lacking this time around, with the story concentrating on the friendship between boy and beast. As much fairy tale as hor-ror story, *Ben* sacrifices dramatic reality by attempting the transcendental kind: Its likable rodent is merely trying to lead its misunderstood "people" to a little food and living space. The syrupy title tune, a love song to a rat, became a no. one hit.

CREDITS

Director Phil Karlson; *Producer* Mort Briskin; *Screenplay* Gilbert A. Ralston, based on characters created by Stephen Gilbert; *Photographer* Russell Metty; *Special Effects* Howard A. Anderson Co., Bud David; *Music* Walter Scharf; *Animal Trainer* Moe Di Sesso

CAST

Danny Garrison, Joseph Campanella, Arthur O'Connell, Rosemary Murphy, Meredith Baxter, Kaz Garas

THE BLACK SLEEP

Film   1956   U.S. (United Artists/Bel Air)
81 minutes   Black & white

Hollywood's faded horror stars deserved a better reunion than this grisly rubbish. Victorian surgeon Basil Rathbone makes monsters out of Akim Tamiroff, Lon Chaney Jr. and John Carradine. Bela Lugosi, looking withered after enduring a cure for drug addiction, comes off best, as Rathbone's mute butler.

CREDITS

Director Reginald LeBorg; *Producer* Howard W. Koch; *Screenplay* John C. Higgins; *Photographer* Gordon Avil; *Art Director* Bob Kinoshita; *Special Effects* Jack Rabin, Louis De Witt; *Makeup* George Bau; *Music* Les Baxter

CAST

Basil Rathbone, Akim Tamiroff, Lon Chaney, Jr., John Carradine, Bela Lugosi, Phyllis Stanley, Tor Johnson

BLACK ZOO

Film   1962   U.S. (Allied Artists)
88 minutes   Eastmancolor   Panavision

Animals in a private Los Angeles zoo savage the enemies of their keeper. Passable chiller, with Michael Gough pulling out all the stops as a demented Dr. Doolittle.

CREDITS

Director Robert Gordon; *Producer* Herman Cohen; *Screenplay* Aben Kandel, Herman Cohen; *Photographer* Floyd Crosby; *Art Director* William Glasgow; *Special Effects* Pat Dinga; *Music* Paul Dunlap

CAST

Michael Gough, Rod Lauren, Jeanne Cooper, Virginia Grey, Jerome Cowan, Elisha Cook, Jr., Marianna Hill

THE BOOGIE MAN WILL GET YOU

Film   1942   U.S. (Columbia)   66 minutes
Black & white

Wartime whimsey conceived as a vehicle for Karloff, who had recently shown a flair for comedy in Broadway's *Arsenic and Old Lace.* Karloff and Lorre trade quips as mad scientists attempting to create supersoldiers in the cellar of a busy country hotel.

CREDITS

Director Lew Landers; *Producer* Colbert Clark; *Screenplay* Edwin Blum; *Photographer* Henry Freulich; *Art Director* Robert Peterson; *Musical Director* Morris Stoloff

CAST

Boris Karloff, Peter Lorre, Maxie Rosenbloom, Larry Parks, Jeff Donnell, Don Beddoe

BRIDE OF THE MONSTER

Film   1956   U.S. (Rolling M)   70 minutes
Black & white

The wonderfully abysmal "science fiction" classic, directed, produced and co-written by transvestite Edward D. Wood, Jr. Mad scientist Bela Lugosi dabbles with radiation to create a race of atomic supermen, several of whom are fed to a giant killer octopus before the lab is blown to bits by a nuclear explosion. (The film is definitely *against* the arms race.) Woods' atomic-ray machine looks suspiciously like an old photographic enlarger, and the apocalyptic finale is obviously government newsreel footage of an H-bomb test. It might have been funnier if not for the sad spec-

tacle of Lugosi, seriously ill and undergoing a breakdown, gamely trying to wrap fake rubber tentacles around his body.

CREDITS

Director/Producer Edward D. Wood, Jr.; *Screenplay* Edward D. Wood, Jr., Alex Gordon; *Photographer* William C. Thompson; *Special Effects* Pat Dinga; *Music* Frank Worth

CAST

Bela Lugosi, Eddie Parker (Lugosi's double), Tony McCoy, Loretta King, William Benedict, Tor Johnson

The Brood: Children born of psychotic rage savage their natural "sister" (Cindy Hinds).

THE BROOD

Film   1979   Canada (New World)
91 minutes   Color

Cult favorite David Cronenberg has something to say about loss of love in the American family, and it's authentically soul-freezing. The scene is the Somafree Institute of Psychoplasmics in Toronto, where Dr. Hal Raglan (Oliver Reed) teaches patients to liberate their psi powers and manifest mental disorders physically as welts and bruises. The technique eventually gets out of control, however, and one patient grows an analagous tumor that dangles cancerously from his throat. Raglan's star patient, with whom he is in love, is a beautiful but hopelessly insane redhead (Samantha Eggar) who was badly beaten by her mother as a child. Although she seems to have improved, her incurable psychosis has spawned a liberating brood of murderous children from a womblike growth on her body. The startling creatures, which resemble snow-suited elves, attack the woman's mother by jumping from a kitchen cabinet and later murder her father by crawling from under the bed while he's removing his shoes.

As in THE PARASITE MURDERS (1975) and *Rabid* (1977) Cronenberg displays a morbid fascination with disease as a metaphor for moral corruption. His fondness of disgusting, taboo images of lesions, growths and open sores undoubtedly have a lot to do with his own psyche. But they are also a highly effective way of scaring hell out of the "me" generation by showing that fit bodies can change overnight into our enemies by natural forces beyond our control. And Cronenberg's mad scientist—a clever variation on the old role Karloff and Atwill used to play—personifies every primal quack who ever came out of the 1960s.

CREDITS

Director/Screenplay David Cronenberg; *Producer* Claude Heroux; *Photographer* Mark Irwin; *Art Director* Carol Spier; *Makeup* Shonagh Jabour; *Special Effects Makeup* Jack Young, Dennis Pike; *Music* Howard Shore

CAST

Oliver Reed, Samantha Eggar, Art Hindle, Cindy Hinds, Nuala Fitzgerald, Henry Beckman

CAPTIVE WILD WOMAN

Film   1942   U.S. (Universal)   61 minutes
Black & white

A glandular specialist transplants his nurse's brain into the body of a circus ape named Cheela, who begins to look like sultry Acquanetta, the studio's second-string Dorothy Lamour. She becomes jealous when her trainer takes a fiancee, however, and has to be destroyed. An atmospheric, lightly likable programmer that emphasizes the physical attributes of its sarong-clad star, with animal footage lifted from *The Big Cage* (1933). Sequels: JUNGLE WOMAN (1944) and JUNGLE CAPTIVE (1945).

CREDITS

Director Edward Dmytrk; *Producer* Ben Pivar; *Screenplay* Henry Sucher, Griffin Jay; *Story* Ted Fithian, Neil

P. Varnick, Maurice Pivar; *Photographer* George Robinson; *Art Director* John B. Goodman; *Makeup* Jack Pierce; *Music* Hans J. Salter

CAST

Acquanetta, John Carradine, Evelyn Ankers, Milburn Stone, Lloyd Corrigan, Fay Helm

CIRCUS OF HORRORS

Film   1960   G.B. (Lynx/Independent Artists)
91 minutes   Eastmancolor

A straightforward well-knit chiller about a plastic surgeon who botches an operation and hides out in a circus peopled by criminals whose faces he has altered. When several of his mutilated performers rebel, he almost gets away with murder by staging a series of circus accidents: a knife-thrower misses, a trapeze rope breaks, etc. Not a new idea but a serviceable one.

CREDITS

Director Sidney Hayes; *Producers* Julian Wintle, Leslie Parkyn; *Screenplay* George Baxt; *Photographer* Douglas Slocombe; *Art Director* Jack Shampan; *Makeup* Trevor Crole-Rees; *Music* Franz Reizenstein, Muir Mathieson

CAST

Anton Diffring, Yvonne Monlaur, Donald Pleasence, Erika Remberg, Jack Gwylim, Jane Hylton, Kenneth Griffith

THE CLAW MONSTERS

Film   1966   U.S. (Republic)
100 minutes   Black & white

A mad chemist guarding his African diamond mine with crawfish grown to giant size is undone by a female Tarzan and her big-game hunter boyfriend. Antique camp culled from the lively 12-episode cliffhanger *Panther Girl of the Congo* (1955), Republic's final serial.

CREDITS

Director Franklin Adreon

CAST

Phyllis Coates, Myron Healey, Arthur Space, John Day, Mike Ragan

CORRIDORS OF BLOOD

Film 1958 G.B. (Producers Assoc.)
87 minutes Black & white

Two legendary horror stars met onscreen for the first time in this tidy little thriller: Boris Karloff and Christopher Lee, his successor as the Frankenstein Monster. Karloff is up to form as a humanitarian doctor who discovers an anesthetic, then slips round the bend when he becomes addicted to it. Lee is a body snatcher who supplies the doctor with research materials. The film was released in the United States in 1962.

CREDITS

Director Robert Day; *Producer* John Croydon; *Screenplay* Jean Scott Rogers; *Photographer* Geoffrey Faithful; *Art Director* Anthony Masters; *Music* Buxton Orr

CAST

Boris Karloff, Christopher Lee, Finlay Currie, Betta St. John, Frank Pettingell, Adrienne Corri

CURSE OF THE FLY

Film 1965 G.B. (20th Century-Fox)
85 minutes Black & white

The second sequel to THE FLY (1958), also in black and white, is considerably more interesting than its predecessor, RETURN OF THE FLY (1959). Brian Donlevy and George Baker are the final members of the Delambre clan to plug away on the old matter-transmitter, and, as usual, people and things get horribly transmogrified during the journey—between London and Montreal this time. We've seen it before, so the film concentrates on the mentally unstable Mrs. Delambre, fresh out of one madhouse and married into another, who's somewhat startled by the monstrosities in her husband's toolshed. Spalding's script intriguingly suggests their relationship is not the healthy one it appears to be.

CREDITS

Director Don Sharp; *Producers* Robert L. Lippert, Jack Parsons; *Screenplay* Harry Spalding, based on characters created by George Langelaan; *Photographer* Basil Emmett; *Special Effects* Harold Fletcher; *Makeup* Eleanor Jones; *Music* Bert Shefter

CAST

Brian Donlevy, George Baker, Carol Gray, Jeremy Wilkins, Michael Graham, Stan Simmons (the creature)

THE DEADLY DREAM

TV film 1971 U.S. (ABC) 75 minutes
Color

Burned out from long hours spent manipulating genes to enhance intelligence, a biochemist suffers tortured nights dreaming he is the defendant in a strange, ritualistic trial that condemns his "immoral" experiment. An intriguing bit of sleight of hand that'll keep you wondering if it's really only a nightmare.

CREDITS

Director Alf Kjellin; *Producer* Stan Sheptner; *Screenplay* Barry Oringer; *Photographer* Jack Marta; *Music* Dave Gruson

CAST

Lloyd Bridges, Janet Leigh, Leif Erickson, Don Stroud, Carl Betz, Richard Jaeckel

THE DEVIL BAT

Film 1940 U.S. (PRC) 69 minutes
Black & white

Lugosi and a devil bat? Sounds like a vampire movie, but it's actually a mad-scientist programmer, with Lugosi sending out a killer bat trained to respond to a shaving lotion, given to executives of a cosmetics company. The sequel, in name only, is DEVIL BAT'S DAUGHTER (1946). The original story turned up again in *The Flying Serpent* (1946), with George Zucco caging the bird-god Chetzequtel and ordering it to kill anyone wearing a certain feather.

CREDITS

Director Jean Yarbrough; *Producer* Jack Gallagher; *Screenplay* John Thomas Neville; *Photographer* Arthur Martinelli; *Art Director* Paul Palmentola; *Music* David Chudnow

CAST

Bela Lugosi, Dave O'Brien, Suzanne Kaaren, Guy Usher, Yoland Mallott

DEVIL BAT'S DAUGHTER

Film   1946   U.S. (PRC)   67 minutes
Black & white

The long unawaited sequel to THE DEVIL BAT (1940), concerning a murderous psychiatrist who tries to frame a female patient by claiming she's a self-styled vampire.

CREDITS

Director/Producer Frank Wisbar; *Screenplay* Griffin Jay; *Photographer* James S. Brown, Jr.; *Art Director* Edward C. Jewell; *Makeup* Bud Westmore; *Music* Alexander Steinert

CAST

Rosemary La Planche, John James, Molly Lamont, Michael Hale, Nolan Leary

THE DEVIL COMMANDS

Film   1941   U.S. (Columbia)   66 minutes
Black & white

Karloff is pure gold as Dr. Julian Blair, a scientist/psychic attempting to make contact with his beloved late wife. To prove his theory that the dead leave their brainwaves behind them, he robs a graveyard and uses the old electrical spark-gap trick to make the bodies act as mediums. Karloff seems not to notice how threadbare some of the sets look, or how incredible his experiment is. He's all business seating his daughter among corpses helmeted with wired steel cones and telling her not to be nervous.

CREDITS

Director Edward Dmytryk; *Producer* Wallace MacDonald; *Screenplay* Robert D. Andrews, Milton Gunzburg, based on the novel *The Edge of Running Water* by William Sloane; *Photographer* Allen Siegler; *Special Sound Effects* Phil Faulkner; *Musical Director* Morris Stoloff

CAST

Boris Karloff, Amanda Duff, Anne Revere, Richard Fiske, Ralph Penney, Dorothy Adams

THE DEVIL DOLL

Film   1936   U.S. (MGM)   79 minutes
Black & white

A banker convicted of a crime he didn't commit returns to Paris from Devil's Island with a serum which can reduce human beings to the size of dolls. Disguised as a motherly old toy peddler, he visits the apartment houses of the men who framed him and gives each a murderous living doll. Creaky now, but still impressive are the miniaturization effects—the first used in a feature film—achieved with traveling mattes and oversized sets. Lionel Barrymore is great fun as the banker in drag (although his voice wouldn't fool anyone), as is his aide-de-camp Rafaela Ottiano, excitedly clucking during an experiment, "We'll make the whole world *small!*" Tod Browning left the genre after this film, which recalls his *The Unholy Three*, a 1925 silent in which Lon Chaney dressed as a woman and burglarized houses with a midget disguised as a baby. The tiny people were seen previously in BRIDE OF FRANKENSTEIN (1935) (see Monsters). The 1964 *Devil Doll*, an unrelated British production, has a ventriloquist out of DEAD OF NIGHT (see Anthologies) injecting a human soul into his puppet.

CREDITS

Director Tod Browning; *Producer* E. J. Mannix; *Screenplay* Garrett Fort, Guy Endore, Erich von Stroheim, based on the novel *Burn Witch Burn* by Abraham Merritt; *Photographer* Leonard Smith; *Art Director* Cedric Gibbons; *Music* Franz Waxman

CAST

Lionel Barrymore, Maureen O'Sullivan, Frank Lawton, Henry B. Walthall, Rafaela Ottiano, Pedro de Cordoba

DR. BLOOD'S COFFIN

Film   1960   G.B. (United Artists)
92 minutes   Black & white

Biochemist Peter Blood intends to resurrect great minds of the past with hearts transplanted from executed criminals, but he gets only as far as the husband of the widow who spurned him. Despite a successful surgery with gleaming scalpels, the corpse is still rotten—just like this movie.

CREDITS

Director Sidney J. Furie; *Producer* George Fowler; *Screenplay* Jerry Juran; *Photographer* Stephen Dade; *Special Effects* Les Bowie, Peter Nelson; *Music* Buxton Orr

CAST

Kieron Moore, Hazel Court, Ian Hunter, Kenneth J. Warren, Gerald C. Lawson

DR. JEKYLL AND MR. HYDE

Film   1920   U.S. (Famous Players-Lasky)
63 minutes   Black & white (silent)

Matinee idol John Barrymore, then at the peak of his movie popularity, took the genre a giant step forward with his meaty portrayal of Robert Louis Stevenson's fragmented mad scientist. Although grainy and primitive by today's standards, the film retains the vigor of its source, and Barrymore makes an impressively fanged and taloned Hyde. Given to highly theatrical roles, the actor managed to please both his feminine admirers as the dashing Dr. Jekyll and himself as the character's appallingly fantastic alter ego (these sequences were originally tinted green). Clara Berenger's script, an adaptation of a play version by Thomas R. Sullivan, introduces a Freudian element into the story by giving Jekyll/Hyde two girlfriends, one virtuous, the other promiscuous, to dramatize his dual nature and sexually fragmented personality. A low-budget ripoff of the Barrymore film was released later that year, with Sheldon Lewis dreaming it all in New York (where both films were shot) rather than London. The producer of the ripoff was former junk dealer Louis B. Mayer, later to become head of MGM.

Undoubtedly the cinema's most popular mad scientist (outranking even Dr. Frankenstein, who often isn't in his Monster's films), Jekyll/Hyde has appeared on the screen at least 25 times. The first version was 1908's *Dr. Jekyll and Mr. Hyde*, a 15-minute film record of a touring company performing a theatrical adaptation on a Chicago stage. The play was written by the above-mentioned Thomas R. Sullivan in 1887 and had starred popular favorite Richard Mansfield in New York, wearing a ghoulish-green makeup. Next came 1910's *Den Skebnesvangre Opfindelse*, made in Denmark. In 1912 another American version starred James Cruze, who went on to become a successful director. This one is unique in that it used two actors for the title role. The year 1913 brought a bumper crop, including the German *Der Januskopf*, which pirated the story to avoid copyright fees; a British *Dr. Jekyll and Mr. Hyde*, shot in an early color process called Kineto-Kinemacolor; and an American version from Universal. Foremost among the silents, however, is the prestige production that starred Barrymore.

Sound versions of the strange duo include DR. JEKYLL AND MR. HYDE (1932), considered the definitive filmization; DR. JEKYLL AND MR. HYDE (1941); SON OF DR. JEKYLL (1951); *Abbott and Costello Meet Dr. Jekyll and Mr. Hyde* (1953); *Daughter of Dr. Jekyll* (1957); MONSTER ON THE CAMPUS (1958); *The Ugly Duckling* (1959); THE TWO FACES OF DR. JEKYLL (1960); *Le Testament du Dr. Cordelier* (1961); *The Nutty Professor* (1963), a Jerry Lewis comedy; I, MONSTER (1970); DR. JEKYLL AND SISTER HYDE, *Dr. Jekyll and the Wolfman* (both 1971); *Dr. Black, Mr. Hyde* (1975); *Dr. Jekyll's Dungeon of Death* (1979); *Dr. Hekyll and Mr. Hype* (1980), a parody starring Oliver Reed and directed by Charles B. Griffith; and *Jekyll and Hyde . . . Together Again* (1982), an unfunny comedy starring Mark Blankfield as a doctor-turned-punk. Paramount never released it theatrically.

On television, the story has been aired on the *Climax* series (1954–58), with Michael Rennie as Jekyll/Hyde. TV films include *Dr. Jekyll and Mr. Hyde* (1973), a musical (!) version starring Kirk Douglas, directed by David Winters and filmed in England; THE STRANGE CASE OF DR. JEKYLL AND MR. HYDE (1974); *The Darker Side of Terror* (1979); and *Dr. Jekyll and Mr. Hyde* (1980), a BBC-TV movie starring David Hemmings.

CREDITS

Director John S. Robertson; *Producer* Adolph Zukor; *Screenplay* Clara Berenger, based on the play by Thomas R. Sullivan, adapted from the novella by Robert Louis Stevenson; *Photographer* Roy Overbaugh; *Art Directors* Robert Hass, Charles O. Sessel

CAST

John Barrymore, Nita Naldi, Brandon Hurst, Martha Mansfield, Louis Wolheim, George Stevens

DR. JEKYLL AND MR. HYDE

Film   1932   U.S. (Paramount)
90 minutes   Black & white

The cinema's definitive Jekyll/Hyde, this robust remake was nominated for several Academy

Dr. Jekyll and Mr. Hyde (1932): Frederic March and Miriam Hopkins still smolder as the sadistic Hyde and bad girl Ivy.

Awards and won Frederic March the genre's only Oscar for best actor. March, giving a remarkable performance, metamorphoses from Dr. Jekyll to Mr. Hyde in full view and assumes a totally different walk, posture and voice. (The well-guarded transformation "secret" was accomplished partially in-camera with red and blue lens filters which, when removed, revealed lines and hollows painted on March's face; the fangs, hair and heavy brow were added in stages and smoothed with dissolves. The effect was later duplicated in Paramount's Jerry Lewis parody, *The Nutty Professor* [1963]).

While March's bestial Neanderthal is a movie invention, the concept is faithful to Stevenson's implication that man's evil evolved from his animal heritage rather than from the religious concept of original sin. In the novel Hyde is a younger, handsome version of Jekyll, and his vile nature is suggested by his attitude rather than by his appearance. (The film's idea of a monstrous Hyde points up the story's subconscious link to the werewolf legend.) And Jekyll wasn't quite the respectable healer usually seen in the movies. Rather, he was a man as fascinated by his libertine, aggressive side as he was repulsed by it. In an attempt to free himself of what he naively believed to be his "extraneous evil," Dr. Jekyll concocted an elixir which

instead created a nasty alter ego called Mr. Hyde. Prowling through London by night, he enjoyed the perverse pleasures of the flesh and finally committed murder. When he decided to end the experiment, Jekyll found that the antidote no longer worked, and that he had permanently changed into Hyde. Wanted by the police and no longer able to disguise himself, he committed suicide by drinking a beaker of poison. In this film version, he changes back into Jekyll, establishing the movie tradition of monsters returning to their normal appearance.

Filmmaker Rouben Mamoulian—who had directed Garbo in *Queen Christina* and helmed such classics as *Applause* and *Love Me Tonight*—creates an evocative visual equivalent of Stevenson's story with fogbound London sets, unexpected camera angles and a dizzying, hallucinogenic 360-degree pan during the transformation scene. Especially effective is Mamoulian's use of sound as an instrument of psychological terror. The amplified heartbeat, remembered by everyone who sees the film, was Mamoulian's own. Surprisingly steamy are the love scenes between Hyde and bad-girl Ivy (Miriam Hopkins), which were cut by censors when Hollywood established a production code during the mid-1930s.

CREDITS

Director/Producer Rouben Mamoulian; *Screenplay* Samuel Hoffenstein, Percy Heath, based on the novella by Robert Louis Stevenson; *Photographer* Karl Struss; *Art Director* Hans Dreier; *Makeup* Wally Westmore; *Music* Schumann

CAST

Frederic March, Miriam Hopkins, Rose Hobart, Holmes Herbert, Halliwell Hobbes, Edgar Norton, Arnold Lucy, Tempe Piggott

DR. JEKYLL AND MR. HYDE

Film   1941   U.S. (MGM)   127 minutes
Black & white

MGM's high-gloss remake has a lot of things going for it—an all-star "golden age" cast, lush Victorian decor and a romantic score by Franz Waxman—but terror isn't one of them. Lead Spencer Tracy chose to play Hyde with a minimum of makeup, and as a result the character comes across as more mean-spirited than malevolent. The deficiency was noted by writer Somerset Maugham, who reportedly asked while visiting the set, "Which one is he playing now?" Tracy's transformation

Dr. Jekyll and Mr. Hyde (1941): A drug-induced high barely alters Spencer Tracy's appearance in MGM's lavish remake.

scenes are augmented by a cliche montage sequence used to show his Freudian confusion, which seems to suggest that the potion has hallucinogenic qualities. Director Victor Fleming, fresh off the plantation after *Gone with the Wind* (1939), wisely cast Ingrid Bergman against type as Ivy, the bad girl, her favorite role.

CREDITS

Director/Producer Victor Fleming; *Screenplay* John Lee Mahin, based on *The Strange Case of Dr. Jekyll and Mr. Hyde* by Robert Louis Stevenson; *Photographer* Joseph Ruttenberg; *Art Director* Cedric Gibbons; *Montage Effects* Peter Ballbusch; *Special Effects* Warren Newcombe; *Makeup* Jack Dawn; *Music* Franz Waxman

CAST

Spencer Tracy, Ingrid Bergman, Lana Turner, Donald Crisp, Ian Hunter, C. Aubrey Smith, Sara Allgood

DR. JEKYLL AND SISTER HYDE

*Film   1971   G.B. (Hammer)   97 minutes
Technicolor*

More and more folks seemed to be switching sexes during the liberated sixties, a phenomenon not unnoticed at Hammer which was then shopping for new drag for its horror veterans. The title gives away the plot, but you might be surprised to find present Jack (or more properly, Jill) the Ripper and body snatchers Burke and Hare. Leads Bates and Beswick look enough alike to bring off the transformation, although they are less successful at playing the script's sly comedy. Best moment comes when the good doctor, courting a brother and sister as his twin selves, forgets his sex and makes a play for the brother. The scene is usually edited from TV screenings.

CREDITS

Director Roy Ward Baker; *Producers* Albert Fennell, Brian Clemens; *Screenplay* Brian Clemens; *Photographer* Norman Warwick; *Makeup* John Wilcox; *Music* David Whitaker

CAST

Ralph Bates, Martine Beswick, Gerald Sim, Lewis Fiander, Susan Broderick

DR. X

*Film   1932   U.S. (Warner Bros.)
82 minutes   Two-strip Technicolor*

A fiendish cannibalistic killer, who strikes only during the full moon, leads detectives to a spooky gabled mansion at Blackstone Shoals, perched atop a Long Island cliff. A horror whodunit, the film alternately tantalizes, titillates and terrifies before finally revealing the murderer's identity (you'll probably guess who but not why). Based on a Broadway Gothic, the film shows its theatrical origins, but Curtiz's direction is brisk and there's barely a dull moment. On hand is the incomparable Lionel Atwill in the title role, Fay Wray shrieking her way to a date with KING KONG (see Monsters), Preston Foster as an amputee scientist who grows a synthetic arm and Lee Tracy slinging wisecracks as a nosy reporter. The *piece de resistance* is a bizarre laboratory with secret panels designed by expressionist art director Anton Grot.

This is the first genre film to be shot in Technicolor, although Chaney's THE PHANTOM OF THE

OPERA (1925) (see Crazies and Freaks) included several scenes in the two-strip process. After honoring a commitment to the Technicolor Corporation, studio head Jack Warner decided it was good enough to succeed without the added expense of color and, except for initial prestige bookings, subsequent prints were released in black and white—the only version available to television. In 1939 Warner followed up with RETURN OF DR. X (see Vampires), a sequel in name only.

CREDITS

Director Michael Curtiz; *Producer* Hal Wallis; *Screenplay* Robert Tasker, Earl Baldwin, based on the play by Howard W. Comstock, Allen C. Miller; *Photographer* Richard Tower, Ray Rennahan; *Art Director* Anton Grot; *Makeup Special Effects* Max Factor; *Musical Director* Leo F. Forbstein

CAST

Preston Foster, Lionel Atwill, Fay Wray, Mae Busch, Lee Tracy, John Wray, Arthur Edmund Carewe, Robert Warwick

EMBRYO

Film   1976   U.S. (Cine Artists)
105 minutes   DeLuxe

A medical researcher experimenting with a growth hormone brings an aborted fetus to term, then finds he can't stop the growth process. The baby quickly grows into a beautiful 25-year-old woman who, upset at the prospect of a short life span, becomes a vengeful murderer. For all its high-tech ambience and professional gloss *Embryo* ultimately fails because of its obsolete premise, popularized in the silent film *Alraune* (1928). That a human being created "artificially" would be soulless and inherently evil seems quaintly remote in an era of fetal transplants and test-tube babies.

CREDITS

Director Ralph Nelson; *Producers* Arnold H. Orgolini, Anita Doohan; *Screenplay* Anita Doohan, Jack W. Thomas; *Photographer* Fred Koenkamp; *Art Director* Joe Alves; *Special Effects* Roy Arbogast, Bill Shourt; *Music* Gil Melle

CAST

Rock Hudson, Diane Ladd, Barbara Carrera, Roddy McDowall, Anne Schedeen

FIRESTARTER

Film   1984   U.S. (Dino De Laurentiis/Universal)
115 minutes   Technicolor   Dolby Stereo

Stephen King's overheated word processor may have given him the idea for this hokey science fiction effort. Little Charlene—nicknamed Charlie—possesses the power of pyrokinesis, the result of government-sponsored experiments on the pituitary glands of her parents. Her fires are stylishly staged, but the story is as preposterous as THE FURY, which was directed by Brian De Palma, who also helmed CARRIE (see Crazies and Freaks), another King story about terrible, emotionally spawned psychic powers. Drew Barrymore, the winsome child of *E.T. The Extra-Terrestrial* (1982), is first-rate, but George C. Scott goes over the top as a one-eyed villain with a gray pony tail.

CREDITS

Director Mark L. Lester; *Producer* Frank Capra, Jr.; *Screenplay* Stanley Mann, based on the novel by Stephen King; *Photographer* Guiseppe Ruzzolini; *Art Director* Giorgio Postiglione; *Pyrotechnics* Jeff Jarvis; *Music* Tangerine Dream

CAST

David Keith, Drew Barrymore, Martin Sheen, George C. Scott, Freddie Jones, Heather Locklear, Louise Fletcher, Moses Gunn, Art Carney

THE FLY

Film   1958   U.S. (20th Century-Fox)
94 minutes   Eastmancolor   CinemaScope

Contemporary audiences expecting the usual fifties giant insect fare were treated instead to a well-made, grisly joke on the old crazy-experiment-gone-wrong idea. Young scientist David Hedison invents a matter transmitter, that science fiction standby which changes people and things into energy and reconstitutes them in a receiver (think of the Transporter Room of *Star Trek*). All goes well until he tries to transmit his own body across the laboratory. The fly in the ointment is that there is a fly in the teleportation cabin. When they rematerialize, neither is one or the other: He has the fly's arm and head, and the fly has his. At the end of the film, the scientist kills himself with the help of his wife by squashing the grotesque head in a hydraulic press. Nobody bothers to explain how

The Fly: A botched experiment creates marital problems for researcher David Hedison and wife Patricia Owens.

he is able to retain his human brain, or why the man's head on the fly's body is able to speak. But no matter. The implausibilities are compensated by a galvanizing climax in which the fly, trapped in a spider's web on the scientist's patio, cries in a faint squeak, "Help me! Help me!"

The film's source is a story by George Langelaan, published in *Playboy* magazine, which had become an increasingly important showcase for horror writers. Intended as a quick-buck programmer to exploit the market developed by AIP and Britain's Hammer studio, the film drew viewers in droves. Consequently, Fox, traditionally a non-horror studio, made two sequels: RETURN OF THE FLY (1959) and CURSE OF THE FLY (1963). Ben Nye's alarming fly mask—consisting of plastic beads, painted turkey feathers, clay and sponge rubber—appears in the first sequel only. A remake was scheduled for 1986.

CREDITS

Director/Producer Kurt Neumann; *Screenplay* James Clavell; *Story* George Langelaan; *Photographer* Karl Struss; *Art Directors* Lyle R. Wheeler, Theobald Holsopple; *Special Effects* Lyle B. Abbott; *Makeup* Ben Nye; *Music* Paul Sawtell

CAST

David Hedison, Patricia Owens, Vincent Price, Herbert Marshall, Charles Herbert, Kathleen Freeman

FROM HELL IT CAME

Film   1957   U.S. (Allied Artists)
71 minutes   Black & white

A witch doctor unjustly executed by his tribe reincarnates as a vengeful tree-man with mobile roots. The mythical African monster, called a Nabonga, is unique—and it's also hilarious as depicted here.

CREDITS

Director Dan Milner; *Producer* Jack Milner; *Screenplay* Richard Bernstein; *Photographer* Bryon Baker; *Art Director* Rudi Field; *Tree Costume* Paul Blaisdell; *Music* Darrell Calker

CAST

Tod Andrews, Tina Carver, Linda Watkin, Gregg Palmer, John McNamara

THE FURY

Film   1978   U.S. (20th Century-Fox)
118 minutes   De Luxe

A government superspy locks horns with a secret government agency which has kidnapped his superpsychic son to harness the boy's telekinetic powers. Writer John Farris attempts to make the special effects believable by accelerating the post-Watergate paranoia of his best-seller, while discarding some important story bits. Director De Palma fills the plot holes with a parade of violent CARRIE-like scenes (see Crazies and Freaks) each more shocking, and less effective, than the last. The ending, although stunning, is so badly timed that when John Cassavetes explodes, you're compelled to laugh in disbelief. Rick Baker created the convincing dummy head, and Cassavetes's woeful blood-discharging eyes are the work of Morton K. Greenspoon, Hollywood's special effects optometrist.

The story's comic possibilities were explored in a clunker, *Zapped* (1983), which plays like a near-parody of *The Fury*. In this one, directed by Howard Schuster and scripted by Bruce Rubin and Robert J. Rosenthal, teen telekinetic Scott Baio pops open the blouses of beautiful girls and whips off their dresses. Highlight of the film is a vomiting contest at an amusement park. For some really terrifying telekinetics, see CARRIE and SCANNERS.

CREDITS

Director Brian De Palma; *Producer* Frank Yablans; *Screenplay* John Farris, based on his novel; *Photographer* Richard H. Kline; *Production Designer* Bill Malley; *Special Effects* A. D. Flowers; *Makeup* William Tuttle; *Special Effects Makeup* Rick Baker; *Music* John Williams

CAST

Kirk Douglas, John Cassavetes, Carrie Snodgress, Charles Durning, Andrew Stevens, Amy Irving, Fiona Lewis

THE HAND OF DEATH

Film   1961   U.S. (20th Century-Fox)
60 minutes   Black & white

Researcher John Agar contaminates himself with a nerve gas that imparts a poisonous touch. Director Gene Nelson showed more talent as a dancer in such films as *Oklahoma* (1955).

CREDITS

Director Gene Nelson; *Producer/Screenplay* Eugene Ling; *Photographer* Floyd Crosby; *Art Director* Harry Reif; *Makeup* Robert Mark; *Music* Sonny Burke

CAST

John Agar, Paula Raymond, Roy Gordon, Steve Dunne, John Alonzo

HORROR HOSPITAL

Film   1973   G.B. (Noteworthy Films)
91 minutes   Color

Michael Gough camps it up—as only Michael Gough can—playing a nutty doctor who disguises his nefarious laboratory as a health spa. The satire is blunt-edged, but Gough and an impudent dwarf assistant furnish a chuckle or two.

CREDITS

Director Anthony Balch; *Producer* Richard Gordon; *Screenplay* Alan Watson; *Photographer* David McDonald; *Art Director* David Bill; *Music* De Wolfe

CAST

Michael Gough, Vanessa Shaw, Robin Askwith, Ellen Pollock, Skip Martin, Dennis Price

I BURY THE LIVING

Film   1957   U.S. (Maxim)   76 minutes
Black & white

A cemetery overseer discovers he can kill people by sticking pins in a map, and uses his power to settle old scores. It's a so-so attempt to reprise the Karloff thrillers of the 1930s, and the ending is a disappointment, but you'll feel something when Richard Boone shoves in those pins.

CREDITS

Director Albert Band; *Producers* Albert Band, Louis Garfinkle; *Screenplay* Louis Garfinkle; *Photographer* Frederick Gately; *Art Director* E. Vorkapich; *Music* Gerald Fried

CAST

Richard Boone, Theodore Bikel, Peggy Maurer, Herbert Anderson, Howard Smith

I, MONSTER

Film   1970   G.B. (Amicus)
75 minutes   Eastmancolor

An intelligent, faithful adaptation of Robert Louis Stevenson's *The Strange Case of Dr. Jekyll and Mr. Hyde* (1886) but with the names of the characters inexplicably changed. Christopher Lee is effective, although he lacks the charisma of earlier Jekyll/Hydes. Filmed in 3-D but released flat.

CREDITS

Director Stephen Weeks; *Producer/Screenplay* Milton Subotsky; *Photographer* Moray Grant; *Art Director* Tony Curtis; *Makeup* Harry Frampton, Peter Frampton; *Music* Carl Davis

CAST

Christopher Lee, Peter Cushing, George Merritt, Susan Jameson, Richard Hurndall, Mike Raven

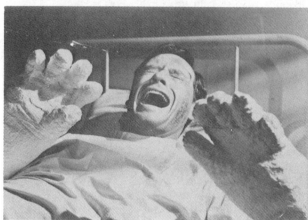

The Hands of Orlac: Clockwise, from left, top: Conrad Veidt examines his new digits in Robert Wiene's **Orlacs Haende** (1925); Peter Lorre performs the operation in MGM's remake, **Mad Love** (1935); and pianist Mel Ferrer inherits the murderer's hands in Britain's **The Hands of Orlac** (1960).

THE HANDS OF ORLAC/Les Mains d'Orlac

U.S. title: Hands of a Strangler

Film   1960   France/G.B. (Riviera/Pendennis)
105 minutes   Black & white

This is the better of two disappointing versions of Maurice Renard's novel *Les Mains d'Orlac* filmed in the early sixties. (The second, a U.S. product directed by Newton Arnold and released in 1962, had nearly the same title in American release: *Hands of a Stranger.*) Renard's story of a pianist with the transplanted hands of an executed murderer was effectively realized in ORLACS HAENDE (1925) and MAD LOVE (1935). Here the filmmakers apparently thought the supernatural pivot would no longer play, so Orlac's fears have become the result of hypnotic suggestion by a tawdry nightclub magician who is also a blackmailer.

CREDITS

Director Edmond T. Greville; *Producers* Steven Pallos, Don Taylor; *Screenplay* John Baines, Edmond T. Greville; *Photographer* Desmond Dickinson; *Art Director* John Blezard; *Music* Claude Bolling

CAST

Mel Ferrer, Christopher Lee, Dany Carrel, Donald Wolfit, Felix Aylmer

THE INCREDIBLE TWO-HEADED TRANSPLANT

Film   1971   U.S. (AIP)   81 minutes   Color

A young mad scientist grafts the head of a murderer onto the body of a moronic strong man and creates a schizophrenic monster. An occasionally hilarious spoof of 1950s monster movies, but the real gem is AIP's follow-up, THE THING WITH TWO HEADS.

CREDITS

Director Anthony Lanza; *Producer* John Lawrence; *Screenplay* James G. White, John Lawrence; *Photographers* John Steely, Glen Gano, Paul Hipp; *Makeup* Barry Noble; *Special Effects* Ray Dorn; *Music* John Barber

CAST

Bruce Dern, Pat Priest, Casey Kasem, Barry Kroeger, Albert Cole

The Invisible Man: "Suddenly I realized the power I held . . . to make the world grovel at my feet."

THE INVISIBLE MAN

Film   1933   U.S. (Universal)   71 minutes
Black & white

If he hadn't minded being invisible until the end of the film, it would have been Karloff who said, "Suddenly I realized the power I held, the power to rule, to make the world grovel at my feet." Just as Lugosi had paved the way for Karloff by turning down FRANKENSTEIN (see Monsters), Karloff's decision gave Claude Rains a chance to become a big star. Rains, whose distinctive British voice is recognizable anywhere (unlike the actors of today), convincingly fleshed out a character seen mostly wrapped in bandages and hidden behind sunglasses, when seen at all.

The plot, based on the famous H.G. Wells novel, has Rains playing a chemist who discovers an invisibility serum called monocane. The potion works remarkably well but has the unexpected side-effect of producing a megalomanic desire to rule the world. (It's Wells's warning against the perils of scientific discovery.) Director James Whale brings his usual wit and vitality to the invisible man's mischief, which includes robbing banks, derailing trains, murdering people and generally turning the world upside down. The effects, which are nothing short of miraculous, were achieved by John P. Fulton with a stunt man and a black velvet background. While the camera turned, the stunt man—dressed from head-to-toe in matching black velvet—unrolled the bandages, which appeared on film as if being manipulated by an unseen presence. The final scene, in which Rains is first "seen" as a depression in his death bed and gradually reappears, was shot directly in-camera in a series of stop-motion shots: A skeleton was photographed, followed by another skeleton fleshed-out with nerves and muscles, and so on, ending with the Invisible Man being made visible again. The one mistake Fulton made was to show shoe prints in the snow rather than bare footprints, when the supposedly naked scientist is finally cornered.

The popularity of the film prompted Universal to make five sequels, all of lesser quality. First came *The Invisible Man Returns* (1940), directed by Joe May and scripted by Curt Siodmak, with Vincent Price swallowing a dose of monocane to trap the killers who framed him. *The Invisible Woman* (1940), scripted by Siodmak, merely exploited the title to allow mad scientist John Barrymore to make Virginia Bruce invisible in a ray machine. High point of the sequels came with *Invisible Agent* (1940), also scripted by Siodmak. Hero Jon Hall, a member of the original scientist's family, has no ill effects from monocane, ingested before he parachutes into Germany on a top-secret spy mission. On hand to stop him is Peter Lorre as a Japanese officer attached to the Gestapo, who sets a trap with a silk net bordered in grappling hooks. Next came *The Invisible Man's Revenge* (1944), written by Bertram Milhauser. Jon Hall, hero of the previous film, is now a convicted murderer who, after escaping from jail, is chewed up by an invisible Great Dane. Last in the series is ABBOTT AND COSTELLO MEET THE INVISIBLE MAN (1951).

Television adaptations include both a British *Invisible Man* (1958–60) and an American version telecast by the NBC network (1975–76). The latter starred David McCallum as a transparent government scientist who destroys the formula rather than let the military have it. He spent 13 weeks searching for an antidote but never found it. The series was revamped late in 1976 with Ben Murphy having his DNA molecules rearranged by an underground explosion in a secret government lab. This invisible man was a right-winger who worked as a security agent for INTERSECT (International Security Technics). The title was *The Gemini Man* but the syndicated pilot film is called *Code Name: Minus One*.

CREDITS

Director James Whale; *Producer* Carl Laemmle, Jr.; *Screenplay* R.C. Sheriff, Philip Wylie, based on the novel by H.G. Wells; *Photographer* Arthur Edeson; *Art Director* Charles D. Hall; *Special Effects* John P. Fulton

CAST

Claude Rains, Gloria Stuart, William Harrigan, Henry Travers, E.E. Clive, Una O'Connor, Dudley Digges, Holmes Herbert, Forrester Harvey

THE ISLAND OF DR. MOREAU

Film   1977   U.S. (AIP)   98 minutes   Color

H.G. Wells's seminal mad scientist returned with this sedate remake of the 1932 Charles Laughton classic, THE ISLAND OF LOST SOULS, under the original title. Middle-aged Burt Lancaster is a less malevolent but equally obsessed experimenter, who eschews Wells's vivisection in favor of chromosome rearrangement to change animals into human beings. Shot in lush color in the Virgin Islands, this version lacks the baneful atmosphere of its predecessor and comes close to resembling a vacation brochure. Best are John Chambers's "humanimal" prosthetic masks, which are fully mobile and can withstand closeups, the best since *Planet of the Apes* (1968), also the work of Chambers. A tie-in novelization of the screenplay was issued in 1977, apparently to generate royalties from the out-of-copyright Wells original.

CREDITS

Director Don Taylor; *Producers* John Temple-Smith, Skip Steloff; *Screenplay* John Herman Shaner, Al Ram-

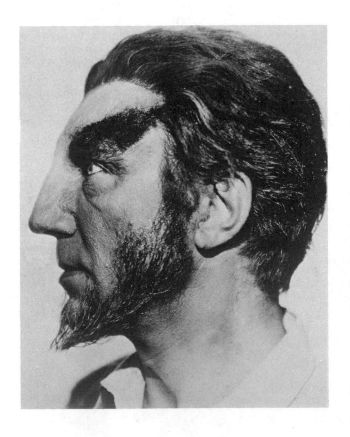

Humanimals: Left, Bela Lugosi is The Sayer of the Law in **Island of Lost Souls** (1932); Richard Basehart plays the head beast in the remake, **The Island of Dr. Moreau** (1977).

rus, based on the novel by H.G. Wells; *Photographers* Gerry Fisher, Ronnie Taylor; *Production Designer* Philip Jeffries; *Special Effects* Cliff Wenger; *Makeup* John Chambers, Dan Striekpeke, Tom Burman, Ed Butterworth, Walter Schenck; *Animal Trainer* Carl Thompson; *Music* Laurence Rosenthal

CAST

Burt Lancaster, Michael York, Barbara Carrera, Nigel Davenport, Richard Basehart, Nick Cravat, Bob Ozman, John L. Sullivan

THE ISLAND OF LOST SOULS

Film   1933   U.S. (Paramount)   72 minutes
Black & white

H.G. Wells denounced it as a "mutilation" of his seminal mad scientist novel, *The Island of Dr. Moreau* (1896), but Paramount's version is a fairly tingly thriller all the same, with a venerable over-the-top performance from Charles Laughton as Moreau. Deported from England because of his cruel experiments on pet dogs, he sets up shop on a remote tropical island and polishes his scalpels. Moreau's calling is to change animals into human beings, or close facsimiles, which he does by performing unbearably painful vivisections. The leader of his "humanimals" is the Ape Man (Bela Lugosi) who tries hard to forget his beastly nature by reciting a quasi-religious chant Moreau has imposed on his brood: "Not to eat meat . . . Not to chase other men . . . Not to go on all fours . . . Not to gnaw the bark off trees . . . That is the Law!" After teaching him to be gentle, Moreau makes the mistake of ordering him to commit a murder, thus precipitating a rebellion that ends with the doctor being dragged into his own House of Pain for some nasty surgery.

While the film takes liberties with Wells's story, it manages to reflect some of the author's message that knowledge and self-awareness can only be gained at the cost of paradise lost. Director Erle C. Kenton brings a steamy hothouse ambience to the story, which was shot on California's Catalina Island. The film also contributed to the world a famous catchphrase, uttered by Laughton at a dinner party in his island fortress. Glancing into the dark jungle, from which guttural murmurs and beating drums can be heard, he turns to his guests and says, "The natives are restless tonight." Years later the rock group Devo, extolling a message of de-evolution, paid homage to Moreau in their song "Are We Not Men?" titled after the cry of the humanimals. A sequel made in 1977, THE ISLAND OF DR. MOREAU, only proves that special effects aren't everything.

CREDITS

Director Erle C. Kenton; *Screenplay* Waldemar Young, Philip Wylie; *Photographer* Karl Struss; *Makeup* Wally Westmore

CAST

Charles Laughton, Bela Lugosi, Richard Arlen, Kathleen Burke, Leila Hyams, Alan Ladd

JUNGLE CAPTIVE

Film   1945   U.S. (Universal)   64 minutes
Black & white

Mad biochemist Otto Kruger revives the Ape Woman, mercifully for the last time, in this third sequel to CAPTIVE WILD WOMAN (1943), with Vicky Lane replacing Acquanetta as the passionate hirsute beauty.

CREDITS

Director Harold Young; *Producer* Ben Pivar; *Screenplay* M. Coates Webster, Dwight V. Babcock; *Photographer* Maury Gertsman; *Art Directors* John B. Goodman, Robert Clatworthy; *Music* Paul Sawtell

CAST

Vicky Lane, Otto Kruger, Amelia Ward, Jerome Cowan, Rondo Hatton

JUNGLE WOMAN

Film   1944   U.S. (Universal)   54 minutes
Black & white

J. Carroll Naish subs for John Carradine, another of the studio's second-string horror stars, in this sequel to and reprise of CAPTIVE WILD WOMAN (1943).

CREDITS

Director Reginald LeBorg; *Producer* Will Cowan; *Screenplay* Bernard Schubert, Henry Sucher, Edward Dein; *Photographer* Jack McKenzie; *Art Directors* John B. Goodman, Abraham Grossman; *Music* Paul Sawtell

CAST

Acquanetta, Evelyn Ankers, Lois Collier, J. Carroll Naish, Milburn Stone

Das Kabinett von Dr. Caligari: An expressionist nightmare from defeated Germany.

DAS KABINETT VON DR. CALIGARI/The Cabinet of Dr. Caligari

Film 1919 Germany (Decla-Bioscop)
52 minutes Black & white (silent)

To the unitiated, silent movies seem exaggerated and jerky and fit only for campy laughs. Which is a pity since there are so many silent genre films still able to raise a hackle or two. Topping the list of the early silents is *The Cabinet of Dr. Caligari*, horror's first masterpiece and its first international hit. If you can catch this one at a film retrospective or on public television, you'll see where Hollywood's classic films of the 1930s and 1940s came from.

It's the story of Dr. Caligari, a sideshow mesmerist who exhibits a hypnotized subject named Cesare (Conrad Veidt) in a cabinet. When a town refuses him permission to play there, he sends out the zombielike Cesare to commit a series of murders. Cesare finally rebels when ordered to kill the girl he loves, and he carries her off instead (the scene would be repeated in scores of later films). Chased by the townspeople across the roofs, he finally drops dead from exhaustion and Caligari puts him into a straitjacket. The writers intended the film to end here as a denouncement of the powers-that-be that had sent Germany's youth to a devastating war, but the producer added a softer ending that has the story being told by a madman.

What makes *Caligari* so durable is its expressionist design. Veidt, who became the cinema's first genre star in the film, seems to always be off-balance as he walks through doors that appear to slant inward, through snakey corridors that make a fun house look normal and past bizarre shadows (which were painted on the ground). The effect, as director Robert Wiene intended, is as if you yourself are the madman watching the film in a trance.

This film is the first to fully incorporate expressionism, a style of art that reached its peak in Germany during the period 1918–33. The style is characterized by an amalgam of distorted sets and props, harsh lighting and disturbing camera movements. Its esthetic is the subjective expression of emotion, especially fear, hatred and anxiety. Among the genre films that reflect the style are DER GOLEM (1915) (see Monsters), *Homunkulus* (1916), *Nosferatu* (1922), ORLACS HAENDE (1925), *Metropolis* (1926) and FRANKENSTEIN (1931) (see Monsters). Expressionism had nearly run its course when Nazi Germany suppressed the movement in 1933, but its far-reaching influence can be seen in the films of Eisenstein, Hitchcock and Orson Welles.

CREDITS

Director Robert Wiene; *Producer* Erich Pommer; *Screenplay* Carl Mayer, Hans Janowitz; *Photographer* Willy Hameister; *Art Directors* Herman Warm, Walter Rohring, Walter Reimann; *Costumes* Walter Reimann

CAST

Conrad Veidt, Werner Krauss, Friedrich Feher, Lil Dagover, Hans H. Von Twardowski, Rudolf Klein-Rogge, Rudolf Lettinger

THE LITTLE SHOP OF HORRORS

*Film   1960   U.S. (Santa Clara/AIP)
70 minutes   Black & white*

Inspired by the reception of A BUCKET OF BLOOD (see Crazies and Freaks), a comedy-horror film he shot in five days, Roger Corman topped himself by knocking off this little gem in a record two days. According to Corman, the leftover sets were due to be torn down any minute, and "at 9:00 in the morning on the first day of shooting the production manager informed us that we were already behind schedule." The plot centers around a plant store on skid row owned by the obnoxious Gravis Mushnik, boss of schlemiel Seymour Krelboin and father of his true love Audrey. Unable to marry until he buys his hypochondriac mother an iron lung, Seymour schemes for advancement by crossing a butterwort and a Venus's-fly-trap to produce a new prize plant.

The result is a cheesy-looking cloth vegetable with a voracious appetite for people. Named Audrey, Jr., after Seymour's girlfriend, the man-eating plant grows ever larger with each response to its memorable demand (spoken in a male voice) of

"Feed me! Feed me!" and, once, "I want some chow!" Jack Nicholson, then an unknown, appears briefly as the masochistic Wilbur Force, who reads *Pain* magazine and goes to the dentist for kicks. Funnier than ever today, although some of the topical humor has been lost, this energetic, witty spoof of low-budgeters was turned into a prize-winning Off-Broadway musical in 1982.

CREDITS

Director/Producer Roger Corman; *Screenplay* Charles B. Griffith; *Photographer* Arch Dalzell; *Art Director* Daniel Haller; *Music* Fred Katz

CAST

Jonathan Haze, Jackie Joseph, Mel Welles, Dick Miller, Jack Nicholson, Myrtle Vail, Leola Wendorff

THE MAD DOCTOR OF MARKET STREET

*Film   1942   U.S. (Universal)   61 minutes
Black & white*

Lionel Atwill does his Dr. Moreau thing on an exotic South Seas island, where he declares himself a god and dabbles in suspended animation. Tedious.

CREDITS

Director Joseph H. Lewis; *Producer* Paul Malvern; *Screenplay* Al Martin; *Photographer* Jerome Ash; *Art Director* Joseph Otterson; *Musical Director* Hans J. Salter

CAST

Lionel Atwill, Una Merkel, Nat Pendleton, Anne Nagel, Claire Dodd, Richard Davies, Noble Johnson

MAD LOVE

Also titled: The Hands of Orlac

*Film   1935   U.S. (MGM)   84 minutes
Black & white*

MGM, largely passed by during Hollywood's shock wave of the 1930s, took another stab at scaring money out of customers with an elaborately macabre version of Maurice Renard's French thriller *The Hands of Orlac*. Pure Grand Guignol, the film casts Peter Lorre in his first American role as the bulging-eyed, totally bald Dr. Gogol. A surgeon, Gogol falls in love with a beautiful performer at Paris's Theatre des Horreurs, where acts of torture and dismemberment are simulated with live actors and their wax counterparts. (A female passerby describes it as "a place where they make you scream and faint.") Although spurned by the leading lady, Gogol nevertheless performs an operation for her husband, a famous concert pianist named Stephen Orlac (Colin Clive), in which he replaces the man's accidentally mangled hands with a guillotined murderer's.

Obsessed with his mad love for the woman, Gogol attempts to drive the pianist mad by showing up in a pair of grotesque metal hands and pretending to be the ghost of the executed murderer. Meanwhile Gogol commits several knife killings (the dead criminal's *modus operandi*), leaving a trail that leads to Orlac. With Orlac safely in jail, the surgeon attempts to make love to Orlac's wife, but when she refuses he begins to strangle her with her own hair. Orlac arrives just in time with the police and neatly dispatches Gogol by throwing a knife into his body, a skill his hands apparently still possess.

The bizarre nature of the film is signaled by the opening credits, in which the names unroll on a frosted glass that looks through to the rooftops of Paris. A fist suddenly lurches out, shattering the glass, and the story begins. The acting is a bit histrionic by today's standards, and the idea of body transplants no longer seems innately perverse, but the film nevertheless has aged well and in many ways seems curiously up-to-date. *Mad Love* was the last directorial outing of Karl Freund, the great German cameraman of such classics as Fritz Lang's *Metropolis* (1926) and who had previously directed and shot Boris Karloff in THE MUMMY (1932) (see Mummies). Freund subsequently went back behind the cameras and later worked in television. The previous version of Renard's novel is Robert Wiene's memorable ORLACS HAENDE, a 1925 silent made in Austria.

CREDITS

Director Karl Freund; *Producer* John W. Considine, Jr.; *Screenplay* Guy Endore, P.J. Wolfson, John Balderston, based on the novel *Les Mains d'Orlac* by Maurice Renard; *Photographers* Chester Lyons, Gregg Toland; *Music* Dimitri Tiomkin

CAST

Peter Lorre, Colin Clive, Frances Drake, Isabel Jewell, Ted Healy, Keye Luke, Sara Haden

THE MAN IN HALF MOON STREET

Film 1944 U.S. (Paramount) 91 minutes
Black & white

A conventional, occasionally chilling screen adaptation of Barre Lyndon's popular play of the same title, concerning a 104-year-old surgeon who stays young by periodically transplanting a vital gland removed from a murdered donor. Hammer's version, titled THE MAN WHO COULD CHEAT DEATH (1959), is the one with the juice.

CREDITS

Director Ralph Murphy; *Producer* Walter MacEwan; *Screenplay* Charles Kenyong, adapted from Barre Lyndon's play by Garret Fort; *Photographer* Henry Sharp; *Art Directors* Hans Dreier, Walter Tyler; *Makeup* Wally Westmore; *Music* Miklos Rozsa

CAST

Nils Asther, Helen Walker, Paul Cavanaugh, Reinhold Schunzel, Edmond Breon

MAN MADE MONSTER

G.B. title: The Electric Man

Film 1941 U.S. (Universal) 68 minutes
Black & white

Lon Chaney, Jr., making an inauspicious horror debut, plays a sideshow freak supercharged with electricity who is framed for murder by mad scientist Lionel Atwill. Sent to the electric chair, he awakens as an angry killer with a high-voltage touch. The roles were originally intended for Boris Karloff and Bela Lugosi, who had appeared in the similar but far more enjoyable Universal scarer, *The Invisible Ray* (1936).

CREDITS

Director George Waggner; *Producer* Jack Bernhard; *Screenplay* Joseph West, based on story "The Electric Man" by H.J. Essex, Sid Schwartz and Len Golos; *Photographer* Elwood Bredell; *Art Director* Jack Otterson; *Special Effects* John P. Fulton; *Makeup* Jack Pierce; *Musical Director* Charles Previn

CAST

Lionel Atwill, Lon Chaney, Jr., Anne Nagel, Frank Albertson, Samuel S. Hinds, Ben Taggart

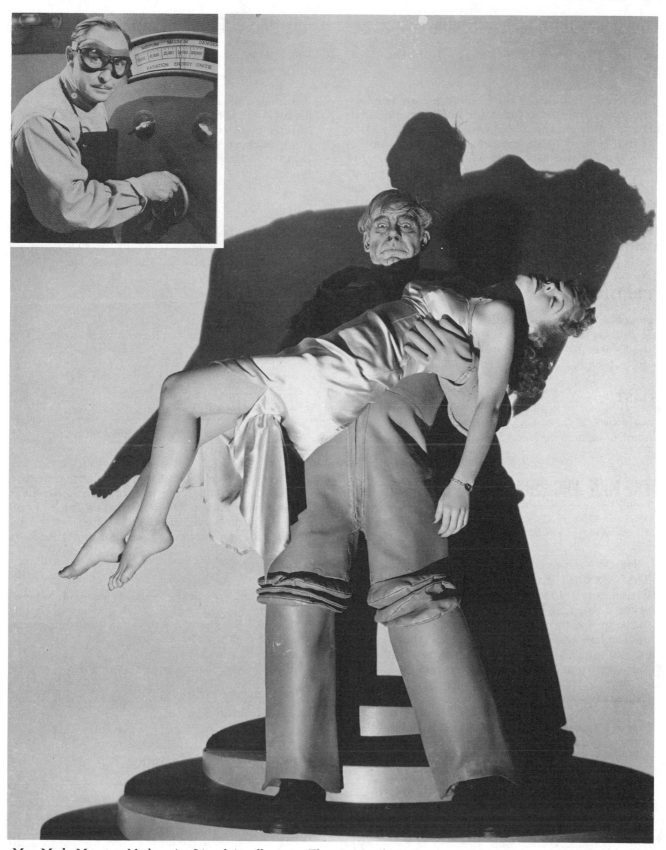

Man Made Monster: Mad genius Lionel Atwill creates Electric Man from the corpse of Lon Chaney, Jr.

THE MAN THEY COULD NOT HANG

Film 1939 U.S. (Columbia) 72 minutes
Black & white

Karloff's initial film for Columbia casts him as a surgeon wrongly executed for botching the installation of a mechanical heart, which is used to revive him. Bent on revenge, he gleefully invites the people who convicted him to his booby-trapped house, where they are summarily disposed of. Directed with mordant vitality by Nick Grinde, the film was successful enough for the studio to cast Karloff in a series of mad scientist vehicles, including *Before I Hang* (1940), THE DEVIL COMMANDS (1941) and THE BOOGIE MAN WILL GET YOU (1942).

CREDITS

Director Nick Grinde; *Producer* Wallace MacDonald; *Screenplay* Karl Brown, from a story by Leslie White and George Sayre; *Photographer* Benjamin Kline; *Music* Morris Stoloff

CAST

Boris Karloff, Lorna Gray, Robert Wilcox, Roger Pryor, Ann Doran, Don Beddoe

THE MAN WHO COULD CHEAT DEATH

Film 1959 G.B. (Hammer/Paramount)
83 minutes Technicolor

Hammer's adaptation of Barre Lyndon's play, THE MAN IN HALF MOON STREET, filmed by Paramount in 1944, scraps the romantic bravura in favor of elegant horror splashed with the studio's most gruesome colors. Anton Diffring's ageless doctor has a wax fruit malevolence that suggests eternal evil, as he goes about filching glands from murdered donors to stay looking young.

CREDITS

Director Terence Fisher; *Producer* Anthony Hinds; *Screenplay* Jimmy Sangster, based on the play *The Man in Half Moon Street* by Barre Lyndon; *Photographer* Jack Asher; *Art Director* Bernard Robinson; *Makeup* Roy Ashton; *Music* Richard Rodney Bennett

CAST

Anton Diffring, Hazel Court, Christopher Lee, Arnold Marle, Francis De Wolff, Delphi Lawrence

THE MAN WITHOUT A BODY

Film 1957 G.B. (Filmways) 80 minutes
Black & white

A crackpot surgeon revives the head of 16th-century prophet Nostradamus for an American businessman, who plans to make a killing in the stock market. A lunatic version of Curt Siodmak's *Donovan's Brain*, filmed first as *The Lady and the Monster* (1944).

CREDITS

Directors W. Lee Wilder, Charles Saunders; *Producer* Guido Coen; *Screenplay* William Grote; *Photographer* Brendan Stafford; *Makeup* Jim Hydes; *Music* Robert Elms

CAST

Robert Hutton, George Coulouris, Michael Golden, Kim Parker, Julie Arnall

THE MONSTER MAKER

Film 1944 U.S. (PRC) 64 minutes
Black & white

A love-smitten biologist, experimenting with a cure for acromegaly, transforms his girlfriend's disapproving father into a misshapen freak. Typical low-grade horror from PRC, almost saved by Naish's title performance as a smarmy psychopath.

CREDITS

Director Sam Newfield; *Producer* Sigmund Neufeld; *Screenplay* Pierre Gendron, Martin Mooney; *Photographer* Robert Kline; *Art Director* Paul Palmentola; *Music* Albert Glasser

CAST

J. Carrol Naish, Ralph Morgan, Tala Birell, Wanda McKay, Glenn Strange

MONSTER ON THE CAMPUS

Film 1958 U.S. (Universal-International)
77 minutes Black & white

Director Arnold attempts to build terror through characterization in this unsteady retelling of *Dr.*

Jekyll and Mr. Hyde; he might have succeeded with a better script and a more talented actor. Arnold's hero/monster is a sensitive college professor turned into a lustful Neanderthal when infected by a mysterious enzyme from the sharp scales of a coelacanth. Unaware that the transformation has taken place, he leads police on a search for the beast who has been ravaging female college students.

CREDITS

Director Jack Arnold; *Producer* Joseph Gershenson; *Screenplay* David Duncan; *Photographer* Russell Metty; *Art Director* Alexander Golitzen; *Special Effects* Clifford Stine; *Makeup* Bud Westmore; *Musical Director* Joseph Gershenson

CAST

Arthur Franz, Joanna Moore, Troy Donahue, Eddie Parker, Whit Bissell, Helen Westcott

MURDERS IN THE RUE MORGUE

Film 1932 U.S. (Universal) 75 minutes Black & white

Patterned after the radically innovative DAS KABINETT VON DR. CALIGARI (1919), this prestige Universal production stars Bela Lugosi as the curly-haired Dr. Mirakle, a leering carnival performer with a pet ape. After the show, Mirakle sends out his gorilla to kidnap young women to

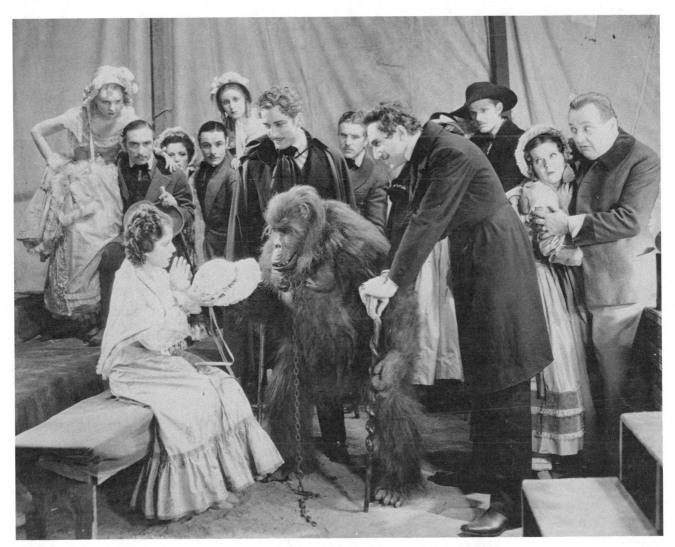

Murders in the Rue Morgue: Carnival magician Dr. Mirakle (Bela Lugosi) has big plans for the lady and the ape.

crossbreed them with the animal and produce a perfect human being. The experiments fail, of course, and the doctor must slowly bleed several women to death until he gets it right. Deemed too gruesome in its time, the film today seems less so and very much of its period. What endures is the emotionally jarring expressionist style of director Robert Florey, who got the film as a consolation prize for losing out on FRANKENSTEIN (1931) (see Monsters). Lugosi, overdoing the sadism bit, is so slimy he practically leaves a trail across the floor. The remakes have even less to do with the Poe short story: PHANTOM OF THE RUE MORGUE (1954) and MURDERS IN THE RUE MORGUE (1971) (see Crazies and Freaks).

CREDITS

Director Robert Florey; *Producer* Carl Laemmle, Jr.; *Screenplay* Tom Reed, Dale Van Every; *Additional Dialogue* John Huston; *Photographer* Karl Freund; *Art Director* Charles D. Hall; *Special Effects* John P. Fulton; *Makeup* Jack Pierce

CAST

Bela Lugosi, Sidney Fox, Leon Waycoff (Leon Ames), Bert Roach, Noble Johnson, Brandon Hurst, D'Arcy Corrigan

THE MUTATIONS

Film 1974 *G.B. (Columbia/Getty)* 91 minutes *Eastmancolor*

By day Donald Pleasence is a respected biochemistry teacher, but by night he is a closet mad-scientist who transforms freaks from a traveling sideshow into hybrid people. His creatures, including a Venus flytrap-man (nicely made-up by Charles Parker), inevitably extract their revenge. A line in the script sums up the nonsense: "You make it sound like bad science fiction."

CREDITS

Director Jack Cardiff; *Producer* Robert D. Weinbach; *Screenplay* Robert D. Weinbach, Edward Mann; *Photographer* Paul Beeson; *Makeup* Charles Parker; *Music* Basil Kirchin

CAST

Donald Pleasence, Tom Baker, Brad Harris, Julie Ege, Michael Dunn, Jill Haworth

NIGHT MONSTER

G.B. title: House of Mystery

Film 1942 *U.S. (Universal)* 73 minutes Black & white

Doctors stranded in a formidable old mansion are victimized by a mad amputee who creates new legs with the power of his mind. A disposable horror programmer from the Universal factory, helmed by serial director Ford Beebe (*Flash Gordon's Trip to Mars, Buck Rogers*).

CREDITS

Director/Producer Ford Beebe; *Screenplay* Charles Upson Young; *Photographer* Charles Van Enger

CAST

Ralph Morgan, Bela Lugosi, Lionel Atwill, Irene Hervey, Don Porter, Leif Erickson

NOTHING BUT THE NIGHT

Film 1972 *G.B. (Rank/Charlemagne)* 90 minutes *Eastmancolor*

Orphans on a remote Scottish island murder the orphanage's trustees after being injected with their "life essences," in a successful experiment in immortality. The specious but dramatically feasible idea that genetic material can be used to control a living host was handled to better effect in the TV movie *Hauser's Memory* (1970).

CREDITS

Director Peter Sasdy; *Producer* Anthony Nelson Keys; *Screenplay* Brian Hayles; *Photographer* Ken Talbot; *Special Effects* Les Bowie; *Makeup* Eddie Knight; *Music* Malcolm Williamson

CAST

Christopher Lee, Peter Cushing, Diana Dors, Georgia Brown, Duncan Lamont

ORLACS HAENDE/The Hands of Orlac

Film   1925   Austria (Pan-Film)   62 minutes
Black & white (silent)

Severed crawling hands, the villains of many good horror films, got their start here. Conrad Veidt, who made a specialty of corrupted heroes in postwar Germany and Austria, is a concert pianist who loses his hands in a railway accident. When a surgeon replaces them with the hands of a murderer, he becomes convinced that the murderer still owns them. It's only a figment of his imagination, however, suggested by the mesmeric surgeon, who wants to drive him crazy. Veidt is outstanding as the nervously gaunt musician but director Robert Wiene (who worked with the actor previously in DAS KABINETT VON DR. CALIGARI) makes the story rather tedious. Best version of the Maurice Renard novel is MGM's MAD LOVE (1935), with Peter Lorre. Other hand movies include the remakes THE HANDS OF ORLAC (1960) and *Hands of a Stranger* (1962); and THE BEAST WITH FIVE FINGERS (1947) (see Crazies and Freaks), *The Crawling Hand* (1963), DR. TERROR'S HOUSE OF HORRORS (1965) (see Anthologies), *The Hand* (1969), *The Hand* (1981) and *Demonoid* (1982). A severed hand also figured in BLOOD FROM THE MUMMY'S TOMB (1971) (see Mummies).

CREDITS

Director Robert Wiene; *Screenplay* Ludwig Nerz, based on the novel by Maurice Renard; *Photographers* Hans Androschin, Gunther Krampf; *Art Directors* Stefan Wessely, Hans Rovc, Karl Exner

CAST

Conrad Veidt, Alexandra Sorina, Carmen Cartellieri, Fritz Kortner, Paul Askonas, Fritz Strassny, Homma

THE PARASITE MURDERS

U.S. title: They Came from Within

G.B. title: Shivers

Film   1975   Canada (Trans-American)
94 minutes   Movielab

A wormlike parasite, released by a crank scientist, infests an isolated apartment complex whose

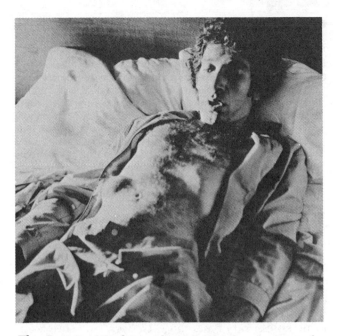

The Parasite Murders: Alan Migicovsky monitors the progress of a sexually transmitted parasite.

residents pass it along via a network of sexual contacts. The contagious parasite—described as a cross between "an aphrodisiac and a venereal disease"—slips into the body of a beautiful lesbian (Barbara Steele) through her vagina while she's taking a bath. Transmitted to her lover during a soul kiss (its subtle outline moves from throat to throat), the parasite, after a long journey, bursts from the stomach of a young man and mutilates the face of his panicked friend.

By turns repulsive, horrifying, hilarious and amateurish, this is the film that earned David Cronenberg a cult following (members include director John Carpenter and novelist Stephen King). Cronenberg, carefully calculating his first commercial effort, apparently tailored the film to the profitable splatter and sexploitation market. While satisfying the requirements of both subgenres, he also manages to transcend them by probing an exposed contemporary nerve with a parodic but graphic depiction of the hazards of sexual promiscuity. What makes this subtext so effective is Cronenberg's expert handling of the barf-bag scenes involving the parasite (which could be viewed as a prophetic metaphor for the disease AIDS). Unfortunately, he doesn't know how to end the story and lets it fall apart halfway through with repetitious scenes of the sex-crazed Yuppies and Muppies slaughtering the building's uninfected tenants.

CREDITS

Director/Screenplay David Cronenberg; *Producer* Ivan Reitman; *Photographer* Robert Saad; *Art Director* Erla Gilserman; *Special Effects, Makeup* Joe Blasco; *Music* Ivan Reitman

CAST

Barbara Steele, Paul Hampton, Lynn Lowry, Susan Petrie, Alan Migicovsky

PETER QUILL

Radio series   1940–41   U.S. (Mutual)
30 minutes (weekly)

Peter Quill, a heroic hunchback scientist-detective, specialized in outwitting sinister wartime spies, saboteurs and traitors and bringing them to justice. His helpers were the athletic, romantically involved team of Captain Dom and Gail. Marvin Miller, better known on TV's *The Millionaire* (1955–60) as Michael Anthony, played Quill. Miller also did the wailing opener, "Peeeeee-terrrr Quillllll . . . . . . !" by aiming a falsetto through the strings of a piano.

CREDITS

Director/Writer Blair Walliser

CAST

Marvin Miller, Alice Hill, Ken Griffin

PHANTOM OF THE RUE MORGUE

Film   1954   U.S. (Warner Bros.)   84 minutes
Warnercolor 3-D

Usually shown "flat" on television, this color remake of MURDERS IN THE RUE MORGUE (1932) has to be experienced in stereo to fully appreciate its killer ape clambering over the rooftops of Paris. Otherwise, it's a conventional mad scientist story—no more faithful to Poe than the previous film—energized by a few graphic murders and the atypical casting of Karl Malden.

CREDITS

Director Roy Del Ruth; *Producer* Henry Blanke; *Screenplay* Harold Medford, James R. Webb, based on the story "Murders in the Rue Morgue" by Edgar Allan Poe; *Photographer* J. Peverell Marley; *Art Director* Bertram Tuttle; *Music* David Buttolph

CAST

Karl Malden, Patricia Medina, Claude Dauphin, Steve Forrest, Allyn McLerie, Merv Griffin, Charles Gemora (gorilla)

THE RAVEN

Film   1935   U.S. (Universal)   60 minutes
Black & white

Karloff and Lugosi even the score by reversing the roles they had played in their previous encounter, THE BLACK CAT (1943) (see Ghosts, Witches and Demons). Lugosi, in the heftier part, is Dr. Vollin, a plastic surgeon with a fondness for the torture devices described by Edgar Allan Poe. Among these are a cell whose walls squeeze perilously together, a bedroom that descends into a dungeon, and the razor-sharp pendulum from Poe's tale of the Spanish Inquisition, "The Pit and the Pendulum." Karloff lends support in a relatively sympathetic role as an escaped murderer horribly disfigured by Vollin's botched operation. Former cliff-hanger director Louis Friedlander (who later changed his name to Lew Landers) moves briskly through the creaky, sadistic nonsense, and Lugosi and Karloff are in top form.

CREDITS

Director Louis Friedlander; *Associate Producer* David Diamond; *Screenplay* David Boehm; *Photographer* Charles Stumar; *Art Director* Albert S. D'Agostino; *Musical Supervisor* Gilbert Kurland

CAST

Bela Lugosi, Boris Karloff, Lester Matthews, Irene Ware, Samuel S. Hinds, Inez Courtney

THE RAVEN

Film   1963   U.S. (Alta Vista/AIP)   86 minutes
Pathecolor   Panavision

One of the last of the Poe series, which Corman decided to play for laughs since he felt "the pictures were in danger of beginning to look and feel alike." Mad magician Price is on the trail of

RETURN OF THE FLY

Film   1959   U.S. (20th Century-Fox)
78 minutes   Black & white   CinemaScope

Virtually the same plot as THE FLY (1958), with the squashed scientist's son (Brett Halsey) reactivating the matter-transmitter and having no more success in working out the bugs. Vincent Price is again on hand, as Uncle Delambre, and there's an unfortunate happy ending. The trilogy was completed with the superior, British-made CURSE OF THE FLY (1965).

CREDITS

Director/Screenplay Edward Bernds; *Producer* Bernard Glasser; *Photographer* Brydon Baker; *Art Director* Lyle R. Wheeler; *Makeup* Hal Lierly; *Music* Paul Sawtell

CAST

Brett Halsey, Vincent Price, John Sutton, Danielle DeMetz, David Frankenham

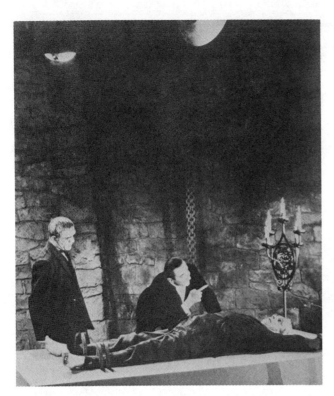

The Raven (1935): The malevolent Dr. Vollin (Bela Lugosi) prepares a victim for a razor-sharp pendulum with the unwilling assistance of Boris Karloff.

Lenore, his lover, with aide-de-camp Lorre, who occasionally transmutes into a peculiar black bird. Matheson's script parodies Corman, not Poe, and the cast has a great time improvising in-jokes that send up the series. When Price says to Lorre, for example, "My wife's body is buried in a crypt beneath the house," and Lorre replies, "Where else," the reference is to a convention of the Poe films which had the deceased entombed in crypts under the house—never in a graveyard. Although the dialogue lacks true wit, it's hilarious all the same, and the climactic wizard's duel between Price and Karloff is a masterpiece of comedy special effects.

CREDITS

Director/Producer Roger Corman; *Screenplay* Richard Matheson; *Photographer* Floyd Crosby; *Art Director* Daniel Haller; *Special Effects* Pat Dinga; *Music* Les Baxter; *Raven Trainer* Moe DiSesso

CAST

Vincent Price, Peter Lorre, Boris Karloff, Hazel Court, Jack Nicholson, Olive Sturges

SCANNERS

Film   1981   Canada (Avco Embassy)
102 minutes   Color

Another mind-blower, quite literally, from Canada's David Cronenberg, the Tod Browning of our time. Cronenberg's scanners are normal-looking mutants with the power to bend, twist and physically destroy people with a casual flick of the mind. The film opens with an out-of-work drifter (Stephen Lack) who wanders into a restaurant and, unaware he's a scanner, sends a woman eyeing him with disgust into terrible convulsions. Vicious corporate intrigue provides the plot, with Lack joining an underground group of scanners battling the ominous Comsec Corporation, which wants to co-opt scanning for military use.

Among the film's many spectacular moments is a long-range cybernetics duel between Lack and a computer, which throws an electronic temper tantrum rather than allow the scanner to read its mind. In another scene two scanners have a mind-off and fire mental rockets at each other, burning smoking craters into their bodies. The battle ends with the head of one scanner bloodily exploding in

Scanners: Scanner Michael Ironside vanquishes a rival using nuclear brain power.

a cloud of electrical haze. *Scanners* crackles with Cronenberg's energy and social and political ideas, of which there are perhaps too many for clarity's sake. (Cronenberg's drifter, a symbol of anyone who has ever felt powerless and was unaware of his inner powers, is also a symbol of our explosive anxieties.) But causes really aren't what he's up to, only mythic scares—the kind that knock your socks off.

CREDITS

Director/Screenplay David Cronenberg; *Producer* Claude Heroux; *Photographer* Mark Irwin; *Art Director* Carol Spier; *Special Makeup* Dick Smith; *Makeup* Chris Walas, Tom Schwartz, Stephen Dupius; *Incendiary Effects* Gary Zeller

CAST

Stephen Lack, Jennifer O'Neill, Patrick McGoohan, Lawrence Dane, Adam Ludwig, Michael Ironside, Victor Desy

SCREAM AND SCREAM AGAIN

*Film   1969   G.B. (AIP/Amicus)   95 minutes
Eastmancolor*

Price, Lee and Cushing joined forces for the first time in this gory little thriller, which has become something of a cult item. Price surgically stitches together "perfect" human beings from body parts excised from murdered locals, and the police are soon on his tail. There's a subplot of political intrigue which has little to do with the nonstop bloodletting—the film's true subject (the most startling effect is of a hand torn away at the wrist). The producers could only afford the big three for a few days' work, so most of the plot is carried forward by two unknowns. The trio got together again in *House of the Long Shadows* (1983).

CREDITS

Director Gordon Hessler; *Producers* Max J. Rosenberg, Milton Subotsky; *Screenplay* Christopher Wicking, based on the novel *The Disoriented Man* by Peter Saxon; *Photographer* John Coquillon; *Production Designer* Bill Constable; *Art Director* Don Mingaye; *Music* David Whittaker

CAST

Vincent Price, Christopher Lee, Peter Cushing, Judy Bloom, Christopher Matthews, Uta Levka, Anthony Newlands

THE SHADOW

*Radio series   1931–56   U.S. (Mutual)
60 minutes (weekly)*

"Who knows what evil lurks in the hearts of men? The Shadow knows!" Thus began this phenomenally popular Sunday afternoon series, accompanied by the Shadow's knowing laugh and an organ theme. Essentially a crime-solver, the Shadow was described as having "a strange and mysterious secret . . . the hypnotic power to cloud men's minds so they cannot see him." Announcing his presence with an eerie, disembodied laugh, he vanquished a succession of mad scientists who could revive dead bodies, turn day into night, ignite volcanoes, and the like. The Shadow's rival radio magicians were *The Avenger*, PETER QUILL and the righters-of-wrongs of *Latitude Zero*.

The character debuted in 1930's *Detective Story*, which featured dramatizations from Street & Smith's pulp detective magazine. Initially the show's announcer, then the narrator, he became so popular that he was written into the program. The publisher then launched a magazine called *The Shadow*, which varied somewhat from the radio persona. One of the first crimefighters to have a dual identity, in this case Lamont Cranston, a wealthy young man-about-town, the Shadow was a model for such celebrated crimefighters as Superman, Batman and Captain Marvel, who also lived two lives. The Shadow's identity, of course, was known only to his "ardent and constant friend" Margot Lane. Among the actors who portrayed the character is Orson Welles.

The Shadow made his movie debut in the summer of 1931 as the narrator of a series of six two-reel shorts of mysteries adapted from the pages of *Detective Story*. He reappeared in more recognizable form in the 1937 feature *The Shadow Strikes*, with Rod La Rocque in the title role. La Rocque played it again in *International House* (1938), then Columbia Pictures gave the part to Victor Jory in a 15-chapter serial titled *The Shadow* (1940). Kane Richmond next starred as the Shadow in a trio of "B" films released by Monogram in 1946. These include *The Shadow Returns, Behind the Mask* and *The Missing Lady*. The character was last seen on the screen in the person of Richard Derr, who starred in Republic's *Invisible Avenger* (1958), which was later re-released as *Bourbon Street Shadow*.

CREDITS

Creators Harry Charlot, Dave Chrisman, Bill Sweets; *Directors* John Cole, Harry Ingram, Chick Vincent, Bill Sweets, William Tuttle, Dana Noyes; *Writers* Joe Bates Smith, Nick Kogan, Peter Barry, Max Ehrlich, Jerry McGill, Robert Arthur, Stedman Coles; *Musical Theme* "Omphale's Spinning Wheel" by Saint-Saens

CAST

James LaCurto (1931), Frank Readick, Robert Hardy Andrews, Orson Welles (1937–38), Bill Johnstone, Bret Morrison (1944–56) (The Shadow); Agnes Moorehead, Majorie Anderson, Gertrude Warner, Grace Matthews, Lesley Woods (Margot Lane); Kenny Delmar, Keenan Wynn, Everett Sloane; *Announcers* Ken Roberts, Sandy Becker, Carl Caruso, Andre Baruch

SHANKS

Film 1974 *U.S. (Paramount)* 93 minutes
Color

Inspired by the macabre stories of E.T.A. Hoffman, this eccentric comedy stars French mime Marcel Marceau in a dual role as an elderly alchemist and a deaf-mute puppeteer to whom the former teaches the secret of turning dead people into androids. Before long Shanks has assembled a contingent of living puppets, soon to be joined by his young fiancee after her brutal death at the hands of a motorcycle gang. The film's juxtaposition of violence and fey humor jarred studio execs, and *Shanks* never saw a wide release.

CREDITS

Director William Castle; *Producer* Steven North; *Screenplay* Ronald Graham; *Photographer* Joseph Biroc; *Special Effects* Richard Albain; *Puppets* Robert Baker; *Music* Alex North

CAST

Marcel Marceau, Cindy Eilbacher, Phillipe Clay, Larry Bishop, Don Calfa

SHE DEMONS

Film 1958 *U.S. (Astor)* 77 minutes
Black & white

An ex-Nazi doctor holed up in a South American jungle tries to revive his aging wife's beauty with skin grafts forcibly obtained from native girls. A botched job all way around.

CREDITS

Director Richard E. Cunha; *Producer* Arthur A. Jacobs; *Screenplay* Richard E. Cunha, H.E. Barrie; *Special Effects* David Koehler; *Makeup* Carlie Taylor; *Music* Nicholas Carras

CAST

Irish McCalla, Tod Griffin, Gene Roth, Victor Sen Yung, Leni Tana, Billy Dix, Bill Coontz

THE SIXTH SENSE

TV series 1972 *U.S. (ABC)*
60 minutes (weekly) *Color*

A parapsychologist who teaches at a major university moonlights as a psychic detective who solves conventional murder mysteries with psi powers. This uneventful program was canceled at the end of the year, and its 25 episodes were trimmed to 30 minutes (which considerably improved them) and rebroadcast on ROD SERLING'S NIGHT GALLERY (1970–73) (see Anthologies). The pilot movie was titled SWEET, SWEET RACHEL.

CAST

Gary Collins, Catherine Farrar

SON OF DR. JEKYLL

Film   1951   U.S. (Columbia)   77 minutes
Black & white

Edward, son of Henry, conducting a routine investigation to prove that Dad wasn't two-faced, comes up with some not very surprising news. (Dracula, also unmarried, had a movie son and daughter too.)

CREDITS

Director Seymour Friedman; *Screenplay* Edward Huebsch, Jack Pollexfen, Mortimer Braus; *Photographer* Henry Freulich; *Art Director* Walter Holscher; *Makeup* Clay Campbell; *Music* Paul Sawtell

CAST

Louis Hayward, Jody Lawrence, Alexander Knox, Gavin Muir, Lester Matthews, Paul Cavanagh

THE STRANGE CASE OF DR. JEKYLL AND MR. HYDE

TV tape   1974   G.B. (ITC)   150 minutes
Color

An elegantly mounted, videotaped British adaptation of Robert Louis Stevenson's tale of a divided doctor, shown on two consecutive nights in the U.S. on the ABC network. The cast is first-rate, but star Jack Palance unfortunately looks sinister even without his Mr. Hyde makeup.

CREDITS

Director Charles Jarrot; *Producer* Dan Curtis; *Screenplay* Ian M. Hunter; *Novel* Robert Louis Stevenson; *Art Director* Trevor Williams; *Special Effects* Karl Moelhausen; *Makeup* Dick Smith, Niki Balch; *Music* Robert Colbert

CAST

Jack Palance, Billie Whitelaw, Denholm Elliott, Tessie O'Shea, Torin Thatcher, Oscar Homolka, Leo Genn

THE STRANGE DR. WEIRD

Radio serial   1944–47   U.S. (Mutual)
15 minutes (M/W/F)

A reduntantly titled early evening serial narrated by Dr. Weird, a magician of sorts who conjured up continuing occult-oriented mysteries. Maurice Tarplin starred as the doctor. Jock MacGregor directed and Robert A. Arthur wrote the scripts.

SUPERNATURAL

Film   1933   U.S. (Paramount)   67 minutes
Black & white

Carole Lombard fans and art deco buffs may enjoy this glossy antique, made before Lombard found stardom as a comedienne. Lombard, paying her dues, is miscast as an ingenue possessed by the spirit of an electrocuted murderess. Director Victor Halperin, who made his genre debut the year before with WHITE ZOMBIE (see Zombies), labors for horrific effect but elicits mostly yawns and giggles.

CREDITS

Director Victor Halperin; *Producers* Victor Halperin, Edward Halperin; *Screenplay* Harvey Thew, Brian Marlow; *Story* Garnett Weston; *Photographer* Arthur Martinelli; *Art Director* Hans Dreier

CAST

Carole Lombard, Randolph Scott, Vivienne Osborne, H.B. Warner, Allan Dinehart, William Farnum

SWEET, SWEET RACHEL

TV film   1971   U.S. (ABC)   74 minutes
Color

Psychic powers blandly wielded by an ESP professional solve the riddle of poor, wealthy Rachel's ghoulish visions: A madman is using mental telepathy to kill people. This is the pilot for the short-lived series THE SIXTH SENSE, which replaced lead Alex Dreier with Gary Collins.

CREDITS

Director Sutton Roley; *Producer* Stan Shpetner; *Screenplay* Anthony Lawrence; *Photographer* James Crabe; *Art Director* Paul Sylos; *Music* Laurence Rosenthal

CAST

Alex Dreier, Stefanie Powers, Pat Hingle, Louise Latham, Brenda Scott, Chris Robinson

TERROR IS A MAN

Film   1959   U.S. (Allied Artists)   89 minutes
Black & white

Cast adrift after a shipwreck, a young seaman reaches a remote island inhabited by a mysterious doctor attempting to surgically transform a panther into a human being. Surprisingly suspenseful, despite its deja-vu plot.

CREDITS

Director/Musical Director Garry DeLeon; *Screenplay* Harry Paul Harber; *Photographer* Emmanuel I. Rojas

CAST

Richard Derr, Francis Lederer, Greta Thyssen, Flory Carlos

THE THING WITH TWO HEADS

Film   1972   U.S. (AIP)   90 minutes   Color

Considered a treasure by collectors of rotten films, this low-budget black comedy has a white racist doctor awakening from death to find his head grafted onto the shoulders of a husky black convict. While prowling through town attempting to prove the latter's innocence, the monstrosity engages in some of the most ludicrous racial bantering ever heard on the screen. In long and medium shots, the extra heads are obvious dummies, but in close-up the stars hunch over each other, trying to pretend they are joined together by more than a desire to make a fast buck.

CREDITS

Director Lee Frost; *Producer* Wes Bishop; *Screenplay* Lee Frost, Wes Bishop, James G. White; *Photographer*

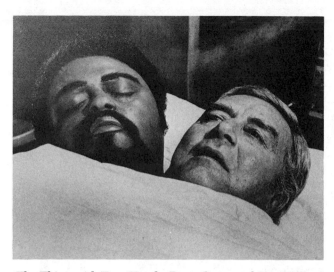

The Thing with Two Heads: Rosie Greer and Ray Milland pretend to be joined at the neck.

Jack Steely; *Heads* Dan Striepke, Tim Burman, Gail Brown, Charles Schram, James White, Pete Peterson; *Music* Robert O. Ragland

CAST

Ray Milland, Rosie Greer, Don Marshall, Roger Perry, Kathy Baumann, Chelsea Brown

THE TWILIGHT PEOPLE

Film   1972   U.S. (Dimension)
83 minutes   Color

A mad scientist on a remote island creates flesh-and-blood hybrids of people and animals. When his wife questions the scientist's dubious contribution to humanity, she gets turned into a tree-woman. H.G. Wells must be spinning.

CREDITS

Director Eddie Romero; *Producer* John Ashley; *Screenplay* Jerome Small; *Photographer* Fredy Conde; *Special Effects* Richard Abelardo; *Music* Ariston Avelino

CAST

John Ashley, Jan Merlin, Pam Grier, Pat Woodell, Ken Metcalfe, Eddie Garcia

THE TWO FACES OF DR. JEKYLL

U.S. title: House of Fright

*Film   1960   G.B. (Hammer/AIP)   89 minutes
Color   Megascope*

Stevenson's tired warhorse takes a refreshing turn, with Dr. Jekyll portrayed as a bearded misanthrope who recalls his lost youth and evil desires in the handsome, smooth-cheeked Mr. Hyde. Terence Fisher directs with a heady erotic tension, but his work is undermined by lackluster performers (particularly Paul Massie as Jekyll/Hyde) and a script weighted with subplots and displaced shock effects.

CREDITS

Director Terence Fisher; *Producer* Michael Carreras; *Screenplay* Wolf Mankowitz; *Photographer* Jack Asher; *Art Directors* Bernard Robinson, Don Mingaye; *Makeup* Roy Ashton; *Music* Monty Norman, David Heneker

CAST

Paul Massie, Dawn Addams, Christopher Lee, David Kossoff, Francis de Wolff, Oliver Reed

THE UNEARTHLY

*Film   1957   U.S. (Republic)   73 minutes
Black & white*

Horror handyman John Carradine is back in the laboratory, this time as a surgeon looking for the secret of eternal life. He messes up the job, with help from the director and scriptwriter.

CREDITS

Director/Producer Brook L. Peters; *Screenplay* Geoffrey Dennis, Jane Mann; *Photographer* Merle Connell; *Art Director* Daniel Hall; *Music* Henry Varse, Michael Terr

CAST

John Carradine, Allison Hayes, Myron Healy, Marilyn Buferd, Tor Johnson, Sally Todd

THE VULTURE

*Film   1966   U.S./G.B./Canada (Paramount)
91 minutes   Black & white*

An aging scientist, gamely manipulating the controls of a nuclear-powered apparatus, "beams up" a pirate's treasure sunk off the coast of Cornwall, England. Like his predecessor in THE FLY (1958), he hasn't gotten the hang of the improbable device, and he inadvertently brings up a feathered 200-year-old pirate whose molecules have been mixed with those of his pet vulture. A fairly suspenseful SF thriller, despite its silly premise.

CREDITS

Director/Producer/Screenplay Lawrence Huntington; *Photographer* Stephen Dade; *Art Director* Duncan Sutherland; *Makeup* Geoffrey Rodway; *Music* Eric Spear

CAST

Broderick Crawford, Akim Tamiroff, Robert Hutton, Diane Clare, Monty Landis

The Walking Dead: Karloff returns from the grave to even the score.

THE WALKING DEAD

*Film   1936   U.S. (Warner Bros.)   66 minutes
Black & white*

The plural title suggests a platoon of zombies, but only one dead man walks, and not until the last half of the film. Karloff, electrocuted for a crime he didn't commit, is resurrected by Dr. Edmund Gwenn (the Santa Claus of 1947's *Miracle on 34th Street*) to take revenge on the gangsters who framed him. Looking hollow-eyed and cadaverous, Karloff forces them into situations that, one by one, induce their own violent deaths. Karloff could be just as frightening in a sympathetic role, especially when he had a lucid script to work from and a capable, visually savvy director like Michael Curtiz. The plot is similar to a later Karloff programmer, THE MAN THEY COULD NOT HANG.

CREDITS

Director Michael Curtiz; *Producer* Lou Edelman; *Screenplay* Ewart Adamson, Peter Milne, Robert Andrews, Lillie Hayward; *Story* Ewart Adamson, Joseph Fields; *Photographer* Hal Mohr; *Art Director* Hugh Reticker

CAST

Boris Karloff, Ricardo Cortez, Edmund Gwenn, Warren Hull, Marguerite Churchill, Barton MacLane

Willard: Bruce Davison's trained rats are about to gnaw nasty employer Ernest Borgnine to death.

WILLARD

Film   1971   U.S. (Cinerama/Bing Crosby)
95 minutes   DeLuxe

Rats are more loyal than people, according to this pulpy revenge fantasy, which owes much of its

impact to Bruce Davison's performance as a put-upon mama's boy named Willard. To even the score, he eliminates his insensitive boss and other meanies with an army of trained rats given orders to "tear 'em apart!" The rat attacks, augmented by sound effects of thundering little paws and tiny gnashing teeth, are initially horrifying, but under Daniel Mann's uninspired direction, the rodents gradually take on the characteristics of furry pets. A surprise hit, *Willard* inspired several films featuring tiny, unsuspecting monsters, including FROGS (see Cataclysmic Disasters) and NIGHT OF THE LEPUS (see Cataclysmic Disasters), an unbelievable dog about killer bunnies, and a sequel, BEN, starring Willard's best friend.

CREDITS

Director Daniel Mann; *Producer* Mort Briskin; *Screenplay* Gilbert A. Ralston, based on the novel *Ratman's Notebooks* by Stephen Gilbert; *Photographer* Robert B. Hauser; *Special Effects* Howard A. Anderson Co., Bud David; *Music* Alex North; *Rat Trainer* Moe di Sesso

CAST

Bruce Davison, Sondra Locke, Elsa Lanchester, Ernest Borgnine, Michael Dante, Jody Gilbert

THE WIZARD

Film   1927   U.S. (Fox)   60 minutes
Black & white (silent)

A mad surgeon sews together a murderous ape man, then falls victim to his own creation. One of the silent era's last horror films, a well-made period piece marred by an excess of cornball humor.

CREDITS

Director Richard Rosson; *Screenplay* Harry O. Hoyt; Adapted from the play *Balaoo* by Gaston Leroux; *Photographer* Frank B. Good; *Titles* Malcolm Stuart Boylan

CAST

Edmund Lowe, Leila Hyams, Gustav von Seyffertitz, George Kotsonaros, Norman Trevor

WOMANEATER

U.S. title: The Woman Eater

Film   1957   G.B. (Fortress)   71 minutes
Black & white

Can you believe carnivorous trees fed female bodies by a mad scientist who plans to distill the sap into an antideath elixir? The real horror is seeing character actor George Coulouris brought low after a distinguished career that included *Citizen Kane* (1941).

CREDITS

Director Charles Saunders; *Producer* Guido Coen; *Screenplay* Brandon Fleming; *Photographer* Ernest Palmer; *Art Director* Herbert Smith; *Makeup* Terry Terrington; *Music* Edwin Astley

CAST

George Coulouris, Vera Day, Peter Wayn, Joy Webster, Sara Leighton, Jimmy Vaughan

"X" THE MAN WITH THE X-RAY EYES

G.B. title: The Man with the X-Ray Eyes

Film   1963   U.S. (AIP)   86 minutes
Pathecolor   Spectarama

A surgeon experimenting with the nature of vision develops eye drops that enable him to see through matter. At first he's pleased with the results (among the unexpected advantages are the ability to see through clothing and to predict winning numbers in Las Vegas). But his supersight continues to increase, torturing him with more truth than he can bear, until at last he gazes into the very heart of the universe. Near madness, his eyes now black disks, he stumbles into the Nevada desert and pleads for salvation from a traveling evangelist. "If thine eye offend thee, pluck it out," advises the preacher, quoting from the Bible and setting the scene for the film's devastating finale. Handled with uncommon care by Roger Corman, "X" is a terrifying, occasionally moving metaphor for mankind's perilous quest for knowledge, marred only by dated humor and spotty special effects.

CREDITS

Director/Producer Roger Corman; *Screenplay* Robert Dillon, Ray Russell; *Story* Ray Russell; *Photographer*

"X" The Man with the X-Ray Eyes: Carnival huckster Don Rickles offers to exhibit supersighted Ray Milland.

Floyd Crosby; *Art Director* Daniel Haller; *Special Effects* Butler-Glouner, Inc; *Makeup* Ted Coodley; *Music* Les Baxter

CAST

Ray Milland, Diana Van Der Vlis, Don Rickles, John Hoyt, Harold J. Stone, John Dierkes

LES YEUX SANS VISAGE/Eyes Without a Face

Also titled: The Horror Chamber of Dr. Faustus

Film   1959   France (Champs Elysees)
90 minutes   Black & white

Much admired in esoteric cult circles for his unusual style and his mordant humor, director Georges Franju might have become France's premier splatter-chef if not for his formidable talent and his larger purpose. In the documentary short that launched his career, *Le Sang des Betes/Blood of the Beasts* (1948), Franju took his camera into a Paris slaughterhouse for an uncompromising look at conveyor-belt death. Typical of his work, the film juxtaposes images of lyric beauty with blunt horror, and, typically, it outraged middle-class audiences, who didn't want to know where their hotdogs and hamburgers came from.

In *Les Yeux sans Visage*, Franju is out for the audience's metaphoric blood once again. Franju's hero is a famous surgeon who finds himself on the horns of a medical dilemma. Disturbed because he was responsible for the disfigurement of his daughter, he abandons the Hippocratic Oath and kidnaps a beautiful young woman in order to transfer her face to his daughter. Despite his great skill, the fleshy mask is horrifyingly rejected by the body, and he has to repeat the operation again and again, slicing off the facial tissue of his victims and carefully molding the features to the girl's obliterated face. Although faked, the surgical scenes appear to be unnervingly real, and as a result the film was almost universally shunned by distributors. Badly dubbed and reedited, it turned up in the United States as *The Horror Chamber of Dr. Faustus*, double-billed in grind houses with such mindless splatter fare as BLOOD FEAST (see Splatter). But even in its truncated form (the only version available for TV showings), the film retains a tingling duality that both pleases the eye and provokes the mind. Especially haunting is the poetic figure of the mutilated girl, her face covered by a fairy-tale china mask, with only her eyes capable of expressing the torment of her lonely prison.

CREDITS

Director Georges Franju; *Producer* Jules Borkon; *Screenplay* Georges Franju, Jean Redon, Claude Sautet, Pierre Boileau, Thomas Narcejac; based on the novel by Jean Redon; *Photographer* Eugen Schuftan; *Art Director* Auguste Capelier; *Music* Maurice Jarre

CAST

Pierre Brasseur, Alida Valli, Juliette Mayniel, Edith Scob, Francois Guerin, Beatrice Altariba

III
Monsters

All horror antagonists are monsters in the general sense of the word, but specific monsters are characterized by their bigness. There are small monsters too, of course, whose size is compensated for by their enormously disproportionate powers. As native to the human mind as fear and curiosity, the concept of monsters is rooted in the murky depths of the subconscious. Psychologist C.G. Jung theorized that we possess a collective racial memory, revealed in historical archetypes such as deluges, redeemers, heroes, monsters and the like. Jung's theory may account for our willingness to believe in allegedly real creatures like the Loch Ness Monster and the Abominable Snowman.

Monsters first appeared in English literature in the epic adventure *Beowulf*, written in verse over a thousand years ago. A fighter of monsters, Beowulf slays the water troll Grendel and then kills the creature's even more terrible mother. He is eventually done in by a dragon, one of those wonderfully imaginative monsters stabled in medieval bestiar-

ies. Others of the species include the winged griffin and sphinx, the gorgon, the manticore and the yale, the latter an antelopelike beast that escaped predators by jumping off high cliffs and landing on the shock-absorber tips of its horns. (The delightful beasts of burden of the *Star Wars* series comprise a modern bestiary.)

Bestiaries are closer to science fiction than to horror, however, since they express a boundless curiosity about the world. Horror, on the other hand, exploits our collective xenophobia—a survival-oriented response which dates from our Paleolithic past, when it made good sense not to trust unfamiliar animals or people.

The first significant movie monster appeared in DER GOLEM (1920). The golem was an uncontrollable man-made giant created from clay by a medieval rabbi. Golem lore traces back to the Bible, in a reference to Adam, and to the branch of Jewish mysticism known as the Cabbalah. The old legend turned up in Mary Shelley's *Frankenstein*

(1818), whose famous Monster, conceived at the beginning of the industrial age, was given life by science rather than by supernatural means. The golem further influenced our conception of the humanoid monster by providing a model for Boris Karloff in the 1931 movie of FRANKENSTEIN. Shelley's novel is actually a mad scientist story, but the film shifted the emphasis to Dr. Frankenstein's more interesting Monster.

Mammoth prehistoric creatures became another popular threat after THE LOST WORLD (1925), which featured tyrannosauruses and brortosauruses brought to life by stop-motion animator Willis O'Brien. In 1933, KING KONG became the greatest throwback of them all when he rescued Fay Wray from a prehistoric menagerie, before embarking on a city-wrecking tour of civilization. Both the Frankenstein Monster and the giant ape brought a new popularity to movie monsters by dwelling on their inner torment. The characterization brought a sympathetic ambivalence to our usual response of repugnance and fear.

Until 1945, the cinema had to make do with these creatures, and a handful of berserk robots, medical mutants and the self-created monsters of mad scientists Dr. Jekyll and the Invisible Man. The fears triggered by the atom bomb revived long-dormant prehistoric reptiles like GODZILLA and THE BEAST FROM 20,000 FATHOMS, which had powers undreamed of by their prewar predecessors. Throughout the 1950s, nuclear radiation and other ecological tampering resulted in a plethora of disastrous creatures, whose careers are discussed in the category Cataclysmic Disasters.

ABBOTT AND COSTELLO MEET FRANKENSTEIN

Film   1948   U.S. (Universal-International)
83 minutes   Black & white

Universal's famous monsters had skidded into a stall at the box office, prompting the studio to cast them as supporting players in a parody series starring the money-making comedy team of Abbott and Costello. This is the first and best of the lot, with the pair impersonating clumsy porters in an old mansion who inadvertently revive the Frankenstein Monster (Strange) and Dracula (Lugosi). The latter plans to donate Costello's brain to The Monster and keep the blood for himself, but before he can complete the task the Wolf Man (Chaney) comes to the rescue. He grabs the vampire bat in his hairy paws and jumps to their mutual destruction. The Monster, meanwhile, is destroyed in a fire, the fourth in his 17-year career. After this outing, the trio

went into cold storage for a decade to await recycling by England's Hammer studios.

The film marks Lugosi's second and final portrayal of the bloodthirsty Count. It also contains an unforgivable blunder: Dracula's image is reflected in a mirror, which, as everyone knows, is impossible. At the fade-out, Vincent Price is heard as the Invisible Man, but it's Arthur Franz who plays him in the subsequent film.

Others in the series include *Abbott and Costello Meet the Invisible Man* (1951), *Abbott and Costello Meet Dr. Jekyll and Mr. Hyde* (1953), and ABBOTT AND COSTELLO MEET THE MUMMY (1955) (see Mummies).

CREDITS

Director Charles T. Barton; *Producer* Robert Arthur; *Screenplay* John Grant, Frederic I. Rinaldo, Robert Lees; *Photographer* Charles Van Enger; *Art Directors* Bernard Herzbrun, Hilyard Brown; *Special Effects* David S. Horsley, Jerome H. Ash; *Makeup* Bud Westmore; *Music* Frank Skinner

CAST

Bud Abbott, Lou Costello, Lon Chaney, Jr., Glenn Strange, Bela Lugosi, Lenore Aubert, Jane Randolph

THE ADDAMS FAMILY

TV series   1964–66   U.S. (ABC)
30 minutes (weekly)   Color

Macabre programs had never fared well on television because of censorship problems and interruptions by commercials that precluded sustaining an appropriate mood. To capitalize on the current boom in Gothic horror inaugurated by Britain's Hammer studio and sustained by Roger Corman's Poe series at AIP, television decided to parody its monsters in two situation "ghoulcoms." First came CBS's THE MUNSTERS, followed that year by ABC's *The Addams Family*. Both were variations on the top-rated *My Favorite Martian* (1963–66), with Ray Walston playing a Martian stranded on Earth—as was *Bewitched* (1964–72), starring Elizabeth Montgomery as an ordinary housewife who happened to be a witch.

The series was based on the *New Yorker* cartoons of Charles Addams about a peculiar family who lived in an old Gothic house and perpetrated such fiendish pranks as dropping a kettle of boiling oil (or, rather, preparing to) on the heads of a group of Christmas carolers. While the scripts never equaled Addams's deliciously sinister wit,

The Addams Family: From left, John Astin, Lisa Loring, Carolyn Jones, Ted Cassidy (standing behind chair) and Ken Weatherwax.

the characters were sharply drawn and expertly played. Mistress of the household was Morticia (Carolyn Jones), beautifully somber in a long black dress. Her wild-eyed husband Gomez (John Astin) and Uncle Fester (Jackie Coogan) resembled psychopaths in remission. The couple's children, Pugsley and Wednesday, seemed to be pint-sized zombies. Lurch, the butler, could pass for Boris Karloff at a distance (a similarity noted by Karloff in his foreword to *Drawn and Quartered,* a 1942 collection of Addams's drawing). The house was filled with bizarre objects, including a disembodied hand kept in a box and called Thing, and cousin Itt, a midget ball of hair. Aristocratic and always socially correct, the Addams family relaxed by cultivating man-eating plants and stretching each other out on a rack in the basement.

The series is still in syndication, as is its Saturday morning "kidvid" animated spinoff (1973–75).

CREDITS

Directors Nat Perrin, Sidney Lanfield, Jean Yarbrough, Jerry Hopper, Sidney Solkon, Sidney Miller; *Producer* Nat Perrin; *Executive Producer* David Levy; *Music* Vic Muzzey

CAST

Carolyn Jones, John Astin, Jackie Coogan, Ted Cassidy, Lisa Loring, Ken Weatherwax, Blossom Rock, Felix Silla, Margaret Hamilton, Ellen Corby

ALIEN

Film   1979   *U.S. (20th Century-Fox)*
124 minutes   *Eastmancolor   Panavision*
Dolby Stereo

Director Ridley Scott brings a stunning new vitality to the cliche monster-from-outer-space movie. Set in a corporate-owned space tanker returning from a long mission in outer space, the plot has the crew stopping off to answer a distress signal from an uncharted planet covered with ovoid pods growing in the soil. Bursting open, one of the pods disgorges a yellow crab-like creature that lodges in the helmet of an astronaut. Brought on board the spacecraft, the creature dies, but not before leaving its parasitic offspring in the man's body. How the Alien escapes is one of the big shocks—and the most talked about scene—in the movie. From then on, it's hold-your-breath time as the creature picks off the crew one by one from its hiding place in the air ducts.

As usual in such films, the crew behaves rather stupidly in order to provide some effective cat-and-mouse jolts. But Ridley's whirlwind pace and wily misdirection make it all worthwhile; the film is as dazzling and as mesmerizing as a flashing strobe light. Among *Alien's* bizarre pleasures are

Alien: Three astronauts approach the orifice-like entrances to a strange derelict ship.

the "biomechanical" sets, by Swiss artist H. R. Giger, which resemble organs of the human body. The constantly metamorphosing monster—probably the most repulsive ever put on the screen—is the work of Carlo Rambaldi, who also built the lovable *E.T. The Extra-Terrestrial* (1982). The plot is roughly similar to *It!—The Terror from Beyond Space* (1958), a well-made low-budgeter directed by Edward L. Cahn. In the latter film, the crew inadvertently picks up a scaly bloodsucker on Mars which pursues them section by section to a dead end in the nose cockpit. Roger Corman remade the film in 1966 as *Queen of Blood*, with footage culled from a Russian science fiction movie, *The Heavens Call*. All three films owe an unacknowledged debt to A. E. van Vogt's novel *Voyage of the Space Beagle* (1950). (Horror buffs will note that the alien landscape was constructed at England's Bray studios, once the home of Hammer productions.)

CREDITS

Director Ridley Scott; *Producers* Gordon Carroll, David Giler; *Screenplay* Dan O'Bannon; *Story* Dan O'Bannon, Ronald Shusett; *Photographer* Derek Vanlint; *Production Designer* Michael Seymour; *Alien Design* Carlo Rambaldi (Academy Award); *Small Alien* Roger Dicken; *Special Effects* Brian Johnson, Nick Allder, Denys Ayling (Academy Awards); *Alien Landscape* H. R. Giger (Academy Award); *Music* Jerry Goldsmith

CAST

Tom Skerritt, Sigourney Weaver, Veronica Cartwright, Harry Dean Stanton, John Hurt, Ian Holm, Yaphet Kotto

THE BRAIN FROM PLANET AROUS

*Film   1958   U.S. (Howco)   71 minutes
Black & white*

A camp classic, with one of the nuttiest plots ever. John Agar, the most wooden of horror heroes, is perfectly cast as a scientist "taken over" by an evil invisible brain dropped off by a flying saucer. When Agar/brain starts to lust after our women, he/it must be stopped before it's too late. Fortunately, a good brain arrives on the scene, but all it can muster is the body of a dog. The inevitable showdown is not to be missed.

CREDITS

Director Nathan H. Juran; *Producer* Jacques Marquette; *Screenplay* Ray Buffum; *Music* Walter Greene

CAST

John Agar, Joyce Meadows, Robert Fuller, Ken Terrell

Bride of Frankenstein: Elsa Lanchester thinks she can do better.

BRIDE OF FRANKENSTEIN

*Film   1935   U.S. (Universal)   80 minutes
Black & white*

More faithful to its source than the first film, this sequel to FRANKENSTEIN (1931) also has a better script, more impressive sets, music—and a sprightly sense of humor. *Bride* opens with author Mary Shelley, husband Percy and their friend Lord Byron seated around a fireplace. They discuss her novel *Frankenstein* and express disappointment at its ending. Shelley explains that the creature did not die but had survived the flames by falling into a pool under the old mill. A dissolve reprises the scene, and the Monster escapes into a forest, badly frightening a goggle-eyed old lady and immediately establishing the humorous tone of the film.

As was the case in the book, the Monster wants companionship. Understanding his deep need, wizened old Dr. Pretorius, a dabbler in artificial life himself, kidnaps Victor Frankenstein's fiancee (Valerie Hobson) and blackmails his former student into creating a female monster. The "bride," of course, turns out to be Elsa Lanchester (who also plays Mary Shelley) in lightning-hair makeup based on ancient sculptures of the Egyptian queen Nefertiti. No one had thought to ask *her* opinion of the idea, however, and when the Monster reaches out to tenderly pat her hand she releases the most soul-freezing scream and hiss in horror movie history. Karloff nevertheless invests the scene with great pathos as he mutters, with a tear in his eye, "We belong dead," before pulling a lever that blows up the lab.

One of the film's high points is the elegantly fussy performance of Ernest Thesiger as Pretorius, a monster in his own right. Commenting to Victor that "while you were playing with dead flesh, I went to the original seed," he displays bottles filled with tiny homunculi dressed as kings, dancers and the like. Later, the Monster gets to laugh, smoke a cigar and talk, the latter a mistake in Karloff's view since it has the effect of making the creature look stupid rather than uncanny. The scenes with the old hermit, who teaches him friendship and kindness, are embarrassingly sentimental, a failure demonstrated in Mel Brooks's brilliant parody in YOUNG FRANKENSTEIN (1974).

This is the film that created the error that Frankenstein is the name of the Monster instead of its creator. The title had some logic in an early draft of the script, which had the doctor's bride being killed by Dwight Frye to provide a heart for the female creature, an idea nixed by Universal. Originally to have been titled *The Return of Frankenstein*, the film is available in several versions, most with the prologue shortened and without the scene in which the Monster murders a burgermeister. The scene in which the Monster strokes the cheek of a dead girl whose parts are to be used in the Bride was cut by censors in England.

CREDITS

Director James Whale; *Producer* Carl Laemmle, Jr.; *Screenplay* John Balderston, William Hurlbut; *Photographer* John J. Mescall; *Art Director* Charles D. Hall; *Special Effects* John P. Fulton; *Electrical Effects* Kenneth Strickfaden; *Makeup* Jack Pierce; *Music* Franz Waxman

CAST

Boris Karloff, Colin Clive, Valerie Hobson, Ernest Thesiger, Elsa Lanchester, Una O'Connor, E.E. Clive, Dwight Frye

CALTIKI, THE IMMORTAL MONSTER

Film   1959   Italy/U.S. (Galatea/Vailati)
76 minutes   Black & white

Nosy archaeologists disturb the sacred ruins of a Mayan temple and awaken the angry god Caltiki, who looks something like the Blob. Reviewers blamed Hollywood for this film, having been misled by the English-sounding names listed in the credits. Such pseudonyms have since become the norm for genre films emanating from Italy and Spain.

CREDITS

Director Robert Hampton (Riccardo Freda); *Producer* Bruno Vailati; *Screenplay* Philip Just (Fillipo Sanjust); *Photographer* John Foam (Mario Bava); *Music* Robert Nicholas (Roman Vlad)

CAST

John Merivale, Didi Perego, Daniela Rocca, Daniele Vargas, Gerard Herter

CREATURE FROM THE BLACK LAGOON

Film   1954   U.S. (Universal-International)
79 minutes   Black & white   3-D

U-I reassembled the production team that had made a hit of its previous 3-D movie *It Came from Outer Space* (1953), and the result was Hollywood's first postwar superstar monster. The serviceable plot has an archaeological expedition cruising up a tributary of the Amazon to a black lagoon occupied by a missing link between man and amphibian. Before long the male members of the expedition find themselves competing with the savage gill-man for the affections of heroine Julie Adams.

Director Jack Arnold keeps the fantasy elements of the story under control, and cooly builds suspense with an accretion of realistic detail. His eerie, shadowy jungle setting suggests the creature's prehistoric past, even though it is the studio's standing jungle set. The underwater photography by James C. Haven still looks good, notably in a scene in which the white-suited Adams swims across the lagoon, her movements matched by the creature in an underwater display of erotic longing.

The creature was designed by Bud Westmore and Jack Kevan and modeled after the Motion Picture Academy's Oscar award. Ricou Browning handled the swimming scenes and Ben Chapman and Tom Hennessy wore the sponge-rubber costume on land. Although the actors recall being ashamed of being in the low-budget film, it was a phenomenal success and spawned two sequels: *Revenge of the Creature* and THE CREATURE WALKS AMONG US. A sympathetic, appealing monster in the tradition of King Kong (even Marilyn Monroe felt

Creature from the Black Lagoon: Julie Adams plays beauty to Ricou Browning's beast.

sorry for him, in *The Seven Year Itch*), the creature was planning a big-screen color comeback in 1986.

CREDITS

Director Jack Arnold; *Producer* William Alland; *Screenplay* Harry Essex, Arthur Ross; *Story* Maurice Zimm; *Photographer* William E. Snyder; *Underwater Photographer* James C. Havens; *Production Designers* Bernard Herzbrun, Hilyard Brown; *Makeup* Bud Westmore, Jack Kevan; *Special Effects* Charles S. Welbourne

CAST

Richard Carlson, Julie Adams, Richard Denning, Antonio Moreno, Nestor Paiva, Ricou Browning, Ben Chapman, Tom Hennessy

THE CREATURE WALKS AMONG US

Film   1956   U.S. (Universal-International)
78 minutes   Black & white

Having gotten free at the climax of *Revenge of the Creature* (1955), the popular gill-man was brought back for an emasculating farewell, badly in need of the powerful imagery and erotic tension director Jack Arnold had brought to the previous films. Burned accidentally during recapture, the amphibian undergoes an emergency operation which saves its life but deprives it of its gills and scales. Now a vulnerable, air-breathing land animal, locked in an outdoor cage like a zoo curiosity, it musters enough strength to break through a fence to rescue the assaulted heroine. Its noble intentions misunderstood once again, it drags its bullet-riddled body instinctively, and fatally, into the sea.

CREDITS

Director John Sherwood; *Producer* William Alland; *Screenplay* Arthur Ross; *Photographer* Maury Gersman; *Special Effects* Clifford Stine; *Makeup* Bud Westmore; *Music* Joseph Gershenson

CAST

Jeff Morrow, Rex Reason, Leigh Snowden, Gregg Palmer, Ricou Browning (the sea Creature), Don Megowan (the land Creature)

THE CURSE OF FRANKENSTEIN

Film 1957 G.B. (Hammer) 83 minutes
Eastmancolor

Britain's little Hammer studios flexed its muscle as a major genre force with this zippy color remake of Universal's 1931 FRANKENSTEIN, which spawned Gothic horror's post-war revival. As before, it's not really Shelley's story, but Sangster's script offers some interesting interpolations. The lab has gone back to its rightful place in Switzerland, with an unsympathetic Dr. Frankenstein (Peter Cushing) deliberately murdering people to obtain body parts for his Monster (Christopher Lee). He then dispatches it to commit even more murders. Karloff's Frankenstein makeup was protected by Universal's copyright, so Lee looks rather like a green-faced, badly scarred zombie. The story is told in flashback, with the imprisoned Frankenstein trying to convince authorities that the Monster committed the crimes he is accused of. But since the creature had been dissolved in acid, there is no proof he ever existed and Frankenstein has to take the rap.

The prototype of Hammer's subsequent output, this film mixes equal parts of suspense, jiggly sex and sadism, all liberally sprinkled with blood (which was only a foretaste of what was to come). Critics hated the garish gore but audiences responded by throwing money, and the film was an international hit. Hammer had even more success with its next horror, DRACULA (1958) (see Vampires), and by the 1960s its formula had become a genre standard. Much of Hammer's product continued to star Lee and Cushing, who had come along just in time to prevent our favorite monsters from becoming the camp menaces of such films as I WAS A TEENAGE FRANKENSTEIN (1957). The studio spun off a series of increasingly explicit sequels, including THE REVENGE OF FRANKENSTEIN (1958), THE EVIL OF FRANKENSTEIN (1964), FRANKENSTEIN CREATED WOMAN (1967), FRANKENSTEIN MUST BE DESTROYED! (1969), THE HORROR OF FRANKENSTEIN (1970), and FRANKENSTEIN AND THE MONSTER FROM HELL (1973).

CREDITS

Director Terence Fisher; *Producer* Anthony Hinds; *Screenplay* Jimmy Sangster; *Photographer* Jack Asher; *Production Designer* Ted Marshall; *Makeup* Phil Leaky, Roy Ashton; *Music* James Bernard

CAST

Peter Cushing, Christopher Lee, Hazel Court, Robert Urquhart, Valerie Gaunt, Noel Hood

DUEL

TV film 1971 U.S. (Universal)
73 minutes Color

The automobile may have been designed for our convenience, but it also kills and maims thousands of us every year while spewing poisonous fumes into the air. Rather than being our savior, it sometimes seems as if the car will lead to our extinction. Director Steven Spielberg, then at the beginning of his career, brilliantly exploits our deep-rooted fear of these robotlike extensions of ourselves in terms of a chase movie like *Bullitt* or *The French Connection*.

Richard Matheson's script is set in a no-man's-land highway where Dennis Weaver, alone in a compact car, is besieged without motive by a hulking black gasoline tanker with an unseen driver. Howling with fumes and rage, the technological dragon tailgates him at 100 miles per hour, shoves him into the oncoming lane, and slams him onto a railway crossing where a train is about to pass. At the finale, Weaver jams the accelerator with a rock and watches the two vehicles lunge together, like dinosaurs locked in mortal combat. It's every motorist's nightmare made real, directed with a nerve-wracking, escalating mood of paranoia, totally satisfying our wish-fulfillment of speed and danger. Spielberg uses the TV medium to his advantage, structuring the story to provide logical cliffhanging breaks for the insertion of commercials, which usually tend to dissipate good horror. One of the best, this one didn't vanish like most made-for-TV movies. It was released theatrically abroad (with additional scenes depicting Weaver's home life) and at home in 1982, after Spielberg had become a marquee name with such films as JAWS (1975) and *E.T. the Extra-Terrestrial* (1982).

Among the movies that have pitted man against his favorite machine is television's *Killdozer* (1974), based on a story by Theodore Sturgeon, in which construction workers on a Pacific island battle a homicidal bulldozer possessed by an alien intelligence. Director/producer was Robert Aldrich. *The Car* (1977), a theatrical film directed by Elliott Silverstein, cast James Brolin as a driver pursued by a black car possessed by the devil. Its best shot is the car itself—designed by George Barris and driven by Everett Creach—described by Stephen King as looking like "a squatty airport limo from one of Hell's used car lots." Another is King's jealous *Christine* (1984). France's contribution is the cerebral *Weekend* (1967), in which *auteur* filmmaker Jean-Luc Godard imagines the end of the world as a massive traffic jam. And from Australia comes the gruesome comedy *The Cars That Ate Paris* (1974). The title refers not to the French capital but to an outback town whose citizens make a living by enticing cars off the highway and recycling their parts and drivers.

CREDITS

Director Steven Spielberg; *Producer* George Eckstein; *Screenplay* Richard Matheson, based on his short story; *Photographer* Jack A. Marta; *Art Director* Robert S. Smith; *Music* Billy Goldenberg

CAST

Dennis Weaver, Tim Herbert, Charles Steel, Eddie Firestone, Lucille Benson, Gary Loftin

THE EVIL OF FRANKENSTEIN

Film   1964   G.B. (Hammer/Universal)
94 minutes   Technicolor

Hammer's third Frankenstein feature, following THE REVENGE OF FRANKENSTEIN (1958), retains Peter Cushing as the baron who has a yen for creating life from death. This episode has the doctor returning to the Balkans (Switzerland in Shelley's novel) and recovering the Monster from a glacier. Its brain has been damaged, so Frankenstein has the creature revived by a sinister carnival mesmerist who usurps the baron's control. Universal finally gave permission to use its copyrighted makeup, so this Monster looks more like Boris Karloff's, but, as portrayed by Kiwi Kingston, it lacks Karloff's subtle, pathetic mime. Production credits are up to Hammer's high standards and the script has a central logic, but the Monster takes too long to get moving and writer Elder has little new to offer. The American TV version has added an unnecessary prologue.

CREDITS

Director Freddie Francis; *Producer/Screenplay* John Elder (Anthony Hinds); *Photographer* John Wilcox; *Art Director* Don Mingaye; *Special Effects* Les Bowie; *Makeup* Roy Ashton; *Music* Don Banks

CAST

Peter Cushing, Sandor Eles, Peter Woodthorpe, Kiwi Kingston, Katy Wild, Duncan Lamont

FRANKENSTEIN

Film   1931   U.S. (Universal)   71 minutes
Black & white

The most famous and one of the most influential genre films, James Whale's *Frankenstein* raised American horror to the level of art. Mary Shelley's novel, *Frankenstein, or a Modern Prometheus* (1818), had been filmed twice before. In 1910 there was Thomas Edison's *Frankenstein*, a film that has since vanished, but whose stills show a wild-maned hunchbacked Monster played by Charles Ogle. In 1915 came the Ocean Film Corporation of New York's *Life Without a Soul*, which featured Percy Darrell as a human-looking Monster who, in the film's program notes, was described as "awesome but never grotesque." The latter film revealed Dr. Frankenstein's experiment to have been a terrible nightmare—a typical cop-out ending of the period.

Karloff defined the role permanently, becoming a major star in the process as well as inspiring scores of imitators. Although its movements are derived from Wegener's DER GOLEM (1920), the creature's superb sense of mime and powerful range of facial expressions are Karloff's own. Equally innovative is the cosmetic creation of Jack Pierce, who updated Shelley's Monster into a pseudo-scientific one, based on "research in anatomy, surgery, criminology, ancient and modern burial customs, and electro-dynamics." The two metal studs that stick out from the sides of Karloff's neck are inlets for electricity, according to Pierce, "plugs, not bolts. The Monster was an electrical gadget and lightning was his life force."

The direct source of the film is a play by Peggy Webling, which introduced the dramatic conflict—not in Shelley's novel—of the Monster accidentally receiving a criminal's brain. (The novel had first been dramatized in London, in 1823, as *Presumption! or, the Fate of Frankenstein*.) French director Robert Florey had written a script based on the play at the behest of Universal, which was anxious to follow up its first sound genre film, DRACULA (1931) (see Vampires). Florey's script further altered Shelley's story by borrowing from Germany's HOMUNKULUS DER FUHRER and DER GOLEM, and having Dr. Viktor Frankenstein (Henry in the film) take a back seat to his Monster. After Bela Lugosi turned down the role because it was a nonspeaking part and required a heavy disguise, the film was reassigned to the more accomplished English director James Whale. Whale's choice was a little-known 44-year-old character actor working under the stage name of Boris Karloff. He was tall, with long arms, and not important enough to balk at the daily four-hour makeup requirements. (Karloff later recalled that

Top: Boris Karloff in **Frankenstein** (1931). Opposite, from top, left, clockwise: Lon Chaney, Jr. in **The Ghost of Franken-stein** (1942); Bela Lugosi in **Frankenstein Meets the Wolf Man** (1943); Glenn Strange in **House of Frankenstein** (1944); Christopher Lee in **The Curse of Frankenstein** (1957); and Dave Prowse—better known as Darth Vader in the *Star Wars* series—in **The Horror of Frankenstein** (1970).

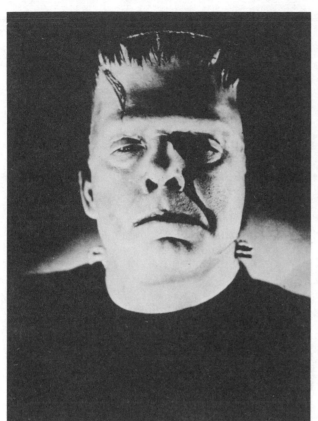
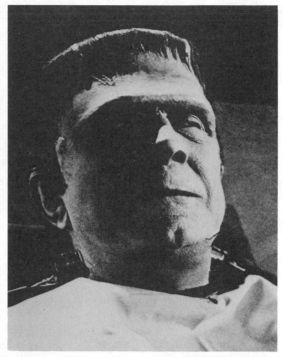
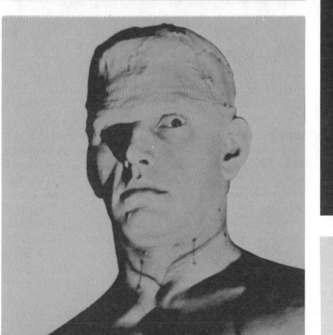
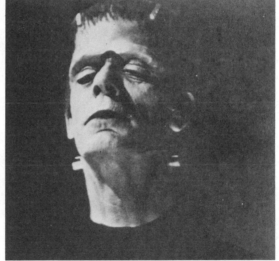
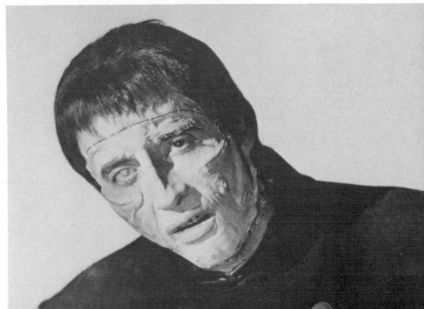

he was delighted to be paid the princely sum of $125 a week for the back-breaking job.)

The film was initially shown in large metropolitan theaters tinted green—the symbolic color of horror—which had the frightening effect of making the lips and hollows on the face of the Monster turn black. Removed from the final release print were two scenes that preview audiences objected to. One of them shows the Monster meeting a little girl in the countryside who is throwing flowers into a stream. Joining in the fun, but unable to discriminate between a flower and a human life, he tosses the girl into the water. The other was the euphoric line of Dr. Frankenstein (Colin Clive) in which he exclaims, "Now I know what it feels like to be God!" A further cut was made in England, of the scene in which the Monster replies to Dwight Frye's taunting by hanging him. A huge success, the film was one of the first to be accompanied by a publicity campaign that warned the "weak-hearted" to stay away—an enticement that continues to this day.

The sequels are BRIDE OF FRANKENSTEIN (1935); SON OF FRANKENSTEIN (1939); THE GHOST OF FRANKENSTEIN (1942); FRANKENSTEIN MEETS THE WOLF MAN (1943); HOUSE OF FRANKENSTEIN (1944); HOUSE OF DRACULA (1945) (see Vampires); and ABBOTT AND COSTELLO MEET FRANKENSTEIN (1948). Britain's Hammer studio inaugurated a color Frankenstein series with THE CURSE OF FRANKENSTEIN (1957).

CREDITS

Director James Whale; *Producer* Carl Laemmle, Jr.; *Screenplay* John L. Balderston, Garrett Fort, Francis Edward Faragoh, Robert Florey (uncredited), based on the play by Peggy Webling, adapted from the novel by Mary Shelley; *Photographer* Arthur Edeson; *Art Director* Charles D. Hall; *Sets* Herman Rosse; *Special Effects* John P. Fulton; *Makeup* Jack Pierce; *Electrical Effects* Kenneth Strickfaden; *Music* David Broekman

CAST

Boris Karloff, Colin Clive, Mae Clarke, Dwight Frye, John Boles, Edward Van Sloan, Frederick Kerr, Lionel Belmore, Michael Mark

FRANKENSTEIN

TV film   1973   U.S. (ABC)   145 minutes Color

While Hammer was phasing out its tired movie series with 1973's FRANKENSTEIN AND THE MON-

STER FROM HELL, television stepped into the breach with two literary adaptations of the Mary Shelley story. (A previous abridgement of the Universal classic had been aired live in 1952 on TALES OF TOMORROW (see Anthologies), with Lon Chaney, Jr. as the Monster). Originally broadcast on two consecutive nights on ABC's late-night *Wide World of Mystery*, it stars pensive Robert Foxworth as Victor Frankenstein and lanky Bo Svenson walking tall as the Monster. Although closer to the novel's text than was FRANKENSTEIN: THE TRUE STORY, the other Shelley adaptation televised that year, this one is no more frightening and considerably less polished. Producer Dan Curtis showed a surer touch with the contemporary Gothic horrors of *The Night Stalker,* which launched the KOLCHAK series (see Anthologies).

CREDITS

Director Glenn Jordan; *Producer* Dan Curtis; *Screenplay* Sam Hall (Part 1), Richard Landau (Part 2); *Photographer* Ben Colman; *Art Director* Trevor Williams; *Music* Robert Cobert

CAST

Robert Foxworth, Susan Strasberg, Bo Svenson, John Karlen, Heidi Vaughn, Philip Bourneuf, Rosella Olson

FRANKENSTEIN

Play   1981   U.S. (Broadway)   2 Acts

Like other fading screen stars, the Frankenstein Monster hoped to revive his career by starring in a big Broadway show. Dracula had scored a smash hit in 1977, and Frank Langella had gone on to star in a lavish movie remake, so why not he? The difference was that *Dracula* on Broadway had a suspenseful script, an eerie wit and a strong central performance. In *Frankenstein* the play merged scenes from James Whale's 1931 film with random thoughts from Mary Shelley's novel, producing an amalgam that had the preachy quality of a PBS documentary. Faithful to the author, the lead-footed Monster learned to talk, and talk he did, even while murdering a lovable little boy and his cute little dog.

The sets were impressive, however, in their massive depiction of a snowy Swiss valley, a garish graveyard and a laboratory filled with gushing neon tubes and sparking wires. What the producers had gambled on were the special effects (the show was promoted as the first special effects play), handled by Bran Ferren, the man responsible for the terrifying transformation sequences of ALTERED STATES (1980) (see Werewolves and Other Shape-Shifters). But no matter how showy and convincing Ferren's blizzards and lightning bolts, they couldn't quite match the magic tricks that can be conjured up on film. Critics agreed that the play's the thing, and the show closed in one night, registering a $2 million loss. It remains Broadway's most catastrophic flop, the theatrical equivalent of Michael Cimino's *Heaven's Gate*, which lost $36 million the year before.

CREDITS

Director Tom Moore; *Producer* Marvin A. Krauss; *Play* Victor Gialanella; *Costumes and Puppets* Carrie F. Robbins; *Special Effects and Sound Effects* Bram Ferren; *Sets* Douglas W. Schmidt; *Music* Richard Peaslee; *Presented by* Terry Allen Kramer, Joseph Kipness, James M. Nederlander, Stewart F. Lane, in association with 20th Century-Fox Productions

CAST

David Dukes (Victor Frankenstein); Keith Jochim (the Monster), John Seitz, John Glover, John Carradine, Scott Schwartz, Dennis Bacigalupi, Dianne Weist, Jill P. Rose

FRANKENSTEIN AND THE MONSTER FROM HELL

Film   1973   G.B. (Hammer)   99 minutes
Color

Peter Cushing returns as Dr. Frankenstein, operating in a secret lab at the insane asylum he had been sentenced to for the crime of "sorcery." Aided by a young disciple committed for a similar offense, the doctor stitches together a new Monster from the amputated body parts of inmates, much the same as he did in THE REVENGE OF FRANKENSTEIN (1958). Predictably, the creature is disassembled by a mob of foaming inmates, sending Victor back to his anatomy texts to spawn a sequel that was never to be. Cushing and director Fisher seem to be played out, and the Monster (impersonated by Dave Prowse, Darth Vader of *Star Wars*) is more to be pitied than feared. It was Fisher's final film and the end of Hammer's series.

CREDITS

Director Terence Fisher; *Producer* Roy Skeggs; *Screenplay* John Elder (Anthony Hinds); *Photographer* Brian

Probyn; *Art Director* Scott MacGregor; *Makeup* Eddie Knight; *Music* James Bernard

CAST

Peter Cushing, Shane Briant, Dave Prowse, Madeline Smith, Bernard Lee, John Stratton

FRANKENSTEIN CONQUERS THE WORLD

Film   1964   Japan (Toho)   87 minutes
Tohoscope

A battle to the death between Baragon, a horned reptile with a freezing ray, and a boy made mammoth by eating the Frankenstein Monster's heart (which really didn't belong to him anyway). From the folks who gave us GODZILLA.

CREDITS

Director Inoshiro Honda; *Producer* Tomoyuki Tanaka; *Screenplay* Kaoru Mabuchi; *Photographer* Hajime Koizumi; *Art Director* Takeo Kita; *Special Effects* Eiji Tsuburaya

CAST

Nick Adams, Tadeo Takashima, Jumi Mizuno, Yoshio Tsuchiya

FRANKENSTEIN CREATED WOMAN

Film   1967   G.B. (Hammer)   92 minutes
Color

Looking remarkably fit after his fatal beating in THE REVENGE OF FRANKENSTEIN, the irrepressible baron (Peter Cushing again) performs the ultimate medical miracle—a transsexual body transplant. In attempting to prove that the soul survives after death, he revives the shapely corpse of a blonde suicide (clad only in a gauze bikini) by giving her the soul of a man wrongly executed for murder. Hinds's screenplay has some interesting implications, but it stretches the myth nearly to the breaking point. Hammer took the idea to a more ridiculous—and enjoyable—extreme in DR. JEKYLL AND SISTER HYDE (see Mad Scientists).

CREDITS

Director Terence Fisher; *Producer* Anthony Nelson Keys; *Screenplay* John Elder (Anthony Hinds); *Photographer*

Arthur Grant; *Production Designer* Bernard Robinson; *Special Effects* Les Bowie; *Makeup* George Partleton; *Music* James Bernard

CAST

Peter Cushing, Susan Denberg, Thorley Walters, Duncan Lamont, Robert Morris, Peter Blythe

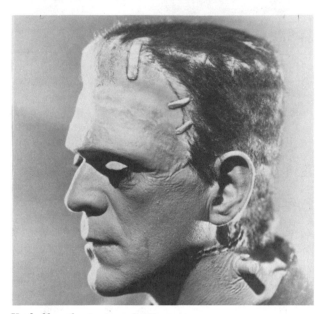

Karloff as the immortal Monster.

FRANKENSTEIN MEETS THE WOLF MAN

Film   1943   U.S. (Universal)   74 minutes
Black & white

Billed by Universal as the "Clash of the Century," this was at least a major social event of monsterdom. An improvement over the previous year's THE GHOST OF FRANKENSTEIN, it's actually a sequel to THE WOLF MAN (1941) (see Werewolves and Other Shape-Shifters). The Monster, playing the first of his supporting roles, is inadvertently revived by mad scientist Lionel Atwill in a failed attempt to wire Larry Talbot's lycanthropy into the Monster's corpse. Playing musical chairs, Lon Chaney, Jr., the Monster in the previous outing, is back in his original role as the Wolf Man. Lugosi, formerly the hunchback Ygor, is now the Monster (he was right to have turned the role down originally). Chaney, meanwhile, also had appeared that year in Lugosi's trademark role as SON OF DRACULA (see Vampires). Got it? The fiendish trio would be united for the first time in the next year's HOUSE OF FRANKENSTEIN. Diminishing box office returns indicated that none of the trio was strong enough to stand on his own.

CREDITS

Director Roy William Neill; *Producer* George Waggner; *Screenplay* Curt Siodmak; *Photographer* George Robinson; *Special Effects* John P. Fulton; *Makeup* Jack Pierce; *Music* Hans Salter

CAST

Bela Lugosi, Lon Chaney, Jr., Lionel Atwill, Patric Knowles, Ilona Massey, Maria Ouspenskaya, Eddie Parker (Monster stunt double)

FRANKENSTEIN MUST BE DESTROYED!

Film   1969   G.B. (Hammer)   97 minutes
Color

Hammer's fifth Frankenstein feature has Cushing back in the lab as the experimental scientist, now dabbling in brain surgery. Director Fisher takes a spirited trip through very familiar terrain, while expanding the limits of movie gore ad nauseam. There are several choice pulse-quickening effects, including a corpse forced up from the mud by a broken waterpipe.

CREDITS

Director Terence Fisher; *Producer* Anthony Nelson Keys; *Screenplay* Bart Batt; *Photographer* Arthur Grant; *Art Director* Bernard Robinson; *Makeup* Eddie Knight; *Music* James Bernard

CAST

Peter Cushing, Simon Ward, Veronica Carlson, Freddie Jones, Thorley Walters, Maxine Audley, George Pravda

FRANKENSTEIN 1970

Film   1958   U.S. (Allied Artists)   83 minutes
Black & white   Anamorphic

Hammer's successful Gothic horror revival inspired this deliberately campy, and ultimately awful, exploitation item from the little studio that used to be Monogram, the former prince of poverty row. Karloff, playing Baron Frankenstein for the first and only time, creates a new monster from body parts acquired from a film crew shooting a horror movie at Castle Frankenstein. Among the script's novel notions is having the creature sparked to life by an atomic reactor. It should have been hilarious.

CREDITS

Director Howard W. Koch; *Producer* Aubrey Schenck; *Screenplay* Richard Landau, George Worthing Yates; *Photographer* Paul Guthrie; *Makeup* Gordon Bau; *Music* Paul Dunlap

CAST

Boris Karloff, Tom Duggan, Jana Lund, Mike Lane, Donald Barry

FRANKENSTEIN: THE TRUE STORY

TV film   1973   G.B. (MCA)   200 minutes Color

Its title notwithstanding, this prestige American TV production (which was shot in London) owes as much to the febrile imagination of writers Christopher Isherwood and Don Bachardy as it does to Mary Shelley's. One of the script's accurate touches—and a refreshing departure from the Universal/Hammer approach—is its characterization of the Monster as a *tabula rasa* named Adam. Unlike Karloff's brutish creature (who has a criminal's brain), Adam (Michael Sarrazin) is a complex being who becomes a killer only after the normal world rejects him. The double-edged title, smacking of scandal-sheet revelations, underlines the film's novel suggestion that Victor Frankenstein (Leonard Whiting) is a latent homosexual whose creation is a narcissistic version of himself.

Among the script's baffling revisions is the introduction of a manipulative scientist named Dr. Polidori (James Mason)—apparently meant as a tribute to Shelley's partner at the famous ghost writing session. Here, it's Polidori, rather than the Monster himself, who pressures young Frankenstein into creating a bride for the Monster. And the bungled ending has the doctor sailing to Antarctica to escape the creature rather than chasing him there. Polite and prettified and never really terrifying, the film at least indicates a growing respect for the genre, and it's superior to the other TV FRANKENSTEIN aired earlier in 1973. An abridged version of this two-parter was released theatrically in Europe after its initial broadcast.

CREDITS

Director Jack Smight; *Producer* Hunt Stromberg, Jr.; *Screenplay* Christopher Isherwood, Don Bachardy, based on the novel by Mary Shelley; *Photographer* Arthur Ibbetson; *Art Director* Wilfrid Shingleton; *Special*

Effects Roy Whybrow; *Makeup* Roy Ashton; *Music* Gil Melle

CAST

Leonard Whiting, Michael Sarrazin, James Mason, Jane Seymour, David McCallum, Agnes Moorehead, Margaret Leighton, Ralph Richardson, Tom Baker, John Gielgud

GARGOYLES

TV film   1972   U.S. (Tomorrow Entertainment) 74 minutes   Color

Fifties science fiction nonsense about a nest of prehistoric creatures threatening to take over the world, uncovered by a spelunking anthropologist and his daughter. The "gargoyles"—part man, part bird and part reptile—won Emmies for makeup artists Ellis Berman and Ross Wheat, but in the clumsy hands of director Norton they're more funny than frightening.

CREDITS

Director B.W.L. Norton; *Producers* Robert W. Christiansen, Rick Rosenberg; *Screenplay* Stephen and Elinor Karpf; *Photographer* Earl Rath; *Makeup* Ellis Berman, Ross Wheat; *Music* Robert Prince

CAST

Cornel Wilde, Jennifer Salt, Grayson Hall, Bernie Casey, Scott Glenn

THE GHOST OF FRANKENSTEIN

Film   1942   U.S. (Universal)   68 minutes Black & white

Frankenstein's second son Ludwig takes up where his brother Wolfgang left off in 1939's SON OF FRANKENSTEIN. Lugosi returns as the crazy hunchback Ygor, having inexplicably recovered from his death in the previous film. He reclaims the Monster from the castle's sulphur pit and coerces Dr. Ludwig (Cedric Hardwicke) into replacing the creature's defective criminal brain with his own. Although successful, the operation blinds the Monster/Ygor, who expresses his displeasure by wrecking the lab and setting it afire. For all its nostalgic appeal, this one is the weak link in the series, and has neither the Gothic vigor of the first three films nor the spirited pace of subsequent episodes. Replacing Karloff, Lon Chaney, Jr., plays the Monster as a robotlike beast, with little of the innate sympathy his predecessor brought to the role. The final scenes set the stage for Lugosi to play the Monster in the next sequel, FRANKENSTEIN MEETS THE WOLF MAN (1943).

CREDITS

Director Erle C. Kenton; *Producer* George Waggner; *Screenplay* W. Scott Darling; *Story* Eric Taylor; *Photographers* Milton Krasner, Woody Bredell; *Art Director* Jack Otterson; *Makeup* Jack Pierce; *Special Effects* John P. Fulton; *Music* Charles Previn

CAST

Lon Chaney, Jr., Bela Lugosi, Cedric Hardwicke, Lionel Atwill, Evelyn Ankers, Ralph Bellamy, Dwight Frye

THE GIANT CLAW

Film   1957   U.S. (Columbia)   76 minutes
Black & white

A giant alien buzzard wings into New York and nips off the top of the Empire State Building. Bird droppings.

CREDITS

Director Fred Sears; *Producer* Sam Katzman; *Screenplay* Samuel Newman, Paul Gangelin; *Photographer* Benjamin Kline; *Art Director* Paul Palmentola; *Music* Mischa Bakaleinikoff

CAST

Jeff Morrow, Mara Corday, Morris Ankrum, Morgan Jones, Robert Shane

GODZILLA, KING OF THE MONSTERS

Film   1954   Japan (Toho)   80 minutes
Black & white

Japan's first full-fledged science fiction film brought to the world the titanic dinosaur called Godzilla—the apotheosis of fifties schlock titles. (In Japan he is known, phonetically, as *Gojira*, a blend of the English word *gorilla* and the Japanese word ku*jira*, meaning whale.) Toho studios conceived the creature as its answer to the popular American movie, THE BEAST FROM 20,000

FATHOMS (1953). The story has the 400-foot-high Jurassic monster being revived by Pacific H-bomb tests, then angrily laying waste to Tokyo with his giant tromping feet, flailing reptilian tail and his radioactive breath, the most lethal halitosis known to mankind.

The talented duo behind this camp masterpiece was director Inoshiro Honda and special effects artisan Eiji Tsuburaya (who died in 1970). The creature itself was impersonated until 1972 by actor Haruo Nakajima in a 100-pound monster suit; for closeups of Godzilla firing his atomic breath, a mechanical head was used. During his 30-year career he has varied in size relative to his miniature cities; he appears tall and thin in some movies and bottom-heavy in others. Modern weaponry can't stop him, only a power equal to his own can do that. This time it's an "oxygen destroyer," a secret weapon so terrible that its inventor commits hari-kari rather than release it to the world.

Something of a national hero at home, akin to America's King Kong, he has evolved from the most evil of creatures to the protector of the world. Semioticists claim the first film is a reflection of no-nuke Japan's nuclear jitters (one character does exclaim, "First Nagasaki, now I have to be in Tokyo when this happens"). But it's doubtful that any of the kids who enjoyed the movie took it seriously.

Godzilla's 16 movies include: *Gigantis, the Fire Monster* (1955) (his name was changed by Warner Bros. because another studio owned the rights to it); KING KONG VS. GODZILLA (1962) (his first in color and wide-screen); *Godzilla vs. the Thing* (1964); *Ghidra, the Three-Headed Monster* (1965); *Monster Zero* (1965); *Godzilla vs. the Sea Monster* (1966); SON OF GODZILLA (1967); *Destroy All Monsters!* (1968); *Godzilla's Revenge* (1969); *Godzilla vs. the Smog Monster* (1971); *Godzilla on Monster Island* (1972); *Godzilla vs. Megalon* (1973); *Godzilla vs. the Cosmic Monster* (1974) (in which he battles a robot duplicate of himself called Mechagodzilla); *Terror of Godzilla* (1976). Toho released a new *Godzilla* in 1985. His kidvid TV series was *The Godzilla Power Hour* (1978–79).

CREDITS

Director Inoshiro Honda; *Producer* Tomoyuki Tanaka; *Screenplay* Takeo Murata, Inoshiro Honda, from a story by Shigeru Kayama; *English-language version* Terry Morse; *Photographers* Masao Tamai, Guy Roe; *Special Effects* Eiji Tsuburaya, Kuichiko Kishida, Akira Watanabe; *Music* Akira Ifukube

CAST

Raymond Burr, Takashi Shimura, Momoko Kochi, Akira Takarada, Akihiko Hirata, Sachio Sakai

DER GOLEM, WIE ER IN DIE WELT KAM/ The Golem, and How He Came into the World

Film 1920 Germany (UFA) 75 minutes
Black & white (silent)

Although others had preceded it, the Golem is the cinema's first important monster and set the standard for later generations of movie monsters.

The great German actor and filmmaker Paul Wegener plays the creature, a huge clay statue built by a 16th-century rabbi in Prague to protect his people from a pogrom. Brought to life by placing a Star of David on its chest, the creature eventually goes out of control and rampages violently through the ghetto. A brave little girl finally de-animates the soulless Golem by removing the Star from its doublet. Many of the plot elements, as well as Hans Poelzig's abstract set design and Karl Freund's camera style, became genre standards in Hollywood during the 1930s and 1940s. And

Der Golem: The prototype for Frankenstein movie monsters.

Wegener's sympathetic portrayal—and his hulking, clay-covered strut—can be seen in Karloff's 1931 FRANKENSTEIN and all those who followed.

Wegener filmed two previous versions of the story, set in the present day: *The Golem* (1915), released in the U.S. as *The Monster of Fate* (in the same week, unfortunately, that the U.S. severed diplomatic relations with Germany) and *The Golem and the Dancing Girl* (1917). All that remains of both films are a few still photographs. This version is adapted from a 1916 novel by Gustav Meyrink, recounting the famous Jewish legend of Rabbi Loew, a Talmudic scholar of 16th-century Prague. Falsely accused of baking the blood of Christians in their matzohs, the ghetto Jews rallied behind a golem named Yoseph, created by Rabbi Loew's sacred Hebrew incantations.

Subsequent film treatments of the legend include France's *Le Golem* (1936), directed by Julien Duvivier; Czechoslovakia's *The Emperor and the Golem* (1951), a comedy directed by Mac Fric; and IT! (1966), an exploitation item from Great Britain. There are several dramatizations, including H. Leivick's *The Golem*, revived in 1984 by the New York Shakespeare Festival.

CREDITS

Directors Paul Wegener, Carl Boese; *Screenplay* Paul Wegener, Henrik Galeen, based on the novel *Der Golem* by Gustav Meyrink; *Photographers* Karl Freund, Guido Seeber; *Assistant Photographer* Edgar G. Ulmer; *Production Designer* Hans Poelzig; *Art Director* Kurt Richter

CAST

Paul Wegener, Albert Steinruck, Lyda Salmonova, Ernst Deutsch, Hanns Sturm, Otto Gebuhr, Lothar Muthel, Loni Nest

GREMLINS

Film   1984   U.S. (Warner Bros.)   105 minutes
Technicolor   Dolby Stereo

Another blockbuster from the prolific Steven Spielberg, and one of the top three box-office draws of 1984. (Numbers one and two were Ivan Reitman's GHOSTBUSTERS (see Ghosts, Demons and Witches) and Spielberg's *Indiana Jones and the Temple of Doom*.) Star of the film is a small, furry, teddy bear–like creature called a mogwai, which has big bunny ears and a nose like Bambi's. Purchased in San Francisco by a visiting inventor and brought home to his family in the comically idealized town of Kingston Falls, U.S.A., the fictitious mogwai soon begins to reproduce itself.

Unlike their cuddly progenitor, the second-generation mogwais—the gremlins of the title—are small devilish creatures that resemble the imps of Hieronymous Bosch. At first they are mischievous, self-absorbed pets, but they eventually turn mean and attack the spacey 20-year-old hero Billy (Zach Galligan) with a chainsaw and shoot an arrow into his shoulder with a spear gun. Mom meanwhile attempts to keep their increasing numbers under control by decapitating one gremlin with a chopping knife and shoving another into a food proces-

Gremlins: Nasty implike pets get their final comeuppance in a movie theater.

sor. The small evildoers finally get their comeuppance when Billy blows up a movie theater, where they are packed inside and enjoying—like a kiddie matinee audience—a screening of *Snow White and the Seven Dwarfs.*

Gremlins is more typical of the cartoon black comedy style of director Joe Dante than the optimistic Peter Pan vision of Spielberg, who had a similar relationship with Tobe Hooper, the director of his spectacular ghost story POLTERGEIST (1982) (see Ghosts, Witches and Demons). As in his episode of *Twilight Zone—The Movie* (1983) and in *Piranha* (1978) and THE HOWLING (1981) (see Werewolves and Other Shape-Shifters), Dante is so preoccupied with movie in-jokes and having nasty fun that he fails to provide a consistent narrative. Chris Walas' mechanical gremlins are everything they should be, however, and they predictably spawned a line of tie-in toys.

This is one of the PG movies of 1984 that prompted parents and critics to complain that special effects were becoming too frightening for small children—for whom *Gremlins* is obviously intended (the *New York Times* called it "kiddie gore"). As a result, the Motion Picture Association of America established the new category of PG-13, which puts some movies off limits to children under 13 unless they are accompanied by a parent or another adult.

CREDITS

Director Joe Dante; *Producer* Michael Finnell; *Executive Producers* Steven Spielberg, Frank Marshall, Kathleen Kennedy; *Screenplay* Chris Columbus; *Photographer* John Hora; *Production Designer* James A. Spencer; *Special Effects* Chris Walas; *Music* Jerry Goldsmith

CAST

Zach Galligan, Hoyt Axton, Frances Lee McCain, Phoebe Cates, Polly Holliday, Scott Brady, Dick Miller, Keye Luke, Jonathan Banke, John Louie, Harry Carey, Jr.

GRIZZLY

Television title: *Killer Grizzly*

Film　1976　U.S. (Film Ventures)　90 minutes
Movielab　Todd AO-35

"From *Jaws* to Claws," ballyhooed the ads, promising "18 feet of gut-crunching, man-eating terror." Since the $100,000 mechanical bear didn't

work, what you get is a tame 12-foot grizzly pretending to be a thawed prehistoric monster, while nuzzling confused, ketchup-stained actors.

CREDITS

Director William Girdler; *Producers/Screenplay* David Sheldon, Harvey Flazman; *Photographers* William Asman, Tom Spaulding; *Special Effects* Phil Corey; *Music* Robert O. Ragland; *Bear Trainer* Lloyd Beebe

CAST

Christopher George, Andrew Prine, Richard Jaeckel, Joan McCall, Joe Dorsey

HOMUNKULUS DER FUHRER/ Homunculus the Leader

Film serial　1916　Germany (Bioscop)
6 episodes　Black & white (silent)

A huge success in wartime Germany, this influential serial depicts a handsome, brilliant young man who becomes embittered when he discovers he was born from chemicals in a test tube. Deciding to revenge himself on the human race, he turns to the last refuge of politics and becomes a cold-blooded dictator with plans to destroy everyone in a global war. Divine intervention stops him in the final reel, in the form of a lightning bolt. The title derives from medieval alchemists whose goal it was to create artificial life, which they called a homunculus. (The same creatures are concocted by Mephistopheles in Goethe's *Faust*.) Director Rippert was apparently also inspired by Mary Shelley's *Frankenstein*. The film's expressionist design influenced later German horror films, including DAS KABINETT VON DR. CALIGARI (1919) (see Mad Scientists). As prophecy it foresaw the rise of Hitler and the concept of Aryan superiority.

CREDITS

Director Otto Rippert; *Screenplay* Otto Rippert, Robert Nuess, based on a novel by Robert Reinert; *Photographer* Carl Hoffman

CAST

Olaf Fonss, Frederick Kuhn, Theodor Loos, Mechtild Their, Maria Carmi

THE HORROR OF FRANKENSTEIN

*Film 1970 G.B. (Hammer) 95 minutes
Technicolor*

Hammer laid a box-office egg with this garishly plumed renovation—the sixth in its Frankenstein series. Filmmaker Sangster sets the story in promiscuous present-day London, where young Dr. Frankenstein murders disco patrons to get body parts for his latest creation. The energetic gore is undermined by Sangster's constant winks at the audience, and the result is neither black comedy nor horror. Ralph Bates, filling in for Cushing, plays the bird-loving baron, and Dave Prowse is the Monster.

CREDITS

Director/Producer Jimmy Sangster; *Screenplay* Jimmy Sangster, Jeremy Burnham; *Photographer* Moray Grant; *Art Director* Scott MacGregor; *Makeup* Tom Smith; *Music* James Bernard

CAST

Ralph Bates, Kate O'Meara, Veronica Carlson, Dave Prowse, Graham James, Dennis Price

HOUSE OF FRANKENSTEIN

*Film 1944 U.S. (Universal) 71 minutes
Black & white*

Inevitably, the success of 1943's FRANKENSTEIN MEETS THE WOLF MAN inspired Universal to add more fiends to its predictable witch's brew. (At one point the Mummy was included, and the film was to be titled *Chamber of Horrors.*) Now a mad magician, Karloff and his hunchback servant (J. Carrol Naish) are conveniently freed from prison by a lightning bolt. Establishing a traveling freak show, they exhibit the skeleton of Dracula, who materializes in a series of double exposures as John Carradine when Karloff pulls the stake from between his ribs. The Monster doesn't appear until the last half hour, discovered by Karloff frozen in ice with the Wolf Man (Lon Chaney, Jr.) after their previous watery demise. Former wrestler Glenn Strange, coached by the master, plays the first of his three Monsters, which duplicates Karloff's record. Although flimsy and predictable, it's an enjoyable monster mash, and if the creatures aren't very frightening, it's because by now they had begun to assume the familiarity of old friends.

CREDITS

Director Erle C. Kenton; *Producer* Paul Malvern; *Screenplay* Edward T. Lowe; *Story* Curt Siodmak; *Photographer* George Robinson; *Special Effects* John P. Fulton; *Makeup* Jack Pierce; *Music* Hans J. Salter

CAST

Boris Karloff, Lon Chaney, Jr., John Carradine, J. Carrol Naish, Lionel Atwill, Anne Gwynne, George Zucco, Glenn Strange, Sig Ruman, Elena Verdugo

I WAS A TEENAGE FRANKENSTEIN

*Film 1957 U.S. (AIP) 74 minutes
Black & white and color sequence*

Herman Cohen's follow-up to his trend-setting I WAS A TEENAGE WEREWOLF (1957) (see Werewolves and Other Shape-Shifters) is more selfconsciously outrageous and in many ways less dated than its predecessor. Whit Bissell is back as the mad scientist, this time setting up shop near an American high school campus so he can appropriate body parts from deceased hot-rodders and other adolescent accident victims. Towering teen Monster Gary Conway—who looks like a fullback hit in the face with pancake batter—soon develops a liking for fast cars, girls in pony tails, and rock and roll music. This was the first film to pry into the creature's private life by referring obliquely to his formidable private parts. It contains the doctor's famous line, "Answer me, you fool! I know you have a civil tongue in your head. I sewed it there myself!"

CREDITS

Director Herbert L. Strock; *Producer* Herman Cohen; *Screenplay* Kenneth Langtry; *Photographer* Lothrop Worth; *Makeup* Philip Scheer; *Music* Paul Dunlap

CAST

Whit Bissell, Gary Conway, Phyllis Coates, Robert Burton, John Cliff, George Lynn

THE INDESTRUCTIBLE MAN

*Film 1956 U.S. (Allied Artists) 70 minutes
Black & white*

Electrocuted for a crime he didn't commit, a small-time thug revives and sparks through town pulling the plugs on the guys who framed him. Juiceless.

CREDITS

Director/Producer Jack Pollexfen; *Screenplay* Sue Bradford, Vy Russell; *Photographer* John Russell, Jr.; *Musical Director* Albert Glasser

CAST

Lon Chaney, Jr., Marian Carr, Ross Elliott, Robert Shayne

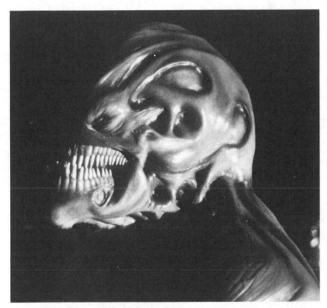

The Intruder Within: A primeval creature floats up from the ocean floor.

THE INTRUDER WITHIN

TV film   1981   U.S. (ABC)   104 minutes Color

A primeval creature "from the dark recesses of time" picks off workers on an oil rig floating in the Arctic Ocean, one by one. The drilling has released the stone-like eggs of a 14-million-year-old monster from suspended animation under the icy ocean floor. A crew member adopts one of the embryonic creatures, which quickly grows into a vicious killer—just like the creature in the film ALIEN (1979), the inspiration for this derivative potboiler. Its original titles were *Panic Offshore* and *The Lucifer Rig*.

CREDITS

Director Peter Carter; *Producer* Neil T. Maffeo; *Screenplay* Ed Waters; *Photographer* James Pergola; *Creature Design* James Cummins, Henry Golas; *Special Effects* Don Powers; *Music* Gil Melle

CAST

Chad Everett, Joseph Bottoms, Jennifer Warren, Rockne Tarkington, Paul Larson

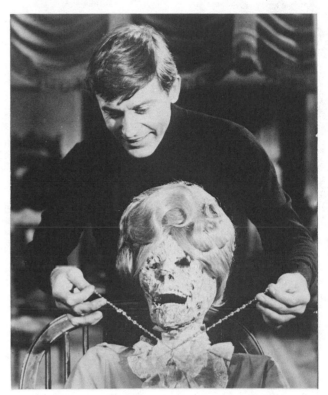

It: Roddy McDowall fastens a stolen necklace to his mother's corpse.

IT!

Film   1966   G.B. (Seven Arts/Goldstar) 97 minutes   Color

Juvenile remake of DER GOLEM (1920), with Roddy McDowall as a nutty museum curator who revives the mystical Hebrew monster and uses it to kill his rivals. Cheap special effects and McDowall's outrageous mugging undermine the script's basic premise.

CREDITS

Director/Producer/Screenplay Herbert J. Leder; *Executive Producer* Robert Goldstein; *Photographer* David

Bolton; *Art Director* Scott McGregor; *Music* Carlo Martelli

CAST

Roddy McDowall, Jill Haworth, Paul Maxwell, Ian McCulloch, Noel Trevarthen

Jaws: A great white shark overturns a sailboat and zeroes in on one of its passengers.

JAWS

Film   1975   U.S. (Universal)   125 minutes Technicolor   Panavision

Everything you could hope for and more in a sea-going adventure fantasy. Simply sketched, the story has a giant white shark preying on the resort community of Amity, Long Island, and driving away the summer business. Three men are called in to play Captain Ahab: the inadequate chief of police (Roy Scheider), an eager young shark expert (Richard Dreyfuss) and Quint (Robert Shaw), the shark boat owner and the leader of the group. In keeping with the trend toward increasingly graphic horror effects, *Jaws* shows people being eaten alive by the razor-mouthed monster, which also rams apart a boat and chomps on a limb or two. Director Steven Spielberg, who wrote his own ticket after this blockbuster, melts us into silly putty, with a little help from editor Verna Fields and John Williams' musical score. Bruce, the head mechanical shark, was built by Bob Mattey, who

won an Oscar for the giant squid of Walt Disney's *20,000 Leagues Under the Sea* (1954). Rechristened Brucette, the shark reappeared as a pregnant female in the sequel, JAWS 2 (1978). You had to take a snorkel to *Jaws 3-D* (1983), to protect yourself from the shark vomit floating off the screen.

CREDITS

Director Steven Spielberg; *Producers* Richard D. Zanuck, David Brown; *Screenplay* Peter Benchley, Carl Gottlieb, based on the novel by Peter Benchley; *Photographer* Bill Butler; *Underwater Photographer* Rexford Metz; *Shark Footage* Ron and Valerie Taylor; *Production Designer* Joseph Alves, Jr.; *Special Effects* Bob Mattey; *Music* John Williams

CAST

Roy Scheider, Robert Shaw, Richard Dreyfuss, Lorraine Gary, Murray Hamilton, Carl Gottlieb, Peter Benchley

JAWS 2

Film   1978   U.S. (Universal)   116 minutes Technicolor   Panavision   Dolby Stereo

If you were stranded on the North Pole and managed to miss JAWS (1975), you might enjoy this "Beach Blanket" sequel, which is essentially a 1950s' monster movie with a big-budget veneer. This time out the great white shark invades a posh Long Island resort to gobble up teenagers, the favorite diet of the omnivorous—and far more entertaining—Blob a generation earlier. Director Jeannot Szwarc provides a few high-tension scenes, but compared to Steven Spielberg's original, the film is a minnow.

CREDITS

Director Jeannot Szwarc; *Producers* Richard D. Zanuck, David Brown; *Screenplay* Carl Gottlieb, Howard Sackler, Dorothy Tristan; *Photographers* Michael Butler, David Butler, Michael McGowan; *Production Designer/ Second Unit Director* Joe Alves; *Special Mechanical Effects* Bob Mattey, Roy Arbogast; *Makeup* Rick Sharp, Ron Snyder, Bob Jiras; *Music* John Williams

CAST

Roy Scheider, Lorraine Gary, Murray Hamilton, Joseph Mascolo, Colin Wilcox, Jeffrey Kramer

JESSE JAMES MEETS FRANKENSTEIN'S DAUGHTER

*Film   1966   U.S. (Embassy)   88 minutes
Color*

Enjoyably hokey Western/horror pastiche that follows Dr. Frankenstein's daughter to the American Southwest, where she falls in love with outlaw Jesse James and turns his sidekick into the Frankenstein monster. Director Beaudine's style is an almanac of 1940s B-picture cliches.

CREDITS

Director William Beaudine; *Producer* Carroll Case; *Screenplay* Carl Hittleman; *Photographer* Lothrop Worth; *Art Director* Paul Sylos; *Makeup* Ted Coodley; *Music* Raoul Kraushaar

CAST

Narda Onyx, John Lupton, Steven Geray, Cal Bolder, Estelita

KING KONG

*Film   1933   U.S. (RKO)   100 minutes
Black & white*

The cinema's greatest fairy tale, outside animated movies. There had been many Darwinian gorilla plays and movies before *King Kong*, including *Balaoo, the Demon Baboon* (1913); *The Gorilla*, with Walter Pidgeon going ape in both the 1927 and 1930 movies of Ralph Spence's play; *Go and Get It* (1920), with Bull Montana as a humanoid ape; *A Blind Bargain* (1922), with Lon Chaney being deformed by grafted monkey glands; *The Wizard* (1927), which had George Kotsonaros sprouting hair everywhere but on his face; and Poe's *Murders in the Rue Morgue* (1914 and 1932). Kong was no mindless savage, however, nor was he a brute trained to extract revenge on the helpless at the behest of a human master. Kong was designed to be noble and lovable. If he seemed to be perversely fascinated by a human female the size of his fist, we know his motives were pure and honorable.

The deceptively simple story begins with producer Carl Denham (Robert Armstrong) planning to make a movie on a remote island where prehistoric monsters have been discovered. Armstrong—playing a role modeled on adventurous, Barnum-like co-director Cooper—hires a desperate, out-of-work actress named Ann Darrow (Fay Wray) to star in the movie. Arriving by ship on Skull Island, the expedition finds it inhabited by a tribe of natives, who have built a mammoth wall to keep out the prehistoric creatures. The natives, having never seen a blonde woman, decide Wray would be perfect as the next virgin sacrifice for the giant gorilla who lives next door.

Unlike many subsequent giant monster movies, which bring on their monsters almost immediately, *King Kong* deliciously builds suspense by showing no unusual animal for its first half hour. When Kong finally comes to claim his prize, instead of killing the girl, he becomes smitten with her. As he carries Wray back to his cave, he proves his devotion by defending her against various prehistoric creatures, including a tyrannosaur and a pterodactyl. Armstrong, springing to the rescue, immobilizes the ape with gas bombs and decides to shanghai him for a money-making exhibit in New York.

Billed as the "eighth wonder of the world," Kong finally rebels and breaks his chains during a picture-taking session with Wray (he thinks the flashbulbs are harming her) and runs amok in Manhattan. Reclaiming Wray, he scales the brand-new Empire State Building which, to him, represents the safety of the highest tree. Air Force biplanes shoot the great furry monarch of beasts from his perch, and he falls, fatally wounded, to the street below—but not before tenderly depositing Wray in a safe place. "Well, Denham, the airplanes got him," says a policeman to Armstrong. The producer shakes his head knowingly and delivers the film's famous last lines: "Oh, no—it wasn't the airplanes. It was beauty killed the beast!"

Although his fur occasionally ripples and his movements are sometimes awkward, Kong is unforgettable. His quizzical, bewildered expressions project the torment of the friendless outsider in the same way that Karloff expressed the horror of discovering the world considered him a monster in FRANKENSTEIN. Kong, of course, was in reality a steel-skeletoned doll only 18 inches high. It was given living, breathing movement by stop-motion animator Willis O'Brien, who painstakingly moved the dyed rabbit fur–covered model against a miniature landscape a fraction of an inch for each frame-photograph. A full-scale mechanical arm and a bearhide-covered head and shoulders were used for the scenes with Wray. Scenes showing a giant foot pulverizing the natives were cut from the film before its release. (An alternative ending had Kong being trapped and shot down in Yankee Stadium.)

Originally titled *The Beast*, then *The Eighth Wonder* and then simply *Kong* before the "King" was added, the film enchanted critics and moviegoers alike. It was the only feature to play simultaneously at Radio City Music Hall and The Roxy, then New York's largest theaters. Fay Wray's immortal screams, combined with the ape's thunderous growls (provided by sound effects man Murray Spivack) were among the era's most thrilling sounds (as was the dynamic musical score by Max Steiner). RKO had wisely refused MGM's offer to buy the movie for $400,000 over its negative cost of $672,000 before its release, for *King Kong* went on to earn a formidable—and continuous—profit.

Less than a year later Cooper, Schoedsack and O'Brien produced SON OF KONG, whose mother had been conspicuously missing in the first film, in which Kong is described as being millions of years old. The team reworked the formula in 1949's MIGHTY JOE YOUNG, a juvenile fairy tale that lacks Kong's universal appeal. More recently there was Dino De Laurentiis's unnecessary 1976 remake, parodied in Britain's *Queen Kong* (1976), which has a female gorilla climbing to the top of the London Post Office with Ray Faye.

CREDITS

Directors/Producers Merian C. Cooper, Ernest B. Schoedsack; *Executive Producer* David O. Selznick; *Screenplay* James Creelman, Ruth Rose; *Story* Merian C. Cooper, Edgar Wallace; *Photographers* Edward Lindon, Vernon L. Walker, J. O. Taylor; *Art Directors* Carroll Clark, Al Herman; *Stop Motion Effects* Willis O'Brien, Marcel Delgado, Fred Reefe, Orville Goldner, Carroll Shephird; *Sound Effects* Murray Spivack; *Makeup* Mel Berns; *Music* Max Steiner

CAST

Robert Armstrong, Fay Wray, Bruce Cabot, Frank Reicher, Sam Hardy, Noble Johnson, Steve Clemente, James Flavin, Victor Wong, Sandra Shaw, Merian C. Cooper, Ernest B. Schoedsack

KING KONG

TV series   1966-69   U.S. (ABC)
30 minutes (weekly)   Color

The mythic gorilla retooled as a Saturday morning TV cartoon character akin to a giant teddy bear. He lives happily as the friend of a human anthropologist on the island of Mondo, where the diabolical Dr. Who (no relation to the BBC-TV Time Lord) constantly attempts to capture him.

King Kong: Fay Wray is the girl in the hairy paw in the 1933 original, top; Jessica Lange took over in the 1976 remake.

KING KONG

Film   1976   U.S. (De Laurentiis/Paramount)
135 minutes   Metrocolor   Panavision
Dolby Stereo

By the 1970s King Kong had become a bona fide cultural hero. He had turned up in literature

(Thomas Pynchon's *Gravity's Rainbow*), in serious journalism (*New York Times* editorial page), and in the various plastic, graphic and performing arts. Like any celebrity, his personal life had been nosed into, notably in *The Girl in the Hairy Paw*, a collection of Kong memorabilia which includes an essay titled "How Big Is Kong's Penis?" Meanwhile, he continued to turn a profit for kidvid television, Japanese moviemakers, advertising agencies and toy manufacturers.

Mogul Dino De Laurentiis, aware that the original film had not been circulated since 1956, when it was sold to television, decided that the time was right to gamble $24 million on an epic color remake (the 1933 *Kong* had cost all of $672,000). Writer Lorenzo Semple, Jr., who had written many of the scripts for TV's campy *Batman* series in the 1960s, updated the original screenplay with a knowing erotic wink. Kong's lady love (Jessica Lange) has become a no-nonsense feminist, again offered to the ape as a sacrifice (although no longer a virgin sacrifice) when she visits Skull Island with an expedition of greedy oil-company despoilers. Taken back to the U.S. in an empty supertanker, Kong makes a brave last stand atop the twin towers of Manhattan's World Trade Center.

Because Willis O'Brien's original composite stop-motion technique was no longer economically feasible, De Laurentiis commissioned special effects craftsman Carlo Rambaldi to build a giant mechanical ape. Trouble was, the robot ape wouldn't answer its cues, so makeup artist Rick Baker was hastily called in to impersonate Kong in his own monkey costume, a role he had previously played in *Schlock* (1973), a creature-feature spoof directed by John Landis. While the film is entertaining, the star is not *our* King Kong. Nor is Jessica Lange an adequate substitute for Fay Wray. And why desert the Empire State Building?

CREDITS

Director John Guillermin; *Producer* Dino De Laurentiis; *Screenplay* Lorenzo Semple, Jr., based on the screenplay by James Creelman and Ruth Rose, from a story by Merian C. Cooper and Edgar Wallace; *Photographer* Richard H. Kline; *Production Designers* Dale Hennessy, Mario Chiari; *Special Effects* Carlo Rambaldi, Frank Van Der Veer, Glen Robinson; *Makeup Effects* Rick Baker; *Music* John Barry

CAST

Jeff Bridges, Charles Grodin, Jessica Lange, John Randolph, Rene Auberjonois, John Agar, Julius Harris

KING KONG ESCAPES

Film 1967 *Japan (Toho)* 96 minutes
Color Tohoscope

The great ape journeys from his Pacific hideaway to Tokyo, where he has a gargantuan battle with MechniKong, a robot double with burning rays. Also getting a drubbing are a sea monster and assorted Cenozoic creatures.

CREDITS

Director Inishiro Honda; *Producer* Tomoyuki Tanaka; *Screenplay* Kaoru Mabuchi; *American version* William J. Kennan; *Photographer* Hajime Koizumi; *Special Effects* Eiji Tsuburaya; *Music* Akira Ifukube

CAST

Rhodes Reason, Linda Miller, Mie Hama, Akira Takarada, Eisei Anamoto

KING KONG VS. GODZILLA

Film 1962 *Japan (Toho)* 90 minutes
Color Anamorphic

They had to meet sooner or later for a special effects showdown—the first movie for both in color and wide screen. After several tag-team matches, they tumble from a mountaintop into the sea below. Not one of the giant lizard's better outings.

CREDITS

Director Inishiro Honda; *Screenplay* Takeshi Kimura; *Photographer* Isamu Ashida; *Special Effects* Eiji Tsuburaya; *Music* Akira Ifukaube

CAST

Michael Keith, James Yagi, Tadao Takashima, Mie Hama

KONGA

Film 1961 *G.B. (AIP)* 90 minutes
Eastmancolor

In his classroom Michael Gough is a model of rectitude, but in the lab, heh-heh-heh, it's another story. He's tinkering with a strange man-eating plant whose sap contains a hormone capable of doubling and tripling the size of any living thing. When university officials object to the unorthodox experiments, Gough, eyebrows arched like porcupines on the attack, injects the stuff into a cute çhimp named Konga and transforms the beast into a killer ape. At the finale Gough gets his comeuppance Fay Wray style when king Konga, who won't stop growing, shoots through the roof with Gough in its hairy paw. Filmmaker Herman Cohen, who gave the world I WAS A TEENAGE WEREWOLF (see Werewolves and Other Shape-Shifters) and I WAS A TEENAGE FRANKENSTEIN (both 1957), reportedly wanted to title this one *I Was a Teenage Gorilla*. Asked why the professor's girlfriend is murdered for no apparent reason, Cohen explained: "I wanted to use my carnivorous plants. She was a very pretty girl and very sexy, and I thought the audience would get a big kick out of seeing her killed rather than Margo Johns or Michael Gough."

CREDITS

Director John Lemont; *Producer* Herman Cohen; *Screenplay* Aben Kandel, Herman Cohen; *Photographer* Desmond Dickinson; *Art Director* Wilfred Arnold; *Music* Gerard Schurmann

CAST

Michael Gough, Margo Johns, Jess Conrad, Claire Gordon, Austin Trevor

THE LIFT

Film   1983   Netherlands (Sigma/Warner)
99 minutes   Eastmancolor

A wry little Dutch movie with an appealingly unconventional villain: a homicidal elevator. A mutated microchip causes a lift in a high-rise office building to go berserk and resourcefully snuff several passengers in various fatal "accidents." One hurried businessman gets his head severed when he attempts to slip between the closing automated doors. In a mordantly misleading scene, the "killevator" plays an up-and-down game with a child holding a teddy bear. The dubbing is atrocious, however, and the duel between man and machine is interminably delayed by some heavy groping in the cabin between the hero and his girlfriend.

CREDITS

Director/Screenplay/Music Dick Maas; *Producer* Matthijs Van Heinjningen; *Photographer* Marc Felperlaan; *Art Director* Harry Ammerlaan

CAST

Huub Stapel, Willeke Van Ammelrooy, Piet Romer, Josine Van Dalsum, Gerard Thoolen, Hans Veerman

THE LOST WORLD

Film   1925   U.S. (First National)   100 minutes
Black & white, with tinted sequences (silent)

The kitsch stop-motion menagerie created by Willis H. O'Brien is the show, but without the requisite grunts, roars and squeaks his creatures aren't very terrifying. A relatively faithful adaptation of Arthur Conan Doyle's novel of the same title—the first in his Professor Challenger series—the film ploddingly follows an English expedition to a lost world in South America inhabited by ape men, dinosaurs and other vanished species. The expedition returns home with a brontosaurus egg (a pterodactyl egg in the book) which hatches in London and grows into a monster that tears apart the city. The scene, a sensation in its time, has since become a science fiction cliche, repeated to better effect in O'Brien's KING KONG (1933). It has also been seen often in Japanese productions, notably in that country's GODZILLA series.

CREDITS

Director Harry O. Hoyt; *Producers* Earl Hudson, Watterson R. Rothacker; *Screenplay* Marion Fairfax; *Special Effects* Willis H. O'Brien; *Models* Marcel Delgado; *Photographer* Arthur Edeson

CAST

Wallace Beery, Lewis Stone, Bessie Love, Lloyd Hughes, Bull Montana (the ape man)

THE MANSTER

G.B. title: The Split

Film   1959   U.S./Japan (United Artists)
72 minutes   Black & white

Two directors are credited for this sleep-inducing science fantasy about an American journalist transformed into a two-headed monster by a Japanese doctor. The pair eventually splits, which is not such a bad idea.

CREDITS

Directors George P. Breakston, Kenneth G. Crane; *Producer/Story* Kenneth G. Crane; *Screenplay* Walter J. Sheldon; *Photographer* David Mason; *Art Director* Nobori Miyakuni; *Music* Hirooki Ogawa

CAST

Peter Dyneley, Satoshi Nakamura, Jane Hylton, Terri Zimmern, Toyoko Takechi

MIGHTY JOE YOUNG

*Film 1949 U.S. (RKO) 94 minutes
Black & white*

Billed as being "Mightier than King Kong!", this great ape is actually closer in spirit to the forgotten SON OF KONG than to the potently malevolent giant. Made by the same team that produced *Kong*, the film is essentially a trivialized smaller-scale remake of the 1933 original. Robert Armstrong, still the fast-talking showman, finds the ape in Africa where he is the docile pet of orphan Terry Moore. Transported to Hollywood, Joe becomes the star attraction of Armstrong's "super-colossal" nightclub (a masterpiece of high camp), where he demonstrates his strength and Moore plays his favorite song "Beautiful Dreamer" on a grand piano. When nightclub patrons harass him, he tears through the templelike auditorium, providing customers with a totally involving, spectacular encore. Joe later redeems himself by rescuing children from a burning orphanage, and then returns to Africa to live happily, and platonically, ever after with Moore.

Although the erotic implications of the earlier film are missing, and Young is much too nice for

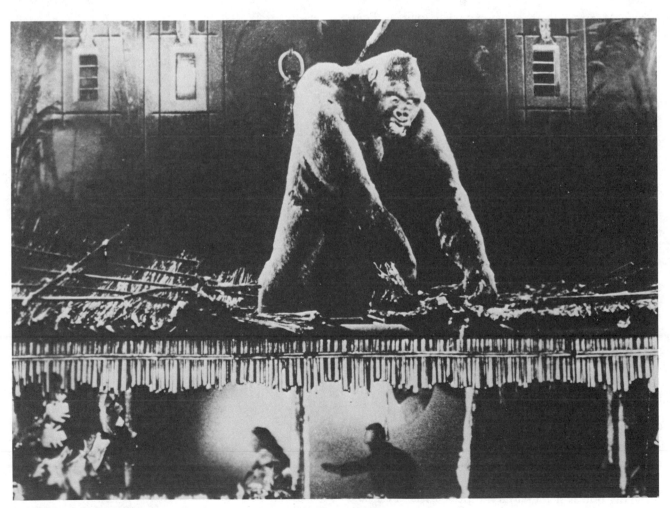

Mighty Joe Young: More friendly than Kong but just as destructive.

his own good, the film is lively and polished, and succeeds as a juvenile adventure show. O'Brien's stop-motion effects are more supple than the original, and there is some interesting footage from his unfinished prehistoric epic, *Gwangi*. Most of the animation was reportedly done by Ray Harryhausen, since O'Brien was busy planning and supervising the production. The pair shared an Academy Award that year for special effects.

CREDITS

Director Ernest B. Schoedsack; *Producer/Story* Merian C. Cooper; *Executive Producer* John Ford; *Screenplay* Ruth Rose; *Photographer* J. Roy Hunt; *Photographic Effects* Harold Stine, Bert Willis; *Art Director* James Basevi; *Stop-Motion Effects* Willis H. O'Brien, Ray Harryhausen, Marcel Delgado, Peter Peterson, George Lofgren, Linwood G. Dunn, Fitch Fulton; *Music* Roy Webb

CAST

Terry Moore, Robert Armstrong, Ben Johnson, Frank McHugh, Lora Lee, Nestor Paiva, Regis Toomey, Douglas Fowley

THE MONSTER AND THE GIRL

Film   1941   U.S. (Paramount)   65 minutes Black & white

A gorilla implanted with the brain of a man executed for a crime he didn't commit goes on a vengeful rampage. You're likely to fall asleep long before justice is done.

CREDITS

Director Stuart Heisler; *Producer* Jack Moss; *Screenplay* Stuart Anthony; *Photographer* Victor Milner; *Musical Director* Sigmund Krumgold

CAST

Ellen Drew, Robert Paige, Onslow Stevens, George Zucco, Paul Lukas, Rod Cameron, Philip Terry

THE MONSTER OF PIEDRAS BLANCAS

Film   1958   U.S. (Vanwick)   71 minutes Black & white

This one is a legendary reptile living in a cave and tended by a nearby lighthouse keeper. As usual, the huge beast is ungrateful.

CREDITS

Director Irvin Berwick; *Producer* Jack Kevan; *Screenplay* C. Haile Chace; *Photographer* Philip Lathrop; *Art Director* Walter Woodworth

CAST

Les Tremayne, John Harmon, Forest Lewis, Frank Arvidson, Wayne Berwick

THE MOST DANGEROUS MAN ALIVE

Film   1961   U.S. (Columbia)   82 minutes Black & white

Convict sentenced for a crime he didn't commit escapes from jail and happens into an exploding cobalt bomb, which turns his tissues into steel and enables him to punish those who framed him. Veteran director Allan Dwan brings a brooding intensity to the cliches.

CREDITS

Director Allan Dwan; *Producer* Benedict Bogeaus; *Screenplay* James Leicester, Phillip Rock, based on the novel *The Steel Monster* by Phillip Rock; *Photographer* Carl Carvahal; *Music* Louis Forbest

CAST

Ron Randell, Debra Paget, Morris Ankrum, Joel Donte

THE MUNSTERS

TV series   1964–66   U.S. (CBS) 30 minutes (weekly)   Color

Universal revamped its famous movie monsters of the 1930s for this prime-time sitcom, which presented them as a somewhat offbeat suburban American family of the 1960s. Herman Munster was a ringer for the Frankenstein Monster, his wife Lily appeared to be a zombie, his 10-year-old son looked like a werewolf cub, and old Grandpa was the spitting image of Count Dracula. The Munsters kept trying to make friends with their frightened neighbors, completely unaware of the effect they had on them, a situation that was initially hilarious but eventually became routine and predictable. The quartet nevertheless was popular enough to star in a mediocre theatrical movie, *Munster, Go Home* (1966). A similar series, THE ADDAMS FAMILY, had more comic verve.

The Munsters: Yvonne DeCarlo and Fred Gwynne.

CREDITS

Directors Norman Abbott, Charles Barton, Earl Bellamy, Seymour Burns, Lawrence Dobkin, Joseph Pevney, Ezra Stone and others; *Producers* Joe Connelly, Bob Mosher; *Music* Jack Marshall

CAST

Fred Gwynne, Yvonne DeCarlo, Butch Patrick, Al Lewis, and Debbie Watson, Paul Lynde, John Carradine

ORCA—KILLER WHALE

Film   1977   U.S. (Paramount/De Laurentiis)
92 minutes   Technicolor   Panavision
Dolby Stereo

It took a small army of technicians to float poor Orca, the vengeful mate of a harpooned pregnant female, and all they could manage was JAWS without teeth.

CREDITS

Director Michael Anderson; *Producer* Luciano Vincenzoni; *Screenplay* Luciano Vincenzoni, Sergio Donati;

Photographers Ted Moore, J. Barry Herron, Ron Taylor, Vittorio Dragonetti; *Production Designer* Mario Garbuglia; *Special Effects* Frank Van Der Veer, Alex C. Weldon, Rinaldo Campoli, Jim Hole, Guiseppe Carozza; *Music* Ennio Morricone

CAST

Richard Harris, Charlotte Rampling, Will Sampson, Keenan Wynn, Bo Derek, Robert Carradine

PANIC ON THE TRANSIBERIAN

U.S. title: Horror Express

Film   1972   Spain/G.B. (Granada/Benmar)
90 minutes   Color

Lee and Cushing, cast as stuffy Edwardian anthropologists, have a jolly awful time transporting a deep-frozen Neanderthal to a London museum aboard the Transiberian Express (a model built for *Nicholas and Alexandra*). Scarcely out of the station, the apeman thaws and begins skulking through the train killing passengers and sucking the wrinkles from their brains. Turns out the creature is a space alien, accidentally iced millennia ago, and it is absorbing human intelligence to learn how to build a spaceship and get back home. A neat trick since it would take another 50 years to work out the technology.

CREDITS

Director Eugenio Martin; *Producer* Bernard Gordon; *Screenplay* Armand d'Usseau, Julian Halvey; *Photographer* Alejandro Ulloa; *Art Director* Ramiro Gomez Guardiana; *Special Effects* Pablo Perez; *Music* John Cacavas

CAST

Christopher Lee, Peter Cushing, Telly Savalas, Silvio Tortosa

PHANTOM FROM SPACE

Film   1953   U.S. (United Artists)   72 minutes
Black & white

By the 1950s, creatures from outer space rivaled the mad scientist and his monsters as the horror film's most malevolent menace. This one is an invisible alien who arrives on Earth in the standard flying saucer and quickly busies himself killing innocent bystanders. When he finally succeeds in breaking into a nearby observatory, the canny astronomers are ready with an infrared lamp that reveals the intruder to be—gasp—a muscle-man wearing a futuristic shower cap. The director/producer is mainstream filmmaker Billy Wilder's brother.

CREDITS

Director/Producer W. Lee Wilder; *Screenplay* William Raynor, Myles Wilder; *Story* W. Lee Wilder; *Special Effects* Alex Welden, Howard Anderson; *Music* William Lava

CAST

Ted Cooper, Jim Bannon, Noreen Nash, Michael Mark

THE PHANTOM FROM 10,000 LEAGUES

Film 1956 U.S. (AIP) 81 minutes Black & white

A mutant sea creature rises from the ocean depths and terrorizes bathers. AIP released this tadpole version of CREATURE FROM THE BLACK LAGOON (1954) as the second half of a double bill with *The Day the World Ended*, whose stars had appeared in the *Creature* series. The idea was to spark the memories of ticket buyers.

CREDITS

Director Dan Milner; *Producers* Jack Milner, Daniel Milner; *Screenplay* Lou Rusoff; *Photographer* Bryden Baker; *Music* Ronald Stein

CAST

Kent Taylor, Cathy Downs, Michael Whalen

Q

Film 1982 U.S. (United Film) 93 minutes Color

Remember THE GIANT CLAW that nested atop a cardboard model of the Empire State Building back in 1957? This one's a bird god called Q, otherwise known as the tongue-twisting Quetzalcoatl of the Aztec and Toltec cultures. Brought to life by worshippers repeating ancient rituals, the god is envisioned, albeit not very effectively, as a dragon-

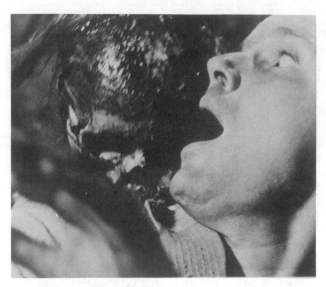

Q: An Aztec serpent holes up in New York's Chrysler Building.

like serpent with a savage set of talons. Larry Cohen's wild plot has the creature holing up in Manhattan's Chrysler Building alongside an unsuspecting gangster on the lam. Meanwhile Q snatches people from midtown rooftops, flaying and beheading its victims and spilling body parts onto startled pedestrians. Best are the miniatures and location shots of the Chrysler Building (whose design motif is art deco Aztec), Manhattan's second most beautiful skyscraper.

CREDITS

Director/Producer/Screenplay Larry Cohen; *Photographer* Fred Murphy; *Special Effects* David Allen; *Music* Robert O. Ragland

CAST

David Carradine, Richard Roundtree, Michael Moriarty, Tony Page, John Capodice

REPTILICUS

Film 1961 Denmark (Saga) 90 minutes Color

Released in the U.S. 1963 (AIP)

Denmark's gift to monsterdom is a wonderfully obvious puppet called Reptilicus, which dangles from wires and menaces tabletop sets. His live-action victims are never in the same shot (there was no budget for split-screen work or mattes), adding to the hilarity. Reptilicus starts out as a piece of tail found in the drill bit of oil surveyors. Regenerated, it escapes from university scientists and slithers into the Baltic Sea, heading perhaps for Japan.

CREDITS

Director Poul Bang; *Screenplay* Ib Melchior, Sidney Pink; *Photographer* Aage Siltrup; *Production Designers* Otto Lund, Helge Hansen, Kai Koed

CAST

Asbjorn Anderson, Mimi Heinrich, Ann Smyrner, Carl Ottosen

THE REVENGE OF FRANKENSTEIN

Film   1958   G.B. (Hammer)   89 minutes Technicolor

For its follow-up to THE CURSE OF FRANKEN-STEIN, Hammer commissioned an original story which established the pattern for the remainder of the series. Rather than focus on the Monster, as had the Universal series, Hammer brought the mad scientist to the fore. Cushing is back as Dr. Frankenstein, having escaped from prison to work under an alias at a charity hospital in Carlsbruck, where he has an unlimited supply of organs and limbs. Before long, the obsessed doctor has fabricated a new creature, animated by the brain of his hunchback assistant. Initially rational and normal-looking, the Monster (Michael Gwynn replacing Christopher Lee) turns ugly and murderously resentful when its brain begins to transform it into a misshapen cripple. The killings lead to Dr. Frankenstein, who is fatally beaten by charity patients when they discover his identity.

Prepared by now for such occupational hazards, the doctor is wheeled into surgery for a body transplant at the hands of his skilled assistant. Although played straight and produced with the usual Hammer aplomb, the film is more humorous than horrifying and is best enjoyed as black comedy.

CREDITS

Director Terence Fisher; *Producer* Anthony Hinds; *Screenplay* Jimmy Sangster; *Photographer* Jack Asher;

Art Director Bernard Robinson; *Makeup* Phil Leakey; *Music* Leonard Salzedo

CAST

Peter Cushing, Francis Matthews, Michael Gwynn, Eunice Gayson, Lionel Jeffries, John Welsh, Oscar Quitak

ROBOT MONSTER

Also titled: Monster from the Moon, Monster(s) from Mars

Film   1953   U.S. (Astor)   63 minutes Black & white (3-D)

There are terrible movies and there are terrible movies . . . and then there is *Robot Monster*, an also-ran of the 3-D craze of the mid-1950s. What can you say about a movie so unimaginative, so incompetent and so moth-eaten in its production values, except to admire the chutzpa of the people who made it? The story, which makes *Cat Women of the Moon* look like Academy Award material, has a nasty "Ro-Man" arriving on Earth from somewhere in outer space (the location depends on which title is being used) and murdering everyone save six people. He's about to finish the job when the narrator awakens and reveals that it has all been a horrible dream. The monster, beloved by junk movie fans as one of the worst ever, looks exactly like what it is: a man in a gorilla suit topped with a diving helmet and bobbing antennae. Unable to afford a real robot costume, resourceful filmmaker Phil Tucker talked his friend George Barrows into appearing gratis in his own costume for the entire three-day shooting schedule. To really appreciate *Robot Monster*, it must be seen in its original glaucoma-producing anaglyphic process—if you can find a pair of glasses with one red lens and one green one.

CREDITS

Director/Producer Phil Tucker; *Screenplay* Wyatt Ordung; *Photographer* Jack Greenhaigh; *Special Effects* Jack Rabin, David Commons; *Music* Elmer Bernstein

CAST

George Nader, Claudie Barrett, Pamela Paulson, Gregory Moffett

The Rocky Horror Picture Show: Tim Curry is Dr. Frank N. Furter, host to a convention from the planet Transsexual in the galaxy Transylvania.

THE ROCKY HORROR PICTURE SHOW

Film   1975   G.B. (20th Century-Fox)
101 minutes   Color

The audience is the show in this camp partnership, described as the "queen" of the Midnight Movie circuit. Tim Curry is spectacular as transvestite Transylvanian Dr. Frank'n'Furter, who brings to life handsome stud Rocky Horror while seducing a pair of newlyweds who have wandered in from Denton, Ohio. The movie evolved from a deliberately tatty-looking London play originally titled *They Came from Denton High*. Music impresario Lou Adler brought the show to Hollywood, where it did boffo business, prompting Fox to finance a movie version shot in London. The play meanwhile failed to find an audience in New York, where it closed after only 45 performances. Critics blasted the spanky-clean movie version, and it seemed doomed until booked into a late-night Greenwich Village cinema. Championed by trend-setting gays, it eventually attracted a more diverse crowd of closet singers and dancers, who still strut their stuff in merry widows as the high-heeled Curry flickers on the screen behind them. The phenomenon has been documented in the movie *Fame* (1980). You should see it to find out what all the fuss is about, although you might wonder what you're doing there.

CREDITS

Director Jim Sharman; *Producer* Michael White; *Screenplay* Jim Sharman, Richard O'Brien, from the stage musical by Richard O'Brien; *Photographer* Peter Suschitzky;

Art Director Terry Ackland; *Special Effects* Wally Veevers; *Makeup* Peter Robb King; *Choreography* David Toguri; *Songs* Richard O'Brien; *Musical Director* Richard Hartley

CAST

Tim Curry, Barry Bostwick, Susan Sarandon, Richard O'Brien, Jonathan Adams, Neil Campbell, Peter Hinwood, Meatloaf, Patricia Quinn; *Narrator* Charles Gray

RODAN

Film   1956   Japan (Toho)   83 minutes
Color

The worldwide success of GODZILLA prompted Honda and Tsuburaya to invent *Rodan*, which Japanese critics consider the finer film. The title creature, a giant pterodactyl revived from an ancient slumber in a coal mine by H-bomb tests, creates devastating air currents with its 250-foot wingspan while leveling several metropolises. The impressive finale, composed entirely of long shots, generates a surprising amount of pathos. The creature has also appeared in *Ghidra, the Three-Headed Monster* (1965) and *Destroy All Monsters* (1968).

CREDITS

Director Inoshiro Honda; *Producer* Tomoyuki Tanaka; *Screenplay* Takeshi Kimura, Takeo Murata; *Photographer* Isamu Ashida; *Special Effects* Eiji Tsuburaya; *Music* Akira Ifukube

CAST

Kenji Sahara, Akihiko Hirata, Yumi Shirakawa, Akio Kabori

SON OF FRANKENSTEIN

Film   1939   U.S. (Universal)   95 minutes
Black & white

After the disappointing returns of DRACULA'S DAUGHTER (1936) (see Vampires), Hollywood made no terror films for three years. Audiences had apparently tired of the genre, but when the profitable 1938 re-release of DRACULA (see Vampires) and FRANKENSTEIN on a double bill proved there was still a market for exciting films, the studios swung back into action. *Son's* plot is strictly formula, but it's played to the hilt, and the castle

Son of Frankenstein: Ygor (Bela Lugosi) convinces Dr. Frankenstein's son (Basil Rathbone) to revive the monster (Karloff).

set is a real showplace this time. (The castle would have looked even better in color, as was the studio's original intention, but tests showed that Karloff's makeup began to melt under the hot lights.)

Returning to the family home 25 years later, son Wolfgang Frankenstein (Basil Rathbone) gazes out the train window and sees the countryside gradually changing from a happy pastoral to one that is misty and lifeless. Entering this foreboding world—and taking the audience right along with him—he encounters the Monster's faithful friend Ygor (Bela Lugosi), a wooly shepherd with a deformed neck broken during a failed execution by hanging. (In the first film the doctor's helper is named Fritz and played by Dwight Frye.) The old dynamos are cranked up again, reviving Karloff for a final go-round as the Monster, which he plays with the machinelike menace of his original portrayal. At the climax, with everyone invading the lab, the Monster tears off the terrible clicking and jerking steel arm of police inspector Lionel Atwill before sinking into the castle's sulphur pit. Lon Chaney, Jr. replaces Karloff in the next film, THE GHOST OF FRANKENSTEIN (1942).

CREDITS

Director/Producer Rowland V. Lee; *Screenplay* Willis Cooper; *Photographer* George Robinson; *Art Directors* Jack Otterson, Richard Riedel; *Makeup* Jack Pierce; *Music* Frank Skinner; *Musical Director* Charles Previn

CAST

Boris Karloff, Bela Lugosi, Basil Rathbone, Lionel Atwill, Josephine Hutchinson, Donnie Dunagan, Gustav von Seyffertitz

SON OF GODZILLA

Film   1967   Japan (Toho/AIP)   86 minutes Color

Papa is obviously touched as he witnesses the birth (from an egg) of little Godzilla, a diminutive dinosaur as frolicsome as a puppy. Mama, unidentified, is not around to defend Junior from predatory monsters, so the task falls to house-husband Godzilla.

CREDITS

Director Jun Fukuda; *Producer* Tomoyuki Tanaka; *Screenplay* Schinichi Sekizawa, Kazue Shiba; *Photographer* Kazuo Yamada; *Special Effects* Sadamas Arikawa, Eiji Tsuburaya; *Music* Masuro Sato

CAST

Tadeo Takashima, Akira Kabo, Kenji Sahara, Bibari Maeda

SON OF KONG

Film   1933   U.S. (RKO)   69 minutes Black & white

Children who haven't seen KING KONG might enjoy this affectionate little fantasy, which deserves to be judged on its own terms. But viewers expecting the gargantuan thrills of the earlier film will be disappointed. The plot begins some time after Kong's demise, as showman Robert Armstrong sets sail for exotic shores to avoid debts and lawsuits connected with the ape's Manhattan rampage. Accompanied by several drifters and ingenue Helen Mack, he returns to Skull Island just in time to rescue Kong's prepubescent son Kiko from a quicksand bog. The white-furred ape, a pint-sized 30 feet tall, is no chip off the primordial block. As likable as a teddy bear, Kiko returns the favor several times over, then sacrifices his own life to save Armstrong's. Unfortunately, Kong, Jr., is given only a scant 20 minutes or so of screen time. RKO rushed the film into production to cash in on Kong's phenomenal box-office appeal, and animator Willis O'Brien didn't have time for a full-length feature.

CREDITS

Director Ernest B. Schoedsack; *Producer* Merian C. Cooper; *Screenplay* Ruth Rose, adapted from the film *The Enchanted Island*; *Photographers* Edward Lindon, Vernon L. Walker; *Art Directors* Van Nest Polglase, Al Herman; *Special Effects Animation* Willis O'Brien, with Marcel Delgado, E.B. Gibson, Carrol Shephird, Fred Reefe, W.G. White; *Makeup* Mel Burns; *Sound Effects* Murray Spivack; *Music* Max Steiner

CAST

Robert Armstrong, Helen Mack, John Marston, Frank Reicher, Victor Wong, Ed Brady, Noble Johnson

SPACE MONSTER

Film   1965   U.S. (AIP)   81 minutes   Color

Giant crabs menace a space probe from Earth on a planet covered with water. The monster lives in a waterproof lair and has a face that resembles latex dropped on a hot griddle (in special effects you get what you pay for).

CREDITS

Director/Screenplay Leonard Katzman; *Producer* Burt Topper; *Makeup* Don Post Studios; *Music* Marlin Skiles

CAST

Russ Bender, Baynes Barron

Struck by Lightning: Jeffrey Kramer, left, and Jack Elam in a TV sitcom based on the Frankenstein legend.

STRUCK BY LIGHTNING

TV series   1979   U.S. (CBS)
30 minutes (weekly)   Color

Ted Stein, a meek young science teacher, inherits a ramshackle New England inn that turns out to be the converted castle of his great-great grandfather, Dr. Frankenstein. In residence is crusty old caretaker Frank, actually the Monster. The one-joke scripts hinge on Ted's attempts to escape while Frank does everything inhumanly possible to make him recreate the formula that keeps Frank alive. Short-lived, this prime-time series failed to capture the whimsical malice of its prototype, CBS's THE MUNSTERS.

CREDITS

Director Joel Zwick and others; *Producer* Marvin Miller; *Writer* Bryan Joseph and others; *Idea* Terry Keegan; *Photographer* Keith Smith; *Art Director* Arch Bacon

CAST

Jack Elam, Jeffrey Kramer, Millie Slavin, Bill Erwin, Jeff Cotler

TENTACOLI/Tentacles

Film 1976 Italy (A-Esse) 102 minutes
Technicolor Technovision

Some top Hollywood stars pretend to be alarmed by a hungry octopus with giant tentacles which pluck surfers from a California beach (actually a beach outside Rome). JAWS revisited, and it shouldn't have been played straight.

CREDITS

Director Oliver Hellman (Sonia Assonia); *Producer* E.F. Doria; *Screenplay* Jerome Max, Tito Carpi, Steve Carabatsos, Sonia Moltemi; *Photographer* Roberto d'Etore Piazzoli; *Special Effects* G.K. Majors; *Music* S.W. Cipriani

CAST

Shelley Winters, John Huston, Henry Fonda, Bo Hopkins, Claude Akins, Cesare Danova

THE TERMINATOR

Film 1984 U.S. (Orion) 105 minutes
DeLuxe

In an era of super-fitness and macho movie fantasies, what better hero than behemoth Arnold Schwarzenegger? Only here he's the villain, not the comparatively benign Conan the Barbarian, his trademark role. Cast as the computerized robot of the title, Schwarzenegger is a zombie-like killing machine, more powerful than the Frankenstein monster and more vicious than Rambo. A product of the year 2029, the Terminator is sent back to 1984 to assassinate a young waitress. The mission and its meaning are highly unlikely, which is how director James Cameron plays it, and the fun is in the car chases, bloody shootouts and Schwarzenegger's hulking, unstoppable brutality. The role fits him like his studded leather glove.

CREDITS

Director James Cameron; *Producer* Gale Ann Hurd; *Screenplay* James Cameron, Gale Anne Hurd; *Photographer* Adam Greenberg; *Special Makeup Effects* Stan Winston

CAST

Arnold Schwarzenegger, Michael Biehn, Linda Hamilton, Paul Winfield, Lance Henriksen, Rick Rossovich

UNEARTHLY STRANGER

Film 1963 G.B. (Independent Artists/AIP)
74 minutes Black & white

A member of a top-secret government project slowly comes to realize that his wife is a space alien who has murdered several of his colleagues—and that he is next on her list. The power of human love saves him, however, when the woman sacrifices herself instead in a scene bathed in horrific pathos: When she attempts to cry, her acidic tears dissolve her beautiful, humanlike face.

CREDITS

Director John Krish; *Producer* Albert Fennell; *Screenplay* Rex Carlton; *Photographer* Reg Wyler; *Music* Edward Williams

CAST

John Neville, Gabriella Licudi, Phillip Stone, Patrick Newell, Jean Marsh

WITHOUT WARNING

Film 1980 U.S. (Filmways) 89 minutes
Movielab

Hungry space aliens with bulbous craniums terrorize the residents of a small American town by immobilizing them with a wormlike "weapon," then settling down for a warm meal. A poor substitute for the genuinely frightening creature seen in ALIEN (1979), the reason for this parasitic feature.

CREDITS

Director/Producer Greydon Clark; *Screenplay* Lyn Freeman, Daniel Grodnik, Ben Nett, Steve Mathis; *Music* Dan Wyman

CAST

Martin Landau, Jack Palance, Tarrah Nutter, Christopher S. Nelson, Cameron Mitchell

X FROM OUTER SPACE

Film 1967 Japan (Schochika) 89 minutes
Color

A devastating monster arrives on Earth as a spore attached to a space probe returning from Mars. Called Gilala (or Guilala in Japan), the hitchhiker swells into a giant bird-reptile by absorbing energy from nuclear devices sent aloft to destroy it. Grade Z.

CREDITS

Director Kazui Nihonmatsu; *Screenplay* Eibi Montomorochi, Moriyoshi Ishida, Kazui Nihonmatsu; *Special Effects* Hiroshi Ikeda; *Music* Taku Izumi

CAST

Franz Gruber, Peggy Neal, Eiji Okada

YOG—MONSTER FROM SPACE

Film 1970 Japan (Toho) 77 minutes
Color Anamorphic

The Japanese, no slouches at dealing with assorted monsters threatening their homeland, beam ultrasonic sound waves at gigantic animals controlled by an alien intelligence. It's very loud and garish and suspiciously similar to the RKO film *Killers from Space* (1954).

CREDITS

Director Inoshiro Honda; *Producer* Tomoyuki Tanaka, Fumio Tanaka; *Screenplay* Ei Ogawa; *Photographer* Yascuichi Sunokura; *Special Effects* Sadamesa Arikawa; *Music* Akira Ifukube

CAST

Akira Kubo, Kenji Sahara, Koshi Tsuchiya

YOUNG FRANKENSTEIN

Film 1974 U.S. (20th Century-Fox)
108 minutes Black & white

Only a comedic genius like Mel Brooks could have conceived this inspired but loving send-up of Universal's horror films of the 1930s. The plot, a pastiche of SON OF FRANKENSTEIN and BRIDE OF FRANKENSTEIN, has the baron's flighty grandson (Gene Wilder) visiting the ancestral home in Transylvania, where he decides to make a new living creature himself. Peter Boyle is close to perfection as a zipper-necked Monster who smokes, drinks, sings and tap dances, not to mention Madeline Kahn as the lightning-haired "not-on-the-lips" Bride and Marty Feldman as the bug-eyed hunchback Ygor.

Brooks peppers the film with knowing gags—some of which are screamingly funny and some of which fall flat—but he plays fair and never lets the humor trample on tradition. Just as ingenious is the copycat look of the movie, which Brooks shot in black and white to avoid the blood-thrill imagery of a Hammer Gothic. The sets are near-duplicates of the originals, and the electrical props are the ones Kenneth Strickfaden designed for the Universal series. Brooks' expressionistic camera set-ups are intended both as a parody of and an homage to director James Whale (he considers his films "cinematic masterpieces"), whose trademark trucking shots were simulated with a very slow zoom lens.

CREDITS

Director Mel Brooks; *Producer* Michael Gruskoff; *Screenplay* Gene Wilder, Mel Brooks; *Photographer* Gerald Hirschfeld; *Art Director* Dale Hennessy; *Special Effects* Hal Millar, Henry Miller, Jr.; *Makeup* William Tuttle; *Music* John Morris

CAST

Gene Wilder, Peter Boyle, Madeline Kahn, Cloris Leachman, Marty Feldman, Terri Garr, Kenneth Mars, Gene Hackman, Richard Hayden

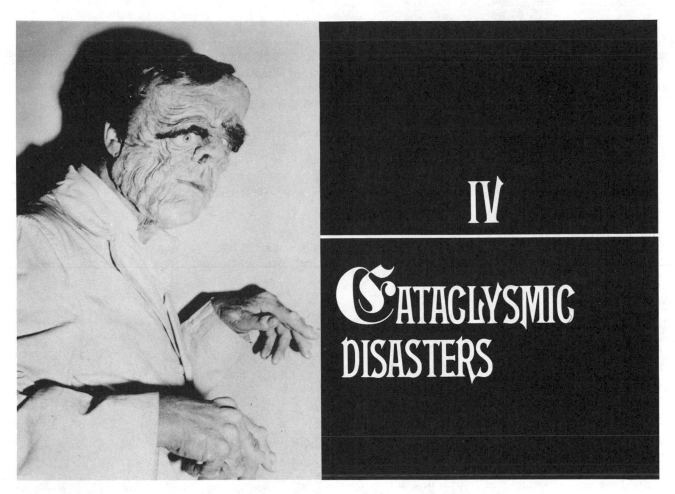

Tarantula: Researcher Leo G. Carroll and an unsuspecting tarantula get splashed with a synthetic growth nutrient.

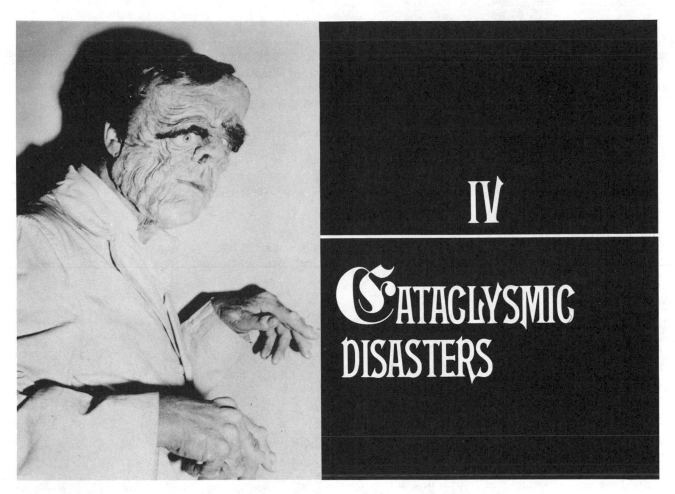

IV

Cataclysmic Disasters

Cataclysmic disasters, like the mad scientists (q.v.) who cause many of them, trespass the boundary between horror and science fiction. These hybrid fantasies came into their own during the 1950s, when the public began to realize that science could drastically alter their lives, not only as individuals, but as a species. Providing the inspiration for scores of dream catastrophes were the atomic bomb, chemical pollution and the dramatic increase in the world's population and its consequent destruction of the natural environment.

Chief among these concerns was the bomb, which spawned a cycle of cautionary post-holocaust thrillers, launched by Arch Oboler's *Five* (1951). The cycle came to an end in 1963 with Stanley Kubrick's *Dr. Strangelove: Or, How I Learned to Stop Worrying and Love the Bomb*, which played the subject for campy black comedy. Another go-round was signaled in 1977 by the horrific *Damnation Alley*, accompanied by Bible-thumping predictions that Armageddon was nigh, and the stirrings of an international grass-roots

movement of antinuclear activists. That the subject still had currency was indicated by the high ratings of television's *The Day After* (1983), which simulated the deadly effects of a nuclear war on the Everymen of Kansas City.

More fantastic and consistently entertaining is the ongoing menagerie of creature features, introduced by THE BEAST FROM 20,000 FATHOMS (1953) (see Monsters) and followed by such outsized atomic giants as THEM! (1954), TARANTULA (1955) and THE AMAZING COLOSSAL MAN (1957) (see Monsters). UFOs had been sighted with increasing frequency in the postwar world, incubating the thought that two-way traffic between Earth and the rest of the universe was possible—if it had not already begun. When the feared extraterrestrials finally arrived at the movies, they were, as expected, hostile trespassers. The vegoid menace from outer space called THE THING (1951) brought with it a new breed of monster which, unlike its earthly cousins, was more intelligent than humans and required a team effort if the species were to survive and perpetuate. The mass alien invasion from Mars predicted by H.G. Wells in 1898 finally arrived onscreen in color with state-of-the-art special effects in WAR OF THE WORLDS (1953), a story whose durable xenophobic appeal had been demonstrated by Orson Welles's panic radio broadcast of 1938.

Man-made cataclysms involving the effects of ecological breakdown and overpopulation asserted their popularity in the 1970s. Looking ahead, filmmakers predicted a variety of hopeless and miserable dystopian futures, which had already been anticipated by Aldous Huxley's *Brave New World* (1932) and George Orwell's *1984* (1949). Science fiction films in this category include *Soylent Green* (1973) and *Logan's Run* (1976), both of which solve the population problem by institutionalized murder, and, most startling of all, the future world slum of BLADE RUNNER (1982).

Unmistakably American in attitude and setting, cataclysm movies arrived with the emergence of the United States as the world leader in the field of scientific research. The position had formerly been occupied by Germany, a country that had supplied Hollywood horror with its initial themes, visual style and personnel. But the transatlantic shift had begun in the 1930s, when the term "science fiction" was coined. Unlike purer examples of the genre, the science fiction/horror film tends to accommodate fear and ignorance of controlling forces of modern life, on a curve of hysteria. These hybrids rise and fall with the trends of anxiety, and what touched a nerve yesterday is likely to tickle the funny bone tomorrow.

THE AMAZING COLOSSAL MAN

Film   1957   U.S. (AIP)   80 minutes
Black & white

Nonbuffs often confuse this with ATTACK OF THE 50-FOOT WOMAN, made a year later by a different filmmaker. Both are quintessential junk-food movies of the 1950s, but *Woman* is the Big Mac of the pair. (Too bad they never got together.) This one reflects a postwar atom-bomb angst, at least initially, and there's an attempt at real science fiction (the human heart can't cope with such an enormous body mass). Logic quickly goes down the tubes, however, when Lieutenant Colonel Manning, having been exposed to nuclear radiation, begins growing at the rate of ten feet a day. As bad as they are, the special effects (mostly split-screen and rear projection) can't compare to the scaled-down and scaled-up props. When the Colossal Man goes on a mad rampage, for example,

instead of shooting him with a tranquilizer dart from a high-powered rifle, several foolhardy volunteers try to ram a mammoth hypodermic syringe into his towering shin.

CREDITS

Director/Producer/Special Effects Bert I. Gordon; *Screenplay* Bert I. Gordon, Mark Hanna; *Photographer* Joseph Biroc; *Music* Albert Glasser

CAST

Glenn Langan, Cathy Downs, Judd Holdren, James Sealy, William Hudson, Larry Thor

Attack of the Crab Monsters: They came from poverty row.

ATTACK OF THE CRAB MONSTERS

Film   1957   U.S. (Allied Artists)   70 minutes
Black & white

Mutant crabs as large as elephants (the result of atomic fallout) scuttle across a former Pacific test site dining on cracked human heads. Seems the predators absorb individual intelligences into group minds, making them impossible to defeat. Fledgling director Roger Corman takes your mind off the unconvincing crustaceans by playing for suspense and editing at breakneck speed. Recalls Corman: "This was the first time I used market research to come up with a title. The picture was very successful. It was made for about $70,000 and grossed over a million."

CREDITS

Director/Producer Roger Corman; *Screenplay* Charles Griffith; *Photographer* Floyd Crosby; *Music* Ronald Stein

CAST

Richard Garland, Pamela Duncan, Leslie Bradley, Mel Welles, Richard Cutting

ATTACK OF THE 50-FOOT WOMAN

Film   1958   U.S. (Allied Artists)   65 minutes Black & white

Like hula hoops, this disposable artifact of the 1950s has since become a nostalgic treasure, cherished by collectors of bad movies. Who can forget the ever-lovely Allison Hayes as a wronged giant— conveniently enlarged by a passing UFO—who stampedes through town flicking off the roofs of papier-mache houses, calling for her philandering husband in an amplified baritone?

CREDITS

Director Nathan Hertz; *Producer* Bernard Woolner; *Screenplay* Mark Hanna; *Photographer* Jacques Marquette; *Music* Ronald Stein

CAST

Allison Hayes, William Hudson, Yvette Vickers, Roy Gordon, Ken Terrell, George Douglas

ATTACK OF THE GIANT LEECHES

G.B. title: Demons of the Swamp

Rerelease title: The Giant Leeches

Film   1959   U.S. (AIP)   62 minutes Black & white

Nuclear pollution from Cape Canaveral leaks into a nearby swamp, creating a strain of giant killer leeches. Minor league science fiction, inept in every department, especially in its rubber-suited leeches.

CREDITS

Director Bernard L. Kowalski; *Producer* Gene Corman; *Screenplay* Leo Gordon; *Photographer* John Nicholaus, Jr.; *Art Director* Daniel Haller; *Music* Alexander Laszlo

CAST

Ken Clark, Yvette Vickers, Michael Emmett, Jan Shepperd

THE BEAST FROM 20,000 FATHOMS

Film   1953   U.S. (Warner Bros.)   80 minutes Sepia-tone

Thawed from a ten-million-year Arctic deep freeze by A-bomb tests, a mammoth dinosaur heads for its old breeding grounds, now occupied by New York City. Confused, the creature walks up Fifth Avenue and bites off the head of an equally bewildered traffic cop, then heads for the roller coaster at Coney Island. A grand fantasy adventure, enhanced by early stop-motion effects from master Ray Harryhausen, this is the film that introduced Hollywood's postwar science-created monster cycle. The story is nominally based on Ray Bradbury's "The Foghorn," published in *The Saturday Evening Post*, about a prehistoric sea serpent that hears a mating call in a lighthouse foghorn.

Director Lourie, a former set designer who worked on such classics as Abel Gance's *Napoleon* (1927) and Jean Renoir's *The Rules of the Game* (1939), made two more prehistoric monster movies, in England. *Behemoth, the Sea Monster/The Giant Behemoth* (1958) is a virtual replay, with the reptile rampaging through London. The stop-motion effects of Willis O'Brien, creator of *King Kong*, leave much to be desired, and were obviously hampered by his low budget. Lourie picked up with *Gorgo* (1960), an enjoyable Technicolor fantasy about a baby "gorgosaurus" kidnapped from its North Sea home and sold to a London circus. The creature, like Godzilla, is a man in a monster suit.

CREDITS

Director/Art Director Eugene Lourie; *Producer* Hal Chester, Jack Dietz; *Screenplay* Lou Morheim, Fred Freiberger; *Photographer* Jack Russell; *Special Effects* Ray Harryhausen; *Music* David Buttolph

CAST

Paul Christian, Paula Raymond, Kenneth Tobey, Cecil Kellaway, King Donovan, Donald Woods, Lee Van Cleef

THE BEAST WITH A MILLION EYES

Film 1955 U.S. (American Releasing Corp.)
78 minutes Black & white

This vervy ultracheap programmer helped launch the little studio soon to become better known as American International Pictures (AIP). As with all the studio's early product, the title came first (picked for "marquee allure"), followed by a story, then a trailer that made the film look like the shocker of all time. In this case the title refers to an alien being from outer space which possesses animals and people (the eyes are apparently theirs).

The beast is the work of Paul Blaisdell, a former art director for a science fiction magazine, who created the fondly remembered schlock monsters for 16 movies between 1955 and 1959. Here, his two special effects consist of an immobile alien with a big head and batwings—described by a later viewer as "exuding all the lifelike qualities of a pet rock"—and a spaceship built from army surplus. The ingenious Blaisdell, something of an actor, also appeared in many of his own costumes.

CREDITS

Director David Kramarsky; *Producer* Roger Corman; *Screenplay* Tom Filer; *Photographer* Everett Baker; *Special Effects* Paul Blaisdell; *Music* John Bickford

CAST

Paul Birch, Lorna Thayer, Chester Conklin, Leonard Tarver, Donna Cole

THE BEGINNING OF THE END

Film 1957 U.S. (Republic) 74 minutes
Black & white

In 1957 the unstoppable Bert I. Gordon rushed out three schlockers about science-created giants. *Beginning of the End*, his second, has big grasshoppers heading for Chicago and being lured into Lake Michigan with electronic mating sounds. Gordon, the most penny-pinching of filmmakers, saved a bundle by scooping up grasshoppers in a California field and prodding them forward on

photos of Chicago skyscrapers. There's a terrific scene in which a bug hops to the pinnacle of a building and onto a photographed cloud.

CREDITS

Director/Producer/Special Effects Bert I. Gordon; *Screenplay* Fred Freiberger, Lester Gorn; *Photographer* Jack Marta

CAST

Peter Graves, Peggie Castle, James Seay, Morris Ankrum

THE BIRDS

Film 1963 U.S. (Universal) 119 minutes
Technicolor

In a small coastal town in northern California, birds—a normally benign species that vastly outnumbers our own—begin to attack people. Center of the onslaught is the home of a young lawyer whose houseguest is an impetuous, spoiled playgirl singled out by swooping gulls and sparrows. Before long the birds have swarmed over the town, attacking pedestrians and making it unsafe to go outside. Hitchcock never explains why man's feathered friends have turned against him. He leaves us with the suggestion that the event is just another phenomenon of unpredictable nature, whose violence and anarchy lie just below the surface.

CREDITS

Director/Producer Alfred Hitchcock; *Screenplay* Evan Hunter, based on the novel by Daphne du Maurier; *Photographer* Robert Burks; *Special Effects* Lawrence A. Hampton, Ub Iwerks; *Sound Consultant* Bernard Herrmann

CAST

Rod Taylor, Tippi Hedren, Jessica Tandy, Suzanne Pleshette, Ethel Griffies

THE BLACK SCORPION

Film 1957 U.S. (Warner Bros.) 88 minutes
Black & white

A volcanic eruption in Mexico uncovers a nest of giant scorpions, a species thought to have been

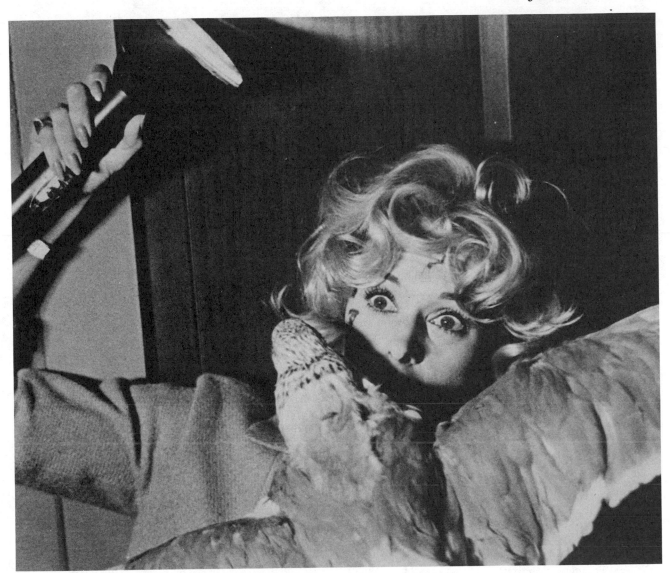

The Birds: Tippi Hedren shouldn't have opened the bedroom door.

extinct since the Triassic era. The film is merely routine, but of interest are the stop-motion scorpion effects by Willis O'Brien, creator of KING KONG (see Monsters). Some of the prehistoric-life sequences are from O'Brien's never-completed epic *Gwangi* (1942). And the scene in which a scorpion wrecks a train is similar to Kong's rampage through a Manhattan subway station.

The other big giant-bug movie that year was Universal's *The Deadly Mantis*, directed by William Alland and written by Martin Berkeley. This insect has none of the real-life menace of the lethal and people-loving (like mice and rats) scorpions. Unthawed from an Arctic deep freeze, in a fashion similar to THE BEAST FROM 20,000 FATHOMS (1953), the photographically enlarged praying mantis is eventually sealed up in Manhat-

tan's Holland Tunnel, which is then fumigated with poison gas. For two superior examples of this subgenre, see THEM! (1954) and TARANTULA (1955).

CREDITS

Director Edward Ludwig; *Producers* Frank Melford, Jack Dietz; *Screenplay* David Duncan, Robert Blees; *Story* Paul Yawitz; *Photographer* Lionel Lindon; *Special Effects* Willis O'Brien, Peter Peterson; *Music* Paul Sawtell, Peter Peterson

CAST

Richard Denning, Mara Corday, Carlos Rivas, Mario Navarro, Carlos Muzquiz, Fanny Schiller

BLADE RUNNER

Film 1982 U.S. (Warner Bros.) 124 minutes
Technicolor Panavision Dolby Stereo

Harrison Ford is the blade runner, one of many bounty hunters of the year of 2019, hired to track down and kill rebellious androids. The machine-made creatures are perfect human doubles, except that they lack emotion. Ford lurches viciously through the macho plot, shooting replicants in backs and bellies in several eye-popping gore scenes. He ultimately discovers that his occupation is dehumanizing, which is the only theme to survive Ridley Scott's confusing adaptation of Philip K. Dick's famous novel *Do Androids Dream of Electric Sheep?* (1968).

Visually, however, the film is a tour de force, the best and most comprehensive vision of a future dystopia ever put on film. Los Angeles has become a garish, derelict city choked with pollution and populated by the dregs of humanity. Space travel is common, and everyone with the wherewithal has moved out. Police tour the city's neon-lit canyons in "spinner cars" that move vertically as well as horizontally. According to Scott, director of the memorable ALIEN, "Background can be as important as the actors. The design of the film is the script." Which is exactly what's wrong with his film.

CREDITS

Director Ridley Scott; *Producer* Michael Deeley; *Screenplay* Hampton Fancher, David Peoples, based on a novel by Philip K. Dick; *Photographer* Jordan Cronenweth; *Production Designer* Lawrence D. Paull; *Special Effects* Douglas Trumbull, Richard Yuricich, David Dryer, Matthew Yuricich; *Music* Vangelis

CAST

Harrison Ford, Rutger Hauer, Sean Young, Edward James Olmos, M. Emmet Walsh, Daryl Hannah, William Sanderson

BUG

Film 1975 U.S. (Paramount) 101 minutes
Movielab

Strange black insects climb through a fissure opened by an earthquake and swarm over a small American town. A few are captured by a biologist who crossbreeds them with a common cockroach, resulting in a strain of intelligent bugs that set people and things on fire by rubbing their rear appendages together. The message is, don't trifle with things you know nothing about; the medium is shrill, creepy-crawly horror. Not for the faint of heart.

CREDITS

Director Jeannot Szwarc; *Producer* William Castle; *Screenplay* William Castle, Thomas Page, based on Page's novel *The Hephaestus Plague*; *Photographer* Michael Hugo; *Insect Photographer* Ken Middleham; *Electronic Music* Charles Fox

CAST

Bradford Dillman, Joanna Miles, Patty McCormack, Richard Gilliland, Jamie Smith Jackson

CHOSEN SURVIVORS

Film 1974 U.S. (Columbia) 98 minutes
Color

Visitors to an underground bomb shelter during a flash nuclear war discover they are the ten "chosen survivors" of the human race. While they slowly come to accept the inevitable, a cloud of madly fluttering vampire bats shriek into the shelter from a nearby cavern, causing mass panic. The Darwinian struggle raises a few goose bumps, but these are quickly dispelled by a limp ending that reveals the horror to be only a psychological test of human reactions to conditions of nuclear war.

CREDITS

Director Sutton Roley; *Producer* Charles Fries; *Screenplay* H.B. Cross, Joe Reb Moffly; *Photographer* Michael Torres; *Music* Fred Karlin

CAST

Alex Cord, Jackie Cooper, Richard Jaeckel, Diana Muldaur, Pedro Armendariz, Jr., Bradford Dillman

A CLOCKWORK ORANGE

Film 1971 Great Britain (Warner Bros.)
136 minutes Color

Stanley Kubrick is a cinema magician who can juggle three genres and never drop one of them: A case in point is *A Clockwork Orange*, which qualifies as prophetic science fiction, garish horror and political black comedy. Kubrick's (and author Burgess') fantasy child of the future is Alex De-Farge (stunningly played by Malcolm McDowell), the progeny of the pot-smoking, self-involved "let-it-all-hang-out" generation of the late 1960s.

The leader of a vicious youth gang called the Droogs, Alex spends most of his time in a bar that serves only a selection of drugs, or in fighting gang wars and beating up old drunks for the fun of it. After murdering an avant garde artist with her own phallic sculpture, he is forced to undergo a painful aversion therapy which conditions him to become ill when exposed to violence—or to Beethoven's Ninth Symphony. Later, when authorities decide it's politically expedient to restore him to his former self, Alex looks into the camera with a knowing smirk, promising worse "horrorshows" (his argot for mayhem) to come—at least as much as the state has inflicted on him.

Although the shock and horror is relentless, Kubrick isn't gratuitous. In order to understand Alex and to care about him, we must attempt to share the perverse glee taken in what we find so abhorrent. In handling scenes of sex and violence Kubrick neutralizes the sensationalism by a poetic use of fast-motion and slow-motion and unexpected injections of humor. We may be awash with muggers, terrorists, gunmen and thrill-seeking punks, Kubrick seems to be saying, but robbing them of their free will is not the solution to the problem. Abused though they are, it is the power to think and choose freely that separates us from other animals. *A Clockwork Orange* is a difficult film that severely tests preconditioned notions and our vision of compassion.

CREDITS

Director/Screenplay Stanley Kubrick; *Producer* Bernard Williams; *Novel* Anthony Burgess; *Photographer* John Alcott; *Production Designer* John Barry; *Erotic Sculptures* Herman Makkink; *Music* Walter Carlos

CAST

Malcolm McDowell, Michael Bates, Adrienne Corri, Patrick Magee, Warren Clarke

DAY OF THE ANIMALS

Film   1976   U.S. (Film Ventures Int.)
95 minutes   DeLuxe   Todd-AO 35

Ecological disaster time again, with wild animals turning on campers in the High Sierras, an unlikely

event caused by aerosol pollution of the Earth's ozone layer. Only the nastiness is convincing.

CREDITS

Director William Girdler; *Producer* Edward L. Montoro; *Screenplay* William and Eleanor Norton; *Photographer* Robert Sorrentino; *Special Effects* Sam Burney, Fred Brown, Don Record; *Makeup* Graham Meech-Burkestone; *Music* Lalo Schifrin; *Animal Trainers* Lou Schumacher, Monty Cox

CAST

Christopher George, Leslie Nielsen, Lynda Day George, Richard Jaeckel, Michael Ansara, Ruth Roman

THE DAY THE WORLD ENDED

Film   1956   U.S. (American Releasing Corp.)
81 minutes   Black & white   SuperScope

James H. Nicholson, co-founder of the little studio soon to command attention as AIP, came up with the exploitive title, then got writer Lou Russoff, brother-in-law of his partner, to fill in the details. The plot concerns a testy group of World War III survivors holed up in a ranch house. It bears a suspicious resemblance to Arch Oboler's *Five* (1951), Hollywood's initial anti-Bomb science fiction film, except that Russoff has a three-eyed mutant carry off the girl. It's Corman's first genre film as director.

CREDITS

Director/Producer Roger Corman; *Screenplay* Lou Russoff; *Photographer* Jack Feindel; *Special Effects* Paul Blaisdell; *Music* Ronald Stein

CAST

Richard Denning, Lori Nelson, Adele Jergens, Touch (Mike) Connors; Paul Blaisdell (Monster)

EARTH VS. THE FLYING SAUCERS

G.B. title: Invasion of the Flying Saucers

Film   1956   U.S. (Columbia)   83 minutes
Black & white

Aliens bungle an attempt to contact Earth in Curt Siodmak's fifties paranoia fantasy, rushed out to exploit the growing science fiction market. This being a Sam Katzman production, costs were kept to a bare minimum, and some of the battles you see were taken from George Pal's Technicolor WAR OF THE WORLDS (1953). Still remarkable are Ray Harryhausen's saucer models and detailed miniatures of Washington, D.C., landmarks, destroyed by painstaking stop-motion photography (there was no money for a high-speed camera and explosive charges).

CREDITS

Director Fred Sears; *Producer* Charles Schneer; *Executive Producer* Sam Katzman; *Screenplay* George Worthing Yates, Raymond Marcus; *Story* Curt Siodmak; *Special Effects* Ray Harryhausen; *Musical Director* Mischa Bakaleinikoff

CAST

Hugh Marlowe, Joan Taylor, Morris Ankrum, Donald Curtis

EMPIRE OF THE ANTS

*Film   1977   U.S. (AIP/Cinema 77)
89 minutes   Movielab*

A follow-up to Bert I. Gordon's FOOD OF THE GODS (1976), the versatile schlockmeister's previous trashing of H.G. Wells. Nominally based on Wells's seminal novel about biology gone mad (it introduced the theme), *Empire* follows a hive of mutant ants from a Florida swamp to a swarming rampage of—gasp!—a small shopping center. It's not quite up to the enjoyably abysmal standards of Gordon's earlier exploration of giantism, VILLAGE OF THE GIANTS (1965), although the ant mock-ups come close.

CREDITS

Director/Producer/Special Effects Bert I. Gordon; *Screenplay* Jack Turley, Bert I. Gordon; *Photographer* Reginald Morris; *Music* Dana Kaproff; *Ant Coordinator* Warren Estes; *Ant Consultant* Charles L. Hogue

CAST

Joan Collins, Robert Lansing, John David Carson, Albert Salmi, Brooke Palance

FOOD OF THE GODS

*Film   1976   U.S. (AIP)   88 minutes
Movielab*

The awesome Bert I. Gordon claims he based this bird dropping "on a portion of" H.G. Wells's *The Food of the Gods* (1904), the portion evidently being the four words of the title. (Gordon's previous "adaptation" was the hilarious VILLAGE OF THE GIANTS.) Wells's classic novel chronicles the disastrous effects of mankind's misuse of the principle of growth. Gordon's fantasy concerns a Canadian farm where chickens peck at a mysterious substance oozing from the earth and grow to mammoth size. Not unexpectedly, news of 50-pound fryers brings forth biologists and businessmen, who fail to anticipate that rats, worms and other vermin also may have fed on the stuff.

CREDITS

Director/Producer/Screenplay/Special Effects Bert I. Gordon; *Makeup* Tom Burman; *Music* Elliot Kaplan

CAST

Ida Lupino, Ralph Meeker, Marjoe Gortner, Pamela Franklin, Jon Cypher

FROGS

*Film   1972   U.S. (AIP)   90 minutes
Movielab*

If you're frightened out of your wits by slimy creepy-crawly creatures (and who isn't), then this is your film. Setting is a remote island in the South, where plantation owner Ray Milland sprays the wetlands with a new chemical to eliminate pests. As he sits on the veranda surveying his domain, the familiar croaks, chirps and gurgles escalate into an angry crescendo, and the creatures begin to crawl toward the house. Before long, the plantation is infested with killer leeches, snakes, turtles, toads, lizards, snapping turtles—and frogs. Novice director George McCowan exploits rather than explores the theme of ecological disaster, but his bravado handling of the tried-and-true shock effects will leave you gasping. AIP promoted the film with the appealingly hokey slogan: "Today—the Pond! Tomorrow—the World!"

CREDITS

Director George McGowan; *Producers* George Edwards, Peter Thomas; *Screenplay* Robert Hutchinson, Robert Blees; *Photographer* Mario Tosi; *Electronic Special Effects* Joe Sidore; *Music* Lex Baxter

CAST

Ray Milland, Sam Elliott, Joan Van Ark, Adam Roarke, Judy Pace, Mae Mercer, Lynn Borden

THE HORROR OF PARTY BEACH

Film	1964	U.S. (20th Century-Fox)
72 minutes	Black & white	

Fish exposed to radiation from waste containers leaking on the ocean floor mutate into angry monsters which resemble the Creature from the Black Lagoon. Their prey, not unexpectedly, is a group of bikini-clad teens making out and rocking and rolling on a California beach. Although inept in every department, the film when seen today evokes an unsettling feeling because of its subtext: the human consequences of the careless disposal of dangerous wastes.

CREDITS

Director/Producer Del Tenny; *Screenplay/Photographer* Richard Hilliard; *Music* Bill Holmes

CAST

John Scott, Allen Laurel, Alice Lyon, Eulabelle Moore, The Del Aires

HUMANOIDS FROM THE DEEP

G.B. title: Monster

Film	1980	U.S. (New World)	81 minutes
Color			

Although Roger Corman isn't credited with this sexist prank, released by his company, it bears his stamp from beginning to end. His frenzied monsters are Pacific salmon contaminated with an experimental DNA that spirals them up the evolutionary ladder. To move to the top rung, the fishy humanoids attempt to mate with human women—while ripping apart their husbands and boyfriends. In addition to rape scenes and a sprinkling of soft-core porn, there are borrowings from every mon-

ster movie in recent memory. Feminist groups have complained, but Corman had covered himself: The director is a woman.

CREDITS

Director Barbara Peeters; *Producer* Martin B. Cohen; *Screenplay* Frederick James; *Photographer* Daniel Lacambre; *Underwater Photographer* Ted Boehler; *Art Director* Michael Erler; *Special Effects* Roger George; *Creature Design* Rob Bottin; *Makeup* Marla Manalis; *Music* James Horner

CAST

Doug McClure, Vic Morrow, Ann Turkel, Cindy Weintraub, Anthony Penya, Lynn Theel, Denise Galik

INVASION OF THE ANIMAL PEOPLE

Film	1960	G.B. (ADP)	73 minutes
Black & white			

Released 1962 U.S. (Favorite Films)   55 minutes

Narrator John Carradine was called in to salvage this science fiction programmer, which lost 18 minutes and several key scenes when released in the U.S. The animal people are space aliens unleashed in Finland.

CREDITS

Directors Arthur Warren, Virgil Vogel; *Producer* Arthur Warren; *Screenplay* Arthur C. Pierce; *Music* Allan Johannson, Harry Arnold

CAST

Robert Burton, Barbara Wilson, Ake Gronberg, Bengt Blomgren, Stan Gester

INVASION OF THE BODY SNATCHERS

Film	1956	U.S. (Allied Artists)	80 minutes
Black & white	Anamorphic		

This much-analyzed science fiction/horror classic retains its power to thrill and provoke thirty years after its release. Intended as a routine programmer by Allied Artists, the "prestige" arm of poverty-row's Monogram studios, the film had the good fortune to be directed by Don Siegel and have an assist by Sam Peckinpah. A parable of creeping

Invasion of the Body Snatchers: Kevin McCarthy torches an alien pod in the 1956 classic. Donald Sutherland doesn't suspect that rare flowers are turning his friends into "pods" in the 1978 color remake.

conformity in the age of *The Lonely Crowd* and *The Organization Man*, it tells the story of vegetable pods which arrive in a small California town and grow replicate replacements of the citizens. Treacherous, the humanoids will allow no deviation from their norm; everyone must become emotionless and "sensible." When they are defied by a young couple determined to retain their humanity, the normals organize search parties and hunt them down.

Liberal critics have claimed the film is an indictment of anti-communist witch hunts of the 1950s, but conservative-minded theorists have just as glibly countered that the pod-people can be seen as communist infiltrators. On a more elemental level, the movie is a tour de force of paranoia (and an important link in the history of horror cinema) which reflects an alienating fear that forces beyond our control are creating "monsters" that look just like ourselves.

In 1978 Phillip Kaufman filmed a technicolor remake for United Artists which hewed closely to the concept of the original. Kaufman alternated goose-bumps with satire and changed the locale to San Francisco. More self-enlightened than their 1956 counterparts, the pods of the me-decade began their take-over with a mind-bending rhetoric of "self-realization" and "total happiness" that was all too recognizable in an era of religious cults and short-cut routes to nirvana. The cast includes Donald Sutherland, Leonard Nimoy, Brooke Adam, Jeff Goldblum, Veronica Cartwright and Kevin McCarthy, reprising the end of the earlier film. Director Don Siegel makes a cameo appearance as a cab driver.

CREDITS

Director Don Siegel; *Producer* Walter Wanger; *Screenplay* Daniel Mainwaring, Sam Peckinpah (uncredited), based on the novel *The Body Snatchers* by Jack Finney; *Photographer* Ellsworth Fredericks; *Special Effects* Milton Rice; *Music* Carmen Dragon

CAST

Kevin McCarthy, Dana Wynter, Larry Gates, King Donovan, Carolyn Jones, Virginia Christine, Sam Peckinpah

ISLAND OF TERROR

*Film   1966   G.B. (Planet/Universal)
89 minutes   Eastmancolor*

Cancer researchers on a remote North Sea island botch an experiment and produce giant mutant viruses. The creatures, resembling slugglish piles of silly putty, slither around corners and up stairways in search of human bone marrow, which they suck from the bodies of unwary villagers. Played straight, the script might have worked as a metaphor for cancer as a malignant evil self-created by man. But screams and shudders are what director Fisher has in mind, and he gets a fair share of both.

CREDITS

Director Terence Fisher; *Producer* Tom Blakeley; *Screenplay* Edward Andrew Mann, Alan Ramsen; *Photographer* Reg Wyer; *Special Effects* John St. John Earl; *Music* Malcolm Lockyer

CAST

Peter Cushing, Carole Gray, Edward Judd, Eddie Byrne, Nial MacGinnis

IT CAME FROM BENEATH THE SEA

*Film   1955   U.S. (Columbia)   77 minutes
Black & white*

An octopus mutated to giant size by an atomic bomb test—as were so many film creatures during the 1950s—demolishes the Golden Gate Bridge and other San Francisco landmarks before being destroyed in a battle with a submarine. The only thing that distinguishes this one from period schlock is some fine stop-motion animation by Ray Harryhausen. The big in-joke is that the beast has only five tentacles, which, at $10,000 per, were all the budget would allow.

CREDITS

Director Robert Gordon; *Producer* Charles H. Schneer; *Executive Producer* Sam Katzman; *Screenplay* George Worthing Yates, Hal Smith; *Photographer* Henry Freulich; *Special Effects* Ray Harryhausen, Jack Erickson; *Musical Director* Mischa Bakaleinikoff

CAST

Faith Domergue, Kenneth Tobey, Donald Curtis, Dean Maddox, Jr., Ian Keith, Harry Lauter

IT'S ALIVE

*Film 1975 U.S. (Larco) 90 minutes
Color*

A mutated newborn baby, the result of chemical poisoning, murders the doctor and nurses in its delivery room, then jumps out a skylight and escapes into the city. Although the plot is absurd and director Cohen teases and cheats quite a bit before delivering the goods, the film nevertheless packs quite a wallop. "There's something wrong with the Davis baby!" ballyhooed the advertising campaign, which, like the film, plays on a contemporary fear, especially among parents, of the unknown effects of pollution, inadequately tested drugs, food additives and other possibly harmful chemicals. Star of the film is the repulsive infant, created by makeup artist Rick Baker. To bring the creature to life, Baker alternated a foam rubber, baby-size dummy with a movable adult-size mask worn by an actor.

CREDITS

Director/Producer/Screenplay Larry Cohen; *Photographer* Fenton Hamilton; *Special Effects* Robert Biggart, Patrick Somerset; *Makeup* Rick Baker; *Music* Bernard Herrmann

CAST

John Ryan, Sharon Farrell, Andrew Duggan, Guy Stockwell, Michael Ansara, James Dixon

IT'S ALIVE II

Also titled: It Lives Again

*Film 1978 U.S. (Larco/Warner Bros.)
91 minutes Color*

Rick Baker's hideously deformed baby isn't given much to work with in this misconceived sequel to IT'S ALIVE. The overwritten script has the genocidal infant, and others like it, being raised in a secret nursery by scientists who believe "these babies are the next step in evolution so we can survive the pollution of the planet." As usual, Cohen teeters on the brink of laughability, and this time he plunges in, feet first.

CREDITS

Director/Producer/Screenplay Larry Cohen; *Photographer* Fenton Hamilton; *Makeup* Rick Baker; *Music* Bernard Herrmann; *Additional Music* Laurie Johnson

CAST

Frederic Forrest, Kathleen Lloyd, Andrew Duggan, John P. Ryan, John Marley

KILLERS FROM SPACE

*Film 1954 U.S. (RKO) 71 minutes
Black & white*

Alien invaders go on a house-cleaning spree with giant people-gobbling bugs, reptiles and other abhorrent creatures. Humanity is saved, however, when a crafty earthling locates their atomic breeding machine. It's a toss-up which is more irresistible: the special effects or the aliens with Ping-Pong ball eyes, dressed in Flash Gordon pajamas.

CREDITS

Director/Producer W. Lee Wilder; *Screenplay* Bill Raynore; *Story* Myles Wilder; *Photographer* William Clothier; *Special Effects* Consolidated Film Industries; *Music* Manuel Compinsky

CAST

Peter Graves, Barbara Bestar, John Merrick, James Seay, Frank Gerstle

KINGDOM OF THE SPIDERS

*Film 1977 U.S. (Arachnid/Dimension)
95 minutes Color*

No one much noticed in the year of *Star Wars*, but while ants were turning Florida into the EMPIRE OF THE ANTS, spiders were busy across the country establishing a kingdom in Arizona. The spiders are normal-size and infinitely more convincing than their distant cousins, although they share a common science fiction malady: mutation caused by chemical pollution. Crawling out of the desert, countless tarantulas, crabs, tunnel-webs and what-have-you invade a small town and wrap its panicked citizens in silken cocoons to munch on later. William Shatner, about to reboard the Enterprise, lends authority to his role as a veterinarian, and the swarming spider effects will make you think twice the next time you're caught in a cobweb.

CREDITS

Director John Cardos; *Producers* Igo Kantor, Jeffrey M. Sneller; *Screenplay* Richard Robinson, Alan Caillou;

Photographers John Morrill, John Wheeler; *Special Effects* Greg Auer, Cy Cidjurgis; *Makeup* Ve Neill, Kathy Agron; *Musical Director* Igo Kantor; *Spider Handlers* Lou Schumacher, Jim Brockett

CAST

William Shatner, Tiffany Bolling, Woody Strode, David McLean, Lieux Dressler

THE MONSTER FROM GREEN HELL

Film   1957   U.S. (DCA)   70 minutes
Black & white

Insects sent aloft in an experimental space shot are turned into mutant monsters when the capsule crashlands in an African jungle and splashes them with radioactive fuel. The insects, mainly giant wasps, are kept from reaching civilization by a handy volcano rented from a film library. The borrowed footage includes long shots of Spencer Tracy and Walter Brennan in *Stanley and Livingstone* (1939).

CREDITS

Director Kenneth Crane; *Producer* Al Zimbalist; *Screenplay* Louis Vittes, Andre Boehm; *Photographer* Ray Flin; *Special Effects* Jess Davison, Jack Rabin, Louis DeWitt

CAST

Jim Davis, Barbara Turner, Eduardo Ciannelli, Robert E. Griffin, Dan Morgan

THE MONSTER THAT CHALLENGED THE WORLD

Film   1957   U.S. (United Artists)   83 minutes
Black & white

H-bomb tests trigger an earthquake in the South Pacific and release mammoth sea slugs who think the world is their oyster. Passable cautionary science fiction film reflecting 1950s' atomic anxiety.

CREDITS

Director Arnold Laven; *Producers* Jules Levy, Arthur Gardner; *Screenplay* Pat Fielder; *Story* David Duncan; *Photographer* Lester White; *Underwater Photographer* Scotty Welborn; *Music* Heinz Roemheld

CAST

Audrey Dalton, Tim Holt, Hans Conreid, Casey Adams, Mimi Gibson

THE NAVY VS. THE NIGHT MONSTERS

G.B. title: Monsters of the Night

Film   1966   U.S. (Standard Club of California)
88 minutes   Color

Navy scientists at an island research station replant vegetation gathered from Antarctica and watch it grow into a forest of man-eating trees that scoot about on rubbery roots. An insult to the Murray Leinster novel on which it is based, but if you're a connoisseur of really bad films, you'll love it.

CREDITS

Director/Screenplay Michael Hoey; *Producer* George Edwards; Based on the novel *Monster from Earth's End* by Murray Leinster; *Photographer* Stanley Cortez; *Special Effects* Edwin Tillman; *Makeup* Harry Thomas; *Music* Gordon Zahler

CAST

Mamie Van Doren, Anthony Eisley, Bobby Van, Walter Sande, Philip Terry, Pamela Mason

NIGHT OF THE LEPUS

Film   1972   U.S. (MGM)   88 minutes
Metrocolor

A lab lepus (Latin for hare) injected with an experimental serum to control breeding escapes into the wild and spawns a species of carnivorous rabbits as big and as hungry as lions. This tired premise is what's left of Russell Braddon's novel *The Year of the Angry Rabbits* (1964), after MGM excised most of its satire and science fiction (and changed the location from Australia to Arizona). Director William Claxton, allegedly inspired by Alfred Hitchcock's THE BIRDS, is at the mercy of photographically enlarged bunnies who look more cute than terrifying as they thump across the desert to the accompaniment of a soundtrack apparently recorded at a buffalo stampede.

CREDITS

Director William F. Claxton; *Producer* A.C. Lyles; *Screenplay* Don Holiday, Gene R. Kearney; *Photographer* Ted Voigtlander; *Special Effects* Howard A. Anderson Company; *Music* Jimmie Haskell; *Animal Trainers* Lou Schumacher, Henry Cowl

CAST

Stuart Whitman, Janet Leigh, Rory Calhoun, DeForrest Kelley, Paul Fix, Chuck Hayward

NOSUTORADAMASU DAIYOGEN

English titles: Prophecies of Nostradamus; Catastrophe 1999

*Film   1974   Japan (Toho)   90 minutes
Tohocolor   Tohoscope*

Shown only once in the U.S. during a Japanese science fiction festival in New York in 1979, this excited disaster film depicts the end of the world as predicted by the French astrologer Nostradamus in the 16th century. The cause, not anticipated by the prophet, is pollution, a reflection perhaps of Japan's concern with the recent ecological horror at Minimata.

CREDITS

Director Toshio Masuda; *Screenplay* Toshio Yasuma; *Photographer* Rokuro Nishigaki; *Special Effects* Teruyoshi Nakano; *Music* Isao Tomina

CAST

Tetsuro Tanba, Toshio Kurasawa, So Yamamura, Kaoru Yumi

PATRIA

*Film serial   1916–17   U.S. (Pathe-International)
13 episodes   Black & white (silent)*

Probably the most jingoistic movie ever, *Patria* depicts the successful invasion of America by a massive army of Mexicans and Japanese. Dancer Irene Castle stands at the Mexican border with a front-line of tanks (a weapon recently introduced to warfare) to repel Japanese troops with flame-guns. Warner Oland, later to play Charlie Chan, is Baron Huroki, dictator of the United States. The film's sponsor was William Randolph Hearst, who reportedly thought Pancho Villa's attacks on U.S. border towns threatened his landholdings in Mexico. *Patria* stirred so much hostility against Japanese and Mexicans that the President was forced to denounce the film, and scenes identifying countries were deleted.

PAWNS OF MARS

*Film   1915   U.S. (Broadway Star)   3 reels
Black & white (silent)*

Not the planet Mars but the Roman god of war is referred to in the title. The pawns are Mapadonia and Cosmotania, two great city-states of the future, battling for dominance with prophetic aircrafts and missile bombs detonated by an invisible ray. *Pawns* is one of a number of moralizing science fiction/horror films that reflect American attitudes and anxieties about World War I.

CREDITS

Director Theodore Marston; *Screenplay* Donald I. Buchanan

CAST

Charles Kent, James Morrison, Dorothy Kelly

PIRANHA

*Film   1978   U.S. (New World)   94 minutes
Metrocolor*

A scientist inadvertently releases a vicious strain of saw-toothed piranhas developed for the Vietnam War into a Texas river, where they bite off the extremities of several famous character actors. John Sayles's quirky script is meant to satirize big-budget disaster films like JAWS (see Monsters). Director Joe Dante is apparently in on the joke, but his emphasis on gore and shock effects nearly obliterates Sayles's subtly pertinent comedy. The net effect is of a big-budget drive-in movie offering an abundance of thrills reminiscent of Roger Corman's early years at AIP. John Cameron directed the idiotic sequel *Piranha II* (1983), made by a different studio with a no-name cast.

CREDITS

Director Joe Dante; *Producers* Jon Davison, Chako Van Leeuwen; *Screenplay* John Sayles; *Story* Richard Robinson, John Sayles; *Photographer* Jamie Anderson; *Optical Effects* Pat O'Neill; *Photographic Effects* Peter Kuran, Bill Hedge; *Special Effects* Jon Berg; *Creature Design* Phil Tippett; *Animation* Adam Beckett; *Makeup* Rob Bottin, Vincent Prentice; *Sound Effects* Richard Anderson, Dave Yewdale, Terry Ekton; *Art Directors* Bill Mellin, Kerry Mellin; *Mechanical Effects* Doug Barnett, Dave Morton; *Music* Pino Donaggio

CAST

Bradford Dillman, Kevin McCarthy, Heather Menzies, Barbara Steele, Keenan Wynn, Dick Miller, Belinda Belaski

THE SLIME PEOPLE

Film   1963   U.S. (Hansen)   76 minutes
Black & white

Disgusting creatures worm their way to the surface of the Earth through the sewers of Los Angeles. They envelop the city in a dome of dense fog to create an environment that will allow them to populate the world. Fortunately, help arrives—about 75 minutes too late for most viewers.

CREDITS

Director Robert Hutton; *Producer* Joseph F. Robertson; *Screenplay* Vance Skarstedt; *Photographer* William Troiano; *Special Effects* Charles Duncan; *Music* Lou Foman

CAST

Robert Hutton, Susan Hart, Les Tremayne, Robert Burton

SQUIRM

Film   1976   U.S. (The Squirm Co.)
92 minutes   Movielab

A bizarre electrical storm causes a power blackout and sparks an attack of man-hungry bloodworms. The spaghettilike creatures trap the occupants of an isolated house and slowly wriggle inside under doors and through windows, pipes and heating ducts. Tyro writer-director Jeff Lieberman reaches for fifties camp science fiction and claustrophobic panic but eventually gets entangled in his own rambling construction. The elements rarely jell, although there are a few choice moments film buffs will appreciate, including a shower scene out of PSYCHO (see Crazies and Freaks), with the showerhead raining down slimy worms when a young woman turns on the spigot. And later, when the hero opens the bathroom door, a mountain of worms tumbles out in a sequence that recalls the hilarious stateroom scene in *A Night at the Opera*.

CREDITS

Director/Screenplay Jeff Lieberman; *Producer* George Manasse; *Photographer* Joseph Mangine; *Art Director* Henry Shrady; *Special Effects* Bill Milling, Don Farnsworth, Lee Howard; *Makeup Design* Rick Baker; *Makeup* Norman Page; *Music* Robert Prince

CAST

John Scardino, Patricia Pearcy, R.A. Dow, Jean Sullivan, Peter MacLean

TARANTULA

Film   1955   U.S. (Universal-International)
80 minutes   Black & white

Since spiders jelly the spines of nearly everyone, what better monster than a giant version of one of the ugliest species of all, the relatively harmless but hairy tarantula? In this variation on the 1950s' giant-bug theme, a tarantula is accidentally splashed with a growth hormone developed in a desert laboratory by an elderly scientist, who has already been made into a grotesque mutant by the solution. The spider, which grows to the size of a small building, terrorizes local Arizona residents in some good creature-on-the-loose effects before being brought down by Air Force fire bombs (young Clint Eastwood is one of the pilots). The transformation is biologically impossible, of course, since a spider that size would collapse under its own weight. But the film sticks in the mind because of its accretion of realistic details and the bleakly primeval *mise en scene* of director Jack Arnold (THE CREATURE FROM THE BLACK LAGOON), who plays the story as a metaphor for the conflict between science and nature. Arnold had directed an abridged version of the story earlier that year for TV's *Science Fiction Theater*.

The part of the spider is played by a real tarantula, "directed" with the help of air jets to spur it on, and combined with the live action by master matte artist Clifford Stine. Probably as frightened as the actors pretended to be, the primarily insect-eating spider has gotten a bad shake throughout history. In medieval Europe, its bite was thought to cause the mass hysteria of tarantism, which is an uncontrollable desire to dance. The notion supposedly originated in the southern Italian town of Taranto, where the symptoms were put to music in a six-eight rhythm which has come to be known as the tarentella.

CREDITS

Director Jack Arnold; *Producer* William Alland; *Screenplay* Robert M. Fresco, Martin Berkley, based on "No Food for Thought," an episode of TV's *Science Fiction Theater*, by Robert Fresco; *Photographer* George Robinson; *Production Designer* Alexander Golitzen, Alfred Sweeney; *Special Effects* Clifford Stine; *Makeup* Bud Westmore; *Music* Henry Mancini, Joseph Gershenson

CAST

John Agar, Leo G. Carroll, Mara Corday, Nestor Paiva, Ross Elliott, Clint Eastwood

THEM!

Film 1954 U.S. (Warner Bros.) 94 minutes
Black & white

One of the best of the science-created-disaster films of the 1950s, made credible by its under-

stated, documentary-style approach. The title refers to ants mutated to giant size by atomic bomb tests in a New Mexican desert. Swarming into the Los Angeles sewers, the creatures give their hiding place away by draining a freight car of its cargo of sugar and leaving a trail of sweet-smelling formic acid. The subtext is man's battle with nature, symbolized by a small town perched precariously on the edge of a desert and which could be easily swept away by the encroaching sand and the mysterious creatures that live there. James Arness, the vegoid of THE THING (1951) and later star of TV's *Gunsmoke* (1955–75), plays one of the soldiers who dispatch the insects with flame throwers.

CREDITS

Director Gordon Douglas; *Producer* David Weisbart; *Screenplay* David Sherdeman; *Story* George Worthing Yates; *Photographer* Sid Hickox; *Art Director* Stanley Fleischer; *Special Effects* Ralph Ayers; *Sound Effects* William Mueller, Francis J. Scheid; *Music* Bronislau Kaper; *Ant Mockups* Dick Smith

CAST

James Whitmore, Edmund Gwenn, Joan Weldon, Onslow Stevens, James Arness, Fess Parker

THE THING

Also titled: The Thing from Another World

Film 1951 U.S. (RKO) 87 minutes
Black & white

Like the metamorphosing creature of its source material, John W. Campbell's novella *Who Goes There?* (1938), this superb, unpretentious movie gave the horror film a new identity. The genre had been put on hold shortly after World War II when it became apparent that audiences were no longer frightened by traditional Gothic terrors. *The Thing* differed from what had gone before in that it drew its inspiration from actual events: the recent arrival of atomic energy, faster-than-sound air travel, and flying saucers, which had been sighted increasingly in the postwar world. Moreover, it explored science fiction from the point of view of horror, updating the old fantasy themes of mutation, dismemberment and monsters.

Although Christian Nyby is credited as director, the film belongs to producer Howard Hawks. His themes are manifest in every frame of the movie: the importance of professionalism, the admiration of group effort and of facing danger with detach-

CAST

Kenneth Tobey, Margaret Sheridan, Robert Cornthwaite, Dewey Martin, James Arness [as the vegoid], Bill Self

THE THING

*Film   1982   U.S. (Universal)   108 minutes
Color   Panavision   Dolby Stereo*

John Carpenter's expensive "revision" of Howard Hawks' science fiction classic may be more faithful to John W. Campbell's story, but it never quite manages to overtake the original version. Carpenter makes several brief allusions to the earlier film, then goes his own way with a dazzling display of the most startling makeup effects ever showcased in a horror film. Makeup artist Rob Bottin and his 40-person crew have supplanted Hawks' super-carrot with an approximation of Campbell's polymorphous creature, which was impossible to bring off in the 1950s. The new alien invader turns its victims into pulsating globs of grotesque ectoplasm before assuming their identities so that it can hide among the staff of a remote military installation (now placed in Antarctica).

Carpenter's punchy choreography renders each eye-popping effect more potent than the one before, which is the film's major problem. Despite scenes in which a man transmogrifies into a spider, worm-like tentacles emerge from the mouth of a severed head, and bodies fuse together covered in red, fetal-like muck, the viewer's interest tends to wander since characterization and dramatic tension is nearly absent. Moviegoers stayed away from *The Thing*, perhaps having been warned off by critics like TV's Roger Ebert, who dismissed it as a "barf-bag movie."

CREDITS

Director John Carpenter; *Producer* David Foster and Lawrence Turman; *Screenplay* Bill Lancaster, based on the novella by John W. Campbell; *Photographer* Dean Cundey; *Production Designer* John J. Lloyd; *Special Effects* Albert Whitlock, Roy Arbogast; *Special Effects Makeup* Rob Bottin; *Music* Ennio Morricone

CAST

Kurt Russell, A. Wilford Brimley, T. K. Carter, Keith David, David Clennon

The Thing (1951): James Arness as the memorable "vegoid" from outer space.

ment and valor. The startling opener, brilliantly edited by Roland Gross, takes place at an army research station in the Arctic where a strange object has been found embedded in the ice. The men fan out on its perimeter and while determining its size and shape, they—and the audience—simultaneously discover they are standing over an immense flying saucer. Its hulking pilot turns out to be an alien "vegoid" with an arm the dogs chew off "just like a carrot." It is capable of regenerating limbs, however, and reproducing itself by dropping seeds into soil fertilized with human blood, which it obtains in the approved monster manner at the isolated outpost.

The film was originally released as *The Thing from Another World*, a title that proved to be too long for most exhibitors, who omitted the last three words from marquees. Its tag line was "Watch the skies!"

CREDITS

Director Christian Nyby; *Producer* Howard Hawks; *Screenplay* Charles Lederer; *Photographer* Russell Harlan; *Special Effects* Linwood Dunn, Donald Stewart; *Music* Dimitri Tiomkin

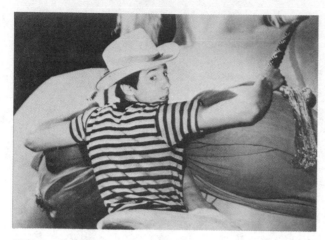

Village of the Giants: A teen thrill-seeker clings to a pair of giant breasts.

VILLAGE OF THE GIANTS

*Film   1965   U.S. (Embassy)   80 minutes
Color*

No one can make bad movies with quite the inept panache of Bert I. Gordon, and *Village of the Giants* is undoubtedly his masterpiece. Gordon's adolescent rebellion fantasy depicts a clique of wild teenagers looking for "kicks" who glom an experimental growth food and swell into giants. After popping out of their clothing (providing an opportunity to leer at nubile female bodies), the kids take over the town and wreak havoc on the square adult world. The special effects are awful and consist mostly of huge seam-lined papier-mache dummies. Among the memorable sights is a normal-size boy slipping between a pair of mammoth breasts, and an eight-foot-high duck twisting and frugging at the Whiskey-a-Go-Go. Gordon, who always went for class, maintains that his source was the H.G. Wells novel *The Food of the Gods,* a title he subsequently misappropriated for his upscale FOOD OF THE GODS (1976).

CREDITS

Director/Producer/Special Effects Bert I. Gordon; *Screenplay* Allan Caillou; *Art Director* Franz Bachelin; *Photographer* Paul C. Vogel; *Special Effects Assistant* Flora Gordon; *Music* Jack Nitzche

CAST

Tommy Kirk, Ronny Howard, Beau Bridges, Johnny Crawford, Tisha Sterling, The Beau Brummels

WAR OF THE COLOSSAL BEAST

G.B. title: The Terror Strikes

*Film   1958   U.S. (AIP)   68 minutes
Black & white, with color sequence*

The death rattle of the 60-foot-tall army colonel exposed to nuclear radiation in THE AMAZING COLOSSAL MAN (played by another actor). For his *final* final demise, he grabs a pair of high-voltage wires that look even more phony in electrifying color.

CREDITS

Director/Producer/Special Effects Bert I. Gordon; *Screenplay* George Worthing Yates; *Story* Bert I. Gordon; *Photographer* Jack Marta; *Music* Albert Glasser

CAST

Dean Parkin, Sally Fraser, Roger Pace, Russ Bender, George Becwar, Charles Stewart

WAR OF THE WORLDS

*Film   1953   U.S. (Paramount)   85 minutes
Technicolor*

Spectacular special effects, the best of their time, highlight this entertaining adaptation of H. G. Wells' classic novel. The action has been shifted from Victorian England to contemporary Los Angeles and in the process Wells' theme of an "assault on human self-satisfaction" has vanished. The Martian spacecraft and their destruction of miniature American cities are the show.

CREDITS

Director Byron Haskin; *Producer* George Pal; *Screenplay* Barre Lyndon; *Photographer* George Barnes; *Special Effects* Gordon Jennings, Wallace Kelley, Paul Perpae; *Art Directors* Hal Pereira, Albert Nozaki, Charles Gemora

CAST

Gene Barry, Ann Robinson, Les Tremayne, Jack Kruschen, Cedric Hardwicke

War of the Worlds: A Martian, unmasked.

X, THE UNKNOWN

Film   1956   G.B. (Hammer/Warner Bros.)
81 minutes   Black & white

In this disquieting little SF thriller, an intelligent blob of radioactive mud seeps from the Earth's core and begins to geometrically increase in size by feeding on nuclear energy from a British research station. Those who try to stop it are instantly dissolved into its radioactive mass. Directed with a nervous intensity and photographed in a smoky chiaroscuro, the film has been described as conveying "cold war hysteria more tellingly than a dozen documentaries."

CREDITS

Director Leslie Norman; *Producer* Anthony Hinds; *Screenplay* Jimmy Sangster; *Photographer* Gerald Gibbs; *Special Effects* Les Bowie, Jack Curtis; *Music* James Bernard

CAST

Dean Jagger, Leo McKern, Edward Chapman, Anthony Newley, Edward Judd, Mariane Brauns

V

GHOULS

Texas Chain Saw Massacre: Leatherface (Gunnar Hansen) and Grandpa (John Dugan) wear masks of tanned skin.

Ghoul, in movie parlance, can refer to any repulsive creature. But strictly speaking the term applies to defilers of the dead—those who rob graves and/or feed on human flesh. Named after the flesh-eating demons of Oriental legend, ghouls can also be vampires and their werewolf relatives. In Russian folklore, for example, vampires ate their own flesh to survive while buried, then feasted on the corpses of neighboring graves before making their way into the countryside. More recently—and less legitimately—zombies developed the habit in THE NIGHT OF THE LIVING DEAD (1968) (see Zombies).

Cannibalism has, of course, been around as long as man. Throughout history, the strong have survived through the weak, especially in times of plague, persecution and famine (the most recent example being 16 Uruguayan rugby players who survived a 1972 plane crash in the Andes by eating their dead companions). But the horror film is more interested in cannibalism as a mental aberra-

tion, broken down by psychologists into *necrophagy*, the eating of a dead body; *necrophilia*, the taking of sexual pleasure from a dead body; and *necrostuprum*, body stealing. All the above are manifested in the genre's most convincing ghoul movie, Tobe Hooper's taboo-shattering THE TEXAS CHAIN SAW MASSACRE (1974), which was anticipated by a host of inept splatter movies.

But most films have portrayed ghouls as body stealers (whose number includes Dr. Frankenstein and scores of other mad scientists). Their prototype is the real-life career of William Burke and William Hare, who inspired Robert Louis Stevenson's "The Body Snatchers," filmed by RKO in 1944, James Bridie's play the *Anatomist* and Dylan Thomas's screenplay of THE DOCTOR AND THE DEVILS. Professional grave-robbers, called Resurrection Men, flourished in 19th-century Britain—a period when medical research was in the ascendant and the supply of cadavers was limited by law. Eschewing the hard labor of digging through six feet of earth, Burke and Hare began their ghastly career in 1827 when a lodger in Hare's boarding house died, owing him money. With the help of Burke, another lodger, he took the corpse to Dr. Robert Knox, who bought it for his anatomy school, no questions asked. When another boarder fell ill, the pair helped him along by smothering him with a pillow to pick up more ready cash.

They murdered some 14 to 28 prostitutes, cripples, drunks and derelicts in the boarding house during their two-year career. The end came when Knox gave a lecture with the body of a beautiful 18-year-old girl whom many of the students had slept with and, consequently, recognized. Burke was hanged before a crowd of 30,000 (proving there's nothing like a good show), and was himself dissected at a medical school following his hanging. Hare managed to escape on a technicality. A popular street song of the day went:

Up the close and down the stair
But and ben with Burke and Hare,
Burke's the butcher, Hare's the Thief.
Knox the boy that buys the beef.

The story has a happy ending of sorts: As a result of their murders, the laws were modified, making it easier for medical schools to get bodies without having to steal them. Burke's name subsequently entered the dictionary in the expression *burking*, which means to murder by smothering so as not to leave marks or evidence.

THE BODY SNATCHER

*Film   1945   U.S. (RKO)   78 minutes
Black & white*

Another sterling effort from the Val Lewton unit, based on the Robert Louis Stevenson short story inspired by the murderous Burke and Hare. The studio brought in big names Karloff and Lugosi to boost the box office of the series, but Henry Daniell has the leading role. Karloff, not wasted for once, shows what he can do as a reptilian cab driver in 1831 Edinburgh providing cadavers (some of his own manufacture) to the head of a prominent medical school (Daniell). Lugosi, playing a blackmailer, is murdered by Karloff early on.

The increased budget is apparent in the carefully evoked period sets and the moody low-key photography. Daniell is good but it's Karloff who keeps it perking, on one hand snatching girls off the dark city streets, and on the other treating children and his horse with great tenderness. Portrayed as an essentially good man, Karloff's grave-robber is overcome by an obsessive need to rise above his station, which drives him to torment the well-intentioned doctor. (Both villains are, after all, providing an invaluable service to medical science.)

A quiet genre film that prefers to tell a strong dramatic story, *The Body Snatcher* saves its big shock for the finale. Having killed Karloff, Daniell goes mad while driving through a thunderstorm with the stolen body of a woman. His guilt causes him to see Karloff's body beside him instead. Falling out of its shroud, the naked corpse encircles him with its waxen arms while Karloff's voice repeats his earlier threat on the sound track: "You'll never get rid of me, never get rid of me, never. . . ."

CREDITS

Director Robert Wise; *Producer* Val Lewton; *Screenplay* Philip MacDonald, Carlos Keith (Val Lewton), based on the short story by Robert Louis Stevenson; *Photographer* Robert de Grasse; *Art Directors* Albert S. D'Agostino, Walter E. Keller; *Music* Roy Webb

CAST

Boris Karloff, Bela Lugosi, Henry Daniell, Edith Atwater, Rita Corday, Russell Wade, Sharon Moffett, Robert Clarke

BURKE AND HARE

*Film   1971   G.B. (Shipman/Armitage)
91 minutes   De Luxe*

A lackluster reprise of the career of the gruesome twosome, adapted to better effect in THE BODY SNATCHER (1945) and THE FLESH AND THE FIENDS (1960). Director Sewell attempts to beef up the story with gratuitous sex scenes in a 19th-century Edinburgh brothel, which only heighten the boredom. Harry Andrews is a splendid Dr. Knox, but the no-name leads are disastrous.

CREDITS

Director Vernon Sewell; *Producer* Guido Coen; *Screenplay* Ernie Bradford; *Photographer* Desmond Dickinson; *Art Director* Scott MacGregor; *Special Effects* Pat Moore; *Music* Roger Webb

CAST

Derren Nesbitt, Glynn Edwards, Harry Andrews, Yootha Joyce, Dee Sjenderey, Alan Tucker

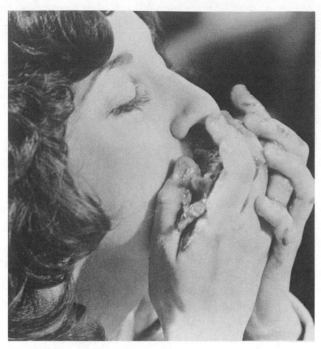

Cannibal Girls: Today's blue plate special.

CANNIBAL GIRLS

Film   1972   Canada (Scary Pictures)
84 minutes   Color

Once upon a time in the Aquarian Age, three groovy ghoulies materialized in a highway hangout, looking for a warm meal. The blue plate special that day happened to be a traveling rock musician and his lady, but they weren't hip to the idea, and ran away into the woods. It was all really far out, said some avant-garde critics—almost like an LSD high. AIP liked the movie too, and released it in the United States accompanied by a loud warning bell that rang before "scenes of supershock." Dated now but worthy of mention as the film that inspired David Cronenberg to make his first commercial film, THE PARASITE MURDERS (see Mad Scientists), which director Reitman produced. Reitman later hit the big time with GHOSTBUSTERS (see Ghosts, Demons and Witches).

CREDITS

Director Ivan Reitman; *Producer* Daniel Goldberg; *Screenplay* Robert Sandler (dialogue developed by the cast); *Photographer* Robert Saad; *Special Effects* Richard Whyte, Michael Lotosky; *Music* Doug Riley

CAST

Eugene Levy, Andrea Martin, Randall Carpenter, Ronald Ulrich, Bonnie Nelson, Mira Pawluk

DEATHLINE

U.S. title: Raw Meat

Film   1973   G.B. (AIP)   88 minutes   Color

When a high-ranking official disappears in the London Underground, a search uncovers the existence of a shaggy hulk of a man living in an abandoned tunnel. The last survivor of a group of people trapped by a cave-in during the subway's construction in 1892, he supplements his diet of rats with an occasional lone passenger. The only clue to his whereabouts is a voice calling, "Mind the doors!" with which he attracts his prey. Often quite as funny as it intends to be, the film is handled with finesse, and the scenes of the cannibal affectionately tending his dead partners have an interesting psyched-out pathos.

CREDITS

Director Gary Sherman; *Producer* Paul Maslansky; *Screenplay* Ceri Jones; *Photographer* Alex Thompson; *Art Director* Denis Gordon-Orr; *Special Effects* John Horton; *Makeup* Harry and Peter Frampton; *Music* Jeremy Rose, Will Malone

CAST

Donald Pleasence, Christopher Lee, David Ladd, Norman Rossington, Sharon Gurney, Hugh Armstrong (the survivor), June Turner

THE DOCTORS AND THE DEVILS

Film   1985   Great Britain (20th Century-Fox)
92 minutes   Color

A slick, classy version of the William Burke and William Hare case, adapted by Ronald Harwood from an original screenplay by the late poet Dylan Thomas. The names have been changed and the time has been moved up to the late 19th century, but in all other ways the movie remains faithful to the classic story. Timothy Dalton is especially winning as Thomas Rock, a character based on Robert Knox, who describes the heart as "an elaborate physical organ and not the seat of love." This is the most candid version yet of a real-life story that is inherently gory.

CREDITS

Director Freddie Francis; *Producer* Jonathan Sanger; *Screenplay* Ronald Harwood, based on a screenplay by Dylan Thomas; *Photographers* Gerry Turpin and Normann Warwick; *Production Designer* Robert Laing; *Music* John Morris

CAST

Timothy Dalton, Jonathan Pryce, Twiggy, Beryl Reid, Julien Sands, Stephen Rea

Eating Raoul: Mary and Paul lure Chicano hustler named Raoul into their grisly spider's web.

EATING RAOUL

Film   1982   U.S. (20th Century-Fox)
87 minutes   Color

Paul and Mary Bland have a dream. Paul, a wine connoisseur, wants to leave his job in a skid-row liquor store, and Mary plans to quit hers as a hospital dietitian so they can open a gourmet restaurant called Chez Bland. Both agree that sex is "dirty," a point of view brought home by the nonstop orgies taking place in the Los Angeles singles apartment building they live in. Fortune finally smiles on the Blands when a drunk swinger breaks into their apartment and attempts to rape Mary. Paul kills the intruder with a professional-quality skillet and empties the man's wallet before stuffing him into the garbage compactor. The ready cash is the solution to their financial problems, so the couple place an ad in a swingers' newspaper to lure to their apartment, in Paul's words, "horrible sex-crazed perverts that nobody will miss anyway."

As much a put-down of the Silent Majority as a send-up of horror movies, *Eating Raoul* works its comic wonders quietly and there are few belly laughs. Filmmaker Bartel, who plays Paul, deliberately paces the film in the deadpan style of its protagonists: two very ordinary Southern Californians who find no moral conflict in their attitudes about sex, murder and cannibalism. Bartel's previous credits include a marvelously kinky comedy about paranoia, *Secret Cinema*, about a young woman who believes—quite accurately—that someone is making a film of her private life. His other films are *Private Parts* and *Death Race 2000*.

CREDITS

Director Paul Bartel; *Producer* Anne Kimmel; *Screenplay* Richard Blackburn, Paul Bartel; *Photographer* Gary Thietges; *Music* Arlon Ober

CAST

Paul Bartel, Mary Woronov, Robert Beltran, Buck Henry, Richard Paul, Susan Saiger, Dan Barrows, Ralph Brannen

THE FLESH AND THE FIENDS

Also titled: The Fiendish Ghouls, Mania

Film   1960   G.B. (Regal/Triad)   97 minutes
Black & white   Anamorphic

Greedy grave robbers Burke and Hare turn to murder to keep anatomist Dr. Robert Knox supplied with fresh cadavers. The real murders weren't nearly so gruesome or eventful (the *modus operandi* was suffocation), nor were the murderers so winningly nasty. George Rose and Donald Pleasence have a good time with the respective characters, locking stylistic horns with steely Peter Cushing as Dr. Knox, who functions as a kind of straight man. The recreation of 1820 Edinburgh has an interesting Hogarthian quality, which masks the low-budget studio settings. Ten minutes or so of gore are usually excised for television, where the film is usually shown under the title *The Fiendish Ghouls*.

CREDITS

Director John Gilling; *Producers* Robert S. Baker, Monty Berman; *Screenplay* John Gilling, Leon Griffiths; *Photographer* Monty Berman; *Art Director* John Elphick; *Music* Stanley Black

CAST

Peter Cushing, George Rose, Donald Pleasence, June Laverick, Billie Whitelaw, Dermot Walsh, Renee Houston

THE GHOUL

Film   1933   G.B. (Gaumont)   79 minutes
Black & white

When Universal launched Hollywood's first major horror cycle in the early 1930s, British studios followed suit with a series of genre films, often featuring American stars. *The Ghoul*, one of the first of these, has Karloff making his British debut as the eccentric Professor Moriant, a dabbler in occult Egyptiana who dies and is buried with a priceless jewel called The Eternal Light. When the gem is stolen from his body by disgruntled heirs and colleagues, he rises from the grave at midnight—in the best Hollywood tradition—to punish the defilers of his tomb. Looking grotesquely cadaverous, he recovers the jewel, then carves occult symbols on his chest (a scene considered strong stuff in its time) before dying again for the final time.

Thought to have been lost for many years, the film—which resembles *The Mummy*—turned up in mint-condition in Eastern Europe in 1969. Although slow-moving and far from the classic it was alleged to be, it's a satisfying slice of well-aged baloney, served with style and wit. Some film historians mistakenly identify Karloff as the title character, but the ghoul, or more accurately, ghouls, are the thieves who desecrated his coffin. A comedy remake featuring the British "Carry-On" gang surfaced in 1962 under the titles *What a Carve Up/No Place Like Homicide*.

CREDITS

Director T. Hayes Hunter; *Producer* Michael Balcon; *Screenplay* Frank King, Leonard Hines, L. DuGarde Peach, Roland Pertwee, based on the novel by Frank King; *Photographer* Gunther Krampf; *Art Director* Alfred Junge; *Makeup* Heinrich Heitfeld; *Music* Alfred Junge

CAST

Boris Karloff, Cedric Hardwicke, Ernest Thesiger, Ralph Richardson, Dorothy Hyson, Anthony Bushell

THE GHOUL

Film   1975   G.B. (Tyburn)   87 minutes
Eastmancolor

Not a remake of the 1933 Karloff film but an *Old Dark House* slasher story, Hammered out by veteran hands Freddie Francis and Anthony Hinds. Setting is the 1920s' British home of a clergyman visited by a group of stranded travelers, who become tasty tidbits for the minister's cannibal son. There's lots of swirling fog-machine atmosphere, a ripe performance from Cushing as the violin-playing father, and a properly putrid bald-headed ghoul.

CREDITS

Director Freddie Francis; *Producer* Kevin Francis; *Screenplay* John Elder (Anthony Hinds); *Photographer* John Wilcox; *Art Director* Jack Shampam; *Makeup* Roy Ashton; *Music* Harry Robinson

CAST

Peter Cushing, John Hurt, Gwen Watford, Alexandra Bastedo, Veronica Carlson, Don Henderson (the Ghoul)

MOTEL HELL

Film   1980   U.S. (United Artists)
102 minutes   Technicolor   Dolby Stereo

A witty little black comedy made all the more delicious by its lapses into bad taste. "Motel Hell" is a neon sign outside a motel which ominously misfunctions and leaves out the final "O". The owners are good ole country boy Farmer Vincent (Rory Calhoun) and his slovenly sister Ida (Nancy Parsons). They waylay motorists, then chloroform them, sever their vocal cords and plant them alive in their garden. The victims are later slaughtered, smoked and wrapped in sanitary plastic to be sold as Vincent's famous country-fresh sausage. The climax parodies THE TEXAS CHAIN SAW MASSACRE, with Vincent snorting through a pig mask as he and Sheriff Bruce stage a chainsaw duel.

CREDITS

Director Kevin Connor; *Producers/Screenplay* Steven-Charles Jaffe, Robert Jaffe; *Photographer* Thomas Del Ruth; *Art Director* Joseph M. Altadonna; *Special Effects* Adams R. Calvert; *Makeup* Marie Carter; *Music* Lance Rubin

CAST

Rory Calhoun, Paul Linke, Nancy Parsons, Nina Axelrod, Wolfman Jack, Elaine Joyce, Dick Curtis

Motel Hell: Farmer Rory Calhoun and sister Nancy Parsons, purveyors of delicious farm-fresh "sausage."

SWEENEY TODD, THE DEMON BARBER OF FLEET STREET

Film 1936 G.B. (King) 68 minutes Black & white

The first sound version of George Dibdin-Pitt's durable comic melodrama about a barber who slits the throats of his customers and cooks them into meat pies sold at the bake shop next door. You probably won't see it unless you visit the British Film Institute. The play's source is *The String of Pearls*, a "penny dreadful" written in 1847 for a popular London magazine by Thomas Preskett Prest, author of the early vampire tale *Varney the Vampire*. The story was retold in a 1971 British TV version titled *Sweeney Todd* and as BLOODTHIRSTY BUTCHERS, a 1969 British splatter movie (see Splatter). Stephen Sondheim put it to music as Broadway's SWEENEY TODD.

CREDITS

Director/Producer George King; *Screenplay* Frederick Hayward, H.F. Maltby, based on the play by George Dibdin-Pitt

CAST

Tod Slaughter, Eve Lister, Bruce Seton, Stella Rho, Ben Soutten

SWEENEY TODD, THE DEMON BARBER OF FLEET STREET

Musical comedy 1979 U.S. 2 Acts

This potent bit of revisionist Victoriana made history on Broadway for attempting to bridge the gap between musical theater and opera. Far removed from traditional show-biz musical comedy, the Grand Guignol plot has barber Sweeney Todd escaping from a penal colony in Australia and returning to London to avenge himself on the crooked judge who framed him and ravished his wife. Teaming up with the bizarre Mrs. Lovett, who runs a pie shop in Fleet Street, he slits the throats of his corrupt customers (thus providing a razor-sharp, absolving social comment). The corpses drop neatly through a trap door beneath the barber's chair and end up inside Mrs. Lovett's suddenly very delicious meat pies. There is also a love story and, of course, a happy ending where the bad get their just desserts, so to speak, and old wrongs are more or less righted.

Composer/lyricist Stephen Sondheim based his work on a 1973 London play by Christopher Bond, who had reworked the original, *The String of Pearls, or the Fiend of Fleet Street*, written by George Dibdin-Pitt in 1847. Over the years, the story has been dramatized several times, and there has been at least one literary sequel. A British film version was made in 1936 (see listing above), and a British TV adaptation aired in 1971. Sondheim's musical version was taped for cable television, and in 1982 was taken into the repertories of the New York City Opera and the Houston Grand Opera.

CREDITS

Director Hal Prince; *Music/Lyrics* Stephen Sondheim; *Book* Hugh Wheeler, based on a play by Christopher Bond; *Scenery Designer* Eugene Lee; *Costumes* Franne Lee; *Lighting* Ken Billington; *Conductor* Jonathan Tunick

CAST

Len Cariou, Angela Lansbury, Merle Louise, Jack Eric Williams, Ken Jennings, Victor Garber, Sarah Rice

THE TEXAS CHAIN SAW MASSACRE

Film   1974   U.S. (Vortex)   81 minutes Color

Still one of the most terrifying movies ever, violent and stomach-turning but also stylish and witty. A group of kids visit the old family home in backwoods Texas, now occupied by a family of inbred cannibals and surrounded by abandoned automobiles. Head of the family is Grandpa, who appears to be well into death and who once slaughtered 60 "cattle" in five minutes. His pride and joy is the shy Leatherface, a squealing maniac wearing a mask that once was a human face and

carrying a McCulloch chain saw. Marilyn Burns is the girl suffering through it all. Hung on a meat hook, she forcibly watches her boyfriend being sliced into filet mignons and is later sat in a chair with human arms, surrounded by folk art made of bones and body parts.

The exploitive title, which already has your fear glands pumping before you enter the theater, effectively stirs a non-Southerner's latent paranoia about the out-of-the-way South. The rather discreet horrors of *Easy Rider* (1969) and *Deliverance* (1972)—and perhaps even the murders of civil rights workers during the 1960s—are nothing compared to the carnage described here. If *Chain Saw* seems unnervingly real, it's because the actors were actually in pain. Most were feuding with each other and/or director Hooper (one threatened to kill him) while filming in 110-degree Texas heat. Leading lady Burns was actually bleeding from injuries suffered during a chase sequence.

Source of the story is the ghoulish career of Ed Gein, a reclusive handyman in Plainfield, Wisconsin, who tanned the skins of corpses and wore them as clothing. Two other films inspired by Gein are PSYCHO (1960) (see Crazies and Freaks) and DERANGED (1974). Hooper has since hit the Hollywood bigtime with such movies as TV's 'SALEM'S LOT (1979) (see Vampires) and POLTERGEIST (1982) (see Ghosts, Witches and Demons).

CREDITS

Director/Producer Tobe Hooper; *Screenplay* Kim Henkel, Tobe Hooper; *Photographers* Daniel Pearl, Tobe Hooper; *Makeup* Dorothy Pearl; *Grandpa Makeup* W. E. Barnes; *Music* Tobe Hooper, Wayne Bell

CAST

Marilyn Burns, Allen Danzinger, William Vail, Paul A. Partain, Teri McGinn, Edwin Neal, John Dugan; *Narrator* John Larroquette

TRAITMENT DE CHOC

U.S. title: Shock

G.B. title: The Doctor in the Nude

Film   1972   France/Italy (Lira/AJ) 91 minutes   Color

Self-conscious but often amusing, this barbed Gallic satire is set in a swank rejuvenation spa, where an aging capitalist discovers the shocking truth about her youth-restoring injections. They are a distillation of the clinic's macerated male Portuguese servants.

CREDITS

Director/Screenplay Alain Jessua; *Producers* Raymond Danon, Jacques Dorfmann; *Photographer* Jacques Robin; *Art Director* Yannis Kokkos; *Special Effects* Andre Pierdel; *Music* Rene Koering, Alain Jessua

CAST

Alain Delon, Annie Girardot, Michel Duchaussoy, Bernard Hirsch

WELCOME TO ARROW BEACH

Also titled: Tender Flesh

Film   1973   U.S. (Brut)   108 minutes Color

The late actor/director Laurence Harvey strikes out on both counts in this slow-moving "ghoulie," his last film. Harvey is a closet cannibal who lives with his protective sister and combs their beach-front property looking for girls to chop up in a basement abattoir. Seems he developed a taste for human flesh after having survived a bomber crash by eating the cadavers of his colleagues. This is an ill-conceived attempt to capitalize on a true-life horror story of the year before, when 16 Uruguayan athletes kept from starving to death in the high Andes by eating fellow passengers killed in a plane crash.

CREDITS

Director Laurence Harvey; *Producer* Jack Cushingham; *Screenplay* Wallace C. Bennett, Jack Gross; *Photographer* Gerald Perry Finnerman; *Music* Tony Camillo

CAST

Laurence Harvey, Joanna Pettet, Stuart Whitman, John Ireland, Meg Foster, Gloria Le Roy

VI

GHOSTS, DEMONS AND WITCHES

Fear No Evil: Lucifer (Stefan Arngrim) comes to Earth.

Through linking occult themes, ghosts, demons and witches somehow merged into one subgenre during the 1960s. But ghosts, the materialized spirits of dead individuals, belong in a category of their own. One of the great themes of Gothic literature, ghosts often appeared in silent films, but with the advent of sound and the cinema's greater realism, filmmakers thought audiences would find them laughable rather than believable. Ghosts occasionally haunted the screen during the early sound era, notably in two versions of Charles Dickens's *A Christmas Carol*, but it wasn't until World War II that they made a movie comeback. The deaths of loved ones in Europe and the Far East made the idea of a communicable afterlife acceptable and even desirable. Great Britain, directly threatened by the war, inaugurated the trend with a number of macabre romantic fantasies, including *A Matter of Life and Death/Stairway to Heaven* (1945). Out of this ghostly revival came two of the cinema's most memorable genre offer-ings: England's DEAD OF NIGHT (1945) (see Anthologies) and Hollywood's THE UNINVITED (1944).

More suitable for our age perhaps is the poltergeist, a boisterous ghost studied by parapsychologists, who have so far unsuccessfully attempted to move the occult into the realm of science. Mischief-makers all, poltergeists like to lob objects through the air, knock over bottles, open and shut doors and generally make nuisances of themselves. Particularly favored by neo-occult horror novelist Stephen King is the fire poltergeist, which can ignite flammable objects, and its human cousin, who can do the same thing with psychokinesis, or the power of mind over matter.

The occult moved into the cinema mainstream with the release of ROSEMARY'S BABY (1968), a film that both exploited and encouraged a wave of fascination with things magical that began with an astrology boom in the early 1960s. During the troubled Aquarian Age, this fascination extended from Satanism and witchcraft to the periphery of science, as in Astronaut Edgar Mitchell's experiment in extrasensory perception from aboard Apollo 14. The era produced so many genre books and movies that today the word occult, denoting hidden knowledge or secret arts, no longer seems appropriate, since what once seemed mystical has long since emerged from the underground.

The stars of these films, whether seen or unseen, were evil spirits, otherwise known as demons, in the service of Satan, the biggest demon of them all. First limned on the damp walls of a paleolithic cave in southern France, the horned, winged creature with claws dates at least as far back as ancient Mesopotamia, where Pazuza reigned as "king of the evil spirits in the air"—the demon featured in the precedent-setting THE EXORCIST (1973).

Still sporting his prehistoric horns and tail, the Devil has terrified and tempted, leered, mocked and romped through 20 centuries of Christianity. For centuries belief in demons was widely prevalent as an explanation for many of our misfortunes. As the Church became a world power, it relegated the old pagan religion of witchcraft to the status of an underground cult, as Christianity had been in the ancient world. Previously, witches were tolerated for centuries, as indicated in the Old Testament when Saul visited the witch of Endor to conjure up the spirit of Samuel.

Witchcraft had in fact been a relatively innocuous form of nature worship, in which villagers gathered four times a year to mark the change in seasons (Halloween marked the arrival of autumn) and to ensure the fertility of fields, rivers, livestock and womenfolk. As the women approached with their broomsticks—a symbol of domestic order—they would sit astride the brooms to imitate the horsemen riding into the assembly. During the Middle Ages, the Church mounted an inquisition against all forms of heresy, and witches were singled out as being in league with the Devil. Among their blasphemous rites was the sabbat, a feast day in which witches gathered allegedly to pay Satan his due.

Christianity's image of the Devil and his witch mistresses endures in the popular imagination, long after the 18th-century British empiricist Thomas Hobbes dismissed them as "phantoms of the brain." The Church subsequently dropped "demonology" as an approved course of study, but its definition of the nature of good and evil lives on in the works of H.P. Lovecraft, Ambrose Bierce and the black magician Aleister Crowley, and in Faust's fiendish friend Mephistopheles, one of literature's great protagonists. That man still seems to need his devil in the same way he needs his God is made apparent by the occult movie.

The Amityville Horror: Yuppies move into a haunted house.

THE AMITYVILLE HORROR

*Film   1979   U.S. (AIP)   118 minutes
Color*

Critics wanted to waste it, but this was the big shock hit of 1979. *Amityville* is based on the bestseller by Jay Anson about a young family who became possessed by their colonial-style house. The story, purportedly a true one, documents the 28-day nightmare of the Lutzes in their new Long Island home, recently the scene of a gruesome multiple murder. The murders, headlined at the time, had been committed by young Ronald DeFeo, who claimed that God had asked him to walk through the house and fire a high-powered rifle into the heads of his sleeping mother, father, brothers and sisters.

In the film George and Kathleen Lutz (James Brolin and Margot Kidder) are besieged by strange rappings and cold drafts almost as soon as they move in. Flies attack them, black puke gushes out of the toilets, the dog growls at nothing, and Lutz begins to act like the murderer. Called in to exorcise the place, priest-psychic Rod Steiger (practically gnawing at his crucifix) is struck deaf and dumb. You're never quite sure of what's happening or why, and it isn't very frightening, but the story works well on an elemental level. Stripped of its EXORCIST-inspired effects, it's essentially a haunted house tale told in the classic bated-breath manner.

Lutz later admitted he had made up many of the incidents, but that didn't stop Orion (which had purchased Filmways after Filmways bought AIP) from producing the shoddy *Amityville II—The Possession* (1982). As directed by Damiano Damiani, this prequel changes the DeFeos to the Montellis and claims that the devil made him do it.

In *Amityville 3-D* (1983) an unmarried couple move in, apparently after the Lutzes have sold the house, and find the gateway to Hell in the basement. The hook derives from the secret room found in the first movie and from 1976's THE SENTINEL. Except for a flashy cremation scene in an automobile, the film, directed by Richard Fleisher, has only a lot of flying objects going for it. Seen on television under the title *Amityville—The Demon*, the effects don't make much sense. Mercifully, the house exploded at the film's climax, bringing an end to the series.

CREDITS

Director Stuart Rosenberg; *Producers* Ronald Saland, Elliot Geisinger; *Screenplay* Sandor Stern, based on the book by Jay Anson; *Photographer* Fred J. Koenkamp; *Art Director* Kim Swados; *Special Effects* William Cruse, Delwyn Rheaume; *Makeup* Steve Abrums; *Music* Lalo Schifrin

CAST

James Brolin, Margot Kidder, Rod Steiger, Don Stroud, Natasha Ryan, Murray Hamilton, K.C. Martel, Meeno Peluce

AND NOW THE SCREAMING STARTS

Film   1973   G.B. (Amicus)   91 minutes
Color

A pregnant bride has more than a few shocks in store when she moves into Fengriffen manor house and triggers a family curse. Director Baker is in fine Gothic fettle, but he plays his hand too soon, so to speak. Before we have a chance to get comfortable with the characters, a bloodied fist bursts from a painting, undermining the surprises that follow.

CREDITS

Director Roy Ward Baker; *Producers* Milton Subotsky, Max J. Rosenberg; *Screenplay* Roger Marshall, based on the novel *Fengriffen* by David Case; *Photographer* Denys Coop; *Art Director* Tony Curtis; *Makeup* Paul Rabinger; *Music* Douglas Gamley

CAST

Peter Cushing, Herbert Lom, Patrick Magee, Stephanie Beacham, Ian Ogilvy, Geoffrey Whitehead

THE BLACK CAT

Also titled: House of Doom; The Vanishing Body

Film   1934   U.S. (Universal)   65 minutes
Black & white

Hollywood's most famous fiends teamed for the first time in this bizarre, slow-moving tale of devil worship. Instead of the usual dank castle, the story takes place in an ultramodern house, strikingly designed by art director Charles D. Hall and director Edgar G. Ulmer (uncredited). In the film the house's designer and owner is an Austrian named Hjalmar Poelzig (an homage to Hans Poelzig, set designer of the 1920 version of *Der Golem*), who has set aside a room for black masses. Loosely based on real-life devil-dabbler Aleister Crowley, Hjalmar was a traitor during World War I whose treachery resulted in the 15-year imprisonment of his friend, Dr. Vitus Verdegast. While Verdegast (Lugosi) was in jail, Poelzig (Karloff) married his wife, then killed her, and now keeps her preserved body in the house.

Into this explosive setup stumble a naive young American couple enjoying their honeymoon, totally unaware of the festering undercurrents of necrophilia and sadism. Karloff decides the girl would be just right for his next human sacrifice, but Lugosi intervenes just in time and rescues her from the Bauhaus temple and its overturned double cross. At the finale Lugosi has bound up Karloff and prepares slowly to skin him alive. Karloff's authentic-sounding invocation to Satan, it might be mentioned, consists of innocuous Latin phrases: *in vino veritas*, in wine there is truth; *cave canum*, beware of the dog; *cum grano salis*, with a grain of salt, and so forth.

The title has nothing to do with Poe's short story; it refers to Lugosi's phobic "all-consuming horror—of cats." Poe's story is more faithfully rendered in *The Living Dead* (1934), directed by Thomas Bent-

The Black Cat: Karloff and Lugosi decide the fate of the heroine by a game of chess.

ley, and TALES OF TERROR (1962) (see Anthologies). The 1941 *The Black Cat*, directed by Albert S. Rogell, is an old house murder mystery, presided over by Basil Rathbone. Japan's 1968 *The Black Cat*, directed by Kaneto Shindo, has to do with two wraiths who return from the dead to punish the Samurai who raped and murdered them.

CREDITS

Director Edgar G. Ulmer; *Producers* Carl Laemmle, Jr., E. M. Asher; *Screenplay* Peter Ruric; *Story* Edgar G. Ulmer, Peter Ruric; *Photographer* John J. Mescall; *Art Director* Charles D. Hall; *Music* Schumann, Liszt, Tschaikovsky; *Musical Director* Heinz Roemheld

CAST

Boris Karloff, Bela Lugosi, David Manners, Jacqueline Wells, Lucille Lund, John Carradine, Egon Brecher, Harry Cording

THE BLACK TORMENT

Film   1964   G.B. (Compton-Tekli)
85 minutes   Eastmancolor

Ghosts from the past suddenly appear in the mansion of an 18th-century English peer. Are they real or is he going mad? (Look for a third explanation.) An agreeable if uninspired Gothic spooker.

CREDITS

Director/Producer Robert Hartford-Davis; *Screenplay* Donald Ford, Derek Ford; *Photographer* Peter Newbrook; *Art Director* Alan Harris; *Music* Robert Richards

CAST

John Turner, Heather Sears, Peter Arne, Ann Lynn, Raymond Huntley, Joseph Tomelty

THE BROTHERHOOD OF SATAN

Film 1970 U.S. (Columbia) 93 minutes Techniscope

A witches' coven operating in a small Southwestern town needs one more child to make its latest sacrificial gift to the devil. This is an unusually chilly small-scale film and one of the best of the ROSEMARY'S BABY imitators that flooded the occult-oriented 1970s. Welch's script shows what can be done when a serious craftsman brings flair and originality to a cliche subject. A clever touch is to have the kids' toys used as murder weapons.

CREDITS

Director Bernard McEveety; *Producers* L.Q. Jones, Alvy Moore; *Screenplay* William Welch; *Story* Sean MacGregor; *Photographer* John Arthur Morril; *Art Director* Ray Boyle; *Music* Jaime Mendoza-Nava

CAST

Strother Martin, L.Q. Jones, Charles Bateman, Anna Capri, Charles Robinson, Alvy Moore, Geri Reischi

BURNT OFFERINGS

Film 1976 U.S. (United Artists/PEA/Curtis) 115 minutes De Luxe

TV horror maven Dan Curtis (*Dark Shadows, Kolchak*) brings his expertise to bear in this screen translation of Robert Marasco's best-selling novel and actually improves on it. The story has Oliver Reed, wife Karen Black and family moving into a summer home, rented incredibly cheaply, which turns out to be occupied by a living creature of sorts that "feeds" on the inhabitants. There are too many red herrings perhaps, and not all the surprises (of which there are many) are credible. But Curtis creates a convincing big-screen atmosphere of terror in the offbeat Gothic setting, a peeling and splintering Victorian mansion in Northern California. Bette Davis, not playing a crazy for once, is superfluous.

CREDITS

Director/Producer Dan Curtis; *Screenplay* William F. Nolan, Dan Curtis, based on the novel by Robert Marasco; *Photographer* Jacques Marquette; *Production Designer* Eugene Lourie; *Special Effects* Cliff Wenger; *Music* Robert Cobert

CAST

Oliver Reed, Karen Black, Bette Davis, Burgess Meredith, Eileen Heckart, Dub Taylor, Lee Montgomery

CAUCHMARS/Nightmares

U.S. title: Cathy's Curse

Film 1976 France/Canada (Makifilms/Agora) 91 minutes Color

CARRIE (see Crazies and Freaks) meets THE EXORCIST, and it's a head-on collision. Cathy's curse is the demonic spirit of her dead aunt, which has taken possession of the eight-year-old. Horror buffs may be amused; thrill-seekers will be disappointed.

CREDITS

Director Eddy Matelon; *Producer* Nicole Mathieu Boisvert; *Screenplay* Alain Sens-Cazenave, Eddy Matelon, Myra Clement; *Photographers* Jean-Jacques Tarbes, Richard Cuipka; *Special Effects* Eurocitel; *Makeup* Julia Grundy; *Music* Didier Vasseur

CAST

Alan Scarfe, Beverley Murray, Randi Allen, Roy Witham, Dorothy Davis, Mary Porter

THE CHANGELING

Film 1980 Canada (AFD) 113 minutes Color

Shattered by the deaths of his wife and daughter in an automobile accident, Manhattan composer George C. Scott attempts to make a new start in Seattle. He takes a lease on a Victorian gingerbread mansion and before long he is awakened by water taps that turn on by themselves, a self-playing piano and an unearthly drumbeat that shakes the house violently. Attempting to communicate with him is the spirit of an invalid six-year-old boy who had been murdered by his father. A healthy orphan child—the changeling—was substituted for him, and this child who bears his name is now a wealthy 78-year-old senator (Melvyn Douglas).

Shot in Seattle and Vancouver, British Columbia, the film calculates its effects with stunning economy. The house, designed by Trevor Williams, is one of the best Gothic mansions ever, with fore-shortened corridors, a cobwebbed stairway and a sealed-off door leading to a secret attic. Heroine Trish Van Devere is led to the room by a series of muffled sounds in a mesmerizing scene that culminates in the boy's empty wheelchair suddenly spinning around and chasing her down the stairs. Director Medak overdoes the low- and high-angle shots, however, and the exposition is overlong. The film has the makings of a masterpiece, but nothing in it cuts very deep.

CREDITS

Director Peter Medak; *Producers* Joel B. Michaels, Garth Drabinsky; *Screenplay* William Gray, Adrian Morrall, Alan Scott, Christopher Bryant; *Photographer* John Coc-quillon; *Production Designer* Trevor Williams; *Photographic Effects* James R. Connell, Rod Parkhurst, Joe Valentine

CAST

George C. Scott, Trish Van Devere, Melvyn Douglas, John Colicos, Barry Morse, Jean Marsh, Bernard Behrens

CHI SEI/Beyond the Door

G.B. title: The Devil Within Her

Film 1974 Italy (A.R. Cinematografica) 109 minutes Color

Poor Juliet Mills! Knocked up by the Devil and she doesn't even remember it. All she knows is that her demonic fetus can turn on toys, open and close doors and make her shout obscenities and vomit into the camera. Satan, it's finally explained, wants to replace a dying human disciple with a new one. ROSEMARY'S BABY and THE EXORCIST were big hits in Italy.

CREDITS

Director Oliver Hellman (Sonia Assonitis); *Producers* Ovidio Assonitis, Giorgio C. Rossi; *Screenplay* Sonia Molteni, Antonio Troisio, Giorgio Marini, Aldo Crudo, Robert D'Ettorre Piazzoli; *Photographer* Robert D'Ettorre Piazzoli; *Music* Franco Micalizzi

CAST

Juliet Mills, Richard Johnson, Barbara Fiorini, Gabriele Lavia, David Colin, Jr.

CHILDREN OF THE CORN

Film 1984 U.S. (New World/Cinema Group) 93 minutes Color

A lackluster version of one of Stephen King's short stories, which bears more than a passing resemblance to Shirley Jackson's "The Lottery." The farm kids band together under the supernatural influence of evil Old Nick and sacrifice their parents to the "Corn God." The children are amateurish and so is the script and direction.

CREDITS

Director Fritz Kiersch; *Producers* Donald P. Porchers, Terence Kirby; *Screenplay* George Goldsmith, based on a story by Stephen King; *Photographer* Raoul Lomas; *Art Director* Craig Stearns; *Music* Jonathan Elias

CAST

Peter Horton, Linda Hamilton, R.G. Armstrong, John Franklin, Courtney Gains, Robby Kiger, AnneMarie McEvoy

CITY OF THE DEAD

U.S. title: Horror Hotel

Film 1960 G.B. (Vulcan) 76 minutes Black & white

Lots of shuddery surprises await a young woman visiting a small Massachusetts town dominated by a secret society of witches. Leader of the coven, played to malicious perfection by Patricia Jessel, is still angry for having been burned at the stake in 1692. (In reality, the women convicted of witchcraft were all hanged.) Director Moxey fills the kettle and keeps it bubbling.

CREDITS

Director John L. Moxey, *Producer* Donald Taylor; *Screenplay* George Baxt; *Story* Milton Subotsky; *Photographer* Desmond Dickinson; *Special Effects* Cliff Richardson; *Music* Douglas Gamley, Ken Jones

CAST

Christopher Lee, Patricia Jessel, Betta St. John, Venetia Stevenson, Dennis Lotis

CRY OF THE BANSHEE

*Film   1970   G.B. (AIP)   87 minutes
Movielab*

A fanatical 16th-century witch hunter is cursed by a dying old hag (the banshee), who conjures up the Devil as his new young colleague. Producer/director Gordon Hessler grapples clumsily with the Irish legend, and Price is pure canned ham, American-style.

CREDITS

Director/Producer Gordon Hessler; *Screenplay* Tim Kelly, Christopher Wicking; *Photographer* John Coquillon; *Music* Les Baxter

CAST

Vincent Price, Elisabeth Bergner, Patrick Mower, Hugh Griffith, Essy Persson, Sally Geeson

CURSE OF THE CRIMSON ALTAR

Also titled: The Crimson Altar, The Crimson Curse

*Film   1968   G.B. (Tigon/AIP)   89 minutes
Eastmancolor*

Karloff, looking worn but vital at age 80, proves he can still deliver the goods, even if the filmmakers can't. The script, pasted together from a horror scrapbook, casts him as the savior of a family terrorized by an ancient witch burned at the stake by its ancestors. Karloff got through four more films that year, his last, with the help of an oxygen mask to alleviate his chronic emphysema.

CREDITS

Director Vernon Sewell; *Producer* Tony Tenser; *Screenplay* Mervyn Haisman, Henry Lincoln; *Photographer* John Coquillon; *Music* Peter Knight

CAST

Boris Karloff, Christopher Lee, Barbara Steele, Rupert Davis, Michael Gough, Mark Eden

Curse of the Demon: A creature better left to the viewer's imagination?

CURSE OF THE DEMON

Also titled: Night of the Demon

*Film   1956   G.B. (Sabre)   95 minutes
Black & white*

A perfect example of genre craftsmanship from director Jacques Tourneur, returning to the subtly powerful style of horror he had pioneered 14 years before with CAT PEOPLE (see Werewolves and Other Shape-Shifters) and other Val Lewton films. Dana Andrews is an American psychologist who becomes involved with a group of Satanists in Britain. The cult possesses an ancient runic parchment said to be capable of summoning up a demon. At first Andrews doesn't believe the story, until the parchment causes several deaths. The owner of the document is the sinister, goateed Nial MacGinnis, whom Andrews initially doubts, then fears, and finally opposes. Tourneur complained when the producer decided to show the demon at the climax (filmed by the producer), but the monster is a convincing one, and it doesn't spoil the film.

CREDITS

Director Jacques Tourneur; *Producer* Frank Bevis; *Screenplay* Charles Bennett, Hal E. Chester, based on the story "Casting the Runes" by M.R. James; *Photographer* Ted Scaife; *Art Director* Ken Adam; *Special Effects* George Blackwell, Wally Veevers; *Special Photographic Effects* S.D. Onions; *Music* Clifton Parker

CAST

Dana Andrews, Peggy Cummins, Niall MacGinnis, Maurice Denham, Athene Seyler, Liam Redmond, Reginald Beckwith, Ewan Roberts

DARK PLACES

Film   1973   G.B. (Sedgled/Glenbeigh)
90 minutes   Color

Christopher Lee, as a mentally unstable heir to an old dark house, finds himself compelled to duplicate a mass murder. Not his or director Sharp's best effort, but the supporting cast of British loonies keeps the mischief moving.

CREDITS

Director Don Sharp; *Producer* James Hannah, Jr.; *Screenplay* Ed Brennan, Joseph Van Winkle; *Photographer* Ernest Steward; *Art Director* Geoffrey Tozer; *Makeup* Basil Newall; *Music* Wilfred Josephs

CAST

Christopher Lee, Robert Hardy, Joan Collins, Herbert Lom, Jane Birkin, Jean Marsh, Carleton Hobbs

THE DARK SECRET OF HARVEST HOME

TV film   1978   U.S. (Universal)   240 minutes
Color

The suspense is bearable in this drawn-out version of Tom Tryon's best-seller *Harvest Home*, originally aired in two parts. Setting is a rustic New England village where a commercial artist and his family have resettled to escape the trials and tribulations of life in New York City. Expecting kindness and charm, they find instead a ritualistic network of Yankee occultists who seem to be offering human sacrifices to Satan. Bette Davis is the Widow Fortune, a dowager with ominous talents. So much for life in the country.

CREDITS

Director Leo Penn; *Producer* Jack Laird; *Screenplay* (Part 1) Jack Guss, (Part 2) Charles E. Israel; *Photographers* Charles Correll, Frank V. Phillips, Ken Dickson; *Art Director* Philip Barber; *Music* Paul Chihara

CAST

Bette Davis, David Ackroyd, Rosanna Arquette, Rene Auberjonois, John Calvin, Michael O'Keefe

DEADLY MESSAGES

TV film   1985   U.S. (ABC)   100 minutes
Color

A fairly effective Lewtonesque thriller about a young woman who, locked out of her apartment building, climbs up the fire escape and witnesses a murder taking place in her living room. Hysterical, she calls police, who find nothing amiss and no body. The rest of the story has her being stalked by a mysterious stranger (the swimming pool scene is a lift from CAT PEOPLE [see Werewolves and Other Shape-Shifters]) and trying to convince her boyfriend she's not imagining things. Director Bender makes it believable with an accretion of mid-1980s Yuppie details, and the liberated heroine, playing with a full deck of credit cards, has some amusing scenes in a video dating service.

The deadly messages of the title are delivered on an Ouija board, a divining instrument invented in the 1880s in Baltimore by one C.W. Kennard. The device is related to the "dowsing rod" used to find underground springs and traces back to the ancient Roman practice of dangling a pendulum above letters to spell out auguries and portents. Coined from the French *oui* and the German *ja*, "ouija" translates into English as "yes, yes." Ouija boards first became popular during World War I and returned to haunt us during World War II and the Vietnam War (which was also the time of the great occult revival), when sales reached a record high.

CREDITS

Director Jack Bender; *Producer* Paul Pompian; *Screenplay* Bill Bleich; *Photographer* Rexford Metz; *Art Directors* Ross Bellah, Robert Purcell; *Music* Brad Fiedel

CAST

Kathleen Beller, Michael Brandon, Dennis Franz, Scott Paulin, Elizabeth Huddle, Charles Tyner

DEATH MOON

TV film   1978   U.S. (Gimbel/EMI)
104 minutes   Color

Mild occult chills in Hawaii, where a vacationing businessman battles an island curse inflicted on a woman he has begun an affair with.

CREDITS

Director Bruce Kessler; *Producer* Jay Benson; *Screenplay* George Schenck; *Photographer* Jack Whitman; *Music* Paul Chihara

CAST

France Nuyen, Robert Foxworth, Joe Penny, Barbara Trentham, Dolph Sweet

DEVIL DOG: THE HOUND OF HELL

TV film   1978   U.S. (Zeitman-Landers-Roberts)
99 minutes   Color

A mutt inhabited by Satan's spirit takes control of a suburban family. Throw it a bone!

CREDITS

Director Curtis Harrington; *Producer* Lou Morheim; *Screenplay* Stephen and Elinor Karpf; *Photographer* Gerald Perry Finnerman; *Music* Artie Kane

CAST

Richard Crenna, Yvette Mimieux, Kim Richards, Victor Jory, Martine Beswick

THE DEVIL RIDES OUT

U.S. title: The Devil's Bride

Film   1967   G.B. (Hammer)   95 minutes
Technicolor

Christopher Lee, atypically a hero, battles a coven of 1920s Satanists for two young souls, playing Dennis Wheatley's psychic investigator de Richleau. Scriptwriter Matheson distills the essence of Wheatley's famous but verbose novel, and director Fisher escalates the terror like a nonstop elevator. Among the heart-pounders is a scene in which the protagonists cling together inside a par-

quet pentacle while Lee's adversary conjures up such specters as a giant tarantula and a lascivious image of a child. One of the best occult features of the sixties, the film failed to benefit from the Aquarian Age interest in black magic, which exploded with ROSEMARY'S BABY the following year.

CREDITS

Director Terence Fisher; *Producer* Anthony Nelson Keys; *Screenplay* Richard Matheson, based on the novel by Dennis Wheatley; *Photographer* Arthur Grant; *Art Director* Bernard Robinson; *Special Effects* Michael Stainer-Hutchins; *Choreography* David Toguri; *Music* James Bernard

CAST

Christopher Lee, Charles Gray, Leon Greene, Nike Arrighi, Patrick Mower, Gwen Francon-Davies, Sarah Lawson

THE DEVIL'S DAUGHTER

TV film   1973   U.S. (Paramount)   74 minutes
Color

A more appropriate title might be *Rosemary's Baby Gets the Shaft.* Shelley Winters, weighing in at 160 pounds and arching her eyebrows like Byzantine serpents, is a demon passing herself off as a dotty hausfrau. She's sold a young girl's soul to the Devil at birth, and now that the girl has grown up Satan wants payment. Jonathan Frid, former star of the TV series DARK SHADOWS (see Vampires), plays the small role of the butler. The producer/writer team, on the way up, later collaborated on the movie comedies *Silver Streak* and *Foul Play.*

CREDITS

Director Jeannot Szwarc; *Producers* Thomas L. Miller, Edward K. Miklis; *Screenplay* Colin Higgins; *Photographer* J.J. Jones; *Art Director* William Campbell

CAST

Shelley Winters, Belinda J. Montgomery, Robert Foxworth, Jonathan Frid, Joseph Cotten, Martha Scott, Diane Ladd, Abe Vigoda

THE DEVIL'S RAIN

Film   1975   U.S. (Bryanston)   86 minutes
Color

Yet another occult potboiler in a field that was already overcrowded by 1975. A cast of veteran stalwarts attempt to make sense of their roles as contemporary Satanists searching for a "sacred book of names." Best scenes are the transformation of Ernest Borgnine into a goatlike version of Satan and a rainstorm finale that melts them all away.

CREDITS

Director Robert Fuest; *Producer* Sandy Howard; *Screenplay* Gabe Essoe, James Ashton, Gerald Hopman; *Photographer* Alex Phillips, Jr.; *Special Effects* Film Effects of Hollywood, Cliff Wenger, Carol Wenger; *Makeup* The Burman's Studio; *Music* Al de Lory

CAST

Ernest Borgnine, Ida Lupino, Eddie Albert, William Shatner, Keenan Wynn, John Travolta, Tom Skerritt

DIE, MONSTER, DIE!

Also titled: Monster of Terror

Film   1965   G.B./U.S. (AIP)   81 minutes
Color   Anamorphic

H.P. Lovecraft's favorite story, "The Color Out of Space," has been reshaped into a Karloff monster vehicle with a damsel-in-distress subplot. Karloff is Nahum Witley, the discoverer of a meteorite from space which he takes to be a supernatural omen from his late father. After the rock deliquesces Mrs. Witley and causes some ghastly mutations, he splits it in two with an axe, releasing "the color out of space" into his own body. Debuting director Daniel Haller (Corman's art director on his Poe series) shows an instinct for visual horror, and the makeup effects are eye-popping. What's wrong is Sohl's vapid script, which thumbs its nose at Lovecraft's more ambitious horror. Karloff's energetic mutant scenes were handled by a double.

CREDITS

Director Daniel Haller; *Producer* Pat Green; *Screenplay* Jerry Sohl; *Photographer* Paul Beeson; *Art Director* Colin Southcott; *Special Effects* Les Bowie; *Makeup* Jimmy Evans; *Music* Don Banks

CAST

Boris Karloff, Nick Adams, Suzan Farmer, Freda Jackson, Patrick Magee, Terence de Marney

DON'T BE AFRAID OF THE DARK

TV film   1973   U.S. (Lorimar)   74 minutes
Color

Goblins infesting an old mansion attempt to claim as their own a young housewife, whose husband thinks she is seeing things. The goblin makeup is startling, but director John Newland, of television's ONE STEP BEYOND (see Anthologies), seems to have nodded off.

CREDITS

Director John Newland; *Producer* Allan S. Epstein; *Screenplay* Nigel McKeand; *Photographer* Andrew Jackson; *Art Director* Ed Graves; *Music* Billy Goldenberg

CAST

Kim Darby, Jim Hutton, William Demarest, Barbara Anderson, Pedro Armendariz, Jr.

DON'T LOOK NOW

Film   1973   G.B./Italy (Casey/Eldorado)
110 minutes   Technicolor

A haunting, visually brilliant enigma as gloomy and ornate as its setting, wintertime Venice. At heart the film is a suspense story about a young British couple who encounter two mediums claiming to have made contact with the spirit of their dead child. A nonbeliever, the husband nevertheless thinks he glimpses the red-coated little girl in dark corridors along the canals. When he finally catches up with "her," he meets his own startling end. Director Roeg relies less on plot than on cumulative episodes united by a common theme, apparently the futility of hope and the finality of death. His technique annoyed viewers used to more conventional genre forms. Virtuosos Christie and Sutherland provide much of what is missing in the script.

CREDITS

Director Nicolas Roeg; *Producer* Peter Katz; *Screenplay* Allan Scott, Chris Bryant; *Story* Daphne du Maurier;

Photographer Anthony Richmond; *Art Director* Giovanni Soccol; *Music* Pino D'Onnagio

CAST

Donald Sutherland, Julie Christie, Hilary Mason, Massimo Serrato, Clelia Matania, Renato Scarpa

THE DUNWICH HORROR

Film   1969   U.S. (AIP)   90 minutes
Movielab

Those who haven't read H.P. Lovecraft's hair-raising short story might enjoy this slick adumbration; those who have, probably won't. Dean Stockwell is beyond redemption as the demon-driven warlock Wilber Whately, and Sandra Dee, the most unlikely of horror heroines, seems to be playing Gidget goes to the Devil. Director Daniel Haller diffuses whatever horror remains with slow motion and fog effects.

CREDITS

Director Daniel Haller; *Producer* James H. Nicholson; *Executive Producer* Roger Corman; *Screenplay* Curtis Lee, based on the story by H.P. Lovecraft; *Photographer* Richard C. Glouner; *Art Director* Paul Sylos; *Special Effects* Roger George; *Music* Les Baxter

CAST

Dean Stockwell, Sandra Dee, Ed Begley, Sam Jaffe, Lloyd Bochner

ENTITY

Film   1983   U.S. (20th Century-Fox)
105 minutes   Color   Dolby Stereo

The story, supposedly a true one, has the lurid fascination of a *National Enquirer* article. A young woman claims she has been repeatedly raped by an unseen entity (that old medieval bugaboo the incubus, dressed for the space age), and the "fact" is confirmed by parapsychologists. Director Furie, a big-league craftsman, initially attempts a character study of the troubled woman, but the exploitive nature of the material gets the better of him. As in THE INVISIBLE MAN (1933) (see Mad Scientists), only the monster's actions are shown. When Barbara Hershey's breasts appear to be kneaded and her hips and body move under the weight of an unseen presence, the illusion is so startling and

well-realized that one's attention wanders from the story to the special effects. (It was a model cast from Hershey's body and manipulated from inside. She supplied the head from a slant board hidden under the fiberglass mold.) Fox, put off by the film, kept it on the shelf for two years.

CREDITS

Director Sidney J. Furie; *Producer* Harold Schneider; *Screenplay* Frank DeFelitta, based on his novel; *Photographer* Stephen H. Burum; *Production Designer* Charles Rosen; *Special Effects* William Cruse, Joe Lombardi; *Body Sculpture* Stan Winston; *Music* Charles Bernstein

CAST

Barbara Hershey, Ron Silver, Jacqueline Brooks, Alex Rocco, David Labiosa, Margaret Blye

EQUINOX

Film   1969   U.S. (Tonylun)   82 minutes
Color

Demons materialize from the underworld to reclaim an ancient book of witchcraft found by teenagers exploring a forest. Special effects luminaries Dennis Muren, David Allen and Jim Danforth cut their creative teeth on the stop-motion spooks (best is a horned, bat-winged devil). Although not up to their later standards, these are superior to the script, direction and acting. Noted genre novelist Fritz Leiber appears briefly as a geologist.

CREDITS

Director/Screenplay Jack Woods; *Producer* Jack H. Harris; *Story* Mark Thomas McGee; *Photographer* Mike Hoover; *Special Effects* Dennis Muren, David Allen, Jim Danforth; *Music* John Caper

CAST

Edward Connell, Frank Boers, Jr., Barbara Hewitt, Robin Christopher, Fritz Leiber

EVILSPEAK

Film   1982   U.S. (Moreno)   89 minutes
Color

Another reworking of CARRIE (1976) (see Crazies and Freaks), with pudgy orphan Clint Howard getting back at the students and teachers who torment him at a ritzy military academy. He comes by his powers when he finds the devilish diary of Estabar while being punished with the job of cleaning out the basement. A clever touch is to have Howard translating the book on a computer, which hooks him up to Satan. Howard makes you care about the wimp, and by the time his tormentors slaughter the cute dog, you're rooting for the Devil to give him a hand.

CREDITS

Director Eric Weston; *Producers* Sylvio, Eric Weston; *Screenplay* Joseph Garofalo, Eric Weston; *Photographer* Irv Goodnoff

CAST

Clint Howard, Joseph Cortese, R.G. Armstrong, Claude Earl Jones, Don Stark, Haywood Nelson

THE EXORCIST

Film 1973 U.S. (Warner Bros.) 122 minutes
Metrocolor

All hell broke loose when *The Exorcist* opened the day after Christmas. Most critics and religious leaders panned it, but audiences responded immediately. Lines snaked outside theaters, where crowds waited in the cold for hours to be shocked, emotionally pummeled and physically sickened. Stories flowed from the press and television of people fainting and vomiting (most allegedly after the masturbation scene). In Berkeley, California, a man raged at the screen to "get the demon." And in suburban Chicago, a Catholic priest had to turn hundreds away from his *Exorcist* sermon, concluding, "It's a social and religious phenomenon."

The reaction had a precedent in the opening in November 1931 of FRANKENSTEIN (see Monsters). One of the first films to be ballyhooed as an awesome shocker, it also premiered with well-publicized incidents of people who ran screaming from the movie or had to be revived with smelling salts. Like *Frankenstein*, *The Exorcist* cleverly tapped the atavistic fears of thrill-hungry moviegoers. But where the former film left the story's gruesome details to the imagination, the latter splashed them across the color screen in special-effects detail.

The most expensive genre film up to that time, it brought to nauseating life William Peter Blatty's best-seller about a Catholic priest whose faith is tested by Satan. The film begins with middle-aged priest Max Von Sydow unearthing a statue in Iraq and releasing a middle-rank demon who eventually settles into the body of little Regan MacNeil (Linda Blair), who lives with her mother (Ellen Burstyn) in Georgetown, Washington, D.C. After urinating on the floor in front of company, the sweet little girl begins to turn nasty. She levitates over her bed, makes sexual advances to her mother, masturbates with a crucifix and begins to look like a putrid, boil-covered demon. Unresponsive to doctors and the latest medical equipment, Regan continues to get worse. Finally, exorcist Max Von Sydow is summoned to respond to Regan's cry for help, written in welts on her stomach.

While the story is obtuse and simple-minded, director William Friedkin tells it with a jolting kineticism that underlines the script's atypical and absolute belief in its lurid psychodrama. Adding to the believability are the first-rate performances of Ellen Burstyn and Jason Miller and especially Max Von Sydow as a latter-day Van Helsing who wins the battle against Satan, but only at the expense of his own life. Linda Blair's memorable performance is due in part to the demon's voice provided by veteran actress Mercedes McCambridge and the state-of-the-art makeup effects of Dick Smith, whose work is the star of the film.

On a less obvious but more powerful level, the film held a hyperbolic mirror up to the then-current generation gap, which may account for its appeal to both young and old and to both believers and scoffers. Young viewers were entranced by Regan's iconoclastic teen tantrums, as when she tells a priest that "your mother sucks cocks in hell," and orders her mother to "eat pussy." When Regan's catharsis finally comes and she is freed of her rebellious spirit—as were, ultimately, thousands of campus demonstrators—her mother breathes a deep sigh of relief. She had caused the death of three men and turned the adult world upside down, but the devil made her do it. This subtext was apparently not a conscious one, since it was lacking in the sequel, EXORCIST II, which failed to connect with moviegoers.

CREDITS

Director William Friedkin; *Producer/Screenplay* William Peter Blatty, based on his novel; *Photographers* Owen Roizman, Billy Williams; *Production Designer* Bill Malley; *Optical Effects* Mary Ystrom; *Special Effects* Marcel Vercoutere; *Makeup* Dick Smith, Rick Baker; *Sound Effects* Ron Nagle, Doc Siegel, Gonzalo Gavira, Bob Fine; *Music* Krysztof Penderecki, Hans Warner Henze, George Crum, Anton Webern, Mike Oldfield, David Borden

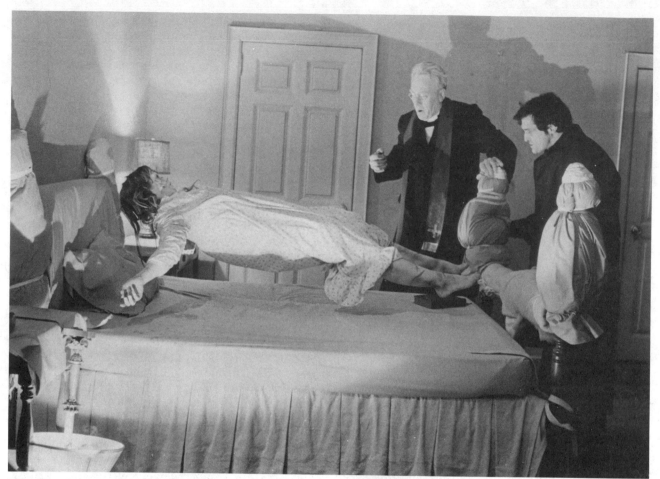

The Exorcist: Levitation is only one of the tricks Satan has in store for a possessed 12 year old (Linda Blair). The exorcists are Max von Sydow and Jason Miller.

CAST

Ellen Burstyn, Max Von Sydow, Lee J. Cobb, Linda Blair, Jason Miller, Kitty Winn, Jack MacGowran, Mercedes McCambridge (voice of the demon)

EXORCIST II: THE HERETIC

Film   1977   U.S. (Warner Bros.)   117 minutes Technicolor

Stanley Kubrick was on the right track when he reportedly advised producer Richard Lederer that the long-awaited sequel to THE EXORCIST would have to "outvomit" the original, "perhaps by having the characters vomit in rainbow colors." Instead, director John Boorman opted for a transcendental psychological study which, while techni-

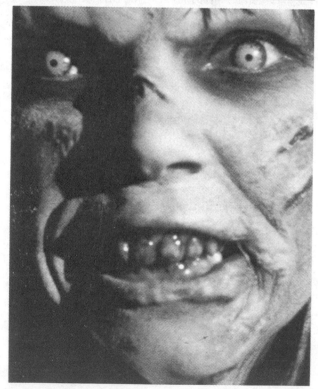

cally brilliant, evokes more yawns than shudders as the new priest, Richard Burton, ponderously exorcises the same old demon from a giggling and smirking Linda Blair. "An extremely nervous and tension-filled audience came and wasn't rewarded," Lederer lamented. "So they responded with derision and couldn't wait to tell other people not to come." The film was withdrawn and re-edited, with no noticeable improvement, and has gone down in movie history as one of Hollywood's most expensive flops.

CREDITS

Director John Boorman; *Producer* Richard Lederer; *Screenplay* William Goodhart, based on characters created by William Peter Blatty; *Photographer* William A. Fraker; *Special Effects* Albert J. Whitlock, Van der Veer, Chuck Gaspar, Wayne Edgar, Jim Blount, Roy Kelly; *Production Designer* Richard MacDonald; *Makeup* Dick Smith; *Sound Effects* Jim Atkinson; *Music* Ennio Morricone

CAST

Richard Burton, Linda Blair, Louise Fletcher, Max Von Sydow, Kitty Winn, Paul Henreid, James Earl Jones, Ned Beatty, Vladek Sheybal (voice of Pazuzu)

FEAR NO EVIL

TV film   1969   U.S. (Universal)   98 minutes Color

The genre's first made-for-television movie features Louis Jourdan as a psychic investigator/psychiatrist who becomes involved with a young woman who communicates with her dead fiancee in an antique mirror. Paul Wendkos directs a first-rate cast with tingly economy, and the film is a model of its kind. The climax, involving the full-length mirror, is genuinely startling. Jourdan repeated the role in a sequel, *Ritual of Evil* (1970), directed by Robert Day, in which he investigates the mysterious death of an heiress involved in black magic.

CREDITS

Director Paul Wendkos; *Producer* Richard Alan Simmons; *Screenplay* Richard Alan Simmons, based on a story by Guy Endore; *Photographer* Andrew J. McIntyre; *Art Director* Howard E. Johnson; *Music* Billy Goldenberg

CAST

Louis Jourdan, Carroll O'Connor, Bradford Dillman, Wilfrid Hyde-White, Lynda Day, Marsha Hunt, Katharine Woodville

FEAR NO EVIL

Film   1981   U.S. (Avco Embassy)   92 minutes Color

Talented newcomer Frank LaLoggia shot this tale of demonic zombies in his home town of Rochester and at a deserted castle on an island in the St. Lawrence River. Reminiscent of THE EXORCIST (see Ghosts, Demons and Witches), CARRIE (see Crazies and Freaks) and THE NIGHT OF THE LIVING DEAD, the film has Lucifer raising an army of corpses, followed by the arrival on Earth of three Archangels—reborn as ordinary mortals—to vanquish him. LaLoggia's script doesn't always make sense, but his suspenseful direction rarely flags. Special effects expert Peter Kuran, who worked on *Star Wars*, *Star Trek—The Motion Picture* and *The Dark*, created the spectacular demonic lightning and Lucifer's dazzling demise at the hand of God.

CREDITS

Director/Screenplay Frank LaLoggia; *Producers* Frank LaLoggia, Charles M. LaLoggia; *Photographer* Fred Goodich; *Art Director* Carl Zollo; *Special Effects* Peter Kuran, Chris Casady, Susan Turner, Kathy Kean; *Music* Frank LaLoggia, David Spear

CAST

Stefan Arngrim, Elizabeth Hoffman, Kathleen Rowe McAllen, Frank Birney, Daniel Eden, Jack Holland, Barry Cooper, Alice Sachs

THE FOG

Film   1979   U.S. (Avco Embassy) 89 minutes   Color

The small California town is celebrating its 100th anniversary, and seated on the beach is old salt John Houseman, telling a circle of rapt kids a scary story. Years ago a foundering brigantine, carrying wealthy lepers to a new colony, smashed against a rock and sank when local residents moved the fog lights. When the mysterious fog returns, Houseman predicts, "The ghosts from that ship will rise from their watery graves. . . ." After this perfect opener,

The Fog: Long-dead lepers invade a California church. Mother and daughter Janet Leigh and Jamie Lee Curtis are among those terrorized.

a fog coalesces offshore and moves on the wind toward the town. The decaying lepers are coming back to avenge themselves on descendants of the settlers, who caused the shipwreck and used the gold to found the town.

Like so many supernatural genre stories, *The Fog* is about nature being perverted by the overwhelming power of human malice. The ghosts resemble Armando de Ossorio's Knights Templars, a secret Christian military society of the 14th century, denounced to the Inquisition when the King of France decided to appropriate its wealth. Comfortably old-fashioned, the film updates traditional Gothic strategies by making the ghosts palpably terrifying, without sacrificing a sense of the fantastic. Carpenter's poetically phosphorescent fog, which seems to have a life of its own, is as much a faceless dread as the hooded lepers. The cast includes mother and daughter Janet Leigh (PSYCHO) and Jamie Lee Curtis (HALLOWEEN) (see Crazies and Freaks). Carpenter appears in a Hitchcock-like cameo as the janitor.

CREDITS

Director John Carpenter; *Producer* Debra Hill; *Screenplay* John Carpenter, Debra Hill; *Photographer* Dean Cundey; *Production Designer* Tommy Wallace; *Special Photographic Effects* James F. Liles; *Special Effects* Richard Albain, Jr., Rob Bottin, Dean Cundey; *Special Effects Makeup* Rob Bottin; *Sound Effects* Frank Serafine, Mag City; *Music* John Carpenter

CAST

Adrienne Barbeau, Hal Holbrook, Janet Leigh, Jamie Lee Curtis, John Houseman, Tom Atkins, Charles Cyphers, Nancy Loomis

GHOST OF DRAGSTRIP HOLLOW

Film 1959 U.S. (AIP/Alta Vista) 65 minutes Black & white

Teen hot rodders headquarter in a haunted house that offers more yawns than scares. Watchable only for AIP's hyperbolic vision of 1950s' American teenagers.

CREDITS

Director William Hole, Jr.; *Producer/Screenplay* Lou Rusoff; *Photographer* Gil Warrenton; *Art Director* Daniel Haller; *Music* Ronald Stein

CAST

Jody Fair, Martin Braddock, Russ Bender, Elaine Dupont, Leon Tyler, Paul Blaisdell

GHOST STORY

Film 1981 U.S. (Universal) 110 minutes Color

Readers of Peter Straub's deliberately complex but compelling Gothic novel will hate this movie; others will probably be bored after the first 30 minutes or so. Lawrence D. Cohen has cut into the heart of the story and reduced it to a clumsily plotted mystery that unravels well before the disappointing payoff. Melvyn Douglas (in his last role), Douglas Fairbanks, Jr., Fred Astaire and John Houseman meet every two weeks to tell ghost stories and share a few shivers before doddering back to their homes. The group—which they call the Chowder Society—also shares an unspeakable secret crime committed in their youth. The wronged spirit hasn't forgotten, however, and vengeance from beyond the grave is the crux of the mystery. The cast works hard but only Alice Krige as the revenant Alma Mobley manages to suggest the icy destructive terror of Straub's book.

CREDITS

Director John Irvin; *Producer* Burt Weissbourd; *Screenplay* Lawrence D. Cohen, based on the novel by Peter

Straub; *Photographer* Jack Cardiff; *Makeup Effects* Dick Smith; *Music* Philippe Sarde

CAST

Melvyn Douglas, Fred Astaire, Douglas Fairbanks, Jr., John Houseman, Patricia Neal, Craig Wasson, Alice Krige, Jacqueline Brooks

GHOSTBUSTERS

Film 1984 U.S. (Columbia) 107 minutes Metrocolor Dolby Stereo

Just as Hollywood's first horror cycle had ended with its monsters playing straight-men in *Abbott and Costello Meet Frankenstein* (1948), the spooks and demons conjured up in the late sixties reached their natural conclusion in this wise-guy parody.

Comedians Bill Murray, Dan Aykroyd and Harold Ramis (the latter two wrote the screenplay) are psychic investigators who open an office in an old Manhattan firehouse and advertise their services on television.

Murray is hilarious as the woman-chasing Dr. Peter Venkman, whose investigations of things that go bump in the night eventually lead to the gleaming, hell-haunted refrigerator of a beautiful lady in distress (Sigourney Weaver). When Weaver is subsequently possessed by a demon, Murray attempts to describe her ravening appearance by saying, "I think we could get her a guest spot on *Wild Kingdom*."

Not a great movie by any criteria, *Ghostbusters* is largely hit and miss, like an episode of *Saturday Night Live*, and its story is as gossamer as the ectoplasmic phantasms. What makes the film so enjoyable are its star performers and the special effects of Richard Edlund, who provides a chilling finale on a rooftop demonic altar. Especially ap-

Ghostbusters: Ectoplasmic exterminators Bill Murray, left, and Dan Aykroyd, center, have just evicted some uninvited guests from a swank hotel.

pealing is a chubby green ghost discovered in a hotel corridor snitching food from a room-service tray. The ghost escapes by "sliming" Murray, and is later seen gorging itself with hot dogs stolen from a sidewalk vendor. For all its demerits, the script is a knowing one, and treats its apparitions with a playful respect.

CREDITS

Director/Producer Ivan Reitman; *Screenplay* Dan Aykroyd, Harold Ramis; *Photographer* Laszlo Kovacs; *Production Designer* John de Cuir; *Visual Effects* Richard Edlund; *Music* Elmer Bernstein

CAST

Bill Murray, Dan Aykroyd, Sigourney Weaver, Harold Ramis, Rick Moranis, Annie Potts, William Atherton, Ernie Hudson, David Margulies

THE GORGON

Film   1964   G.B. (Hammer)   83 minutes
Technicolor

A competent and occasionally genuinely frightening "who-is-it" about a bizarre series of deaths in a Central European village. Someone in the village is a Gorgon, a creature out of Greek mythology, hideous and snake-haired, who turns anyone who looks at it to stone. Fisher directs with a straight face and gets a fine-honed performance out of Cushing, playing a villain. The rather unconvincing Gorgon is, wisely, given a minimum of screen exposure.

CREDITS

Director Terence Fisher; *Producer* Anthony Nelson Keys; *Screenplay* John Gilling; *Story* J. Llewellyn Devine; *Photographer* Michael Reed; *Art Director* Bernard Robinson, Don Mingaye; *Special Effects* Syd Pearson; *Makeup* Roy Ashton; *Music* James Bernard

CAST

Peter Cushing, Christopher Lee, Barbara Shelley, Michael Goodliffe, Richard Pasco, Patrick Troughton

THE HAUNTED PALACE

Film   1963   U.S. (AIP)   85 minutes
Pathecolor   Panavision

Here's one to give you nightmares. The title is from a Poe verse, but the story is an adaptation of

H.P. Lovecraft's *The Case of Charles Dexter Ward*. It's the first film based on Lovecraft, and, though far from perfect, it's also the best. Vincent Price, for once properly subdued by director Corman, musters a virtuoso dual performance as a New England warlock burned at the stake and the descendant his spirit takes possession of. Truly intimidating are the deformed mutant children, part of the epic plan of the banished Ancient Ones, who are constantly scheming to come back "home." And wait until you see the thing in the well.

CREDITS

Director/Producer Roger Corman; *Screenplay* Charles Beaumont, based on *The Case of Charles Dexter Ward* by H.P. Lovecraft; *Photographer* Floyd Crosby; *Art Director* Daniel Haller; *Makeup* Ted Coodley; *Music* Ronald Stein

CAST

Vincent Price, Debra Paget, Lon Chaney, Jr., Elisha Cook, Jr., Leo Gordon, Frank Maxwell, John Dierkes

THE HAUNTING

Film   1963   G.B. (MGM/Argyle)   112 minutes
Black & white   Panavision

"Hill House, not sane, stood by itself against its hills, holding darkness within; it had stood so for eighty years . . . whatever walked there, walked alone." So begins Shirley Jackson's opalescent novel *The Haunting of Hill House* (1959), which is not the traditional ghost story its title implies. Instead, it focuses on the effects of fear on four investigators who risk staying in the old teutonic Boston mansion. There are no clutching hands or shrouded ghosts, only a pervasive, escalating mood of unspeakable dread. Director Wise respects Jackson and underplays his hand, obtaining his scares with atmospheric touches, weird sounds and the reactions of an excellent cast. Many of the novel's subtleties are beyond the camera's scope, but Wise offers some compensatory visuals, including a pounding door that bulges grotesquely inward. A *frisson* of Freudianism is provided by roommates Claire Bloom and Julie Harris, respectively a lesbian and a repressed virgin, who are tuned into each other's thoughts.

Lewton alumnus Wise, who had directed THE BODY SNATCHER (1945) (see Ghouls), said boo! for the last time with this triumph, and went on to the schmaltzy glories of *The Sound of Music* (1965).

Other major ghost movies include DEAD OF NIGHT (1945) (see Anthologies); THE INNOCENTS

(1961); THE LEGEND OF HELL HOUSE (1973), THE UNINVITED (1944) and THE CHANGELING (1980).

CREDITS

Director/Producer Robert Wise; *Screenplay* Nelson Gidding, based on the novel *The Haunting of Hill House* by Shirley Jackson; *Photographer* David Boulton; *Production Designer* Elliot Scott; *Special Effects* Tom Howard; *Music* Humphrey Searle

CAST

Julie Harris, Claire Bloom, Richard Johnson, Russ Tamblyn, Rosalie Crutchley, Lois Maxwell, Fay Compton, Valentine Dyall

HAXAN

Also titled: Witchcraft Through the Ages

Film   1921   Sweden (Svensk)   83 minutes Black & white (silent)

A still horrifying "documentary" history of witchcraft from the Middle Ages to the 1920s, staged with licentious vigor by Benjamin Christiansen, who appears as the Devil. Static lectures introduce outrageous depictions of black masses, nude orgies and other diabolical practices, which caused the film to be banned in many countries. It is available today only in film museums.

CREDITS

Director/Screenplay Benjamin Christiansen; *Photographer* Johan Ankerstjerne

CAST

Clara Pontoppidan, Oscar Stribolt, Elith Pio, Karen Winther, Tora Teje, Benjamin Christiansen

THE HERMIT'S CAVE

Radio series   1936-?   U.S. 30 minutes (weekly)

Ghost stories from The Hermit, noted for his crackling laughter and mordant wit. He introduced each uncanny tale of murder and treachery by ordering listeners to "Turn out your lights. TURN THEM OUT!" The Hermit's sign-off was "Listen again next week for our hounds howling when I'll tell you the story of—Heh, heh, heh, heh!" Presenter was The Mummers in the Little Theater of the Air.

HEX

Film   1973   U.S. (20th Century-Fox) 90 minutes   Color

Fox shelved this engaging misfit after preview audiences turned thumbs down. Set in the early 1900s, it follows a group of vintage hippies on an *Easy Rider* cycle trip that brings them to an isolated ranch inhabited by two young women. Part of the problem is the film's jarring shift from idyllic pastoral to occult horror, with the women turning out to be Indian witches who conjure up killer owls, mysterious bogs and so forth.

CREDITS

Director Leo Garen; *Producer* Clark Paylow; *Screenplay* Leo Garen, Steve Katz; *Story* Doran William Cannon, Vernon Zimmerman

CAST

Keith Carradine, Scott Glenn, Robert Walker, Jr., Hilarie Thompson, Tina Herazo, Mike Combs

HOUSE ON HAUNTED HILL

Film   1958   U.S. (Allied Artists)   75 minutes Black & white

Gimmick-meister William Castle premiered this enjoyably hokey creeper in a "process" called Emergo, which turned out to be the old magic show trick of having an illuminated skeleton swing over the heads of the audience. The skeletons produced more laughter than screams, however, and the device was soon abandoned. (The fear of living skeletons dates back to the medieval belief that skeletons rise in the spring in a dance of death to commemorate the dying of winter. Witch doctors in primitive cultures still prophesy the future from casting human bones on the ground. Hence the call of crapshooters to "Shake them bones!")

The story has millionaire Price inviting five guests to his house, supposedly haunted, and offering them $10,000 each to spend the night. The skeleton, related to the action, is one of the tricks of a mad killer, who also produces ghostly visions, levitating sheets and doors and windows that slam open of their own accord. The forbidding house, actually a Los Angeles residence designed by

Frank Lloyd Wright, was also seen in *Day of the Locust* and BLADE RUNNER (see Cataclysmic Disasters).

CREDITS

Director/Producer William Castle; *Screenplay* Robb White; *Photographer* Carl Guthrie; *Art Director* David Milton; *Special Effects* Herman Townsley; *Makeup* Dick Jack Dusick; *Theme Song* Richard Kayne, Richard Loring; *Music* Von Dexter

CAST

Vincent Price, Carol Ohmart, Richard Long, Elisha Cook, Jr., Alan Marshall, Carolyn Craig

THE INNOCENTS

Film   1961   G.B. (20th Century-Fox)
99 minutes   Black & white   CinemaScope

It's probably impossible to find a dramatic equivalent for Henry James's literary conundrum of a ghost story, *The Turn of the Screw* (1895), judging from various ambitious attempts made over several decades. In 1949 composer Benjamin Britten set the novel to music as a chamber opera, and in 1950 William Archibald's dramatization played in London's West End and on Broadway. Ingrid Bergman made her American TV debut in a 1959 teleplay by James Costigan under the direction of John Frankenheimer, and Lynn Redgrave starred in a 1974 TV movie titled TURN OF THE SCREW. While all are respectful, intelligent adaptations, none communicate a Jamesian feeling of neurotic sexual tension or capture the novel's Victorian ambience as well as *The Innocents*.

Deborah Kerr is the prim governess Miss Giddens, hired to care for two children in a remote country estate by their handsome guardian, for whom she feels a repressed sexual attraction. Both the estate and the children seem picture-perfect at first, but the screw inevitably begins to turn when the governess learns that young Miles was expelled

Dramatizations of Henry James's classic ghost story include **The Innocents** (1961) and TV's **The Turn of the Screw** (1959), with Ingrid Bergman as the haunted governess.

from boarding school as "an injury to the others." Miles and his sister Flora had become involved in the sadistic love affair of the former governess Miss Jessel and Quint, a servant. The couple had died under mysterious circumstances, and Kerr begins seeing their ghosts around every corner. Convinced that the depraved lovers have possessed the children, she attempts to exorcise Miles, who dies in her arms. The novel's ambiguous ending lets the reader decide whether it was the governess or the ghosts who caused the boy's heart to stop.

Truman Capote's script, an adaptation of William Archibald's 1950 play *The Innocents*, is less open-ended than the novel, and the suggestion is that the ghosts are the product of the governess's sex-starved hysteria. The interpretation reportedly came from director Clayton, who had discovered that James had a great interest in Freud's work. Taken on its own terms, however, the film is an impeccable, dignified chiller, evocatively photographed in velvety black and white by Freddie Francis. Compared to the fast-food pleasures of such recent shockers as THE AMITYVILLE HORROR and GHOST STORY, *The Innocents* seems more than ever like vintage wine. For a bizarre prequel to the story, see THE NIGHTCOMERS (1971).

CREDITS

Director/Producer Jack Clayton; *Screenplay* Truman Capote and William Archibald, based on the Henry James novel *The Turn of the Screw*; *Additional Dialogue* John Mortimer; *Photographer* Freddie Francis; *Art Director* Wilfrid Shingleton; *Makeup* Harold Fletcher; *Music* Georges Auric

CAST

Deborah Kerr, Megs Jenkins, Michael Redgrave, Pamela Franklin, Martin Stephens, Peter Wyngarde, Clytie Jessop, Isla Cameron

THE LEGACY

Film   1979   G.B. (Universal/Pethurst)
100 minutes   Technicolor   Dolby Stereo

Lured by a $50,000 fee, a beautiful American designer takes along her live-in boyfriend for a hellish week in an old English mansion. In addition to fierce black dogs, a psychic white cat and sinister servants, there are deaths by: 1. a shattering mirror; 2. an exploding shotgun; 3. a swallowed chicken bone (by rock star Roger Daltrey), to mention a few. If those cliches aren't enough, wait until you

The Legacy: Katharine Ross is startled by a pair of mottled hands.

see the master of the house, all tubes and bottles, who's made a pact with Lucifer.

CREDITS

Director Richard Marquand; *Producer* David Foster; *Screenplay* Jimmy Sangster, Patrick Tilley, Paul Wheeler; *Photographers* Dick Bush, Alan Hume; *Underwater Photographer* Michel Gemmell; *Special Effects* Ian Wingrove; *Makeup* Robin Grantham; *Music* Michael J. Lewis

CAST

Katharine Ross, Sam Elliott, John Standing, Ian Hogg, Lee Montague, Hildegarde Neil, Margaret Tyzack, Roger Daltrey

THE LEGEND OF HELL HOUSE

Film   1973   G.B. (20th Century-Fox)
94 minutes   DeLuxe

Something terrible has taken up residence in the Gothic estate of depraved millionaire Emeric Belasco. Evil manifestations have already caused the deaths of several psychic researchers foolish enough to disturb the musty quietude of Hell House. And now four more ghostbusters have arrived to spend a week there, lured by the prospect of determining whether the house can prove the existence of life after death. Unlike its movie predecessors, the specter turns out to have some very earthly desires, which it satisfies by seducing

Pamela Franklin, grown up since her previous haunting in THE INNOCENTS.

Richard Matheson's screenplay (based on his novel) builds rather mechanically to its climax, but there are some really frightening stretches along the way. The film may not be up to the high standards of THE UNINVITED and THE HAUNTING, but time after time our bones turn to jelly and our scalps tingle with the feeling that dreadful things are about to happen. (They always do.)

CREDITS

Director John Hough; *Producers* Albert Fennell, Norman T. Herman; *Screenplay* Richard Matheson, based on his novel *Hell House*; *Photographer* Alan Hume; *Art Director* Robert Jones; *Special Effects* Tom Howard, Roy Whybrow; *Electronic Music* Brian Hodgson, Delia Derbyshire

CAST

Pamela Franklin, Roddy McDowall, Clive Revill, Roland Culver, Gayle Hunnicutt, Michael Gough

THE MASQUE OF THE RED DEATH

Film   1964   U.S. (AIP)   86 minutes
Pathecolor   Anamorphic

Corman shot his sixth Poe imagining in England on a five-week schedule (as opposed to the usual three weeks), and the care and attention show. This one has more of Poe's text than a title, with a bit of padding from another story, "Hop-Frog." Price, playing a full-fledged villain for a change rather than a jittery neurotic, is Prince Prospero, a devil-dabbling sadist waiting out the plague in his 12th-century Italian castle. To keep away Death, he throws an orgiastic party, attended by a young virgin abducted from a nearby village.

Corman overreaches himself occasionally, as in the final danse macabre of the afflicted guests, which strives for Ingmar Bergman (one of Corman's idols) but is closer in spirit to Classic Comics. What unifies the film is Corman's vigorous staging and highly defined visual style. Especially stunning is the kaleidoscope of macabre reds, yellows and purples seen in the chambers of Prospero's castle. The photographer is Nicolas Roeg who later directed the intriguing DON'T LOOK NOW.

CREDITS

Director Roger Corman; *Producer* George Willoughby; *Screenplay* Charles Beaumont, R. Wright Campbell

based on stories of Edgar Allan Poe; *Photographer* Nicolas Roeg; *Art Director* Robert Jones; *Special Effects* George Blackwell; *Makeup* George Partleton; *Choreography* Jack Carter; *Music* David Lee

CAST

Vincent Price, Hazel Court, Jane Asher, David Weston, Patrick Magee, Skip Martin, Nigel Green

THE MEPHISTO WALTZ

Film   1971   U.S. (20th Century-Fox)
109 minutes   DeLuxe

A devil-dabbling concert pianist stricken with cancer outwits death by transferring his soul into the body of a young journalist. Curt Jurgens and Alan Alda are believable in their stereotypical roles, but director Wendkos apparently never heard the story before and his scares are pretty much old hat. It's based on the best-selling novel by Fred Mustard Stewart, and the title is from a Liszt waltz.

CREDITS

Director Paul Wendkos; *Producer* Quinn Martin; *Screenplay* Ben Maddow, based on the novel by Fred Mustard Stewart; *Photographer* William W. Spencer; *Art Director* Richard Haman; *Special Effects* The Howard A. Anderson Co.; *Music* Jerry Goldsmith; *Pianist* Jakob Gimpel

CAST

Alan Alda, Jacqueline Bisset, Curt Jurgens, Barbara Parkins, Bradford Dillman, William Windom, Kathleen Widdoes

NECROMANCY

Film   1971   U.S. (Cinerama)   82 minutes
Color

Two young visitors to a small town dominated by a factory that manufactures occult devices discover that one of them is to be sacrificed by a friendly coven of witches. Necromancy (witchcraft) may be the explanation for the presence of Orson Welles in this lifeless thriller, directed, produced and written by Hollywood schlock king Bert I. Gordon.

CREDITS

Director/Producer/Screenplay Bert I. Gordon; *Executive Producer* Sidney L. Caplan; *Photographer* Winton Hoch; *Art Director* Frank Sylos; *Special Effects* William Vanderbyl; *Music* Fred Karger

CAST

Orson Welles, Pamela Franklin, Michael Ontkean, Lee Purcell, Harvey Jason, Lisa James, Sue Bernard

Night of the Eagle: Peter Wyngarde suffers the consequences of not believing in witchcraft.

NIGHT OF THE EAGLE

U.S. title: Burn, Witch, Burn

Film   1962   G.B. (Independent Artists)
87 minutes   Black & white

If you consider witchcraft a figment of the mind, you may have second thoughts after screening *Night of the Eagle*. As in CURSE OF THE DEMON (1958), Jacques Tourneur's superb Lewtonesque thriller from Britain, the hero is a contemporary scientist whose skepticism unleashes an occult evil. Discovering his wife is a witch who protects his university tenure with magic, he throws her paraphernalia into the fireplace and thereby liberates the powers of a rival promoting the career of her own husband. The script by suspense masters Richard Matheson and Charles Beaumont is among their best, and director Hayers replays an eerie

trick from Dreyer's VAMPYR (see Vampires) by showing a cemetery from the point of view of a coffin. Margaret Johnston is memorable as the nasty witch who brings to life a huge granite bird to chase the hero through the school grounds.

The American title of this film has given rise to some confusion. *Burn, Witch, Burn* is the title of a novel by Abraham Merritt which was filmed in 1936 as THE DEVIL DOLL (see Mad Scientists). This one is based on an American novel called *Conjure Wife* by Fritz Leiber. The story was previously filmed in 1944 as *Weird Woman*—with Lon Chaney, Jr.—one of the studio's *Inner Sanctum* mysteries, inspired by the radio program.

CREDITS

Director Sidney Hayers; *Producer* Albert Fennell; *Screenplay* Charles Beaumont, Richard Matheson, George Baxt, based on the novel *Conjure Wife* by Fritz Leiber; *Photographer* Reginald Wyer; *Art Director* Jack Shampan; *Music* William Alwyn

CAST

Janet Blair, Peter Wyngarde, Margaret Johnston, Colin Gordon, Anthony Nicholls, Kathleen Byron

THE OMEN

Film   1976   U.S. (20th Century-Fox)
111 minutes   De Luxe   Panavision

Another epic massaging of Christianity's dark underside, derivative of but as effective as THE EXORCIST (1973). Both films locate evil in the usual dwelling place of innocence—in children. When Lee Remick loses a baby at birth, a priest convinces husband Gregory Peck to substitute a child born at the same time to prevent a nervous breakdown. It soon becomes apparent that the angelic-looking boy is not what he seems to be, especially after his supernatural anger results in the decapitation of omen-finder David Warner. In one of the film's heart-pounding scenes, Peck finds himself chased by a pack of demonic dogs through a cemetery while searching for the real mother's grave. Opening her coffin, he looks at the preserved remains of what looks like a humanoid jackal. The child, of course, is the Antichrist, born of Satan and destined to set "man against his brother . . . till man exists no more."

Scriptwriter David Seltzer borrows his premise from the Bible's Book of Revelations, which predicts the coming of Armageddon, the final battle on Earth between good and evil. Director Richard

The Omen: Hounds of Hell attack Gregory Peck as he tries to prove his adopted son is the Antichrist. The son of Satan (Jonathan Scott-Taylor) grew into adolescence in **Damien-Omen II.**

Donner handles the set pieces like the veteran craftsman he is and brings a lingering sense of hopelessness to Peck's battle against overwhelming evil. Production credits are Hollywood's best, including Jerry Goldsmith's jangly musical score. A major commercial success, the film inspired two sequels. In *Damien: Omen II* (1978) the boy has grown into a cadet in a military school, where he continues his efforts to control the world. William Holden and Lee Grant are the new parents, and Don Taylor directed from a script by Stanley Mann. In *The Final Conflict* (1980), the least of the trio, Damien has grown into adulthood as the U.S. ambassador to London. The plan is to murder the son of God, whose Second Coming is supposed to take place somewhere around London. Sam Neill is Damien.

CREDITS

Director Richard Donner; *Producer* Harvey Bernhard; *Screenplay* David Seltzer; *Photographer* Gilbert Taylor;

Art Director Carmen Dillon; *Dog Trainer* Ben Woodgate, Joan Woodgate; *Special Effects* John Richardson; *Music* Jerry Goldsmith

CAST

Gregory Peck, Lee Remick, David Warner, Billie Whitelaw, Harvey Stephens, Leo McKern, Patrick Troughton, Martin Benson, Holly Palance

ONIBABA

Alternate titles: The Demon, The Hole

Film   1964   Japan (Kindai Eiga Kyokai/
Tokyo Eiga)   104 minutes   Black & white
Tohoscope

Jealousy in medieval Japan separates a mother and daughter holdup team when the girl falls in love with a soldier they had intended to murder for his armor. To frighten her into submission, the mother puts on a hideous demon mask, which when removed reveals her true, shocking nature. A strange but mesmerizing allegory from a country where ghosts are rampant, directed and photographed by the team responsible for the uniquely poetic film *The Island* (1961).

CREDITS

Director/Screenplay/Art Director Kaneto Shindo; *Photographer* Kiyoshi Kuroda; *Music* Hikaru Hayashi

CAST

Nobuko Otowa, Jitsuko Yoshimura, Kei Sato, Taiji Tonomura

THE OTHER

Film   1972   U.S. (20th Century-Fox)
100 minutes   DeLuxe

Actor-turned-novelist Tom Tryon wrote the script based on his best-selling novel, which, like the movie, is targeted at the largely female audience who buy Gothic romances. It's a major Hollywood production, refined, and suspensefully directed by mainstreamer Robert Mulligan. The plot involves twin brothers who exchange identities (one of them is the "other"). There are curses, insanity, visions, murders—and a neat surprise twist that you probably won't see coming. Setting is a Connecticut farm, circa 1935, and to tell more would be giving the game away.

CREDITS

Director/Producer Robert Mulligan; *Screenplay* Thomas Tryon, based on his novel; *Photographer* Robert L. Surtees; *Production Designer* Albert Brenner; *Music* Jerry Goldsmith

CAST

Uta Hagen, Diana Muldaur, Chris Udvarnoky, Martin Udvarnoky, Victor French, Portia Nelson, John Ritter

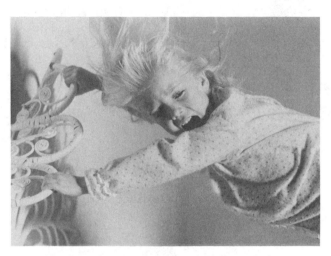

Poltergeist: Carol Anne Freeling screams for her parents when violent supernatural spirits attempt to capture her.

POLTERGEIST

Film   1982   U.S. (MGM/UA)   115 minutes
Technicolor   Dolby Stereo

Like a ride on a loop-the-loop roller coaster, *Poltergeist* elicits the cathartic kind of screams let loose by people on a dizzying joy-ride. There are creepy, crawly things that lunge from the shadows, ectoplasmic figures marching down a living room staircase, coffins that pop up out of the ground, a tree that comes viciously to life—and even a gateway to another dimension. The setting is an average middle-class home in a California housing tract (where all the homes look alike). The paranormal phenomena enter through the family's TV set ("They're here," says the ten-year-old daughter, who senses their arrival). Initially, the manifestations are rather like playful pets, but when they turn nasty a parapsychologist is called in, followed by a diminutive exorcist.

Producer Steven Spielberg and director Tobe Hooper surprisingly complement their respective styles. Spielberg (who reportedly directed some scenes) tempers Hooper's tendency toward stomach-churning gore, and Hooper brings an undertow of Grand Guignol to Spielberg's playful, child-like script. The performances are first-rate, and the characters are more fully developed than one usually finds in the genre. The full-blown special effects, by George Lucas's Industrial Light & Magic, carry the film to its blockbuster climax.

CREDITS

Director Tobe Hooper; *Producers* Steven Spielberg, Frank Marshall; *Screenplay* Steven Spielberg, Michael Grais, Mark Victor; *Photographer* Matthew F. Leonetti; *Production Designer* James H. Spencer; *Special Effects* Industrial Light & Magic; *Special Makeup Effects* Craig Reardon; *Sound Effects* Art Rochester; *Music* Jerry Goldsmith

CAST

Craig T. Nelson, JoBeth Williams, Beatrice Straight, Dominique Dunne, Oliver Robins, Heather O'Rourke, Zelda Rubinstein, Michael McManus

THE POSSESSION OF JOEL DELANEY

Film   1971   U.S. (ITC/Haworth)   105 minutes Eastmancolor

Upscale New Yorker Shirley Maclaine struggles to free kid brother Perry King from the spirit of a dead Puerto Rican decapitator, before a group of Spanish occultists can get their hands on him. Harrowing exorcism scenes and disquieting location shots can't make up for a patulous script that tries to blend horror and social commentary. Producer Martin Poll had his name removed from the credits.

CREDITS

Director Waris Hussein; *Screenplay* Matt Robinson, Grimes Grice, based on the novel by Ramona Stewart; *Photographer* Arthur J. Ornitz; *Production Designer* Peter Murton; *Music* Joe Raposo

CAST

Shirley Maclaine, Perry King, Michael Hordern, David Ellacott, Lovelady Powell

THE REINCARNATION OF PETER PROUD

Film   1974   U.S. (Avco Embassy/Bing Crosby) *104 minutes   Technicolor*

Visions of the recent past flash through the mind of a young history professor, who eventually comes to believe—while watching a TV documentary—that he was murdered in a previous existence. Its cumbersome flashbacks leave room for only a *frisson* or two, and the shock finale is a long time coming.

CREDITS

Director J. Lee Thompson; *Producer* Frank P. Rosenberg; *Screenplay* Max Ehrlich, based on his novel; *Photographer* Victor J. Kemper; *Art Director* Jack Martin Smith; *Music* Jerry Goldsmith

CAST

Michael Sarrazin, Jennifer O'Neal, Margot Kidder, Córnelia Sharpe, Paul Hecht

ROSEMARY'S BABY

Film   1968   U.S. (Paramount)   137 minutes Technicolor

The Aquarian Age of the 1960s kindled a new interest in magic and the occult, accompanied by a legion of demonic novels unmatched since the initial burst of Gothic literature nearly 200 years before. First among these was Ira Levin's blockbuster *Rosemary's Baby*. Written during the time of the God-is-dead controversy, when the existence of the Almighty was being seriously questioned, the novel, paradoxically, had no trouble at all convincing readers of the reality of Satan.

Rights to the novel were acquired by movie merchandiser William Castle, previously known for such gimmicky B fare as THE HOUSE ON HAUNTED HILL and 13 GHOSTS. Castle had the good sense to hand the property over to Polish expatriate Roman Polanski, who had made several genre films abroad. Polanski's screenplay blunts the novel's serio-comic edge somewhat and denies viewers a glimpse of the devilish baby, which Levin described in comic-book cliches as having horns, claws and a tail. Eschewing graphic details, Polanski plays the story as a slick soap opera and lets the terror build slowly from an accretion of details and the performances of his stars.

Young Rosemary (Mia Farrow) and her husband, an underemployed actor, move into a Gothic

Rosemary's Baby: Newlywed Mia Farrow doesn't yet suspect husband John Cassavetes of being in league with the devil.

apartment building in Manhattan (in reality the Dakota, where John Lennon was murdered), next door to a strange but friendly old couple. Suspecting she has been drugged by the garrulous wife (Ruth Gordon), she begins to have strange ritualistic dreams involving other neighbors in the building. She awakens one morning with mysterious scratches on her body and shows them to her husband (John Cassavetes). "It's all right," he explains, displaying his fingernails. "I cut them this morning." Meanwhile, his career suddenly takes a turn for the better. Rosemary eventually comes to the realization that her normal-appearing neighbors are all witches, and that her husband has made a pact with the Devil. Pregnant now, she has no choice but to surrender to her solicitous new "friends" and bear Satan's child.

Deceptively simple, the story connected powerfully with its audience, and the novel and film were the biggest money-makers of their time. In essence *Rosemary's Baby* is a woman's picture, not from a sexist point of view, but because only the birth-giver can know how it feels to have life inside you and to fear, as here, that the infant may be a monster. (The thalidomide tragedies and concern about the effects of recreational drug-taking had recently pointed up this possibility.) On another level it can be seen as a religious film: Rosemary, a lapsed Roman Catholic, has conveniently provided an opening for the Devil. It's also a tale of urban alienation in which nothing is as it appears to be, where people you think you can trust are plotting against you.

In 1976 Paramount released a bland TV movie sequel, *Look What Happened to Rosemary's Baby*, which was subsequently retitled *Rosemary's Baby II* in syndication. The plot has Patty Duke Astin and George Maharis continuing where Farrow and Cassavetes left off. Gordon, who won an Oscar for her role, is back as the dotty neighbor. Adrian, the half-devil, half-human child, grows up and finds his evil nature constantly in conflict with his good one. Director is Sam O'Sheen, one of the editors of the original film. See also THE OMEN.

CREDITS

Director/Screenplay Roman Polanski; *Producer* William Castle; *Photographer* William Fraker; *Production Designer* Richard Sylbert; *Special Effects* Farciot Edouart; *Makeup* Allan Snyder; *Music* Krzysztof Komeda

CAST

Mia Farrow, John Cassavetes, Ruth Gordon, Sidney Blackmer, Maurice Evans, Ralph Bellamy, Patsy Kelly, Elisha Cook, Jr., Charles Grodin, Angela Dorian

SATAN'S SCHOOL FOR GIRLS

TV film 1973 U.S. (Spelling/Goldberg)
73 minutes Color

During the 1970s Satan seemed to be in so many places at once he was almost underfoot. In a quieter moment, he even worked as an art teacher at a private girls' school attended by undercover preppie witches. He didn't stay long, however, after he discovered that sacrificial virgins were in short supply.

CREDITS

Director David Lowell Rich; *Producers* Aaron Spelling, Leonard Goldberg; *Screenplay* Arthur A. Ross; *Photographer* Tim Southcott; *Art Director* Tracy Bousman; *Music* Laurence Rosenthal

CAST

Pamela Franklin, Roy Thinnes, Kate Jackson, Lloyd Bochner, Jo Van Fleet, Cheryl Jean Stoppelmoor (Cheryl Ladd)

SATAN'S SKIN

Also titled: Blood on Satan's Claw

Film 1970 G.B. (Tigon/Chilton) 93 minutes Eastmancolor

Thanks to director Piers Haggard, this occult thriller about a juvenile witchcraft cult in 17th-century England manages to avoid the cliches common to such plots and keeps you guessing throughout. The kids, turning diabolical when they unearth a skull with one living eye, lock horns, so to speak, with a savvy aristocrat whose hobby is exorcism. Period details are exemplary, and there are some startling makeup effects, including a girl who grows claws.

CREDITS

Director Piers Haggard; *Producers* Peter L. Andrews, Malcolm B. Heyworth; *Screenplay* Robert Wynne-Simmons; *Additional Material* Piers Haggard; *Photographer* Dick Bush; *Art Director* Arnold Chapkis; *Makeup* Eddie Knight; *Music* Marc Wilkinson

CAST

Patrick Wymark, Linda Hayden, Barry Andrews, Avice Landon, Simon Williams, Tamara Ustinov

THE SAVAGE HUNT OF KING STAKH

Film 1982 U.S.S.R. (Sovexportfilm) 129 minutes Color

Like a chill wind from the steppes of Russia, this relentlessly gloomy Gothic blew into the United States for a brief showing during a 1982 Soviet film festival in Manhattan. Its promising story, set in 19th-century Byelorussia, has a deadpan ethnographer journeying to the palace of a feudal lord to investigate reports of ghosts in the area. The cheap color stock is mostly blue and gray, and the repetitive, syrupy musical score is unnerving for the wrong reason. High points of the film are the horrific ghost effects, which are a comedown from the polished illusions of the Soviet science fiction masterpiece *Solaris* (1972).

CREDITS

Director Valery Rubinchink; *Producer* Byelorusfilm; *Screenplay* Vladimir Korotkevich, Valery Rubinchink; *Photographer* Tatyana Logineva; *Music* Yevgeny Glabov

CAST

Boris Plotnikov, Albert Filozov, Yelena Dimitrova, Boris Khmelnitsky, Valentina Chendrikova, Igor Kluss

THE SENTINEL

Film 1976 U.S. (Universal) 92 minutes Technicolor

A grandiose, big-budget version of Jeffrey Konvitz's bestselling spooker about a fashion model who moves into a chic Brooklyn townhouse, peopled by peculiar tenants and animated corpses. As it happens, the building is the gateway to hell, and her boyfriend is the Devil's sentinel. Director Winner and co-scripter Konvitz reshuffle the novel's pages, discarding some and adding new ones, but fail to deal a winning hand. There's a feeling of condescension to the material, partially redeemed by some EXORCIST-style effects and atmospheric camera work.

CREDITS

Director Michael Winner; *Producers/Screenplay* Michael Winner, Jeffrey Konvitz, based on the novel by Jeffrey Konvitz; *Photographer* Dick Kratina; *Special Effects* Albert Whitlock; *Production Designer* Philip Rosenberg; *Makeup* Dick Smith, Bob Laden; *Music* Gil Melle

CAST

Cristina Raines, Chris Sarandon, Martin Balsam, Ava Gardner, Arthur Kennedy, John Carradine, Jose Ferrer, Burgess Meredith, Eli Wallach, Sylvia Miles, Deborah Raffin

THE SEVENTH VICTIM

Film 1943 U.S. (RKO) 71 minutes Black & white

Editor Mark Robson made an auspicious directorial debut with this prophetic psychological thriller, which begins with a quotation from John Donne's Holy Sonnet VII: "I run to Death, and Death meets me as fast, and all my Pleasures are like Yesterdays." As in many of Lewton's films, the plot unfolds from the viewpoint of an innocent stumbling into a half-world of menace and perversity. Kim Hunter, fresh from Broadway, plays a young woman visiting Manhattan to find her missing sister, who, lonely and alienated, had become involved with a cult of devil-worshippers known as the Palladists. Because she had revealed the cult's identity to her psychiatrist (Tom Conway, repeating his *Cat People* role), the sister was pressured into commiting suicide, thus becoming the Palladists' seventh victim.

Populated by a gallery of complex characters and suffused with a mood of bitter melancholy (an affliction common to RKO *noir* movies of the forties), the film proved inaccessible to contemporary audiences and was a critical and popular failure. Viewed today, from the perspective of cult murders and the mass Guyana suicides of 1978, it has an unsettling impact and often seems curiously up-to-date. There are several stunning set pieces: a nocturnal subway scene in which a corpse is deposited in a train by two men pretending to be carrying a drunk; a gathering of Satanists in a Greenwich Village apartment. Although the film has a stagey studio-bound look (the opening scene's staircase was used in *The Magnificent Ambersons*), it evokes the anonymous terror of a large city at night, the feeling that nameless dangers lay around every corner. The ending, unfortunately, is a cop-out in which the Palladists are shamed into repentance by a recital of The Lord's Prayer.

CREDITS

Director Mark Robson; *Producer* Val Lewton; *Screenplay* Charles O'Neal, DeWitt Bodeen; *Photographer* Nicholas Musuraca; *Art Directors* Albert D'Agostino, Walter E. Keller; *Music* Roy Webb

CAST

Tom Conway, Jean Brooks, Kim Hunter, Isabel Jewell, Evelyn Brent, Hugh Beaumont, Erford Gage

THE SHINING

Film   1980   G.B. (Warner Bros.)
146 minutes   Color   Dolby Stereo

If Stanley Kubrick had preserved the values of Stephen King's scary novel instead of spending it all on technical perfection, he might have produced a great horror film instead of a mesmerizingly beautiful one. It's the most expensive genre film yet, but the story might have been written for an old *Twilight Zone* episode. Jack Nicholson and Shelley Duvall play a couple with a young son who become caretakers of an isolated—and, as it happens, a haunted—hotel. Solitude and ghosts from the past turn Nicholson into a homicidal maniac,

The Shining: Shelley Duvall begins to sense she is no longer safe from husband Jack Nicholson.

and he spends the latter half of the film trying to kill his wife and son.

Where Kubrick succeeds is in his use of architectural space as a negative emotional force. There is a throat-grabbing chase through a maze of snow-shrouded evergreens, followed breath for icy breath by a Steadicam camera, and a startling moment of realization when the wife peeks at her writer-husband's manuscript and sees that he's been typing only geometric patterns. Nicholson, an emigre from low-budget horror, is both hilarious and terrifying as he announces, "Wendy, I'm home," while axing a bathroom door and intending to chop her into little pieces. Much of the story doesn't make sense, however. The "shining," a psychic power, is never adequately explained, and the black cook who has it can't spot a killer standing six feet away. According to King, "Neither Stanley Kubrick nor his screenwriter Diane Johnson had any knowledge of the genre. It was like they had never seen a horror movie before, so they did a lot of things audiences had seen before."

CREDITS

Director/Producer Stanley Kubrick; *Screenplay* Stanley Kubrick, Diane Johnson, based on the novel by Stephen King; *Photographers* John Alcott, Douglas Milsome, MacGillivray Freeman; *Production Designer* Roy Walker; *Makeup* Tom Smith, Barbara Daly; *Music* Bela Bartok, Gyorgy Ligeti, Krzysztof Penderecki, Wendy Carlos, Rachel Elkind

CAST

Jack Nicholson, Shelley Duvall, Danny Lloyd, Scatman Crothers, Barry Nelson, Anne Jackson, Joe Turkel, Philip Stone, Lia Beldam

THE SKULL

Film	1965	G.B. (Amicus)	83 minutes
Techniscope	Color		

Amicus, keeping the Hammer stable busy on off days, cast Peter Cushing as a collector of occult objects who buys the skull of the Marquis de Sade at an auction. The spirit of the notorious marquis still inhabits the skull, of course, and before long it also takes up residence in Cushing's. Scriptwriter Subotsky makes mincemeat of Bloch's story, but director Francis skips over the inadequacies at a shuddery pace.

CREDITS

Director Freddie Francis; *Producers* Milton Subotsky, Max J. Rosenberg; *Screenplay* Milton Subotsky, based on the story "The Skull of the Marquis de Sade" by Robert Bloch; *Photographer* John Wilcox; *Art Director* Bill Constable; *Special Effects* Ted Samuels; *Music* Elisabeth Lutyens

CAST

Peter Cushing, Christopher Lee, Patrick Wymark, Jill Bennett, Michael Gough, George Coulouris, Patrick Magee, Nigel Green

STRANGER IN OUR HOUSE

TV film	1978	U.S. (Inter Planetary Pictures/	
Finnegan)	104 minutes	Color	

Linda Blair, who never quite recovered from THE EXORCIST, is typecast as a young girl who battles a visiting witch (her cousin) intent on dominating the family. The film premiered on Halloween night opposite a more interesting "possession" dud titled DEVIL DOG: THE HOUND OF HELL.

CREDITS

Director Wes Craven; *Producers* Pat Finnegan, Bill Finnegan; *Screenplay* Max A. Keller, Glenn M. Benest, based on the novel *Summer of Fear* by Lois Duncan;

Photographer William K. Jurgensen; *Music* Michael Lloyd, John D'Andrea

CAST

Linda Blair, Lee Purcell, Carol Lawrence, Jeremy Slate, Macdonald Carey, Jeff McCracken

THE STRANGER WITHIN

TV film	1974	U.S. (ABC)	72 minutes
Color			

Richard Matheson's slow-moving screenplay, an amalgam of ROSEMARY'S BABY and THE EXORCIST, follows the predicament of a young woman who becomes pregnant even though her husband is sterile. He believes she's been unfaithful, until the fetus takes control of the woman and makes her do bizarre things. The demon "father" turns out to be a force from outer space.

CREDITS

Director Lee Philips; *Producer* Neil T. Maffeo; *Screenplay* Richard Matheson; *Photographer* Michael Margulies; *Art Director* Hilyard Brown; *Music* Charles Fox

CAST

Barbara Eden, George Grizzard, Joyce Van Patten, David Doyle, Nehemiah Persoff

STUDENT VON PRAG/The Student of Prague

Film	1913	Germany (Bioscop)	75 minutes
Black & white (silent)			

One of the earliest movies about a pact with Satan, this was also the genre's first feature-length production. The student of the title is an ambitious young man named Baldwin (Paul Wegener), who sells his mirror image to the wizard Scapinelli, a representative of the Devil, in return for love, money and fame. The Faustian bargain turns out to be no bargain, of course. Although granted his ambitions, the student eventually becomes distraught and murders Scapinelli, an act that causes the mirror to break and destroy him body and soul.

The film brilliantly brings to life a favorite theme of Gothic literature—especially in Germany—the doppelganger, a ghostly double of a living person. The sets and lighting are evocative of Baldwin's state of mind, and the location shots are well-integrated into the eerie story. For the first time, the split-screen technique inaugurated by French magician Georges Melies becomes a storytelling device rather than a trick used for its own sake. The story was filmed successfully again in 1926 by Henrik Galeen, with Conrad Veidt as Baldwin. The later version emphasizes the student's battle with his other self rather than with his supernatural double. The expressionist studio landscape underlines his inner conflict. An inferior 1935 sound version, directed by Arthur Robison and starring Anton Walbrook, includes operetta music and dismisses Scapinelli as a jealous lover.

CREDITS

Director Stellan Rye; *Screenplay* Hanns Heinz Ewers; *Photographer* Guido Seeber; *Art Directors* Robert A. Dietrich, Kurt Richter

CAST

Paul Wegener, John Gottowt, Lyda Salmonova, Greta Berger, Lothar Korner

SUPERSTITION

Radio series   1943–46   U.S. (ABC)
30 minutes (weekly)

Ralph Bell was the Voice of Superstition, a mysterious presence that told of the tragic consequences of superstitious beliefs and, occasionally, the dire consequences of not believing. Robert Sloane directed and wrote many of the scripts.

THE TERROR

Film   1963   U.S. (AIP/Filmgroup)
81 minutes   Pathecolor

This is one of Corman's ingenious afterthoughts, slapped together because THE RAVEN (see Mad Scientists) finished ahead of schedule. Karloff owed two more days on his contract, so Corman—taking a break in his Poe cycle—put him to work as a mysterious baron who shares his castle with a beautiful, vengeful ghost. Unfortunately, the bur-

The Terror: AIP's standing graveyard set, designed by Daniel Haller, often seen in the studio's Poe series.

den of the film falls on the neophyte shoulders of young Jack Nicholson, playing a Napoleonic officer who follows the ethereal beauty home. Scenes fluctuate between campiness and Gothic splendor, which is no surprise, considering how the film was made. Eager beavers Francis Ford Coppola, Monte Hellman and Jack Hill shot Nicholson's additional scenes over a three-month period on sets borrowed from other films. The graveyard belongs to THE PREMATURE BURIAL (see Crazies and Freaks), the castle hall to *The Raven*, and the torture chamber to THE PIT AND THE PENDULUM (see Crazies and Freaks). Background footage was culled from HOUSE OF USHER (see Crazies and Freaks). Corman, whose motto must be "waste not, want not," gave the cuts to director Peter Bogdanovich five years later to use in his debut film TARGETS (see Crazies and Freaks).

CREDITS

Director/Producer Roger Corman; *Location Director* Monte Hellman; *Associate Producer* Francis Ford Coppola; *Screenplay* Leo Gordon, Jack Hill; *Photographer* John Nikolaus; *Art Director* Daniel Haller; *Music* Ronald Stein

CAST

Boris Karloff, Jack Nicholson, Sandra Knight, Richard Miller, Dorothy Neumann, Jonathan Haze

13 GHOSTS

Film   1960   U.S. (Columbia/Castle)
88 minutes   Technicolor

Thirteen proved to be an unlucky number for gimmicky filmmaker William Castle, who had produced the far more lively fright flick THE TINGLER the year before. The juvenile story of this one revolves around a penniless academic who inherits an old house with a fortune hidden somewhere among the gingerbread and knickknacks. There are ghosts in the house too, which you could look at or not in the film's original run. The gimmick was "Illusion-O", a pair of paper glasses with a blue lens and a red one that enabled you to see the specters, if you weren't too scared. Featured is housekeeper Margaret Hamilton, the witch from *The Wizard of Oz*, wearing a makeup as close to her original role as Castle could get away with.

CREDITS

Director/Producer William Castle; *Screenplay* Robb White; *Photographer* Joseph Biroc; *Art Director* Cary

Odell; *Color Special Effects* Butler-Glouner Inc.; *Makeup* Ben Lane; *Music* Von Dexter

CAST

Charles Herbert, Martin Milner, Jo Morrow, Rosemary DeCamp, Margaret Hamilton, Donald Woods

THE TINGLER

Film   1959   U.S. (Columbia/Castle)
82 minutes   Black & white

After the flying skeletons failed to perform as expected in his HOUSE ON HAUNTED HILL, master showman William Castle decided to bring a new verity to the cliche expression "spinetingling." Vincent Price plays a scientist who has discovered that fear manifests itself as a parasitic scorpionlike monster, which will sever the spinal column unless released by a scream.

To keep audiences on the edge of their seats, Castle arranged to have the film shown in obliging theaters with a gimmick called "Percepto," in which certain seats were wired to produce tangible electric shocks. At one point the screen went blank as Price announced, "Ladies and gentlemen, please do not panic, but scream. Scream for your lives! The Tingler is loose in this theater. If you don't scream it may kill you." This signaled theater employees to turn on the juice and begin accompanying recorded voices shouting things like "Help, it's on me!" and "Look under your seat!" Actually, the film is one of Castle's better efforts, with Price cementing his position as America's leading genre star. Judith Evelyn gives a good performance as a deaf-mute unable to scream when she finds her death certificate in a medicine cabinet and, later, when she sees a hand reaching out from her blood-filled bathtub (filmed in color).

CREDITS

Director/Producer William Castle; *Screenplay* Robb White; *Photographer* Wilfrid M. Cline; *Art Director* Phil Bennett; *Music* Von Dexter

CAST

Vincent Price, Judith Evelyn, Philip Coolidge, Darryl Hickman, Patricia Cutts, Pamela Lincoln

TO THE DEVIL...A DAUGHTER

Film   1976   G.B./Germany (EMI/Hammer/Terra)
93 minutes   Technicolor

Hammer's sign-off feature is a ponderous, choppy version of Dennis Wheatley's 1953 novel. In the pruned storyline, an American occultist visits Germany to protect the daughter of a friend from a Satanist cult. By now Hammer had lost ground to the majors, which had taken up the little studio's innovations in such films as THE EXORCIST. Hammer, sticking to the tried and true, found itself locked in a dead-end formula.

CREDITS

Director Peter Sykes; *Producer* Roy Skeggs; *Screenplay* Chris Wicking; *Photographer* David Warkin; *Art Director* Don Picton; *Makeup* Eric Allwright, George Blackler; *Special Effects* Les Bowie; *Music* Paul Glass

CAST

Richard Widmark, Christopher Lee, Nastassia Kinski, Honor Blackman, Denholm Elliott, Michael Goodliffe

THE TOMB OF LIGEIA

Film   1964   G.B./U.S. (AIP)   81 minutes
Eastmancolor   CinemaScope

Corman climaxed his Poe series with a grand flourish, reprising his past glories in a Victorian English setting, far from his cramped Hollywood studio. The crew is a British one, but Vincent Price is still on hand with the same troubled fears about conjuring up the implacable dead he exhibited in the inaugural film, 1960's HOUSE OF USHER (see Crazies and Freaks). Ligeia, the deceased first wife of drug addict Price, returns from death to haunt him as a black cat, and then possesses the body of his delicately lovely second spouse, Lady Rowena.

More Corman than Poe, as usual, the film is an engaging but occasionally confusing blend of necrophilia, black magic and Gothic atmosphere. The Byzantine love story was written by Robert Towne, a Corman protege soon to make his mark in the mainstream with such films as *Chinatown* (1974). Corman, feeling he had nowhere left to go with the series, exited the genre after this outing and returned to topical youth-oriented films. AIP finished the Poe cycle with other directors. It was an honorable departure, and Corman could take satisfaction in the knowledge that he had left the American horror film better than he had found it.

CREDITS

Director Roger Corman; *Producer* Pat Green; *Screenplay* Robert Towne, based on "Ligeia" by Edgar Allan Poe; *Photographer* Arthur Grant; *Art Director* Colin Southcott; *Special Effects* Ted Samuels; *Makeup* George Blackler; *Music* Kenneth V. Jones

CAST

Vincent Price, Elizabeth Shepherd, John Westbrook, Derek Francis, Oliver Johnston, Richard Vernon

TURN OF THE SCREW

TV film   1974   U.S. (Dan Curtis/ABC)
144 minutes   Color

Originally broadcast on two consecutive nights, this videotape-to-film production makes a laudable attempt to dramatize the Henry James novella for the home screen. Lynn Redgrave gives a bravura performance as the protective/possessive Victorian governess whose charges seem to be haunted by the ghosts of two dead servants. The screenplay by William F. Nolan preserves the story's dark ambiguities and wisely makes no attempt to explain whether the ghosts are real or imagined. The direction is stagey, however, and the sets and decor are not up to par.

CREDITS

Director/Producer Dan Curtis; *Screenplay* William F. Nolan, based on the novel by Henry James; *Photographer* Ben Colman; *Art Director* Trevor Williams; *Music* William Cobert

CAST

Lynn Redgrave, Eva Griffith, Jasper Jacob, Megs Jenkins, John Barton, Anthony Langdon

THE UNCANNY

Film   1977   Canada/G.B. (Cinevideo/Tor)
85 minutes   Color

After an earlier association with holiness, cats were demoted to devil's helper by medieval Christians, who thereby provided horror with one of its most durable symbols. In this lively low-budgeter—made under the title *Brrrr!*—three contemporary felines nastily avenge their murdered owners while writer Peter Cushing tries to convince a London publisher that his stories (told in flashback) are true. Local cats, apparently tired of bad publicity, savage Cushing when he leaves the publisher's office and will the publisher to destroy Cushing's manuscript.

CREDITS

Director Denis Heroux; *Producers* Claude Heroux, Rene Dupont; *Screenplay* Michel Parry; *Photographers* Harry Waxman, James Bawden; *Special Effects* Michael Albrechtsen; *Makeup* Tom Smith; *Music* Wilfred Josephs

CAST

Peter Cushing, Ray Milland, Joan Greenwood, Donald Pleasence, Samantha Eggar, Alexandra Stewart, John Vernon, Susan Penhaligon

THE UNINVITED

Film   1944   U.S. (Paramount)   98 minutes Black & white

Hollywood has never been comfortable with serious ghost stories, allegedly because audiences won't come to see them, and the subgenre generally has been the province of European studios. An exception came during the years of World War II, when idealized spirits helped soften the blow of wartime losses. Among Hollywood's output during this period were *A Guy Named Joe* (1943), in which Spencer Tracy comes back from the dead to make Van Johnson a better pilot, *The Canterville Ghost* (1944), a serio-comic revision of Oscar Wilde's story about a ghost (Charles Laughton) redeemed by child actress Margaret O'Brien, and this bona fide classic.

Ray Milland and Ruth Hussey are a brother and sister who buy the stately house of Windwood on the Cornish coast and become involved with its two spirits (one good and one bad). The key to the mystery seems to be troubled young Gail Russell, whose fragile dark beauty is underscored by the romantic theme song Victor Young dedicated to her character ("Stella by Starlight"). The unnatural events that eventually compel the girl to the edge of a cliff are so skillfully rendered that one can almost smell the ghost's giveaway scent of mimosa and feel the cold spot in the artist's studio upstairs. Candles flicker, pages of a book turn of their own accord and flowers wilt in seconds, suggesting unknown terrors that would later be realized by special effects. An A production, the film is as satisfying and as creamily consistent as a bar of Lindt chocolate, down to its surprise happy end-

ing, which reassures us that laughter is the best defense against evil spirits.

CREDITS

Director Lewis Allen; *Producer* Charles Brackett; *Screenplay* Frank Partos, Dodie Smith, based on the novel *Uneasy Freehold* by Dorothy Macardle; *Photographer* Charles Lang; *Art Director* Hans Dreier, Ernst Fegte; *Special Effects* Farciot Edouart; *Music* Victor Young

CAST

Ray Milland, Ruth Hussey, Gail Russell, Donald Crisp, Cornelia Otis Skinner, Dorothy Stickney, Alan Napier, Barbara Everest

THE WICKER MAN

Film   1973   G.B. (British Lion)   86 minutes Eastmancolor

A cult favorite, whose script is based on Iron Age tribal rituals in which selected members of the community were annually sacrificed to Mother Earth to ensure a bountiful harvest. The film has the practice continuing in secret on a small island off the coast of Scotland, where a policeman arrives from the mainland to investigate the disappearance of a young girl. There are two plots, both carefully conceived by writer Anthony Shaffer, and it's not until the last few minutes that the policeman—and the viewer—learn the truth is much different than it appears to be. Director Robin Hardy, during a visit to the United States in 1978, reported that the distributor severely edited the film for its American release.

CREDITS

Director Robin Hardy; *Producer* Peter Snell; *Screenplay* Anthony Shaffer; *Photographer* Harry Waxman; *Art Director* Seamus Flannery; *Music* Paul Giovanni

CAST

Edward Woodward, Diane Cilento, Christopher Lee, Britt Ekland, Ingrid Pitt, Lindsay Kemp

WITCHCRAFT

Film   1964   G.B. (Lippert)   79 minutes Black & white

Land developers uncover the unmarked grave of a 17th-century witch, who returns to terrorize the latest generation of the family that did her in. Director Sharp maneuvers through the spider web with a deft Lewtonesque hand, and delivers an effective, unassuming chiller.

CREDITS

Director Don Sharp; *Producers* Robert Lippert, Jack Parsons; *Screenplay* Harry Spaulding; *Photographer* Arthur Lavis; *Art Director* George Provis; *Music* Carlo Martelli

CAST

Lon Chaney, Jr., Jack Hedley, David Weston, Jill Dixon, Marie Ney, Viola Keats

THE WITCHFINDER GENERAL

U.S. title: The Conqueror Worm

Film 1968   G.B. (Tigon British)   87 minutes
Eastmancolor

Vincent Price is awesomely intimidating as the infamous Matthew Hopkins, a real-life English witch hunter who made a fortune sending witches to the gallows during the 17th century. Hopkins's favorite methods of torture were "swimming" and "pricking." The former involved dropping a roped suspect into a river or pond to see if he or she would float; the latter consisted of puncturing the witch's devil's mark (usually a mole or a flap of skin) with a long pointed instrument to see if it would bleed. A fearsome fanatic, Hopkins testified during various witch trials that he had seen witches talking to their dogs, cats and other pets, which he claimed were their "familiars," or contacts with the Devil. Public outrage ultimately ended his career and forced authorities to reduce the crime of witchcraft to a misdemeanor (which remained on England's law books until 1951).

Many of Hopkins's sickening tortures are accu-rately depicted in this no-holds-barred film, and to enjoy it you're forced to run the gauntlet. Most of the gore is justified, however, and it's not a gratuitous splatter flick. Director Reeves, who promised to become a major genre force, died of a barbiturate overdose the following year.

CREDITS

Director Michael Reeves; *Producer* Arnold L. Miller; *Screenplay* Michael Reeves, Tom Baker, based on the novel by Ronald Bassett; *Photographer* John Coquillon; *Special Effects* Roger Dicken; *Music* Paul Ferris

CAST

Vincent Price, Ian Ogilvy, Hilary Dwyer, Rupert Davies, Robert Russell, Patrick Wymark, Wilfrid Brambell, Nicky Henson

THE WITCH'S TALE

Radio series 1934–?   U.S. (Mutual)
30 minutes (weekly)

Old Nancy, the Witch of Salem, and Satan, the wise black cat, "are waiting, waiting for you now," an eerie voice would announce as organ music wafted from the background, followed by thunder and a howling wind. Nancy would then introduce "weird, blood-chilling tales" liberally drenched in gallows humor. The program opened and closed with a tolling tower clock.

CREDITS

Director Alonzo Deen Cole, Roger Bower; *Writer* Alonzo Deen Cole

CAST

Adelaide Fitz-Allan, Miriam Wolfe, Martha Wentworth (Old Nancy); *Host* Mark Smith, Marie Flynn, Alonzo Deen Cole

VII

Vampires

Dracula (1931): Bela Lugosi remains the screen's preeminent vampire.

The vampire is the royalty of horror. In addition to possessing a hereditary title and/or unlimited wealth (enabling it to indulge in unholy cravings), the vampire outranks other monsters by its natural superiority as a literary and movie menace. A creature of many parts, it has been consistently popular since being introduced in English Gothic literature over 150 years ago. There have been more than 100 vampire movies and scores of television and radio plays and stage dramatizations.

On a fundamental level, the vampire represents our mythical fascination with blood. From prehistory, the precious life-sustaining fluid has been the focal point of many rituals and taboos. The therapeutic use of transfusions in modern medicine restates the cultural equation of blood and life. The connection was also restated in the wave of public apprehension that accompanied the diagnosis in the early 1980s of the mysterious disease called AIDS, which is carried in the blood and transmitted through sexual contact (both aspects of vampire mythology).

Vampires came into their own during the Middle Ages, when the Black Death swept out of Asia and into the heartland of Europe, claiming 75 million lives. In blind panic, people blamed the disease of bubonic plague on vampires and witches. Christianity gave both a new legitimacy by recognizing them as agents of the Devil, God's avowed enemy. Those condemned to vampirism were considered physically dead but unable to relinquish their souls because they had died either as suicides, excommunicated Catholics, heretics, fornicators, homosexuals, witches or werewolves. Only professional vampire hunters and priests, armed with holy water, consecrated communion wafers, garlic and the like, had the necessary expertise to fight vampires.

The king of vampires, as everyone knows, is Dracula, the title character of Bram Stoker's 1897 novel. Stoker cast his vampire in the mold of the romantic outsider, so beloved in 19th-century Gothic fiction. Dracula's closest male ancestor is the sympathetic Lord Ruthven, the central character of John Polidori's short novel *The Vampyre* (1819). The idea was suggested to Polidori by Lord Byron during Shelley's famous ghost-writing session at Geneva, Switzerland, in 1816. The most famous literary product of that rainy-day activity was *Frankenstein*, written by Shelley's bride-to-be, Mary Godwin.

Another of Stoker's influences was *Varney the Vampire*, a 220-chapter "penny dreadful" (meaning a story filled with dread that could be bought for a penny), attributed to Thomas Preskett Prest, best remembered as the source of SWEENEY TODD (see Ghouls). Significantly, Prest incorporated many of the superstitions of Central Europe into his story and introduced the now-obligatory scene in which the vampire takes advantage of a sleeping young virgin.

Stoker also read *Carmilla* (1872), an atmospheric, heady tale inspired by Elizabeth Bathory, a criminal psychopath of the 16th century who liked to bathe in the blood of virgins. Written by an Irishman with the unlikely name of Sheridan Le Fanu, *Carmilla* is the prototype of the female vampire. Set in Austria, the story relates the vampiric seduction of the lonely blonde Laura by the exquisitely dark Carmilla. Le Fanu's romantic terror is heightened by the almost lesbian relationship between the women. When Stoker sat down to write *Dracula*, he transferred the novel's eroticism to his Transylvanian seducer.

Stoker chose Transylvania as his setting, as he explained in the novel's introduction, because "every known superstition in the world is gathered into the horseshoe of the Carpathians as if it were the center of some sort of imaginative whirlpool." His vampire's name came from an obscure 15th-century despot called Vlad Tepes, known to his countrymen by the nickname Dracul, which is Romanian for devil. Further creative input was supplied by the murders of Jack the Ripper, who terrorized London prostitutes for several months in 1888. Synthesized into the story was Stoker's own libido, expressed in the only way it could be in Victorian England. "He wrote one of the most erotic novels ever published," stated Daniel Farson, the author's great-nephew and biographer. "The vampire superstition is riddled with sexuality; indeed, it is dependent on it, with all the sucking, the flowing of blood and the love-biting."

ATOMIC AGE VAMPIRE

Film   1961   Italy (Topaz)   87 minutes
Black & white

A love-smitten doctor rejuvenates a disfigured beauty with blood drained from dead women, whose corpses soon begin to pile up. Below par melodramatics, badly dubbed.

CREDITS

Director Richard McNamara; *Producer* Mario Bava; *Screenplay* Piero Monviso, Gino deSantis, Alberto Bevilacqua, A.G. Majano, John Hart; *Photographer* Aldo Giordano; *Special Effects* Ugo Amadoro; *Music* Armando Trovajoli

CAST

Alberto Lupo, Susanne Loret, Roberto Berta, Sergio Fantoni

Billy the Kid vs. Dracula: John Carradine with cowboy victim Chuck Courtney.

BILLY THE KID VS. DRACULA

Film   1965   U.S. (Circle)   84 minutes
Color

A companion piece to JESSE JAMES MEETS FRANKENSTEIN'S DAUGHTER (see Monsters), a far more enjoyable attempt at deliberate camp. The aging John Carradine, one of Universal's Draculas, does an amusing parody, but it's sad to watch. Hollywood's previous genre mixer was CURSE OF THE UNDEAD.

CREDITS

Director William Beaudine; *Producer* Carroll Case; *Screenplay* Carl Hittleman; *Photographer* Lothrop Worth; *Art Directors* Paul Sylos, Harry Reif; *Makeup* Ted Coodley; *Music* Raoul Kraushaar

CAST

John Carradine, Chuck Courtney, Melinda Plowman, Walter Janovitz, Virginia Christine, Olive Carey, Harry Carey, Jr.

BLACULA

Film   1972   U.S. (AIP)   93 minutes
Movielab

Bitten by Dracula during an 1815 visit to Transylvania ("I curse you with my name! You will become Blacula the vampire"), African prince Mumawalde is subsequently revived by two gays and shipped off to Los Angeles. Eyebrows and sideburns sprouting like mini-Afros, he indulges in the familiar mayhem and grapples with the traditional Christian iconography. One of the genre's sympathetic vampires, he infects his girlfriend (Vonetta McGee), but only to keep her from dying after she is shot. When she is finally destroyed by a black Van Helsing, he takes his own life in the manner of Varney the Vampire, by walking into the sun. The title performance by suave William Marshall makes it fairly scary.

The sequel, *Scream, Blacula, Scream*, released the same year, made the racial angle more explicit. Revived by a voodoo ritual, the vampire (Marshall) slaughters two black pimps who laugh at his reproaches for exploiting their brothers and sisters. Trapped in an alienating contemporary world, a slave to his malady, the African prince no longer seeks a cure as he did in the first film. Finally staked, he reels around the room in a frustrating circle of despair while the camera looks down and freeze-frames his unyielding black anger.

Both films were popular successes and spawned a short-lived series of black monster movies. In the forgettable *Blackenstein* (1973), directed by William Levey, a mad doctor turns a Vietnam War casualty into the Monster. *Dr. Black and Mr. Hyde* (1975), directed by William Crain, has Dr. Henry Pride (Bernie Casey) operating out of a clinic in Watts and driving a Rolls Royce. When his elixir brings out the beast in him, he recalls a childhood phobia and begins slaughtering local prostitutes. There is also *Abby* (1974), with Marshall as a black exorcist and SUGAR HILL (1974) (see Zombies).

CREDITS

Director William Crain; *Producer* Joseph T. Naar; *Screenplay* Joan Torres, Raymond Koenig; *Photographer* John Stevens; *Art Director* Walter Herndon; *Special Effects* Roger George; *Makeup* Fred Phillips; *Music* Gene Page; *Songs* Wally Holmes, performed by The Hues Corporation

CAST

William Marshall, Vonetta McGee, Denise Nichols, Thalmus Rasulala, Charles Macaulay (Dracula), Gordon Pinsent, Elisha Cook, Jr., Emily Yancy

BLOOD OF DRACULA

Also titled: Blood Is My Heritage, Blood of the Demon

Film   1957   U.S. (AIP)   69 minutes
Black & white

This one should have been titled *I Was a Teenage Vampire*, since it completed Herman Cohen's trilogy, which began with I WAS A TEENAGE WEREWOLF (see Werewolves and Other Shape-Shifters), followed by I WAS A TEENAGE FRANKENSTEIN (see Monsters). Once again puberty is abused (although not as amusingly), by a nasty chemistry teacher who transforms a delinquent girl into a bloodsucker.

CREDITS

Director Herbert L. Strock; *Producer* Herman Cohen; *Screenplay* Ralph Thorton; *Photographer* Monroe Askins; *Art Director* Leslie Thomas; *Makeup* Philip Scheer; *Music* Paul Dunlap

CAST

Sandra Harrison, Louise Lewis, Jerry Blaine, Gail Ganley, Heather Ames, Malcolm Atterbury

BLOOD OF DRACULA'S CASTLE

TV title: Dracula's Castle

Film   1969   U.S. (Crown Int.)   84 minutes
Color

Count and Countess Dracula refuse to be evicted by the new owner of their castle. A lurid and low-brow parody that tries to have it both ways, graced by John Carradine's authoritative presence.

CREDITS

Director Al Adamson; *Producers* Al Adamson, Rex Carlton; *Screenplay* Rex Carlton; *Photographer* Laszlo Kovacs; *Makeup* Kenny Osborne; *Music* Lincoln Mayorage

CAST

John Carradine, Paula Raymond, Alex D'Arcy, Robert Dix, Gene O'Shane, Vicky Volante

BLOOD OF THE VAMPIRE

Film 1958 G.B. (Universal/Eros)
85 minutes Color

A doctor afflicted with vampirism bleeds patients in a mental hospital. No longer as gruesome as it once seemed, and even more stilted and solemn.

CREDITS

Director Henry Cass; *Producer* Robert S. Baker; *Screenplay* Jimmy Sangster; *Photographer* Geoffrey Seaholme; *Art Director* John Elphick; *Makeup* Jimmy Evans; *Music* Stanley Black

CAST

Donald Wolfit, Vincent Ball, Barbara Shelley, Victor Maddern, William Devlin, Andrew Faulds

BRIDES OF DRACULA

Film 1960 G.B. (Hammer/Universal)
85 minutes Technicolor

After making his mark in Hammer's 1958 remake of DRACULA, Christopher Lee turned his back on the role for fear of being typecast, so the studio cast David Peel in this misleadingly titled but eminently satisfying follow-up. Filling in for Dracula, Peel is an atypical blond vampire named Baron Meinster whose "disease" is described as a result of his degenerate life-style. Kept locked in his castle bedroom on a silver chain, the lavender-caped baron escapes with the help of a beautiful but dim-witted visitor, leaving behind the blood-drained body of his hated old mother. Cushing returns, cruciform in hand, giving his most energetic impersonation of Professor Van Helsing, splashing the epicene baron with holy water and instantly raising oozing blisters on his skin. Later bitten by

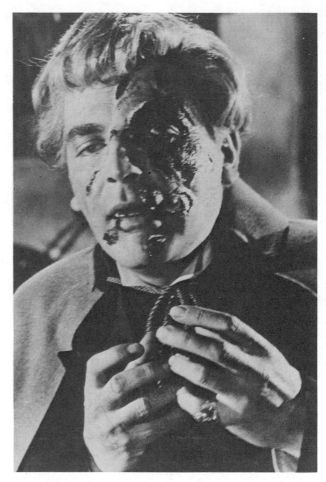

Brides of Dracula: David Peel receives a bracing splash of holy water.

the vampire, he cauterizes the wounds himself with a poker heated on a blacksmith's forge. Everything comes together in this one: Transylvania has never looked more threatening, and the old icons have never seemed more powerful. The icing on the cake is the vampire's comeuppance on a huge fiery cross fashioned from the blades of a windmill.

CREDITS

Director Terence Fisher; *Producer* Anthony Hinds; *Screenplay* Jimmy Sangster, Peter Bryan, Edward Percy; *Photographer* Jack Asher; *Art Director* Bernard Robinson, Thomas Goswell; *Special Effects* Sydney Pearson; *Makeup* Roy Ashton; *Music* Malcolm Williamson

CAST

Peter Cushing, David Peel, Yvonne Monlaur, Freda Jackson, Martita Hunt, Mona Washbourne, Andree Melly, Henry Oscar

CAPTAIN KRONOS—VAMPIRE HUNTER

Film   1972   G.B. (Hammer)   91 minutes
Color

By the 1970s, Hammer's classic vampire format was no longer paying off, so the studio recast the mold and came up with this likable sword-and-sorcery fable. Captain Kronos, a spiritual forebear of the Jedi Knights of *Star Wars*, is a handsome Nordic type with a stoic presence and a mysterious past. He chants and meditates (he's apparently a student of Zen culture) and occasionally smokes an Oriental herb in cigar form.

Setting is an early 19th-century European village, which summons Kronos and his faithful sidekick Professor Grost, a hunchback, to eliminate a local member of the undead. This species is indifferent to the cross and the stake, however. Only silver will do the job, prompting Kronos and Grost to forge a sword from a large crucifix—a symbol of righteous strength and moral health.

Kronos was to be the first in a series, but audiences were confused by its mixing of genres, and the film, unfortunately, has all but disappeared from sight (although it is available on cassette). The producer/director team is Albert Fennell and Brian Clemens, known for the horror-oriented TV series *The Avengers* (1962–68).

CREDITS

Director/Screenplay Brian Clemens; *Producers* Albert Fennell, Brian Clemens; *Photographer* Ian Wilson; *Music* Roy Skeggs

CAST

Horst Janson, John Carson, Shane Briant, Caroline Munro, John Cater, Ian Hendry

CARMILLA

Chamber opera   1976   U.S. (La Mama Co.)
13 scenes

This avant-garde off-off-Broadway production sang Le Fanu's poetic novella to an amplified chamber quartet, which played everything from rock to Gregorian chant. Director Wilford Leach eschewed love bites and crosses and preserved the original delicate, romantic horror of the story. The lesbian angle was left properly ambiguous, although in the portrayal by Nancy Heikin, Carmilla's intent was all too apparent. The setting was essentially a sinuously carved blood-red Victorian settee, behind which films of crypts and corpses were projected. In all, a surprisingly effective and unusual retelling, a *coup de theatre*.

CREDITS

Director/Script Wilford Leach, based on the novel by Sheridan Le Fanu; *Music* Ben Johnston; *Lighting* Carol Mullins; *Musical Direction* Zizi Mueller

CAST

Margaret Benczak, Nancy Heikin, Tony Azito, Cayce Blanchard, Donald Harrington

EL CONDE DRACULA/Count Dracula

Film   1970   Spain/Germany/Italy
(Fenix/Corona/Towers of London)   100 minutes
Color   Panavision

After completing Hammer's DRACULA HAS RISEN FROM THE GRAVE, Christopher Lee played the count in this low-budget European co-production, filmed in Spain. The script follows Stoker's story more closely than any other film, and Dracula is accurately depicted as a gray-haired, gray-mustached old man who grows progressively younger with each blood transfusion. Large chunks of dialogue come from Stoker, but this has the unfortunate effect of underscoring the triteness of scriptwriter Towers. Although the film is very respectful of its source, it lacks definition and seems to exist in a limbo between romantic fantasy and horror. Director Franco attempts to supply the latter with an excess of scare zooms and annoying shock cuts. Reportedly, this is Lee's favorite version of Dracula.

CREDITS

Director Jess (Jesus) Franco; *Producer* Harry Alan Towers; *Screenplay* Peter Welbeck (Harry Alan Towers), Jess Franco, based on the novel by Bram Stoker; *Photographer* Manuel Marino; *Art Director* Karl Schneider; *Music* Bruno Nicolai

CAST

Christopher Lee, Herbert Lom (Van Helsing), Klaus Kinski (Renfield), Frederick Williams, Maria Rohm, Soledad Miranda, Jack Taylor

CONDEMNED TO LIVE

Film   1935   U.S. (Invincible)   65 minutes
Black & white

Subdued but surprisingly effective, this minor gem has survived the crumbling inventory of Invincible studios, one of Hollywood's forgotten poverty-row movie factories. Middle-aged Ralph Morgan (brother of Frank Morgan of *The Wizard of Oz*) is impressive as a kindly professor unaware he's a vampire, and the script and photography are better than they have any right to be.

CREDITS

Director Frank Strayer; *Producer* Maury M. Cohen; *Screenplay* Karen DeWolf; *Photographer* M.A. Anderson; *Musical Director* Abe Meyer

CAST

Ralph Morgan, Russell Gleason, Maxine Doyle, Mischa Auer, Pedro de Cordoba

COUNT DRACULA

TV miniseries   1978   G.B. (BBC)
165 minutes   Color

An eloquent, opulent and involving version of Stoker—everything that Universal's 1979 DRACULA hoped to be and wasn't. The locales look authentic and the sets and houses seem genuinely lived in. As in the novel, Dracula changes into a dog, a steamy mist and, of course, a bat (he is shown grotesquely climbing down a wall with his batwings). Louis Jourdan isn't exactly Stoker's Dracula (who is?), but he's a better actor than Lugosi and has more animal magnetism than Lee. Jourdan, who naturally projects a detached self-involvement, is a perfect vampire for the late 20th century: amoral, cunning and interested only in what benefits him directly. Addressing Van Helsing (Frank Finlay), he almost convinces you he has a right to live because he's the ultimate predator, the top of the food chain.

The program was originally aired in the United States over public television on three consecutive nights during Halloween in 1979. The impressive opening credits, which establish an appropriate mood for terrors to come, are a video effect transferred to film.

CREDITS

Director Philip Saville; *Producer* Morris Barry; *Screenplay* Gerald Savory; *Production Designer* Michael Young; *Special Effects* Tony Harding; *Makeup* Suzan Broad; *Music* Kenyon Emrys-Roberts

CAST

Louis Jourdan, Frank Finlay, Susan Penhaligon, Judi Bowker, Mark Burns, Jack Shepherd

COUNT YORGA—VAMPIRE

Film   1970   U.S. (Erica/AIP)   90 minutes
Movielab

Count Yorga emigrates from Transylvania to contemporary Los Angeles, where he zips along the freeways in a station wagon, looking for blood donors. One of this film's many problems is its inability to reconcile vampire lore with a modern setting. Director/writer Bob Kelljan attempts to overcome disbelief by having characters mouth lines like "You've got to be kidding—a vampire," and piling on the exploitive distractions of sex and violence. A surprise hit, the film inspired an equally dismal sequel, *The Return of Count Yorga*, again starring the capable Robert Quarry as a beefy bloodsucker.

CREDITS

Director/Screenplay Bob Kelljan; *Producer* Michael Macready; *Photographer* Arch Archambault; *Music* William Marx

CAST

Robert Quarry, Roger Perry, Michael Murphy, Michael Macready, Donna Anders; *Narrator* George Macready

COUNTESS DRACULA

Film   1970   G.B. (Hammer)   93 minutes
Color

Having blatantly deceived audiences with BRIDES OF DRACULA (1960), Hammer did another fast shuffle with this unconventional vampire film. Unrelated to Dracula, the mortal Countess Nadasdy owes her existence to the real-life Elizabeth Bathory, a 17th-century Hungarian countess who is the female equivalent of the psychopathic

Vlad the Impaler. At age 40 Elizabeth began a ten-year beauty ritual that involved bathing in the blood of virgins and sometimes showering in it by hanging a girl overhead in an inwardly spiked iron cage. Eventually, relatives of the girls who had been "milked" complained to authorities, and Elizabeth was arrested and walled up inside her bedroom. In Hammer's version of the story, Ingrid Pitt transforms herself from a blonde beauty to an old hag whenever the treatment begins to wear off. The script has some good twists and turns, but director Sasdy makes it more gruesome than gratifying.

Other versions of the Bathory story include *Daughters of Darkness* (1971); *Immoral Tales* (1974), a four-parter written and directed by Walerian Borowczyk and starring Paloma Picasso (daughter of Pablo) as Elizabeth; and *Mamma Dracula* (1980), a Belgian-French spoof directed by Boris Szulzinger, with Louise Fletcher bemoaning the short supply of virgins in contemporary times.

CREDITS

Director Peter Sasdy; *Producer* Alexander Paal; *Screenplay* Jeremy Paul; *Photographer* Ken Talbot; *Makeup* Tom Smith; *Music* Harry Robinson

CAST

Ingrid Pitt, Nigel Green, Sandor Eles, Maurice Denham, Lesley-Anne Downe, Patience Collier

CURSE OF THE UNDEAD

*Film   1959   U.S. (Universal)   79 minutes
Black & white*

A Spanish vampire disguised as a gunfighter is dispatched with a silver bullet reinforced by a splinter from "the true cross." Quirky but inconsequential, *Curse* is one of many misguided Hollywood attempts to breathe new life into the genre after Universal discontinued its Dracula series in the late 1940s. For another vampire Western, see BILLY THE KID VS. DRACULA.

CREDITS

Director Edward Dein; *Producer* Joseph Gershenson; *Screenplay* Edward Dein, Mildred Dein; *Photographer* Ellis W. Carter; *Art Directors* Alexander Golitzen, Robert Clatworthy; *Makeup* Bud Westmore; *Music* Irving Gertz

CAST

Eric Fleming, Michael Pate, Kathleen Crowley, John Hoyt, Edward Binns, Bruce Gordon

Dark Shadows: Jonathan Frid, TV's longest-running vampire, with costar Kathryn Leigh Scott.

DARK SHADOWS

*TV serial   1966–71   U.S. (ABC)
30 minutes (M/T/W/Th/F)   Color*

A cultural oddity, *Dark Shadows* is television's only horror soap opera, and it holds the medium's record for the number of genre episodes aired. Originally conceived as a Gothic romance for the medium's daytime, predominantly female audience, the serial was about to be cancelled when producers Dan Curtis and Robert Costello switched to kitsch horror and introduced an offbeat new character. As the gaunt-faced yet attractive vampire Barnabas Collins, actor Jonathan Frid captivated millions of housewives and teenagers just home from school, and turned the show into a smash hit.

The continuing story focused on young Victoria Winters (Alexandra Moltke), who had come to the Maine coast to live in an old Gothic mansion as governess to ten-year-old David Collins. The occupants included nominal star Joan Bennett as matriarch Elizabeth Collins Stoddard and Frid as the

175-year-old black-cloaked Barnabas. The characters included werewolves, witches and practitioners of black magic. During the serial's last year, the cast traveled back to the 19th century—via black magic—and played their ancestors. Rare among soap operas, it had a significant run in syndication and spawned two MGM movies: HOUSE OF DARK SHADOWS (1970) and NIGHT OF DARK SHADOWS (1971).

CAST

Joan Bennett, Alexandra Moltke, Jonathan Frid, Nancy Barrett, Louis Edmonds, Grayson Hall, Kathryn Leigh Scott, Lara Parker, Chris Pennock, Thayer David, David Selby, Kate Jackson, John Karlen

DEATH SHIP

Film   1980   Canada/G.B. (Bloodstar)
91 minutes   Color

Pleasure boaters investigate a decrepit Nazi ship gliding through the Caribbean and find a cargo of decaying bodies. Turns out the old tub is possessed by its sadistic past as an SS torture chamber. It remains "alive" by feeding on the blood of unwary explorers. After an atmospheric beginning, the film lurches into a steep dive—down to the depths of its script and direction.

CREDITS

Director Alvin Rakoff; *Producers* Derek Gibson, Harold Greenberg; *Screenplay* John Robbins; *Story* Jack Hill, David P. Lewis; *Photographers* Rene Verzier, Peter Benison; *Special Effects* Mike Albrechtsen, Peter Hughes; *Makeup* Joan Isaacson; *Music* Ivor Slaney

CAST

George Kennedy, Richard Crenna, Nick Mancuso, Sally Ann Howes, Kate Reid

THE DEATHMASTER

Film   1972   U.S. (RF/World Entertainment)
88 minutes   Color

An almost unwatchable vanity vehicle for Robert Quarry (doing his COUNT YORGA thing), about a vampire pretending to be a California guru. The beaded and bloodied young actors are inept, to put it mildly, and the hippie dialogue was moldy then.

CREDITS

Director Ray Danton; *Producers* Fred Sadoff, Robert Quarry; *Screenplay* R.L. Grove; *Photographer* Wilmer C. Butler; *Special Effects* John L. Oliver; *Makeup* Mark Bussan; *Music* Bill Marx

CAST

Robert Quarry, Bill Ewing, John Fiedler, Brenda Dickson, Betty Anne Rees, William Jordan

Dracula (1931): Lugosi turns on the charm for Frances Dade.

DRACULA

Play   1924   G.B.   3 acts

In 1897 Bram Stoker had arranged a one-time theatrical reading of his novel *Dracula* in London to establish his copyright of the story (which would be purloined in 1922 by the film *Nosferatu*). This is the first true dramatization, however, and it was written by Irish actor-manager Hamilton Deane. Opening in June 1924 in London, with 22-year-old Raymond Huntley in the title role, the play was a huge popular success, despite almost unanimous critical disapproval. It made its way across the Atlantic in 1927 to Broadway, where the producers had it revised by John Balderston and cast an out-of-work immigrant bit player named Bela Lugosi as Dracula.

Playing the part with a continental elan that had made him a star in Germany, Lugosi came across as an elegant, overaged lecher whose lust for the ladies did not end with their blood. By adding his own erotic qualities to the character, he also brought an indelible new tension to the story that amplified its implicit sexuality. A contemporary viewer noted that Lugosi seemed openly scornful of audience sympathy, and when he looked into the auditorium, theatergoers felt as threatened as the victims onstage. Not surprisingly, critics panned the play, just as a generation earlier they had dismissed Stoker's novel as a potboiler. Particularly objectionable to critics was the producer's "gimmick" of having a nurse in attendance at every performance. Reportedly, the nurse was there for more than show, since people fainted or became emotionally disturbed during most performances.

Slick and perfectly timed, *Dracula* was aided immeasurably by the use of magicians' props. Smoke bombs provided the mist the vampire turned himself into, eerie cries and howls emanated from concealed loudspeakers, and a battery-operated bat with eyes lighted red darted unexpectedly across the stage. The cleverest effect of all was the destruction of Dracula in his coffin. As Van Helsing (Edward Van Sloan) staked the vampire through the heart, his body hid Lugosi's reclining figure for a brief moment, giving the actor an opportunity to activate two side flaps. As the stake was driven home, Lugosi disappeared into the coffin, and a cloud of clay dropped onto the closed flaps above him. To the audience it looked as if Dracula had instantly turned to dust.

The play ran for a year on Broadway and two years on tour, then a record for a traveling production. Lugosi again toured with it in 1940, and took it to Great Britain in 1951. Frank Langella starred in a smash hit, slyly mocking Broadway revival of the play in 1977, which used many of the stage tricks of the 1927 original. The production was wittily designed by Victorian caricaturist Edward Gorey and spawned two American touring companies and a subsequent long run in London.

CREDITS

Adaptation Hamilton Deane and John Balderston; *Producer* Horace Liveright

CAST

Bela Lugosi, Nedda Harrington, Terrence Neill, Herbert Bunston, Edward Van Sloan, Bernard Jukes, Alfred Frith, Dorothy Peterson

DRACULA

Film 1931 U.S. (Universal) 83 minutes Black & white

If not for the hand of fate, we'd probably have quite a different conception of the world's most famous vampire. In 1929 Universal bought the rights to a popular dramatization of the Stoker novel, with the intention of turning it into a vehicle for Hollywood horror king Lon Chaney, who had previously played a vampire in the silent film LONDON AFTER MIDNIGHT. When Chaney died of cancer in 1930, Paul Muni was considered, but the role fell to Bela Lugosi, the Hungarian-born actor who had played it on Broadway. Lugosi's sinister personality was even more shuddery onscreen, and when he announced, "I am . . . Dracula," there were few who could doubt it. Lugosi defined the role for all time and, to his professional regret, became permanently identified with it. The film also established the characterizations of Renfield in Dwight Frye's hyperbolic performance as Dracula's half-crazed servant, and Dr. Van Helsing in Edward Van Sloan's portrayal of the wise old exorcist of vampires.

Shot in stark monochrome by Karl Freund, Lugosi's old acquaintance from Germany, the film begins with a stunning shot of Dracula's bleak castle in the Carpathian Mountains, accompanied by a theme from Tchaikovsky's *Swan Lake*. Renfield is journeying to meet Dracula and to arrange his purchase of an English country estate (Transylvania is running out of victims). Fatally bitten, Renfield becomes the vampire's tortured helper, subsisting on a diet of bugs and small animals. Unexpected comedy touches are cleverly placed to catch the audience off-guard. Offered a glass of wine, Lugosi demurs, his eyes glowing. "I never drink—wine," he says, as only Lugosi can.

After the first 20 minutes or so, however, when the action moves to Carfax Abbey in England, the incipient mood of Gothic terror begins to dissipate. The rest of the story is told mostly in dialogue, betraying the film's theatrical origin. Other than the use of pin-spots to light Lugosi's eyes and a startling scene in which his guests discover that the count casts no reflection in a mirror, opportunities for visual horror are missed entirely. Lucy's transformation into a vampire and Dracula's arrival as a red mist occur offscreen. And when Dracula is staked through the heart, the only evidence is a groan. In comparison, the special effects of the Deane/Balderston play were said to be breathtaking.

But in its time the film enraptured the public, which turned out in record numbers after it opened on Valentine's Day, billed as "The Strangest Love Story of All." Critics were more enthusiastic than they had been for the stage version, and a reviewer for the *Hollywood Filmograph* summed up the film's appeal when he wrote: "There are times when the force of the evil vampire seems to sweep from him beyond the confines of the screen and into the minds of the audience. His cruel smile, hypnotic glance, slow, stately tread, they make Dracula. . . ."

Although sound had previously been introduced in Warner Brothers' THE TERROR (1928) (see Crazies and Freaks), *Dracula* was the first genre film to use the medium effectively. It rescued Universal from its precarious financial position in Depression-era Hollywood, and launched the studio on its course as the premier maker of genre films for the next two decades. Universal's immediate follow-up was FRANKENSTEIN (see Monsters), released later that year. The studio's Dracula sequels include DRACULA'S DAUGHTER (1936), SON OF DRACULA (1943), HOUSE OF FRANKENSTEIN (1944) (see Monsters), HOUSE OF DRACULA (1945) and ABBOTT AND COSTELLO MEET FRANKENSTEIN (1948) (see Monsters). Britain's Hammer studios revived the series in 1958 with a color version of DRACULA, based directly on the Stoker novel.

A Spanish version was filmed back-to-back with the 1931 film, using the same sets. Carmen Villarias subbed for Lugosi, and the director was George Melford.

CREDITS

Director Tod Browning; *Producer* Carl Laemmle, Jr.; *Screenplay* Garret Fort and Dudley Murphy, based on the play by Hamilton Deane and John Balderston, adapted from the Bram Stoker novel; *Photographer* Karl Freund; *Art Director* Charles D. Hall; *Makeup* Jack Pierce; *Music* Tchaikovsky

CAST

Bela Lugosi, Helen Chandler, Dwight Frye, David Manners, Edward Van Sloan, Frances Dade, Herbert Bunston, Moon Carroll

DRACULA

U.S. title: The Horror of Dracula

Film 1958 G.B. (Hammer) 82 minutes Technicolor

Following its previous remake THE CURSE OF FRANKENSTEIN (1957) (see Monsters), England's Hammer studio cemented its position as the premier genre filmmaker of its time with the first color version of *Dracula*. Hammer returned to Stoker's novel rather than use the stage play on which Lugosi's 1931 classic movie is based, and for the first time the story was told in the same bloodthirsty spirit as the author had written it. Towering Christopher Lee, making his debut as the vampire, brings a primitive animal dynamism to the role, tempered by a refreshing note of sympathy. His adversary, the steely-eyed Professor Van Helsing, is deftly sketched by Peter Cushing, who alternated the role with appearances as Dr. Frankenstein.

While previous versions featured only as much blood as could be squeezed from a cat scratch, this one broke the old barriers against on-screen gore and was the first to show bright red stage blood spurting from punctured throats and impaled chests. Still beautiful to look at, the film is graced with Bernard Robinson's richly detailed sets and Hammer's mandatory low-cut, bosomy heroines. Director Terence Fisher makes no attempt to capture the stylized mood of the Tod Browning film and opts instead for lightning-paced visceral action. There are a number of back-stiffening scenes, as when Dracula, red-eyed and snarling, rescues Harker from one of his wives by flinging the woman sadistically to the ground, and the tautly edited, thrilling showdown at dawn. Chased up the mountain to his castle, the vampire disintegrates into dust at the first shaft of sunlight, an ending equaled only in DRACULA HAS RISEN FROM THE GRAVE (1968). The effect was achieved not by the usual double-exposed transformation, but by a rapid succession of quick-cut action shots. Deemed excessively sexy and sadistic at the time of its release, the film plays like family fare today and is usually shown uncut on television.

After the worldwide success of this film, Universal gave Hammer the go-ahead to remake its old Karloff-starrer THE MUMMY (1932) (see Mummies) and to spawn a series of Dracula sequels. These include BRIDES OF DRACULA (1960), in which Lee did not appear; DRACULA, PRINCE OF DARKNESS (1965); DRACULA HAS RISEN FROM THE GRAVE (1968); TASTE THE BLOOD OF DRACULA and *Scars of Dracula* (both 1970); THE SATANIC RITES OF DRACULA (1973).

CREDITS

Director Terence Fisher; *Producer* Anthony Hinds; *Screenplay* Jimmy Sangster, based on the novel by Bram Stoker; *Photographer* Jack Asher; *Art Director* Bernard Robinson; *Makeup* Phil Leakey; *Special Effects* Les Bowie; *Music* James Bernard

Four Draculas

From top, right, clockwise: Bela Lugosi in a 1940s stage revival of **Dracula;** Christopher Lee in Hammer's color remake (1958); Louis Jourdan as a French seducer in the BBC-TV's **Count Dracula** (1978); Frank Langella repeated his stage role without fangs in a lavish 1979 retelling of the Stoker novel.

CAST

Peter Cushing, Christopher Lee, Michael Gough, Melissa Stribling, Carol Marsh, John Van Eyssen, Valerie Gaunt

DRACULA

TV film   1974   U.S./G.B. (Universal)
100 minutes   Color

As portrayed by movie villain Jack Palance, Dracula is an anguished, brooding vampire, given to expressing his moods by shifting back his hairline and soft-focus reminiscences about his mortal past as a great lover. Richard Matheson's interesting script identifies Dracula as Vlad Tepes, Stoker's real-life Transylvanian prototype, and the narrative has a journal-like progression that suggests the novel. Shot on location in Yugoslavia and England and peopled with a sterling cast of British actors, the film conjures an authentically portentous atmosphere but rarely catches fire. Part of the problem is American TV censorship, which, like vampire-destroyer Van Helsing, has considerably cramped Dracula's style. Dan Curtis's other Gothic TV misfires include FRANKENSTEIN (1973) (see Monsters) and THE STRANGE CASE OF DR. JEKYLL AND MR. HYDE (1974) (see Mad Scientists).

CREDITS

Director/Producer Dan Curtis; *Screenplay* Richard Matheson, based on the novel by Bram Stoker; *Photographer* Oswald Morris; *Art Director* Trevor Williams; *Special Effects* Kit West; *Music* Robert Cobert

CAST

Jack Palance, Simon Ward, Nigel Davenport, Pamela Brown, Fiona Lewis, Murray Brown, Sarah Douglas, Virginia Wetherall

DRACULA

Film   1979   U.S./G.B. (Universal)
112 minutes   Technicolor   Panavision
Dolby Stereo

History seemed to be repeating itself when Frank Langella starred in a hit Broadway version of the 1927 play by Hamilton Deane and John Balderston, then repeated his performance in a Universal film. Alas, Langella proves to be no Lugosi, and most of the black magic of the play has been supplanted by sumptuous atmospherics that sug-

gest a permeating, overripe decadence. Langella, looking too clean and blow-dried to have slept in a coffin, is a lonely, misunderstood ladies' man who spends his waking hours searching for physical sustenance—and the ideal mate. Constantly thwarted by professional vampire hunters, he must resort to violence from time to time, even though it's against his sensitive nature. Judging from a Victrola that plays tango records and a vintage automobile that sputters through the English countryside, the time period has been moved up to about 1920.

CREDITS

Director John Badham; *Producer* Walter Mirisch; *Screenplay* W. Richter, based on the play by Hamilton Deane and John L. Balderston, adapted from the novel by Bram Stoker; *Photographer* Gilbert Taylor; *Production Designer* Peter Murton; *Art Director* Maurice Binder; *Special Effects* Albert Whitlock, Roy Arbogast; *Makeup* Peter Robb-King; *Music* John Williams

CAST

Frank Langella, Laurence Olivier, Donald Pleasence, Kate Nelligan, Trevor Eve, Jan Francis, Tony Haygarth, Teddy Turner

DRACULA AD 1972

Film   1972   G.B. (Hammer/Warner Bros.)
95 minutes   Eastmancolor

Cushing, on leave from Hammer's faltering Frankenstein series, rejoins the fold after a 12-year absence as vampire-destroyer Professor Van Helsing. Scriptwriter Houghton, desperate for new ideas for an old series, focuses on a Manson-like cult of dropouts who revive ancestor Dracula/Lee in contemporary "mod" London. Dracula, becoming more and more of a background character, seems woefully out of place in an era of discos, drugs and promiscuous sex. Best scene—and a reminder of Hammer's past glories—is the flashback opener, a thrilling struggle aboard an out-of-control coach, in which Van Helsing stabs Dracula through the heart with a broken wheel spoke.

CREDITS

Director Alan Gibson; *Producer* Josephine Douglas; *Screenplay* Don Houghton; *Photographer* Richard Bush; *Art Director* Don Mingaye; *Special Effects* Les Bowie; *Makeup* Jill Carpenter; *Music* Michael Vickers

CAST

Christopher Lee, Peter Cushing, Michael Coles, Stephanie Beacham, Christopher Neame, Marsha Hunt, William Ellis

Dracula Has Risen from the Grave: Christopher Lee unstakes himself in this Hammer production.

DRACULA HAS RISEN FROM THE GRAVE

Film 1968 G.B. (Hammer) 92 minutes Technicolor

Hammer pulled out the stops for this powerhouse sequel to DRACULA, PRINCE OF DARKNESS (1965). It's one of the best and bloodiest of the series (the neck bites have become large infected wounds now). Dracula, discovered in his icebound castle, revives when a defrocked priest injures his mouth and drips blood on the vampire's lips. Later, Dracula survives impalement by leaping from his coffin and yanking a king-sized stake from his perforated chest. The film ends in a flourish of religious symbolism, with Dracula being impaled on a huge cross. Writer Hinds cunningly reworks Transylvanian tradition—and the nature of good and evil—by presenting Dracula's disciple as a priest and his enemy as an agnostic.

CREDITS

Director Freddie Francis; *Producer* Aida Young; *Screenplay* John Elder (Anthony Hinds); *Photographer* Arthur Grant; *Art Director* Bernard Robinson; *Special Effects* James Bernard; *Makeup* Heather Nurse, Rosemarie McDonald Peattie

CAST

Christopher Lee, Rupert Davies, Veronica Carlson, Barry Andrews, Barbara Ewing, Michael Ripper

DRACULA, PRINCE OF DARKNESS

Film 1965 G.B. (Hammer/Warner Bros.) 90 minutes Techniscope

Christopher Lee, back in the fold after opting out of Hammer's superior BRIDES OF DRACULA (1960), retains much of the demonic intensity of his 1958 DRACULA, of which this film is considered the sequel. The story begins with two vacationing English couples who happen onto Dracula's castle in the Carpathian Mountains. A servant invites them to dinner, explaining that the owner had made provisions to entertain visitors after his death because, "My master died without issue, sir . . . in the accepted sense of the word." None suspect that within a few screen minutes, one of them will be hung upside-down with his throat slit, bleeding into Dracula's great stone sarcophagus to revive the vampire's ashes. Fisher later has Dracula clawing open his own veins for a blood fix. Cushing's Van Helsing (seen in a reprise of the ending of DRACULA) is replaced by Andrew Keir as Father Sandor, who forces his quarry onto the broken ice of his castle moat and into an underwater demise. As everyone knows, vampires can't stand—gulp!—running water.

CREDITS

Director Terence Fisher; *Producer* Anthony Nelson Keys; *Screenplay* John Sansom; *Idea* John Elder (Anthony Hinds); *Photographer* Michael Reed; *Production Designer* Bernard Robinson; *Special Effects* Bowie Films; *Makeup* Roy Ashton; *Music* James Bernard

CAST

Christopher Lee, Andrew Keir, Barbara Shelley, Francis Matthews, Suzan Farmer, Charles Tingwell, Thorley Walters

Dracula's Daughter: The screen's first female vampire.

DRACULA'S DAUGHTER

Film 1936 U.S. (Universal) 70 minutes Black & white

Inexplicably, Universal neglected to capitalize on the immense popularity of DRACULA (1931), and waited five years before producing this informal sequel, minus Lugosi. The story picks up after the death of Dracula, with his daughter stealing his body from a London morgue and burning it in a moonlit ritual to exorcise her "tendencies." A reluctant vampire who regards herself as a normal woman afflicted by a hereditary disease, the countess later enlists the aid of a handsome psychiatrist she is attracted to. Nothing works, however, and she's soon imitating daddy, saying things like "I never drink—wine," and mesmerizing females with a magic ring to satisfy her unquenchable bestiality. Unlike her predecessor, she's dispatched not by Professor Van Helsing (Edward Van Sloan again), but by a Transylvanian peasant with a bow and arrow, an inventive variation on the old sharpened stake that would become a fixture of later Hammer epics. All plot and mood, the film failed to satisfy the contemporary thrill-quotient, despite a highly charged performance from lead Gloria Holden and some atmospheric camera work. (One of the sets is Ming's lab, borrowed from the *Flash Gordon* serials.) Consequently, the studio shelved its horror series until 1939, when the re-release of FRANKENSTEIN (see Monsters) and *Dracula* proved there was still a market for out-and-out villainous thrills.

CREDITS

Director Lambert Hillyer; *Producer* E.M. Asher; *Screenplay* Garett Fort; *Story* John L. Balderston; *Idea* Oliver Jeffries; *Photographer* George Robinson; *Art Director* Albert D'Agostino; *Special Effects* John P. Fulton; *Music* Heinz Roemheld

CAST

Gloria Holden, Otto Kruger, Edward Van Sloan, Irving Pichel, Marguerite Churchill, Hedda Hopper, Nan Grey

DRACULA'S DOG

G.B. title: Zoltan . . . Hound of Dracula

Film 1977 U.S. (Vic) 88 minutes Color

The count has apparently committed other crimes against nature according to this garish programmer, which revives Dracula, his manservant and dog for a blood feast in contemporary Los Angeles. Zoltan's vicious but uncomfortable looking fangs are the handiwork of makeup artist Stan Winston, who deserves some kind of an award for having to fit Doberman pinschers with false teeth.

CREDITS

Director Albert Band; *Producer* Albert Band, Ray Perilli; *Screenplay* Frank Ray Perilli; *Photographers* Bruce Logan, Ron Johnson; *Special Effects* Sam Shaw; *Makeup* Stan Winston; *Music* Andrew Belling

CAST

Michael Pataki, Jan Shutan, John Levin, Libbie Xhase, Jose Ferrer, Reggie Nalder

ET MOURIR DE PLAISIR/Blood and Roses

Film 1960 France/Italy (Eger/Documento) 87 minutes Technirama

Roger Vadim uses only fragments of *Carmilla*, Sheridan Le Fanu's 1872 novel, and he's decidedly more interested in the story's lesbianism than its vampirism. Wife number two Annette Vadim (between Brigitte Bardot and Jane Fonda) is a winsome Carmilla, and the photography by Claude Renoir (son of the painter) is stunning, but the story is awkwardly handled and more likely to provoke heavy breathing than shivers. Vadim claims that Paramount snipped out 13 minutes of the more erotic scenes for the film's American release, and that further cuts for television showings have bowdlerized it. Stay with Hammer's THE VAMPIRE LOVERS (1970).

CREDITS

Director Roger Vadim; *Producer* Raymond Eger; *Screenplay* Claude Brule, Claude Martin, Roger Vadim, based on *Carmilla* by Sheridan Le Fanu; *Photographer* Claude Renoir; *Art Director* Jean Andre; *Music* Jean Prodromides

CAST

Annette Vadim, Elsa Martinelli, Mel Ferrer, Marc Allegret, Camilla Stroyberg, Jacques-Rene Chauffard

Et Mourir de Plaisir/Blood and Roses: Roger Vadim's erotic version of Le Fanu's *Carmilla*.

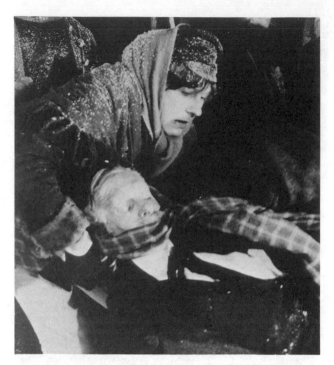

The Fearless Vampire Killers or Pardon Me, But Your Teeth Are in My Neck: Director Roman Polanski (in white pants) cast himself as a dim-witted assistant.

THE FEARLESS VAMPIRE KILLERS, OR PARDON ME BUT YOUR TEETH ARE IN MY NECK

Also titled: Dance of the Vampires, The Fearless Vampire Killers

Film 1967 G.B./U.S. (MGM/Cadre/Filmways) 124 minutes Metrocolor Panavision

As the title indicates, this one is a send-up of vampire movies, Hammer's in particular. Director/co-writer Roman Polanski plays the bumbling assistant of Professor Ambronsius (a Van Helsing figure), whose misguided attempts to stop vampirism end up spreading the disease even farther. Although considered labored and clumsy by nonbuffs, the film is often hilarious for the way it toys with vampire lore. The vampire in question turns out to be Jewish, for example, and he brushes aside the mandatory crucifix with the line: "Oy vey, have you got the wrong vampire!" Later, he chases his quarry down a snow-covered slope using his coffin as a sled. There are several brilliant set pieces which make one wonder what Polanski would have done with a straightforward vampire story. The scenes Polanski plays with his wife Sharon Tate, murdered in 1969 by Charles Manson and his followers, add an unsettling quality to the film, which Polanski has disowned because of changes made by the distributor.

CREDITS

Director Roman Polanski; *Producer* Gene Gutowski; *Screenplay* Roman Polanski, Gerard Brach; *Photographer* Douglas Slocombe; *Production Designer* Wilfrid Shingleton; *Makeup* Tom Smith; *Music* Krzysztof Komeda

CAST

Jack MacGowran, Roman Polanski, Sharon Tate, Jessie Robbins, Alfie Bass, Fiona Lewis, Ferdy Mayne

THE HAND OF NIGHT

U.S. title: Beast of Morocco

*Film   1966   G.B. (Associated British-Pathe)
73 minutes   Color*

Nicely photographed Hammer-style rubbish about a nervous male tourist who falls in love with a beautiful Moroccan vampire.

CREDITS

Director Frederic Goode; *Producer* Harry Field; *Screenplay* Bruce Stewart; *Photographer* William Jordan; *Art Director* Peter Moll; *Special Effects* Biographic Films; *Choreography* Boscoe Holder; *Music* John Shakespeare, Joan Shakespeare

CAST

William Sylvester, Diane Clare, Edward Underdown, Aliza Gur, Terence de Marney

HORROR OF THE BLOOD MONSTERS

*Film   1971   U.S. (Independent International)
85 minutes   Color*

An epidemic of vampirism is found to originate from a virus wafting to Earth from a war-torn planet populated by grotesque humanoids. Why not send this film there?

CREDITS

Director/Producer Al Adamson; *Screenplay* Sue McNair; *Music* Mike Velarde

CAST

John Carradine, Bruce Powers, Vicki Volante, Robert Dix; *Narrator* Brother Theodore

HOUSE OF DARK SHADOWS

*Film   1970   U.S. (MGM)   98 minutes
Color*

MGM gives television's phenomenally successful DARK SHADOWS the full glamour treatment in this feature-length spinoff. The familiar cast also gives it their all, and creator Curtis has added an extra measure of violence and gore (taboo on the small screen). The sequel is NIGHT OF DARK SHADOWS.

CREDITS

Director/Producer Dan Curtis; *Screenplay* Sam Hall, Gordon Russell; *Photographer* Arthur Ornitz; *Production Designer* Trevor Williams; *Makeup* Dick Smith, Robert Layden; *Music* Robert Cobert

CAST

Jonathan Frid, Joan Bennett, Grayson Hall, Kathryn Leigh Scott, Roger Davis, Thayer David

HOUSE OF DRACULA

*Film   1945   U.S. (Universal)   67 minutes
Black & white*

This *House* belongs to the Wolf Man more than anyone, but Dracula was better box office and Frankenstein had lent his name to the previous *House* (see Monsters). Setting is Castle Frankenstein, where the Wolf Man and Dracula are treated by mad doctor Onslow Stevens to cure them of their respective maladies. Dracula's vampirism is traced to a parasite in his blood, and Larry Talbot suffers from a pressure on the brain. Accidents will happen, and the doctor gets infected by giving the vampire a transfusion with his own blood.

Talbot (Lon Chaney, Jr.), promoted to hero, is finally cured by the vampire doctor, who nevertheless must be destroyed for the common good. Showing up late, the Frankenstein Monster (Glenn Strange) stands by until called upon to attack the former Wolf Man and die again in a laboratory fire. Talbot, having atoned for his previous full-moon murders, finally gets the girl and a happily-ever-after ending—at least until the trio meet again for the last time in ABBOTT AND COSTELLO MEET FRANKENSTEIN (1948) (see Monsters).

Interestingly, this was one of the first films to portray a male vampire as genuinely longing for a release from his bloodthirsty affliction, an idea that was also used in the low-budget programmer THE VAMPIRE'S GHOST, made the same year. The science fiction angle was also new, and would be exploited more fully during the 1950s and 1960s. John Carradine, playing Dracula for the second time, wears an elderly, graying makeup closer in conception to the Stoker original. Director Kenton, who helmed the previous three-ring circus, is more spirited in this one and evokes something of the Gothic style of the earlier films (shown in a montage sequence).

CREDITS

Director Erle C. Kenton; *Producer* Paul Malvern; *Screenplay* George Bricker, Dwight V. Babcock, Edward T. Lowe; *Photographer* George Robinson; *Makeup* Jack Pierce; *Special Effects* John P. Fulton; *Music* Edgar Fairchild

CAST

Lon Chaney, Jr., John Carradine, Onslow Stevens, Lionel Atwill, Glenn Strange, Martha O'Driscoll, Jane Adams

THE HUNGER

Film   1983   G.B. (MGM/UA)   98 minutes
Color

A sleek, chic upscale updating of a vampire classic. Catherine Deneuve is Miriam, who emerged from Egypt millennia ago and fell in love with John (David Bowie) in England in the 18th century. Today John and Miriam Blaylock live on Manhattan's East Side in a posh Bloomingdale's tomb of an apartment. Young and beautiful, they spend most of their time searching for fresh young blood. When John's aging process begins to accelerate (a transfusion from a disco pickup hasn't worked), Miriam visits a brilliant young gerontologist (Susan Sarandon) for medical help, then decides to trade in John for the doctor. The lesbian scenes are done tastefully, which is to say that the action is shot through soft-focus lenses and fog filters. John, meanwhile, is slated to take his place among Miriam's other past loves, who are stored in coffins in the attic.

Based on Whitley Strieber's novel, *The Hunger* is essentially an offbeat tongue-in-cheek remodeling of Le Fanu's *Carmilla*, filmed previously as THE VAMPIRE LOVERS and LE ROUGE AUX LEVRES (both 1970). Exquisitely framed by Tony Scott, a British director of TV commercials and brother of Ridley Scott (*Alien*), it dazzles the eye with enigmatic visual sensations but often confuses the mind by neglecting narrative logic. The look is that of a Chanel commercial, but one so wildly fashionable and outre that only mythical beings could live there. It's one of the few genre films in which vampires seem completely at home in a contemporary setting. Deneuve and Bowie are outstanding as the screen's most elegantly mannered and handsome undead couple, who nevertheless manage to suggest a deep fatigue lurking beneath their veneer. Equally impressive are the makeup illusions by Dick Smith and Carl Fullerton, in which Bowie ages from 30 to 85 before our very eyes while waiting to see the doctor.

CREDITS

Director Tony Scott; *Producer* Richard A. Shepherd; *Screenplay* Ivan Davis, Michael Thomas, based on the novel by Whitley Strieber; *Photographer* Stephen Goldblatt; *Production Designer* Brian Morris; *Makeup Effects* Dick Smith, Carl Fullerton, Dave Allen, Roger Dicken; *Music* Michel Rubini, Denny Jaeger

CAST

Catherine Deneuve, David Bowie, Susan Sarandon, Cliff de Young, Beth Ehlers, Dan Hedaya, Rufus Collins, Suzanne Bertish, James Aubrey

ISLE OF THE DEAD

Film   1945   U.S. (RKO)   72 minutes
Black & white

In 1912 a mixed bag of travelers is quarantined by a plague on a Greek island, where they are gradually being picked off by a *vrykolaka*—a Balkan vampire. One of Val Lewton's most underrated films (see Horror-Makers), *Isle of the Dead* suffers when seen on non-cable television, whose commercial interruptions destroy Lewton's subtly orchestrated symphony of offscreen terror. Building slowly, the film blossoms into a fully gratifying catharsis in its final reels when one of the travelers, the patrician wife of a British foreign service officer, suffers a "cataleptic" fit and is mistaken for dead. Having previously learned that the woman's greatest fear is of being buried alive, the viewer is drawn into her predicament: The camera pulls in for a tight closeup that reveals a slight twitch to her nostrils, unnoticed by the others. The scene is punctuated only by the creak of wood, a mournful wind—and her silent scream.

CREDITS

Director Mark Robson; *Producer* Val Lewton; *Screenplay* Ardel Wray, Josef Mischel; *Photographer* Jack Mackenzie; *Art Directors* Albert D'Agostino, Walter E. Keller; *Music* Leigh Harline

CAST

Boris Karloff, Ellen Drew, Alan Napier, Helene Thimig, Marc Kramer, Katherine Emery, Jason Robards, Sr.

INCENSE FOR THE DAMNED

U.S. title: Bloodsuckers

Film 1970 G.B. (Lucinda/Titan Int.)
87 minutes Color

How a sexually troubled Oxford don with establishment connections got involved with a trendy black magic cult in Greece and became a vampire (from the bite of a hippie beauty). Photographer Desmond Dickinson's evocative images make one wish the talky script and pedestrian direction were up to his standards.

CREDITS

Director Michael Burrowes (Robert Hartford-Davis); *Producer* Graham Harris; *Executive Producer* Peter Newbrook; *Screenplay* Julian More, from the novel *Doctors Wear Scarlet* by Simon Raven; *Photographer* Desmond Dickinson; *Production Designer* George Provis; *Music* Bobby Richards

CAST

Peter Cushing, Patrick Macnee, Johnny Sekka, Alex Davion, Madeline Hinde, Imogen Hassall, Patrick Mower

ISLAND OF THE DOOMED

Film 1966 Germany/Spain (Orbital)
87 minutes Color

Released 1968 U.S. (Allied Artists)

A latter-day Dr. Moreau crossbreeds plants with animals and comes up with a vampire tree that wraps its thirsty branches around unsuspecting visitors. Dead wood.

CREDITS

Director Mel Welles; *Producer* George Ferrer; *Screenplay* Stephen Schmidt; *Story* Ira Meltcher, F.V. Theumer; *Photographer* Cecilio Paniagua; *Music* Anto Abril

CAST

Cameron Mitchell, Kay Fischer, Elisa Montes, Ralph Naukoff

KISS OF THE VAMPIRE

U.S. title: Kiss of Evil

Film 1962 G.B. (Hammer/Universal)
87 minutes Eastmancolor

Since Christopher Lee was still refusing to wear the black satin cape after his 1958 debut, Hammer came up with this Draculoid thriller featuring Noel Willman as a surrogate blood drinker named Dr. Ravna. A polished and urbane medical researcher, Ravna owed his condition to a bungled experiment in "evil science." The soul-chilling opener has a mourning father interrupting his daughter's funeral by stabbing a garden spade into her coffin, thereby eliciting one of the nastiest blood spurts and most ear-splitting moans in movie history. From then on the film tails off to detail the search for a young bride last seen in Ravna's castle. Director Sharp ties up the loose ends with a satisfying ending in which a cavern full of vampires is eliminated by hordes of bats (a scene reminiscent of Hitchcock's *The Birds*), dispatched by Professor Zimmer, the Van Helsing figure.

CREDITS

Director Don Sharp; *Producer* Anthony Hinds; *Screenplay* John Elder (Anthony Hinds); *Photographer* Alan Hume; *Production Designer* Bernard Robinson; *Art Director* Don Mingaye; *Special Effects* Les Bowie; *Makeup* Roy Ashton; *Music* James Bernard

CAST

Clifford Evans, Noel Willman, Jennifer Daniel, Edward de Souza, Barry Warren, Jaqui Wallis

LAKE OF DRACULA

Also titled: Bloodthirsty Eyes, Dracula's Lust for Blood

Film   1971   Japan (Toho)   82 minutes
Color   TohoScope

How worldwide genre conventions have become is apparent in this lyrical, beautifully photographed item from Japan. The innocent heroine is troubled by the recurring memory of an attack by a handsome Asian vampire who is, of course, shrouded in black, and has pale skin and fangs.

CREDITS

Director Michio Yamanoto; *Screenplay* Ei Ogawa; *Photographer* Rokuro Nishigaki

CAST

Mori Kishida, Midori Fujita, Osahide Takahasri, Kaku Taskashina

THE LAST MAN ON EARTH

Film   1964   U.S./Italy (AIP)   86 minutes
Black & white

Filmed twice within a decade, Richard Matheson's restlessly paranoid novel *I Am Legend* adroitly broke with the past and set vampirism free (almost) of its ties with Christian mythology by providing a believable science fiction explanation for the malady. While neither movie version succeeded in capturing Matheson's allegorical intensity, this hastily assembled production, made in Italy, comes closer than the second, THE OMEGA MAN (1971). Vincent Price, in an atypical non-villain role, is the only human untouched by a future plague which has killed most of the population and turned those who are left into blood-drinking parasites. Hunted by night, Price barricades himself in his house and plays phonograph records to drown out voices of the creatures calling him by name. A hunter by day, he roams the streets and destroys the vampires where they sleep, in the traditional manner, with sharpened stakes and a hammer. The film, like the book, ends with a reverberating note of political horror. Price, captured by the vampires, learns that they consider themselves the "normals" and him the anomaly, the "vampire" who must be killed for the good of the ruling majority.

CREDITS

Director Sidney Salkow; *Producer* Robert L. Lippert; *Screenplay* Logan Swanson, William P. Leicester; *Photographer* Franco Della Colli; *Art Director* Giorgio Giovannini; *Makeup* Piero Mecacci; *Music* Paul Sawtell, Bert Shefter

CAST

Vincent Price, Franco Bettoia, Emma Danieli, Giacomo Rossi-Stuart, Umberto Rau

THE LEECH WOMAN

Film   1960   U.S. (Universal)   77 minutes
Black & white

To periodically restore her youth and beauty, an old crone kills men and injects herself with their brain hormones. When she murders the fiancee of a man she has fallen in love with, she makes the fatal mistake of using the girl's brain fluids in the formula (the recipe calls for no substitutions). An unintentionally hilarious mating of DRACULA with H. Rider Haggard's classic fantasy *She*.

CREDITS

Director Edward Dein; *Producer* Joseph Gershenson; *Screenplay* David Duncan; *Story* Ben Pivar, Francis Rosenwald; *Photographer* Ellis Carter; *Makeup* Bud Westmore; *Music* Irving Gertz

CAST

Coleen Gray, Philip Terry, Grant Williams, Gloria Talbot

THE LEGEND OF THE 7 GOLDEN VAMPIRES

U.S. title: The Seven Brothers Meet Dracula

Film   1974   G.B./Hong Kong (Hammer/Shaw)
89 minutes   Eastmancolor   Panavision

The fist meets the fang in this martial arts–vampire movie, made to capitalize on the kung fu craze of the 1970s. Peter Cushing is back as Dr. Van Helsing, riding down an unfamiliar Dracula (John Forbes Robertson) and hordes of undead in turn-of-the-century China. U.S. audiences liked this preposterously fast-paced mix of gore and gymnastics, and it hit the jackpot.

CREDITS

Director Roy Ward Baker; *Producers* Don Houghton, Vee King Shaw; *Screenplay* Don Houghton; *Photographers* John Wilcox, Roy Ford; *Special Effects* Les Bowie; *Makeup* Wu Hsu Ching; *Martial Arts Sequences* Tang Chia, Liu Chia Liang; *Music* James Bernard

CAST

Peter Cushing, John Forbes Robertson, Julie Ege, David Chiang, Robin Stewart, Shih Szu, Robert Hann

LET'S SCARE JESSICA TO DEATH

Film   1971   U.S. (Paramount)   89 minutes
Color

Released from an asylum after a nervous breakdown, Jessica goes back to her Connecticut farm with her husband for a long convalescence—or so she thinks. Is she going out of her mind, or are there really vampires and zombies haunting the countryside? Director Hancock gets more out of this minor-league chiller than you would suppose, and you're hardly aware until the climax that the plot is a rehash of *Invasion of the Body Snatchers*. The surrealistic nightmare sequences are impressive, but what holds it all together is the performance of Zohra Lampert, an actress who can express the conflicting emotions of hope and terror with a simple look and gesture.

CREDITS

Director John Hancock; *Producer* Charles B. Moss, Jr.; *Screenplay* Norman Jonas, Ralph Rose; *Photographer* Bob Baldwin; *Electronic Music* Walter Stear; *Music* Orville Stoeber

CAST

Zohra Lampert, Barton Heyman, Kevin O'Connor, Alan Manson, Gretchen Corbett, Mariclare Costello

LONDON AFTER MIDNIGHT

Film   1927   U.S. (MGM)   61 minutes
Black & white (silent)

In his last great horror role, Lon Chaney plays a detective posing as a vampire to frighten a murderer into confessing. A formula whodunit, the

London After Midnight: Lon Chaney is only fooling.

film is of interest for Chaney's frizzy-haired vampire, who, except for his black cloak, is totally unlike the sophisticated nobleman Bela Lugosi brought to the Broadway stage that year. Chaney's top-hatted vampire has an insane, unkempt look and a mouthful of very sharp teeth. To effect the disguise, Chaney gouged thin wires into his cheeks to make his eyes bulge and wore a set of animal teeth which were so painful they could only be inserted for an hour at a time. Our conception of Dracula might have been quite different if Chaney had fulfilled his wish to star in the movie. (He died in 1930.) Tod Browning went on to direct DRACULA with Lugosi, who also appeared in the sound remake of this one, THE MARK OF THE VAMPIRE (1935).

CREDITS

Director/Producer/Story Tod Browning; *Screenplay* Waldemar Young; *Photographer* Merrit B. Gerstad; *Art Directors* Cedric Gibbons, Arnold Gillespie; *Titles* Joe Farham

CAST

Lon Chaney, Henry B. Walthall, Conrad Nagel, Marceline Day, Polly Moran, Edna Tichenor, Claude King

Vampire Comedies

From top, clockwise: In 1973 David Niven portrayed **Old Dracula,** while Harry Nilsson became the **Son of Dracula** (with Ringo Starr as Merlin the Magician); George Hamilton and Susan Saint James danced the night away in **Love At First Bite** (1979); but Carol Lawrence and Dick Shawn failed to make the grade in TV's **Mr. and Mrs. Dracula** (1980).

LOVE AT FIRST BITE

Film   1979   U.S. (AIP)   93 minutes   Color

Ordered by the Romanian government to leave Transylvania for giving the place a bad name, Dracula settles in present-day Manhattan and becomes a member of the after-dark disco set. Looking quite at home in his new "anything goes" environment, the elegantly attired vampire wins the affections of a scatterbrained model, who is impressed with his title and trendy love bites. The fun begins when his coffin is mistakenly shipped to a Harlem funeral home, and the count is mugged trying to get home to his posh digs at the Plaza Hotel. There's also a midnight raid on a blood bank and the hilarious sight of Dracula, cape swirling, doing the hustle to "I Like the Night Life." Coproducer George Hamilton, whose patent leather hair and embalmed good looks are perfect for the role, displays an unexpected flair for comedy and a pretty good Lugosi accent. And Arte Johnson does a winning takeoff on Renfield. Director Stan Dragoti plays fast and loose with the count's legend, but Robert Kaufman's script respects it, and the result is the most hilarious vampire spoof yet.

CREDITS

Director Stan Dragoti; *Producer/Screenplay* Robert Kaufman; *Photographer* Edward Rosson; *Art Director* Serge Krizman; *Special Effects* Allen Hall; *Makeup* William Tuttle; *Music* Charles Bernstein

CAST

George Hamilton, Susan Saint James, Richard Benjamin, Arte Johnson, Dick Shawn, Isabel Sanford

LUST FOR A VAMPIRE

TV titles: Love for a Vampire; To Love a Vampire

Film   1970   G.B. (Hammer)   95 minutes Technicolor

An exclusive girls' school now occupies the old Karnstein Castle in this hand-me-down sequel to Hammer's well-received THE VAMPIRE LOVERS, released earlier that year. Carmilla, reincarnated as a beautiful student anagrammatically named Mircalla (Yutte Stensgaard), terrorizes nubile girls while reprising the blood-and-boobs goings-on of the previous film. Best moment comes when a vampire, desperate for a blood fix, assaults an unwary drunk who is relieving himself behind a public house. The film's lustier scenes have been excised by TV censors, who also insisted on a title change.

CREDITS

Director Jimmy Sangster; *Producers* Harry Fine, Michael Style; *Screenplay* Tudor Gates, based on the novel *Carmilla* by Sheridan Le Fanu; *Photographer* David Muir; *Art Director* Don Mingaye; *Makeup* George Blackler; *Music* Harry Robinson

CAST

Ralph Bates, Barbara Jefford, Suzanna Leigh, Yutte Stensgaard, Mike Raven, Helen Christie, Michael Johnson

LE MANOIR DU DIABLE

U.S. titles: The Devil's Castle, The Haunted Castle

Film   1896   France (Warwick)   3 minutes Black & white (silent)

Legendary movie magician Georges Melies introduces the vampire to films. This was his 68th production of 1896, his most elaborate up to that time. The 1901 catalog of Warwick Film (Melies's distributor) describes the plot as follows:

"The picture shows a room in a medieval castle; carved stone pillars, low doors and vaulted ceiling. A huge bat flies in and circles around. It is suddenly transformed into Mephistopheles. He walks around, makes a magic pass, and a large cauldron appears and out of it, in a great cloud of smoke, there emerges a beautiful lady. . . . Cavaliers, ghosts, a skeleton and witches appear and disappear at a sign from the Evil One. Finally one of the cavaliers produces a cross, and Mephistopheles throws up his hands and disappears in a cloud of smoke."

THE MARK OF THE VAMPIRE

Film   1935   U.S. (MGM)   60 minutes Black & white

The year 1935 was a busy one for Hollywood terror. In addition to a score of lesser films from minor studios, Universal had in release BRIDE OF FRANKENSTEIN (see Monsters) with Karloff and THE RAVEN (see Mad Scientists) with Karloff *and* Bela Lugosi. Metro also had a hit that year with

Peter Lorre in MAD LOVE (see Mad Scientists), which prompted the studio to revamp Lon Chaney's quasi-vampire movie LONDON AFTER MIDNIGHT (1927). Chaney's old role has been divided into separate parts for Lionel Barrymore as the inspector and Bela Lugosi as the vampire, duplicating his Dracula image as Count Mora. Obviously made to capitalize on the memory of Universal's 1931 film, the movie avoids copyright problems by making no direct reference to Stoker's characters, and the locale has been changed from Transylvania to Czechoslovakia. Browning, who directed both the Chaney and Lugosi films, gets more explicit in this one, and the vampire's "bride" (Carol Borland) is actually shown flying on bat wings like a malevolent White Rock girl. Although photographed with nightmarish bravura by James Wong Howe on obviously expensive sets, the film cancels out its supernatural shudders by revealing the vampires were only actors hired to trap a murderer.

CREDITS

Director Tod Browning; *Producer* E.J. Mannix; *Screenplay* Guy Endore, Bernard Schubert; *Adaptation* Guy Endore, from the film *London After Midnight*; *Photographer* James Wong Howe; *Art Director* Cedric Gibbons

CAST

Lionel Barrymore, Bela Lugosi, Lionel Atwill, Carol Borland, Elizabeth Allen, Jean Hersholt, Donald Meek

LA MASCHERA DEL DEMONIO/Black Sunday

Also titled: Revenge of the Vampire

Film   1960   Italy (Galatea/Jolly)   83 minutes
Black & white

This stylishly malefic Italian effort was one of the first European sound movies to break Hollywood's stranglehold and play to a mass American audience. It also established the international cult reputation of Barbara Steele, the horror queen of the 1960s. Steele plays a dual role: the beautiful vampire–witch princess Asa, and Katia, her brother's descendant. The film opens in 1630 with Asa being put to death by her brother, who hammers a spiked witch's mask into her beautiful face. Cut to 1830. A scientist opens her tomb, and while he is gazing at her decomposed face, a bat cuts the man's hand. His dripping blood revives Asa (in the manner Dracula was revived in

Hammer's 1965 film DRACULA, PRINCE OF DARKNESS), and she revives her erstwhile lover to keep her supplied with fresh blood. Meanwhile, Asa attempts to put the bite on innocent Katia, whose blood will make her immortal.

The late Mario Bava, Italy's premier vampire specialist, has never been better. His mobile camera insistently probes the film's claustrophobic Gothic world, constantly surprising and provoking the viewer. In her resurrection scene, for example, the camera tracks through the empty tomb until it stops on Asa's face, shown crawling with maggots and covered by holes from the spikes. (Steele's transformation was accomplished by the filter trick devised for the 1932 *Dr. Jekyll and Mr. Hyde*.) *Black Sunday* was released in the U.S. in 1961 by AIP, which paired the film in some locations with Corman's THE LITTLE SHOP OF HORRORS (see Mad Scientists). The dubbing job, unfortunately, is one of the worst, and the lip-synching rarely matches the dialogue. A score by Les Baxter replaced the original by Roberto Nicolosi.

CREDITS

Director Mario Bava; *Producer* Massimo De Rita; *Screenplay* Ennio De Concini, Mario Bava, Marcello Coscai, Mario Serandrei, based on *The Vij* by Nikolai Gogol; *Photographers* Ubaldo Terzano, Mario Bava; *Art Director* Giorgio Giovannini; *Music* Roberto Nicolosi

CAST

Barbara Steele, John Richardson, Ivo Garrani, Andrea Checchi, Arturo Dominci, Clara Bindi, Enrico Olivieri, Mario Passante

MR. AND MRS. DRACULA

TV pilot   1980   U.S. (ABC)   25 minutes
Color

Comedian Dick Shawn squeezed a few chuckles out of this pilot for a rejected sitcom, which surfaced during the summer reruns for a one-time showing. Settling in New York's decaying South Bronx, Dracula and his wife sleep in twin coffins, listen to the music of the Grateful Dead and dine on steaks very rare, preferably still alive. The idea, apparently, was to rework the old ADDAMS FAMILY (see Monsters) formula in the slick, spoofy style of LOVE AT FIRST BITE (in which Shawn also appeared).

CREDITS

Director Doug Rogers; *Producer/Creator/Writer* Robert Klane; *Production Designer* Frank Stiefel; *Music* Ken Luber

CAST

Dick Shawn, Carol Lawrence, Barry Gordon, Anthony Battaglia, Gail Mayron

La Maschera del Demonio: Scream queen Barbara Steele is a vampire-witch.

NIGHT OF DARK SHADOWS

*Film   1971   U.S. (MGM)   96 minutes
Metrocolor*

The second movie spinoff from the popular 1960s TV soap, DARK SHADOWS (the first was HOUSE OF DARK SHADOWS), minus matinee idol vampire Barnabas Collins, focus of the series. The pastiche story, something about a Collins descendant who is "taken over" by his late ancestor and made to menace his new bride, plays like bits and pieces of discarded horror scripts. Architecture buffs might enjoy a tour of the old Gould mansion in Tarrytown, New York, where the film was entirely shot.

CREDITS

Director/Producer Dan Curtis; *Screenplay* Sam Hall; *Photographer* Richard Shore; *Associate Producer/Art Director* Trevor Williams; *Makeup* Reginald Tackley; *Music* Robert Cobert

CAST

David Selby, Kate Jackson, Grayson Hall, Lara Parker, John Karlen, Nancy Barrett, James Storm

NOSFERATU—EINE SYMPHONIE DES GRAUENS

*Film   1922   Germany (Prana)   72 minutes
Silent*

This is the first movie version of Bram Stoker's *Dracula*, albeit a pirated one. Although the filmmakers changed the names of some characters and story details, Stoker's widow sued nevertheless, and the film was withdrawn from distribution and most copies were destroyed. More creepy than horrific, it moves sluggishly through the familiar plot but is worth seeing for the grotesque beauty of director F.W. Murnau's staging and the obsessional central performance of Max Schreck as the vampire Orlock. Orlock, with his rat-like face and taloned fingers, would not have been able to pass as a normal man as Dracula did, but he's authentically unsettling as he scuttles through the back streets of town under the weight of the coffin carried on his back.

Murnau and screenwriter Henrik Galeen ignored an important fact of vampire mythology—that vampires cast no shadows—and thus created the often imitated image of Orlock's hand moving in shadow toward the victim's bed. In another departure from its literary model, the film introduced the idea that sunlight is fatal to vampires. Stoker's Dracula could shop for sustenance day or night.

CREDITS

Director F.W. Murnau; *Screenplay* Henrik Galeen; *Photographers* Fritz Arno Wagner, Cunther Krampf; *Art Director* Albin Grau

CAST

Max Schreck, Alexander Granach, Gustav von Waggenheim, Greta Schroder-Matray, G.H. Schnell, Ruth Landshoff

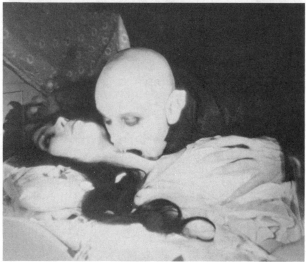

Nosferatu: Top, Max Schreck is a fanged and taloned vampire in the 1922 film; Klaus Kinski dons the same makeup in the 1979 color remake.

NOSFERATU THE VAMPYRE

Film   1979   West Germany/France (20th Century-Fox)   107 minutes   Color

Werner Herzog's remake of F.W. Murnau's pirated *Dracula* (see listing above) is beautiful to look at, but it barely raises a goose-pimple. More a tribute to Murnau than to Stoker, the film makes little sense unless you've seen the original. Best is Klaus Kinski as the kinky Nosferatu (meaning the "undead") in a copy of Max Schreck's fiendish, snaggle-toothed makeup and his peculiar hunched-over gait. Kinski plays the vampire—now called Dracula since Stoker's copyright had expired—as a

half-tamed animal unable to resist his craving for human blood. The ending offers an interesting twist, with Lucy offering herself to Dracula to save husband Jonathan's life.

CREDITS

Director/Producer/Screenplay Werner Herzog; *Photographer* Jorg Schmidt-Reitwein; *Production Designers* Henning von Gierke, Ulrich Bergfelder; *Special Effects* Cornelius Siegel; *Makeup* Reiko Kruk, Dominique Ansambl Gordela; *Music* Popol Vuh, Florian Flicke

CAST

Klaus Kinski, Isabelle Adjani, Bruno Ganz, Roland Topor, Walter Ladengast, Dan Van Husen, Jan Groth, Werner Herzog

NOT OF THIS EARTH

Film   1956   U.S. (Allied Artists)   72 minutes Black & white

A macabre space alien, who hides his albino pupils behind sunglasses, makes a lot of people scream as he fusses with tubes and bottles while accumulating blood for the poisoned folks back home. One of Roger Corman's early jokes.

CREDITS

Director/Producer Roger Corman; *Screenplay* Charles Griffith, Mark Hanna; *Special Effects* Paul Blaisdell; *Music* Ronald Stein

CAST

Paul Birch, Beverly Garland, Morgan Jones, Jonathan Haze

OLD DRACULA

Also titled: Vampira

Film   1973   G.B. (World Film/Columbia) 88 minutes   Color

Dracula is nearly as old as the jokes in this broad lampoon, which dances over the old traditions with two left feet. The plot has Dracula luring magazine centerfold models to his drafty castle for fresh blood to revive his wife Vampira, who comes back to life as a black woman. Debonair David

Niven has a few good moments drinking blood from a crystal glass, filled from a cellar stocked from skiing fatalities and other accidents.

CREDITS

Director Clive Donner; *Producer* John H. Weiner; *Screenplay* Jeremy Lloyd; *Photographer* Tony Richmond; *Art Director* Philip Harrison; *Music* David Whitaker, Anthony Newley

CAST

David Niven, Teresa Graves, Jennie Linden, Peter Bayliss, Nicky Henson, Linda Hayden

THE OMEGA MAN

Film   1971   U.S. (Warner Bros.)   98 minutes
Technicolor   Panavision

This is the second screen adaptation of Richard Matheson's superb novel *I Am Legend* (1954), and it's less true to the story than the first, THE LAST MAN ON EARTH (1964). Gone are Matheson's vampires, replaced by plague-carrying mutant survivors of a 1977 Sino-Soviet germ war who prowl the streets of Los Angeles at night in dark robes like demented monks. During the day, when the mutants are inactive (their albino eyes are sensitive to light), healthy scientist Charlton Heston goes around killing them not with a sharpened stake and hammer but with an up-to-date machine gun. What the film has on its mind soon becomes apparent with Heston's repeated viewings of an old print of his favorite movie, *Woodstock*, whose message of peace and love had obviously gone unheeded. The film occasionally captures something of Matheson's harrowing vision of a post-apocalyptic world, but it's essentially a slick action-adventurer cast in the Heston image.

CREDITS

Director Boris Sagal; *Producer* Walter Seltzer; *Screenplay* John William Corrington, based on the novel *I Am Legend* by Richard Matheson; *Photographer* Russell Metty; *Art Director* Arthur Loel; *Makeup* Gordon Bau; *Music* Ron Grainer

CAST

Charlton Heston, Rosalind Cash, Anthony Zerbe, Paul Koslo, Lincoln Kilpatrick

RETURN OF DR. X

Film   1939   U.S. (Warner Bros.)   62 minutes
Black & white

Warner Brothers, impressed by the profits of Universal's SON OF FRANKENSTEIN (see Monsters), released that year, produced this slipshod programmer to satisfy the renewed public demand for genre films. Related in title only to the studio's previous DOCTOR X (see Mad Scientists), it's of interest only for the offbeat casting of Humphrey Bogart as a child killer brought back from the dead and kept alive with fresh blood from unwilling donors. Bogart, in his only horror role, is a sight, with pallid face, rouged lips and hair streaked malevolently white like Elsa Lanchester's in BRIDE OF FRANKENSTEIN (see Monsters).

CREDITS

Director Vincent Sherman; *Producer* Bryan Foy; *Screenplay* Lee Katz, based on *The Doctor's Secret* by William J. Makin; *Photographer* Sid Hickox; *Art Director* Esdras Hartley; *Makeup* Perc Westmore; *Music* Bernhard Kaun

CAST

Humphrey Bogart, Rosemary Lane, Wayne Morris, Dennis Morgan, John Litel, Huntz Hall, Glen Langan

RETURN OF THE VAMPIRE

Film   1943   U.S. (Columbia)   69 minutes
Black & white

Lugosi, fresh from his portrayal of the Monster in Universal's FRANKENSTEIN MEETS THE WOLF MAN (see Monsters), revisits his trademark role in this likable kitsch revenge fantasy. Resurrected by workmen who discover its remains during the London Blitz of World War II, the vampire proceeds to put the bite on descendants of the family that had previously staked him. Columbia, borrowing from Universal's formula of pairing monsters, provides Lugosi with a werewolf servant.

CREDITS

Director Lew Landers; *Producer* Sam White; *Screenplay* Griffin Jay; *Story* Kurt Neumann; *Photographer* John Stumar, L.W. O'Connell; *Art Director* Lionel Banks; *Special Effects* Aaron Nadley; *Music* Mario Tedesco

CAST

Bela Lugosi, Nina Foch, Frieda Inescort, Roland Varno, Miles Mander, Matt Willis (werewolf)

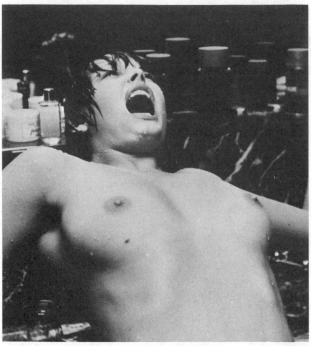

Le Rouge aux Levres/Daughters of Darkness: While Delphine Seyrig seduces young bride Daniele Ouimet, her handmaiden Andrea Rau is accidentally killed by Ouimet's errant husband.

LE ROUGE AUX LEVRES/Daughters of Darkness

Film 1970 Belgium/France/West Germany (Maya/Gemini/Maron) 87 minutes Color

One of the kinkiest of vampire films, this elegantly mounted co-production mixes equal portions of Sheridan Le Fanu's *Carmilla* and the history of Elizabeth Bathory, the so-called blood countess of 17th-century Hungary. Delphine Seyrig, looking fetchingly pale, her lips layered with blood-red lipstick (a visual pun on the French title), plays an ageless beauty whose lusts include a craving for lesbian encounters. A seducer rather than an attacker, Elizabeth becomes enamored of a young bride she meets in an exclusive spa and orders her servant girl Ilona to seduce the husband so that she may do the same to the wife. Dragged nude into the shower by the errant husband (who is revealed to be a sadist), Ilona recoils violently at the touch of water and falls onto a straight razor that penetrates her heart. Seyrig, nonplussed, later confides that her amazingly durable good looks are due to "diet and lots of sleep." (See also THE VAMPIRE LOVERS, COUNTESS DRACULA.)

CREDITS

Director Harry Kumel; *Producers* Alain Guillaume, Paul Collet; *Screenplay* Harry Kumel, Pierre Drout; *Photographer* Eddy van der Enden; *Art Director* Francoise Hardy; *Music* Francois de Roubaix

CAST

Delphine Seyrig, John Karlen, Andrea Rau, Daniele Ouimet, Paul Esser

'SALEM'S LOT

TV film 1979 U.S. (CBS) 198 minutes Color

Stephen King's best-seller about vampirism running rampant in modern-day New England gets the deluxe treatment in this two-part CBS miniseries. David Soul stars as a novelist who returns to his hometown, drawn by the memory of a mysterious old house, now owned by antiques dealer James Mason. Also involved in the sinister community are a young career woman (Bonnie Bedelia), looking for—ha!—a little peace and quiet, and a local teenager (Lance Kerwin) whose interest in the occult borders on the obsessive. Director Tobe Hooper (*The Texas Chain Saw Massacre*) proves he doesn't need gore and body parts to startle and provoke, and the film is remarkably effective for a TV production. The abridged version, shown on cable television without commercials, is even better.

CREDITS

Director Tobe Hooper; *Producer* Richard Kobritz; *Executive Producer* Stirling Silliphant; *Screenplay* Paul Monash, based on the novel by Stephen King

CAST

David Soul, Lance Kerwin, James Mason, Bonnie Bedelia, Reggie Nalder, Lew Ayres, Elisha Cook, Jr., Julie Cobb, Ed Flanders, George Dzundza

THE SATANIC RITES OF DRACULA

U.S. title: Dracula and His Vampire Bride

Film   1973   G.B. (Hammer)   88 minutes Technicolor

Christopher Lee and Peter Cushing square off for a final round as Dracula and Van Helsing (although both went on to play the roles opposite others). It's a lackluster farewell, more mystery thriller than Gothic chiller, with Van Helsing gumshoeing the source (Dracula) of a virus sweeping through contemporary London. Lee's portrayal of the vampire as a ruthless big-business czar is interesting, but the script's premise doesn't hold water: Would Dracula endanger his blood supply by depopulating the world with a plague? Hammer couldn't find American distribution for this one until 1978, when Broadway's DRACULA sparked a mini–vampire revival.

CREDITS

Director Alan Gibson; *Producer* Roy Skeggs; *Screenplay* Don Houghton; *Photographer* Brian Probyn; *Art Director* Lionel Couch; *Special Effects* Les Bowie; *Makeup* George Blackler; *Music* John Cacavas

CAST

Christopher Lee, Peter Cushing, Michael Coles, Freddie Jones, William Franklyn, Joanna Lumley

SCARS OF DRACULA

Film   1970   G.B. (Hammer/EMI) 96 minutes   Technicolor

For its sixth Dracula film, (Lee's fifth), Hammer added a few gruesome shocks, although not as many as were originally called for. A scene in which the Count was to lick blood from a dungeon floor was never shot, and another in which his servant saws apart a female victim was trimmed back shortly before the Christmas release date. Christopher Lee is called upon mostly to stab and whip a young couple on the run who don't know enough to stay away from Castle Dracula. The special effects are variable (even the bat wires are visible), except for a vivid nighttime climax on the castle walls that has Dracula impaled on a metal spike which attracts a *coup de grace* of lightning. The film is faithful to the Bram Stoker novel in at least one respect: Dracula is shown crawling along his castle wall face down.

CREDITS

Director Roy Ward Baker; *Producer* Aida Young; *Screenplay* John Elder (Anthony Hinds); *Photographer* Moray Grant; *Art Director* Scott MacGregor; *Special Effects* Roger Licken; *Makeup* Wally Schneidermann; *Music* James Bernard

CAST

Christopher Lee, Dennis Waterman, Jenny Hanley, Patrick Troughton, Christopher Matthews, Wendy Hamilton

SON OF DRACULA

Film   1943   U.S. (Universal)   79 minutes Black & white

Having followed in Karloff's footsteps as the Frankenstein Monster and the Mummy, Lon Chaney, Jr., tried on Lugosi's cape and a fake mustache for the second sequel to DRACULA. Chaney, whose own trademark role is the Wolf Man, looks a bit too well-fleshed to be playing the gaunt count, but he's passable, and so is the film. The title character turns out to be the old man himself, disguised as Count Alucard (spell it backward) and resettled near a Georgia swampland because, as he explains, "This young virile country can provide me with what I want; what I crave; what I must have!"

Especially good are John Fulton's special effects, the first to realize the magical qualities of Stoker's novel. In one spellbinding scene, a coffin emerges from Universal's backlot swamp—also seen in the MUMMY series (see Mummies), vapor rises from the lid, and Dracula coalesces into human form. He then floats across the water standing upright on his coffin. He is also seen changing into a bat—a transformation never shown in the Lugosi film. Writer Siodmak adds an original touch, later incorporated into the genre, by having a lady victim welcome the vampire's advances.

CREDITS

Director Robert Siodmak; *Producer* Ford Beebe; *Screenplay* Eric Taylor; *Story* Curt Siodmak; *Photographer* George Robinson; *Art Director* John B. Goodman; *Special Effects* John P. Fulton; *Makeup* Jack Pierce; *Music* Hans J. Salter

CAST

Lon Chaney, Jr., Louise Albritton, Robert Paige, Evelyn Ankers, J. Edward Bromberg, Frank Craven

SON OF DRACULA

Film   1973   G.B. (Apple)   90 minutes
Color

Producer Ringo Starr cooked up this affectionate spoof, which is the most rara of avis—a rock and roll vampire movie. Songs are by Harry Nilsson, who stars as Count Downe, son of the late Count Dracula, with former vampire-destroyer Professor Van Helsing as his aide-de-camp. Also on hand are Starr as Merlin the Magician and club members Keith Moon, Peter Frampton and John Bonham in cameo roles. Director Francis, who isn't right for this kind of material, attempts to keep the party under control, but he hasn't a chance against his self-indulgent cast.

CREDITS

Director Freddie Francis; *Producer* Ringo Starr; *Screenplay* Jay Fairbank (Jennifer Jayne); *Photographer* Norman Warwick; *Art Director* Andrew Sanders; *Makeup* Jill Carpenter; *Music* Harry Nilsson

CAST

Harry Nilsson, Ringo Starr, Freddie Jones, Dennis Price, Peter Frampton, Suzannah Leigh, Keith Moon, Shakira Baksh, John Bonham

LA SORELLA DI SATANA/Satan's Sister

U.S. title: The She-Beast

G.B. title: The Revenge of the Blood Beast

Film   1965   Italy/Yugoslavia (Europix/Leith)
76 minutes   Color   Anamorphic

A crazy quilt of a movie, by turns ridiculous, horrifying and hilarious, but always fascinating. The nonsensical story has Barbara Steele and Ian Ogilvy (in his pre-*Saint* days) motoring through present-day Transylvania when their car is mysteriously drawn into a lake. Turns out a witch was executed there centuries before (shown in the prologue), and she wants Steele's young body. While the villagers are being ripped apart by Steele/witch, a subplot evolves concerning a very Slavic-looking innkeeper having problems with local wenches and the Communist bureaucracy. Director Reeves, working on a dime, had better luck with THE WITCHFINDER GENERAL (1968) (see Ghosts, Demons and Witches).

CREDITS

Director Michael Reeves; *Producer* Paul Maslansky; *Screenplay* Michael Reeves, Tom Baker; *Idea* John Burke; *Photographer* Stanley Long; *Art Director* Tony Curtis; *Music* Paul Ferris

CAST

Barbara Steele, Ian Ogilvy, John Karlsen, Mel Welles, Jay Riley, Richardson Watson

TASTE THE BLOOD OF DRACULA

Film   1970   G.B. (Hammer)   95 minutes
Technicolor

Hammer's fifth Dracula outing reprises the famous impalement scene that climaxed DRACULA HAS RISEN FROM THE GRAVE. All that's left of the vampire are a handful of ashes and his trademark series props—a signet ring and a red-lined cape. Again, Dracula is revived by human blood, mixed into his powdery remains in a scalp-tingling ritual which gets the film off to a very promising start. Dramatically, it's downhill from then on, however, with the action shifting to three Victorian peers dabbling in sex and Satanism. As in much of his Hammer product, scriptwriter Hinds seems less interested in traditional horrors than in the Freudian kind. His Dracula is essentially a catalyst who leads the children of the hypocritical peers to patricide when they discover their fathers had been indulging in sexual perversions while restraining their kids' own healthy libidos. Director Sasdy, making his debut, leaves no doubt as to the nature of the vampire's soul bite this time around: The response of his beautiful young victims is unmistakably orgasmic.

CREDITS

Director Peter Sasdy; *Producer* Aida Young; *Screenplay* John Elder (Anthony Hinds); *Photographer* Arthur Grant; *Art Director* Scott MacGregor; *Special Effects* Brian Johncock; *Makeup* Gerry Fletcher; *Music* James Bernard

CAST

Christopher Lee, Geoffrey Keen, Gwen Watford, Ralph Bates, Linda Hayden, Peter Sallis, Roy Kinnear, Michael Ripper

TEMPI DURI PER I VAMPIRI

U.S. title: Uncle Was a Vampire

Film 1959 Italy (Embassy) 81 minutes
Color

A vampire complicates the life of his impoverished nephew, a former baron now employed as a hotel porter, in this good-natured Italian spoof, dubbed in English. Robust fun for those who can't take vampire films seriously.

CREDITS

Director Stefano Steno; *Screenplay* Alessandro Continenza, Dino Verde; *Photographer* Marco Scarpelli; *Art Director* Andrea Tomassi

CAST

Renato Rascel, Sylva Koscina, Christopher Lee, Lia Zoppelli, Kay Fisher, Susanne Loret

TERRORE NELLO SPAZIO

U.S. title: Planet of the Vampires

Film 1965 Italy/U.S. (AIP) 85 minutes
Color Anamorphic

Italian horror specialist Mario Bava offers a surfeit of shivers in this elegantly photographed coupling of science fiction and vampirism. The setting is a distant planet where a crew of astronauts begins murdering each other shortly after their arrival. Recovering their senses, they bury their dead, marking the graves with scrap-metal crosses. After they are gone, the markers slowly tumble from the soil and the corpses burst through, still wrapped in plastic body bags. Eventually, the entire crew become space vampires animated by alien beings, who head for home as an advance invasion force.

CREDITS

Director Mario Bava; *Producer* Fulvio Lucisana; *Screenplay* Castillo Cosulich, Antonio Roman, Rafael J. Salvia, Mario Bava; *English-language version* Ib Melchior, Louis M. Heyward; *Music* Gino Marinuzzi

CAST

Barry Sullivan, Norman Bengell, Angel Aranda, Ivan Rasimov, Evi Morandi

TWINS OF EVIL

Film 1971 G.B. (Rank/Hammer)
87 minutes Eastmancolor

Peter Cushing, looking more emaciated than ever, is at the top of his form as a fanatical witch hunter out of Hawthorne whose twin nieces become involved with a vampire cult. One of the better entries in Hammer's vampire series, seasoned with lesbianism (borrowed from CARMILLA), nudity and eye-popping gore.

CREDITS

Director John Hough; *Producers* Harry Fine, Michael Style; *Screenplay* Tudor Gates, based on characters created by Sheridan Le Fanu; *Photographer* Dick Bush; *Art Director* Roy Stannard; *Special Effects* Bert Luxford; *Makeup* George Blackler, John Webber; *Music* Harry Robinson

CAST

Peter Cushing, Mary Collinson, Madeleine Collinson, Dennis Price, Kathleen Byron, Damien Thomas

THE VAMPIRE

Film   1957   U.S. (Gramercy)   73 minutes
Black & white

Laborious 1950s' drive-in fare that offers a lame science fantasy excuse for vampirism: bat-serum pills accidentally swallowed by a researcher.

CREDITS

Director Paul Landres; *Producers* Arthur Gardner, Jules Levy; *Screenplay* Pat Fielder; *Photographer* Jack McKenzie; *Makeup* Don Robertson; *Music* Gerald Fried

CAST

John Beal, Coleen Gray, Kenneth Tobey, Dabbs Greer, Lydia Reed

THE VAMPIRE BAT

Film   1933   U.S. (Majestic)   63 minutes
Black & white

Poverty row's assembly lines retooled for horror product after Universal released DRACULA and FRANKENSTEIN (see Monsters) in 1931. This is one of the period's more interesting footnotes, largely because of its cast. There's no vampire, only crazy chemist Lionel Atwill killing people to find a "blood substitute" and shifting the blame to Dwight Frye's pet bat. Melvyn Douglas and Fay Wray see that justice is served.

CREDITS

Director Frank Strayer; *Producer* Phil Goldstone; *Screenplay* Edward T. Lowe; *Photographer* Ira Morgan; *Art Director* Dan Hall

CAST

Lionel Atwill, Dwight Frye, Fay Wray, Melvyn Douglas, Maude Eburne

VAMPIRE CIRCUS

Film   1971   G.B. (Hammer)   87 minutes
Color

Circuses have always been perfect settings for genre movies, and this later Hammer offers a three-ring big-top of terror. There are enough characters to populate a Victorian novel, but what the plot boils down to is an allegorical conflict between a vampire family and the townspeople who destroyed one of their members. Disguised as circus gypsies, a troupe of the undead throws up a tent near a Serbian village, circa 1812, and amuses audiences with a dazzling display of their supposed trick shape-shiftings: a tumbler leaps into the air and turns into a panther; others turn into bats, etc. There are hints of bestiality and incest, and a clever schematic interplay between the real and the illusionary. But while the film captures something of Hammer's early excitements, Robert Young's feverish direction fails to take advantage of the script's subtler horrors, and it's not the classic it should have been.

CREDITS

Director Robert Young; *Producer* Wilbur Stark; *Screenplay* Judson Kinberg; *Story* George Baxt; *Photographer* Moray Grant; *Art Director* Scott MacGregor; *Music* David Whittaker

CAST

Adrienne Corri, Laurence Payne, Thorley Walters, John Moulder Brown, Dave Prowse, Elizabeth Seal, Lynn Frederick

THE VAMPIRE LOVERS

Film   1970   G.B. (Hammer/AIP)   91 minutes
Technicolor

Hammer may have been faltering with its Dracula series, but it came up with a winner in this striking and sensual adaptation of Sheridan Le Fanu's *Carmilla*. Intelligently plotted and mounted with a throbbing erotic intensity, the film boasts a full-blooded performance by Polish actress Ingrid Pitt as Carmilla/Mircalla. Hungry and restless, given to a compulsive desire for her own sex (although she takes male victims as well), the aggressively beautiful Pitt is perhaps the cinema's most effective female vampire yet.

The film opens with a scene in which a vampire hunter grimly searches through the Karnstein Castle, staking and decapitating its undead residents. Carmilla, hidden in a safe place, escapes the blood-drenched crowbar, and later returns to avenge her decimated family. At the finale the Vampire Lover is impaled and beheaded herself, while a nearby portrait reflects her rapid 300-year-old decay. In between, Carmilla indulges in a bare-bosomed bedroom frolic with Laura, who receives the vampire's love bite not on her throat but on a blue-veined breast. Director Baker keeps the heavy breathing under control by getting down to matters at hand and abruptly switching to the supernatural. The sequels are LUST FOR A VAMPIRE (1970) and TWINS OF EVIL (1971).

CREDITS

Director Roy Ward Baker; *Producers* Harry Fine, Michael Style; *Screenplay* Tudor Gates; *Adaptation* Harry Fine, Tudor Gates, Michael Style, based on the novel *Carmilla* by Sheridan Le Fanu; *Photographer* Moray Grant; *Art Director* Scott MacGregor; *Music* Harry Robinson

CAST

Ingrid Pitt, Pippa Steele, Madeleine Smith, Peter Cushing, George Cole, Dawn Addams, Jon Finch, Kate O'Mara

THE VAMPIRE'S GHOST

**Film   1945   U.S. (Republic)   54 minutes
Black & white**

By the mid-1940s vampires had been overexposed in dozens of trivial "B" movies, produced by studios that had neither the time nor the money to do the subject justice. Still of interest is the redundantly titled *The Vampire's Ghost*, scripted by John K. Butler and Leigh Brackett, the latter a science fiction writer on her way to a major career with such films as *The Big Sleep* (1946) and *The Empire Strikes Back* (1980). Although dramatically wanting, the screenplay offers a rare (for its time) sympathetic vampire, whose mythology borrows from two works that influenced Stoker's *Dracula*: Polidori's *The Vampyre* (1819) and Prest's *Varney the Vampire* (1847). Like Polidori's Lord Ruthven, Brackett's vampire—the owner of a seedy bar in remote Africa—can operate by day or night, wearing only dark glasses to suggest his sensitivity to light. And like Varney, his affliction is a punishment for committing an abominable crime.

CREDITS

Director Lesley Selander; *Producer* Ruday Abel; *Screenplay* Leigh Brackett, John K. Butler; *Story* Leigh Brackett; *Photographers* Bud Thackeray, Robert Pittack; *Musical Director* Richard Cherwin

CAST

John Abbott, Charles Gordon, Peggy Stewart, Adele Mara, Roy Barcroft, Grant Withers

VAMPYR

Also titled: Castle of Doom; The Strange Adventure of David Gray

*Film   1932   France/Germany (Dreyer)
65 minutes   Black & white*

When *Vampyr* opened in Berlin, Carl Dreyer, Denmark's major contribution to cinema, was lashed by critics for choosing a genre that was beneath him. The public rejected the film as well, finding it turgid and obscure when compared with the excitements of FRANKENSTEIN (see Monsters) and DRACULA, then in release in Europe and America. Posterity has since made amends, but the film remains heavy going for anyone but the serious buff.

Dreyer's source material is Sheridan Le Fanu's 1872 short novel *Carmilla*, although he borrows only its premise of a vampirical woman feeding on another woman. Unlike Le Fanu's beautiful bloodsucker, Dreyer's is a gray-haired crone surviving on the energies of a young girl. David Gray, a traveler, happens into the village where this is taking place, and, feeling threatened by the vampire, he has a hallucinatory vision of his own death. In the film's famous burial scene, the action is shot from his point of view inside the coffin. In a state of mute shock, he looks up through the glass window of the lid to see the old woman peering down at him, dripping wax from a candle.

As a story *Vampyr* is economically austere, a gentle version of a medieval morality play, but its impact lies in the way Dreyer tells it. Shot through a layer of gauze at dawn and dusk (so that the time would seem neither day nor night), the film has the surreal resonance of a remembered nightmare. Like the couple who escape the vampire at the end, one leaves it feeling the fetid breath of superstition at one's back. Dreyer, making his first sound movie, had complete control of the production, which was financed by his friend Dutch Baron Nicolas de Gunzberg, so he could play the leading role.

CREDITS

Director Carl Dreyer; *Producers* Carl Dreyer, Nicholas de Gunzberg; *Screenplay* Carl Dreyer, Christian Jul, suggested by Sheridan Le Fanu; *Photographer* Rudolph Mate, Louis Neet; *Art Directors* Hermann Warm, Hans Bittmann, Cesare Silvani; *Music* Wolfgang Zeller

CAST

Julian West (Nicolas de Gunzburg), Henriette Gerard, Sybille Schmitz, Jan Hieronimko, Maurice Schutz, Rena Mandel

VAMPYRES

Film   1974   G.B. (Essay Films)   84 minutes Color

"The blood flows like Mogen David at a well-attended Bar-Mitzvah," wrote a *Variety* critic in his review of *Vampyres*, a soft-core sex fantasy that has a few offbeat surprises. The title refers to a pair of lesbian vampires who masquerade as hitch-hikers and lure various motorists to their swinging crypt for a drink, some sex and a predictably grue-some end. The X-rated version was tidied-up to an R and re-released as *Vampyres—Daughters of Darkness*. (*The* hardcore vampire film is *Dracula Sucks* [1978]).

CREDITS

Director Joseph (Jose) Larraz; *Producer* Brian Smedley-Aston; *Screenplay* D. Daubeney; *Photographer* Harry

Vampyres: Lesbian vampires Marianne Morris and Anulka have fun with Murray Brown.

Waxman; *Art Director* Ken Bridgeman; *Music* James Clarke

CAST

Marianne Morris, Anulka, Murray Brown, Brian Deacon, Sally Faulkner

THE VELVET VAMPIRE

Film 1971 U.S. (New World) 80 minutes Metrocolor

Velvet entices a young couple to her desert lair for some bedroom gymnastics, but her real objective is you-know-what. Basically an R-rated nudie shocker, directed by, surprisingly, a woman.

CREDITS

Director Stephanie Rothman; *Producer* Charles S. Swartz; *Screenplay* Maurice Jules, Charles S. Swartz, Stephanie Rothman; *Photographer* Daniel Lacambre; *Music* Clancy B. Grass III, Roger Dollarhide

CAST

Michael Blodgett, Sherry Miles, Jerry Daniels, Celeste Yarnell, Gene Shane

VIERGES ET VAMPIRES/Virgins and Vampires

U.S. title: Caged Virgins

Film 1972 France (ABC Films) 91 minutes Color

In recent years, filmmakers in Europe have fixed on the sexual aspects of vampire mythology, usually by graphically depicting what had formerly been left so deliciously to the imagination. Carry-

ing this trend to the point of parody are the bizarre sadomasochistic fantasies of Jean Rollin, France's gift to porno-horror. Typical of his *oeuvre* is *Virgins and Vampires*, which offers two full-frontal escapees from a girl's reformatory hiding out in an abandoned castle, populated by monsters and a male vampire whose libido apparently never sleeps.

CREDITS

Director/Screenplay Jean Rollin; *Producer* Sam Selsky; *Photographer* Renan Pooes

CAST

Marie Pierre Castle, Mireille D'Argent, Philippe Gaste, Olivier Francois

THE WASP WOMAN

Film 1960 U.S. (Allied Artists) 60 minutes Black & white

An aging cosmetics queen overdoses on a beauty potion of wasp enzymes that turns her into an insect-faced monstrosity capped by jiggling antennae. To reverse the damage she must prowl the streets at night looking for stray blood donors. Rusty junk from the Corman fast-movie factory.

CREDITS

Director/Producer Roger Corman; *Screenplay* Leo Gordon; *Story* Kinta Zertuche; *Photographer* Harry Newman; *Art Director* Daniel Haller; *Music* Fred Katz

CAST

Susan Cabot, Michael Mark, Fred Eisley, Frank Wolff, William Roerick

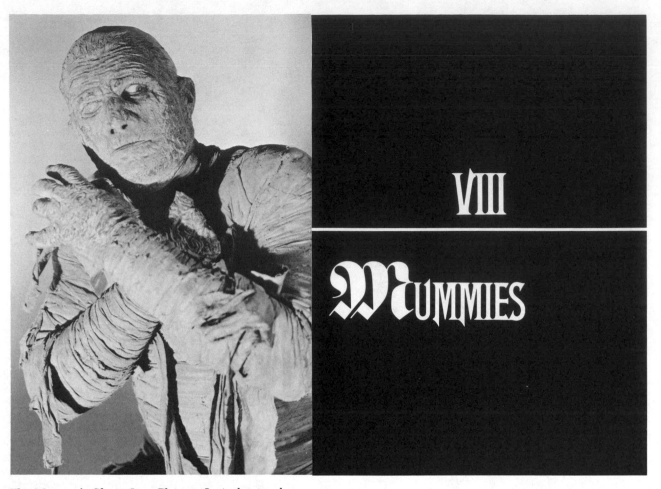

VIII

Mummies

The Mummy's Ghost: Lon Chaney, Jr. is the murderous monster Kharis.

In terms of output, the mummy is a minor genre figure. But in terms of movie fame, he ranks with the Frankenstein Monster, Dracula and the Wolf Man. The mummy actually predates the big three in cinema by having debuted in the 1909 film *The Mummy of King Ramses*. There already had been a number of popular romance novels about mummies and their ghosts, who returned from the dead to wreak vengeance on the desecrators of their tombs. The most durable of these is the short story "The Mummy's Foot" (1863), by French fantasy writer Theophile Gautier. This undistinguished and largely forgotten literary tradition derives from the archaeological discoveries made during Napoleon Bonaparte's Egyptian campaign at the turn of the 19th century.

People were as fascinated 180 years ago as they are now by the majesty and mystery of the ancient past. Discovered in the centers of labyrinthine stone pyramids were sealed chambers containing sarcophagi with the mummified remains of the honored dead, wrapped in bandages to resist cor-

ruption in their airless confinement. The ancient Egyptians never envisioned that their pharaohs would rise from the dead, however. They preserved their remains in the belief that the physical body was essential to the human personality and that a person could not go on to an afterlife without it. Even if mummies had wanted to, revival would have been difficult since the embalming process required that internal organs be removed and replaced with packing. Brain tissue was painstakingly excised through the nose, for example, and eyes were replaced with glass substitutes.

In 1922 the mummy made a striking comeback when a team of British archaeologists, led by Howard Carter and Lord Carnarvon, discovered the tomb of King Tutankhamen in the Valley of the Kings. The grandson of the great Nefertiti (whose fabled tomb has yet to be found), King Tut had been buried with priceless treasures largely found intact. The headlined event had the romantic appeal of discovering a lost city, and Tut's artifacts spawned a fashion trend which can still be seen in the remaining ochre-and-gold-ornamented art deco movie palaces of the period.

But what interested Universal studios were the curses found in the tomb, one of which warned, "Death will slay with its wings whoever disturbs the peace of the pharaoh." During the 1920s, a number of people connected with the expedition had died of seemingly inexplicable causes, beginning with financer Lord Carnarvon, who expired soon after falling ill at the excavation site. The official verdict was death probably "due to inhalation of dust containing the fungus histoplasma from dried bat droppings," but newspaper reports suggested that what had been laughed off as an ancient superstition seemed to have come true. Universal, then establishing itself as the home of the horror film, assigned Nina Wilcox Putnam and John L. Balderston, who had co-authored the stage version of *Dracula*, to come up with a what-if version of the discovery.

The result was THE MUMMY (1932), which recast the old horror vengeance myth as a tragic love story and borrowed elements from the mythology of Dracula, a fellow member of the undead. Both were cursed and forced to live out their destinies (in the best Judaeo-Christian tradition), and both were obsessed with the idea of eternally possessing their lovers. Moreover, both crumbled to dust when finally vanquished. Mummies proved to be less versatile than vampires, however, and after several sequels Universal reached a dead end with its restricted and repetitious love-story format. When Hammer revived the series in 1959, it also found that the storyline quickly became as stereotyped as the Western but with less story possibilities.

Mummies made a brief return to the screen in 1980, when the publicity resulting from the first American tour of King Tut's treasures reminded people of the curse. Television aired Philip Leacock's mystery *The Curse of King Tut's Tomb*, which explained away most of the deaths as the work of burnoosed villain Raymond Burr. Theatrically, there was THE AWAKENING, a new version of Bram Stoker's novel *The Jewel of the Seven Stars*, and a forgettable gore movie titled *Dawn of the Mummy*.

ABBOTT AND COSTELLO MEET THE MUMMY

Film 1955 *U.S. (Universal-International)*
90 minutes *Black & white*

The weakest link in Abbott and Costello's "meet-the-monster" series, with the clowns trading petrified quips as stranded tourists involved in an Egyptian treasure hunt.

CREDITS

Director Charles Lamont; *Producer* Howard Christie; *Screenplay* John Grant; *Photographer* George Robinson; *Art Directors* Alexander Golitzen, Bill Newberry; *Special Effects* Clifford Stine; *Makeup* Bud Westmore; *Musical Director* Joseph Gershenson

CAST

Bud Abbott, Lou Costello, Eddie Parker, Marie Windsor, Michael Ansara, Dan Seymour

The Awakening: Charlton Heston, as an Egyptologist obsessed with an ancient mummy, performs a ritual to bring it back to life.

THE AWAKENING

Film 1980 *G.B. (Solofilm/Orion)*
105 minutes *Color*

Bram Stoker's *The Jewel of the Seven Stars* (1903) was given the royal treatment in this second screen adaptation of his novel (the first was Hammer's BLOOD FROM THE MUMMY'S TOMB). Charlton Heston is the obsessed archaeologist who, while excavating the tomb of a 3000-year-old Egyptian queen, ignores the inscription "Do Not Approach the Nameless One Lest Your Soul Be Withered!" Director Newell rations the horror effects for maximum impact, as when Heston opens the ancient portal: With each blow of the hammer, the film cuts to Heston's pregnant wife doubling over in pain. Like THE EXORCIST (see Ghosts, Demons and Witches), the film tries to find a scientific explanation for its supernatural events. When the queen's spirit first manifests its presence 18 years later, for example, Heston's daughter visits a psychiatrist, complaining, "I don't feel like me anymore."

CREDITS

Director Mike Newell; *Producer* Robert Solo; *Screenplay* Allan Scott, Chris Bryant, Clive Exton, based on the novel *The Jewel of the Seven Stars* by Bram Stoker; *Photographer* Jack Cardiff; *Production Designer* Michael Stringer; *Special Effects* John Stears; *Makeup* George Frost; *Music* Claude Bolling

CAST

Charlton Heston, Susannah York, Jill Townsend, Stephanie Zimbalist, Patrick Drury, Bruce Myers

Blood from the Mummy's Tomb: Archaeologists Rosalie Crutchley, Hugh Burden, center, and James Villiers examine the severed hand of a mummy which is still dripping blood.

BLOOD FROM THE MUMMY'S TOMB

Film   1971   G.B. (Hammer)   94 minutes Technicolor

Not a mummy but the spirit of one (a queen), which possesses the daughter of an archaeologist 20 years after he has opened an ancient Egyptian tomb. A fresh, inventive handling of Bram Stoker's novel, *The Jewel of the Seven Stars*, directed by Seth Holt, who died shortly before the film was completed (Michael Carreras tied up the loose ends). Even better was THE AWAKENING (1980).

CREDITS

Director Seth Holt; *Producer* Howard Brandy; *Screenplay* Christopher Wicking, based on the novel *The Jewel*

of the Seven Stars by Bram Stoker; *Photographer* Arthur Grant; *Art Director* Scott Macgregor; *Special Effects* Michael Collins; *Makeup* Eddie Knight; *Music* Tristram Cary

CAST

Andrew Keir, Valerie Leon, James Villiers, George Coulouris, Hugh Burden, Mark Edwards, Rosalie Crutchley

CURSE OF THE FACELESS MAN

Film   1958   U.S. (Vogue)   66 minutes Black & white

Archaeologists at Pompeii uncover a petrified, 1900-year-old gladiator, who springs back to life. Amateur actors tangle with a script that confuses the Golem with the Mummy.

CREDITS

Director Edward L. Cahn; *Producer* Robert E. Kent; *Screenplay* Jerome Bixby; *Photographer* Kenneth Peach; *Art Director* Herman Schoenbrun

CAST

Richard Anderson, Elaine Edwards, Adele Mara, Gar Moore, Luis vann Roote

CURSE OF THE MUMMY'S TOMB

Film   1964   G.B. (Hammer/Swallow) 80 minutes   Technicolor

The Mummy, unable to keep a grip on his horrible temper, strangles the archaeologists who dared defile his holy resting place—or so it seems. Scriptwriter Younger attempts to liven up the kitsch by introducing a surprise heavy, but what's so surprising is how dull the film is. Christopher Lee turned the role over to Dickie Owen, who passed it to the equally anonymous Eddie Powell for the second sequel, THE MUMMY'S SHROUD.

CREDITS

Director Michael Carreras; *Screenplay* Henry Younger; *Photographer* Otto Heller

CAST

Ronald Howard, Terence Morgan, Fred Clark, Jeanne Roland, Dickie Owen, Michael Ripper

THE MUMMY

Film 1932 U.S. (Universal) 72 minutes Black & white

While this is the seminal mummy movie, it's not the first. France's *The Mummy of King Ramses* (1909) claims that distinction, followed by the American-made *The Mummy* (1911) and *The Dust of Egypt* (1915). Like its predecessors, the film is a movieland fantasy but one that is still able to move and disturb us more than 50 years later. The story opens in 1921 (the year before the headlined discovery in Egypt of King Tutankhamen's tomb). An expeditionary team from the British Museum finds the mummified body of Im-ho-tep, a lesser priest of the Temple of the Sun at Karnak, in a pyramidal tomb. Buried with him is the scroll of Thoth, inscribed with the words with which Isis raised Osiris from the dead.

Also contained in the sarcophagus is the warning: "Death and punishment for anyone who opens this casket." Despite Edward Van Sloan's cautionary advice to his colleagues that "The spells are weaker but still potent," a young scientist stays behind in the tomb and reads the scroll, alone. The camera conveniently faces the eager scientist so that we can see, but he cannot, that the eyes of the moldy, gauze-wrapped creature behind him have slowly reopened, and that the crossed, emaciated arms are stirring to life. The Mummy's exit from the tomb is shown only by the bands of his shroud slowly trailing the floor and the hysterical reaction of his foolhardy revivifier.

The film then jumps to 1932. The British scientists have returned to Egypt, where they are visited by a strange, parchment-skinned man named Ardath Bey (Boris Karloff), who is, of course, the ancient Im-ho-tep. Bey is instantly attracted to the half-Egyptian daughter (Zita Johann) of the British governor of the Sudan, and she finds herself mysteriously returning his interest. She is, Bey determines, the direct descendant and reincarnation of the Princess Anck-es-en-Amon, his lover of 3700 years before. In a flashback sequence, Bey recalls how he was so crazed with grief that he stole the Scroll of Thoth from the temple in order to bring her back to life. As punishment, the high priests had him embalmed alive and sealed into his sweetheart's tomb with the scroll, so that no one would ever again attempt such a thing. Now that science has restored him, Bey plans to give his lover immortality, a process that requires her death. In the rather hastily paced climax, Johann's fiance (David Manners) saves her life, and Im-ho-tep/Bey horrifyingly disintegrates into his natural condition of dust and ashes.

Apart from its unsatisfying conclusion and some pedestrian performances, *The Mummy* is a potent film that imparts a feeling of being suspended in time. Karloff, firmly establishing himself as Lon Chaney's successor, gives a hypnotic performance very different from his recent Frankenstein Monster. He seems to glide rather than walk, and his facial muscles never move. Only his eyes express his profound inner turmoil, as in the burial scene, when the tapes are drawn across his mouth and nose, leaving open his wild eyes to face the prospect of eternal sleep. The disguise, another of Jack Pierce's brilliant makeups, took eight hours to apply. Pierce literally cooked the cloth to give it the appearance of having rotted away centuries ago. He then wrapped it around Karloff's body in three directions to keep the layers from separating, and caked them with dried mud and glue. When Karloff opened his eyes and stepped from the coffin, the cloth disintegrated on camera. Sustaining the film's strange undercurrents is the angular photography of Charles Stumar, working under German director Karl Freund, who had previously photographed DER GOLEM (1920) (see Monsters) and DRACULA (1931) (see Vampires).

Although the film addresses the conflict between death and immortality and the idea that one must live out his destiny, it is, at its purest level, a love story, as are the majority of Mummy films that followed. Karloff's obsessive devotion, the script suggests, is a sickness that only love can bring. Bey is every anguished lover whose sacrifice, fidelity and true feeling, as painful as they are, make him feel alive and active. "All this I endured for thee," he tells Johann, reflecting a timeless belief in the curative power of love.

The sequels are THE MUMMY'S HAND (1940); THE MUMMY'S TOMB (1942); THE MUMMY'S GHOST, THE MUMMY'S CURSE (1944); and ABBOTT AND COSTELLO MEET THE MUMMY (1955). Two previous comedies are *Mummy's Boys* (1936) and *Mummies Dummies* (1948), the latter with the The Three Stooges. Britain's Hammer studio began a short-lived series in 1959 with Christopher Lee as the Mummy.

CREDITS

Director Karl Freund; *Producer* Stanley Bergerman; *Screenplay* John L. Balderston; *Story* Nina Wilcox Putnam, Richard Schayer; *Photographer* Charles Stumar; *Art Director* Willy Pogany; *Makeup* Jack Pierce

CAST

Boris Karloff, Zita Johann, Edward Van Sloan, David Manners, Arthur Byron, Bramwell Fletcher, Noble Johnson, Leonard Mudie, Eddie Kane, Katheryn Byron

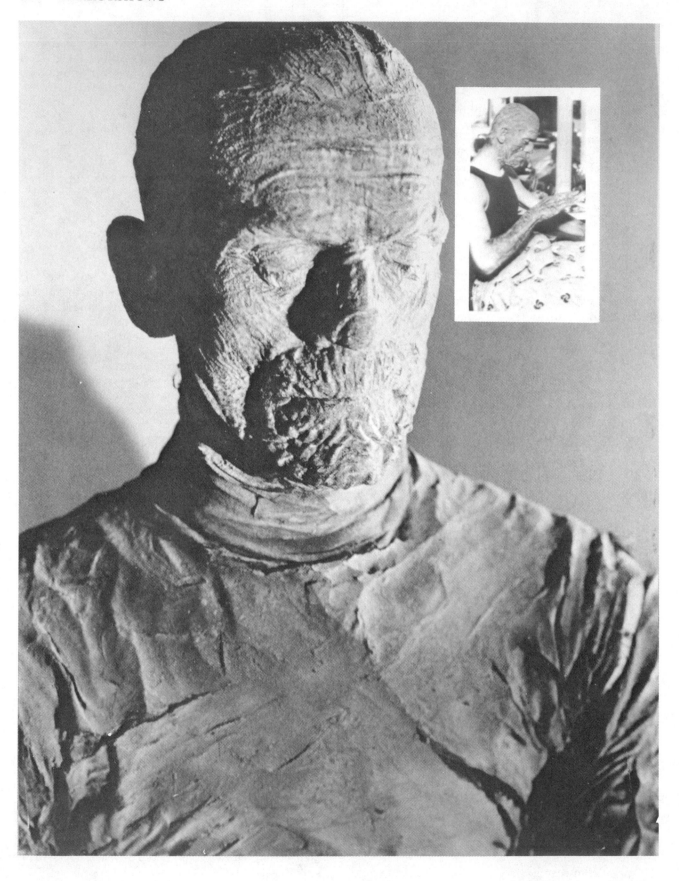

The Mummy (1932): Karloff, in a dual role as the Mummy (left) and a mysterious Egyptologist, finds a reincarnated princess in Zita Johann. Inset: Karloff being made-up in Jack Pierce's studio.

The Mummy (1959): Peter Cushing drives a spear into Christopher Lee's festering body in Hammer's color remake.

THE MUMMY

*Film   1959   G.B. (Hammer)   88 minutes
Technicolor*

Encouraged by the popularity of Hammer's full-blooded color remakes of DRACULA (see Vampires) and FRANKENSTEIN (see Monsters), Hollywood released the rights to other classic chillers, including DR. JEKYLL AND MR. HYDE (1932) (see Mad Scientists), *The Hound of the Baskervilles* (1939) and THE PHANTOM OF THE OPERA (1943) (see Crazies and Freaks). First on the agenda was Universal's *Mummy* series, with all-purpose monster Christopher Lee being wrapped in the mildewed gauze bandages. The title is from Karloff's initial film, but the plot resembles the sequels THE MUMMY'S HAND (1940) and THE MUMMY'S GHOST (1944). When the tomb of Princess Ananka is opened by snoopy Peter Cushing and a team of scientists, Kharis the mummy, her royal guard, gets *very* angry and keeps up the mischief in Victorian London. Not a very bloody or scary outing for Hammer, although things get moving in the last half hour. The real treat lies in stars Lee and Cushing, the Sade/Masoch of horror films. The sequel is CURSE OF THE MUMMY'S TOMB (1964).

CREDITS

Director Terence Fisher; *Producer* Michael Carreras; *Screenplay* Jimmy Sangster, based on the screenplay by Nina Wilcox Putnam and Richard Schayer, adapted from the story by John L. Balderston; *Photographer* Jack Asher; *Art Director* Bernard Robinson; *Makeup* Roy Ashton; *Music* Frank Reizenstein

CAST

Christopher Lee, Peter Cushing, Yvonne Furneaux, Eddie Byrne, Felix Aylmer, Raymond Huntley, George Pastel

THE MUMMY'S CURSE

Film   1944   U.S. (Universal)   62 minutes
Black & white

The Mummy and his princess wake up in a Louisiana swamp, after having been last seen in New England (THE MUMMY'S GHOST). Universal rolled up its gauze bandages after this hollow effort— The Mummy's fifth movie—except for a forgettable comedy outing in ABBOTT AND COSTELLO MEET THE MUMMY (1955).

CREDITS

Director Leslie Goodwins; *Producers* Ben Pivar, Oliver Drake; *Screenplay* Leon Abrams, Dwight V. Babcock; *Photographer* Virgil Miller; *Art Director* John B. Goodman; *Special Effects* John P. Fulton; *Makeup* Jack Pierce; *Musical Director* Paul Sawtell

CAST

Lon Chaney, Jr., Eddie Parker, Virginia Christine, Peter Coe, Kay Harding

THE MUMMY'S GHOST

Film   1944   U.S. (Universal)   60 minutes
Black & white

Kharis goes to college, where he finds the reincarnation of his 3000-year-old love—a search begun in THE MUMMY'S TOMB (1942). After repeatedly resisting his advances, the girl finally accedes and, properly withered and whitened, mutely follows The Mummy into a fog-shrouded swamp. Unfortunately, this surprisingly gloomy finale—rare in horror films—did not signal the end of the series. The pair returned later that year, inexplicably transported to a Southern bayou, for an unrequested curtain call in THE MUMMY'S CURSE.

CREDITS

Director Reginald Le Borg; *Producers* Joseph Gershenson, Ben Pivar; *Screenplay* Griffin Jay, Henry Sucher, Brenda Weisberg; *Photographer* William Sickner; *Art Directors* John B. Goodman, Abraham Grossman; *Makeup* Jack Pierce; *Musical Director* Hans J. Salter

CAST

Lon Chaney, Jr., Ramsay Ames, John Carradine, Robert Lowery, Barton MacLane, Eddie Parker

The Mummy's Hand: Cowboy actor Tom Tyler filled in for Karloff in Universal's first sequel to *The Mummy*.

THE MUMMY'S HAND

Film   1940   U.S. (Universal)   67 minutes
Black & white

Universal's low-budget follow-up to THE MUMMY (1932) brought forth a new mummy called Kharis. Not only buried alive, Kharis also had his tongue cut out for stealing some valuable tana leaves (he had no interest in the Scroll of Thoth). When archaeologists remove the 3000-year-old mummy of the princess Ananka, high priest George Zucco revives Kharis with some tana-leaf tea and takes him along to America so that he can return her body to the Hill of Seven Jackals. Given superhuman strength by heavy doses of the stuff, Kharis has several good scenes murdering some startled New Englanders before being destroyed by fire. Played by cowboy actor Tom Tyler in his one and only monster role (remember Glenn Strange as the Frankenstein Monster?), Kharis was brought back for three more go-arounds, with Lon Chaney, Jr., in the role: THE MUMMY'S TOMB (1942), THE MUMMY'S GHOST (1944) and THE MUMMY'S CURSE (1944).

CREDITS

Director Christy Cabanne; *Producer* Ben Pivar; *Screenplay* Griffin Jay, Maxwell Shane; *Story* Griffin Jay; *Photographer* Elwood Bredell; *Art Directors* Jack Otterson, Ralph M. De Lacy; *Makeup* Jack Pierce

CAST

Tom Tyler, Dick Foran, Peggy Moran, George Zucco, Eduardo Ciannelli, Wallace Ford, Cecil Kellaway

THE MUMMY'S SHROUD

Film   1966   G.B. (Hammer)   84 minutes
Color

The corpse of a former palace guard goes on a vengeful grope when the remains of the pharaoh and his wife are disturbed. Hammer sent its Mummy back to the tomb forever after this tattered and musty third outing, which, at the very least, had a winning advertising slogan: "Beware the beat of the cloth-wrapped feet!" The studio's next mummy feature, BLOOD FROM THE MUMMY'S TOMB, offered a refreshing variation on the theme by reviving an Egyptian princess in her full unearthly beauty.

CREDITS

Director/Screenplay John Gilling; *Producer* Anthony Nelson Keys; *Story* John Elder (Anthony Hinds); *Photographer* Arthur Grant; *Production Designer* Bernard

The Mummy's Shroud: Roger Delgado, as a direct descendant of a pharoah's personal guard, attempts to revive the remains of a former monarch.

Robinson; *Special Effects* Bowie Films; *Makeup* George Partleton; *Music* Don Banks

CAST

John Phillips, Elizabeth Sellars, Andre Morell, Michael Ripper, Maggie Kimberley, Eddie Powell (the Mummy); *Narrator* Peter Cushing

THE MUMMY'S TOMB

Film   1942   U.S. (Universal)   61 minutes *Black & white*

Lon Chaney, Jr., the world's paunchiest mummy, tries on Karloff's moldy bandages for this second sequel to THE MUMMY (1932), which also begins a new series. Footage from THE MUMMY'S HAND (1940) pads out the short running time, with Kharis being revived by a high priest to murder the archaeologists who previously desecrated his tomb. Stunt man Eddie Parker did all the strenuous work in the Chaney series—each of diminishing quality— and finally got the part in ABBOTT AND COSTELLO MEET THE MUMMY (1955).

CREDITS

Director Harold Young; *Producer* Ben Pivar; *Screenplay* Griffin Jay, Henry Sucher; *Photographer* George Robinson; *Art Director* Jack Otterson; *Makeup* Jack Pierce; *Musical Director* Hans J. Salter

CAST

Lon Chaney, Jr., Elyse Knox, Dick Foran, John Hubbard, Turhan Bey, George Zucco, Wallace Ford, Eddie Parker

PHARAOH'S CURSE

Film   1956   U.S. (Bel-Air)   66 minutes *Black & white*

Archaeologists disturb an ancient Egyptian tomb and rouse the wrathful spirit of the pharaoh's high priest. Only if you've nothing better to do.

CREDITS

Director Lee Sholem; *Producer* Howard W. Koch; *Screenplay* Richard Landau; *Photographer* William Margulies; *Art Director* Bob Kinoshita; *Special Effects* Jack Rabin, Louis DeWitt; *Makeup* Ted Coodley; *Music* Les Baxter

CAST

Mark Dana, Ziva Shapir, Diane Brewster, Alvaro Guillot, George Neise, Ben Wright

WRESTLING WOMEN VS. THE AZTEC MUMMY

Film   1965   Mexico (Calderon)   88 minutes *Black & white*

The Aztec Mummy, Mexico's own, goes to the mat. Part of a goofy series that includes *Robot vs. the Aztec Mummy* (1959) and *Wrestling Women vs. the Murderous Robot* (1969).

CREDITS

Director Rene Cardona

CAST

Lorena Velasquez, Armand Sylvestre

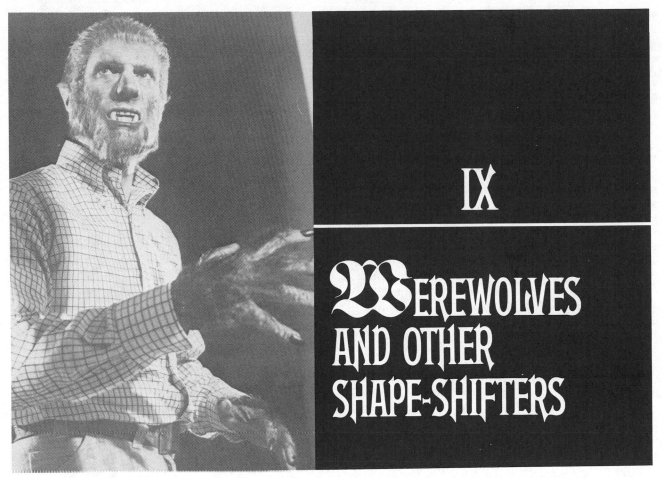

IX

WEREWOLVES AND OTHER SHAPE-SHIFTERS

Moon of the Wolf: Bradford Dillman's creature was more effective on the small screen.

Next to the vampire, werewolf mythology is the most widespread in the world. (The prefix *were* comes from the old Roman word *vir*, which means man.) In countries where there are no wolves, other strange man-beasts have exhibited a craving for human flesh: South American Indians, for example, have were-jaguars, polar Eskimos have were-whales, and the Chinese have were-crocodiles.

The ancient Greeks were one of the first to come up with a werewolf legend. The historian Ovid recounts the story of Lycaeon, the ghoulish king of Arcadia, who served a "hash of human flesh" to his banquet guests and was punished by the god Zeus, who turned him into a wolf. From the ruler's name comes the modern word "lycanthropy," which describes the condition of werewolfism. Habits of werewolves were well-documented in the Middle Ages, when belief in lycanthropy was widespread. Werewolves were thought to be sorcerers in league with Satan, who helped transform them into vicious animals. The legend owes its origins to the fear-

some appearance and savage cunning of the wolf, whose predation of shepherds, peasants and travelers made it easy to foster the superstitious belief that a bestial killer was in their midst.

Some werewolves were said to accomplish their bloody attacks by projecting themselves as astral bodies while asleep in their beds, in an occult practice known as doubling. If wounded or killed while searching for human meat in graveyards or a fresher supply on highways, the astral body's wounds were duplicated on the sleeper. Others were thought to make the transformation by turning their skins inside out to expose a lining of fur between skin and muscle. The belief in this manifestation was so widespread that during a werewolf scare in Europe in the late 16th century thousands of suspects were skinned alive in a futile search for wolf hairs.

Unlike the vampire, the werewolf is very much alive—although after his death he may go on to become a vampire as punishment for his crimes. Lycanthropy can have many causes, including

211

drinking water from a bewitched spring, wearing clothing that had belonged to a werewolf and, of course, having been bitten by one. The transformation always takes place at night and reverses itself at dawn, just as the vampire has to return to his tomb at sunrise. Werewolves can only be killed by a silver blade or bullet, and not necessarily wielded by a loved one as in the classic movie, THE WOLF MAN (1941).

The werewolf, surprisingly, had rarely turned up in literature, and the only two works of note are *The Were-Wolf* (1890), a Gothic thriller by Clemence Housman, the sister of poet A.E. Housman, and Guy Endore's *The Werewolf of Paris* (1933), a tale of psychological distortion with strong Freudian overtones. Author Endore contributed to the scripts of two horror films: MAD LOVE (1935) and THE DEVIL DOLL (1936) (see Mad Scientists). Having no literary tradition to draw on, Universal studios relied on the old Balkan legends and invented some of their own when they initially brought the creature to the screen in THE WEREWOLF OF LONDON (1935). The filmic model has a symbolic kinship with Robert Louis Stevenson's *Dr. Jekyll and Mr. Hyde*, in which the amoral, animalistic part of man's evolutionary heritage emerges and reasserts its original shape. Most other movie shape-shifters adhered to this model when they changed into various wild animals, ranging from panthers to snakes.

Werewolf movies declined in quality after the subgenre was co-opted by Hollywood's poverty row studios in the 1940s, but the creature periodically returns with new vigor, as in Hammer's CURSE OF THE WEREWOLF (1961) and, more recently, in THE HOWLING (1981) and AN AMERICAN WEREWOLF IN LONDON (1980), two witty but terrifying outings that show the most convincing transformations yet.

THE ALLIGATOR PEOPLE

Film   1959   U.S. (20th Century-Fox)
74 minutes   Black & white   Anamorphic

Typical science fantasy kitsch from the 1950s, with a biologist developing a serum to grow limbs for amputees which has reptilian side effects. For a change, the doctor isn't a conscienceless maniac.

CREDITS

Director Roy Del Ruth; *Producer* Jack Leewood; *Screenplay* O.H. Hampton; *Story* O.H. Hampton, Charles O'Neal; *Photographer* Karl Struss; *Art Director* Lyle R. Wheeler; *Makeup* Ben Nye, Dick Smith; *Music* Irving Gertz

CAST

George Macready, Bruce Bennett, Lon Chaney, Jr., Beverly Garland, Freda Inescort

ALTERED STATES

Film   1980   U.S. (Warner Bros.)   103 minutes
Technicolor   Panavision   Dolby Stereo

Harvard psycho-physiologist William Hurt attempts to plug into his genetic memory bank by tripping out with peyote buds and immersing himself for long hours in an isolation tank filled with water. The experiment eventually transforms him into his Neanderthal self, and, looking something like the Incredible Hulk, he strips off his clothes and begins ripping the neighbors' throats and generally misbehaving. Director Ken Russell gives *Dr. Jekyll and Mr. Hyde* a wild spin that doesn't amount to much, but the shape-shifting effects—by Dick Smith and Bran Ferren—are exciting, and they take place before your very eyes. The late Paddy Chayefsky, who wrote both the novel and the script, was displeased with Russell's direction and had his name removed from the credits.

CREDITS

Director Ken Russell; *Producer* Howard Gottfried; *Screenplay* Sidney Aaron (Paddy Chayefsky); *Photographer* Jordan Cronenweth; *Visual Effects* Bran Ferren; *Makeup Effects* Dick Smith, Craig Fullerton; *Production Designer* Richard McDonald; *Music* John Corigliano

CAST

William Hurt, Blair Brown, Bob Balaban, Charles Haid, Thaao Penghlis, Charles White Eagle

AN AMERICAN WEREWOLF IN LONDON

Film   1981   G.B. (Universal)   97 minutes
Technicolor

Rick Baker brought a new realism to special effects makeup in this updating of the werewolf legend, and for his troubles won the first Academy Award given in that category. Rewarding as both a parody of the sub-genre and as straight horror, the film has two young American tourists wisecracking their way through a tour of the English countryside. Disregarding a pentagram scrawled on a pub wall, and warnings to stay off the moors at night,

An American Werewolf in London: Lycanthrope David Naughton covers himself with stolen balloons after waking up naked.

they find themselves, of course, on the moors on the night of a full moon.

Jack (Griffin Dunne) is killed by the werewolf but David (David Naughton) survives the savage mauling and becomes a werewolf. While David is convalescing in the care of a beautiful nurse (Jenny Agutter), Jack pays him a visit and explains the rules of werewolfdom. Now a mouldering corpse condemned to walk the earth until the werewolf's line is broken, Jack is still as witty as ever and comments on the fickleness of his girlfriend at his funeral. The transformation effects are accompanied by several versions of the pop standard "Blue Moon" and are shown in tight close-up. For all their wonder, these are held a bit too long, giving the viewer time to think about the mechanics of the effect. But this is a minor flaw in an otherwise engaging and suspenseful movie.

CREDITS

Director/Screenplay John Landis; *Producers* Peter Guber, Jon Peters; *Photographer* Robert Paynter; *Special Effects Makeup* Rick Baker; *Music* Creedence Clearwater Revival, Elmer Bernstein

CAST

David Naughton, Griffin Dunne, Jenny Agutter, John Woodvine

THE APE MAN

G.B. title: Lock Your Doors

Film   1943   U.S. (Monogram)   64 minutes *Black & white*

One of Lugosi's numerous duds, concerning a researcher who becomes his own guinea pig and turns into a furry-muzzled primitive. RETURN OF THE APE MAN, a sequel of sorts, was made the following year.

CREDITS

Director William Beaudine; *Producers* Sam Katzman, Jack Dietz; *Screenplay* Barney A. Sarecky, based on the story "They Creep in the Dark" by Karl Brown; *Photographer* Mack Stengler; *Art Director* David Milton; *Musical Director* Edward Kay

CAST

Bela Lugosi, Wallace Ford, Louise Currie, Henry Hall, Minerva Urecal

THE BEAST MUST DIE

Film   1974   G.B. (BL/Amicus)   93 minutes *Technicolor*

Amicus fired a blank when it attempted to mate *And Then There Were None* with THE MOST DANGEROUS GAME (see Crazies and Freaks) and spawn a werewolf movie. Setting is the isolated mansion of a black big-game hunter who invites several people down for the weekend, knowing that one of them is a lycanthrope. There's an interesting werewolf trap, several gory deaths and a "guess who" break near the finale. The plot's nominal source is James Blish's "There Shall Be No Darkness."

CREDITS

Director Paul Annett; *Producer* Milton Subotsky; *Screenplay* Michael Winder, based on a James Blish story; *Photographer* Jack Hildyard; *Music* Douglas Gamley

CAST

Calvin Lockhart, Peter Cushing, Anton Diffring, Charles Gray, Marlene Clark, Ciaran Madden

BELA LUGOSI MEETS A BROOKLYN GORILLA

G.B. title: The Monster Meets a Gorilla

Film   1952   U.S. (Jack Broder)   75 minutes
Black & white

A mad scientist creates an ape man while playing straight man to a pair of unfunny burlesque comedians. Worth mentioning only for the presence of erstwhile horror star Bela Lugosi.

CREDITS

Director William Beaudine; *Producer* Maurice Duke; *Associate Producer* Herman Cohen; *Screenplay* Tim Ryan; *Photographer* Charles Van Enger; *Art Director* James Sullivan; *Music* Richard Hazard

CAST

Bela Lugosi, Sammy Petrillo, Duke Mitchell, Charlita, Muriel Landers, Milton Newberger

THE BLOOD BEAST TERROR

U.S. title: The Vampire-Beast Craves Blood

Film   1967   G.B. (Tigon)   88 minutes
Eastmancolor

A blood beast yes, a vampire no; specifically, a young beauty capable of transforming herself into a giant death's-head moth, the creation of a Victorian entomologist. Lots of bloodletting and often pretty scary, but the low-budget makeup ruins it.

CREDITS

Director Vernon Sewell; *Producer* Arnold L. Miller; *Screenplay* Peter Bryan; *Photographer* Stanley A. Long; *Art Director* Wilfred Wood; *Special Effects* Roger Dicken; *Makeup* Rosemarie Peattie; *Music* Paul Ferris

CAST

Peter Cushing, Robert Flemyng, Wanda Ventham, David Griffin, Vanessa Howard, John Paul

THE BOY WHO CRIED WEREWOLF

Film   1973   U.S. (Universal/RFK)   93 minutes
Color

A young boy is the only one who believes that daddy is the werewolf terrorizing a summer community. More amusing than scary, especially when scriptwriter Homel attempts to relate lycanthropy to the "me" generation. Best scene: The werewolf tangles with superstitious hippie cultists encamped in a forest.

CREDITS

Director Nathan H. Juran; *Producer* Aaron Rosenberg; *Screenplay* Bob Homel; *Photographer* Michael P. Joyce; *Makeup* Tom Burman; *Music* Ted Stowall

CAST

Kerwin Mathews, Elaine Devry, Scott Sealey, Robert J. Wilke, Susan Foster, Jack Lucas

THE BRIDE AND THE BEAST

Film   1957   U.S. (Allied Artists)   78 minutes
Black & white

A young couple big-game hunting in Africa face a compatibility crisis when the wife regresses into her prehistoric self and runs off in search of her own kind. One of horrordom's all-time stinkers, and absurdly hilarious!

CREDITS

Director/Producer/Story Adrian Weiss; *Screenplay* Edward D. Wood, Jr.; *Photographer* Roland Price; *Special Effects* Gerald Endler; *Makeup* Harry Thomas; *Music* Les Baxter

CAST

Lance Fuller, Charlotte Austin, Steve Calvery, Johnny Roth, William Justine

LA CASA DEL TERROR/The House of Terror

U.S. title: Face of the Screaming Werewolf

Film   1959   Mexico (Diana)   78 minutes
Black & white

El cheapo beans from south of the border featuring, can you believe, a mummy that turns into a werewolf. It's decorated with partially nude females, slapstick gore, corny gags and the embarrassing presence of Lon Chaney, Jr.

CREDITS

Director/Screenplay Gilberto Martinez Solares; *Screenplay* Gilberto Martinez Solares, Fernando de Fuentes;

Photographer Raul Martinez Solares; *Music* Luis Hernandez

CAST

Lon Chaney, Jr., Landa Varle, Raymond Gaylord, D.W. Barron, German "Tin-Tan" Valdes, Agustin Fernandez

THE CAT CREATURE

TV film   1973   U.S. (Screen Gems)
73 minutes   Color

A fan letter to the old Val Lewton B-unit of the 1940s from pros Curtis Harrington and Robert Bloch. The story is a weak witch's brew, but it's a pleasure to see Hollywood's vintage horror players assembled for a class reunion. Gale Sondergaard, off the screen for many years after being black-listed in the 1950s, plays an ancient cat goddess disguised as a mysterious shopkeeper. She's after an amulet stolen from the mummy of an Egyptian princess, and anyone who interferes gets dealt with by one of her mesmerized tabbies. Also present, in cameo roles, are John Carradine, Keye Luke (Charlie Chan's no. one son), Peter Lorre, Jr., and Kent Smith, to remind us of CAT PEOPLE (1942). MGM's Academy-Award winning photographer Charles Rosher was coaxed out of retirement to shoot the film.

CREDITS

Director Curtis Harrington; *Producer* Douglas S. Cramer; *Screenplay* Robert Bloch; *Story* Douglas S. Cramer, Wilford Lloyd Baumes, Robert Bloch; *Photographer* Charles Rosher; *Music* Leonard Rosenman

CAST

Meredith Baxter, David Hedison, Gale Sondergaard, John Carradine, Stuart Whitman, Kent Smith, Keye Luke, Peter Lorre, Jr.

CAT PEOPLE

Film   1942   U.S. (RKO)   73 minutes
Black & white

Producer Val Lewton inaugurated his modest series of B chillers with this unsettling mood piece. Simone Simon is a Serbian-born woman living in Manhattan who fears she will turn into a panther and kill those she loves. Director Jacques Tourneur emulates the great Fritz Lang in avoiding the standard human-into-beast transformation, according to the dictum that nothing the camera can show is as horrible as what the mind can imagine. The story's subtext of sexual repression and sexual-ancestral fears is so understated by today's standards that the effect is dissipated, but Tourneur's

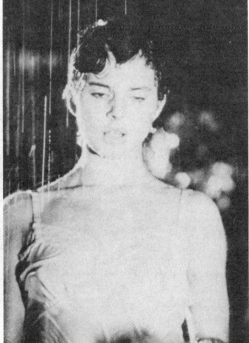

Cat People: Simone Simon (with Tom Conway) is the cat-woman in the Val Lewton original. Nastassia Kinski played the role in the 1982 remake.

use of shadows and distorted sounds to convey unseen terrors is masterful. Especially potent are scenes in which a woman is chased through Central Park by a hidden, snarling horror, and a deserted basement swimming pool is invaded by a similarly nameless beast.

The Curse of the Cat People (1944) is neither a sequel nor a horror film. Except for one scary sequence, the film is a fairy tale focusing on the fertile imagination of a six-year-old girl. Wistful and ambiguous, the film concerns the lonely daughter of the cat woman who dreams up a protective and understanding friend (played by Simone Simon, the original cat woman). Robert Wise directed DeWitt Bodeen's screenplay, and Kent Smith co-starred.

CREDITS

Director Jacques Tourneur; *Producer* Val Lewton; *Screenplay* DeWitt Bodeen; *Photographer* Nicholas Musuraca; *Art Directors* Albert D'Agostino, Walter E. Keller; *Music* Roy Webb

CAST

Simone Simon, Kent Smith, Tom Conway, Jane Randolph, Jack Holt, Alan Napier, Elizabeth Dunne

CAT PEOPLE

Film 1982 U.S. (Universal) 117 minutes
Color

Paul Schrader radically altered Val Lewton's *Cat People* (1942) in this expensive remake, set in New Orleans, and it flopped with critics and audiences alike. Nastassia Kinski (daughter of Klaus) is Irena, brother of the creepy Paul (Malcolm McDowell), whose ancestors mated with black leopards and left behind a family curse. Sexual passion turns them into cat people, so they can safely sleep only with each other. Into this incestuous menage steps John Heard's fearless zookeeper, who falls in love with Irena and decides that a night of love is worth the inevitable outcome. Sluggish and obscure, the film has an air of unintended camp, relieved occasionally by some lively gore (a human arm pops out a panther's innards during an autopsy; another human arm is ripped out its socket). The script is by Alan Ormsby, better known among cultists for CHILDREN SHOULDN'T PLAY WITH DEAD THINGS (1972) (see Zombies).

CREDITS

Director Paul Schrader; *Producer* Charles Fries; *Screenplay* Alan Ormsby; *Photographer* John Bailey; *Visual*

Consultant Ferdinando Scarfiotto; *Special Effects Makeup* Tom Burman; *Special Effects* Albert Whitlock; *Music* Giorgio Moroder, David Bowie

CAST

Nastassia Kinski, Malcolm McDowell, John Heard, Annette O'Toole, Ruby Dee, Ed Begley, Jr.

The Catman of Paris: Gerald Mohr's "werecat" doesn't have a chance against Lenore Aubert.

THE CATMAN OF PARIS

Film 1946 U.S. (Republic) 65 minutes
Black & white

A perfectly valid shape-shifting but not a very good one. Republic's paw prints lead back to THE WEREWOLF OF LONDON (1935) and RKO's CAT PEOPLE (1942). Given a scant transformation scene and a minimum of screen time, the beast is, in the words of a contemporary *New York Times* reviewer, "more to be pitied than feared."

CREDITS

Director Lesley Selander; *Producer* Marek V. Libkov; *Screenplay* Sherman L. Lowe; *Photographer* Reggie Lanning; *Special Effects* Howard and Theodore Lydecker; *Music* Dale Butt

CAST

Carl Esmond, Lenore Aubert, Adele Mara, Douglass Dumbrille, Gerald Mohr, Robert J. Wilke

CRY OF THE WEREWOLF

Film   1944   U.S. (Columbia)   65 minutes
Black & white

During the mid-1940s Hollywood turned tail in a succession of spinoff movies that had women becoming werewolves and men becoming cat people. First came *Cry of the Werewolf*, with Nina Foch as an unlikely gypsy queen named Celeste LaTour, inheriting the curse from her mother. Unfortunately, there wasn't enough money for on-camera transformation scenes, or much else. Its inspiration was obviously CAT PEOPLE (1942), which also bred THE LEOPARD MAN (1943) and THE CATMAN OF PARIS (1946). In 1946 Universal changed its copyrighted lycanthrope into the *She-Wolf of London*, with June Lockhart (later to become Lassie's TV "mother") hyperventilating under Jean Yarbrough's pedestrian direction as a young woman who thinks she's committing ghastly murders in Hyde Park. Probably forgotten at the time was the fact that the screen's original wolf-person was a woman. In *The Werewolf* (1913), based on an old Navajo legend, she returns from death as a wolf to find the man who killed her sweetheart.

CREDITS

Director Henry Levin; *Producer* Wallace MacDonald; *Screenplay* Griffin Jay, Charles O'Neal; *Story* Griffin Jay; *Photographer* L.W. O'Connell; *Musical Director* Mischa Bakaleinikoff

CAST

Nina Foch, Stephen Crane, Osa Massen, Blanche Yurka, Barton MacLane, Ivan Triesault

CULT OF THE COBRA

Film   1955   U.S. (Universal-International)
82 minutes   Black & white

Faith Domergue, a minor cult figure herself, is a mysterious young woman keeping company with a group of ex-GIs who desecrated a snake ritual in the Orient during World War II. When the men begin dropping dead, autopsies reveal the cause to be snake venom. The culprit—a "queen" cobra—is shown only at the finale, when it gets thrown out a high window into the street and makes a flashy transformation into Domergue. Best moments are when the snake is about to strike—indicated by filming from its viewpoint, a technique used previously in the studio's *It Came from Outer Space*. But mostly the film is heavy going and not the camp delight its title would suggest. The idea resurfaced in THE SNAKE WOMAN (1960), THE REPTILE (1966), and *Night of the Cobra* (1972), a Filipino production remarkable only for the names of its stars: Joy Bang and Slash Marks.

CREDITS

Director Francis D. Lyons; *Producer* Howard Pine; *Screenplay* Jerry Davis, Cecil Maiden, Richard Collins; *Photographer* Russell Metty; *Art Director* Alexander Golitzen; *Music* Joseph Gershenson

CAST

Faith Domergue, Marshall Thompson, David Janssen, Richard Long, Kathleen Hughes

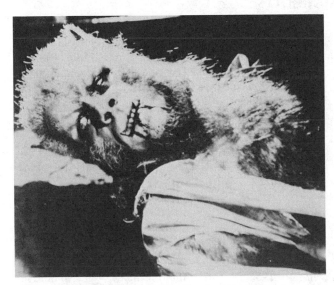

The Curse of the Werewolf: That's Oliver Reed inside the monkey fur.

CURSE OF THE WEREWOLF

Film   1961   G.B. (Hammer/Universal-International)   92 minutes   Technicolor

Hammer's solo werewolf outing is an intelligent reworking of Guy Endore's definitive lycanthropy novel *The Werewolf of Paris* (1933). The setting has been shifted to 1830s' Spain, where a servant girl raped by a vagrant gives birth to an infant marked by an ominous black patch of hairs on his arm. Raised by loving adoptive parents, the boy doesn't become fully aware of his monstrous potential until rejected by the girl he loves. Writer/producer Hinds pays respectful attention to the lycanthrope's folkloric traits, and carefully delineates the psychology of the afflicted young man. Born on Christmas Eve—the birthdate of werewolves—the boy is about to be plunged into the baptismal font when the holy water begins to boil. At the rousing finale in a church steeple, the werewolf (Oliver Reed) is killed by his own stepfather with a silver bullet forged from the family crucifix.

Although not the definitive werewolf movie Hammer had hoped for (one has yet to be made), the film gives a logic and motivation to a subgenre usually thought of as ludicrous and for children only. Blood and violence are used sparingly—but effectively—and the story is told with a fairy-tale richness that suggests RKO's THE HUNCHBACK OF NOTRE DAME (1939) (see Crazies and Freaks). According to director Fisher, "I consider it to be a tragic love story and not fundamentally a horror story."

CREDITS

Director Terence Fisher; *Producer* Anthony Hinds; *Screenplay* John Elder (Anthony Hinds), based on the novel *The Werewolf of Paris* by Guy Endore; *Photographer* Arthur Grant; *Production Designer* Bernard Robinson; *Special Effects* Les Bowie; *Makeup* Roy Ashton; *Music* Benjamin Frankel

CAST

Oliver Reed, Clifford Evans, Yvonne Romain, Catherine Feller, Anthony Dawson, Michael Ripper, Josephine Llewellyn

DAUGHTER OF DR. JEKYLL

Film   1957   U.S. (Allied Artists)   70 minutes Black & white

Greedy relatives attempt to drive naive Janet Jekyll mad by convincing her she is an after-hours werewolf. A listless, low-grade attempt to enliven the old story with the inane introduction of lycanthropy. Director Ulmer finds some visual gold among the dross.

CREDITS

Director Edgar G. Ulmer; *Producer/Screenplay* Jack Pollexfen; *Photographer* John F. Warren; *Art Director* Theobald Holsopple; *Music* Melvyn Leonard

CAST

Gloria Talbot, John Agar, John Dierkes, Arthur Shields, Martha Wentworth

DR. RENAULT'S SECRET

Film   1942   U.S. (20th Century-Fox) 58 minutes   Black & white

The old man-into-ape trick, accomplished neatly by George Zucco, with J. Carrol Naish adding a touch of pathos to the familiar crossbreed. The film is a low-budget, sound remake of Fox's THE WIZARD (1927) (see Mad Scientists).

CREDITS

Director Harry Lachman; *Producer* Sol M. Wurtzel; *Screenplay* William Bruckner, Robert F. Metzler; *Photographer* Virgil Miller; *Art Directors* Nathan H. Juran, Richard Day; *Music* David Raskin, Emil Newman

CAST

J. Carrol Naish, George Zucco, John Shepperd (Shepperd Strudwick), Lynne Roberts, Bert Roach

THE HOWLING

Film   1981   U.S. (Avco Embassy)   91 minutes Color

This is the lesser of two entertaining werewolves who emerged from hibernation in 1981, the other being AN AMERICAN WEREWOLF IN LONDON. John Sayles's campy screenplay has a pretty Los Angeles reporter going for a rest at a clinic, which happens to be a club for werewolf swingers. The double-entendre title also refers to the noise werewolves make while coupling (we get to see a furry couple making love, surely a genre first). Sayles, who wrote *Piranha* for Roger Corman's New World Productions and directed his own Academy-Award nominated *The Return of the Secaucus Seven* (1980), apparently means *The Howling* as a tribute to Corman, Hollywood's great nurturer of unsung talent. Corman himself appears in a walk-on, along with Dick Miller, Walter Paisley of Corman's spoofy A BUCKET OF BLOOD (1959) (see Crazies and Freaks), playing his original character. Also on hand are horror staples John Carradine and Kevin McCarthy doing a reprise of the ending of INVASION OF THE BODY SNATCHERS (1956) (see Cataclysmic Disasters).

Highlight of the film is the incredible transformation effect devised by Rob Bottin (in consultation with Rick Baker of the other werewolf movie). The transformation begins with a throbbing at the temples, followed by jaws elongating before your very eyes, along with hair and fingernails. Once completed, however, the makeup seems less impressive than how it was achieved, especially so since the creatures are played as buffoons.

CREDITS

Director Joe Dante; *Producers* Michael Finnell, Jack Conrad; *Screenplay* John Sayles, Terence H. Winkless, based on the novel by Gary Brandner; *Photographer* John Hora; *Art Director* Robert A. Burns; *Special Effects Makeup* Rob Bottin; *Makeup Consultant* Rick Baker; *Music* Pino Donaggio; *Songs* Rick and Joyce Fienhage, Chris Charney

CAST

Dee Wallace, Patrick Macnee, Dennis Dugan, Christopher Stone, Belinda Balaski, Kevin McCarthy, John Carradine, Slim Pickens, Kenneth Tobey, Dick Miller, The Round Oak String Band

The Howling: Christopher Stone undergoes a startling on-screen transformation

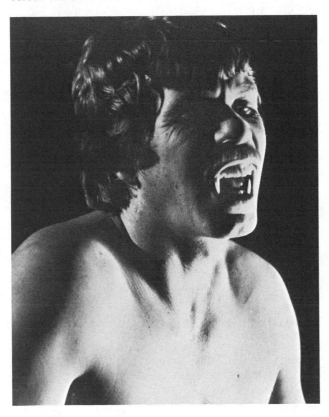

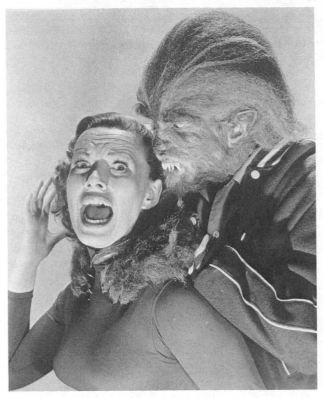

I Was a Teenage Werewolf: Michael Landon's contribution to movie camp. His victim is Dawn Richard.

I WAS A TEENAGE WEREWOLF

*Film   1957   U.S. (AIP)   76 minutes
Black & white*

As absurd now as then—as it was intended to be—this incredibly cheapie film pointed AIP in the direction of horror and launched a flotilla of 1950s teen movies with an anti-establishment theme (later, and more subtly, incorporated into some of Corman's Poe films). More interesting for its reflection of a social trend than for its genre manipulations, the film was the brainchild of 29-year-old producer Herman Cohen, who had read a poll indicating that 70 percent of moviegoers were between 12 and 25 years old. Then coming of age, war babies were groping for their own identities to the anarchic beat of rock and roll and becoming increasingly disaffiliated from their infuriated elders. Wealthier than any previous generation of kids, they represented a vast market that was making its power known via the entertainment industry.

Cohen, taking a cue from such recent song hits as "Teen Angel," concluded that his title could hardly fail at the box office. And he was right. Adolescent audiences relished the film's rebel hero, a juvenile delinquent in the making, misunderstood by parents and teachers alike, who, instead of trying to understand, sent him to a quack psychiatrist. Michael Landon, then in his James Dean period, reverted to his primeval werewolf self under hypnosis, terrorizing grinds and debs in his letter jacket whenever the school bell rang. Played with camp seriousness, the film was both an iconoclastic send-up and a terrifying monster movie of a type not seen since the 1940s. Much of the werewolf's wide appeal undoubtedly had to do with the vicarious thrills he offered revenge-minded students and class straight-arrows, who both saw the story as an object lesson in who and where not to be.

The film took in $2,500,000 on a $150,000 investment, and Cohen followed with I WAS A TEENAGE FRANKENSTEIN (1957) (see Monsters) and BLOOD OF DRACULA (1957) (see Vampires). For a more knowing spoof of the genre, see AN AMERICAN WEREWOLF IN LONDON (1981).

CREDITS

Director Gene Fowler, Jr.; *Producer* Herman Cohen; *Screenplay* Ralph Thornton; *Photographer* Joseph La-Shelle; *Art Director* Leslie Thomas; *Music* Paul Dunlap, Jerry Blain

CAST

Michael Landon, Whit Bissell, Yvonne Lime, Tony Marshall, Dawn Richard, Barney Phillips, Ken Miller, Eddie Marr

INVASION OF THE BEE GIRLS

Film   1973   U.S. (Sequoia)   85 minutes
Color

While experimenting with radioactivity, female scientists in a research lab alter their chromosomes and turn into sexually hungry queen bees who mate their way through a number of unlucky males. Writer Nicholas Meyer, who later scored as a director with *Time After Time* and *Star Trek II*, plays the story for laughs and often succeeds.

CREDITS

Director Denis Sanders; *Screenplay* Nicholas Meyer; *Photographer* Gary Graver; *Special Effects* Joe Lombardi; *Music* Chuck Bernstein

CAST

William Smith, Victoria Vetri, Anitra Ford, Cliff Osmond, Ben Hammer, Wright King

LEGEND OF THE WEREWOLF

Film   1974   G.B. (Tyburn)   90 minutes
Color

The usually dependable Freddie Francis directed this fangless rehash, set in the Paris zoo, where an attendant raised by wolves turns into one. Shots of the real thing are more terrifying.

CREDITS

Director Freddie Francis; *Producer* Kevin Francis; *Screenplay* John Elder (Anthony Hinds); *Photographer* John Wilcox; *Art Director* Jack Shampan; *Special Effects* Charles Staffell; *Makeup* Jimmy Evans, Graham Freeborn; *Music* Harry Robinson

CAST

Peter Cushing, Ron Moody, David Rintoul, Hugh Griffith, Roy Castle

THE LEOPARD MAN

Film   1943   U.S. (RKO)   66 minutes
Black & white

Another goosepimply understatement from the Lewton team. The story is a murder mystery with a Jack the Ripper theme, pivoted on a reporter investigating a rash of savage murders which appear to have been committed by a leopard. The killer turns out to be not a shape-shifter but a psychotic suffering from the mental aberration of lycanthropy (a rare but real form of insanity, according to anthropologists). Although not in a class with Lewton's CAT PEOPLE (1942), the film has its share of memorable moments: a woman hurrying along a deserted nighttime street, sensing she is being followed, startled by a clangorous garbage can lid; an unseen woman being viciously mauled, revealed by blood flowing under a closed door.

CREDITS

Director Jacques Tourneur; *Producer* Val Lewton; *Screenplay* Ardel Wray, based on the novel *Black Alibi* by Cornell Woolrich; *Photographer* Robert de Grasse; *Art Directors* Albert D'Agostino, Walter E. Keller; *Music* Roy Webb

CAST

Dennis O'Keefe, Margo, Jean Brooks, James Bell, Isabell Jewell, Margaret Landry

LYCANTHROPUS

U.S. title: Werewolf in a Girl's Dormitory

G.B. title: I Married a Werewolf

Film   1961   Italy/Austria (Royal)   84 minutes Black & white

Silly, badly dubbed murder mystery concerning a series of grisly murders at a girl's school, where every member of the staff falls under suspicion. (Turns out the superintendent is a wolf man.) The real wolves howling in a nearby forest are more frightening than the sad, debased werewolf depicted here. Theme song is a would-be hit titled "The Ghoul in School."

CREDITS

Director Richard Benson (Paolo Heusch); *Producer* Jack Forrest; *Screenplay* Julian Berry; *Photographer* George Patrick; *Art Director* Peter Travers; *Music* Francis Berman

CAST

Carl Schell, Barbara Lass, Maurice Marsac, Curt Lowens, Maureen O'Connor, Alan Collins

THE MAD MONSTER

Film   1942   U.S. (PRC)   77 minutes Black & white

Glenn Strange, soon to be one of Universal's Frankenstein Monsters, plays an assistant to mad scientist George Zucco, who turns him into a werewolf as the first member of an anti-Nazi army of werewolves. Meanwhile, over at Monogram, a German doctor was putting together a platoon of the "walking dead" to help Hitler in KING OF THE ZOMBIES (see Zombies).

CREDITS

Director Sam Newfield; *Producer* Sigmund Neufield; *Screenplay* Fred Myron; *Special Effects* Gene Stone; *Makeup* Harry Ross; *Music* David Chudnow

CAST

George Zucco, Glenn Strange, Anne Nagel, Henry Hull, Mae Busch, Gordon Demain

THE MAN WHO TURNED TO STONE

Film   1956   U.S. (Columbia)   80 minutes Black & white

Diabolical 200-year-old scientists kidnap and kill young girls to extract a mysterious substance that keeps the old-timers young. Otherwise, they will— and do—turn to stone.

CREDITS

Director Leslie Kardos; *Producer* Sam Katzman; *Screenplay* Raymond T. Marcus; *Photographer* Benjamin H. Kline; *Art Director* Paul Palmentola; *Music* Ross DiMaggio

CAST

Victor Jory, William Hudson, Ann Doran, Paul Cavanaugh, Tina Carver

MASTER MINDS

Film   1949   U.S. (Monogram)   65 minutes Black & white

The Bowery Boys fumble into the laboratory of a nutty doctor who decides to transplant stooge Huntz Hall's brain into the body of his pet ape man. This threadbare burlesque, made when Hollywood's first horror cycle had been played out, offers a convincing creature design by Jack Pierce (see Horror-Makers), creator of Universal's classic monsters. Inside the get-up is Glenn Strange, who wore Pierce's makeup in several Frankenstein movies.

CREDITS

Director Jean Yarbrough; *Producer* Jan Grippo; *Screenplay* Charles R. Marion, Bert Lawrence; *Photographer* Marcel Le Picard; *Makeup* Jack Pierce; *Musical Director* Edward J. Kay

CAST

Leo Gorcey, Gabriel Dell, Huntz Hall, William Benedict, Alan Napier, Glenn Strange

MOON OF THE WOLF

*TV film   1972   U.S. (Filmways)   74 minutes
Color*

Director Petrie pokes through the ashes of Universal's old Wolf Man series and manages to spark a flame or two. His lycanthrope, operating in the misty bayou country of present-day Louisiana, tests its animal cunning against the wiles of a country sheriff. There are some spine-tingling scenes (for television), but you'll probably guess the werewolf's identity long before the fade-out.

CREDITS

Director Daniel Petrie; *Producers* Everett Chambers, Peter Thomas; *Screenplay* Alvin Sapinsley, based on the novel by Leslie H. Whitten; *Photographer* Richard C. Glouner; *Art Director* James G. Hulsey, *Makeup* Tom Tuttle, William Tuttle; *Music* Bernardo Segall

CAST

David Janssen, Barbara Rush, Bradford Dillman, John Beradino, Royal Dano, Claudia McNeil

THE NEANDERTHAL MAN

*Film   1953   U.S. (United Artists)   78 minutes
Black & white*

It's hard to believe that this was made by the same director responsible for the silent masterpiece *Variety* (1925). A cinema oddity, E.A. Dupont left Germany for Hollywood for an undistinguished career that ended with low-budget programmers like this one. In telling the story of a scientist who chemically transforms himself into a prehistoric brute (and his cat into a sabre-toothed tiger), Dupont resorts to the hoariest of monster movie cliches without any understanding of dramatic function. The subject was handled with more originality in ALTERED STATES (1980).

CREDITS

Director E.A. Dupont; *Producers/Screenplay* Aubrey Wisberg, Jack Pollexfen; *Photographer* Stanley Cortez; *Art Director* Walter Koestler; *Special Effects* Jack Rabin; *Music* Albert Glasser

CAST

Robert Shayne, Doris Merrick, Richard Crane, Dick Rich, Robert Long, Jean Quinn

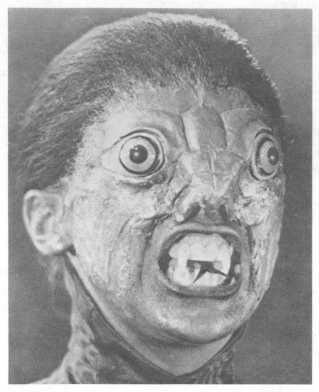

The Reptile: Jacqueline Pearce is a beauty victimized by an old Mayan curse.

THE REPTILE

*Film   1966   G.B. (Hammer)   90 minutes
Technicolor*

Cursed by an arcane Malayan sect, the daughter of a medical researcher turns into a snake from time to time to poison visitors to their remote Cornwall home. Although the makeup isn't entirely convincing and the shocks short-circuit early on, the characterizations are persuasive, and there are several chilling scenes: the girl writhing on a bed to the sinuous song of a Malay servant; her superstitious father frantically thrashing her nightgown, which contains an empty green snakeskin. Director Gilling may have been fatigued by filming THE PLAGUE OF THE ZOMBIES (see Zombies) back-to-back on the same 19th-century sets at the Bray studio.

CREDITS

Director John Gilling; *Producer* Anthony Nelson Keys; *Screenplay* John Elder (Anthony Hinds); *Photographer*

Arthur Grant; *Production Designer* Bernard Robinson; *Special Effects* Bowie Films; *Makeup* Roy Ashton; *Music* Don Banks

CAST

Noel Willman, Jacqueline Pearce, Jennifer Daniel, Ray Barrett, Michael Ripper, John Laurie

RETURN OF THE APE MAN

Film   1944   U.S. (Monogram)   60 minutes
Black & white

A sequel in name only to THE APE MAN (1943), with no plot connection. Lugosi is no longer the ape man but the keeper of frozen Neanderthal John Carradine, into whom he implants a new brain. The composite turns out to be George Zucco, a courtly monster who plays Beethoven's "Moonlight Sonata" on the piano before taking off for a homicidal rampage.

CREDITS

Director Philip Rosen; *Producers* Sam Katzman, Jack Dietz; *Screenplay* Robert Charles; *Photographer* Marcel le Picard; *Art Director* David Milton; *Music* Edward Kay

CAST

Bela Lugosi, George Zucco, John Carradine, Frank Moran, Judith Gibson, Michael Ames

THE SHE-CREATURE

Film   1957   U.S. (AIP)   78 minutes   Color

To prove he can predict murders, an ambitious sideshow hypnotist reverts a female subject to her primeval self and orders her to kill people. Low-budget special effects man Paul Blaisdell is inside the shaggy She-Creature costume.

CREDITS

Director Edward L. Cahn; *Producer* Alex Gordon; *Screenplay* Lou Rosoff; *Story* Jerry Zigmond; *Special Effects* Paul Blaisdell; *Music* Ronald Stein

CAST

Chester Morris, Marla English, Lance Fuller, Tom Conway, Cathy Downs

THE SNAKE WOMAN

Film   1962   G.B. (Caralan)   67 minutes
Black & white

Big-time director Sidney J. Furie was learning the ropes when he slapped together this gloomy nonsense. The title character can turn herself into a snake whenever she gets the itch, thanks to a dose of cobra venom injected into her pregnant mother as an insanity cure. You've never heard of the cast.

CREDITS

Director Sidney J. Furie; *Producer* George Fowler; *Screenplay* Orville Hampton; *Photographer* Stephen Dade; *Art Director* John G. Earl; *Music* Buxton Orr

CAST

Susan Travers, John McCarthy, Geoffrey Danton, Arnold Marle, John Cazabon

THE UNDYING MONSTER

G.B. title: The Hammond Mystery

Film   1942   U.S. (20th Century-Fox)
63 minutes   Black & white

Werewolves were back in business after Universal's THE WOLF MAN (1941), which prompted rival studios to spawn their own hairy beasts. Best of the litter was Fox's *The Undying Monster*, a programmer that belies its lowly origins and offers an object lesson in how to put limited resources to maximum use. The film more or less follows its source, a 1922 novel of the same title by Jessie Douglas Kerruish, an obscure British archaeologist who wrote several popular historical fantasies: A dreadful family curse has manifested itself on successive generations, and a psychic detective discovers that the problem is hereditary lycanthropy.

The action takes place in an ancestral mansion near the Cornwall coast, both stunningly evoked on standing studio sets. Director John Brahm—who would make a name for himself with *The Lodger* (1944), a psychological thriller about Jack the Ripper—plays for undefined terror and keeps the werewolf's appearances to a minimum. The mystery of his identity (he turns out to be one of the stars) was maintained in lobby photos showing a stand-in made-up as the creature. Originally released as a second feature, the film was later paired for genre release with the inferior DR. RENAULT'S SECRET (1942).

CREDITS

Director John Brahm; *Screenplay* Lillie Hayward, Michel Jacoby, based on a novel by Jessie Douglas Kerruish; *Photographer* Lucien Ballard; *Music* Emil Newman, David Raskin

CAST

James Ellison, Heather Angel, John Howard, Bramwell Fletcher, Heather Thatcher

THE WEREWOLF

Film   1956   U.S. (Columbia)   80 minutes
Black & white

Scientists attempting to cure a man exposed to lethal radiation inject an experimental serum that periodically transforms him into a werewolf. An initially suspenseful attempt to bring lycanthropy out of the supernatural that talks its way to tedium long before the predictable ending.

CREDITS

Director Fred F. Sears; *Producer* Sam Katzman; *Screenplay* Robert E. Kent, James B. Gordon; *Photographer* Edwin Linden; *Art Director* Paul Palmentola; *Musical Director* Mischa Bakaleinikoff

CAST

Don Megowan, Steven Ritch, Joyce Holden, Kim Charney, Eleanore Tanin

THE WEREWOLF OF LONDON

Film   1935   U.S. (Universal)   75 minutes
Black & white

Casting around for a new monster to satisfy the demand created by FRANKENSTEIN (see Monsters), DRACULA (see Vampires) and THE MUMMY (see Mummies), Universal rummaged through old mythology books and revamped a Balkan legend about an obscure flower which, when eaten, could turn a man into a wolf. The story is a sedate variation on DR. JEKYLL AND MR. HYDE (see Mad Scientists), with British botanist Henry Hull being bitten by a werewolf while on expedition in Tibet to collect a rare moonlight-blooming flower. Returning to London, he metamorphoses into a howling animal at the next full moon and kills a woman in the back streets of Soho. Unaware of what he has done—and feeling like an alcoholic with a bad hangover—he learns the truth from a

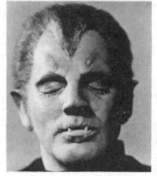

The Werewolf of London: Henry Hull, Hollywood's original werewolf, transformed by Jack Pierce's makeup.

mysterious Japanese named Dr. Yogami (played by Warner Oland of the Charlie Chan films). The good doctor turns out to be the werewolf who bit Hull in Tibet. When Yogami reveals that the only known antidote to the malady is the juice of the *marifasa lupino lumino*, the flower picked by the botanist, the man-beasts fight to the death for the curative drink. The Japanese gets away with the plant, and the ill-fated Hull is killed by a policeman's bullets and reverts to normal human form.

Well-plotted but clumsily acted and by turns suspenseful and tedious, the film at least established the motion picture tradition of the sympathetic werewolf who is more man than animal (and who, incidentally, does not have a tail). Neither Pierce's makeup nor Fulton's special effects are up to their usual standards, allegedly because Hull didn't want his face covered and was impatient with lengthy camera setups. One transformation scene occurs behind an obviously camouflaging series of pillars, allowing the camera to be stopped so that the animal makeup could be applied in stages. The definitive werewolf movie would have to wait for THE WOLF MAN (1941).

CREDITS

Director Stuart Walker; *Producer* Stanley Bergerman; *Screenplay* John Colton; *Story* Robert Harris; *Photographer* Charles Stumar; *Art Director* Albert S. D'Agostino; *Special Effects* John P. Fulton; *Makeup* Jack Pierce

CAST

Henry Hull, Warner Oland, Valerie Hobson, Spring Byington, Lester Matthews, Ethel Griffies

THE WEREWOLF OF WASHINGTON

Film   1973   U.S. (Millco)   90 minutes
Color

On nights of the full moon, a foreign correspondent becomes a werewolf (he was infected on assignment in Transylvania) who stalks Washington's power elite. A fruity, little seen spoof, leavened with political satire, that plays the lycanthropy legend straight and scores a near bull's-eye.

CREDITS

Director, Screenplay Milton Moses Ginsberg; *Producer* Nina Schulman; *Photographer* Bob Baldwin; *Art Director* Nancy Miller-Corwin; *Makeup* Bob Obradovich; *Music* Arnold Freed

CAST

Dean Stockwell, Biff Maguire, Clifton James, Beeson Carroll, Jacqueline Brooks, Thayer David

WEREWOLVES ON WHEELS

Film   1971   U.S. (South Street)   84 minutes
Color

Bikers out on a spree in the California desert take up with a Satanic cult that transforms two of them into werewolves. *Easy Rider* meets *The Wolf Man* on amateur night, and the collision is often hilarious.

CREDITS

Director Michel Levesque; *Producer* Paul Lewis; *Screenplay* David M. Kaufmann, Michel Levesque; *Photographer* Isadore Mankoffsky; *Art Director* Allen Jones; *Music* Don Gere

CAST

Severn Darden, Stephen Oliver, D.J. Anderson, Deuce Berry, Tex Hall, William Gray

THE WOLF MAN

Film   1941   U.S. (Universal)   71 minutes
Black & white

THE WEREWOLF OF LONDON (1935) was a box-office disappointment, so Universal went back to the drawing board and came up with a more

Frankenstein Meets the Wolf Man: Lon Chaney, Jr., the original Wolf Man, rehearses with dog actor Moose.

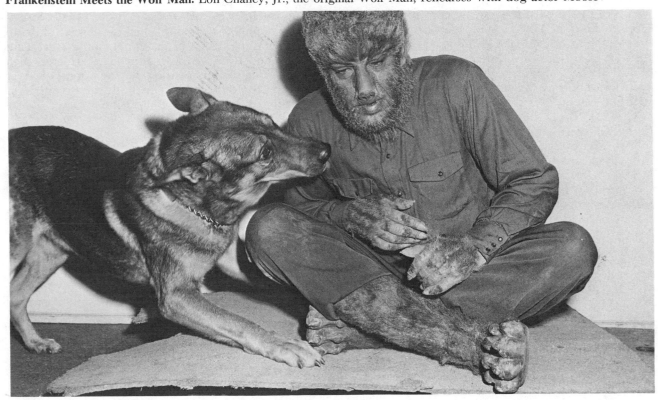

menacing monster. Having no literary model to draw upon, or to get in his way, writer Curt Siodmak defined the canon of movie lycanthropy for all time. The old mysterious flower was discarded in favor of other deterrents, namely a silver bullet or a silver-topped cane wielded by a loved one, and the curse was now manifested by a pentagram appearing in the palm of the hand. But as before, becoming a werewolf, or wolf man (although they had never been called that) was no reflection on one's character. Trembly voiced gypsy Maria Ouspenskaya summed it up in her oft-quoted verse:

Even a man who is pure in heart,
And says his prayers by night,
May become a wolf when the wolfbane blooms,
And the autumn moon is full and bright.

Lon Chaney, Jr. became a major horror star as Larry Talbot, a 26-year-old American college student who visits his ancestral home in Wales and is bitten by a werewolf during a moonlight stroll in the moors. Troubled by dreams that he has killed people, Talbot visits an old gypsy (Ouspenskaya), who explains that he was fanged by her werewolf son (Bela Lugosi) and that he is now one himself. She lays down the ground rules and Talbot begins to dread the coming of the full moon. After the curse drives him to commit several ghastly murders, he confesses to his fiancee and instructs her to stay inside during the next moonlit night. She doesn't, of course, and Talbot's agony is brought to a head, so to speak, when his father (Claude Rains) clubs him with his silver-encrusted cane.

A minor classic, *The Wolf Man* owes much of its success to its superb supporting cast and the ferocious makeup of Jack Pierce, creator of the Frankenstein Monster and the Mummy. Application of the man-beast makeup—far superior to what Pierce had done for *The Werewolf of London*—was a six-hour job requiring Chaney to be fitted with a long wolflike snout of rubber and to have his face covered with yak hair applied a few strands at a time. The remarkable transformation sequences, which reportedly took 22 hours to film, were done in reverse, with Chaney's makeup being removed a little at a time for 21 consecutive shots. Chaney would reposition himself between tiny nails to preserve the film alignment, against draperies that had been starched to remain motionless during the scene. Chaney returned as the Wolf Man in four more films, but never without the support of a stronger monster. These include FRANKENSTEIN MEETS THE WOLF MAN (see Monsters) (1943); HOUSE OF FRANKENSTEIN (1944) (see Monsters); HOUSE OF DRACULA (1945) (see Vampires); and ABBOTT AND COSTELLO MEET FRANKENSTEIN (1948) (see Monsters).

CREDITS

Director/Producer George Waggner; *Screenplay* Curt Siodmak; *Photographer* Joe Valentine; *Art Director* Jack Otterson; *Special Effects* John P. Fulton; *Makeup* Jack Pierce; *Music* Hans J. Salter

CAST

Lon Chaney, Jr., Claude Rains, Evelyn Ankers, Bela Lugosi, Ralph Bellamy, Maria Ouspenskaya, Warren William, Patric Knowles, Fay Helm

WOLFEN

| Film | 1981 | U.S. (Orion) | 115 minutes |
| Technicolor | | Panavision | Dolby Stereo |

Woodstock director Michael Wadleigh, making his feature debut, works up a lot of colorful sound and fury. (Back in 1969 this one would have been called a trip flick.) The plot, adapted from Whitley Strieber's novel, has New York City police detective Albert Finney on the trail of a mysterious murderer who savaged a couple of cocaine-sniffing millionaires in Battery Park. The trail leads to the South Bronx and, eventually, to Brooklyn and a community of American Indians who feel their people have gotten the shaft. A beautifully mounted film, obviously done with care and money, it generates a lot of heat but fails to pay off at the climax. The guilty parties, wolves conjured by or from the Indians (it's never made clear), look like, well, wolves walking down Wall Street. They're only threatening when the camera shifts to their "wolfen" point of view, done on a Steadicam video and transferred to film. The effect, which shows the wolfen reading the emotions of their victims through changes in body temperature, is startling and deserves a better film.

CREDITS

Director Michael Wadleigh; *Producer* Rupert Hitzig; *Screenplay* David Michael Wadleigh, based on the novel by Whitley Strieber; *Photographer* Gerry Fisher; *Art Director* Paul Sylbert; *Special Effects* Robert Blalack, Ronnie Otteson, Conrad Brink; *Makeup* Carl Fullerton; *Animal Technician* George N. Toth; *Sound Effects* Andrew London, Robert Grieve; *Music* James Horner

CAST

Albert Finney, Diane Venora, Edward James Olmos, Gregory Hines, Tom Noonan, Dick O'Neill, Dehl Berti

X

ZOMBIES

I Walked with a Zombie: Jessica (Christine Gordon) has a mysterious illness that has left her speechless and mindless.

Unlike vampires, mummies and other members of the undead, zombies have some basis in fact. Deriving from the occult religion known as voodoo, zombies originated centuries ago on the Caribbean island of Haiti, a country founded on an Afro-slave society. According to superstition, zombies are corpses reanimated by magic spells and potions to provide free labor for sugar cane fields at night and to guard property. Neither inherently evil like vampires nor vengeful like mummies, they are merely docile servants. Anthropologist Francis Huxley speculated that "the folklore surrounding them is partly a reminiscence of plantation days when the Negroes learned to endure forced labor, punishments and whimsical cruelties by acting stupid and not allowing their resentment to show."

A relatively recent addition to the genre, zombies reached Hollywood by way of a highly sensational account of contemporary voodoo in Haiti by William Seabrook in a 1929 book titled *The Magic Island*. Seabrook, who spent a year among the island's voodoo worshippers, claimed that he actually saw the "walking dead" at work in the fields. He described them as remote and mechanical, "with the eyes of a dead man, not blind, but staring, unfocussed, unseeing." As proof that such creatures exist, he cited an article in the Haitian Penal Code that mandates a charge of attempted murder against anyone using "drugs, hypnosis, or any other occult practice which produces lethargic coma or lifeless sleep; if the person has been buried it shall be considered murder no matter what results follow."

After the book's publication, stories began to appear in newspapers and rotogravures certifying the existence of zombies. First to spot the potential of these latent monsters were the independent Halperin brothers, who introduced them to the screen in WHITE ZOMBIE (1932). A major hit, the film lured audiences with lobby posters that included the above quotation from the Penal Code, with the word "zombie" cleverly inserted before "person." From then on, zombies meant only one thing in horror films—animated corpses, usually in

227

the service of a white evildoer. Zombies seemed to be everywhere during the 1930s, even in Orson Welles's 1936 Broadway production of Shakespeare's *Macbeth*, which was set in Haiti and featured a trio of voodoo witches.

In 1942, reporter Inez Wallace wrote a series of newspaper articles titled "I Walked with a Zombie," in which she claimed zombies weren't really dead but had been drugged. (She also pointed out they worked only at night to avoid police inspectors.) The series was purchased by RKO studios, who further compounded the myth in Val Lewton's ambiguous, beautifully wrought movie of the same title. Since then, zombies have become increasingly terrifying and gruesome, a trend that began with George A. Romero's influential NIGHT OF THE LIVING DEAD (1968), in which they developed a ghoulish taste for human flesh.

The truth may be almost as bizarre as fiction, however. In a broadcast of television's *20-20* magazine show in 1985, reporter Geraldo Rivera and a camera crew visited a voodoo ritual in a Haitian jungle purporting to show how zombies are created. As had been cited in previous studies, the condition was inflicted on lawbreakers as a form of native justice. The victims were rubbed with a skin-active potion derived from a pufferfish, which placed them in a deathlike trance. (The elixir, examined by the show's doctors, was found to contain a drug currently used to relax the body during surgery.) The victims were subsequently buried alive for several hours or a day, then exhumed. Most were still alive, but the lack of oxygen resulted in brain damage for many, producing the familiar blank-eyed, feebleminded look we associate with zombies. These of course have no willpower, which is the original Haitian definition of the word "zombie."

CHILDREN SHOULDN'T PLAY WITH DEAD THINGS

Film   1972   U.S. (Major)   101 minutes
Color

For the fun of it, a troupe of fledgling actors stages an occult ritual by lighting candles, rattling their love beads and mumbling incantations. Soon they're knee-deep in flesh-hungry corpses which resemble the zombies of NIGHT OF THE LIVING DEAD (1968). It's a good come-on title, but the film sputters along like an old psychedelic jalopy running out of gas. You're compelled to watch to see if it's going to complete the journey.

CREDITS

Director/Screenplay Benjamin Clark; *Producers* Benjamin Clark, Gary Goch; *Photographer* Jack McGowan; *Art Director* Forest Carpenter; *Makeup* Alan Ormsby; *Music* Carl Zittrer

CAST

Alan Ormsby, Anya Ormsby, Valerie Manches, Jeffrey Gillen, Jane Day, Paul Cronin

CINQUE TOMBE PER UN MEDIUM/ Five Graves for a Medium

U.S. title: Terror-Creatures from the Grave

Film   1965   Italy/U.S. (MBS Cinematografica/ International Entertainment)   90 minutes
Black & white   Anamorphic

Barbara Steele, Europe's favorite scream queen of the 1960s, is always a pleasure to watch, even in a confused genre mixer like this one. Steele plays the wife of a turn-of-the-century ghost, who avenges his murder by recalling 12th-century plague victims from their burial grounds on his villa. Director Pupillo cleverly announces each death with the creaking wheels of an approaching corpse wagon, used to carry away the diseased dead.

CREDITS

Director/Co-producer Ralph Zucker (Massimo Pupillo); *Producer* Frank Merle; *Screenplay* Roberto Natale, Romano Migliorini; *Photographer* Carlo Di Palma; *Music* Aldo Piga

CAST

Barbara Steele, Richard Garret (Ricardo Garrone), Walter Brandt (Walter Brandi), Marilyn Mitchell, Alfred Rice (Alfredo Rizzo), Alan Collins (Luciano Pigozzi)

CREATURE WITH THE ATOM BRAIN

Film   1955   U.S. (Columbia)   69 minutes
Black & white

Sam Katzman, up to his sly old tricks, pulled this mad scientist story out of the studio's files and had it re-dressed for the nuclear age by nimble storyteller Curt Siodmak. The creatures of the misleading title (Katzman thought it read better in the singular) are mindless supermen created by atomic radiation to murder enemies of a convicted gangster. The plot is reminiscent of a series of programmers Karloff made for Columbia, beginning with THE MAN THEY COULD NOT HANG (1939) (see Mad Scientists).

CREDITS

Director Edward L. Cahn; *Producer* Sam Katzman; *Screenplay* Curt Siodmak; *Photographer* Fred Jackman, Jr.; *Musical Director* Mischa Bakeleinikoff

CAST

Richard Denning, Angela Stevens, Michael Granger, S. John Launer, Gregory Gay

DAWN OF THE DEAD

Also titled: Zombie

Film   1979   U.S. (United Film)   125 minutes *Technicolor*

Unlike some of his contemporaries, George A. Romero knew better than to try to top himself with a sequel to his NIGHT OF THE LIVING DEAD (1968). Instead, he opted for an excruciatingly gory black comedy, which piles up the body count to an ingenious new level. Romero's zombie-ghouls are on the move again, rising en masse from their graves and trapping five people inside an antiseptically clean shopping mall outside Pittsburgh. Afflicted with what has been described as "materialism after death," the creatures are determined to get inside, apparently to resume their former buying habits.

The survivors are held prisoner with every creature comfort inside the mall, which is invaded by a motorcycle gang picking off the zombies for fun. Having been instrumental in lowering the barriers against movie violence in his earlier film, Romero is now free to show heads being completely blown off, a zombie sliced into chopped ham by whirling helicopter blades, and full-color closeups of yummy blood feasts. He eventually overdoes it, however, and after the fourth zombie attack the fun and violence aren't much more involving than a video game. Third film in the series is *Day of the Dead*, released in 1985.

CREDITS

Director/Screenplay George A. Romero; *Producer* Richard P. Rubinstein; *Consultant* Dario Argento; *Pho-*

tographer Michael Gornick; *Makeup Effects* Tom Savini; *Explosions* Gary Zeller, Don Berry; *Optical Effects* Exceptional Optics; *Weapons Coordinator* Clayton Hill; *Music* The Goblins

CAST

David Emge, Ken Foree, Scott Reiniger, Gaylen Ross, David Crawford, George A. Romero

THE EARTH DIES SCREAMING

Film   1964   G.B. (Lippert/20th Century-Fox) *62 minutes   Black & white*

Faceless robots from space murder everyone in London and reanimate their pupilless corpses to kill the remaining survivors. This is one of three minor low-budget science fiction thrillers made during the 1960s by Terence Fisher, Hammer's leading horror director. The other two are ISLAND OF TERROR (see Cataclysmic Disasters) and *Night of the Big Heat* (both 1967). The basic plot was previously seen in 1959's THE INVISIBLE INVADERS, which anticipated George Romero's superior NIGHT OF THE LIVING DEAD (1968).

CREDITS

Director Terence Fisher; *Producers* Robert L. Lippert, Jack Parsons; *Screenplay* Henry Cross; *Story* Harry Spaulding; *Makeup* Harold Fletcher; *Music* Elizabeth Lutyens

CAST

Willard Parker, Virginia Field, Dennis Price, Thorley Walters

THE FOUR SKULLS OF JONATHAN DRAKE

Film   1959   U.S. (United Artists)   70 minutes *Black & white*

A good cast sparks this modest occult thriller, which tells the familiar tale of a witch doctor who places a curse on unbelieving foreigners. This time out he has a grand time turning them into shrunken heads to add to his collection in Ecuador.

CREDITS

Director Edward L. Cahn; *Producer* Robert E. Kent; *Screenplay* Orville H. Hampton; *Photographer* Maurey Gertsman; *Art Director* William Glasgow; *Music* Paul Dunlap

CAST

Henry Daniell, Eduard Franz, Valerie French, Paul Cavanagh, Grant Richards

THE GHOST BREAKERS

Film 1940 U.S. (Paramount) 82 minutes
Black & white

A hilarious follow-up to THE CAT AND THE CANARY (see Crazies and Freaks), and its equal in every department. Bob Hope and Paulette Goddard, stars of the earlier film, play a radio performer and an heiress who investigate her haunted castle in Cuba—the site of a buried treasure. The laughs and chills are expertly orchestrated by director Marshall. Best scene: Goddard is chased through dim corridors by pop-eyed zombie Noble Johnson. The script's source is *The Ghost Breaker,* a play by Paul Dickey and Charles W. Gooddard, filmed in 1914 and 1922 and again, less successfully, in 1953 as *Scared Stiff,* a vehicle for comedians Dean Martin and Jerry Lewis.

CREDITS

Director George Marshall; *Producer* Arthur Hornblow, Jr.; *Screenplay* Walter De Leon; *Photographers* Charles Lang, Theodore Sparkuhl; *Process Photography* Farciot Edouart; *Art Directors* Hans Dreier, Robert Usher; *Music* Ernest Hoch

CAST

Bob Hope, Paulette Goddard, Richard Carlson, Paul Lukas, Pedro de Cordoba, Anthony Quinn, Noble Johnson

I EAT YOUR SKIN

Original title: Zombies

Film 1964 U.S. (Iselin/Tenney) 81 minutes
Black & white

Not so spooky doings on a remote Caribbean hideaway, where a mad scientist experimenting with a cure for cancer mindlessly turns human guinea pigs into Hollywood's most unconvincing zombies. Made in 1964, this throwback to poverty row second features of the 1940s finally saw release in 1971 as a companion piece to the far superior I DRINK YOUR BLOOD (see Crazies and Freaks).

CREDITS

Director/Producer/Screenplay Del Tenney; *Associate Producer* Jesse Hartman, Dan Stapleton; *Photographer* Francois Farkas; *Art Director* Robert Verberkmoss; *Makeup* Guy Del Russo; *Music* Lon. E. Norman

CAST

Heather Hewitt, William Joyce, Dan Stapleton, Betty Hyatt Linton, Walter Coy, Robert Stanton

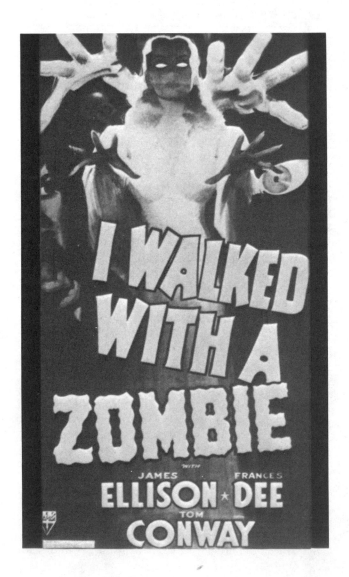

I WALKED WITH A ZOMBIE

Film   1943   U.S. (RKO)   69 minutes
Black & white

One of the great supernatural mood pieces of the cinema, this cult favorite derives from a series of articles written for a Hearst Sunday supplement by Inez Wallace. Initially skeptical, she claimed to have actually seen zombies working as slave labor on a Haitian plantation. Rather than being raised from the dead, however, they were very much alive but had been deprived of their voices and free will by poisonous drugs. Typically, studio brass handed producer Val Lewton the articles and told him to come up with a story to go with the very marketable title. Free to make any movie he wished, Lewton ignored its sensational connotations and opted for a contemporary version of Charlotte Bronte's *Jane Eyre*, set in West Indian voodoo country.

Frances Dee is a private nurse hired by handsome plantation owner Tom Conway to care for his wife, who is suffering from a mysterious illness that has left her mute and in a permanent trance-like state. Her condition has been diagnosed as the result of a prolonged fever, but doctors have been unable to cure her, and natives believe she has been turned into a zombie. In typical Lewton fashion, the film keeps you guessing which diagnosis is true. Like Jane Eyre, the nurse falls in love with her employer, and, to free him of his burden, she takes the woman to a voodoo doctor in the film's heart-pounding climax. Journeying from reason to superstition, the young woman and her charge, clad in spectral white, walk through the sugar plantation, past dangling animal amulets and zombie guards. The scene is nearly silent except for the wind rustling through the reeds, gradually being drowned out by approaching voodoo drums.

Unlike its classic predecessor WHITE ZOMBIE (1932), which believes in zombies, Lewton's film lets you make up your own mind. Paced exquisitely by director Tourneur, the film unravels the motivations of its characters slowly, keeping you slightly off balance while trying to decide if the supernatural is fact or only belief. Adding to the uncanny mood is a calypso score and the amazing Darby Jones as a lofty black zombie you would not want to meet on a dark night.

CREDITS

Director Jacques Tourneur; *Producer* Val Lewton; *Screenplay* Curt Siodmak, Ardel Wray, based on newspaper articles by Inez Wallace; *Photographer* J. Roy Hunt; *Art Directors* Albert D'Agostino, Walter E. Keller; *Music* Roy Webb

CAST

Tom Conway, Frances Dee, James Ellison, Edith Barrett, Christine Gordon, James Bell, Richard Abrams, Teresa Harris, Darby Jones, Sir Lancelot

THE INCREDIBLY STRANGE CREATURES WHO STOPPED LIVING AND BECAME MIXED-UP ZOMBIES

Film   1964   U.S.   Color

Of great historical significance, this neglected exploiter boasts the dual distinction of having the longest title in horror movie history and of being the only movie of any kind shot in "Hypnovision." During its initial run, the film lured in customers with the following poster blurb: "Warning! Unlike Anything Before! You are Surrounded by Monsters! Not 3-D but real FLESH-and-BLOOD Monsters." Once inside, viewers watched a routine story about a fortune-teller who hypnotizes beatniks and turns them into zombies to murder rival carnival beauties. At certain times the action was interrupted by a spiraling "hypnotic" wheel which signaled ushers to put on rubber masks resembling the creatures in the movie, and then to run like hell through the auditorium brandishing cardboard axes. Stars are the ever-lovely Carolyn Brandt and Cash Flagg. Cameramen Laszlo Kovacs and Vilmos Zsigmond worked together again on *Close Encounters of the Third Kind* (1977). Others of the cast and crew have paid us not to be listed.

THE INVISIBLE INVADERS

Film   1959   U.S. (United Artists)   66 minutes
Black & white

This forgotten programmer appeared on drive-in screens nine years before George A. Romero's cult classic NIGHT OF THE LIVING DEAD. The similar plot has a group of people trapped in an isolated house besieged by rather well-fed corpses, animated by the alien force-field that murdered them. Fortunately, blasts of ultra high-frequency sound waves exorcise the cadavers and send the invisible entities on their way to look for another world to conquer. In 1964 Terence Fisher recast the plot for his science fiction thriller THE EARTH DIES SCREAMING.

CREDITS

Director Edward L. Cahn; *Producer* Robert Kent; *Screenplay* Samuel Newman; *Makeup* Phil Scheer; *Special Effects* Roger George

CAST

John Agar, Robert Hutton, John Carradine, Jean Byron, Paul Langton

KING OF THE ZOMBIES

Film   1941   U.S. (Monogram)   68 minutes Black & white

The war years saw a plethora of zombie movies, perhaps because audiences had been conditioned to the idea that human beings could be turned into irresponsible, mindless killers, especially if they were under the thrall of a madman like Adolf Hitler. In this forgotten programmer, a German scientist prepares for Hitler's invasion of America by creating an army of animated corpses from natives and chance visitors to his Caribbean hideaway. John Carradine resumed the experiments in the 1943 sequel *Revenge of the Zombies*, which relocated the lab in the Deep South and had Carradine turning his wife into a zombie to help the cause. Strangely enough, the program was still being implemented as late as 1975 in a movie titled *Shock Waves*, written and directed by Ken Wiederhorn. Former SS officer Peter Cushing, now in possession of the old Caribbean island, spent his days and nights fabricating amphibian Aryan mutants, who popped up from the water like goggled blond Adonises. Also in the cast were Brooke Adam and John Carradine.

CREDITS

Director Jean Yarbrough; *Producer* Linsley Parsons; *Screenplay* Edmund Kelso; *Photographer* Mack Stengler; *Music* Edward Kay

CAST

Dick Purcell, Mantan Moreland, John Archer, Joan Woodbury

THE MAD GHOUL

Film   1943   U.S. (Universal)   65 minutes Black & white

Hollywood's stock mad scientist tampers with the secret of life and comes up with a "death-in-life" gas that works in conjunction with fresh heart transplants to keep the dead from dying. Often effective, with David Bruce adding zest as doctor-turned-zombie.

CREDITS

Director James Hogan; *Producer* Ben Pivar; *Screenplay* Brenda Weisberg, Paul Gangelin; *Story* Hans Kraly; *Photographer* Milton Krasner; *Makeup* Jack Pierce; *Musical Director* Hans Salter

CAST

George Zucco, Evelyn Ankers, Turhan Bey, Milburn Stone, Robert Armstrong, David Bruce

MONSTROSITY

Film   1964   U.S. (Cinema Venture) 70 minutes   Black & white

An old woman with dreams of immortality undergoes a body transplant at the hands of a quack surgeon. The result is a zombie—and this moronic anachronism. The electrical effects are by Ken Strickfaden, creator of the sparks and coils in FRANKENSTEIN (1931) (see Monsters).

CREDITS

Director Joseph Mascelli; *Producers* Jack Pollexfen, Dean Dillman, Jr.; *Screenplay* Vi Russell, Sue Dwiggens, Dean Dillman, Jr.; *Photographer* Alfred Taylor; *Special Effects* Kenneth Strickfaden; *Music* Gene Kauer

CAST

Frank Gerstle, Judy Bamber, Erika Peters, Marjorie Eaton, Frank Fowler

NEITHER THE SEA NOR THE SAND

Film   1972   G.B. (Tigon British)   94 minutes Color

A putrefying zombie kept "alive" by a young woman's love, long after his fatal heart attack, becomes understandably deranged and kills people. An often engrossing oddball hybrid of sentimental romance and horror that reaches for allegory but settles instead for macabre melodrama.

CREDITS

Director Fred Burnley; *Producers* Tony Tenser, Peter J. Thompson; *Screenplay* Gordon Honeycombe, based on his novel; *Photographer* David Muri; *Art Director* Michael Bastow; *Music* Nahum Heiman

CAST

Susan Hampshire, Frank Finlay, Michael Petrovitch, Jack Lambert, Michael Craze, David Garth

NIGHT OF THE LIVING DEAD

Film   1968   U.S. (Reade/Continental)
90 minutes   Black & white

Made to order for local drive-ins, this unheralded landmark movie, shot on a shoestring in Pittsburgh, imposed a cynical new vision on the horror film. Discovered by cult fans, it played on the underground circuit for years, gaining popularity among a generation raised on the nihilism of the Vietnam War, mass murders and assassinations and the Watergate scandal.

Absurd, shoddy and amateurishly acted, the film tells the story of a satellite-carried "radiation" (an explanation brushed aside), which transforms corpses in a cemetery into cannibalistic zombies hungry for the flesh of "normals" trapped in a nearby farmhouse. Where director/photographer George A. Romero departs from tradition is in his breaking of social taboos while mordantly destroying our consoling notions of the world. Characters we have come to identify with commit and suffer

the vilest of brutalities: A dead teen-ager frantically attempts to kill his loving sister; a little zombie girl munches numbly on the corpse of her doting father, devouring him organ by organ. The only survivor, a resourceful black man, is killed by rescuers who mistake him for one of the walking dead.

In Romero's dead society, no one cares about anyone else: Family bonds don't matter, courage is punished, and logic doesn't solve anything. The only response left is either to scream or to laugh. The film provides plenty of opportunities for both.

CREDITS

Director/Photographer George A. Romero; *Producers* Russell Streiner, Karl Hardman; *Screenplay* John A. Russo; *Special Effects* Regis Survinski, Tony Pantanello

CAST

Duane Jones, Russell Streiner, Judith O'Dea, Keith Wayne, Julia Ridley, Karl Hardman, Marilyn Estman

PHANTASM

Film   1978   U.S. (New Breed)   90 minutes
Color

Strange things are happening at the Morningside Mortuary. A voluptuous "lady in lavender" lures

Night of the Living Dead: A girl ghoul munches on human innards in George Romero's seminal film. The zombies returned in color in the sequel **Dawn of the Dead** (right).

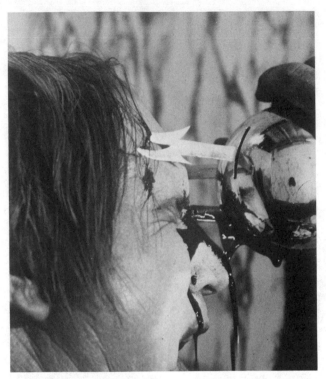

Phantasm: Aliens protect the entrance to their domain with a whirling, brain-eating silver sphere.

men to a nearby cemetery, then rewards them with a stiletto once the act of love is completed. The funerals, of course, are held in the mortuary. Guarding the embalming room is a silver sphere that darts through the air, homing in on intruders with spinning razor-sharp daggers. The corpses— gasp!—are being dwarfed and revived and shipped to another dimension for slave labor.

Former UCLA film student Don Coscarelli handled most of the creative chores on this unsteady but imaginative tomfoolery. The shocks arrive too abruptly for full impact, but he has a sure instinct for combining horror with humor: When a hacked-off finger metamorphoses into a tiny demon, it's destroyed by the only means immediately available—a kitchen garbage disposal.

CREDITS

Director/Producer/Screenplay/Photographer/Editor Don Coscarelli; *Special Effects* Paul Pepperman, Lorane Mitchell, Gene Corso; *Silver Sphere Model* Willard Green; *Makeup* Shirley Mae; *Music* Fred Myrow, Malcolm Seagrave

CAST

Michael Baldwin, Angus Scrimm, Bill Thornbury, Reggie Bannister, Kathy Lester

THE PLAGUE OF THE ZOMBIES

Film   1966   G.B. (Hammer)   91 minutes Technicolor

Corpses are raised from the dead by a voodoo-practicing Cornish squire to provide free labor for his tin mine. Hammer reprises Hollywood's old zombie programmers with its typical panache, even if the script by Peter Bryan lacks invention. A nice change of pace is the film's hero, a charming Van Helsing type. And you'll remember the putrescent zombies wriggling out of their graves. Director Gilling filmed THE REPTILE (see Werewolves and Other Shape-Shifters) back-to-back on the same atmospheric Cornwall sets, designed by Hammer luminary Bernard Robinson.

CREDITS

Director John Gilling; *Producer* Anthony Nelson Keys; *Screenplay* Peter Bryan; *Photographer* Arthur Grant; *Production Designer* Bernard Robinson; *Special Effects* Bowie Films; *Makeup* Roy Ashton; *Music* James Bernard

CAST

Andre Morell, Diane Clare, Brook Williams, Jacqueline Pearce, Michael Ripper, John Carson

PLAN 9 FROM OUTER SPACE

Also titled: Grave Robbers from Outer Space

Film   1958   U.S. (DCA)   79 minutes Black & white

To call *Plan 9* a B-picture is to clothe it in white tie and tails (or, as filmmaker Edward D. Wood, Jr., might have preferred, an evening gown). Wood, a former Marine who claimed to have helped liberate a Pacific island wearing French lingerie under his fatigues, was a colorful Hollywood transvestite who liked to work in nylons, high heels and fluffy sweaters. Star of the film is Bela Lugosi, who had worked for Wood previously in BRIDE OF THE MONSTER (see Mad Scientists) and *Glen or Glenda?* (1953), a plea for the acceptance of transvestites which has become something of a cult item. Since Lugosi had died in 1956 leaving behind only two minutes of footage for the uncompleted *Tomb of the Vampire*, Wood decided to recoup his investment by building this film around the takes, repeating them half a dozen times and having his cloaked chiropractor double for the actor in long shots.

The delirious tangle of a plot has to do with a couple from outer space who—like movie mad scientists of a decade before—plan to conquer humanity by raising a mindless army from its dead. The performers, all friends of Wood, include Tor Johnson, a 400-pound professional wrestler, Vampira, the anorexic hostess of a popular late-night horror-movie TV program in Los Angeles, and Criswell, Mae West's psychic adviser. Their almost total lack of acting ability is complemented by the outrageously cheap improv sets and effects: the same furniture is found in every room; in one shot it's day, in another it's night; a cardboard tombstone topples over in the middle of a scene, and for the grand finale a paper-plate UFO is set aflame and tossed into the air. A masterpiece of its kind, *Plan 9* was elected "The Worst Film of All Time" in a poll taken by Harry and Michael Medved for their book *The Golden Turkey Awards* (1980), which also named Wood "The Worst Director of All Time." Cherished by lovers of movie trash, who delight in glorified amateurism and thrift-shop production values, the film has gone on to make a tidy profit at midnight screenings, raising the question of who is laughing at whom?

CREDITS

Director/Producer/Screenplay Edward D. Wood, Jr.; *Photographer* William C. Thompson; *Music* Cordon Zahler

CAST

Bela Lugosi, Vampira, Tor Johnson, Lyle Talbot, Joanna Lee, Criswell, Gregory Walcott

PSYCHOMANIA

U.S. title: The Death Wheelers

Film   1972   G.B. (Benmar)   91 minutes *Technicolor*

British director Don Sharp does a Roger Corman takeoff in this witty occult bike flick. His immortal motorcycle gang comprises dead men led by a suicide, whose witch of a mother has brought them back for more murder and mayhem. Hollywood star George Sanders, playing a butler, took his own life soon after the film was completed.

CREDITS

Director Don Sharp; *Producer* Andrew Donally; *Screenplay* Arnaud D'Useau; *Story* Julian Halevy; *Photographer*

Ted Moore; *Art Director* Maurice Carter; *Special Effects* Patrick Moore; *Music* David Whitaker

CAST

George Sanders, Beryl Reid, Nicky Henson, Roy Holder, Robert Hardy, Mary Larkin

REVOLT OF THE ZOMBIES

Film   1936   U.S. (Halperin)   65 minutes *Black & white*

The Halperin brothers trashed their own reputations with this patchwork follow-up to WHITE ZOMBIE. Among their many mistakes is shifting the action from the Caribbean to Indochina, where a French planter recruits an army of zombies to fight for the French during World War I. Monogram compounded the lunacy in two wartime programmers that had crazy scientists making zombies for Hitler: KING OF THE ZOMBIES (1941) and *Revenge of the Zombies* (1943).

CREDITS

Director Victor Halperin; *Producer* Edward Halperin; *Screenplay* Howard Higgins, Rollo Lloyd, Victor Halperin; *Photographer* J. Arthur Feindel; *Special Effects* Ray Mercer; *Musical Director* Abe Meyer

CAST

Dean Jagger, Dorothy Stone, Roy D'Arcy, Robert Noland, George Cleveland

SUGAR HILL

Film   1974   U.S. (AIP)   90 minutes   Color

Thankfully, this was the last of AIP's "blaxploitation" horrors, inaugurated by the profitable BLACULA (1972) (see Vampires). It's pegged to the recent 1960s revival of voodoo, but the story is basically *Shaft* in cheap drag, with pneumatic heroine Sugar getting even with the white racketeers who killed her man with zombies recruited from a voodoo priestess. The simple-minded racism is more frightening than its rotund witch god, who runs off with mob king Robert Quarry's struggling red-headed mistress.

CREDITS

Director Paul Maslansky; *Producer* Elliott Schick; *Screenplay* Tim Kelly

CAST

Marki Bey, Robert Quarry, Betty Ann Rees, Richard Lawson, Charles Robinson, Judy Hanson

VALLEY OF THE ZOMBIES

Film 1946 U.S. (Republic) 56 minutes Black & white

No zombies here, only a dead mad doctor animated by blood drained from a colleague. Don't they call them vampires?

CREDITS

Director Philip Ford; *Screenplay* Dorrell McGowan, Stuart McGowan; *Photographer* Reggie Lanning; *Art Director* Hilyard Brown; *Special Effects* Howard Lydecker, Theodore Lydecker; *Makeup* Bob Mark; *Music* Richard Cherwin

CAST

Robert Livingston, Adrian Booth, Ian Keith, Wilton Graff, Earle Hodings

VOODOO HEARTBEAT

Film 1972 U.S. (TWI National) 88 minutes Color

A really awful independent production which deserves to be on everyone's "worst" list. Producer/star Ray Molina tramples every legend in sight as he impersonates a Las Vegan who gulps a magical potion stolen from a voodoo ceremony that ensures eternal youth. Instead, the drink turns him into an ugly old vampire. Need we say more?

CREDITS

Director/Screenplay Charles Nizet; *Producer* Ray Molina

CAST

Ray Molina, Ray Molina, Jr., Ern Dugo, Philip Ahn

THE VOODOO MAN

Film 1944 U.S. (Monogram) 62 minutes Black & white

Dr. Lugosi attempts to cure his wife of zombiedom (she has been laid up for 22 years) by injecting her with the life essence of kidnapped young women. A throwaway programmer that wastes the talents of three horror luminaries.

CREDITS

Director William Beaudine; *Producer* Sam Katzman; *Screenplay* Robert Charles; *Photographer* Marcel Le Picard; *Sets* David Milton; *Music* Edward Kay

CAST

Bela Lugosi, John Carradine, George Zucco, Wanda McKay, Louise Curry, Michael Ames

VOODOO WOMAN

Film 1957 U.S. (AIP) 77 minutes Black & white

Tom Conway, star of I WALKED WITH A ZOMBIE and the Falcon series of the 1940s, finds himself in reduced circumstances as a mad doctor who transforms a native girl into his obedient slave. The medium is a cheapjack jungle thriller and the message is the saronged body of would-be actress Marla English. From the director who gave us ZOMBIES OF MORA TAU.

CREDITS

Director Edward L. Cahn; *Producer* Alex Gordon; *Screenplay* Russell Bender, V.I. Voss; *Art Director* Frederick E. West; *Music* Darrell Calker

CAST

Marla English, Tom Conway, Touch (Chuck) Connors, Lance Fuller, Paul Blaisdell

WHITE ZOMBIE

Film 1932 U.S. (Amusement Securities) 73 minutes Black & white

The prototype for all zombie films, *White Zombie* begins in Port-au-Prince where a young woman

White Zombie: Plantation owner Bela Lugosi is protected by an army of zombies.

(Madge Bellamy) has arrived to marry her fiance. Visiting a church, she notices a body being buried at a crossroads and learns that the practice is to prevent the body from being stolen and turned into an undead slave by the sinister zombie master "Murder" Legendre (Bela Lugosi). Taking a fancy to the girl, Legendre puts her in a trance on her wedding day by squeezing a wax effigy with a piece of her clothing. Now a mindless, speechless shadow totally dominated by the sorcerer, she is sent out into the night to murder for him.

Filmed in an exaggerated silent-movie style that was dated back then, *White Zombie* seems turgid and decrepit to some. But it's this very quality of antique remoteness, aided by the condition of existing prints, that makes the film seem so other-worldly and bizarre. The zombies are first seen as black silhouettes lurching to a field of sugar cane, and Lugosi makes his entrance as a pair of eyes superimposed over his figure as he awaits the ar-

rival of his zombie-driven coach. Dressed in full evening wear, Lugosi (in one of his favorite roles) has never been so sneeringly, sadistically malevolent. The script is little more than a collection of good vs. evil cliches, but the archetypes are so spartanly defined that the film plays rather like a darker version of *Snow White*. The fairy-tale ending, which should be cherished, has the girl reviving (she wasn't a zombie after all, only a victim of a voodoo spell), while Lugosi plunges over a cliff, followed by his "walking dead" lemmings. The Halperin brothers, pioneer independents who usually made throwaway programmers, released a throwaway sequel in 1936, REVOLT OF THE ZOMBIES.

CREDITS

Director Victor Halperin; *Producer* Edward Halperin; *Screenplay* Garnett Weston, suggested by the book *The*

Magic Island by William Seabrook; *Photographer* Arthur Martinelli; *Art Directors* Ralph Berger; *Makeup* Jack Pierce; *Musical Director* Abe Meyer

CAST

Bela Lugosi, Madge Bellamy, Joseph Cawthorn, John Harron, Robert Fraser, Clarence Muse, Brandon Hurst

ZOMBIE ISLAND MASSACRE

Film 1985 U.S. (Troma) 86 minutes
Color

More a slasher movie than a zombie flick, but atrocious as either one. The highlights are some good photography of the island of Jamaica, where it was filmed, and some semidraped shots of Rita Jenrette, a former Congressman's wife who rose to the top by posing in a skin magazine. The title tells the story.

CREDITS

Director John N. Carter; *Producer* David Broadnax; *Screenplay* William Stoddard, Logan O'Neill; *Photographer* Robert M. Baldwin; *Music* Harry Manfredini

CAST

David Broadnax, Rita Jenrette, Tom Cantrell

ZOMBIES OF MORA TAU

G.B. title: The Dead That Walk

Film 1957 U.S. (Clover) 71 minutes
Black & white

Amphibious zombies spook an expedition of divers attempting to raise a sunken treasure off the coast of Africa. It has a novel idea, but that's all.

CREDITS

Director Edward L. Cahn; *Producer* Sam Katzman; *Screenplay* Raymond T. Marcus; *Photographer* Benjamin H. Kline; *Art Director* Paul Palmentola; *Music* Mischa Bakaleinikoff

CAST

Gregg Palmer, Allison Hayes, Joel Ashley, Autumn Russell, Marjorie Eaton, Morris Ankrum

ZOMBIES ON BROADWAY

G.B. title: Loonies on Broadway

Film 1945 U.S. (RKO) 68 minutes
Black & white

Lugosi is billed as the star of this dim-witted farce. But his mad doctor is only a supporting player to two Runyonesque press agents who bring back a zombie from the Caribbean to exhibit in a nightclub.

CREDITS

Director Gordon Douglas; *Producer* Sid Rogell; *Screenplay* Lawrence Kimble; *Photographer* Jack MacKenzie; *Art Directors* Albert D'Agostino, Walter E. Keller; *Music* Roy Webb

CAST

Bela Lugosi, Anne Jeffreys, Wally Brown, Alan Carney, Sheldon Leonard

XI

SPLATTER

Andy Warhol's Frankenstein: Joe Dellasandro and Srdjan Zelenovic (the monster) explore the more perverse implications of the Mary Shelley story.

The term "splatter," which is interchangeable with the term "gore," is currently being used to describe any horror movie featuring explicit bloodshed and sadistic violence. Specifically, however, "splatter" refers to a subgenre of atrocity documentaries purposely designed to shock and sicken. Many of these exaggerated excursions into dismemberment and disembowelment also fall into the category of "idiot horror" because of the crudeness of their scripts, direction, performances and sets. Too explicit to be shown on television (even on cable), splatter movies are usually screened at gore and "worst film" festivals, where they are often paired with such camp fare as BRIDE OF THE MONSTER (see Mad Scientists) and *Ilsa, She-Wolf of the* SS. Many are also available on videocassettes for home viewing.

The father of "gore-nography" is Herschell Gordon Lewis, maker of the infamous BLOOD FEAST (1963), an eye-popping tale of a latter-day Dr. Frankenstein. Gordon, a former English teacher at the University of Mississippi, began his brief film career in 1960 with a series of soft-core sex movies. Noticing that his drive-in audiences seemed to be particularly enthralled by rape scenes, he switched to hard-core violence and made a name of sorts for himself with a butcher's dozen of reactionary splatter movies. Gordon retired from the screen in 1971, after Hammer, AIP and, ultimately, the majors coopted many of his subjects and techniques.

Bloodletting, of course, both real and simulated, has been a popular entertainment for centuries. The ancient Romans packed the Colosseum to enjoy gladiatorial contests; the English of the Jacobean period thrilled to plays featuring sex-crazed murderers; and French Revolutionary crowds sat for hours watching the heads of aristocrats roll from the guillotine.

But splatter's direct ancestor is the Theatre du Grand Guignol, an erstwhile Paris novelty which has given its name to violently bloody melodramas. Established in 1899 by an impresario named Max Maurey, it flourished for more than 60 years in a seedy back street of the Montmartre district. The theater featured ripper murders, decapitations, bloodied rapes and mob vengeance, all enthusiastically and shockingly depicted live and onstage. Among its most popular attractions were juiced-up versions of Poe's "The Murders in the Rue Morgue" and "The Tell-Tale Heart." Also in its repertory were *Le Vampyre*, in the Gothic tradition of castles and costumes, and an abridged version of *The Hands of Orlac*, titled *Duet for Two Hands*. A popular tourist attraction for years, the Grand Guignol was rendered obsolete by changing public tastes and the increasingly graphic *frissons* of the horror film. It closed its doors in 1959.

The most notorious splatter movie of all is a 1973 release titled *Snuff*. Advertised as being "Made in South America—Where Life is Cheap," this perverted film allegedly features the actual torture and murders of several terrified young women, who thought they had been hired to perform in an exploitation sex movie. When the film opened in New York's Times Square, feminists staged a demonstration outside the theater, and the police department confiscated the film. Vice squad viewers found *Snuff* to be an obscure Argentinian programmer, padded with scenes of simulated machete murders shot in New York by a local porno filmmaker. In an attempt to make the film appear to be bona fide, the distributor had deleted the cast and credits. Reportedly, genuine "snuff" movies are available to S&M afficianados via a clandestine network, but investigators have yet to find one.

In reality, most splatter fans don't take these knee-jerk films seriously. The majority of cultists are teenagers, who view the deliberately exaggerrated gore as a send-up of horror movies, in a manner similar to the bad taste humor of *Mad Magazine* and *The National Lampoon*. The ordeal of watching amounts to a war of nerves—perfect for teenagers anxious to prove their mettle—and there is the added enjoyment of outraging their elders. Upsetting is splatter's brutalizing treatment of women, which has been explained as a hysterical male response to feminism. But probably more insidious are television's preoccupation with macho violence and some of Hollywood's "teenie-kill" movies, spawned by the phenomenally successful HALLOWEEN (1978) (see Crazies and Freaks). The natural heirs to splatter, these movies receive wide distribution and are seen by millions.

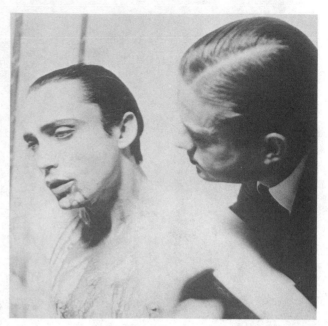

Andy Warhol's Dracula: Count Dracula (Udo Kier) is calmed by his servant after discovering his latest victim not to be a virgin.

ANDY WARHOL'S DRACULA

Also titled: Blood for Dracula

Film   1974   Italy/France (Cinematografica)
103 minutes   Color

When Transylvania begins to run short of virgins, Count Dracula moves to Roman Catholic Italy for a fresh supply. (It's the only kind of blood he can tolerate.) The setting is a posh villa, where his plans to fang-bang three beauties are thwarted by a quick-thinking Brooklyn handyman who deflowers them in the nick of time. This one's not up to the deadpan barf-bag standards of the 3-D ANDY WARHOL'S FRANKENSTEIN (1973), although there is a repulsive scene in which Dracula's arms and legs are brutally amputated. Somehow, master filmmakers Vittorio De Sica and Roman Polanski got talked into showing up.

CREDITS

Director/Screenplay Paul Morrissey; *Producer* Andrew Braunsberg; *Photographer* Luigi Kuveiller; *Production Designer* Enrico Job; *Special Effects* Carlo Rambaldi; *Makeup* Mario Di Salvio; *Sound Effects* Roberto Arcangeli; *Music* Claudio Gizzi

CAST

Udo Keir, Maxime McKendry, Joe Dallesandro, Arno Juerging, Vittorio De Sica, Roman Polanski, Milena Vukotic

ANDY WARHOL'S FRANKENSTEIN

Also titled: Flesh for Frankenstein

Film   1973   Italy/France (EMI/Warhol)
95 minutes   Eastmancolor   3-D

It's a terrific idea to spin the Hammer formula to its natural conclusion while probing taboo implications of the Frankenstein legend, but to bring it off would require more talent than is apparent here. At heart, this is another campy Warhol hetero/homo/bi/transsexual/incest film, dressed up with animal entrails shoved into your face with a 3-D camera. The baron and his sister/wife, the parents of two very weird children, combine talents to produce a perfect man and woman for their personal use, while groping and poking various members of the household. Always in search of new thrills, the baron slices open his beautiful android playmate and pleasures himself with her gallbladder. Lead Udo Keir came back for more in ANDY WARHOL'S DRACULA the following year.

CREDITS

Director/Screenplay Paul Morrissey; *Producer* Andrew Braunsberg; *Executive Producer* Carlo Ponti; *Photographer* Luigi Kuveiller; *Production Designer* Enrico Job; *Special Effects* Carlo Rambaldi; *Makeup* Mario Di Salvio; *Music* Claudio Gizzi

CAST

Udo Keir, Monique Van Vooren, Joe Dallesandro, Arno Juerging, Carla Mancini (female Monster), Srdjan Zelenovic (male Monster), Dalila Di Lazzaro (female zombie)

BASKET CASE

Film   1982   U.S. (Analysis)   90 minutes
Color

Remember SISTERS (see Crazies and Freaks)? This former Siamese twin saves his undeveloped brother Belial (another name for Satan) from a garbage-can death and carries him around in a wicker basket. The pair check into a ratty Manhattan hotel and begin looking up the doctors who performed the operation 10 years before.

The print (blown up from 16 mm) is grainy and the sound awful, but there's a mordant wit at work here, and lead actor Van Hentenryck is ingratiating. The murderous Belial, sporting startling eyes lit from within, is the work of Kevin Haney and

John Caglione, Jr. Haney sculpted the body suit designed by Dick Smith and worn by William Hurt in ALTERED STATES (1980) (see Werewolves and Other Shape-Shifters). *Basket Case* is available in "hard" and "soft" versions, meaning gore not porn.

CREDITS

Director/Screenplay Frank Henenlotter; *Producer* Edgar Ievins; *Photographer* Bruce Torbet; *Special Effects Makeup* Kevin Haney, John Caglione, Jr.; *Music* Gus Russo

CAST

Kevin Van Hentenryck, Terri Susan Smith, Robert Vogel, Beverly Bonner, Diana Browne, Lloyd Price

BLOOD FEAST

Film   1963   U.S. (Box Office Spectaculars)
75 minutes   Color

The granddaddy of them all, this seminal gore feast set in motion the brief genre career of Herschell Gordon Lewis, an exploitation filmmaker who shifted to blood and guts once the majors began to catch up to him on soft-core sex. The plot, something along the lines of Dr. Frankenstein meets the Mummy, involves a nutcase who attempts to revive an ancient Egyptian princess with body parts carved from shapely young women.

It cost only $70,000 to make and looks it, but polish and style are beside the point in a Lewis film. What matters is that we get to see brains and internal organs being scooped out of living bodies, and learn how to tear a tongue out by its roots. (Lewis staged the latter effect with a calf's tongue, cranberries and chunks of raw meat, all sauced with stage blood and crammed into an actress's mouth.) Drive-in audiences vomited—which means they liked it—and the film grossed a small fortune, enabling Lewis to go on to the more ambitious carnage of 2000 MANIACS.

CREDITS

Director/Photographer/Music Herschell Gordon Lewis; *Producer* David F. Friedman; *Screenplay* Allison Louise Downe

CAST

Thomas Wood, Connie Mason, Mal Arnold, Lyn Bolton, Toni Calvert, Scott H. Hall

BLOODSUCKING FREAKS

Film   1976   U.S. (Troma)   88 minutes
Color

Filmed in 1976 as *The Incredible Torture Show*, this tawdry exercise in necrophilia found its natural home at "sleaze" film festivals when it was re-released in 1982 as *Bloodsucking Freaks*. Played for sadistic laughs, the minimal plot concerns an out-of-the-way Manhattan "Theatre of the Maca-bre" run by a gleeful white slaver who likes to guil-lotine nude actresses and/or penetrate their skulls with an electric drill. Similar to the soft-core S&M porn movies of the 1960s, the movie is currently on the hit list of several feminist groups.

CREDITS

Director/Screenplay Joel M. Reed; *Producer* Alan Mar-golin; *Photographer* Gerry Toll; *Makeup and Special Effects* Bob O'Bradovich; *Choreography* Gyles Fon-taine; *Music* Michael Sahl

CAST

Seamus O'Brien, Louie DeJusus, Niles McMaster, Viju Krim, Alan Dellay, Dan Fauci, Ernie Peysher

COLOR ME BLOOD RED

Film   1964   U.S. (Box Office Spectaculars)
74 minutes   Color

A high-flying painter butchers models to obtain just the right shade of vermillion for his canvasses. Part of a triple drive-in bill that included BLOOD FEAST and 2000 MANIACS—the inspiration for John Waters's homage to H.G. Lewis, *Multiple Maniacs* (1970).

CREDITS

Director/Producer/Screenplay Herschell Gordon Lewis; *Photographer* Andy Romanoff

CAST

Don Joseph, Candi Conder, Elyn Warner, Scott H. Hall, Patricia Lee, Jerome Eden

THE CORPSE GRINDERS

Film   1971   U.S. (C.G. Productions)
72 minutes   Color

Trained cats attack people to provide their owner with raw material for a delicious new cat food. A tasty idea served without talent or real wit by all concerned. The conveyor belt scenes are guaranteed to turn your stomach.

CREDITS

Director/Producer/Editor/Music Ted V. Mikels; *Screen-play* Arch Hall, Joseph L. Cranston; *Photographer* Bill Anneman; *Special Effects* Gary Heacock

CAST

Sean Kenney, Monika Kelly, Sanford Mitchell, J. Byron Foster, Warren Ball

DRIVE-IN MASSACRE

Film   1976   U.S. (New American)   78 minutes
Color

It's a busy night at the local drive-in. Before you can say "boo!" a patron reaches out a car window for a speaker, and someone chops off his arm. A mad killer is turning the outdoor arena into a butcher shop! Director/producer Segall tempers the fast-cut splatter scenes by introducing colorful background characters, there that night for their own peculiar reasons. The clever open ending has all the suspects being killed and the theater's P.A. system announcing that a killer is loose in the audience.

CREDITS

Director/Producer Stuart Segall; *Screenplay* John Goff, Buck Flower; *Photographer* Kenneth Lloyd Gibb; *Music* Longjohn Productions

CAST

Jake Barnes, Douglas Gudbye, Adam Lawrence, New-ton Naushaus, Valdesta, Norman Sherlock

FLESH FEAST

Also titled: Time Is Terror

*Film   1970   U.S. (Cine World)   72 minutes
Color*

A woman doctor, recently released from a mental institution, dabbles with maggots and corpses in an effort to find a rejuvenation serum. When Hitler arrives for plastic surgery, she recalls his war crimes against her family and throws the wiggly larvae in his face, cackling with pleasure at his agony. Made in Florida, *Flesh Feast* is the last film of erstwhile Hollywood sex bomb Veronica Lake, who had been rediscovered in the late 1960s working in a Manhattan coffee shop. The actor playing Hitler should be given some kind of an award for enduring a kisserful of live maggots, raised by a makeup man on decaying hamburger.

CREDITS

Producers Brad F. Grinter, Veronica Lake; *Screenplay* Brad F. Grinter, Thomas Casey; *Makeup* Douglas Blake Hobart

CAST

Veronica Lake, Phil Phiburn, Martha Mischon, Heather Hughes, Yanka Mann

FRIGHTMARE

*Film   1974   G.B. (Heritage)   86 minutes
Color*

Released from a long stay in an insane asylum, a husband and wife resume their murderous habits and add cannibalism to their list of heinous crimes. Like most of the works of Peter Walker, who is considered Britain's leading "gore-ophile," this one is technically more polished and several levels above the usual ultra low-budget product of his American colleagues. Dramatically it's no more substantial, however, even with the presence of a few reputable actors and a union cameraman. Walker's output includes *Die, Beautiful Maryanne* (1969), *The Flesh and Blood Show* (1973), *Schizo* (1976), *The Confessional* (1977) (a blackmailing priest tapes the confessions of parishioners) and *The Comeback* (1979). His most well known exploiter is *House of Whipcord* (1974), a slickly sadistic fantasy about women punishing female "offenders" in their own private prison. After percolating for years just below the mainstream,

Walker raised enough money in 1983 to hire Peter Cushing, Christopher Lee and Vincent Price for his *House of the Long Shadows*, an old house story filmed in the Gothic Hammer style.

CREDITS

Director/Producer Peter Walker; *Screenplay* David McGillivray; *Photographer* Peter Jessup; *Art Director* Chris Burke; *Music* Stanley Myers

CAST

Rupert Davis, Deborah Fairfax, Sheila Keith, Paul Greenwood, Kim Butcher

THE GORE-GORE GIRLS

Also titled: Blood Orgy

*Film   1971   U.S. (Lewis Enterprises)
90 minutes   Color*

Herschell Gordon Lewis's last splatter indicates he hadn't learned a thing about filmmaking in eight years. His go-go girls, who dance as awkwardly as they act, get slaughtered after auditioning for kinky disco owners. There's some enterprising sadism (a girl's face is scorched with an iron and pushed into a boiling french-fryer), but Lewis's garish gore eventually palls. Even the drive-in crowd panned this one.

CREDITS

Producer/Director Herschell Gordon Lewis; *Screenplay* Alan Dachman; *Photographer* Eskandar Ameripoor; *Music* Sheldon Seymour (Herschell Gordon Lewis)

CAST

Frank Kress, Amy Farrell, Russ Badger, Hedda Lubin, Nora Alexis, Frank Rice

THE GRUESOME TWOSOME

*Film   1966   U.S. (Mayflower)   81 minutes
Color*

Mom and sonny hit on a novel way to keep down costs in their wig shop. He scalps women stupid enough to date him, and Mom recycles the hair. Filmmaker Lewis has never been better.

CREDITS

Director/Producer/Photographer Herschell Gordon Lewis; *Screenplay* Allison Louise Downe; *Music* Larry Wellington

CAST

Elizabeth David, Chris Martell, Rodney Bedell, Gretchen Welles

I DISMEMBER MAMA

Also titled: Poor Albert and Little Annie

Film   *1972*   *U.S. (Europix)*   *78 minutes* *Color*

Albert, a Hollywood "perv" who likes to carve up "impure women," finds temporary salvation when he falls in love with a nine-year-old girl. The relationship doesn't work out, however, and . . . chop, chop! Greg Mullavey, the husband of TV's *Mary Hartman, Mary Hartman*, plays a detective. Filmmaker Paul Leder's *oeuvre* includes *Please Don't Eat My Mother*, an X-rated version of Roger Corman's *The Little Shop of Horrors*, about a middle-aged mama's boy who watches people making love and feeds them to his man-eating plant.

CREDITS

Director Paul Leder; *Producer* Leon Roth; *Screenplay* William Norton

CAST

Zoey Hall, Geri Reischl, Greg Mullavey

I SPIT ON YOUR GRAVE

Also titled: Day of the Woman

Film   *1980*   *U.S. (Jerry Gross)*   *73 minutes* *Color*

One of a new breed of odious splatters, inspired by FRIDAY THE 13TH (1980) (see Crazies and Freaks), with a smattering of film school pretensions. Pert Camille Keaton (niece of Buster) goes to a quiet upstate village to write a book and gets sodomized on a rock, *Deliverance*-style, and otherwise sexually abused by four smarmy locals. Debased once too often (giving viewers several re-

plays), Camille gets retribution by castrating one pig with outboard motorboat blades, hanging another and finishing off the rest with an axe. It's totally without redemption, a portrayal of rape to stimulate male fantasies. Camille, who appears almost totally nude throughout, makes *Ilsa, She-Wolf of the SS* look like Snow White. Writer and director is macho-minded (to put it mildly) Israeli Meir Zarchi. The Motion Picture Association of America brought suit against the producers for trying to pass this one off with a R rating.

THE ISLAND

Film   *1980*   *U.S. (Universal)*   *113 minutes* *Technicolor*   *Panavision*   *Dolby Stereo*

A vacationing magazine writer and his young son endure sadistic tortures (including splinters through the eyelids) at the hands of pirates time-trapped on an island in the Bermuda Triangle. Slick, mean and brutal, and about as convincing as men's action-adventure pulps of the 1950s. Peter Benchley, author of the novel *Jaws*, wrote the script based on his best-seller.

CREDITS

Director Michael Ritchie; *Producers* Richard D. Zanuck, David Brown; *Screenplay* Peter Benchley, based on his novel; *Photographer* Henri Decae; *Production Designer* Dale Hennesy; *Special Visual Effects* Albert Whitlock; *Special Effects* Cliff Wenger; *Music* Ennio Morricone

CAST

Michael Caine, David Warner, Angela Punch McGregor, Frank Middlemass, Don Henderson, Dudley Sutton, Jeffrey Frank

THE LAST HOUSE ON THE LEFT

Film   *1972*   *U.S.*   *88 minutes*   *Color*

An unbearably gross film which should shame even the most hardcore splatter fans. Director Wes Craven rips off Ingmar Bergman's *The Virgin Spring* (1960) in this contemporary tale of a trio of rapists who are enticed into the home of their victim's family. Mom castrates one of them with her teeth, while Dad takes care of the other two with a chain saw. Craven dwells interminably on the suffering and leaves nothing to the imagination. Sean Cunningham, who later made FRIDAY THE 13TH (see Crazies and Freaks), collaborated with Craven on the script. Craven directed the equally repulsive *The Hills Have Eyes* (1977), which has a vacationing family being burned alive, crucified and similarly abused while on a vacation in a Southwestern desert, and *Deadly Blessing* (1981). He redeemed his reputation somewhat with the comic book adaptation *Swamp Thing* (1982) and the thriller *The Nightmare on Elm Street* (1984).

MONSTER-A-GO-GO

Also titled: Terror at Halfday

Film	1965	U.S. (B&W)	70 minutes
Black & white		

Splatter-meister Herschell Gordon Lewis taped together this minor offering from footage purchased from a bankrupt producer and added a few new close-ups. Released on a double bill with his *Moonshine Mountain*, it resembles a science fiction movie in the way rat turds look like caviar.

CREDITS

Director Bill Rebane; *Producer/Additional Scenes* Sheldon Seymour (Herschell Gordon Lewis); *Screenplay* Jeff Smith, Bill Rebane, Don Stanford; *Photographer* Frank Pfieffer

CAST

Phil Morton, June Travis, Lois Brooke, George Perry, Henry Hite

LA NOVIA ENSANGRENTADA/ The Blood-Splattered Bride

Film   1972   Spain (Morgana)   102 minutes
Color

Sheridan Le Fanu's *Carmilla* (1872), smothered in sadism and soft-core sex (both lesbian and heterosexual) and squeezed of its ethereal horror. Stay with Roger Vadim's ET MOURIR DE PLAISIR (1960) (see Vampires) and Hammer's *Carmilla* films.

CREDITS

Director/Screenplay Vicente Aranda, based on *Carmilla* by Sheridan Le Fanu; *Producer* Jose Lopez Morena; *Photographer* Fernando Arribas; *Production Designer* Juan Alberto Soler; *Special Effects* Antonio Molina; *Makeup* Cristobel Criado; *Music* Antonio Perez Olea

CAST

Maribel Martin, Simon Andrea, Alexandra Bastedo, Dean Selmier, Monserrat Julio

THE RATS ARE COMING! THE WEREWOLVES ARE HERE

Film   1972   G.B. (William Mishkin)
73 minutes   Color

"A gruesome tale of man-eating rats and blood-sucking werewolves," brags the garish, no-frills lobby poster, which, if nothing else, is a model of truth in advertising. Apparently inspired by Hollywood's WILLARD (1971) and BEN (1972) (see Mad Scientists), *Rats* is either the eighth or ninth film of no. 2 splatter celebrity Andy Milligan, the garment industry's gift to exploitation films.

Something of a history buff, Milligan specializes in period gore because—to paraphrase him—such films are less likely to seem dated when retitled and recirculated at sex-strip grind houses and drive-ins. His *oeuvre* includes *The Ghastly Ones* (1966); *Bloodthirsty Butchers* (1969)—a splatter version of *Sweeney Todd–The Body Beneath*; *Torture Dungeon* (1970); *Guru, the Mad Monk* (1971); and *Blood!* (1974), his swan song. Milligan's budgets never exceeded $20,000, a paltry sum which, by comparison, makes Herschell Gordon Lewis look like Cecil B. DeMille. Most were filmed in England and Staten Island—where Milligan lives—with both locales often turning up in a single film. He presently owns a respectable off-Broadway playhouse, and is reportedly thinking of making a comeback in splatter (or, as he prefers, "terror").

CREDITS

Director/Producer/Screenplay/Photographer Andy Milligan

CAST

Hope Stansbury, Jackie Skarvellis, "The Rats of Mooney Manor"

SHE-DEVILS ON WHEELS

Film   1968   U.S. (Mayflower)   83 minutes
Color

H.G. Lewis may have been responding to feminist critics by turning the tables and casting woman as perpetrator rather than as victim, but the sentiment is the same. His sleazy riders are a braless motorcycle gang called "The Man-Eaters." Tooling around the country, the hard-drinking mamas work over a few male chauvinists with brass knuckles and get into some heavy maiming and mutilation. AIP, then making a series of biker films, allegedly wanted to release *She-Devils* nationally, but Lewis thought he could do better. And did. It was his second biggest box-office success (after BLOOD FEAST).

CREDITS

Director/Producer Herschell Gordon Lewis; *Screenplay* Allison Louise Downe; *Photographer* Ray Collodi; *Music* Robert Lewis, Sheldon Seymour (Herschell Gordon Lewis)

CAST

Betty Conell, Nancy Lee Noble, Pat Poston, Christie Wagner, Ruby Tuesday, Rodney Bedell

SUSPIRIA

Film   1976   Italy (Seda Spettacoli)
97 minutes   Eastmancolor   Technovision

Murder and mayhem galore at a chic private school in Europe, complete with thunderstorms, psychopaths and a frenzied stereo sound track. Argento's plot is barely skin deep, but the manipulative way he slits throats and cuts film will leave you gasping.

CREDITS

Director Dario Argento; *Producer* Claudio Argento; *Screenplay* Dario Argento, Dario Nicolodi; *Photographer* Luciano Tovoli; *Music* Dario Argento

CAST

Jessica Harper, Alida Valli, Joan Bennett, Stefania Casini, Udo Kier

A TASTE OF BLOOD

Also titled: The Secret of Dr. Alucard

Film   1967   U.S. (Creative Films)
120 minutes   Color

Dracula today, as seen through the bloodshot eyes of H.G. Lewis. The count's name (spell it backwards) is borrowed from Universal's SON OF DRACULA (see Vampires), and the plot is from hunger. Lewis plays an unconvincing Englishman, a casting coup resulting from a nonprofessional actor (actually, a shop clerk) not showing up on the set. Lewis says that Roger Corman offered him a job in Hollywood after screening this film.

CREDITS

Director/Producer Herschell Gordon Lewis; *Screenplay* Donald Stanford; *Photographer* Andy Romanoff; *Music* Larry Wellington

CAST

Bill Rogers, Elizabeth Wilkinson, Otto Schlesinger, Lawrence Tobin, Eleanor Valli, H.G. Lewis

THE TOOLBOX MURDERS

Film   1977   U.S. (Cal-Am)   95 minutes
Color

A really risible film that boasts the presence of one Hollywood semi-star (Cameron Mitchell) and one soap opera semi-star (Wesley Eure, from *Days of Our Lives*), who play father and sniveling son. The plot has to do with a slasher terrorizing the occupants of an apartment building with various tools, including a large drill and a power nailer. Stephen King, a fan of the film, recommended it for Halloween screenings: "If you show the movie before the guests bob for apples, you can probably save the apples for a pie on Nov. 1."

CREDITS

Director Dennis Donnelly; *Producer* Tony Didio; *Screenplay* Neva Friedenn, Robert Easter, Ann Kindberg; *Photographer* Gary Graver; *Makeup* Ed Ternes; *Music* George Deaton

CAST

Cameron Mitchell, Wesley Eure, Pamelyn Ferdyn, Nicolas Beauvy, Tim Donelly

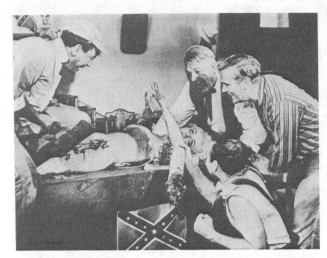

2000 Maniacs: Good ole boys extend a female guest some southern hospitality.

2000 MANIACS

*Film   1964   U.S. (Box Office Spectaculars)
75 minutes   Color*

Northern tourists are delighted with the Southern hospitality of a small Georgia town, where a festivity of some sort is about to take place. Too late they learn it was 100 years ago today that Sherman marched through Georgia and that the villagers are vengeful redneck ghosts. The Yankees begin to get the picture when one of them participates in a barrel race—inside a barrel studded with nails. The stars are ex-*Playboy* playmate Connie Mason and the redoubtable Thomas Wood, fresh from their *succes d'estime* in BLOOD FEAST. To promote the film, H.G. Lewis wrote a lead-in song,

"The South's Gonna Rise Again," and a tie-in novelization of his screenplay. Not a box-office winner, probably because there's less gore than usual in a Lewis production, the film is interesting for the way it pokes through the still-smoldering ashes of Southern resentment against the North.

CREDITS

Director/Screenplay/Photographer Herschell Gordon Lewis; *Producer/Art Director* David F. Friedman; *Music* Larry Wellington and The Pleasant Valley Boys

CAST

Connie Mason, Thomas Wood, Jeffrey Allen, Ben Moore, Vincent Santo, Gary Bakeman

THE WIZARD OF GORE

*Film   1968   U.S. (Mayflower)   96 minutes
Color*

The usual hack job from the movie wizard, with a stage magician turning his illusions into realities (e.g., sawing a woman in half).

CREDITS

Director Herschell Gordon Lewis; *Producer* Fred M. Sandy; *Screenplay* Allen Kahn; *Photographer* Eskandar Ameripoor; *Music* Larry Wellington

CAST

Ray Sager, Judy Cler, Wayne Rattay, Jim Rau, Phil Laurensen, Don Alexander, John Elliott

The Horror Show: Tony Perkins visited the old *Psycho* house while hosting a history of horror movies.

ALFRED HITCHCOCK PRESENTS

TV series   1955-64   U.S. (CBS/NBC)
30/60 minutes (weekly)   Black & white

Already well-known from cameo appearances in his films, Hitchcock became a popular TV star as the host of this weekly horror/suspense anthology. The filmmaker's portly countenance greeted viewers to the strains of Gounod's "Funeral March of a Marionette" as he introduced droll tales of murder and the supernatural with a sardonic "Good ev-en-ing, ladies and gentlemen." Most of the episodes came close to violating television's strict code of ethics by seeming to allow the villain to get away with murder. After tweaking the nose of his sponsors, Hitchcock would explain that a patently silly coincidence had brought poetic justice to the evildoer.

One of the most fondly remembered tales is "Lamb to the Slaughter," which might have ap-peared in the old E.C. comic books. Barbara Bel Geddes is the wife of the chief of police who beats her husband to death with a leg of lamb, then serves the incriminating evidence to police investi-gators. And in "Arthur," Laurence Harvey plays the owner of a chicken farm who gets rid of unfaithful wife Hazel Court by adding an extra ingredient—Court—to the machine that grinds his chicken feed. The popular series shifted between CBS and NBC, and in 1962 it was expanded to 60 minutes and retitled *The Alfred Hitchcock Hour.* Since going off network, its 268 episodes have never been out of syndication.

In 1985 Universal remade four of the original episodes for an NBC TV movie titled *Alfred Hitchcock Presents.* The stories include "Bang! You're Dead"—originally directed by Hitchcock—a prophetic gun control story made prior to the Kennedy assassination; "Incident in a Small Jail," about a man unjustly accused of a crime by a red-neck sheriff, which anticipated films like *Macon*

County Line; and "The Unlocked Window," the story of a group of nurses terrorized by a mad killer, which anticipated HALLOWEEN (1978) and, of course, Hitchcock's seminal slasher movie PSYCHO (1960) (see Crazies and Freaks), filmed on the set of this series. In the cast are Kim Novak and Tippi Hedren, who had appeared, respectively, in Hitchcock's *Vertigo* and *The Birds*, and John Huston, Ned Beatty and Annette O'Toole. Hitchcock turns up as narrator in computer-colored footage from the original shows—an effect previously used in a 25th anniversary airing of THE TWILIGHT ZONE in 1984.

CREDITS

Directors Alfred Hitchcock, Paul Henreid, Boris Sagal, Don Taylor, Ida Lupino, Harvey Hart, Alf Kjellin, Robert Stevens, et al.; *Producers* Joan Harrison, Robert Douglas, Herbert Coleman, Charles Russell, Norman Lloyd; *Executive Producer* Alfred Hitchcock; *Music* Bernard Herrmann, Leonard Rosenman, Frederick Herbert, Lyn Murray

CAST

Guest stars: Steve McQueen, Cara Williams, Hazel Court, Laurence Harvey, Peter Lorre, Charles Bronson, Patrick Macnee, Nehemiah Persoff, Billy Mumy, et al.; *Host* Alfred Hitchcock

ASYLUM

Film 1972 G.B. (Amicus) 88 minutes Eastmancolor

Novelist Robert Bloch (*Psycho*) nimbly recalls the past pleasures of DAS KABINETT VON DR. CALIGARI (see Mad Scientists), DEAD OF NIGHT and other classic films in this likable quartet, Amicus's third anthology film. The framework is a mental institution visited by a job-hunting psychiatrist, who listens to four case histories. In "Frozen Fear," a woman's disassembled body parts come back to haunt her husband; "The Weird Tailor" is commissioned to fashion a suit to revive a corpse; "Lucy Comes to Stay" concerns a woman with a murderous alter ego; and "Mannikins of Terror"—eeriest of the lot—has the former asylum head, now an inmate, making killer dolls and sending them out into the halls. The narrator (Patrick Magee) provides a fifth story, unexpectedly linked with the fourth.

CREDITS

Director Roy Ward Baker; *Producers* Max J. Rosenberg, Milton Subotsky; *Screenplay* Robert Bloch; *Photographer*

Denys Coop; *Art Director* Tony Curtis; *Special Effects* Ernie Sullivan; *Makeup* Roy Ashton; *Music* Douglas Gamley

CAST

Patrick Magee, Robert Powell, Barbara Parkins, Richard Todd, Geoffrey Bayldon, Peter Cushing, Barry Morse, Britt Ekland, Herbert Lom, Charlotte Rampling, Sylvia Syms, Megs Jenkins, James Villiers, Ann Firbank

CIRCLE OF FEAR

TV series 1973 U.S. (NBC) 60 minutes (weekly) Color

When GHOST STORY's mixture of horror and whimsey failed to capture significant ratings, NBC decided to play the series straight under the title *Circle of Fear*. As before, it was a case of good story ideas indifferently executed, and audiences couldn't care less. Among the program's better offerings were "Graveyard Shift," featuring husband-and-wife caretakers of a defunct horror film studio, whose celluloid monsters attempt to survive by possessing the couple's child. They escaped by burning the film. In "Spare Parts" a deceased doctor took control of his eyes, hands and other body parts relinquished for transplants. And in "Death's Head" PSYCHO (see Crazies and Freaks) star Janet Leigh was an adulteress-murderer whose husband returns as a vengeful moth.

CREDITS

Producer William Castle

CAST

Guest stars: Patty Duke Astin, John Astin, Janet Leigh, Rory Calhoun, Gene Nelson, Shirley Knight, Neva Patterson, Susan Oliver

CREEPSHOW

Film 1982 U.S. (Warner Bros.) 122 minutes Color

A valentine to the gleefully grisly E.C. comic books of the 1950s, conceived by horror mavens George A. Romero and Stephen King. Unlike the recent spate of comic book movies—*Popeye, Annie, Swamp Thing, Flash Gordon, Buck Rogers* and *Superman*—this one attempts to integrate film technique with comic book graphics, and succeeds for the most part. The alliance is a natural one, since comic books from the beginning were influenced by the movies. And Romero's visual style, with its exaggerated moves between long shots and extreme closeups, had already seemed like a kinetic extension of comic art. The film tells five stories of varying quality, which require a degree of familiarity with E.C. comics to fully appreciate their sly humor.

Creepshow opens cleverly with an angry father throwing one of his son's E.C. comics into a trash bin. A stormy wind blows open the pages, and cartoon animation leads us into the opening scene of each episode. In "Father's Day" the head of the family returns from the grave as a decaying corpse. "The Lonesome Death of Jordy Verill" has Stephen King playing a dopey hillbilly who becomes totally covered by a green fungus delivered by a meteorite (the character calls it "meteorshit"). "Something to Tide You Over" is another vengeful corpse story, with Leslie Nielsen eliminating his wife and her lover. In "The Crate," scariest of the lot, a 150-year-old ghoul-beast is set free from its cage for several good warm meals. The most repulsive—and best remembered—tale is "They're Creeping Up on You." E.G. Marshall is an eccentric millionaire recluse with a cleanliness fetish whose worst fears come true when hordes of cockroaches invade his penthouse apartment. The insects swarm in through drains, spigots, baseboards and, ultimately, into his body via his mouth, nose and ears. King calls the movie "basically a junk food movie but high class junk food."

For two British adaptations of E.C. comics, see TALES FROM THE CRYPT (1972) and VAULT OF HORROR (1973).

CREDITS

Director George A. Romero; *Producer* Richard Romero; *Screenplay* Stephen King; *Photographer* Michael Gornick; *Special Makeup Effects* Tom Savini; *Artwork* Jack Kamen; *Optical Effects* Dave Stipes, Dave Garber; *Animation* Rick Catizone

CAST

Hal Holbrook, Adrienne Barbeau, Viveca Lindfors, Carrie Nye, E.G. Marshall, Leslie Nielsen, Fritz Weaver, Stephen King

Dead of Night: A classic genre anthology from Great Britain.

DEAD OF NIGHT

Film   1945   G.B. (Ealing)   104 minutes
Black & white

A splendid anthology of occult stories told by five people in a country house visited by a young architect, who had anticipated the scene in a nightmare. Each recounts a bizarre personal tale, and after hearing the last the architect strangles the sole remaining guest, a disbelieving psychiatrist. Awakened next morning, the architect discovers he had dreamed it all, then finds himself keeping an appointment at the same house with the same people.

In "The Hearse Driver," directed by Basil Dearden, a strange hearse nearly causes the death of a racing car driver. "The Christmas Story," directed by Alberto Cavalcanti, casts Sally Ann Howe as a young girl visited by the ghost of a little boy who had been murdered by his sister. Robert Hamer's "The Haunted Mirror," one of the cinema's most gripping ghost stories, concerns an antique mirror that reflects the tortured life of its previous owner—a suicide—and nearly compels its new owner to commit murder. Weakest episode is Charles Crichton's "The Golfing Story," adapted from a short story by H.G. Wells, which has an avid golfer being haunted by his former opponent.

Cavalcanti directed the most famous episode, "The Ventriloquist's Dummy," with Michael Redgrave as a schizophrenic ventriloquist who gradually exchanges personalities with his dummy. The story has been retold many times, notably on TV's THE TWILIGHT ZONE in a 1962 episode titled "The Dummy," scripted by Rod Serling and starring William Shatner, and in "The Glass Eye," an episode of ALFRED HITCHCOCK PRESENTS. In 1978 Richard Attenborough directed William Goldman's version, titled *Magic*, with ventriloquist Anthony Hopkins being turned into a mad slasher by his dummy. Also in the cast are Ann-Margret and Burgess Meredith.

A popular and critical sensation in its time, *Dead of Night* was the first horror film to be released in Great Britain since the beginning of the war. (Censors had banned genre films for the duration as being too violent, and major Hollywood genre items were unseen until 1945.) Obviously patterned after the Val Lewton model, the film evokes rather than depicts horror, and weaves its symmetrical spell with the magic of a good script and expert direction. Contributing in no small measure to the uncanny mood is the ominous, Wagnerian score by Georges Auric, who had written the music for Jean Cocteau's films.

This is the first British genre compendium, a format which later flourished in the factory-polished product of Amicus, launched with DR. TERROR'S HOUSE OF HORRORS (1965). *Dead of Night* is available for TV screenings in two versions: Its original American release print (77 minutes), with "The Christmas Story" and "The Golfing Story" deleted, and a restored print—which reverses the medium's scissor-mad tendency.

CREDITS

Directors Basil Dearden, Alberto Cavalcanti, Robert Hamer, Charles Crichton; *Producer* Michael Balcon; *Screenplay* John Baines, Angus McPhail, T.E.B. Clarke, based on stories by H.G. Wells, E.F. Benson, John Baines, Angus McPhail; *Photographers* Stan Pavey, Douglas Slocombe, Jack Parker, H. Julius; *Makeup* Tom Shenton, Ernest Taylor; *Music* Georges Auric

CAST

Mervyn Johns, Roland Culver, Mary Merrall, Frederick Valk, Hugh Grainger, Miles Malleson, Sally Ann Howe, Googie Withers, Ralph Michael, Esme Percy, Basil Radford, Naunton Wayne, Peggy Bryan, Michael Redgrave, Hartley Power, Allan Jeayes, John Maguire, Magda Kun

Dr. Terror's House of Horrors: Christopher Lee is an art critic pursued by a disembodied hand.

DR. TERROR'S HOUSE OF HORRORS

Film   1965   G.B. (Amicus)   98 minutes Techniscope

After Hammer proved there was a worldwide market for splashy Gothic horror, little Amicus opted for a slice of the pie with a series of well-produced portmanteau features, usually with Hammer players. Like those that followed, *Dr. Terror's House of Horrors* is populated with generic creatures rather than Hammer's name brands, and the format has a sinister narrator relating terrible tales to a group of strangers. Here, Peter Cushing reads tarot cards for five travelers in his railway carriage. In "Werewolf," a surveyor wrestles with the lycanthropic owner of his former home. In "Voodoo," a musician who steals a song from a pagan priest in Haiti gets his comeuppance in London. In "The Crawling Hand," a pompous art critic is chased by an artist's hand he has accidentally severed. "Creeping Vine" has a family being imprisoned by a peculiar outdoor plant. And "Vampire" has Donald Sutherland playing his first featured role as a double-edged member of the undead. A poor debut film, but Amicus did better later with the likes of THE HOUSE THAT DRIPPED BLOOD (1970) and TALES FROM THE CRYPT (1972).

CREDITS

Director Freddie Francis; *Producers* Milton Subotsky, Max J. Rosenberg; *Screenplay* Milton Subotsky; *Photographer* Alan Hume; *Art Director* Bill Constable; *Special Effects* Ted Samuels; *Makeup* Roy Ashton; *Music* Elizabeth Lutyens

CAST

Peter Cushing, Christopher Lee, Michael Gough, Donald Sutherland, Bernard Lee, Max Adrian, Ursula Howells, Jeremy Kemp, Roy Castle, Alan Freeman, Harold Lang

ESCAPE

Radio series   1950–53   U.S. (CBS)
30 minutes (weekly)

One of radio's last prime-time horror programs, *Escape* was designed, in the words of the announcer, "to free you from the four walls of today for a half-hour of high adventure." Its most popular episode was "Three Skeleton Keys," repeated from the SUSPENSE series. Vincent Price starred as one of three men stranded in an island lighthouse being overrun with predatory rats. The program's theme was *A Night on Bald Mountain* by Moussorgsky.

CREDITS

Directors/Producers William N. Robson, Norman Macdonnell; *Sound Effects* Cliff Thorsness, Bill Gould

ANNOUNCERS

William Conrad, Paul Frees

EVERYMAN'S THEATER

Radio series   1938–44   U.S. (NBC)
60 minutes (weekly)

Master radio dramatist Arch Oboler conceived this anthology dramatic package and wrote and directed most of the scripts. Some were romantic historical melodramas: "None But the Lonely Heart" told the story of Tschaikovsky; "Lust for Life" recalled the story of Vincent Van Gogh. But the favorites were Oboler's chillers. In "Two," Joan Crawford starred with Raymond Edward Johnson as the last two people left on Earth after a cataclysmic war; "The Laughing Man" was the tale of a joker looking back from the future and laughing at a generation that had annihilated itself with a monstrous bomb. The most popular episode, repeated five times, was "The Ugliest Man in the World," a sentimental drama about a man initially forced to pay for love.

GUEST STARS

Bette Davis, Joan Crawford, Alla Nazimova, Katherine Hepburn, Raymond Massey, Boris Karloff, Martin Gabel

THE EVIL TOUCH

TV series   1973   Canada
30 minutes (weekly)   Color

Unintentional humor lightened the load of this downbeat series, made in Canada, which aired for one syndicated season. The format was similar to live television's LIGHTS OUT. Narrator Anthony Quayle appeared from a wispy fog to introduce well-known American actors in science fiction/horror tales that illustrated "there is a touch of evil in all of us."

CAST

Susan Strasberg, Darren McGavin, Carol Lynley, Kim Hunter; *Host* Anthony Quayle

FROM BEYOND THE GRAVE

Film   1973   G.B. (Warner/Amicus)
98 minutes   Technicolor

Amicus, which was having a run with anthology films during 1972–73, followed its VAULT OF HORROR with this droll above-average spinoff. Peter Cushing is the owner of a London antiques shop on the wrong side of town who imagines disastrous ends for customers who try to cheat him. The four episodes are based on stories by fantasy writer R. Chetwynd-Hayes (who likes to invent offspring from the coupling of two monsters, such as the "weregoo," a cross between a werewolf and a ghoul).

CREDITS

Director Kevin Connor; *Producer* Milton Subotsky; *Screenplay* Robin Clarke, Raymond Christodoulou, based on stories by R. Chetwynd-Hayes; *Photographer* Alan Hume; *Production Designer* Maurice Carter; *Music* David Gamley

CAST

Peter Cushing, David Warner, Ian Bannen, Donald Pleasence, Diana Dors, Margaret Leighton, Ian Carmichael, Ian Ogilvy, Nyree Dawn Porter

GHOST STORY

TV series   1972   U.S. (NBC)
60 minutes (weekly)   Color

Vampires, witches and mad scientists but very few ghosts were featured in this inaccurately titled series, produced without his characteristic flair by filmmaker William Castle. Rotund actor Sebastian Cabot played droll host Winston Essex, elegantly cradling a brandy snifter as he wandered through his shadowy mansion to introduce stories of the ordinary confronted by the uncanny. The best of these included "Alter Ego" and "The Summer House." The former cast Broadway grande dame Helen Hayes as a teacher who helps a student "return" his evil double, willed into existence as a playmate. In the latter Carolyn Jones of THE ADDAMS FAMILY (see Monsters) had a vision in which her husband murders her, only to have the nightmare nearly come true. Few of the stories could sustain a mood of terror, however, and after 13 weeks a murder-mystery element was introduced. Cabot was dropped from the cast. The program was then called CIRCLE OF FEAR.

CREDITS

Producer William Castle

GUEST STARS

James Franciscus, Elizabeth Ashley, Carolyn Jones, Steve Forrest, Helen Hayes, Jason Robards, Stella Stevens

THE HORROR SHOW: 60 MAGICAL YEARS OF MOVIE MONSTERS, MADMEN AND OTHER CREATURES OF THE NIGHT

TV special   1979   U.S. (CBS)   105 minutes
Color

An intelligent, entertaining capsule history of the horror film, scripted by critic Richard Schickel and hosted by Anthony Perkins. Visiting the house where he lived with his "mother" in Hitchcock's PSYCHO (1960) (see Crazies and Freaks)—now a favorite attraction on Universal's studio tour—Perkins introduced clips from Hollywood's classic genre movies: KING KONG (1933) (see Monsters), THE PHANTOM OF THE OPERA (1925) (see Crazies and Freaks), THE FLY (1958) (see Mad Scientists), DRACULA (1931) (see Vampires), THE OMEN (1976) (see Ghosts, Demons and Witches), JAWS (1975) (see Monsters), THE EXORCIST (1973) (see Ghosts, Demons and Witches) and many others.

THE HOUSE THAT DRIPPED BLOOD

Film   1970   G.B. (Amicus)   102 minutes
Eastmancolor

That you can't judge a film by its trashy title is evidenced by this well-written and expertly directed compendium, chrome-bright with Amicus production values. Robert Bloch's neat-handed "hook" has a mysterious house being visited by a Scotland Yard detective searching for a missing film actor. In the course of his investigation, he recounts the stories of three unfortunates who lived in the dwelling. In "Method for Murder," a horror story writer (not unlike Bloch) materializes a lunatic killer he has created for his latest novel. In "Waxworks," Peter Cushing and a friend are turned into exhibits by the owner of a waxworks museum. And "Sweets to the Sweet" has Christopher Lee being murdered via his daughter's voodoo doll. Story four, "The Cloak," reveals that the actor, a horror star, has become a vampire after buying what is purported to be Count Dracula's cape. The latter is played for hilarious comedy, with Ingrid Pitt, star of THE VAMPIRE LOVERS (see Vampires), giving a "let-it-all-fang-out" performance.

CREDITS

Director Peter Duffell; *Producers* Max J. Rosenberg, Milton Subotsky; *Screenplay* Robert Bloch; *Photographer* Ray Parslow; *Art Director* Tony Curtis; *Makeup* Harry and Peter Frampton; *Music* Michael Dress

CAST

Christopher Lee, Peter Cushing, John Bennett, Jon Pertwee, Ingrid Pitt, Denholm Elliott, Nyree Dawn Porter, Joanna Dunham

I LOVE A MYSTERY

Radio series   1939–52   U.S. (NBC/CBS)
15/30 minutes (daily/weekly)

For years millions of radio listeners cozied up to their Philcos and Radiolas and steeled themselves to test their courage against the bizarre villains of *I Love a Mystery*. The heroes were Jack Packard, Reggie Yorke and Doc Long, three brawling adventurers who had survived a near-fatal bombing in Shanghai and had consequently dedicated themselves to solving weird crimes. Motto of their A-1 Detective Agency was "No job too tough, no mystery too baffling." In "The Decapitation of Jefferson Monk," a typical program, an Eastern mystic was determined to have the head of a businessman as a replacement for the embalmed but decaying head of his high priest, which the executive resembled. Another popular tale, repeated several times, was "The Temple of the Vampire."

The unsung heroes of the program were the sound effects men, who created the appropriate mood and environment for various scenes. An ethereal death melody played on an organ (actually Brahms's *Cradle Song*) signaled that an insane killer was about to strike. The sound of a tinkling collar bell accompanied by the click of thundering paws indicated that the otherwise silent Prometheus, a merciless wolf dog, was approaching. In one two-part episode, listeners were treated to a sound effects striptease, as a lady detective ordered a femme fatale to disrobe "completely." As with later generations of genre films and TV shows, the program and others like it were criticized as being excessively violent. (A 1939 *Newsweek* article referred to "radio gore," and in 1941 *The New Republic* ran the title, "Slaughter, Sponsored by . . .")

Creator of the series was radio pioneer Carlton E. Morse, creator of *One Man's Family* (1932–59), radio's longest-running prime-time soap opera. The series began as a 15-minute program broadcast five nights a week and later expanded to a weekly half hour. Opening and closing theme, preceded by a train whistle, was *Valse Triste* by Jean Sibelius. Columbia studios based three "B" pictures on the program: *I Love a Mystery* (1945) reprised "Jefferson Monk," *The Devil's Mask* (1946) dealt with voodoo and hypnosis and *The Unknown* (1946) took place in a haunted house. Actor Jim Bannon played Jack Packard and Barton Yarborough repeated his radio portrayal as Doc Long. Henry Levin directed.

CREDITS

Director Mel Bailey et al.; *Creator/Writer* Carlton E. Morse; *Writer* Michael Raffetto and others

CAST

Michael Raffetto, Russell Thorson, Jay Novello, John McIntire (Jack Packard); Barton Yarborough, Jim Boles (Doc Long); Walter Paterson, Tony Randall (Reggie Yorke); Gloria Blondell (Gerry Booke); Mercedes McCambridge, Cathy Lewis, Luis Van Rooten

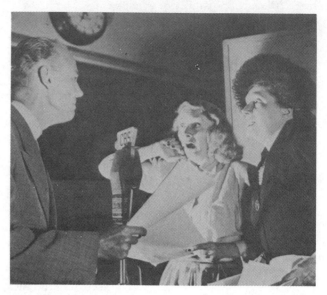

Inner Sanctum: A publicity photo for a 1940s broadcast.

INNER SANCTUM

Radio series   1941–52   U.S. (NBC)
30 minutes (weekly)

Designed to scare the daylights out of listeners, *Inner Sanctum* featured mystery stories that climaxed with a bizarre, occult twist. The program began with a sinister organ theme, followed by the sound of a door squeaking open on rusty hinges and the macabre intonations of the host, who introduced himself simply as Raymond. The closing line was always an insincere, "Until then, good night and . . . pleasant dreams," and the door to the listener's dark imagination swung shut again.

One of the most listened-to programs of the 1940s, the series is credited with launching the tradition of using a peculiar, sardonic host to tell a horror story. The device was subsequently copied in comic books, films and television. When the program made the transition to television for a year-long run in 1954, the squeaking door was seen in all its glory but host Raymond (Paul McGrath) remained off-camera. Universal filmed six minor "Inner Sanctum Mysteries" with Lon Chaney, Jr. as the star. Each story was introduced by a distorted, disembodied head (belonging to David Hoffman). Titles include *Calling Dr. Death* (1943); *Weird Woman* (1944), later remade as *Night of the Eagle*;

Dead Man's Eyes (1944); *Strange Confession* and *The Frozen Ghost* (1945); and *Pillow of Death* (1946).

CREDITS

Producer/Director Himan Brown; *Writers* Robert Sloane, Robert Newman, John Roeburt, Gail and Harry Ingram, Milton Lewis, Sigmund Miller; *Sound Effects* Jack Amerine

HOSTS

Raymond Edward Johnson, Paul McGrath, House James; *Announcer* James Herlihy

IT CAME FROM HOLLYWOOD

Film   1982   U.S.   90 minutes
Black & white and color

A compilation of Hollywood genre worsts, assembled by producers Jeffrey Stein and Susan Strausberg. Guest comedians provide campy introductions to the footage, which is culled into categories: Gilda Radner has "Gorillas and Musical Memories," Dan Aykroyd handles "Brains, Aliens and Troubled Teenagers," and Cheech and Chong appropriately deal with "Getting High at the Movies." The clips would be just as hilarious without the commentary, and there are some wonderful moments from *The Brain That Wouldn't Die*, PLAN 9 FROM OUTER SPACE (see Zombies), *Glen or Glenda? Bride of the Monster, The Flying Disc-man from Mars* and many other trash classics.

KOLCHAK: THE NIGHT STALKER

TV series   1974   U.S. (ABC)
60 minutes (weekly)   Color

One of the few series to convincingly place legendary monsters in the present day, *Kolchak* starred Darren McGavin as an aggressive crime reporter who, instead of tangling with the usual hoods, kept bumping into zombies, demons, werewolves, vampires and other supernatural menaces. This latter-day Van Helsing debuted in a TV movie titled *The Night Stalker* (1972). Richard Matheson's script had an ageless vampire (Barry Atwater) preying on late-night denizens of contemporary Las Vegas. The highest rated TV movie of the year, it was several cuts above most Dan Curtis productions and boasted a good director, John L. Moxey. The cast included Carol Lynley,

Kolchak: The Night Stalker: Darren McGavin as a newsman on the trail of supernatural killers.

Ralph Meeker, Kent Smith, Claude Akins, Elisha Cook, Jr., and Simon Oakland as Kolchak's irate city editor.

The following year Kolchak came back in a sequel, *The Night Strangler*, with another good Matheson script about a centuries-old alchemist (Richard Anderson) who ventures from his underground Seattle laboratory to drain young women of the serum he needs to stay alive. Curtis directed a cast that included Scott Brady, Margaret Hamilton, John Carradine, Wally Cox, Jo Ann Pflug and Oakland.

Despite the popular success of these films, ABC was reluctant to commit to a series because of mounting pressures against TV violence and, reportedly, because network executives had little enthusiasm for what advertisers considered a non-family genre. The ill-fated series finally came to the screen on Friday the 13th of the following year, co-produced by McGavin's company. McGavin's budget precluded hiring writers of the caliber of Richard Matheson, and horror elements had to be softened to appease network censors, so more emphasis was placed on the rumpled, underpaid Kolchak and his running battle with skeptical editor Tony Vincenzo (Oakland), who refused to print his sensational revelations. Most episodes did not live up to the promise of the films, however, although Jimmy Sangster's "Horror in the Heights," an homage to H.P. Lovecraft, came close. Directed by Michael T. Caffrey, the story featured Phil Silvers as an elderly Jew in danger of being gnawed to death by a legendary monster called a Rakshasah, which appears in the guise of a trusted friend. (To Kolchak, it looked like Miss Emily Cowles (Ruth McDevitt), his sweet old friend.) ABC did not promote the series, and it was cancelled after one season.

CREDITS

Creator: Jeff Rice, from his novel *The Kolchak Papers* (1970); *Producers* Paul Playton, Cy Chermak; *Executive Producer* Darren McGavin; *Directors* Vincent McEveety, Don Weiss, Robert Scherer, Alex Grasshoff, Allen Baron, Michael T. Caffrey and others; *Writers* Don Weiss, Michael Kozoll, L. Ford Neale, Zekial Markel, Rudolph Borchert, Paul Playdon, David Chase, Jimmy Sangster and others; *Music* Gil Melle

CAST

Darren McGavin, Simon Oakland, Ruth McDevitt, Jack Grinnage

GUEST STARS

Julie Adams, Nina Foch, Tom Bosley, Dick Van Patten, Cathy Lee Crosby, Victor Jory, Hans Conreid, Dwayne Hickman and others.

LIGHTS OUT

Radio series   1938–50   U.S. (NBC/Mutual)
15/30 minutes (weekly)

One of the genre's great radio anthologies, *Lights Out* used the power of suggestion and sound effects to bring to life creatures and situations that would still be impossible to depict on the screen. Its most notorious story, rebroadcast on the science fiction oriented *Dimension X* (NBC, 1949–57), was "The Chicken Heart That Ate the World." Written by Arch Oboler, radio's foremost thriller dramatist,

Lights Out: Writer Arch Oboler directs a radio broadcast from the control booth.

the story was outrageous enough to elicit giggles from listeners and terrifying enough to chill them to the bone: An ordinary chicken's heart, injected with a growth hormone by a scholarly scientist, begins to grow uncontrollably until it covers the world with "creeping, grasping flesh." In another Oboler tale, a scientist turns himself inside out—a scene made vivid in the mind's eye by a sound-effects man who slowly peeled off a tight rubber glove while an assistant crunched together strawberry boxes to simulate breaking bones.

Originally a 15-minute program, *Lights Out* quickly attracted a large audience, and it was lengthened to 30 minutes. Broadcast time was usually late at night; for many years it was at 10:30 P.M. on Wednesdays. During its last years, when ratings began to wane after the show transferred to television, it was dumped onto the financially shaky Mutual network of affiliated independent stations. The TV series (see listing below) was entertaining, but it never approached the insidious power of its model.

CREDITS

Creator Wyllis Cooper; *Writers* Wyllis Cooper, Betty Winkler, Ted N. Fraser, et al.

CAST

Sidney Ellstrom, Raymond Edward Johnson, Betty Winkler, Ted Maxwell, Templeton Fox, Lou Merrill

LIGHTS OUT

TV series   1949–52   U.S. (NBC)
30 minutes (weekly)   Black & white

This popular series, broadcast live, was a TV translation of the long-running radio series (see listing above). The program—the genre's first—had previously aired in four specials produced in 1946 by Fred Coe. It was abandoned when video technology proved too primitive to achieve the required special effects. After 1950 *Lights Out* always began with a closeup of the candlelit eyes of gaunt host Frank Gallop, followed by his eerie laugh and the words "Lights out, everybody . . . ," as he snuffed out the candle. The self-contained stories dealt with premonitions, hauntings, old houses and other standard horror fare, but occasionally ventured into science fiction. In "Ann Adams Begot," for example (starring *Cat People*'s Kent Smith), an American family was captured by a Neanderthal while exploring a cavern in the south of France. At first the program used only unknown performers, but in 1950 a "guest star" policy was inaugurated to bolster ratings. A 1972 would-be pilot film with this title bore little resemblance to the original series.

CREDITS

Director William Corrigon; *Producers* Herbert Swope, Jr., Ernie Walling; *Music* Fred Howard, Arlo Hults (organ), Paul Lipman (theremin), Doris Johnson (harp)

GUEST STARS

Veronica Lake, Boris Karloff, Josephine Hull, Kent Smith, William Eythe, Burgess Meredith, Raymond Massey, Billie Burke, Yvonne DeCarlo, Leslie Nielsen, Eddie Albert, Basil Rathbone; *Host* Jack LaRue (1949–50), Frank Gallop (1950–52)

THE MERCURY THEATRE ON THE AIR

Radio series   1938–40   U.S. (CBS)
60 minutes (weekly)

This attempt by CBS to bring culture to the airwaves showcased *wunderkind* Orson Welles and his experimental Broadway repertory group, The Mercury Theatre. The program adapted to radio such famous literary properties as Victor Hugo's *Les Miserables* and Charlotte Bronte's *Jane Eyre*, and made two excursions into Gothic horror with Mary Shelley's *Frankenstein* and Bram Stoker's

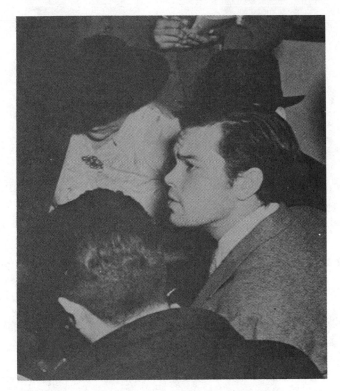

The Mercury Theatre on the Air: Orson Welles attempts to explain his Halloween "prank" to reporters.

Dracula. Welles, who had previously starred on radio's *The Shadow*, usually played the leading roles, supported by such fledgling stars as Joseph Cotten, Richard Widmark and Agnes Moorehead. The program limped along in the Sunday night ratings until Welles came up with his legendary Halloween joke—a hair-raising adaptation of H.G. Wells's *The War of the Worlds*.

Welles cleverly "reported" the story of Martians landing at Grover Mills, New Jersey, as a series of newsbreaks interrupting a program of music and commentary, duping suggestible listeners who thought they were hearing the real thing. Some panicked and took to the roads, while others barricaded themselves in their houses against the coming onslaught. The ruse was reinforced by an announcer who copied the hysterical delivery of a newscaster who had given an on-the-spot description of the explosion of the Hindenburg dirigible the year before. Moreover, people were increasingly relying on remote broadcasts for news from war-shadowed Europe.

Welles's prank more than justified H.G. Wells's prediction of the persuasive power of electronic media, and the FCC promptly banned such broadcasts. Director Joseph Sargent based a 1974 TV movie, *The Night That Panicked America*, on the incident. Recalling the furor 20 years later, co-producer John Houseman wrote the following: "To this day it is impossible to sit in a room and hear the scratched, worn, off-the-air recording of the broadcast without feeling in the back of your neck some slight draft left over from that great wind of terror that swept the nation."

CREDITS

Producer/Director Orson Welles; *Co-producer/Editor* John Houseman; *Writer* Howard Koch; *Musical Director* Bernard Herrmann

CAST

Orson Welles, Fred Readick, Kenneth Delmar, Agnes Moorehead, Joseph Cotten, Martin Gabel, Everett Sloane, Ray Collins, Alice Frost

THE MONSTER SQUAD

TV series   1976   U.S. (NBC)
30 minutes (weekly)   Color

A criminology student paying his tuition as a night watchman in a wax museum brings his crime computer to work. Its oscillations shake to life the figures of Frankenstein, Dracula and the Werewolf, who decide to help him fight crime to atone for their past sins.

CREDITS

Directors Herman Hoffman, James Sheldon; *Producer* Michael McClean; *Executive Producers* William P. D'Angelo, Harvey Bullock, Ray Allen; *Music* Richard LaSalle

CAST

Fred Grandy, Henry Polic II, Buck Kartalian, Michael Lane

THE MYSTERIOUS TRAVELER

Radio series   1943–47   U.S. (Mutual)
30 minutes (weekly)

The Mysterious Traveler always warned listeners to keep a hypodermic handy in case his emotional shocks proved too much for them. Most tales dealt with villains who had supernatural powers or seemed to, and usually revolved around a murder committed in one of the places where he had stopped off. "I take this same train every week at

The Mysterious Traveler: Maurice Tarplin was the character's voice.

this time," was his customary farewell. Lead Tarplin also played THE STRANGE DR. WEIRD (see Mad Scientists).

CREDITS

Director Jock MacGregor; *Writers* David Kogan, Robert A. Arthur; *Sound Effects* Jim Goode, Jack Amerine, Ron Harper

CAST

Maurice Tarplin (The Mysterious Traveler), Lon Clark, Bill Zuckert, Ed Begley, Jack Beck

NIGHT GALLERY

TV film   1969   U.S. (Universal)   98 minutes
Color

This three-part anthology was actually a pilot for the series ROD SERLING'S NIGHT GALLERY. A mixed bag of goose-pimplers, the film is set in a shadowy art gallery whose paintings tell each story. The first tale, directed by Boris Sagal, has a young schemer murdering his rich uncle and being possessed by a family painting. The second episode, which propelled director Steven Spielberg to an important career, concerns a wealthy blind woman (Joan Crawford) who buys the eyes of a man who owes her money to see for 12 hours. In the third story, directed by Barry Shear, a former Nazi war criminal is found hiding in a Buenos Aires art gallery.

CREDITS

Directors Boris Sagal, Steven Spielberg, Barry Shear; *Producer* William Sackheim; *Screenplay* Rod Serling; *Photog-*

raphers Richard Batcheller, William Margulies; *Art Director* Howard E. Johnson; *Music* Billy Goldenberg

CAST

Joan Crawford, Ossie Davis, Richard Kiley, Roddy McDowall, Barry Sullivan, Tom Bosley, Sam Jaffe, George Macready

ONE STEP BEYOND

TV series	1959–61	U.S. (ABC)
30 minutes (weekly)		Black & white

Director John Newland hosted this intriguing excursion into the supernatural, which debuted in the same year as THE TWILIGHT ZONE, to which it was inevitably compared. Unlike the former, *One Step Beyond* claimed to be based on fact, not fantasy. Typical of its subject matter was an episode titled "If You See Sally." The title character was a young girl found walking along a deserted road by a truck driver. Taken home, according to her own directions, the girl vanished from the truck when her parents explained she had been dead for several years. Dozens of viewers reportedly wrote in after the broadcast to report similar experiences. The series occasionally ventured into monster territory, as in "Ordeal on Locust Street," whose half-human, half-fish mutant was kept prisoner in a house. Cancelled because of low ratings, the program continues to attract an audience of buffs in local syndication.

CREDITS

Creator Merwin Gerard; *Producer* Collier Young; *Director* John Newland; *Writers* Michael Plant, Don Mankiewicz, Merwin Gerard, Larry Marcus, Collier Young, Charles Beaumont, Derry Quinn, Paul David and others; *Music* Harry Lubin

GUEST CAST

Luana Anders, Olive Deering, Torin Thatcher, Patrick Macnee, Ron Howard, Joan Fontaine, Warren Beatty, David Opatoshu, Barbara Baxley, Christopher Lee, Peter Wyngarde, Donald Pleasence and others.

THE OUTER LIMITS

TV series	1963–65	U.S. (ABC)
60 minutes (weekly)		Black & white

First-time viewers of this science fiction series were brought to attention by a jumbled image that

The Outer Limits: Shirley Knight and humanoid friend in an episode titled "The Man Who Was Never Born."

appeared on their TV screens at the opening of each episode. An accompanying voice-over quickly explained the problem: "There is nothing wrong with your television set, do not attempt to adjust the picture. We are controlling transmission. . . . You are about to participate in a great adventure . . . which reaches from the inner mind to the Outer Limits." Intelligent and imaginative, the program specialized in bug-eyed monsters from outer space. One of its most absorbing episodes was "The Invisibles," written by the show's producer Joseph Stefano and directed by Gerd Oswald, with George Macready as an extraterrestrial seeking to conquer Earth by attaching superintelligent slugs to human spinal cords. Stefano was replaced during the second season by Ben Brady, who assigned scripts to such leading science fiction writers as Harlan Ellison and David Duncan. Ellison won two Hugos for "Soldier" and "Demon with a Glass Hand," which had to do with an android with a hand encoded with the human race, who was pursued by enemy aliens.

The Outer Limits was a proving ground for many future stars and for cameraman Conrad Hall, who subsequently photographed *In Cold Blood* (1967) and *Butch Cassidy and the Sundance Kid* (1968). A popular success, the program foundered when moved opposite Saturday night's *The Jackie Gleason Show* and was canceled in mid-season.

CREDITS

Directors Byron Haskin, Leonard Horn, Gerd Oswald, Charles Haas, et al.; *Creator/Executive Producer* Leslie Stevens; *Producers* Joseph Stefano, Ben Brady; *Writers* David Duncan, Harlan Ellison, Robert Towne, Jerry Sohl, Jerome Ross, Meyer Dolinsky, Dean Reisner, Joseph Stefano, et al.; *Photographer* Conrad Hall; *Special Effects* The Ray Mercer Company, Projects Unlimited; *Makeup* John Chambers, Wah Chang, Fred Phillips; *Music* Dominic Frontiere, Harry Lubin

GUEST STARS

Robert Culp, Leonard Nimoy, Bruce Dern, William Shatner, Donald Pleasence, Martin Landau, David McCallum, Salome Jens, Grant Williams, et al.

ROD SERLING'S NIGHT GALLERY

TV series   1970-73   U.S. (NBC)
60/30 minutes (weekly)   Color

Rod Serling, creator of THE TWILIGHT ZONE, was less successful with two subsequent series. *The Loner* (1965–66), an adult Western, failed to capture an audience, as did this even more problematical weekly venture into the occult. The series began with a two-hour pilot film, NIGHT GALLERY, followed by an alternating hour-long slot in an NBC series titled *Four in One* (the other shows were *McCloud, San Francisco International Airport* and *The Psychiatrist*). It stayed in the Wednesday lineup by itself for the second season, then was shortened to a half-hour and shifted to Sunday nights.

Serling opened the show in an empty art gallery which had closed for the night. Beginning his narration, he would stroll past the paintings and pause at one that introduced the episode's story. Pitted against CBS's top-rated *Mannix*, the program failed to attract a significant audience, despite Universal's and NBC's injection of shock effects and imitative chase scenes and fights. Serling attempted to leave the series after creative control was taken away from him, but his NBC contract was iron-clad and he was forced to stay on. Still, two of the episodes are among Serling's finest. "The Messiah of Mott Street" stars Edward G. Robinson as an ill old Jew whose grandson attempts to grant his last wish by going in search of the Messiah. In "They're Tearing Down Tim Riley's Bar," a businessman sees an analogy between a neighborhood bar that is being torn down and his own mess of a life.

CREDITS

Directors Douglas Heyes, Jeannot Szwarc, John Astin, Daryl Duke, Steven Spielberg, Theodore Flicker, Jeff Corey, Jack Laird, Don Taylor, Gene Kearney, Leonard Nimoy, John Badham, et al.; *Creator* Rod Serling; *Producer* Jack Laird; *Writers* Rod Serling, Gene Kearney, Alvin Sapinsley, Jack Laird, Theodore Flicker, Halsted Welles, Richard Matheson, Douglas Heyes, et al.; *Makeup* Bud Westmore, John Chambers; *Music* Gil Melle

GUEST STARS

Phyllis Diller, John Astin, Pat Boone, Ray Milland, John Colicos, Kim Stanley, Larry Hagman, Suzy Parker, Joanna Pettet, Buddy Ebsen, Pernell Roberts, William Windom, Edward G. Robinson, et al.

STAY TUNED FOR TERROR

Radio series   1944–45(?)   U.S. (Mutual)
30 minutes (weekly)

This low-budget series never made the grade, despite 39 clever, well-polished scripts by horror writer Robert Bloch. Bloch, who began his career as a disciple of H.P. Lovecraft, had broadened his market by the mid-1940s by writing mysteries and science fantasies as well as genre novels and short stories. The program was presented under the aegis of *Weird Tales*, an unprofitable but influential magazine that began publication in 1923 and had been one of the first to publish the works of the reclusive Lovecraft and the eager Bloch. The most renowned episode was Bloch's adaptation of his short story, "Yours Truly, Jack the Ripper," which brought the mass murderer into the 20th century as a latter-day vampire who maintains his youth by going on intermittent killing sprees. The story was later revised by Bloch for TV's THRILLER (1960–62). Bloch, of course, is the author of the psychological horror story on which Hitchcock based PSYCHO (1960) (see Crazies and Freaks).

SUSPENSE

Radio series   1942-62   U.S. (CBS)
60 minutes (weekly)

One of CBS's most prestigious drama series, *Suspense* was honored by the industry with a Peabody Award and a citation from the Mystery Writers of America. The program specialized in original, eerie sagas of people caught in bizarre

Suspense: The young Grace Kelly in a TV episode titled "50 Beautiful Girls."

the tales aired on this landmark program were preserved on tape, and the best have been rebroadcast on CBS's syndicated *CBS Radio Mystery Theater* (1973–   ), radio's first major revival of drama.

CREDITS

Directors John Peyser, Tony Leader, William Spier, Norman Macdonnell; *Producers* Charles Vanda, Elliott Lewis; *Writers* Sigmund Miller, Joseph Russell, Robert Richards, Ferrin N. Fraser, Joseph L. Green; *Sound Effects* Jack Sixsmith, Ross Murray, Dave Light, Gus Bayz

GUEST STARS

Agnes Moorehead, Orson Welles, Ida Lupino, Lucille Ball, Brian Donlevy, Cary Grant, Vincent Price, et al.; *Narrator* Paul Frees; *Announcer* Truman Bradley

SUSPENSE

TV series   1949–54   U.S. (CBS)
30 minutes (weekly)   Black & white

Suspense was still a top-rated radio program (see listing above) when it made the transition to television. Broadcast live from New York, the program featured, in the announcer's words, "Well-calculated tales to keep you in suspense." The stories dealt with people in perilous situations, real or imagined. A small percentage were radio adaptations of such classic horror stories as *Dr. Jekyll and Mr. Hyde*—telecast in 1950 with Ralph Bell as Stevenson's dual-natured scientist and again in 1951 with Basil Rathbone. Other genre plays included "The Waxworks" with William Prince, "The Tortured Hand" with Peter Lorre and several adaptations of Poe and Lovecraft stories. Most of the performers were seasoned Broadway and Hollywood actors, but a few were talented unknowns who received their first important exposure here. These included Grace Kelly, Cloris Leachman and Mike Wallace, the *60 Minutes* anchor who had previously been an announcer on radio's *The Green Hornet*.

In 1964 *Suspense* was revived as a 30-minute program filmed in color, with Sebastian Cabot as host. Several performers in the original series appeared in the first few episodes, including Basil Rathbone and E.G. Marshall, but audiences failed to tune in, and filming was abruptly canceled. The show played out its run with episodes that had been previously aired on *Schlitz Playhouse of Stars*.

and terrifying situations, which seemed to be (but often weren't) the products of a paranoid imagination.

In "Hitchhiker," for example, Orson Welles played a terrified driver who keeps passing the same man thumbing a ride as he travels across the country. Describing his encounters sotto voce, Welles offers a harrowing portrait of the driver and demonstrates the formidable power of radio to stimulate the imagination. "Sorry Wrong Number," broadcast in 1943, starred Agnes Moorehead as a lonely invalid who accidentally overhears a telephone conversation plotting a murder, which turns out to be her own. One of the series' most popular episodes, it was rebroadcast several times and filmed in 1948 by Anatole Litvak, with Barbara Stanwyck and Burt Lancaster. In another popular tale titled "Three Skeleton Keys," rebroadcast on CBS's ESCAPE, Vincent Price played a man trapped on a rat-infested island. Many of

CREDITS

Director Robert Stevens; *Producers* Robert Stevens, Martin Manulis; *Music* Wilbur Hatch

GUEST STARS

Boris Karloff, John Carradine, Jackie Cooper, Grace Kelly, Thomas Mitchell, Teresa Wright, Victor Jory, Charles Bickford, Lilia Skala, Barry Sullivan, Basil Rathbone, E.G. Marshall, Cloris Leachman, Mike Wallace, Peter Lorre

Tales from the Crypt: Grimsdyke (Peter Cushing) rises from the grave to provide a framework for the movie.

TALES FROM THE CRYPT

Film   1972   G.B. (Metromedia/Amicus)
92 minutes   Eastmancolor

E.C. Comics buffs have mixed feelings about this British incursion into a particularly American genre. Ralph Richardson is too staid as the lascivious fun-punning Crypt-Keeper, and a bit of camp corniness creeps in occasionally, but it's an enjoyable translation that works well enough on its own level. The setting is a catacombs where the hooded Crypt-Keeper predicts hellish futures for each of his captive guests. In "All Through the House," a young mother fights off a slasher dressed as Santa Claus on Christmas Eve. "Blind Alley" has a man trying to find his way out of a maze of razor blades, and "Wish You Were Here" is a variation on "The Monkey's Paw" idea. "Poetic Justice,"

which evokes something of the style of E.C. artist Graham Ingels, has Peter Cushing as a putrid corpse rising from the grave to deliver a vengeful Valentine's Day gift.

While not up to the wonderfully gruesome and grotesque inventiveness of its model, this anthology and its successor, VAULT OF HORROR (1973), at least acknowledge the genre's debt to E.C.'s unique group of splatter-oriented comic books. Conceived in 1950 by William Gaines and Albert Feldstein during the cinema's dry years between Gothic horror and science fiction, the series helped keep horror alive for a generation of future writers and filmmakers, whose ranks include Stephen King and George A. Romero. Influenced by the increasingly bizarre monsters who confronted superheroes in comic books of the 1940s, Gaines and Feldstein debuted with three titles featuring the villain as star: *The Vault of Horror, The Haunt of Fear* and *Tales from the Crypt*. Each had a master of ceremonies, like the narrators of earlier radio thrillers. These were, respectively, The Vault-Keeper, The Old Witch and The Crypt-Keeper (described in an early issue as being the offspring of two sideshow freaks).

Young readers relished the magazines for their ingeniously implausible and expertly illustrated gore stories, which were obviously meant to be amusing rather than emotionally reactive, but parents were outraged. In one typical strip titled "Foul Play," a homicidal baseball player got his comeuppance at the hands of angry team members, who performed a premature autopsy and used his body parts as sporting equipment. E.C.'s death knell came with the publication of Dr. Frederic Wertham's book *Seduction of the Innocent*, which tenuously reasoned that E.C. comics, and their scores of imitators, were contributing to juvenile delinquency. In 1954 the industry reacted to mounting criticism by forming a censorship board called the Comics Code Authority, which finished off macabre comic books by denying them distribution. The film CREEPSHOW is an homage to the E.C. comics.

CREDITS

Director Freddie Francis; *Producer/Screenplay* Milton Subotsky, based on stories in the comic books *Tales from the Crypt* and *The Vault of Horror* by Al Feldstein and William Gaines; *Photographer* Norman Warwick; *Music* Douglas Gamely

CAST

Ralph Richardson, Peter Cushing, Joan Collins, Ian Hendry, Patrick Magee, Richard Greene, Geoffrey Bayldon

TALES OF TERROR

Film   1962   U.S. (AIP)   90 minutes
Pathecolor   Panavision

Moviegoers failed to turn out for Roger Corman's fourth Poe film, probably because of the unfamiliar anthology format, and posterity has been making amends ever since. It's the most inventive of the series, cleverly scripted by Richard Matheson—who expanded three Poe stories, some no longer than three pages—with Corman squeezing the last ounce of Poe-esque effect from his limited resources. In "Morella," a subtly incestuous tale, the spirit of Vincent Price's mummified wife possesses their daughter. In "The Black Cat," Matheson borrows elements from "The Cask of Amontillado" and adds a leavening of humor, as Price and Peter Lorre get memorably drunk tasting wine before one of them is walled up alive in the cellar. In "The Case of M. Valdemar," hypnotist Basil Rathbone puts Price on hold at the moment of death, with Price eventually turning into a pool of "oozing liquid putrescence."

CREDITS

Director/Producer Roger Corman; *Screenplay* Richard Matheson, based on stories of Edgar Allan Poe; *Photographer* Floyd Crosby; *Art Director* Daniel Haller; *Special Effects* Pat Dinga; *Music* Les Baxter

CAST

Vincent Price, Peter Lorre, Basil Rathbone, Debra Paget, Joyce Jameson, Maggie Pierce, Leona Gage

TALES OF THE UNEXPECTED

TV series   1977   U.S. (NBC)
60 minutes (weekly)   Color

This anthology series presented suspense stories with surprise O. Henry endings. Most segments dealt in low-key psychological horror and the occult, and a few were science fiction oriented. Typical was "The Mark of Adonis," the tale of a middle-aged theatrical producer who owed his youthful appearance to a mysterious beauty treatment that had unfortunate side effects. Producer Quinn Martin was more successful with TV's *The Invaders* (1967–68).

GUEST STARS

Robert Foxworth, Marilyn Mason, Van Johnson, Ronny Cox, Roy Thinnes, Christine Belford; *Narrator/Host* William Conrad

TALES OF TOMORROW

TV series   1951–53   U.S. (ABC)
30 minutes (weekly)   Black & white

This live anthology series, a precursor of THE TWILIGHT ZONE, was one of the few science-fiction/horror shows of the period intended for adults. It debuted with a two-part version of Jules Verne's *20,000 Leagues Under the Sea*, starring Thomas Mitchell as Captain Nemo, with Leslie Nielsen as his captive visitor. Stories were adapted from the classics and contemporary genre magazines, and most featured alien invaders from strange planets. Among the program's ambitious attempts to present horror was a reprise of FRANKENSTEIN (see Monsters), with Lon Chaney, Jr., repeating his movie impersonation, and "Dark Angel," about a female Dorian Gray who never ages. Seen today, the series is handicapped by its restrictive live studio sets (special effects were filmed) and a pedantic approach to its material. It was also heard briefly on radio in 1953.

CREDITS

Creator/Producer George F. Foley, Jr.; *Executive Producers* Mort Abrams, Dick Gordon; *Director* Leonard Valenta; *Music* Bobby Christian

GUEST STARS

Boris Karloff, Lon Chaney, Jr., Veronica Lake, Franchot Tone, Lee J. Cobb, Eva Gabor, Sidney Blackmer, Meg Mundy, Thomas Mitchell, Leslie Nielsen

TALES THAT WITNESS MADNESS

Film   1973   G.B. (Amicus/Paramount)
90 minutes   Color

There's barely a shiver in this glossy compendium from Amicus, the little studio that gave us such chillers as TALES FROM THE CRYPT and ASYLUM. The television quality script has a doctor recounting four case histories from his mental clinic. In "Penny Farthing," an antiques dealer travels back in time. "Me" concerns a tree that attacks the wife of its owner. In "Mr. Tiger," a small boy conjures up a tiger to take care of his squabbling parents. And "Luau" involves an American woman and her daughter in cannibalistic rituals on a Pacific island.

CREDITS

Director Freddie Francis; *Producer* Norman Priggen; *Screenplay* Jay Fairbank (Jennifer Jayne); *Photographer* Norman Warwick; *Art Director* Roy Walker; *Makeup* Eric Allwright; *Music* Bernard Ebbinghouse

CAST

Kim Novak, Jack Hawkins, Suzy Kendall, Joan Collins, Donald Pleasence, Georgia Brown, Michael Jayston, Peter McEnery

THRILLER

TV series   1960-62   U.S. (NBC)
60 minutes (weekly)   Black & white

An ambitious, quality series, *Thriller* was expected to compete with THE TWILIGHT ZONE and ALFRED HITCHCOCK PRESENTS, both still in half-hour formats. Its originator was Hubbell Robinson, who had been associated with the prestigious *Studio One* and the occult oriented *Climax*. Horror luminary Boris Karloff was hired to host the program and to act occasionally in episodes. From the first, the series was troubled by a Jekyll-and-Hyde format that left some doubt as to what kind of thrills it had in mind. After *Thriller's* poorly received premiere, producer Maxwell Shane was brought in to handle the crime melodramas, and William Frye was assigned the bone-chillers, which were the better half of the series.

Many of the genre stories were drawn from the pages of the old *Weird Tales* and were scripted by the magazine's alumnus Robert Bloch. Among these was "Yours Truly, Jack the Ripper," which Bloch had previously adapted for the *Weird Tales* radio series STAY TUNED FOR TERROR. Bloch also wrote "The Cheaters," one of the series' best, which was directed by John Brahm of the movie thrillers *The Lodger* (1944) and *Hangover Square* (1945). The story concerns a cursed pair of spectacles which allows its wearers to read people's minds and see other ugly truths, including the final wearer's grotesque, loathsome inner self reflected in a mirror. The makeup, reminiscent of the final scene in *The Picture of Dorian Gray* (1945), was by Jack Barron. Another startling story from *Weird Tales* was Robert E. Howard's "Pigeons from Hell," adapted by John Kneubuhl and directed by

John Newland of the series ONE STEP BEYOND. In this one, teenagers Brandon DeWilde and David Walton spend the night in an abandoned house occupied by a "zuvembie"—a mongrel mix of zombie, vampire and werewolf—which drives an axe into the head of one of them. Also aired was Poe's *The Premature Burial*, with Karloff in the lead role, and "The Ordeal of Dr. Cordell," an adaptation of Stevenson's *Dr. Jekyll and Mr. Hyde*.

CREDITS

Directors Ray Milland, Fletcher Markle, Maxwell Shane, Arthur Hiller, Douglas Heyes, John Newland, John Brahm, Ida Lupino, Lazlo Benedek, et al.; *Executive Producer* Hubbell Robinson; *Producers* Fletcher Markle, Maxwell Shane, William Frye; *Writers* Robert Bloch, Donald S. Sanford, Hugh Walpole, John Kneubuhl, Robert Arthur, Maxwell Shane, Mel Goldberg, et al.; *Makeup* Jack Barron; *Music* Peter Rugolo, Jerry Goldsmith

GUEST STARS

Mary Astor, Mort Sahl, Nehemiah Persoff, Kenneth Haigh, Philip Carey, Guy Stockwell, Constance Ford, Oscar Homolka, Harry Townes, George Grizzard, Boris Karloff, et al.; *Host* Boris Karloff

TORTURE GARDEN

Film   1967   G.B. (Amicus/Columbia)
93 minutes   Technicolor

Good, medium-level tingles for those who like their horror tongue-in-cheek. The wry script is by the prolific Robert Bloch, and the production and performances are up to Amicus's high standards. Framework is a carnival sideshow where a barker named Dr. Diablo predicts disastrous futures for five visitors. First and best story is "Enoch," an adaptation of the *Weird Tales* favorite about a murderer whose head is devoured by a cat. In "Terror Over Hollywood," a nosy starlet learns—to her regret—why a famous star never ages. "Mr. Steinway" has a jealous piano murdering its owner's fiancee. And "The Man Who Collected Poe," weakest of the lot, has Jack Palance hamming it up as a magician who brings Poe back from the dead to write more stories.

CREDITS

Director Freddie Francis; *Producers* Max Rosenberg, Milton Subotsky; *Screenplay* Robert Bloch; *Photographer* Norman Warwick; *Art Directors* Don Mingaye, Scott

Simon; *Makeup* Jill Carpenter; *Music* Don Banks, James Bernard

CAST

Burgess Meredith, Jack Palance, Peter Cushing, Robert Hutton, Michael Ripper, Beverly Adams, John Standing, Michael Bryant

I TRE VOLTI DELLA PAURA/Black Sabbath

Film   1963   Italy/France (Emmepi/Galatea/Lyre)
99 minutes   Color

A lushly decadent trio of tales from Mario Bava, then Italy's leading Hammeresque scare exporter. In "The Drop of Water," a female ghost comes back to reclaim a ring stolen from her body. "The Telephone" has a high-class hooker murdering the heavy breather who has been terrorizing her over the telephone. But the man returns from the dead and continues making the calls. Bava's unnecessary shock cuts and constant zooms are annoying, but less so in "The Wurdalak," adapted from a story by Tolstoy. Karloff, riding into the frame with a severed hand in his fist, is superb as the head of a Russian peasant family cursed by a wurdalak—a vampire.

CREDITS

Director Mario Bava; *Producer* Salvator Billeteri; *Screenplay* Marcello Fondato, Alberto Bevilacqua, Mario Bava, from stories by Anton Chekov, Alexei Tolstoy, Howard Snyder; *Photographer* Ubaldo Terzano; *Art Director* Giorgio Giovannini; *Music* Roberto Nicolosi

CAST

Boris Karloff, Michele Mercier, Jacqueline Pierreux, Susy Anderson, Mark Damon, Glauco Onorato

TWICE TOLD TALES

Film   1963   U.S. (Admiral)   119 minutes
Color

A laudable, if not entirely successful, attempt to adapt Nathaniel Hawthorne's macabre fiction to the screen—not the easiest of tasks—in the manner of AIP's Poe series. In "Dr. Heidegger's Experiment," a physician finds a way of restoring his youth and reviving his dead fiancee. "Rapaccini's Daughter" has a scientist making his daughter poi-

sonous to anyone who touches her. And in the classic "The House of Seven Gables"—much too abridged to be effective—a man searching for a hidden treasure in the old family mansion falls victim to a deadly curse. Vincent Price, a Hawthorne fan, plays all three leads with an uncharacteristic subtlety true to the author's spirit.

CREDITS

Director Sidney Salkow; *Producer/Screenplay* Robert Kent, based on stories by Nathaniel Hawthorne; *Photographer* Ellis W. Carter; *Special Effects* Milton Olsen; *Music* Richard LaSalle

CAST

Vincent Price, Sebastian Cabot, Mari Blanchard, Brett Halsey, Joyce Taylor, Richard Denning, Abraham Sofaer, Beverly Garland

The Twilight Zone: Creator and host Rod Sterling.

THE TWILIGHT ZONE

TV series   1959-64   U.S. (CBS)
30 minutes/60 minutes (weekly)   Black & white

When the late television writer Rod Serling found his socially concerned dramas being forced out by the medium's escapist fare, he journeyed into the Fifth Dimension—originally to be the

Sixth—of *The Twilight Zone*. "Things which couldn't be said by a Republican or Democrat could be said by a Martian," he explained in an interview. Serling wrote many of the stories himself and was the sober, clench-jawed narrator (Orson Welles, among others, had been considered by the network). In "The Eye of the Beholder," for example, he attacked prejudice. A hideously deformed woman undergoes plastic surgery and emerges as a stunning beauty—at least by Earth's standards. As the camera pulls back, we see that her doctors and nurses are reptilian humanoids who recoil in disgust at the sight of the "other." And in "Time Enough at Last," a timid bank clerk hides in a vault to finish reading *David Copperfield*, only to emerge and find himself the lone survivor of a nuclear holocaust—a TV no-no at the time.

But not all episodes dealt in messages; some were genuinely terrifying. Agnes Moorehead starred in "The Invaders," playing a dialogueless role as a farm woman besieged by a miniature flying saucer. Most stories had surprise endings, as in "Stopover in a Quiet Town." A married couple find themselves trapped in a strange desolate town where an empty train keeps bringing them to their point of departure. The sound of a child's laughter causes them to look up, and they discover to their horror that they are pets of a gigantic child in a toy village.

Although somewhat tame by today's graphic, paranoid standards, the series enjoyed a long run in syndication until the recent present. In the fall of 1985 it was supplanted by a new big-budget version of *The Twilight Zone*, presented by CBS. Ironically, the original series had left the air when network executives decided that viewers wanted more sitcoms and action series. By 1985 prime time's formula seemed moribund, and ratings indicated that audiences welcomed back the anthology genre, with its rich vein of stories and styles. Also debuting that season were Steven Spielberg's anthology series *Amazing Stories* and a remake of *Alfred Hitchcock Presents*. In 1983, four episodes were retooled for a disappointing big-budget film, *Twilight Zone—the Movie*.

CREDITS

Creator/Executive Producer/Writer Rod Serling; *Directors* Richard Donner, William Claxton, Ralph Nelson, Buzz Kulik, Christian Nyby, Ted Post, Don Weiss, Perry Lafferty and others; *Writers* Charles Beaumont, Richard Matheson, Ray Bradbury, Earl Hamner and others; *Makeup* William Tuttle; *Music* Bernard Herrmann, Jerry Goldsmith

GUEST CAST

Burgess Meredith, Fay Wray, Dana Andrews, William Shatner, Robert Duvall, Cliff Robertson, Leonard Nimoy, Albert Salmi, Cloris Leachman, Josephine Hutchinson, Robert Redford, Buster Keaton and others

VAULT OF HORROR

Film   1973   G.B. (Metromedia/Amicus)
86 minutes   Eastmancolor

Amicus's follow-up to its TALES FROM THE CRYPT (1972) tackles more of the fondly remembered E.C. horror comics of the 1950s, but with less fidelity to its source. The linkup here is the basement of a strange office building, where five people are stranded during an elevator failure and pass the time recalling horrible nightmares that involve voodoo, black magic, vampirism and grisly murder, all with surprise endings. The final denouement comes when the strangers discover they are all dead. Best episode is "Midnight Mess," in which a male guest at a vampire party supplies the drinks by having a spigot fitted into his jugular vein.

CREDITS

Director Roy Ward Baker; *Producers* Max J. Rosenberg, Milton Subotsky; *Screenplay* Milton Subotsky, based on stories in the comic books *Tales from the Crypt* and *The Vault of Horror* by Al Feldstein and William Gaines; *Photographer* Denys Coop; *Art Director* Tony Curtis; *Makeup* Roy Ashton; *Music* Douglas Gamley

CAST

Daniel Massey, Terry-Thomas, Anna Massey, Glynis Johns, Curt Jurgens, Dawn Addams, Tom Baker, Michael Craig, Edward Judd, Denholm Elliott

DAS WACHSFIGURENKABINETT/Waxworks

U.S. title: Three Wax Men

Film   1924   Germany (Neptun-Film)
62 minutes   Black & white (silent)

Although slow-moving and creakily plotted by today's standards, this initial horror anthology remains watchable for its startlingly grotesque milieu and its legendary stars. Setting is a carnival wax museum whose keeper relates three stories that bring to life the figures of Jack the Ripper, Haroun al Raschid and Ivan the Terrible. "The main action is set at night," writes Lotte Eisner in *The Haunted Screen*, her study of German expressionist cinema. "Tents with mysterious shadows, innumerable electric signs, the merry-go-round and a gigantic wheel turning in a welter of lights, the whole multiplied by the superimpositions which thread across the screen like spiders' webs. . . ." Director/designer Paul Leni deliberately forced perspective to make the actors move abnormally: Doorways have low arches, staircases are narrow and body-bending, and floors slant precipitously. Universal brought Leni to Hollywood on the basis of *Waxworks*, one of the earliest movies set in a wax museum. The list includes *The Mystery of the Wax Museum* (1932), *Midnight at Madame Tussaud's* (1936), *Charlie Chan in the Wax Museum* (1940), *House of Wax* (1953), *Chamber of Horrors* (1966) and *Terror in the Wax Museum* (1973). In 1961 Robert Bloch scripted a TV version of *Waxworks*, broadcast on the THRILLER series.

CREDITS

Director Paul Leni; *Screenplay* Henrik Galeen; *Photographer* Helmar Lenski; *Art Directors* Paul Leni, Ernst Stern, Alfred Junge

CAST

Emil Jannings, Conrad Veidt, Werner Krauss, Wilhelm (William) Dieterle

WAY OUT

TV series   1961   U.S. (CBS)
30 minutes (weekly)   Black & white

English author Roald Dahl hosted this unfortunately brief anthology series, which brought his elegantly macabre, poison-etched stories to the small screen. One memorable program concerned a photographer who could improve the features of his subjects by retouching their pictures. When he accidentally splashed the magical fluid on his own portrait, one side of his face was instantly erased to match the featureless plane in the damaged photograph. What made this chiller so effective was the convincing makeup of Dick Smith, later to make a name with THE EXORCIST (1973) (see Ghosts, Demons and Witches). Although it aired in the half-hour preceding the popular TWILIGHT ZONE, *Way Out* never caught on, and it was canceled after six weeks.

GUEST STARS

Charlotte Rae, Kathleen Widdoes, Rosemary Murphy, Philip Coolidge, William Rogers; *Host* Roald Dahl

George Romero, director of the cult favorite **Night of the Living Dead.**

ANKERS, EVELYN 1918–1985

Actress. Born in Valparaiso, Chile, to British parents. Educated in England at the Royal Academy of Dramatic Arts, she made her debut in the British film *The Bells of St. Mary's* (1936). Ankers appeared on Broadway in *Ladies in Retirement* (1939) and made her Hollywood debut in *Hit the Road* (1940). She launched her brief career as "The Screamer" in the genre comedy *Hold That Ghost* (1941), succeeding Fay Wray as Hollywood's most persecuted (but unruffled) heroine. She also appeared on television in her husband Richard Denning's series *Mr. and Mrs. North* (1952–54) and guest starred on *Ford Theatre* and other live dramatic programs of the 1950s.

FILMS INCLUDE

The Wolf Man (1941); *The Ghost of Frankenstein* (1941); *Sherlock Holmes and the Voice of Terror* (1942); *Cap-*

tive Wild Woman, Son of Dracula, The Mad Ghoul (1943); *Jungle Woman, The Invisible Man's Revenge, Pearl of Death, Weird Woman* (1944); *The Frozen Ghost* (1945); *Queen of Burlesque, The French Key* (1946); *The Lone Wolf in London* (1947); *Tarzan's Magic Fountain* (1949); *The Texan Meets Calamity Jane* (1950); *No Greater Love* (sponsored by the Lutheran Church) (1960).

ARNOLD, JACK 1916–

Director. Born in New Haven, Connecticut. Educated at Ohio State University and the American Academy of Dramatic Arts, Arnold trained as an actor and appeared on Broadway in 1936's *Three Men on a Horse.* During World War II, he served his apprenticeship as a filmmaker under documentary *auteur* Robert Flaherty, who made training films for the U.S. Army Signal Corps. After military service, Arnold acted in films and directed documentaries for the State Department and private industry. In 1953 he was signed by Universal-International and made his feature debut with *Girls in the Night*. His genre debut was the impressive *It Came from Outer Space* (1953), the first science fiction film to be shot in 3-D. Throughout the 1950s, Arnold directed several provocative and unsettling SF-horror features notable for their visual, atmospheric style, which have become classics. Best of these is *The Incredible Shrinking Man* (1957), a metaphoric tale of a mutated man vanishing into infinity, which comes close to capturing the ideological mysticism of literary science fiction. Arnold left genre movies in the late 1950s to produce and direct mainstream product.

OTHER FILMS INCLUDE

It Came from Outer Space (1953); *The Creature from the Black Lagoon* (1954); *Revenge of the Creature, Tarantula* (1955); *The Tattered Dress* (1957); *The Space-Children, Monster on the Campus* (1958); *The Mouse That Roared* (1959); *A Global Affair* (1964); *Boss Nigger* (1975); *The Swiss Conspiracy* (1977).

TV CREDITS INCLUDE

Science Fiction Theatre (1955–57); *Gilligan's Island* (1964–67); *It Takes a Thief* (1968–69); *Holmes and Yo-Yo* (1976); *Sex and the Married Woman* (1977); *The Nancy Drew Mysteries* (1977–78).

ATWILL, LIONEL 1885–1946

Actor. Born in Croydon, England. Atwill entered the theater in 1904, on the suggestion of his friend Lillie Langtry. By the 1920s he had appeared in the West End, on Broadway and in silent movies made in New York. His credits include *The Lodger* (as Jack the Ripper) and *The Silent Witness*, a play that brought him to Hollywood to reprise his role in a 1932 screen adaptation. A talented performer who played both leads and supporting parts in major films, he is remembered primarily for his elegantly snide mad scientists, portrayed usually in the company of Boris Karloff, Bela Lugosi and other select horror stars. During the early 1940s he was involved in a Hollywood sex scandal that resulted in his receiving a suspended jail sentence for perjury. Atwill never regained his career footing, although he continued to enliven low-budget programmers with his lecherous smile and mesmerizing stare. He died of pneumonia while shooting the serial *Lost City of the Jungle*. His remaining scenes were completed by a stand-in.

FILMS INCLUDE

The Marriage Price (1919); *The Silent Witness, Dr. X* (1932); *The Mystery of the Wax Museum, The Sphinx, The Vampire Bat, Murders in the Zoo* (1933); *Nana, The Man Who Reclaimed His Head* (1934); *Mark of the Vampire, The Devil Is a Woman* (1935); *The Great Waltz* (1938); *Son of Frankenstein, The Hound of the Baskervilles, The Gorilla, Balalaika* (1939); *Boom Town* (1940); *Man Made Monster* (1941); *The Mad Doctor of Market Street, The Strange Case of Dr. Rx, The Ghost of Frankenstein, Night Monster* (1942); *Frankenstein Meets the Wolf Man, Sherlock Holmes and the Secret Weapon* (as Moriarty) (1943); *House of Frankenstein* (1944); *House of Dracula, Fog Island* (1945); *Genius at Work, Lost City of the Jungle* (serial) (1946).

BAVA, MARIO 1914–1980

Director and photographer. Born in San Remo, Italy, Bava began his career as an assistant cameraman and graduated to cinematographer in the late 1930s. His genre debut as photographer was *I Vampiri/Lust of the Vampire* (1957), directed by fantasy filmmaker Ricardo Fredo, which inaugurated Italy's vampire cycle. In 1959 he co-directed *La Battaglia di Maratona/The Giant of Marathon*, but was listed only as photographer. His first solo feature was *Black Sunday/La Maschera del Demonio/Revenge of the Vampire* (1960), a strikingly eerie black and white film that has since become a cult classic. He failed to duplicate its success in subsequent genre features, however, many of which are marred by a garish use of color and a deliberate exaggeration of horror cliches. He alternated between Italian beefcake epics, thrillers and genre films, and often collaborated on his scripts under the pseudonyms John Foam and John M. Old.

FILMS INCLUDE

Black Sunday/La Maschera del Demonio/Revenge of the Demon (1960); *Hercules in the Haunted World* (1961); *Evil Eye, Black Sabbath* (1963); *Blood and Black Lace* (1964); *Terrore nella Spazio/Planet of the Vampires* (1965); *Dr. Goldfoot and the Girl Bombs* (1966); *Danger Diabolik* (1968); *Hatchet for a Honeymoon, Blood Brides* (1969); *Blood Bath* (1970); *Four Times That Night* (1973); *Moses* (special effects only) (1976); *Shock, Baby Kong* (1977).

BESWICK, MARTINE 1941–

Actress. Born in Kingston, Jamaica, Beswick paid her way to London with a beauty contest prize and worked briefly as a model before entering films. After appearing in two James Bond movies, she was signed by Hammer which used her sultry, darkly dominant presence to good effect in *Dr. Jekyll and Sister Hyde* (1971). During the early 1970s she relocated to California and appeared often on American television.

FILMS INCLUDE

Saturday Night Out, From Russia with Love (1964); *Thunderball* (1965); *One Million Years B.C.* (1966); *Prehistoric Women, The Penthouse* (1967); *Dr. Jekyll and Sister Hyde* (1971); *Seizure* (1974).

BROWNING, TOD 1880–1962

Director. Born in Louisville, Kentucky. Browning ran away from home at 16 to join a circus, and appeared as a contortionist, an acrobat and a clown. He later moved into vaudeville and toured in an act called "The Lizard and the Coon." Signed by Biograph about 1915, he played small roles in several films and worked as one of D.W. Griffith's assistants on *Intolerance* (1916). His first feature as director was *Jim Bludso* (1919), followed by a formidable output of routine melodramas. The turning point in his career came when MGM allowed him to film his own project, *The Unholy Three* (1925), which starred Lon Chaney as a transvestite criminal, Harry Earles as a dwarf posing as a baby and Victor McLaglen as a strongman. Browning and Chaney went on to collaborate in a succession of films, in which Chaney brought to the screen some of his most remarkable and convincing grotesques.

His stagey direction of *Dracula* (1931)—which had been intended for the recently deceased Lon Chaney—further enhanced his reputation as a money-making filmmaker. The following year he made the notorious *Freaks*, featuring a cast of real-life dwarfs, armless and legless beings and other human anomalies. Fascinated by deformity and the grotesque, Browning so shocked audiences and studio executives with the film's obsessional horror that the film was locked away in MGM's vaults for more than 20 years. His career recovered somewhat with *The Devil Doll* (1936), whose miniaturization effects were a box-office draw, but he never regained his former stature. He retired in comfort in 1939 to a castlelike California home and lived quietly until his death at 82.

FILMS INCLUDE

The Eyes of Mystery, Revenge, The Legion of Death (1918); *The Wicked Darling, Bonnie Bonnie Lassie* (1919); *Outside the Law* (1921); *Drifting* (1923); *Silk Stocking Sal* (1924); *The Unholy Three, The Mystic* (1925); *The Black Bird* (1926); *The Show, The Unknown, London After Midnight* (1927); *West of Zanzibar* (1928); *Where East Is East, The Thirteenth Chair* (1929); *Dracula, The Iron Man* (1931); *Freaks* (1932); *Fast Workers* (1933); *Mark of the Vampire* (1935); *The Devil Doll* (1936); *Miracles for Sale* (1939).

CARPENTER, JOHN 1948–

Director, screenwriter, composer. Born in Bowling Green, Kentucky. While a student at the UCLA film school, he participated in the making of *The Resurrection of Bronco Billy* (1970), winner of an Oscar for best short subject. His first feature was *Dark Star* (1975), an engaging science-fiction spoof that brought him to the attention of Hollywood. In *Assault on Precinct 13*, he paid homage to GEORGE ROMERO's *Night of the Living Dead* (1968) by presenting a youth gang as an army of zombie fanatics who besiege a police station. After several mainstream assignments, he independently produced *Halloween* (1978), a Hitchcockian genre film that cleverly reworked the great horror effects of the past. The movie broke box office records and established him as a leading genre director. A master of carefully controlled suspense, Carpenter has shown a less steady hand in recent films and a tendency to overwork genre conventions. He is married to the actress Adrienne Barbeau who often appears in his movies.

FILMS INCLUDE

Dark Star (1975); *Assault on Precinct 13* (1976); *Eyes of Laura Mars* [script only], *Someone Is Watching Me, Halloween* (1978); *Elvis!* (1979); *The Fog* (1980); *Escape from New York, Halloween II* (1981); *The Thing, Halloween III* (1982); *Starman* (1984).

CHANEY, LON 1886–1930

Actor, director. Born Alonzo Chaney in Colorado Springs. Both his parents were deaf mutes and in learning to communicate with them he developed a skillful mime. Dropping out of school at age 12 to care for his sick mother, Chaney left home several years later and worked at odd jobs before joining his brother's traveling theatrical troupe. He made his way to Hollywood via a vaudeville company and in 1915 was signed as a Universal contract player.

He had directed several films and appeared in others when he made his genre debut in *The Glory* of Love (1919) in which he played the mad owner of a wax museum. Considered too horrific for contemporary audiences, the movie was finally released in 1923 under the title *While Paris Sleeps*. Gaining a reputation for his ingenious—and often painful—disguises, he played Quasimodo in *The Hunchback of Notre Dame* (1923), the first of his classic horror movies. He made a smooth transition from silents to talkies in *The Unholy Three* (1930), playing a criminal ventriloquist who spends most of his time dressed as a woman. He was scheduled to star in Universal's *Dracula* but died before shooting was to begin, and the role fell to Bela Lugosi. Although only a handful of his 150 roles were in genre films, Chaney is considered one of the great horror stars. In 1957 James Cagney played the star and appeared in facsimiles of his disguises in the movie biography *Man of a Thousand Faces*.

FILMS INCLUDE

The Sea Urchin (1913); *A Night of Thrills* (1914); *The Gilded Spider* (1916); *The Kaiser—Beast of Berlin* (1918); *Nomads of the North* (1920); *A Blind Bargain* (1922); *The Hunchback Of Notre Dame, All the Brothers Were Valiant* (1923); *He Who Gets Slapped* (1924); *The Monster, The Unholy Three, The Phantom of the Opera* (1925); *The Unknown, London After Midnight* (1927); *Laugh, Clown, Laugh, West of Zanzibar* (1928); *The Unholy Three* [sound remake] (1930).

CHANEY, LON, JR. 1906–1973

Actor. Born in Oklahoma City. The son of Lon Chaney (who advised him against a show business career), he entered films in 1932 playing bit parts in serials and B pictures under his real name Creighton. He changed his name in the mid-1930s and attracted attention as the lovable, feeble-minded Lennie in *Of Mice and Men* (1940). He also appeared that year as a battle-scarred prehistoric warrior in *One Million B.C.*, prompting Universal to sign him as a horror player.

Chaney made his genre debut as a sideshow "electric-man" in *Man Made Monster* (1941). Later that year he starred in *The Wolf Man*, a trademark role that was his greatest success. During the next seven years he was the studio's resident second-string monster, playing Dr. Frankenstein's creature, Dracula and the Mummy—all roles that had been made famous by Boris Karloff and Bela Lugosi. His limited dramatic range and monotonous delivery kept him from achieving lasting stardom, but he worked continuously in films of all kinds up to the time of his death.

FILMS INCLUDE

Undersea Kingdom [serial] (1936); *One Million B.C., Of Mice and Men* (1940); *Man Made Monster, Billy the Kid, The Wolf Man* (1941); *Ghost of Frankenstein, The Mummy's Tomb* (1942); *Frankenstein Meets the Wolf Man, Crazy House, Son of Dracula, Calling Dr. Death* (1943); *Weird Woman, Cobra Woman, Ghost Catchers, The Mummy's Ghost, Dead Man's Eyes* (1944); *House of Frankenstein, The Mummy's Curse, House of Dracula, The Frozen Ghost, Strange Confession, Pillow of Death* (1945); *My Favorite Brunette* (1947); *Abbott and Costello Meet Frankenstein* (1948); *Behave Yourself* (1951); *High Noon* (1952); *Pardners, The Indestructible Man* (1956); *Cyclops* (1957); *Face of the Screaming Werewolf, The Devil's Messenger, The Alligator People* (1959); *The Phantom* (1961); *The Haunted Palace* (1963); *Witchcraft* (1964); *Dr. Terror's House of Horrors* (1967); *Dracula vs. Frankenstein* (1973).

CORMAN, ROGER 1926–

Director, producer, screenwriter. Born in Los Angeles. Graduated from Stanford University with an engineering degree, Corman entered films as a messenger boy for 20th Century-Fox and was later promoted to reader in the story department. After a term at Oxford University studying English literature, he returned to Hollywood for a job as a literary agent and wrote screenplays in his spare time. Encouraged by the sale of a script for a film titled *Highway Dragnet* (1953) he formed his own movie company and produced *Monster from the Ocean Floor* (1954). The science fiction potboiler cost $11,000 to make and netted a profit of $110,000, pointing the way to his future.

In 1955 he joined forces with a fledgling film company called American International Pictures (AIP), which specialized in cheaply made exploitation movies. He made his directorial debut with *Five Guns West* (1955). Switching easily from genre to genre, Corman became one of Hollywood's most prolific suppliers of campy drive-in programmers. In the 1960s he embarked on a lavish (by his standards) series of Edgar Allen Poe tales that were critical and popular favorites.

Despite his slapdash methods, Corman injected his films with a flamboyant visual energy that captured something of the troubled spirit of his primarily teen-age audiences. He has a keen eye for talent, and his discoveries include directors Martin Scorsese, Francis Ford Coppola and Peter Bogdanovich and actors Jack Nicholson, Robert De Niro and Ellen Burstyn. In the early 1970s, the "King of the Bs" formed his own motion picture company, New World Films. Among the studio's distinguished releases were Ingmar Bergman's

Cries and Whispers (1972) and Werner Herzog's *Fitzcarraldo* (1982). He subsequently sold the company and returned to independent production.

FILMS [AS DIRECTOR] INCLUDE

The Day the World Ended, It Conquered the World (1956); *Not of This Earth, Attack of the Crab Monsters* (1957); *Teenage Caveman* (1958); *A Bucket of Blood, The Wasp Woman* (1959); *Fall of the House of Usher, The Little Shop of Horrors, The Last Woman on Earth* (1960); *The Pit and the Pendulum* (1961); *Tower of London, The Premature Burial, Tales of Terror* (1962); *The Terror, The Comedy of Terrors, X, The Man with the X-Ray Eyes* (1963); *The Masque of the Red Death, The Tomb of Ligeia* (1964); *The Wild Angels* (1966); *Ga-s-s-s, Bloody Mama* (1970); *Von Richthofen and Brown* (1971).

COURT, HAZEL 1926–

Actress. Signed by Gainsborough studios as a teenage contract player in 1944, Court appeared in a succession of forgettable films including *Ghost Ship* (1952), her genre debut. A striking, ladylike redhead with a voluptuous figure, she finally hit her stride as a Gothic heroine in Hammer's color remakes of horror classics, followed by several of Roger Corman's Poe films. She starred in an American TV series, *Dick and the Duchess* (1957–58) and played in a memorable episode of *Alfred Hitchcock Presents*. In semi-retirement since the late 1960s, she lives in California with her husband, actor-director Don Taylor.

FILMS INCLUDE

Champagne Charlie (1944); *Meet Me at Dawn* (1946); *Forbidden* (1949); *Ghost Ship* (1952); *The Curse of Frankenstein* (1957); *Model for Murder* (1958); *The Man Who Could Cheat Death* (1959); *The Shakedown* (1960); *Dr. Blood's Coffin, Mary Had a Little . . .* (1961); *The Premature Burial* (1962); *The Raven* (1963); *The Masque of the Red Death* (1964).

CRONENBERG, DAVID 1943–

Director, screenwriter. Born in Toronto, Canada. A graduate of the University of Toronto, Cronenberg made his genre debut while in college with two short films. His first horror feature was the little-seen *Stereo*, for which he handled most of the production chores. His next, *Crimes of the Future*—made with college friends who doubled as actors

and crew members—delighted cultists with its graphic depiction of the wildly imaginative adventures of a demented dermatologist. His following grew with subsequent films, including *Rabid*, a vampire film starring porno queen Marilyn Chambers that broke box-office records in Canada. He moved into the mainstream with *The Brood*, a horrifyingly vivid chiller that established him as a master of contemporary horror. While most of Cronenberg's films provide abundant nonstop shocks, they are grounded in real experience and leavened with a mordant wit that enhances their impact. In 1985 he was developing a remake of *The Fly*.

FILMS INCLUDE

Stereo (1969); *Crimes of the Future* (1970); *The Parasite Murders* (1975); *Rabid* (1977); *The Brood* (1979); *Scanners* (1981); *Videodrome, The Dead Zone* (1983).

CUSHING, PETER 1913–

Actor. Born in Kenley, Surrey, England. Trained as a surveyor, Cushing became interested in amateur dramatics and studied with the Guildhall School of Music and Drama in London. He made his professional stage debut in *Cornelius* and played in repertory for several years throughout England. Gambling on a Hollywood career, he spent his savings on a one-way ticket to California and made a brief appearance in *The Man in the Iron Mask* (1939), as the recipient of a sword wielded by Warren William.

After appearing in several bit parts, he returned to England with the outbreak of World War II and enlisted in the army theatrical unit. His first notable appearance came in 1948 when Laurence Olivier cast him as Osric in the Old Vic production of *Hamlet*. Other sizable stage and television roles followed, and he became a home screen favorite, winning a 1955 award as Television Actor of the Year. His critically acclaimed impersonation of George Orwell's tormented hero in a live TV version of *1984* led to a starring role as the Baron in Hammer's inaugural horror film, *The Curse of Frankenstein* (1957).

Cushing's sinister, gaunt looks and humorless manner are perfectly suited to genre heavies, and he finally achieved the fame he sought, playing the kind of roles Basil Rathbone had trademarked (including Sherlock Holmes) a generation before. A major post-war horror star, he has been often locked in mortal combat with Christopher Lee, in the manner of their predecessors, Boris Karloff and Bela Lugosi.

FILMS INCLUDE

The Abominable Snowman, The Curse of Frankenstein (1957); *Dracula, The Revenge of Frankenstein* (1958); *The Hound of the Baskervilles, The Mummy* (1959); *The Flesh and the Fiends, The Brides of Dracula* (1960); *The Evil of Frankenstein, The Gorgon, Dr. Terror's House of Horrors* (1964); *She, Dr. Who and the Daleks, The Skull* (1965); *Island of Terror, Daleks—Invasion Earth 2150 A.D.* (1966); *Frankenstein Created Woman, Night of the Big Heat, Torture Garden, The Blood Beast Terror, The Mummy's Shroud* [narrator only] (1967); *Corruption* (1968); *Frankenstein Must Be Destroyed, One More Time, Scream and Scream Again* (1969); *The Vampire Lovers, I, Monster, The House That Dripped Blood, Incense for the Damned* (1970); *Twins of Evil* (1971); *Fear in the Night, Dracula A.D. 1972, Horror Express, Asylum, Dr. Phibes Rises Again, Nothing but the Night, Tales from the Crypt, The Creeping Flesh* (1972); *Frankenstein and the Monster from Hell, The Satanic Rites of Dracula, And Now the Screaming Starts, From Beyond the Grave* (1973); *The Beast Must Die, The Legend of the Seven Golden Vampires, The Seven Brothers Meet Dracula, Madhouse, Tender Dracula, Legend of the Werewolf* (1974); *The Ghoul* (1975); *Shock Waves/Death Corps, The Devil's Men* (1976); *At the Earth's Core, Star Wars, The Uncanny* (1977); *An Arabian Adventure* (1979); *The Mystery of Monster Island* (1980); *House of the Long Shadows* (1983).

DIFFRING, ANTON 1918–

German-born actor. An alumnus of Berlin's Academy of Drama, he performed on the stage in Canada and the United States following World War II, and began his film career in 1950 in Great Britain. He is fluent in several languages and has played numerous character roles in German, French, American and British productions. He specializes in arrogant Nazis and smug villains. Although adept at frightening audiences, he has appeared in only a handful of genre films.

FILMS INCLUDE

State Secret (1950); *I Am a Camera* (1955); *House of Secrets* (genre debut) (1957); *The Man Who Could Cheat Death* (1959); *Circus of Horrors* (1960); *Fahrenheit 451* (1966); *Where Eagles Dare* (1969); *The Beast Must Die* (1974); *Mark of the Devil: Pt. II* (1975); *Valentino* (1977).

FISHER, TERENCE 1904–1980

British director, who inaugurated Hammer's series of remakes of Hollywood horror classics. Born in London, Fisher worked as a merchant seaman and as a window dresser before entering films at London's Lime Grove studios as a trainee at the age of 28. Beginning as a clapper boy, he progressed slowly through the ranks and became a director in 1947. After directing several melodramas and genre items, Fisher was chosen by Hammer studios to helm its first major excursion into the horror market, *The Curse of Frankenstein* (1957), and its follow-up, *Dracula* (1958). Both were ambitious reworkings of the Universal originals of the 1930s, updated for a later generation with graphically depicted full-color gore. Although not well received critically, the films were enormous hits throughout the world, establishing Fisher as a leading genre filmmaker. The films also made stars of Peter Cushing and Christopher Lee, members of Fisher's unofficial stock company, who appeared in many of his films, giving them an interlocking identity.

In retrospect, Fisher was a gifted craftsman whose best films move at a kinetic pace that brings a fresh excitement to his familiar subject matter. A no-nonsense storyteller, he eschewed the subtle art of creating terror by suggestion and concentrated instead on building detailed scenes of sheer physical horror. Fisher directed 17 films for Hammer, embracing monsters, vampires, werewolves, mummies and mad magicians.

HORROR FILMS INCLUDE

Stolen Face (1952); *Four-Sided Triangle* (1953); *The Curse of Frankenstein* (1957); *Dracula, The Revenge of Frankenstein* (1958); *The Hound of the Baskervilles, The Man Who Could Cheat Death, The Mummy, The Stranglers of Bombay* (1959); *The Brides of Dracula, The Two Faces of Dr. Jekyll* (1960); *The Curse of the Werewolf* (1961); *The Phantom of the Opera, Sherlock Holmes and the Deadly Necklace* (1962); *The Horror of It All, The Gorgon* (1964); *Dracula—Prince of Darkness* (1965); *Frankenstein Created Woman, Island of Terror* (1966); *The Devil Rides Out* (1968); *Frankenstein Must Be Destroyed!* (1969); *Frankenstein and the Monster from Hell* (1973).

OTHER FILMS INCLUDE

Colonel Bogey, Portrait From Life (1948); *Marry Me* (1949); *So Long at the Fair* (co-dir.) (1950); *Home to Danger* (1951); *Spaceways* (1953); *The Flaw* (1955); *The Last Man to Hang* (1956); *The Earth Dies Screaming* (1964); *Night of the Big Heat* (1967).

FRANCIS, FREDDIE 1917–

Director and photographer. Born in Islington, London. A former still photographer, he entered films as a clapper boy and progressed to camera assistant. After World War II service with an army cinema unit, he was promoted to cinematographer and handled the camera for a number of important films. These include *Moulin Rouge* (1953), *Moby Dick* (1956), *Room at the Top* (1959) and *The Innocents* (1961). He won an Oscar for the photography of *Sons and Lovers* (1960). He later directed a number of horror and science fiction films, many of them for England's Hammer studio, with less impressive results. He subsequently returned to the camera and shot, among others, the flawed science fiction epic *Dune* (1984). In 1985 he re-emerged as a director with the well-made *The Doctors and the Devils*.

FILMS INCLUDE

The Brain (1962); *Paranoiac, Nightmare* (1963); *The Evil of Frankenstein* (1964); *Dr. Terror's House of Horrors, The Skull* (1965); *The Deadly Bees, They Came from Beyond Space, Torture Garden* (1967); *Dracula Has Risen from the Grave* (1968); *Trog* (1970); *The Creeping Flesh, Tales from the Crypt* (1972); *Tales That Witness Madness* (1973); *The Ghoul, Son of Dracula* (1974); *Legend of the Werewolf* (1975); *The Doctors and the Devils* (1985).

FRYE, DWIGHT 1899–1943

Character actor; featured in Universal's classic horror series of the 1930s and 1940s. Born in Salina, Kansas, he appeared on the stage before arriving in Hollywood in the late 1920s. He made a lasting impression in *Dracula* (1931), his first film, as the half-mad Renfield, a role that permanently typecast him as a jittery grotesque. In 1940 he reprised the part in a revival of the stage version and toured the United States with Bela Lugosi. A favorite of horror buffs, he was paid homage in the 1960s by ghoul-rocker Alice Cooper in the song "Dwight Frye."

FILMS INCLUDE

Dracula, Frankenstein (1931); *The Vampire Bat, The Invisible Man* (1933); *Bride of Frankenstein, The Crime of Dr. Crespi* (1935); *Something to Sing About* (1938); *The Cat and the Canary, Son of Frankenstein* (1939); *Son of Monte Cristo* (1941); *The Ghost of Frankenstein* (1942); *Frankenstein Meets the Wolf Man, Dead Men Walk* (1943).

GALEEN, HENRIK 1882–1949

(Also Henryk and Heinrich) Danish-born director and screenwriter of German films; former stage actor and director with Max Reinhardt's Deutsches Theater. His first important credit was *Der Golem/The Golem* (1914), which he co-scripted and co-directed with its star, Paul Wegener. His work on Wegener's third Golem film led to an offer from director F.W. Murnau to write the screenplay for *Nosferatu*, the cinema's first (unauthorized) adaptation of Bram Stoker's *Dracula*. He later scripted *Das Wachsfigurenkabinett/Waxworks* and wrote and directed a superior remake of *Der Student von Prag/The Student of Prague*. A major voice in the German expressionist movement, Galeen helped chart the course of the modern horror film. He left Germany for the United States after Hitler was named dictator but never worked in movies here and subsequently faded into obscurity.

FILMS INCLUDE

Der Student von Prag/The Student of Prague (assistant director) (1913); *Der Golem/The Golem* (1914); *Peter Schlemihl* (1915); *Der Golem—wie er in die Welt Kam/The Golem* (1920); *Nosferatu—eine Symphonie des Grauens/Nosferatu the Vampire* (1922); *Das Wachsfigurenkabinett/Waxworks* (1924); *Der Student von Prag/The Student of Prague* (1926); *Alraune* (1928); *After the Verdict* (G.B.) (1929).

GORDON, BERT I. 1922–

Producer, director, screenwriter, special effects technician. Born in Kenosha, Wisconsin, and educated at the University of Wisconsin, Gordon made local commercials and industrial films before venturing to Hollywood, where he began his career as a production supervisor of the TV series *Racket Squad* (1951–53). His first film, made with private backing, was *King Dinosaur* (1955), a ludicrous monster movie ground out so cheaply that it managed to earn money. Typical of his *oeuvre*, the film dealt with the theme of giantism, with Gordon handling most of the production chores with equal lack of care. Dubbed a "renaissance man of schlock," he is considered the dean of movie chintz and one of the inspirations for a later generation of deliberately campy moviemakers.

FILMS INCLUDE

King Dinosaur (1955); *The Amazing Colossal Man, The Beginning of the End, Cyclops* (1957); *Attack of the*

Puppet People, War of the Colossal Beast, The Spider (1958); *The Boy and the Pirates, Tormented* (1960); *The Magic Sword* (1962); *Village of the Giants* (1965); *Picture Mommy Dead* (1966); *How to Succeed with Sex* (1970); *Necromancy* (1971); *The Mad Bomber, The Police Connection* (1973); *The Food of the Gods* (1976); *Empire of the Ants* (1977).

GOUGH, MICHAEL 1917–1985

British character actor. Born in the British colony of Malaya and educated at Wye Agricultural College. Schooled at the Old Vic Theatre, he made his London stage debut at the age of 19 and subsequently displayed his versatility by appearing in both leading and supporting roles. His first movie was *Blanche Fury* (1948), a Victorian melodrama, followed by other mainstream films in which he usually played a haughty aristocrat. He made his genre debut in Hammer's remake of *Dracula* (1958), a turning point in his career that led to stardom in a series of mostly routine British horror films. Tall and gaunt, with a suave, elegant demeanor, Gough specialized in hammy mad scientist roles in the tradition of Hollywood's Lionel Atwill and George Zucco.

FILMS INCLUDE

Anna Karenina (1948); *The Man in the White Suit* (1951); *The Sword and the Rose, Rob Roy* (1953); *Richard III* (1955); *Dracula* (1958); *Horrors of the Black Museum* (1959); *The Horse's Mouth* (1959); *Konga* (1961); *The Phantom of the Opera, Black Zoo* (1962); *Dr. Terror's House of Horrors* (1964); *The Skull* (1965); *They Came from Beyond Space, Berserk!* (1967); *Curse of the Crimson Altar* (1968); *Trog, Crucible of Horror, Julius Caesar* (1970); *Horror Hospital, The Legend of Hell House* (1973); *Satan's Slaves* (1976); *The Boys from Brazil* (1978).

GROT, ANTON 1884–1974

(Antocz Franziszek Groszewski) Polish-born art director of American films. A former illustrator and stage designer, he immigrated to the United States in 1909 and began his film career decorating movies shot in New York and New Jersey. In 1927 he signed with First National-Warner Brothers and remained with the studio until retirement in 1948. His eerie foreshortened set design for *Svengali* (1931), his genre debut, won him an Oscar nomination and top studio assignments, often with director Michael Curtiz, who shared Grot's expressionist vision. Versatile and deeply involved in the films he worked on, he left his stamp on virtually every Warner film made during his tenure, from surrealist Busby Berkeley musicals to historical dramas and gangster films. In 1940 he won an Academy Award for inventing a device that creates ripple and wave illusions on water scenes. After retirement, he turned to painting.

FILMS INCLUDE

The Mouse and the Lion (1913); *The Naulahka* (1918); *The Thief of Bagdad* (1924); *Noah's Ark* (1929); *Svengali, Little Caesar, The Mad Genius* (1931); *Dr. X* (1932); *The Mystery of the Wax Museum* (1933); *Gold Diggers of 1935* (1935); *Elizabeth and Essex* (1939); *Mildred Pierce* (1945); *One Sunday Afternoon* (1948); *Backfire* (1950).

HALL, CHARLES D. 1899–1968

Art director, described by film historian Leon Barsacq as the "chief architect of all the greater Transylvanias reared on Universal's back lot." Born in Norwich, England, he designed for the stage before immigrating to Hollywood in 1921. His first credit as an art director came with *Smiling All the Way* (1921), a popular success that led to four movies for Charlie Chaplin and other top filmmakers. As the principal art director for Universal during the late 1920s and 1930s, Hall was influenced by the expressionist ideas of German director Paul Leni (an art director himself), with whom he made three memorable genre films. Leni's tutelage is apparent in the settings created by Hall for several of the studio's key horror features. Among his durable fantasies are the sinuous cobwebbed stairway of *Dracula*, the nightmarishly high laboratory of *Bride of Frankenstein*, and the cold, Bauhaus-style "chapel" where Karloff held black masses in *The Black Cat*.

HORROR FILMS INCLUDE

The Phantom of the Opera (1927); *The Cat and the Canary* (director Paul Leni) (1927); *The Man Who Laughs* (director Paul Leni) (1928); *The Last Warning* (director Paul Leni) (1929); *Dracula, Frankenstein* (with Herman Rosse) (1931); *The Old Dark House* (1932); *The Invisible Man* (1933); *The Black Cat* (1934); *Bride of Frankenstein* (1935); *One Million B.C.* (1940); *The Flying Saucer* (1950); *Red Planet Mars* (1952); *The Unearthly* (1957).

HALPERIN, VICTOR 1895–

Director. Born in Chicago and educated at the University of Wisconsin and the University of Chicago. Originally a stage actor and director, he made his movie debut with *When a Girl Loves* (1924). His first horror film was *White Zombie* (1932), a minor classic played with sadistic gusto by Bela Lugosi. A Hollywood independent, Halperin often directed, co-produced and distributed low-budget programmers with his brother Edward. With the exception of *White Zombie*, his handful of genre films are perfunctory and very much of their time.

FILMS INCLUDE

When a Girl Loves (1924); *The Unknown Lover* (1925); *Party Girl* (1930); *White Zombie* (1932); *Supernatural* (1933); *Revolt of the Zombies* (1936); *Torture Ship* (1939); *Buried Alive* (1940); *Girls Town* (1942).

HARBOU, THEA VON 1888–1954

German novelist, screenwriter and occasional director. An important member of the expressionist movement, she is known for her films with director Fritz Lang, whom she married in 1924 after her divorce from Rudolf Klein-Rogge, one of Lang's favored stars. Von Harbou collaborated on all of Lang's films until his departure from Germany in 1933. They were divorced the following year for ideological and personal differences. She subsequently joined the Nazi party and was named one of the state's official screenwriters. After the war she resumed her career, with limited success.

FILMS INCLUDE

Dr. Mabuse der Spieler/Dr. Mabuse, Phantom (1922); *Metropolis* (1927); *Die Frau im Mond/Rocket to the Moon* (1929); *M* (1931); *Das Testament des Dr. Mabuse/ The Testament of Dr. Mabuse* (1932); *Mutterlied/Mother Love* (1937); *Dr. Holl* (1951).

HATTON, RONDO 1894–1946

American actor. Born in Hagerstown, Maryland. Hatton was a Hollywood oddity and a minimally talented performer who owed his career to physical deformity. Afflicted with acromegaly (an abnormality of the pituitary gland which also afflicted John Merrick, the "Elephant Man"), he had grotesquely enlarged bones in his head, hands and feet. A well-mannered introvert, he was cruelly exploited in several programmers of the 1940s, usually as a mad killer called the Creeper. Hatton required little makeup in the role, and was always lighted from below to heighten his fearsome appearance. The character debuted in *Pearl of Death*, a Sherlock Holmes feature in the Basil Rathbone-Nigel Bruce series, and appeared in *Spider Woman Strikes Back* and *House of Horrors*. Genesis of the Creeper is recounted in *The Brute Man*, released after the actor's death.

HORROR FILMS INCLUDE

The Hunchback of Notre Dame (1939); *Pearl of Death* (1944); *Jungle Captive* (1945); *Spider Woman Strikes Back, House of Horrors, The Brute Man* (1946).

KARLOFF, BORIS 1887–1969

(William Henry Pratt) British-born Hollywood actor whose name is synonomous with horror. The youngest of eight children, Karloff studied for a career in the British foreign service—his family's profession—before leaving home to pursue an earlier ambition, the theater. Immigrating to Canada at the age of 21, he served a 10-year apprenticeship as a character actor with touring theater companies. His travels took him to Hollywood, where he made his screen debut as an extra in *The Dumb Girl of Portici* (1916), which starred Anna Pavlova.

When the influenza epidemic of 1918 forced the cancellation of theater tours, he returned to Hollywood and appeared in bit parts, supporting himself as a truck driver between assignments. He had played in nearly 40 silent and sound films when he scored as a gangster in *The Criminal Code* (1931), a part he had played on the stage the year before. A follow-up role in *Graft* (1931) brought him to the attention of director James Whale, who was looking for an actor to play the Monster in *Frankenstein*, a part that Bela Lugosi had turned down.

Karloff's terrifying yet very human portrayal made the improbable monster believable and propelled the actor to international stardom. Others have tried to fill the lead-weighted boots, but Karloff remains the definitive Frankenstein Monster. During the 1930s he headed Universal's team of horror players and starred in a succession of box-office hits, often paired with Lugosi. A versatile, talented actor, Karloff never regretted being identified with horror films, as Lugosi did. He was able to escape typecasting to a large degree, and played both comedy and high drama. On Broadway he scored personal triumphs in the long-running *Arsenic and Old Lace* (1941) and in *Peter Pan* (1950), the latter as Captain Hook. On television he vocalized in *Hollywood Sings* (1960), a musical special, played Cauchon to Julie Harris's Joan of Arc in *The Lark*, and sleuthed through London in the 1958 series *Colonel March of Scotland Yard*.

Unlike his horror personas, Karloff was a kind, mild-mannered gentleman always ready to support Hollywood charities. He was a founder of the Screen Actors' Guild and one of its most active members (he made approximately 140 movies).

HORROR FILMS INCLUDE

The Unholy Night (1929); *The Mad Genius, Frankenstein* (1931); *The Old Dark House, The Mask of Fu Manchu, The Mummy* (1932); *The Ghoul* (G.B.) (1933); *The Black Cat* (1934); *The Bride of Frankenstein, The Black Room, The Raven* (1935); *The Invisible Ray, The Walking Dead, The Man Who Lived Again* (G.B.) (1936); *The Invisible Menace* (1938); *Son of Frankenstein, The Man They Could Not Hang, Tower of London* (1939); *Black Friday, The Man with Nine Lives, Before I Hang, The Ape, You'll Find Out* (1940); *The Devil Commands* (1941); *The Boogie Man Will Get You* (1942); *The Climax, House of Frankenstein* (1944); *The Body Snatcher, Isle of the Dead* (1945); *Bedlam* (1946); *Abbott and Costello Meet the Killer—Boris Karloff* (1949); *The Strange Door* (1951); *The Black Castle* (1952); *Abbott and Costello Meet Dr. Jekyll and Mr. Hyde, Monster of the Island* (It.) (1953); *Voodoo Island* (1957); *Grip of the Strangler* (G.B.), *Frankenstein 1970, Corridors of Blood* (G.B.) (1958); *The Raven, The Terror, I Tre Volti della Paura/Black Sabbath* (It./Fr./U.S.), *The Comedy of Terrors* (1963); *Die Monster Die!/Monster of Terror* (1965); *The Ghost in the Invisible Bikini, Mad Monster Party* (animated, voice of Baron Frankenstein), *Cauldron of Blood* (Sp./U.S.), *The Sorcerers* (G.B.) (1967); *Targets, Curse of the Crimson Altar* (G.B.), *House of Evil* (U.S./Mex.), *Fear Chamber* (U.S./Mex.), *The Snake People* (U.S./Sp.), *The Incredible Invasion* (U.S./Sp.), (1968).

OTHER FILMS INCLUDE

Scarface (1932), *The Lost Patrol, The House of Rothschild* (1934), *The Secret Life of Walter Mitty, Unconquered* (1947), *Tap Roots* (1948), *The Venetian Affair* (1967).

TV CREDITS INCLUDE

Starring Boris Karloff (series) (1949), *Inside U.S.A.* (1949–50), *Lights Out* (1949–52), *Suspense* (1949–54), *Masterpiece Playhouse* (1950), *Tales of Tomorrow* (1951–53), *The Elgin TV Hour* (1954–55), *A Connecticut Yankee* (1955), *Shirley Temple's Storybook* (1959–61), *Thriller* (series host and star) (1960–62), *Tell Us More* (documentary on his career) (1963).

RADIO CREDITS INCLUDE

Lux Radio Theatre, Inner Sanctum, Everyman's Theatre, Starring Boris Karloff.

THEATER CREDITS INCLUDE

Arsenic and Old Lace, Black Castle, The Linden Tree, Peter Pan, Shop at Sly Corner, The Strange Door, The Virginian.

KATZMAN, SAM 1901–1973

Producer. Born in New York City. A grade-school dropout, Katzman began his career at the age of 13 as a prop boy. At Fox films from 1914 to 1931, he progressed through the ranks to production manager and assistant producer before being laid off by the studio during the Depression. He subsequently produced assembly-line "B" movies for such poverty row studios as Showmen's, Supreme, Victory and Monogram. Hired by Columbia during the late 1940s, he was put in charge of the *Jungle Jim* series starring Johnny Weissmuller, who had grown too paunchy for Tarzan's loincloth. Katzman hit his stride at Columbia during the 1950s and 1960s by churning out quickies whose titles often resembled those of current hits. Although some of his product was relatively effective, he is remembered for a handful of science fiction/horror exploiters, which had their first-runs in drive-in theaters. Inanely plotted and performed and almost totally lacking in production values, these lively films have become icons of low camp, revered by fans of bad movies. Katzman's cinematic heirs are Edward L. Cahn, the early Roger Corman, William Castle and Bert I. Gordon, with whom Katzman worked on his next-to-last picture in a rare meeting of talents.

FILMS INCLUDE

Ship of Wanted Men (1933); *Spooks Run Wild* (1941); *The Corpse Vanishes* (1942); *Voodoo Man* (1944); *Rock Around the Clock, Earth Vs. the Flying Saucers* (1956); *Calypso Heat Wave, Zombies of Mora-Tau, The Giant Claw, The Night the World Exploded* (1957); *The Enemy General* (1960); *Twist Around the Clock* (1961); *The Wild Westerners* (1962); *Get Yourself a College Girl* (1964); *Harum Scarum* (1965); *The Young Runaways* (1968); *How to Succeed with Sex, The Loners* (1972).

LEE, CHRISTOPHER 1922–

Actor. Born in London. Lee studied at Wellington College before volunteering for service with the

Royal Air Force during World War II. Deciding to become an actor after the war, he was initially rejected by an executive at J. Arthur Rank because of his ungainly height of six feet, four inches. Through the intervention of a family friend— producer Filippo del Guidice—he landed a small part in *Corridor of Mirrors* (1947) and went on to play bit parts in dozens of British movies. His gaunt features and tall, skeletal frame were unsuited for leading roles, and he seemed destined to be an also-ran until Hammer cast him as the Frankenstein Monster in its milestone genre movie, *The Curse of Frankenstein* (1957). He followed with the title role in *Dracula* (1958), another color remake of a Hollywood classic, which established him as a major star of the sinister cinema. In both films and many subsequent sequels he was paired with Peter Cushing, with whom he had previously appeared (but not in the same scenes) in *Hamlet* (1948) and *Moulin Rouge* (1952). The only actor to have played the Frankenstein Monster, Dracula, the Mummy, Fu Manchu and detective Sherlock Holmes (in Germany), he has starred in over 100 films of varying quality.

FILMS INCLUDE

A Tale of Two Cities (1958); *The Hound of the Baskervilles, The Man Who Could Cheat Death, The Mummy* (1959); *The Two Faces of Dr. Jekyll/House of Fright, The City of the Dead/Horror Hotel* (1960); *Les Mains d'Orlac, Taste of Fear/Scream of Fear, The Terror of the Tongs, Tempi duri per i vampiri/Uncle Was a Vampire* (1961); *The Longest Day, Sherlock Holmes and the Deadly Necklace* (1962); *The Gorgon* (1964); *Dr. Terror's House of Horrors, The Skull, The Face of Fu Manchu* (1965); *Theatre of Death, Circus of Fear, Night of the Big Heat, The Devil Rides Out* (1967); *Dracula Has Risen from the Grave, Curse of the Crimson Altar* (1968); *The Oblong Box, The Magic Christian* (as Dracula), *Scream and Scream Again, One More Time* (as Dracula) (1969); *Taste the Blood of Dracula, Scars of Dracula, Julius Caesar, The House That Dripped Blood, El Conde Dracula* (1970); *Dracula A.D. 1972* (1972); *Horror Express, The Creeping Flesh, Frankenstein and the Monster From Hell, Death Line, Nothing But the Night, The Satanic Rites of Dracula, The Wicker Man* (1973); *The Legend of the 7 Golden Vampires, The Three, Tendre Dracula* (1974); *In Search of Dracula* (1975); *To the Devil . . . a Daughter, Revenge of the Dead, Dracula Pere et Fils* (1976); *Airport '77, Starship Invasions, End of the World, Meat Cleaver Massacre, Alien Encounter* (1977); *Escape from Witch Mountain* (1978); *Arabian Adventure, 1941, Bear Island, Circle of Iron* (1979); *Goliath Awaits* (1980); *House of the Long Shadows* (1983).

LENI, PAUL 1885–1929

German director and art director. Originally an avant-garde painter, Leni designed theater posters and stage sets for impresario Max Reinhardt before entering films as an art director. A director from 1916, he was instrumental in the development of expressionism in cinema. His *Das Wachsfigurenkabinett/Waxworks* is a seminal genre feature, notable for its use of sets and decor to delineate character, social milieu and plot. The success of the film in America brought an offer from Universal where Leni made four films, all remarkable for their enveloping mood of mystery and terror. It seems likely that Paul would have directed *Dracula* and/or *Frankenstein*, since he pointed the studio in their direction, but he died of blood poisoning in 1929. His immediate influence can be seen in the work of art director Charles D. Hall.

GERMAN FILMS INCLUDE

Das Tagebuch des Dr. Hart (1916); *Patience* (1920); *Hintertreppe/Backstairs* (co-director with Leopold Jessner) (1921); *Das Wachsfigurenkabinett/Waxworks* (1924); *Der Goldene Schmetterling* (directed by Michael Kertesz [Curtiz]) (1926).

U.S. FILMS INCLUDE

The Cat and the Canary (1927); *The Chinese Parrot* (1927); *The Man Who Laughs* (1928); *The Last Warning* (1929).

LEWTON, VAL 1904–1951

Producer. Born Vladimir Ivan Leventon in Yalta, Russia. He was brought to America at age seven by his mother, a sister of famed actress Alla Nazimova, and educated at a military academy and The Columbia School of Journalism. During the late 1920s and early 1930s, he published 16 books of nonfiction and fiction (including an under-the-counter erotic novel). After a brief stint writing publicity for MGM in New York, he was hired as an editorial assistant by producer David O. Selznick and quickly progressed to story editor. He wrote a number of screenplays under the pseudonyms Cosmo Forbes and Carlos Keith before joining RKO as head of a production unit formed to make low-budget horror movies. His debut film was *Cat People* (1942). Highly praised by critics and cinema historians, his horror films relied on suggestion rather than outright horror and seem tame today, but their emphasis on psychological realism marked a turning point in the horror film.

His personal vision, which delineated his films as much as his director's, failed to transfer to his non-genre outings. He died of a heart attack at age 46.

FILMS INCLUDE

Cat People (1942); *I Walked With a Zombie, The Leopard Man, The Seventh Victim, The Ghost Ship* (1943); *Mademoiselle Fifi, The Curse of the Cat People, Youth Runs Wild* (1944); *The Body Snatcher, Isle of the Dead* (1945); *Bedlam* (1946); *My Own True Love* (1949); *Please Believe Me* (1950); *Apache Drums* (1951).

LORRE, PETER 1904–1964

(Laszlo Lowenstein) Actor, born in Rosenberg, Hungary. A former bank clerk, Lorre trained for the stage in Vienna and made his acting debut in Breslau, Germany. For the next seven years he worked steadily in Germany, Austria and Switzerland and played small roles in German films. He was a virtual unknown when the great German director Fritz Lang spotted him at Berlin's Volksbuhne (People's Theater) and cast him as a child murderer in the title role of *M* (1931). Lorre's physical limitations—his sinister yet sympathetic bulging eyes, effeminate baby face and small pudgy body—seemed ideally suited for dangerous neurotics and psychopaths, and the actor exploited these qualities to the limit.

When Hitler came to power, Lorre, a Jew, immigrated to Paris and then London, where he made his English-speaking debut in Alfred Hitchcock's *The Man Who Knew Too Much* (1934). He made his American genre debut in *Mad Love* (1935), a top-drawer MGM remake of *The Hands of Orlac*. His career took another step forward when he was paired with Sydney Greenstreet in *The Maltese Falcon* (1941), which led to a Warner Brothers contract and a succession of important roles. His career declined during the early fifties, but he worked steadily in small character parts until he found stardom once again in Roger Corman's Poe series of the 1960s. Lorre directed, wrote and starred in *Der Verlorene/The Lost One* (1951), a moving film about refugee camps in Germany shortly after World War II. Playing the resident doctor, Lorre comments on the conditions that fostered Nazism, an unusual sentiment for a German film at that time.

FILMS INCLUDE

M (1931); *F.P. 1 Antwortet Nicht/F.P. 1 Does Not Answer* (1932); *The Man Who Knew Too Much* (1934); *Mad Love, Crime and Punishment* (1935); *Think Fast Mr. Moto, Thank You Mr. Moto* (1937); *Mr. Moto Takes a Chance, Mr. Moto of Devil's Island* (1938); *Strange Cargo, You'll Find Out, Island of Doomed Men* (1940); *The Face Behind the Mask, The Maltese Falcon* (1941); *The Boogie Man Will Get You, The Invisible Agent, Casablanca* (1942); *The Mask of Dimitrios, Arsenic and Old Lace, The Conspirators* (1944); *Confidential Agent* (1945); *The Beast with Five Fingers* (1947); *Casbah* (1948); *Rope of Sand* (1949); *Quicksand* (1950); *Der Verlorene/The Lost One* (also director, co-writer) (1951); *Beat the Devil, 20,000 Leagues Under the Sea* (1954); *Around the World in 80 Days* (1956); *Silk Stockings, The Story of Mankind* (as Nero), *Scent of Mystery* (1960); *Voyage to the Bottom of the Sea* (1961); *Tales of Terror, Five Weeks in a Balloon* (1962); *The Comedy of Terrors, The Raven* (1963); *Muscle Beach Party, The Patsy* (1964).

LUGOSI, BELA 1882–1956

Actor. Born Bela Blasko in Lugos, Hungary. After changing his surname to honor his home town, Lugosi began his career with the Royal National Theater in Budapest and became a moderately successful actor there. He returned to Budapest after service with the Hungarian infantry during World War I (he was badly wounded) and graduated to movie roles. With the failure of the communist government of Bela Kun, whom he supported, he emigrated to Germany and appeared there in films as Arisztid Olt. He made his genre debut in F.W. Murnau's *Der Januskopf* (1920), a silent version of *Dr. Jekyll and Mr. Hyde*.

Finding parts difficult to come by, he emigrated to the U.S. in 1921 by working as a deck hand on a cargo ship. He learned to speak English while performing with a Hungarian-speaking touring theater that played to emigre groups and began his American career the following year—at the age of 39—with a small role in a Broadway play. He worked steadily for the next five years, when he achieved "overnight" stardom in the title role of *Dracula*.

His screen impersonation of the tall and suave, mellifluous-voiced vampire—a role originally intended for reigning horror king Lon Chaney, who died before shooting began—brought him worldwide stardom and permanent identification with the part. Earlier that year he had tested as the Frankenstein Monster in full makeup on the set of the uncompleted *Dracula*, but relinquished the role to an unknown named Boris Karloff because, as he put it, "no one will recognize me in that disguise." He later proved his point with an ill-at-ease impersonation of the Monster in *Frankenstein Meets the Wolf Man* (1943). As Hollywood's superstars of horror during the 1930s and early 1940s, Lugosi and Karloff were teamed in a number of successful features, usually as adversaries.

By the mid-1940s Hollywood's first horror cycle had run its course and Lugosi's career was virtually over. Unlike Karloff, he had tarnished his screen image by appearing in second-rate films and had never broadened his range. "I can blame it all on *Dracula*," he once said. "Since then Hollywood has scribbled a little card of classification for me and it looks as if I'll never be able to prove my mettle in any other kind of role."

In 1951 he revived the *Dracula* play for a third touring production and later burlesqued the Count in a nightclub revue. Declaring himself penniless in 1954, he entered a California hospital to cure a long-term addiction to morphine. The cure worked, but he was unable to find suitable roles and ended his career in two films that are considered the worst he ever made. He died in August 1956 and was buried, according to his wishes, in his black vampire cape with the blood-red lining. Although Lugosi's career was a disappointment, his screen presence remains as chilling as ever, and he has left an indelible mark on the horror film.

FILMS INCLUDE

The Silent Command (1923); *Dracula* (1931); *Murders in the Rue Morgue, White Zombie* (1932); *Island of Lost Souls* (1933); *The Black Cat* (1934); *Mark of the Vampire* (1935); *The Invisible Ray* (1936); *S.O.S. Coast Guard* (1937); *The Phantom Creeps, Son of Frankenstein, The Gorilla, Dark Eyes of London, Ninotchka* (1939); *Black Friday, You'll Find Out* (1940); *The Devil Bat, Spooks Run Wild, The Wolf Man* (1941); *The Ghost of Frankenstein, Black Dragons, The Corpse Vanishes, Bowery at Midnight, Night Monster* (1942); *Frankenstein Meets the Wolf Man, The Ape Man, Ghosts on the Loose* (1943); *The Return of the Vampire, Voodoo Man, Return of the Ape Man, The Body Snatcher, Zombies on Broadway* (1945); *Scared to Death* (1947); *Abbott and Costello Meet Frankenstein* (1948); *Mother Riley Meets the Vampire, Bela Lugosi Meets a Brooklyn Gorilla* (1952); *Bride of the Monster* (1955); *The Black Sleep, Plan 9 From Outer Space* (1956) [released in 1959].

NAISH, J. CARROL 1900–1973

(Joseph Patrick Carrol Naish) Character actor. Raised in New York's poor East Harlem area, Naish left home at 16 to enlist in the military. He saw front-line service with the U.S. Army aviation corps during World War I, and remained in Europe after the Armistice, supporting himself with odd jobs while learning several languages. After gaining experience on the Paris stage, he returned to New York for a career on Broadway. He arrived in Hollywood as a featured player in 1930 and made his horror debut in *Return of the Terror* (1934). Although he was of pure Irish descent, Naish's dark complexion and curly black hair typecast him as a swarthy ethnic, usually an Italian or Spaniard. His ability to mimic dialects completed the illusion. He never played an Irishman in his more than 200 movies. He also starred in a popular radio series, *Life with Luigi* (1948–51), a role he repeated in a short-lived TV series, in 1952. His other TV series are *The New Adventures of Charlie Chan* (1957) and *Guestward Ho!* (1960–61), in which he played an American Indian.

FILMS INCLUDE

Good Intentions (1930); *Cabin in the Cotton* (1932); *Return of the Terror* (1934); *The Charge of the Light Brigade* (1936); *Beau Geste, Island of Lost Men* (1939); *Blood and Sand* (1941); *Dr. Renault's Secret* (1942); *Batman* (serial), *Calling Dr. Death* (1943); *Jungle Woman, The Monster Maker, House of Frankenstein* (1944); *The Beast with Five Fingers* (1947); *Joan of Arc* (1948); *The Hanged Man* (1964); *Dracula vs. Frankenstein* (1970).

OBOLER, ARCH 1909–

Radio writer, film director, screenwriter and producer. Born in Chicago. Educated at the University of Chicago. One of the great dramatists of radio, Oboler is a restless man of many interests who has also worked in the legitimate theater and in movies. Among his many radio credits is *Everyman's Theater* (1938–44), *First Nighter* (1929–53) and his horror masterwork, the super-chilling *Lights Out* (1938–50). He later worked in Hollywood where he made science fiction's first anti-bomb movie, *Five* (1951), and launched the brief 3-D movie fad of the 1950s with *Bwana Devil* (1953). He subsequently made a handful of exploitation "gimmick" movies.

Oboler's natural medium was radio, however. His gift for creating exciting drama with voices and sound effects did not transfer well to a visual medium, and his films seem talky and stagebound. In a 1970 interview he recalled the golden age of radio: "'Blind' broadcasting that was only heard was an art form, as unique, as image-provoking as music itself, because the listener gave of himself as he listened; in his own mind he built up pictures evoked by the sounds of words and effects and orchestral accompaniment." For those who want to hear what Oboler was capable of, Capitol has released the lp *Drop Dead! An Exercise in Horror*, produced, written and directed by Oboler.

FILMS INCLUDE

Bewitched, Strange Holiday (1945); *The Arnelo Affair* (1947); *Five* (1951); *The Twonky, Bwana Devil* (1953); *1 + 1: Exploring the Kinsey Report* [based on his play] (1961); *The Bubble* (1966).

O'BRIEN, WILLIS H. 1886–1962

Stop-motion animator; creator of King Kong. Born in Oakland, California. O'Brien worked at a number of jobs—including poultry handler, sports cartoonist and commercial sculptor—before entering films in 1914 with a series of trick shorts. His first important film was *The Dinosaur and the Missing Link* (1915), made on $5000 advanced by a San Francisco bank on the strength of a 60-second thriller he filmed on the building's roof. In 1919 he shot *Curious Pets of Our Ancestors*, a humorous short which anticipated TV's popular Neanderthal family *The Flintstones* by 50 years. He continued to pioneer stop-motion techniques until he was able to combine models with real people in his first major feature *The Lost World* (1925). His next film proved to be his masterwork. In *King Kong* (1933) his special effects set a standard against which all other movie monsters continue to be judged. Others have tried, but so far no one has equaled O'Brien's terrifying yet emotionally vulnerable fur-covered puppet. In 1942 O'Brien began work on a favorite project titled *Gwangi*, set on a Texas mesa where a group of cowboys encounter prehistoric monsters, but RKO canceled the film in favor of less costly projects. Completed scenes later were used in O'Brien's *Mighty Joe Young* (1949), a retelling of the Kong story for which he won a belated Academy Award. Among O'Brien's disciples are Jim Danforth and Ray Harryhausen.

FILMS INCLUDE

The Dinosaur and the Missing Link (1915); *Prehistoric Poultry* (1917); *The Ghost of Slumber Mountain, Curious Pets of Our Ancestors* (1919); *The Lost World* (1925); *King Kong, Son of Kong* (1933); *The Last Days of Pompeii* (1935); *The Dancing Pirate* (1936); *Mighty Joe Young* (1949); *The Beast of Hollow Mountain* (story only), *The Animal World* (1956); *The Black Scorpion* (1957); *The Giant Behemoth* (1959); *The Lost World* (1960); *It's a Mad Mad Mad Mad World* (1963).

PIERCE, JACK 1889–1968

Make-up artist. Born in New York. Pierce arrived at his calling in a roundabout way. A promising baseball shortstop, he had hoped to place with a California team in 1910 but was turned down because he was too light and short. Pierce eventually got a job managing a chain of cinemas owned by Harry Culver, founder of Culver City. After an abortive attempt to make his own movies, Pierce played bit parts for a while, until Fox took him on as an assistant cameraman.

Unions and the strict division of labor were far in the future, and film crews were asked to help out with various tasks, whatever they might be. As a cameraman on *The Monkey Talks*, he was asked for suggestions on making the ape makeup more convincing. Taking over the job, he came up with a more realistic version, which brought offers from other studios for similar tasks. Pierce concentrated on learning the craft, and in 1926 he joined Universal studios to organize its first professional makeup department. A pioneer, he rose to the height of his craft during the 1930s and 1940s by creating all the studio's famous monsters: Dracula, the Frankenstein Monster, the Wolf Man and the Mummy. His creation of the Frankenstein Monster's face and physique was so unique that it was copyrighted by the studio. Pierce's work was, in effect, one of the stars of the film. After Universal's horror cycle had run its course, he left the studio in 1946 to freelance.

FILMS INCLUDE

The Monkey Talks (1925); *Dracula, Frankenstein* (1931); *The Mummy, Murders in the Rue Morgue, The Old Dark House, White Zombie* (1932); *Bride of Frankenstein, The Werewolf of London, The Raven* (1935); *Dracula's Daughter* (1936); *Son of Frankenstein* (1939); *The Mummy's Hand* (1940); *Man-Made Monster, The Wolf Man* (1941); *The Ghost of Frankenstein, The Mummy's Tomb* (1942); *The Phantom of the Opera, Son of Dracula, Frankenstein Meets the Wolf Man, Captive Wild Woman* (1943); *The Mummy's Ghost, The Mad Ghoul, House of Frankenstein, The Mummy's Curse* (1944); *Jungle Captive, House of Dracula, The Spider Woman Strikes Back* (1945); *House of Horrors, The Time of Their Lives* (1946); *Master Minds* (1949); *Teenage Monster* (1957); *The Devil's Hand* (1958); *Giant from the Unknown* (1959); *Beyond the Time Barrier* (1960); *The Creation of the Humanoids* (1962); *Beauty and the Beast* (1963).

PLEASENCE, DONALD 1919–

British character actor. Born in Worksop, England. He began performing in local repertory, in 1939. When Britain went to war, he enlisted in the Royal Air Force and spent the duration in a prisoner-of-war camp in Germany. He returned to London and by the mid-1950s had established himself as a leading stage actor. After many TV appearances he entered films with *The Beachcomber* (1954). His first genre effort was *The Flesh and the Fiends* (1960). He has since specialized in megalomaniacal villains such as Blofeld, James Bond's arch-nemesis, in *You Only Live Twice* (1967). His performances are usually superior to his horror films, and he is at his most convincing as a repressed milquetoast driven over the edge into dangerous psychosis.

FILMS INCLUDE

The Beachcomber (1954); *1984* (1955); *Look Back in Anger* (1959); *The Flesh and the Fiends, Circus of Horrors, The Hands of Orlac* (1960); *What a Carve-Up!* (1961); *Dr. Crippen, The Caretaker* (1963); *Maniac* (1963); *Eye of the Devil, Cul-de-Sac, Fantastic Voyage* (1966); *THX 1138* (1971); *Death Line* (1972); *Tales That Witness Madness, From Beyond the Grave* (1973); *The Mutations, Barry Mackenzie Holds His Own* (1974); *I Don't Want to Be Born, Escape to Witch Mountain, Journey into Fear* (1975); *The Devil's Men* (1976); *The Uncanny* (1977); *The Dark Secret of Harvest Home* [TV film], *Blood Relatives, Meteor, Halloween* (1978); *Dracula* (1979); *The Monster Club* (1980); *Escape From New York, Halloween II, The Thing* (1981).

PRICE, VINCENT 1911–

Actor. Born in St. Louis, Missouri. The son of a wealthy candy manufacturer, Price was graduated from Yale with a degree in art history and English. While in London preparing for his M.A. in fine arts, he played a walk-on part in a West End play titled *Chicago* and decided to become an actor. After a number of supporting roles, he quickly climbed to stardom as Prince Albert in the London production of *Victoria Regina* (1935). After repeating the role on Broadway with Helen Hayes as Queen Victoria, he became a member of Orson Welles' Mercury Theater Workshop. His screen debut came in *Service de Luxe* (1938), followed by his genre debut in *Tower of London* (1939).

Initially cast as a romantic leading man, Price found his niche as an unctuous, prissily effete villain in horror films. His tendency to play many of his roles tongue-in-cheek, with a camp British accent, often causes him to binge on his own image, but he has been genuinely terrifying in such films as *Witchfinder General*. He is also an art expert and master chef and has published several books on these subjects. Unlike other major horror stars, Price rose to the genre's hierarchy without benefit of a continuing character, with the exception of two Dr. Phibes movies. Since 1981 he has been the host of PBS-TV's *Mystery Theater*.

FILMS INCLUDE

The Private Lives of Elizabeth and Essex, Tower of London (1939); *The Invisible Man Returns, The House of the Seven Gables* (1940); *The Song of Bernadette* (1943); *Laura* (1944); *Leave Her to Heaven* (1945); *Abbott and Costello Meet Frankenstein* [as the voice of the Invisible Man] (1948); *House of Wax* (1953); *The Mad Magician* (1954); *The Fly, House on Haunted Hill* (1958); *The Bat, Return of the Fly, The Tingler* (1959); *The House of Usher* (1960); *The Pit and the Pendulum, Master of the World* (1961); *Tales of Terror, Confessions of an Opium Eater, Tower of London* (1962); *The Raven, Diary of a Madman, Beach Party, Twice-Told Tales, The Comedy of Terrors, The Haunted Palace* (1963); *The Masque of the Red Death, The Last Man on Earth, The Tomb of Ligeia* (1964); *Dr. Goldfoot and the Bikini Machine* (1965); *The Jackals* [unreleased] (1967); *Witchfinder General/The Conqueror Worm, Spirits of the Dead* [narrator of English-language version] (1968); *The Oblong Box, The Trouble with Girls, Scream and Scream Again* (1969); *Cry of the Banshee* (1970); *The Abominable Dr. Phibes* (1971); *Dr. Phibes Rises Again* (1972); *Theatre of Blood* (1973); *Percy's Progress, Madhouse* (1974); *Journey into Fear* (1975); *The Monster Club, Romance in the Jugular Vein* (1980); *House of the Long Shadows* (1983).

POLANSKI, ROMAN 1933–

Director. Born in Paris to Polish-Jewish parents who returned to live in Cracow, Poland when he was three. At the age of eight he was left entirely alone after the Nazis sent his parents to a concentration camp. As his father intended, the boy escaped the final liquidation of the ghetto by living with a succession of Catholic families. At 14 the diminutive Polanski got a part on a Marxist radio program for children and subsequently appeared on the stage and in films. His quick study of film technique won him acceptance at the famous Polish Film School at Lodz, where he made *Two Men and a Wardrobe* (1958), a surrealistic short film that won international recognition. In 1962 he made his first feature, *Knife in the Water*, a compelling, mature drama of sexual rivalry, which launched his career in the West.

Polanski's films are characterized by technical skill, a deep pessimism and a preoccupation with sexual psychosis. Many of his features have shown a fascination for explicit gore and violence, qualifying them as horror films although he has avoided a genre label. His most successful film has been *Rosemary's Baby* (1968), a straightforward tale of witchcraft and Satanism that took him to the top of the Hollywood ladder. He was deciding on his next project when he suffered another personal tragedy. In August of 1969 his pregnant actress wife Sharon Tate and three guests were massacred by the Charles Manson "family" in the couple's Beverly Hills mansion while Polanski was in London. Badly shaken, he returned to films in Great Britain with *Macbeth* (1971), a ruthlessly brutal version of Shakespeare's play with several ultra-bloody killings that seemed like replays of the Tate murders.

His career rebounded with *Chinatown* (1974), a polished and evocative political thriller in which Polanski cast himself as a small-time hood who slices open star Jack Nicholson's nostril. In 1977 he was again in the news when the Superior Court of California put him under psychiatric observation after he was arrested for having had "unlawful sexual intercourse" with a 13-year-old girl he had photographed for the French edition of *Vogue*. He subsequently fled to France, where he now lives, and is still wanted by The State of California as a fugitive from justice.

FILMS INCLUDE

Knife in the Water (1962); *The Beautiful Swindlers* ["Amsterdam" episode] (1964); *Repulsion* (1965); *Cul-de-Sac* (1966); *The Fearless Vampire Killers or Pardon Me but Your Teeth Are in My Neck* (1967); *Rosemary's Baby* (1968); *Macbeth* (1971); *What?, Chinatown* (1974); *The Tenant, Diary of Forbidden Dreams* (1976); *Tess* (1979).

QUARRY, ROBERT 1923–

American actor who played a contemporary bloodsucker in *Count Yorga, Vampire* (1970)—his genre debut—and its sequel, *Return of Count Yorga* (1971). Quarry studied at the Actor's Lab in Los Angeles, and made his film debut in Alfred Hitchcock's *Shadow of a Doubt* (1943) playing a juvenile. After a brief contract with Universal, he worked on the stage for many years, while appearing in occasional movies and TV programs. He returned to the screen in the 1970s in an unsuccessful bid to become a horror star.

TV CREDITS INCLUDE

Hollywood Screen Test (series) (1949); *The Millionaire* [movie] (1978).

FILMS INCLUDE

A Kiss Before Dying (1956); *Dr. Phibes Rises Again, The Deathmaster* (1972); *Madhouse, Sugar Hill* (1974).

RATHBONE, BASIL 1892–1967

Actor. Born in Johannesburg, South Africa, to British parents. Educated in England, Rathbone made his professional stage debut there in *The Taming of the Shrew* (1911). After military service during World War I, he appeared in plays on both sides of the Atlantic, usually in classical roles, and made his British film debut in *Innocent* (1921). His first Hollywood film was *Trouping with Ellen* (1924), which led to a series of romantic leading roles in silent movies.

Rathbone's greatest success came after the arrival of sound, however, when his suave voice complemented his icily incisive demeanor and gauntly elegant looks. (Critic Dorothy Parker described him as "two profiles pasted together.") These qualities brought him a long career as a popular Hollywood villain who alternated between genre films and major productions. He is equally well-known as the screen's archetypal Sherlock Holmes in 14 films made during the 1940s.

FILMS INCLUDE

The Last of Mrs. Cheyney (1929); *The Bishop Murder Case* [as detective Philo Vance] (1930); *David Copperfield, Anna Karenina, A Tale of Two Cities, Captain Blood* (1935), *Romeo and Juliet* (1936); *The Adventures of Robin Hood* (1938); *Son of Frankenstein, The Hound of the Baskervilles, The Adventures of Sherlock Holmes, Tower of London* (1939); *The Mad Doctor, The Black Cat* (1941); *Sherlock Holmes and the Secret Weapon* (1943); *The House of Fear* (1945); *Dressed to Kill* (1946); *The Court Jester, The Black Sleep* (1956); *The Last Hurrah* (1958); *Tales of Terror* (1962); *The Comedy of Terrors* (1963); *Queen of Blood, The Ghost in the Invisible Bikini* (1966); *Voyage to a Prehistoric Planet, Autopsy of a Ghost, Hillbillys in a Haunted House* (1967).

RIEDEL, RICHARD H. 1907–1960

American art director; associated with Universal. Although he designed sets for nearly every film genre, Riedel was most at home with horror, fantasy and science fiction. His bizarre expressionist sets for *Son of Frankenstein* (1939)—in collaboration with Jack Otterson—are probably the most stunning of any seen in Universal's horror cycle of the 1930s and 1940s. A contemporary *New York Times* critic described the film as "a paradise of low, brow-bursting beams! Such endless miles of corridors, rendered fascinating by skiddy turns, pneumonic draughts and sudden breakneck stairways." Riedel died in a traffic accident near Rome while scouting locations for a 1961 remake of *Back Street*.

FILMS INCLUDE

Son of Frankenstein (1939); *The Bank Dick* (1940); *Night Monster* (1942); *Flesh and Fantasy* (1943); *Ali Baba and the 40 Thieves* (1944); *The Ghost Steps Out* (1946); *Abbott and Costello Meet the Killer—Boris Karloff* (1949); *Abbott and Costello Meet the Invisible Man* (with Bernard Herzbrun) (1951); *This Island Earth* (1955); *I've Lived Before* (1956); *Imitation of Life* (1959).

ROMERO, GEORGE A. 1940–

Director, producer, screenwriter. Born in the Bronx, New York. After graduation from the Carnegie-Mellon Institute with a B.A. in art, he remained in Pittsburgh (where he still resides) to make commercials for an advertising agency. In 1967 Romero obtained local financing and cast his friends in an ultra low-budget programmer which he hoped would be a ticket to a movie career. The result was *Night of the Living Dead*, a feverish zombie movie whose storyline he borrowed from Richard Matheson's vampire novel *I Am Legend* (filmed twice, as *The Last Man on Earth* and *The Omega Man*).

Dismissed by the few critics who reviewed it (*Variety* saw only "amateurism of the first order"), the film initially played in drive-ins before being rescued and moved indoors by a growing legion of horror buffs. More explicit than anything that had been seen before, it became notorious for its stomach-wrenching scenes of hideously decaying corpses ripping out human entrails and devouring them with hungry pleasure. What Romero had done was to bring horror back into the horror film and to point the genre in its present direction. One of the new breed of filmmakers nourished on old Hollywood genre movies (and the banned E.C. comics), Romero works in the horror-humor tradition. His films often contain subtle political and social subtexts.

FILMS INCLUDE

Night of the Living Dead (1968); *The Crazies* (1973); *Martin* (1978); *Dawn of the Dead* (1979); *Creepshow* (1982); *Day of the Dead* (1985).

SASDY, PETER 1934–

TV and film director, born in Hungary, where he was graduated from the University of Budapest with a theater degree. Sasdy worked as a newspaper critic and stage and film director before

immigrating to Britain during the 1956 uprising. He began his career there as a production assistant with the BBC-TV. His first film, *Taste the Blood of Dracula* (1970), indicated a talent for colorful Freudian horror, displaced by empty shock and dazzle in his later offerings.

FILMS INCLUDE

Countess Dracula (1970); *Hands of the Ripper* (1971); *Doomwatch, Nothing But the Night* (1972); *I Don't Want to Be Born* (1975); *Welcome to Blood City* (1977).

SERLING, ROD 1924–1975

Television dramatist and film writer. Born in Syracuse, New York. After army service as a paratrooper during World War II, Serling enrolled at Antioch College in Ohio on the GI Bill and studied drama. Upon graduation he worked as a writer for a Cincinnati radio station and subsequently created a weekly live drama series for a local television station. Freelance sales of scripts to such early live TV anthology series as *The Hallmark Hall of Fame* and *Kraft Television Theatre* brought him critical praise and network offers.

In 1954 Serling and his family moved to Westport, Connecticut to be near New York City, then the center of TV production. A prolific playwright, he turned out more than 20 original scripts in 1955 alone. He won his first Emmy for *Patterns*, a forceful study of a corporate power struggle, which he adapted for a Hollywood film. He won more kudos for *Requiem for a Heavyweight*, the moving drama of a washed-up boxer, also filmed. As economics forced television to switch production to formated sitcoms and crime series, many of the "golden age" writers left for Hollywood.

Serling stayed on, however, and served as executive producer, host and author of most of the episodes of a unique fantasy series, *The Twilight Zone* (1959–64). The stories covered the landscape of science fiction and soft-core horror and often had ironic endings in the manner of O. Henry. *The Twilight Zone* allowed Serling to continue exploring humanist concerns—e.g. prejudice, despotism, the corruption of fame—which had marked his work in live television. Rating problems plagued the series from the start, and sponsors came and went, but a core audience of sophisticated viewers tuned in weekly. The show won three Emmies and CBS was happy to have a "prestige" series. Ratings dipped, however, and the series was dropped for half a season, only to be resurrected in an hour-long format of lackluster episodes. Its resumption of 30-minute episodes the following year failed to attract a larger audience, and the program was retired in the spring of 1964 after its troubled but successful run.

Serling's two subsequent series also failed in the ratings game. In *The Loner* (1965–66), he attempted to create an adult western with provocative characters and situations. Creative control was denied Serling for his last series, *Night Gallery* (1970–72), whose producers insisted on shock over substance. Embittered by the experience of trying to write original, meaningful drama for a commercial mass medium, he turned to teaching dramatic writing at Ithaca College in upstate New York. A workaholic who chain-smoked four packs of cigarettes a day, Serling died at age 50 following open-heart surgery.

FILMS INCLUDE

The Rack [based on his teleplay], *Patterns* (1956); *Saddle the Wind* (1958); *Incident in an Alley* [story only], *Requiem for a Heavyweight* (1962); *The Yellow Canary* (1963); *Seven Days in May* (1964); *Assault on a Queen* (1965); *Planet of the Apes* (1968); *Night Gallery* [TV pilot movie] (1969); *The Man* (1972); *Deadly Fathoms* [narrator] (1973); *The Outer Space Connection* [narrator], *Encounters with the Unknown* [narrator] (1975).

SPIELBERG, STEVEN 1947–

Filmmaker. Born in Cincinnati, Ohio. Spielberg grew up fascinated by movies. He made his first home movie at the age of 12, and a year later he won a contest with a war feature titled *Escape to Nowhere*. At 17 he completed a lengthy film called *Firefight*, which got him admitted to the film department of California State College. While there he produced five shorts, including *Amblin'*, which was shown theatrically at the 1969 Atlanta Film Festival. The exposure led to a contract with Universal and a string of television assignments. Among his early efforts were Rod Serling's *Night Gallery* (1969), in which he directed veteran superstar Joan Crawford; "L.A. 2017," an episode of *The Name of the Game* series (1970); Richard Matheson's *Duel* (1971), which has become a cult favorite; *Something Evil* (1972); and *Savage* (1973).

Spielberg made his theatrical feature debut with *The Sugarland Express* (1973), which critic Pauline Kael called "one of the most phenomenal directorial debut films in the history of movies." His next film, *Jaws* (1975), was one of the greatest box-office successes of the decade, and established him as a leading filmmaker who could name his own terms. He scored another bull's-eye with *Close Encounters of the Third Kind* (1977), which he fol-

lowed with the amiably nostalgic *I Wanna Hold Your Hand* (1978), as executive producer. His next was the overdone World War II comedy *1941* (1979), which was bombed by the critics and merely broke even at the box office.

In 1980 Spielberg joined forces with George Lucas, maker of the *Star Wars* series, with whom he is allied by age, upbringing and taste. The first Spielberg/Lucas collaboration, *Raiders of the Lost Ark* (1981), an homage to the matinee serials of the 1930s, struck gold, and since then every Spielberg film has been among the top moneymakers of the year. In 1982 he directed *E.T. The Extra-Terrestrial* and produced and co-wrote the horrific *Poltergeist*. "E.T. is what I love and *Poltergeist* is what I fear," Spielberg explained. "One is about suburban good and the other is about suburban evil." In 1983 he produced and directed an episode of *Twilight Zone—The Movie*. His most recent releases are *Indiana Jones and the Temple of Doom* (a sequel to *Raiders*), *Gremlins* (both 1984), *The Goonies, The Color Purple* and *Young Sherlock Holmes* (1985). He also produced the TV anthology series *Amazing Stories* (1985).

Spielberg's best films are characterized by a romantic idealism and a belief that good will always triumph over evil. Most feature children in important or emblematic roles, and many are filled with references to well-known childrens' books and films that he himself grew up with.

STEELE, BARBARA 1938–

British actress, who acquired cult status during the 1960s in European genre films. Born in either Liverpool or Ireland in 1937 or 1938 (her stories vary), Steele studied at the Chelsea Art School in London and the Sorbonne in Paris before debuting in British repertory in the mid-1950s. Signed to a long-term contract by the J. Arthur Rank Organisation, she made her first film appearance in *Bachelor of Hearts* (1958), followed by a color remake of Alfred Hitchcock's classic *The 39 Steps*, directed by Ralph Thomas.

After casting her in several minor roles, the studio sold her contract to 20th Century-Fox. Steele lived in Hollywood for a year without being assigned to a film, and in 1960 departed for Italy to film Mario Bava's *Black Sunday*. Her imposing presence and sculptured features with her prominent cheekbones and large, wild eyes seem made to order for the genre, and she soon established her preeminence as the cinema's first full-time female fiend. (One critic described her as the "only girl in films whose eyelids can snarl.") A multilingual who can speak Italian, Spanish and French as well as

English, Steele subsequently divided her time between the U.S. and Europe, appearing most frequently in Italian films. Although her versatility was demonstrated in such quality films as Fellini's *8½* (1963) and *Young Torless* (1966), by the 1970s she found herself typecast as a sorceress and has worked only sporadically since then.

FILMS INCLUDE

Bachelor of Hearts (1958); *Sapphire* (1959); *Black Sunday/ La Maschera del Demonio/Revenge of the Vampire* (1960); *The Pit and the Pendulum* (1961); *The Horrible Dr. Hitchcock/L'Orrible Segreto del Dr. Hitchcock, 8½/Otto e Mezzo, The Ghost/Lo Spetro* (1963); *Danse Macabre/Danza Macabre/Castle of Blood, The Maniacs, White Voices/Le Voci bianche* (1964); *Nightmare Castle, Terror-Creatures from the Grave, La Sorella di Satana/The She-Beast/Revenge of the Blood Beast* (1965); *Der junge Torless/Young Torless, An Angel for Satan* (1966); *Curse of the Crimson Altar/The Crimson Cult* (1968); *Caged Heat* (1974); *They Came from Within/ The Parasite Murders* (1975); *I Never Promised You a Rose Garden* (1977); *Piranha, La Cle sur la Porte, The Space-Watch Murders* (made for TV) (1978); *The Silent Scream* (1979).

TV CREDITS INCLUDE

Adventures in Paradise (1960); *Alfred Hitchcock Presents* (1961); *Secret Agent* (1965).

TOURNEUR, JACQUES 1904–1977

Director. Born in Paris. The son of fantasy director Maurice Tourneur, he emigrated to the U.S. with his father in 1914 and later became an American citizen. He entered the film industry in 1924 as an office boy at MGM and subsequently worked as an actor and as a script assistant on his father's films. He returned to France with his father in 1928 and directed his first film there. Returning to the U.S. in 1934, he was hired by MGM as the second unit director of *A Tale of Two Cities* and went on to make short subjects for the studio. After several years of directing B pictures, he moved to RKO and emerged as an important genre director with *Cat People* (1942), under the tutelage of producer Val Lewton. At his best, Tourneur was a master of tasteful, low-key horror whose shocks were suggested rather than shown and sustained by an ominous mood. At the end of his career he worked in television.

FILMS INCLUDE

Un Vieux Garcon (1931); *Les Filles de la Concierge* (1934); *They All Came Out, Nick Carter—Master Detective* (1939); *Phantom Raiders* (1940); *Doctors Don't Tell* (1941); *Cat People* (1942); *I Walked With a Zombie, The Leopard Man* (1943); *Experiment Perilous* (1944); *Out of the Past* (1947); *Easy Living* (1949); *The Flame and the Arrow* (1950); *Way of a Gaucho* (1952); *Appointment in Honduras* (1953); *Nightfall, Night of the Demon* (1957); *The Fearmakers* (1958); *The Giant of Marathon* (1959); *The Comedy of Terrors* (1963); *War Gods of the Deep* (1965).

VAN SLOAN, EDWARD 1882–1964

Character actor. Born in San Francisco. Van Sloan worked as a commercial artist before embarking on a stage career in the mid-1900s. He is best known as the vampire-destroyer Professor Van Helsing, a role he originated in the 1927 Broadway production of *Dracula* and repeated in the 1931 film. A white-haired gentleman with wire-rimmed eyeglasses, he made an indelible impression as the vampire's nemesis, armed with only Victorian righteousness, wolfbane, crosses and wooden stakes. He played Van Helsing again in *Dracula's Daughter* and matched wits with other famous Hollywood menaces.

FILMS INCLUDE

Dracula, Frankenstein (1931); *Behind the Mask, The Mummy, The Last Mile, Forgotten Commandments, The Death Kiss* (1932); *Infernal Machine, The Deluge, The Working Man* (1933); *The Scarlet Empress* (1934); *The Last Days of Pompeii, A Shot in the Dark* (1935); *Sins of Man, The Story of Louis Pasteur, Dracula's Daughter* (1936); *Penitentiary* (1938); *The Phantom Creeps* (serial) (1939); *Before I Hang, The Secret Seven* (1940); *The Mask of Dijon* (1946); *Betty Co-Ed, A Foreign Affair* (1947).

VEIDT, CONRAD 1893–1943

Actor. Born in Potsdam, Germany. Veidt studied with Max Reinhardt and made his debut with the impresario's Deutsches Theater in 1913. Entering films in 1917 with *Der Spion*, he rose to prominence as the somnambulist Cesare in *Das Kabinett von Dr. Caligari/The Cabinet of Dr. Caligari* (1919). During the 1920s he specialized in macabre roles that characterized the bizarre, expressionist cinema that flourished in defeated Germany after

World War I. The genre's first star, Veidt appeared during this period in *Der Januskopf* (1920), an adaptation of *Dr. Jekyll and Mr. Hyde*; *Das Wachsfigurenkabinett/Waxworks/Three Wax Men* (1924); *Orlacs Haende/The Hands of Orlac* (1925); and *Student von Prag/The Student of Prague* (1926).

Made world famous by the latter film, he was called to Hollywood where he appeared notably in *The Man Who Laughs* (1928) and two other films. Returning to Germany with the advent of sound, he starred in a series of films, including *Rasputin* and the science fiction success *F.P. 1 antwortet nicht/F.P. 1 Does Not Answer* (both 1932). With the coming of Hitler, he immigrated to England with his Jewish wife and embarked on a succession of romantic roles. Becoming a British citizen, he went back to Hollywood to complete *The Thief of Bagdad* (1940)—which had been interrupted by the outbreak of World War II. He appeared in, among others, *A Woman's Face* and *Whistling in the Dark* (1941). Veidt is probably best remembered by moviegoers as a sneering sadistic Nazi in such films as *Casablanca* and *Above Suspicion* (both 1943). He died of a heart attack in 1943.

WEGENER, PAUL 1874–1948

German actor, director, screenwriter and producer. A national stage idol—akin in his time to Britain's Laurence Olivier—he rose to prominence interpreting classical roles at Max Reinhardt's influential Deutsches Theater in Berlin. He displayed a flair for the macabre in his first film, *Der Student von Prag/The Student of Prague* (1913), and an instinct for film technique in his next, *Der Golem/The Golem* (1914), the first of three versions he directed and starred in. Wegener's imposing physique and commanding theatrical presence were uniquely suited to the Golem, a sort of mystical Jewish Hulk, which he played with a characteristic restraint that makes his performance seem less dated than others of the period. His costume and characterization later provided a model for Universal's Frankenstein Monster. During the Nazi era Wegener was criticized by former co-workers (many of whom had settled in Hollywood) for consenting to be named Actor of the State and for making propaganda films. He was exonerated after the war by the government of East Germany, where he received an honorary university degree.

FILMS INCLUDE

Der Student von Prag/The Student of Prague (1913); *Der Golem/The Golem* (1914); *Der Rattenfanger von*

Hamelin/The Pied Piper of Hamelin (1916); *Der Golem und die Tanzerin/The Golem and the Dancer* (1917); *Der Golem—wie er in die Welt Kam/The Golem* (1920); *The Magician* (U.S., made in France) (1926); *Ramper der Tiermensch/The Strange Case of Captain Ramper, Svengali* (1927); *Alraune/Unholy Love* (1928); *Unheimliche Geschichten/The Living Dead, Horst Wessel* (1933); *Starker als die Liebe/Stronger Than Love* (1938); *Der grosse Mandarin* (1949).

WESTMORE, BUD 1918–1973

Makeup artist. As the successor to Jack Pierce, Westmore took over Universal's makeup department and created the studio's subsequent monsters, the most memorable of which is *Creature from the Black Lagoon* (1954). He was the fifth of six sons who comprised a famed Hollywood dynasty that established the lexicon of movie makeup. In 1935 the brothers branched out to open The House of Westmore, which became the eminent beauty salon to the stars for over 30 years. (One of its early tasks was to change the natural center hair part of contract player Ronald Reagan to his current side part.) Other members of the family, who worked less frequently (or not at all) in horror, are as follows:

Westmore, George (1879–1931): The British-born father of the dynasty. A former barber and wig-maker, he was one of the first to make-up movie actors, who had previously applied their own artifices.

Perc Westmore (1904–68): The twin brother of Ern. His credits include *The Walking Dead* (1936), *The Hunchback of Notre Dame* (1939), *The Return of Dr. X* (1939) and TV's *The Munsters* (1964–66);

Ern Westmore (1904–70);

Monty Westmore: *What Ever Happened to Baby Jane?* (1962);

Wally Westmore (1906–73): *Dr. Jekyll and Mr. Hyde* (1931), *The Most Dangerous Game, The Island of Lost Souls* (1932), *The Man in Half Moon Street* (1943), *Alias Nick Beal* (1949), *The Colossus of New York* (1958), *Robinson Crusoe on Mars* (1964);

Frank Westmore (1923–   ).

FILMS INCLUDE:

The Flying Serpent, Strangler of the Swamp (1945); *Devil Bat's Daughter* (1946); *Abbott and Costello Meet Frankenstein* (1948); *Abbott and Costello Meet the*

Killer, Boris Karloff (1949); *Abbott and Costello Meet the Invisible Man* (1951); *Abbott and Costello Meet Dr. Jekyll and Mr. Hyde, It Came from Outer Space* (1953); *Creature from the Black Lagoon* [with Jack Kevan] (1954); *Revenge of the Creature, This Island Earth, Abbott and Costello Meet the Mummy, Cult of the Cobra, Tarantula* (1955); *The Creature Walks Among Us, The Mole People, The Land Unknown* (1956); *The Monolith Monsters, Man of a Thousand Faces, The Deadly Mantis* (1957); *Monster on the Campus, The Thing That Couldn't Die* (1958); *Curse of the Undead* (1959); *The Leech Woman, The Night Walker* (1964); *Dark Intruder* [made for TV] (1965); *Munster Go Home* (1966); *Games* (1967); *Eye of the Cat* (1969); *Hauser's Memory* [made for TV] (1970); *Skullduggery* (1970).

WHALE, JAMES 1896–1957

Director. Born in Dudley, England. A former newspaper cartoonist, Whale decided on a career in the theater after acting in plays performed in a German prisoner-of-war camp during military service in World War I. He made his professional stage debut in a small role in *Abraham Lincoln*, produced by the Birmingham Repertory Company. He worked on the London stage as an actor, producer and director until 1930 when he was hired by Hollywood to film his stage success, *Journey's End*.

After co-directing *Hell's Angels* with Howard Hughes, Whale, under contract to Universal, was chosen to direct *Frankenstein* (1931). The film launched Whale's career as a horror director and transformed a little known contract player named Boris Karloff into a major star. The pair subsequently worked together in *The Old Dark House* (1932) and *Bride of Frankenstein* (1935). Gifted with a mordant sense of humor, Whale is a seminal genre director whose films are marked by a striking expressionist vision and a discriminating instinct for macabre detail. He also directed a musical (*Show Boat*), a war film (*The Road Back*), several comedies and adventure movies.

He retired in the early 1940s, a wealthy man, to devote his time to painting, but decided on a comeback in 1949 for an episode of *Hello Out There*, a multipart film that was never completed. He was found dead in his swimming pool, apparently having drowned after a mysterious fall.

FILMS INCLUDE

Hell's Angels (1930); *Waterloo Bridge, Frankenstein* (1931); *The Impatient Maiden, The Old Dark House* (1932); *The Kiss Before the Mirror, The Invisible Man, By Candlelight* (1933); *One More River* (1934); *Bride of Frankenstein, Remember Last Night?* (1935); *Show Boat* (1936); *The Road Back, The Great Garrick* (1937); *Sinners in Paradise, Wives Under Suspicion, Port of Seven Seas* (1938); *The Man in the Iron Mask* (1939); *Green Hell* (1940); *They Dare Not Love* (1941).

WRAY, FAY 1907–

Actress. Born in Alberta, Canada, and raised in Los Angeles. Wray began making the casting rounds in her early teens. Soon after graduation from Hollywood High School, she landed a part in *Gasoline Love* (1923) and then worked steadily as an extra and bit player. The turning point in her career came when she was selected from dozens of actresses by director Erich von Stroheim for the lead in Paramount's *The Wedding March*, begun in 1926 and completed in 1928. She subsequently starred opposite the leading men of the day, including Gary Cooper, Fredric March, Ronald Colman, William Powell and, of course, King Kong. "They told me I was going to have the tallest, darkest leading man in Hollywood," she later wrote. "Naturally, I thought of Clark Gable." Her famous scream was heard in several important genre films of the thirties, but by the end of the decade she was being cast in routine films.

Retiring in 1942 after her marriage to screenwriter Robert Riskin, she made a comeback as a character actress in the early 1950s after Riskin was stricken with a fatal illness. Her return to films coincided with the release to television of *King Kong*, which brought her a new generation of fans. She has written several plays, one of which was filmed as the Universal musical *This Is the Life* (1944). In 1971 Wray's daughter Victoria Riskin recreated her mother's famous role in a Volkswagen commercial, which had Kong driving through Manhattan in a giant automobile. Wray herself appeared at a 1976 tribute to the great ape at the Telluride Film Festival.

FILMS INCLUDE

Gasoline Love (1923); *The Coast Patrol* (1925); *Lazy Lightning* (1926); *Spurs and Saddles, The Street of Sin, The Wedding March* (1928); *The Four Feathers* (1929); *Paramount on Parade* (1930); *The Sea God, The Finger Points, Dirigible* (1931); *Doctor X, The Most Dangerous Game* (1932); *The Vampire Bat, Mystery of the Wax Museum, King Kong, Master of Men, The Bowery* (1933); *Viva Villa!, The Affairs of Cellini* (1934); *The Clairvoyant* (1935); *When Knights Were Bold* (1936); *It Happened in Hollywood* (1937); *Smashing the Spy Ring* (1938); *Navy Secrets* (1939); *The Wildcat Bus* (1940); *Adam Had Four Sons* (1941); *Not a Ladies' Man* (1942);

Treasure of the Golden Condor, Small Town Girl (1953); *The Cobweb, Queen Bee* (1955); *Hell on Frisco Bay* (1956); *Rock Pretty Baby, Tammy and the Bachelor* (1957); *Dragstrip Riot* (1958).

TV CREDITS INCLUDE

Pride of the Family (as Natalie Wood's mother) (1953-54); *Damon Runyon Theater, Studio 57* (1955); *The 20th Century-Fox Hour* (1956); *The Jane Wyman Theater* (1957); *Alfred Hitchcock Presents* ("A Dip in the Pool") (1958); *Perry Mason* (1959, 1965); *The Islanders, Hawaiian Eye* (1960); *The G.E. Theater* (1961); *Wagon Train* (1962); *The Eleventh Hour* (1964).

ZUCCO, GEORGE 1886–1960

Character actor, born in Manchester, England. Zucco began his stage career in Canada in 1908, and toured in American stock companies before returning to Britain for military service during World War I. He subsequently alternated between London's West End and Broadway, appearing in both vaudeville and the legitimate theater. His first British movie was *Autumn Crocus* (1930), in which he recreated a stage role. Invited to Hollywood by MGM, he debuted in *After the Thin Man* (1936) and was featured in several top studio productions. He is best remembered, however, for a handful of low-budget horror films made in the 1940s. Gifted with a malevolent baritone, eyes like frozen marbles, and a deceptively cultivated manner, he could usually be found conducting unspeakable medical experiments with the likes of Boris Karloff, Bela Lugosi and Lionel Atwill.

FILMS INCLUDE

Autumn Crocus (1930); *The Man Who Could Work Miracles, After the Thin Man* (1936); *Parnell* (1937); *Marie Antoinette* (1938); *The Adventures of Sherlock Holmes* (as Moriarty), *The Cat and the Canary, The Hunchback of Notre Dame* (1939); *The Mummy's Hand* (1940); *The Monster and the Girl, A Woman's Face* (1941); *Dr. Renault's Secret, The Mad Monster, The Mummy's Tomb* (1942); *Dead Men Walk, The Mad Ghoul* (1943); *The Mummy's Ghost, The Voodoo Man, Return of the Ape Man, House of Frankenstein* (1944); *Fog Island* (1945); *The Flying Serpent* (1946); *Captain From Castile* (1947); *David and Bathsheba* (1951).

BIBLIOGRAPHY

Ashley, Mike, *Who's Who in Horror and Fantasy Fiction*, New York: Taplinger, 1978.

Aylesworth, Thomas G., *Monsters from the Movies*, Philadelphia and New York: Lippincott, 1972.

Barsacq, Leon, *Caligari's Cabinet and Other Grand Illusions*, Boston: New York Graphic Society, 1976.

Basten, Fred E., *Glorious Technicolor*, New York: A. S. Barnes, 1980.

Bawden, Liz-Anne, ed., *The Oxford Companion to Film*, New York: Oxford University Press, 1976.

Baxter, John, *Hollywood in the Thirties*, New York: Paperback Library, 1970.

Baxter, John, *Science Fiction in the Cinema*, New York: Paperback Library, 1970.

Beck, Calvin Thomas, *Scream Queens*, New York: Collier, 1978.

Brooks, Tim and Marsh, Earle, *The Complete Directory to Prime Time Network TV Shows*, New York: Ballantine, 1979.

Brown, Les, *The New York Times Encyclopedia of Television*, New York: Times Books, 1977.

Brownlow, Kevin, *The Parade's Gone By*, New York: Knopf, 1969.

Buston, Frank and Owen, Bill, *The Big Broadcast*, New York: Viking, 1966.

Butler, Ivan, *Horror in the Cinema*, New York: Paperback Library, 1971.

Cagin, Seth and Dray, Philip, *Hollywood Films of the Seventies*, New York: Harper & Row, 1984.

Clarens, Carlos, *An Illustrated History of the Horror Film*, New York: Capricorn, 1968.

Cohen, Daniel, *Magicians, Wizards & Sorcerers*, Philadelphia and New York: Lippincott, 1973.

Daniels, Les, *Living in Fear*, New York: Scribner's, 1975.

Di Franco, J. Philip, ed., *The Movie World of Roger Corman*, New York: Chelsea House, 1979.

Everson, William K., *Classics of the Horror Film*, Secaucus, N.J.: Citadel, 1974.

Frank, Alan, *The Horror Film Handbook*, Totowa, N.J.: Barnes & Noble, 1982.

Gerani, Gary and Schulman, Paul H., *Fantastic Television*, New York: Harmony, 1977.

Haining, Peter, ed., *The Dracula Scrapbook*, New York: Bramhall House, 1976.

Halliwell, Leslie, *Halliwell's Film Guide*, New York: Scribner's, 1984.

Hammond, Paul, *Marvellous Melies*, New York: St. Martin's, 1975.

Higham, Charles and Greenberg, Joel, *Hollywood in the Forties*, New York: A. S. Barnes, 1968.

Katz, Ephraim, *The Film Encyclopedia*, New York: Thomas Y. Crowell, 1979.

King, Stephen, *Danse Macabre*, New York: Berkeley, 1982.

Lee, Walt, *Reference Guide to Fantastic Films*, Los Angeles: Chelsea-Lee Books, 1973.

Marill, Alvin H., *Movies Made for Television*, New York: Da Capo, 1980.

Masters, Anthony, *The Natural History of the Vampire*, New York: Putnam's, 1972.

McCarty, John, *Splatter Movies*, New York: St. Martin's, 1984.

Rottensteiner, Franz, *The Fantasy Book*, New York: Collier, 1978.

Settel, Irving, *A Pictorial History of Radio*, New York: Grosset & Dunlap, 1960.

Shulman, Arthur and Youman, Roger, *How Sweet It Was*, New York: Bonanza, 1966.

Silver, Alain and Ursini, James, *The Vampire Film*, New York: A. S. Barnes, 1975.

Steinbrunner, Chris and Goldblatt, Burt, *Cinema of the Fantastic*, New York: Saturday Review Press, 1972.

Taylor, Al and Roy, Sue, *Making a Monster*, New York: Crown, 1980.

Terrace, Vincent, *Complete Encyclopedia of Television Programs*, New York: A. S. Barnes, 1979.

Truffaut, Francois, *Hitchcock*, New York: Simon and Schuster, 1967.

Weldon, Michael, *The Psychotronic Encyclopedia of Film*, New York: Ballantine, 1983.

INDEX

Note: Entries are categorized as follows: Films; TV Films; TV Programs; Radio Programs; Theater; Authors.